AGATHA CHRISTIE A to Z

The Essential Reference to Her Life & Writings

DAWN B. SOVA, Ph.D.

FOREWORD BY
DAVID SUCHET

INTRODUCTION BY
MATHEW PRICHARD,
Chairman, Agatha Christie Ltd

®Checkmark Books™
An imprint of Facts On File, Inc.

Agatha Christie A to Z: The Essential Reference to Her Life and Writings

First paperback edition 2000

Checkmark Books
An imprint of Facts On File, Inc.
11 Penn Plaza
New York NY 10001

Library of Congress Cataloging-in-Publication Data

Sova, Dawn B.
Agatha Christie A to Z : the essential reference to her life and writings / Dawn Sova ; foreword by David Suchet ; introduction by Mathew Prichard.
p.   cm.
Includes bibliographical references and index.
ISBN 0-8160-3018-9 (hc. : alk. paper). — ISBN 0-8160-4311-6 (pbk. : alk. paper)
1. Christie, Agatha, 1890–1976—Encyclopedias. 2. Women and literature—England—History—20th century—Encyclopedias. 3. Women authors, English—20th century—Biography—Encyclopedias.
4. Detective and mystery stories, English—Encyclopedias.
I. Title.
PR6005.H66Z885   1996   95-48326
823′.912—dc20

Cover design by Nora Wertz
Printed in the United States of America

RRD BVC 10 9 8 7 6 5 4 3 2 1
   (pbk)10 9 8 7 6 5 4 3 2

This book is printed on acid-free paper.

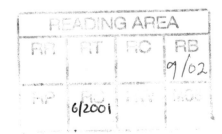

CONTENTS

FOREWORD

The language of the classical theatre has intrigued me ever since my early years on stage. This fascination with language led me into character work, which begins with the text as well as with language. The character actor assumes a *persona,* a term that I perceive in its original meaning—"through sound." In other words, how one speaks and what one says reveals character. Therefore, you can imagine my joy in becoming Hercule Poirot!

In order to do justice to the character, I first read all of the stories and the novels that feature him. Agatha Christie gave details in her works that helped me to draw up a complete dossier of how he spoke, how he moved, and how he thought and behaved. I was given the chance to develop him fully, from a literary figure in the novels and short stories into a living character for the screen.

My goal from the outset was to portray Hercule Poirot in a way that would be truthful and that would honour Agatha Christie's creation. Every story that she wrote made his characterization more specific, maintaining his earlier traits and augmenting them with one or two new ones.

I can understand why he became a *bête noir* to the author, but he has not become that for me, yet. I still very much enjoy portraying him. What attracts me to him, as much as anything else, are his attention to detail and his highly analytical mind. We share the trait of having investigative minds, and he is one of my favorite characters. He does not merely listen to the facts in a case, but goes beyond them to discern the truths.

A book such as this would have pride of place on Hercule Poirot's bookshelf, and not merely for the reason that he appears in many of the entries. Rather, he would have between two covers a source of knowledge about every work and everyone that exists as a result of his own creator—Agatha Christie. Consequently, *Agatha Christie A to Z* will have a pride of place on my own bookshelf.

David Suchet
October 6, 1995

ACKNOWLEDGMENTS

The extensive nature of this project required the assistance and support of many individuals, some of whom will remain unacknowledged in public but to whom my deep and sincere gratitude has been privately made known. One person led to another, much as in an investigation in one of the novels, and I formed many associations in the process. All fans of Agatha Christie, my supporters were generous with their time, their advice and their knowledge of the subject—and I appreciate greatly all of their efforts.

I am grateful for the assistance of Bert Holtje of James Peter Associates, Inc., a friend as well as literary agent. He is a most amazing individual, who talked me through the occasional frustrations and offered a friendly perspective when a brick wall loomed at points in the project. My sincere appreciation belongs to Facts On File, Inc. editors Gary M. Krebs, who conceived the form of the project with me, and Randy Ladenheim-Gil, who molded and guided the growing work. Gary helped to give the project life, and Randy worked hard and succeeded in keeping it healthy and growing to maturity.

Invaluable assistance was provided by numerous library friends upon whom I strongly depended as I aimed to locate every work and identify every character. As many times before, I am grateful to I. Macarthur Nickles, Director of the Garfield (New Jersey) Library, for his professional expertise as well as his efforts in bringing the newest in library technology to my hometown library and for alerting me to increasing research opportunities. Reference experts Kathleen Zalenski and Karen Calandriello sought and found the sources of obscure names and notes, even when the task seemed impossible. I am also very grateful to the many library experts throughout the country who trusted me with their books, sending long-out-of-print references through interlibrary loan and thus aiding me in making the work accurate.

Individuals close to the Christie legend were also generous with their time and talents. Mathew Prichard, Chairman of Agatha Christie Ltd. and grandson of Agatha Christie, identified errors and inaccuracies in the manuscript, which were corrected to make this work the most accurate possible. I am further grateful to Mathew for his assistance in suggesting the subtle touches that set this work apart from all others about Christie. David Suchet, a fine stage and film actor, as well as the definitive Hercule Poirot, brought his magic to the Foreword. Further, Dorothy Carr, president of the Agatha Christie Appreciation Society—Postern of Murder, Inc. (U.S. only), reviewed an early draft of the manuscript and offered numerous suggestions which enhanced the final product.

When time seemed all but gone, Millicent Petrullo and Sammantha Petrullo, my sister and niece respectively, provided the help which greatly extended the mere 24 hours in my day and assisted me in completing the research.

As the piles of books and papers mounted, my personal supporters made the madness manageable. I am forever grateful to my son, Rob Gregor, who joined me as I recaptured my enjoyment of the Christie oeuvre by watching the televised versions and who aided in the research process. My parents, Emil and Violet Sova, make me feel very fortunate for their continued pride in my accomplishments and their unstinting confidence.

Last, but most important, I am grateful for the genius of Agatha Christie. I wish that I could have met her. Her novels, stories and plays created a world apart for my much younger self, allowing me to enter the cozy microcosm of the Christie mystery which, nonetheless, never obscured the reality of the dangers of the real world beyond.

INTRODUCTION

Whenever I visit America, I am always struck by the enormous interest there still is in Agatha Christie. This not only reflects, I am glad to say, on the sales of the books and on the audiences of films and television adaptations of Christie, but on a personal level as well. People want to know more about her books, how and why they came to be written, what sort of person wrote them, where her characters originated, and, in other words, where the legend had its base. In fact, the curiosity about Agatha Christie is limitless. In passing, I would not like you to think that this curiosity is confined to America—it is a worldwide phenomenon!

I was therefore delighted when Dawn Sova told me that it was her intention to write *Agatha Christie A to Z*. I think many people will be fascinated by all the detail concerning Christie's books, films and plays. I suspect that almost everybody will discover that there is something they have not read or did not know about—and I am sure that everybody will find it a valuable companion that will enhance their Christie enjoyment.

Most of all, however, as I leafed through the pages of a proof copy, I was impressed at yet another demonstration of Agatha Christie's ingenuity, the enormous breadth and scope of her characters, and the different kinds of books that she attempted. Dawn's book is a remarkable chronicle of a remarkable literary achievement stretching over 75 years. I congratulate her on her industry and perseverance, and I hope you all enjoy it.

And, by the way, none of the solutions of the plots are revealed, so the real fun is just beginning. . . .

Mathew Prichard
Chairman,
Agatha Christie Ltd.
September 4, 1995

AGATHA CHRISTIE— A BACKGROUND

Agatha Christie remains one of the world's most published writers. With worldwide sales of over two billion copies, only Shakespeare and the Bible have outsold her, and the royalties for her works in the 19 years since her death continue to average in the millions annually. In her lifetime, Agatha Christie wrote 68 mystery novels, 19 plays, and more than 100 short stories which have been translated into 44 languages. In addition, she wrote three books of poetry, six romance novels (under the pseudonym Mary Westmacott), and two nonfiction works. Her works span multiple shelves in bookstores and libraries, and paperback versions of her mysteries can be found in the hands of numerous vacationers on the beach or wherever they might choose to relax and to escape the world's stresses. Her quaint and fluffy Miss Jane Marple and the egotistical Monsieur Hercule Poirot are seen regularly in television broadcasts, and somewhere in the United States and Britain there is always a theatre group presenting a Christie play.

How does an individual prepare for such success? Agatha Christie had her own view regarding why her works are so popular and how she managed to produce so many well-received books. A very private individual, she gave few interviews during her lifetime, and she revealed relatively little of the inner self in her posthumously published *An Autobiography* (1977). Indeed, despite the acclaim, she was modest about her talents, observing that she had never set out to dazzle the literary world. As she once said, "I regard my work of no importance—I've simply been out to entertain." She said that the formula lay in having a happy childhood and one which left her with numerous hours to use her imagination.

Agatha Christie was born in comfortable financial circumstances in Torquay, a seaside town along the English coast in Devonshire. She was the third child of Frederick Alvah Miller and Clarissa Margaret Boehmer, born eleven years after her sister Marjorie (Madge) and ten years after her brother Louis Montant (Monty). Frederick Miller was an independently wealthy American with ties to both the United States

Agatha Christie as she appeared in her writing prime, the mid-1930s. (Photographed by Angus McBean)

and Britain, and Clarissa Boehmer was his stepmother's penniless niece. The two married in 1878 and decided to spend some time at Torquay before moving permanently to the United States. Soon after Madge was born in 1879, the Millers left Torquay for the United States and lived with Mr. Miller's grandparents in New England, where Mrs. Miller gave birth in 1880 to their son Monty. While on a visit to England, Frederick Miller was forced to return to the United States on a business matter, and he asked his wife to find a suitable rental house in the Torquay area for herself and the children. When he returned a short while later, he was surprised to find that she had purchased a home, Ashfield, whose influence would permeate Agatha Christie's life. Still planning to return permanently to the United States, Mr. Miller felt that the house could easily be sold in a year or so, when they would make their move. The beauty of the land surrounding Ashfield combined with the pace of life in Torquay to make the Millers permanent residents of England.

It was at Ashfield, on September 15, 1890, that Agatha May Clarissa Miller was born. She was substantially younger than her brother and sister, who were away at school, so little Agatha was the only child in the house. Mrs. Miller decided that a formal education was not suitable until a certain age, so her youngest daughter was educated at home, teaching herself to read and learning mathematics from her father. For a time, the extremely shy nature of their youngest daughter led the Millers to question whether she might not be mentally slow, but they soon observed that her diffidence masked an intensely curious nature. Her formal education began in 1906, when she attended finishing school in Paris and polished her singing voice and talent for playing the piano. Although she showed early promise, and once considered a career as a concert singer, these interests soon moved into the background, although she would always have a piano wherever she lived.

The gravest unhappiness of Agatha Christie's youth occurred in 1901, when her beloved, easygoing father died. She missed his jocularity, and after his death the family found itself in greatly reduced financial circumstances. To provide her daughter with the appropriate social life, Mrs. Miller occasionally rented Ashfield out while she and Agatha traveled in a discreetly frugal manner. The young woman also attracted several marriage proposals from solid,

stable types, but she seemed to be waiting to be swept off her feet. Engaged in 1912 to a major in the Gunners, she met Captain Archibald Christie in 1913 at a party, and he arrived at Ashfield on his motorcycle several days later. The two became engaged, and Agatha had to write her first fiancé to break off the engagement. The Christies were married eighteen months later, on Christmas Eve, 1914, and Captain Christie went off to war two days later. For two years, Agatha worked as a nursing volunteer at the local hospital, seeing Archibald periodically; then she was transferred to the hospital pharmaceutical dispensary, where she acquired a thorough knowledge of medicines and poisons.

After the war ended, the Christies lived in London, where Archibald Christie worked for a banking firm, and Agatha stayed home. Agatha Christie's only child, Rosalind, was born in 1919. Agatha had written a mystery novel sometime in 1916, to fill the evenings of a lonely wife, but *The Mysterious Affair at Styles* did not find a publisher until 1920. (It came out the following year.) She began to write in earnest, producing a book each year, but her marriage was less successful; the Christies seemed to be growing apart. In 1926, Clara Miller died, and Agatha's world fell apart. Her sister Madge was out of the area, and Agatha took over the task of removing the years of family memories from Ashfield. Her husband stayed in London and, when they came together for Rosalind's birthday, he announced that he wanted a divorce; he had fallen in love with someone else. Agatha was devastated by the news, and the pressures became too much for her to bear. On December 3, 1926, she disappeared, and was not seen for ten days. During those ten days, the newspapers screamed headlines and massive manhunts occurred in the area where her car was found. When she was located, the official medical verdict was amnesia. The author never spoke publicly about her disappearance. (See THE DISAPPEARANCE OF AGATHA CHRISTIE.)

The Christies were divorced in 1928, and Agatha traveled to the Middle East, where she met Max Mallowan, then an assistant to renowned archaeologist, Leonard Woolley, and fourteen years her junior. They were married in September 1930, and shared a forty-six-year partnership and love. Although the author retained her first married name due to its readership recognition, she privately referred to herself as Mrs. Mallowan. She embraced her new life enthusiastically, and she published her nonfiction account of life on the archaeological digs, *Come, Tell Me How You Live*, as Agatha Christie Mallowan. The couple spent time in both England and the Middle East, as Mallowan built his reputation as an archaeologist. Many of Agatha's best works were written while on those digs, despite the fact that she was a busy member of the team, photographing finds, cleaning pottery and learning countless other tasks that gave her a great appreciation for the profession and an increased appreciation for antiquity.

Rosalind Christie had married Hubert Prichard early during World War II, and one of Agatha Christie's happiest moments occurred on September 21, 1943: the birth of her grandson, Mathew Prichard. A year later, Agatha mourned with her daughter when Hubert Prichard was killed in action. She heartily approved when Rosalind married Anthony Hicks in 1949, extremely impressed by his scholarly nature and his ability to read Sanskrit.

After World War II, even though she continued to produce a book per year, Agatha Christie experienced substantial success with her plays. In 1952, the extremely successful West End production of *The Mousetrap* began its run, which continues to this day. *Witness for the Prosecution* appeared onstage the next year, then became a successful movie in 1957.

Both Agatha Christie and Max Mallowan received official recognition for their accomplishments. In 1956, Agatha Christie became a Commander of the British Empire, and Max Mallowan received the same honor in 1961. However, he became Sir Max Mallowan in 1968 when he was knighted. Agatha Christie did not become a Dame of the British Empire until 1971.

Agatha Christie died on January 12, 1976, after enduring failing health for several years. Her husband wrote in the "Epilogue" to *Mallowan's Memoirs* that she died "peacefully and gently" and left him with a great loss for "Few men know what it is to live in harmony beside an imaginative, creative mind which inspires life with zest."

HOW TO USE THIS BOOK

All of Agatha Christie's writings are discussed in the entries that follow. The book is arranged in alphabetical order throughout, and character names and titles of works are cross-referenced, with additional information indicated in parentheses as needed. The entries for the novels appear under the original British title, but publishing history sections within entries include first publication dates for both British and U.S. editions, as well as alternate titles. Each entry for the novels, plays and short stories contains complete publishing and dramatization history, a list of characters and a plot synopsis. If the work is a mystery, a section entitled "Crime Notes" appears at the end of the entry, in which the means of murder in the work is identified. Care has been taken to list characters according to the spelling of their names in British editions. Therefore, a reader might look for Mr. Sanders and find that he is listed as Mr. Saunders. In approaching the entries, a reader must be aware that Agatha Christie frequently chose names for characters that are very similar to each other. One example is the Comte Armaud De La Roche, who appears in *The Mystery of the Blue Train*, and the Count Armand De La Rochefour in "The Plymouth Express." Another, more rare occurrence is the change of a character's name mid-work, as in "The Strange Case of Sir Arthur Carmichael" which was retitled "The Strange Case of Sir Andrew Carmichael" in its U.S. publication, although the character remained Sir Arthur throughout the body of the story.

The entries provide substantial information regarding character and plot, but solutions to the crimes are carefully concealed from readers, even if this means that the summary of final chapters may suffer from brevity. The fun of reading, even rereading, a work written by Agatha Christie is determining "whodunit," and that possibility for fun is not hampered by this reference work.

A

Aarons, Joseph A longtime friend of Hercule POIROT, he uses his theatrical knowledge to aid the great detective in THE BIG FOUR, MURDER ON THE LINKS and THE MYSTERY OF THE BLUE TRAIN.

Abbot, Mr. (1) An attorney and resident of the village of Wychwood in MURDER IS EASY, he is first suspected of the multiple murders.

Abbot, Mr. (2) The amiable grocer in SAD CYPRESS from whose store Mary CARLISLE purchases the fish pastes that are used to make the sandwiches that may have poisoned Mary GERRARD.

A.B.C. Murders, The Mystery novel.

The title of the novel is derived from *The ABC Rail Guide* to British railways, which contains an alphabetical listing of station stops. The plot centers on finding a killer who murders victims in alphabetical order, starting with a victim in Andover whose initials are A.A. By the time the killer reaches letter "D," Hercule POIROT recognizes that all but one of the murders have been committed as mere deceptions meant to mask the truly significant murder.

The novel is a curious mix of Captain HASTINGS's first-person narrative and eight chapters that are identified as "Not from Captain Hastings' Personal Narrative," which, as he tells the reader in the Foreword, contain discussions of incidents and scenes at which he was not present.

PUBLISHING AND DRAMATIZATION HISTORY

The novel was first published in 1936 by William Collins Sons and Co., Ltd., in London and by Dodd, Mead and Company in New York.

The novel was made into a 1966 film named THE ALPHABET MURDERS, starring Tony Randall as Hercule Poirot. In 1992, the novel was adapted for television by London Weekend Television in Britain; the adaptation was shown on the Public Broadcasting Service in the United States.

CHARACTERS

Colonel ANDERSON, Alice ASCHER, Franz ASCHER, Mr. BALL, Mr. BARNARD, Mrs. BARNARD, Elizabeth BARNARD, Megan BARNARD, Nurse CAPSTICK, Sir Carmichael CLARKE, Lady Charlotte CLARKE, Franklin CLARKE, Inspector CROME, Alexander Bonaparte CUST, DEVERIL, Roger Emmanuel DOWNES, Mary DROWER, George EARLSFIELD, Donald FRASER, Thora GREY, Tom HARTIGAN, Captain Arthur HASTINGS, Milly HIGLEY, Commissionaire JAMESON, Chief Inspector JAPP, Dr. KERR, Sir LIONEL, Hercule Poirot, Dr. THOMPSON

PLOT SYNOPSIS
Chapter 1
The novel opens with a meeting between Captain Hastings and Hercule Poirot after years apart during which Hastings has been living with his wife on a ranch in Argentina. As they reminisce about previous cases, Poirot takes out a letter signed by "A.B.C." that challenges him to solve a murder yet to be committed in Andover.

Chapter 2
Not part of Hastings' narrative, this one-page chapter simply introduces Mr. Alexander Bonaparte Cust and provides a physical description of him.

Chapters 3–7
Inspector Japp visits Poirot on the intended day of the first murder and tells him that the message must have been a hoax, because Scotland Yard has received no word from Andover of a murder. Within hours, they learn that a shopkeeper named Alice Ascher has

been murdered, and an opened *ABC Rail Guide* is found face down on the store counter. The police suspect the victim's abusive, alcoholic husband, but Poirot knows that the man was incapable of writing the taunting message. After consulting police, Poirot and Hastings question Mrs. Ascher's niece and neighbors but learn nothing of importance from them.

Chapters 8–13

The first A.B.C. murder produces no clues, and the court returns a verdict of "murder by some person or persons unknown." A month after the first letter, Poirot receives a second taunting letter, which warns that the second murder will be committed in Bex-on-the-Sea. A young woman named Elizabeth "Betty" Barnard of that village is strangled, and an open A.B.C. guide is found under the body. While questioning family and acquaintances of the dead woman, Poirot learns that she was flirtatious and had a jealous fiancé. No clues to the killer are uncovered.

Chapters 14–15

The third letter, apparently misdelivered, arrives on the day of the murder, too late for Poirot to direct police to the intended site of Churston until the murder of Sir Carmichael Clarke has already occurred. Once again, the body is found with an open A.B.C. guide face downwards nearby. Interviews with the victim's brother, secretary and butler yield no clues.

Chapter 16

Not part of Hastings' narrative, this chapter provides a further look at the life of the insignificant-appearing Mr. Cust, who becomes very agitated when reading news reports of the third murder.

Chapters 17–20

As the newspapers sensationalize the murders, Poirot considers the case, and Hastings criticizes him for physical inaction. Relatives of the victims contact the detective, to form a "Special Legion" to pool information and to uncover seemingly insignificant clues. Poirot meets with the fatally ill widow of the third victim, and Lady Clarke provides a vital clue about the stranger at the door on the day of the murder.

Chapter 21

The fourth letter arrives and warns Poirot that the next murder will take place in Doncaster on the day of a heavily attended horse race, the St. Leger. As the Special Legion convenes, Poirot learns that all three murders were preceded by the appearance of a salesman selling silk stockings door-to-door.

Chapter 22

Not part of Hastings' narrative, the chapter identifies Mr. Cust's suspicious behavior and the fact that he has been present at the three previous murder sites. He is now headed toward the fourth site, and his landlady's daughter and her boyfriend have linked him with the murders.

Chapter 23

Poirot and the Special Legion meet in Doncaster and patrol the town in the hope of identifying the murderer.

Chapters 24–26

Not part of Hastings' narrative, the chapters describe the murder that occurs in a Doncaster movie theater and the involvement of Mr. Cust. The victim is stabbed while seated in the theater and an open railway guide is left on the body. Mr. Cust emerges from the same theater and goes to his hotel room at the Black Swan, where he is shocked to find blood on his cuff and a bloody knife in his jacket pocket.

Chapters 27–29

Scotland Yard inspectors take statements from members of the theater audience and learn that the killer made a mistake in choosing the fourth victim. The murdered man is George Earlsfield, rather than the man named Downes who sat only two seats from him. The authorities obtain an important lead when a maid from the Black Swan reports the bloody water in Cust's room.

Chapters 30–35

A.B. Cust turns himself in to the police and is committed for trial, but Poirot remains uncertain that Cust is the killer. To test his doubts, he convenes a meeting of the Special Legion, then later meets with Cust in an interview that confirms Poirot's doubts. After meeting once again with the Special Legion and questioning all members, Poirot identifies the real murderer.

CRIME NOTES

Chapter 3 of this novel contains the plot for CARDS ON THE TABLE, in which Poirot describes the type of crime he would order, if given the choice.

The means of murder in *The A.B.C. Murders* include bludgeoning, strangulation with a belt and stabbing with a long, thin knife.

Abdul   Described as understanding nothing, he is a servant in APPOINTMENT WITH DEATH who discovers Mrs. BOYNTON's body.

Abercrombie, Colonel   A pompous and annoying former military man who is also a patient of the murdered dentist in ONE, TWO, BUCKLE MY SHOE, he aggravates Hercule POIROT to the point that the detective considers him one of those "Englishmen who are altogether so unpleasing and ridiculous that they should have been put out of their misery at birth."

Abernethie, Helen   Childless while married, she has an affair after being widowed and hides the existence of the son born of this relationship to protect her image with her late husband's family in AFTER THE FUNERAL. Her sharp-eyed observance of unusual behavior by another character results in her death; she is hit on the head with a blunt object while making a telephone call to Mr. ENTWHISTLE.

Abernethie, Maude   Officious and physically imposing, she seems to prefer that her husband Timothy remain an invalid as she retains control in her marriage in AFTER THE FUNERAL. She accepts with reluctance the need to employ Miss GILCHRIST as a cook and housekeeper after breaking her ankle.

Abernethie, Timothy   A bitter, spiteful man in AFTER THE FUNERAL who feels that, as sole remaining brother, he is the rightful heir of both his late brother's extensive estate and title as head of the family. He willingly plays the role of a chronic invalid to whom his wife Maude must minister completely. He resents the involvement of Hercule POIROT in the family murders.

Absent in the Spring   Non-mystery novel.

The author claimed in her autobiography that she wrote the third of her non-mystery novels under the pseudonym of Mary WESTMACOTT during a feverishly paced three days. The title is taken from the first line of "Sonnet 98" by William Shakespeare: "From you have I been absent in the Spring." The novel is a psychological exploration of a middle-aged woman's identity crisis, which occurs during a brief period in which she is isolated from both family and friends in Mesopotamia. Given time for introspection, Joan SCUDAMORE realizes that her life has been one of self-deception, and she returns home with a resolve to be more forthright in her relationships.

PUBLISHING AND DRAMATIZATION HISTORY
Absent in the Spring was first published in 1944 by William Collins Sons and Co., Ltd., in London and by Farrar and Rinehart in New York.

The novel has not been adapted for either stage or screen.

CHARACTERS
Michael CALLAWAY, Rupert CARGILL, Miss GILBEY, Blanche HAGGARD, Princess Sasha HOHENBACH SALM, Myrna RANDOLPH, Major REID, Joan Scudamore, Rodney SCUDAMORE, Tony SCUDAMORE, Captain Charles SHERSTON, Leslie SHERSTON, Barbara WRAY, William WRAY

PLOT SYNOPSIS
Chapters 1–4
Prior to returning by train to England after visiting her daughter in Iraq, Joan Scudamore meets a former schoolmate from St. Anne's School, Blanche Haggard, whose present coarse appearance and rootless lifestyle make Joan uncomfortable. Blanche makes seemingly careless comments about unhappiness and scandal in the marriage of Joan's daughter and hints that Joan's husband has had an affair. The remarks unsettle Joan, but she pushes them aside and thanks God silently that she has not deteriorated as Blanche has.

When flooded train tracks strand Joan for a few days in a travelers' rest house at Tell Abu Hamid, near the Turkish border, she is essentially cut off from outside communication. Boredom forces her to review her life, and she recalls the many ways in which she has imposed her will on her husband and children over the years. She also recalls how relieved her husband had appeared to be to see her off at the station.

Chapters 5–8
Joan learns that the original delay has been extended, and her self-examination continues, revealing that she has no intimate memories of her children or of her husband. She can recall only household details,

her children's clothes and the substance of arguments. Through her condescending mind run other memories of her perfect control over both family and servants, which she contrasts with the inabilities of other, less efficient women.

She realizes that she has established no emotional connection with her family and that she has lived her life on the basis of "duty" and compelled others also to do so.

Chapters 9–12
After four days in the rest house, Joan becomes frantic because of her memories and confronts her new awareness that she has been pretentious and self-righteous. Overwhelmed by the fear that she is truly alone, she berates herself that she has failed to be a loving and caring wife and mother despite her carefully created facade. As the train takes her back to England, she seems to have lost her smugness and resolves to begin a new life with her husband. The resolve is short-lived and, once home, Joan resumes her bossy ways and chooses to deny her revelations.

"Accident"   Mystery short story.
The story revolves around the classic situation of a recently purchased life insurance policy and spousal greed.

PUBLISHING AND DRAMATIZATION HISTORY
The short story was first published in 1934 by William Collins Sons and Co., Ltd., in London in the short story collection, THE LISTERDALE MYSTERY (1), and in 1948 by Dodd, Mead and Company in New York in WITNESS FOR THE PROSECUTION AND OTHER STORIES.

The story has not been adapted for stage or screen.

CHARACTERS
Mrs. ANTHONY, Inspector EVANS, Captain HAYDOCK, George MERROWDENE, Margaret MERROWDENE

PLOT SYNOPSIS
Former Central Intelligence Division inspector Evans visits his friend Captain Haydock and meets Haydock's neighbors, Mr. and Mrs. Merrowdene. When introduced, Evans thinks that there is something vaguely familiar about Mrs. Merrowdene, but he fails

to remember what it is until he learns that her husband recently took out a very large insurance policy. At that point, he recalls seeing her photograph in the newspaper several years earlier, when she was acquitted of poisoning her first husband, who had just taken out a large insurance policy. He accepts an invitation to tea but finds that he is too late to prevent the crime.

CRIME NOTES
Although reference is made to arsenic in the story, cyanide administered in tea is the means of murder.

Ackroyd, Mrs. Cecil   The impoverished widow of the black sheep of the Ackroyd family in THE MURDER OF ROGER ACKROYD, she moved with her daughter Flora ACKROYD from Canada to England to live on the charity of her generous brother-in-law. Despite her lack of money, she acts the role of the fine lady and aims for her daughter to marry well.

Ackroyd, Flora   The niece of the title character in THE MURDER OF ROGER ACKROYD, she is a beautiful young woman engaged to Hector BLUNT, who inherits twenty thousand pounds when her uncle is murdered.

Ackroyd, Roger   A man who plays the role of the country squire in THE MURDER OF ROGER ACKROYD, although he acquired a fortune as a manufacturer. He is an old acquaintance of Hercule POIROT. Shortly before his murder, he becomes secretly engaged to Mrs. Ferrars, which adds to the mysteries to be solved in the novel.

Adams, Dr.   A physician in "THE CORNISH MYSTERY" who appears to be the typical country doctor; he becomes irate when his approach to the care of a patient is questioned.

Adams, Carlotta   An excellent impersonator, the actress loses her life in LORD EDGWARE DIES because she is too perfect a mimic. She eagerly accepts ten thousand dollars from Jane WILKINSON to impersonate her at a dinner party, after which she is found poisoned.

Addison, Thomas   A man of action who continues to enjoy outdoor sports despite being color-blind and plagued by the gout, he is a childhood friend of Mr. SATTERTHWAITE and the father of Lily GILLIAT and Maria HORTON in "THE HARLEQUIN TEA SET."

Adventure Inc.   See DIE ABENTEURER G.M.B.H.

"Adventure of Johnnie Waverly, The"   Mystery short story.

The plot centers on the kidnapping of a child and examines the family dynamics of a couple forced to pay ransom.

PUBLISHING AND DRAMATIZATION HISTORY
The story was not published in England, but Dodd, Mead and Company in New York published it in 1950 in the short story collection, THREE BLIND MICE AND OTHER STORIES.

The story was adapted for television in 1989 by London Weekend Television in England and was also shown on the Public Broadcasting Service in the U.S.

CHARACTERS
Miss COLLINS, Captain Arthur HASTINGS, Hercule POIROT, TREDWELL, Ada WAVERLY, Johnnie WAVERLY, Marcus WAVERLY, Miss Jessie WITHERS

PLOT SYNOPSIS
The story places a twist on the usual kidnapping plot. Mr. Waverly has received ransom notes which threaten the kidnapping of his three-year-old son Johnnie unless a demand for fifty thousand pounds is met. Waverly waits until the kidnapping occurs, then contacts Hercule Poirot. The detective interviews the child's nurse and other staff, but his interest is really piqued when he learns that Mrs. Waverly holds the purse strings in the household.

CRIME NOTES
A bottle of chloroform and soaked wool are left behind when the child disappears to suggest their use in the attack.

This short story marks the third use of the name Tredwell for a butler.

"Adventure of the Cheap Flat, The"   Mystery short story.

An international case of stolen submarine plans is solved when Hercule POIROT investigates, simply out of curiosity, the extremely low rent for a flat.

PUBLISHING AND DRAMATIZATION HISTORY
The story appeared in Agatha Christie's first short story collection, POIROT INVESTIGATES, published in 1924 by John Lane, Publishers in London and in 1925 by Dodd, Mead and Company in New York.

The story was adapted for television in 1990 by London Weekend Television Productions in England and was also shown on the Public Broadcasting Service in the U.S.

CHARACTERS
Mr. BURT, Elsa HARDT, Captain HASTINGS, Inspector JAPP, Gerald PARKER, Hercule POIROT, Stella ROBINSON

PLOT SYNOPSIS
Hercule Poirot attends a party and overhears a young couple telling friends of the low rent—80 pounds annually instead of the usual 350 pounds—they are paying for a flat in an expensive apartment building. Intrigued, he decides to investigate and draws Hastings into the case by leasing an apartment in the same building for them. With more information, the detectives realize that the case has international implications as they unmask a German spy with plans to sell stolen American naval plans.

"Adventure of the Christmas Pudding, The"   Mystery short story.

This tale centers on the theft and recovery of an extremely valuable ruby belonging to the prince of a Far Eastern kingdom.

PUBLISHING AND DRAMATIZATION HISTORY
The story appeared as the only original short story in the mystery short story collection THE ADVENTURE OF THE CHRISTMAS PUDDING AND A SELECTION OF ENTREES, published in 1960 by William Collins Sons and Co., Ltd., in London with no American publication. It has also been titled "THE THEFT OF THE ROYAL RUBY."

The story was adapted for television in 1991 by London Weekend Television in Britian and was also

Hercule Poirot (David Suchet) must decide if a crime has actually occurred in "The Adventure of Johnnie Waverly." (Photo courtesy of London Weekend Television)

shown on the Public Broadcasting Service in the U.S. under the title "The Theft of the Royal Ruby."

CHARACTERS

Prince ALI, Annie BATES, Mr. JESMOND, Colin LACEY, Em LACEY, Colonel Horace LACEY, Sarah LACEY, Mr. Desmond LEE-WORTLEY, Hercule POIROT

PLOT SYNOPSIS

A charming young woman, part of a gang of thieves, spends an evening in London with the son of a powerful Middle Eastern ruler, then disappears with a priceless royal ruby. Concerned for the international repercussions of the theft, a government official contacts Hercule Poirot, who manages to identify the young woman and to obtain an invitation to a weekend Christmas party where she is expected.

The famous detective frightens the young woman, who hides the ruby in the pudding prepared for New Year's Day but which is unexpectedly served early. Discreetly, Poirot substitutes a replica of the gem and tricks the thieves into leaving the country.

Adventure of the Christmas Pudding and a Selection of Entrees, The   Mystery short story collection.

The book contains only two new stories among the six in the collection, with a foreword provided by the author. In the foreword, the author reminisces about Christmas celebrations of her youth and relates the stories to the various courses of a holiday dinner.

PUBLISHING AND DRAMATIZATION HISTORY

The Adventure of the Christmas Pudding and a Selection of Entrees was published in 1960 by William Collins Sons and Co., Ltd., in London, but it has not been published intact in the United States. "THE MYSTERY OF THE SPANISH CHEST" and "THE DREAM" were published in THE REGATTA MYSTERY AND OTHER STORIES, "THE UNDER DOG" appeared in THE UNDER DOG AND OTHER STORIES and "FOUR-AND-TWENTY BLACKBIRDS" was published in THREE BLIND MICE AND OTHER STORIES.

"The Adventure of the Christmas Pudding" and "The Mystery of the Spanish Chest" were adapted for television in 1991 by London Weekend Television in England, and were also shown on the Public Broadcasting Service in the U.S. Similarly adapted by the same company were "The Dream" (1989), "Four-and-Twenty Blackbirds" (1989) and "The Under Dog" (1993).

TITLES IN THE COLLECTION

The Adventure of the Christmas Pudding and a Selection of Entrees contains the following stories: "The Adventure of the Christmas Pudding," "The Mystery of the Spanish Chest," "The Under Dog," "Four-and-Twenty Blackbirds," "The Dream" and "Greenshaw's Folly."

"Adventure of the Clapham Cook, The"
Mystery short story.

In this story, Hercule POIROT surprises Captain HASTINGS when he agrees to search for a missing cook.

PUBLISHING AND DRAMATIZATION HISTORY

The story appeared in the short story collection, THE UNDER DOG AND OTHER STORIES, published in 1951 by William Collins Sons and Co., Ltd., in London, and was reprinted by the publisher in the 1974 short story collection, POIROT'S EARLY CASES.

Captain Hastings (Hugh Fraser) and Hercule Poirot (David Suchet) look for a missing domestic in "The Adventure of the Clapham Cook." (Photo courtesy of London Weekend Television)

The story was adapted for television in 1989 by London Weekend Television Productions in England, and was also shown on the Public Broadcasting Service in the U.S.

CHARACTERS
ANNIE, Eliza DUNN, Captain Hastings, Hercule Poirot, Mr. SIMPSON, Mr. and Mrs. TODD

PLOT SYNOPSIS
Mrs. Todd pleads with Poirot to help her find her missing cook, a case which he at first refuses. Once involved, however, he recognizes that the case may well be linked to the disappearance of fifty thousand pounds from a bank and a missing bank employee whose coworker is a lodger in the Todds' home.

"Adventure of the Egyptian Tomb, The"
Mystery short story.

The deaths which Hercule POIROT is retained to investigate may be due to an ancient Egyptian curse, or they might be murder.

PUBLISHING AND DRAMATIZATION
HISTORY
The story appeared in the short story collection, POIROT INVESTIGATES, published in 1924 by John Lane, Publishers, in London, and in 1925 by Dodd, Mead and Company in New York.

The story was adapted for television in 1993 by London Weekend Television in Britain, and was also shown on the Public Broadcasting Service in the U.S.

CHARACTERS
Dr. AMES, Mr. BLEIBNER, Rupert BLEIBNER, Mr. HARPER, Captain HASTINGS, Hercule Poirot, Mr.

SCHNEIDER, Lady WILLARD, Sir Guy WILLARD, Sir John WILLARD

PLOT SYNOPSIS
Within a month of uncovering the tomb of King Men-her-Ra near Cairo, the head archaeologist and a wealthy supporter die of natural causes and a third member of the team shoots himself. Poirot and Hastings are called in to investigate, and they arrive in Cairo in time to learn that the Metropolitan Museum curator has died from tetanus. All clues point to a curse, but Poirot suspects a human killer.

"Adventure of the Italian Nobleman, The"
Mystery short story.

Hercule POIROT must discover who made a mysterious phone call before he can discover the identity of the murderer in this story.

PUBLISHING AND DRAMATIZATION
HISTORY
The story appeared in the short story collection, POIROT INVESTIGATES, published in 1924 by John Lane, Publishers, in London, and in 1925 by Dodd, Mead and Company in New York.

The story was adapted for television in 1993 by London Weekend Television in Britain, and was also shown on the Public Broadcasting Service in the U.S.

CHARACTERS
Signor ASCANIO, Count FOSCATINI, Mr. GRAVES, Captain HASTINGS, Dr. HAWKER, Hercule Poirot

PLOT SYNOPSIS
All thoughts of a quiet evening with friends vanish when Poirot's guest Dr. Hawker receives a frantic call from his housekeeper. She claims that a man who gave his name as Count Foscatini had just called to tell the doctor that he had just been killed. When Poirot and the others arrive at Foscatini's home, they find him dead and there is evidence that three people have been there recently.

"Adventure of the Sinister Stranger, The"
Mystery short story.

The plot centers on the arrival of a letter which may contain information of international importance. The story is another in a series starring Tommy and Tuppence BERESFORD, in which the author parodies popular fictional detectives of her day.

PUBLISHING AND DRAMATIZATION
HISTORY
The story appeared in the short story collection, PARTNERS IN CRIME, published in 1929 by William Collins Sons and Co., Ltd., in London, and by Dodd, Mead and Company in New York.

The story has not been adapted for stage or screen.

CHARACTERS
Albert BATT, Tommy Beresford, Tuppence Beresford, Dr. Charles BOWER, COGGINS, Detective Inspector DYMCHURCH, Inspector MARRIOT

PLOT SYNOPSIS
Tommy and Tuppence Beresford wait anxiously for a letter from Russia which might contain a long-expected clue hidden under the stamp. The letter arrives at almost the same time that a foreign stranger, Dr. Bower, arrives to ask the Beresfords for help in protecting his valuable research on alkaloids. As attempts are made to wrest the letter from the Beresfords before they can look under the stamp, they realize that the letter is important to several groups.

CRIME NOTES
In this story, Tommy and Tuppence assume the mannerisms and relationship of the Okewood brothers, Desmond and Francis, detectives created by writer Valentine Williams (1883–1946), who wrote under the pseudonym Douglas Valentine. The typical Okewood scenario consisted of Desmond becoming embroiled in a difficult situation and being rescued by Francis.

"Adventure of 'The Western Star,' The"
Mystery short story.

The adventure concerns a diamond that has quite a history, and more than one identity.

PUBLISHING AND DRAMATIZATION
HISTORY
The story appeared in the short story collection, POIROT INVESTIGATES, published in 1924 by John Lane, Publishers, in London, and in 1925 by Dodd, Mead and Company in New York.

The impetuous gift of a priceless diamond by an actress (Caroline Goodall) to her lover leads to near-disaster in "The Adventure of the 'Western Star.'" (Photo courtesy of London Weekend Television)

The story was adapted for television in 1990 by London Weekend Television in Britain, and was also shown on the Public Broadcasting Service in the U.S.

CHARACTERS
Captain Arthur HASTINGS, Mary MARVELL, Hercule POIROT, Gregory ROLF, Lady YARDLY, Lord YARDLY

PLOT SYNOPSIS
Movie star Mary Marvell consults with Hercule Poirot after receiving threatening letters that warn her to return her diamond "The Western Star" to its origins. At the same time, Lady Yardly is also highly interested in the diamond, because it is the same gem that she once owned when it was called "The Star of the East." She had an affair and paid off a blackmailer with the diamond, replacing it with a replica. Now her husband wants to sell the stone, which he thinks is the real diamond.

"Affair at the Bungalow, The" Mystery short story.
This is the puzzling case of a young playwright who makes an appointment with a well-known actress to discuss his play and who is later charged with robbery after meeting an imposter.

PUBLISHING AND DRAMATIZATION HISTORY
The story appeared in the short story collection, THE THIRTEEN PROBLEMS, published in 1932 by William Collins Sons and Co., Ltd., in London and in 1933 by Dodd, Mead and Company in New York.
The story has not been adapted for stage or screen.

CHARACTERS
Dolly BANTRY, Sir Herman COHEN, Mr. Leslie FAULKENER, Netta GREEN, Jane HELIER, Miss Mary KERR, Miss Jane MARPLE

PLOT SYNOPSIS
At a meeting of the impromptu crime-solving club, the Tuesday Night Club, actress Jane Helier relates her adventure of having been impersonated in an incident which landed a young playwright in jail on a robbery charge. The young man claimed that a woman posing as her had met him in a bungalow, presumably to talk, then gave him a drink, after which he remembered nothing until awakening with a splitting headache by the side of a road. Police arrested the man on the charge of robbing the bungalow, and no clues exist to exonerate him.

"Affair at the Victory Ball, The" Mystery short story.
A well-publicized society murder is the center of this mystery, in which a young woman is found dead of a cocaine overdose on the same night that her aristocratic fiancé is found stabbed to death.

PUBLISHING AND DRAMATIZATION HISTORY
The story appeared in the short story collection, THE UNDER DOG AND OTHER STORIES, published in 1951 by Dodd, Mead and Company in New York.
The story was adapted for television in 1991 by London Weekend Television in England, and was shown on the Public Broadcasting Service in the U.S.

CHARACTERS
The Honourable Eustace BELTANE, Miss Coco COURTENAY, Lord CRONSHAW, Mrs. DAVIDSON, Mr. Chris DAVIDSON, Captain HASTINGS, Inspector JAPP, Mrs. MALLABY, Hercule POIROT

Tommy and Tuppence Beresford (James Warwick and Francesca Annis) try to solve the dilemma in "The Affair of the Pink Pearl."   (Photo courtesy of London Weekend Television)

PLOT SYNOPSIS

The murder of a young aristocrat and the apparent suicide by drug overdose of his fiancée on the same evening creates a difficult case, and Inspector Japp calls in Hercule Poirot to assist in the investigation. The detective learns that the victims had attended a ball that evening where they and their friends had dressed as figures from *commedia dell'arte*, and one individual had switched costumes during the evening.

CRIME NOTES

Two murders occur in the story. The first is the result of a stab wound and the second is an overdose of cocaine.

"Affair of the Pink Pearl, The"   Mystery short story.

The disappearance of a valuable pink pearl presumed stolen by a houseguest leads the host to contact the International Detective Agency for help. This story is another in the series of Tommy and Tuppence BERESFORD adventures in which the author parodies popular fictional detectives of her day.

PUBLISHING AND DRAMATIZATION HISTORY

The story appeared in the short story collection, PARTNERS IN CRIME, published in 1929 by William Collins Sons and Co., Ltd., in London, and by Dodd, Mead and Company in New York.

The story was adapted for television in 1984 by London Weekend Television Productions in Britain, and was also shown on the Public Broadcasting Service in the U.S.

CHARACTERS

Lady Laura BARTON, Tommy BERESFORD, Tuppence Beresford, Mrs. Hamilton BETTS, Gladys HILL,

Colonel KINGSTON BRUCE, Beatrice KINGSTON BRUCE, Mr. RENNIE

PLOT SYNOPSIS
While staying at the Laurels with the Kingston Bruce family, Mrs. Hamilton Betts discovers that her pink pearl is missing. The concerned hosts recall hearing friends speak of the Beresfords, and they call in the couple to locate the pearl.

CRIME NOTES
In this story, Tommy Beresford imitates the investigative style of the well-known fictional detective, Dr. John Evelyn Thorndyke, a medical detective known for his sharp intelligence, extensive learning and handsome appearance who was created by R. Austin Freeman (1862–1943).

Afflick, Dorothy Socially prominent and reserved, she meets her husband, Jackie AFFLICK, on a cruise in SLEEPING MURDER, and marries despite the great disparity in their social levels and personalities.

Afflick, Jackie High-spirited and coarse in manner, he is the proprietor of "Afflick's Daffodil Coaches," a coach tour service which features bright yellow buses, in SLEEPING MURDER. Although he dresses like a gambler in loud-patterned suits, he marries a socially prominent woman.

After the Funeral Mystery novel.

The novel is dedicated to the author's nephew, James Watt III, "in memory of happy days at Abney." The plot centers on the wealthy Abernethie family, whose gathering after the funeral of the eldest brother sparks talk of murder.

PUBLISHING AND DRAMATIZATION
HISTORY
The novel was published in 1953 by Collins in London and under the title *Funerals Are Fatal* by Dodd, Mead and Company in New York.

The novel was loosely adapted into the 1963 MGM film *Murder at the Gallop*, in which Hercule POIROT was replaced by Miss MARPLE, played by Margaret RUTHERFORD.

CHARACTERS
Helen ABERNETHIE, Maude ABERNETHIE, Timothy ABERNETHIE, Gregory BANKS, Susan BANKS, George CROSSFIELD, Mr. ENTWHISTLE, Miss GILCHRIST, Mr. GOBY, Alexander GUTHRIE, LANSCOMBE, Cora LANSQUENET, Dr. LARRABY, Inspector MORTON, Hercule Poirot, Michael SHANE, Rosamund SHANE

PLOT SYNOPSIS
Chapters 1–3
The Abernethie family gathers for dinner and the reading of the will after the funeral of the eldest brother, Richard, master of Enderby Hall. The arrangements are determined and Richard's sister Cora thoughtlessly blurts out her impression that Richard had been murdered "from what he said." The family hushes Cora, but family solicitor Mr. Entwhistle is disturbed by the remark, although he knew that Richard was ill.

Chapters 4–6
After a sleepless night, Mr. Entwhistle receives a call from a partner in his firm and learns that Cora has been murdered. Miss Gilchrist, her companion, tells him that Cora was killed with a hatchet during a robbery. He also learns that Richard had visited Cora three weeks before his death. When Mr. Entwhistle speaks with the other family members, their concerns are less with their murdered sister than with how her share of the estate will be divided. Timothy is especially adamant that Cora's money should be his, and he adds that Richard's entire estate should also have been his.

Chapters 7–8
The solicitor consults Hercule Poirot, giving him the details of the Abernethie case. The detective asks what each of the family members claims to have been doing when Cora was murdered, and Mr. Entwhistle responds. The solicitor then meets with Dr. Larraby to learn about Richard's medication. He also questions the butler, who tells him that Richard had visited both Tim and Cora not long before his death.

Chapters 9–11
Susan Banks visits Cora's cottage to sort through her possessions with the help of Miss Gilchrist. While she is there, a package containing a piece of wedding cake from "John and Mary" arrives. Miss Gilchrist does not know the senders, but eats some of the cake and later suffers from arsenic poisoning. When she has recovered, Miss Gilchrist is given a position in the home of Timothy and Maude Abernethie.

Costumes are in order in "The Affair at the Victory Ball." (Photo courtesy of London Weekend Television)

Chapters 12–14
Poirot consults with the mysterious Mr. Goby regarding the weak alibis of the Abernethie family members, most of whom had the opportunity to have killed Cora. Poirot also confers with Inspector Morton and interviews the Enderby Hall staff. He plans to gather the family.

Chapters 15–17
The family receives the call to gather and, for various reasons, all decide to accept. Several family members wonder aloud if Miss Gilchrist knows who killed Cora.

Chapters 18–21
The family gathers at Enderby Hall, and they are introduced to Poirot, who masquerades as M. Pontar, a representative of U.N.A.R.C.O., an anagram which no one questions. He claims to be bidding on the house. Unfortunately for him, Rosamund recognizes him and reveals his true identity. Soon after, Helen claims to remember something about the day of Richard's wake, but she is hit over the head and hospitalized before she can call Mr. Entwhistle.

Chapters 22–24
Once again, Poirot calls a family meeting. Miss Gilchrist claims to have overheard Richard tell Cora that he feared for his life. The group is startled when Gregory insists that he murdered Richard, and Susan contradicts him and tells the group that they were both in London when Richard died. Other secrets emerge, but no killer. Poirot finally reveals that they had been misled and that Richard had not been murdered, but that Cora's murderer had been present after the funeral and fooled them all. With his usual sleight of hand, the detective produces not only the murderer but evidence and a logical explanation.

CRIME NOTES
The sole murder in this novel is the result of several blows to the head with a hatchet.

Agatha   Film released in 1979 by Warner Brothers Studios.

The movie is based on Kathleen Tynan's 1978 novel of the same name.

CAST
The cast includes: Alan Badel, Tony Britton, Timothy Dalton, Dustin Hoffman, Helen Morse, Vanessa Redgrave and Timothy West.

PLOT SYNOPSIS
The film purports to explain Agatha Christie's mysterious ten-day disappearance in 1926, which occurred after the death of her mother and her first husband's announcement that he was leaving her for another woman. The film is based on the newspaper reports of the period. Agatha Christie never provided the full story behind the disappearance, any discussion of which she excluded from her posthumously published AN AUTOBIOGRAPHY.

Vanessa Redgrave, in the title role, plays the distraught author who registers at a Harrogate hotel, using the last name of her husband's lover, as did the author. The movie contains a fictional speculation that postulates a suicide attempt by Christie and a brief romantic encounter with an equally fictitious American newspaperman, played by Dustin Hoffman.

CHANGES FROM THE ORIGINAL TEXT
The film retains the plot, characters and setting of the original book.

PRODUCTION NOTES
The period is accurately recreated through carefully stylized costuming and elaborate indoor sets, which reflect the opulence of the resort to which the main characters retreat. Because neither Agatha Christie nor her family ever spoke publicly about the incident, the film can only create an imaginary explanation of the real-life disappearance.

(See also DISAPPEARANCE OF AGATHA CHRISTIE.)

Agrodopolous, Mr.   An old friend of Aristide LEONIDES, the murder victim in CROOKED HOUSE, who is entrusted with a copy of Aristide's final will, which is to be delivered after Aristide's death.

Akhnaton   Non-mystery play.

Written in the same period as DEATH ON THE NILE (2), *Akhnaton* is a dramatization of the Pharaoh AKH-NATON's efforts to create a peaceful, monotheistic Egypt that would worship Aton, the Sun God. The play is set in Egypt from 1375 to 1358 B.C.

THEATRICAL AND PUBLISHING HISTORY
Akhnaton was written in 1937, but the play was not published until 1973, by William Collins Sons and Co., Ltd., in London, and by Dodd, Mead and Co., in New York.

The play has not been produced.

CAST (IN ORDER OF APPEARANCE)
A Woman, A Man, Second Woman, Second Man, Old Woman, Soldier of the Guard, MERIPTAH, Envoy of the King of Mitanni, High Priest, HOREMHEB, Herald, Queen TYI, Akhnaton, Royal Scribe, Nubian Servant, AY, NEFERTITI, NEZZEMUT, PARA, BEK, PTAHMOSE, TUTANKHATON, Captain of Soldiers, Peasant Men and Women, Soldiers, Guards, Young Artists

PLOT SYNOPSIS
Act 1
The act spans three years, from Akhnaton's rise to power to his building of the City of the Horizon. A crowd waits for news of the ailing King Amenhotep, as the High Priest tells Horemheb his fears for Egypt should Amenhotep die. Queen Tyi will rule jointly with Akhnaton, whom the High Priest believes to be mentally unbalanced. Horemheb and Akhnaton meet and vow to remain steadfast friends. Amenhotep dies and Akhnaton becomes ruler.

Three years later, Akhnaton accuses his mother of usurping his power, and decides to rule alone. The queen tries to enlist the aid of Akhnaton's wife, Nefertiti, but she refuses.

A month later, Akhnaton begins building the City of the Horizon, a site dedicated to Aton, where he and Nefertiti will be buried after death.

Act 2
Eight years pass, during which the City of the Horizon is completed. As Lord Governor, Horemheb rules Lower Egypt with an iron hand, a contrast to Akhnaton's lax rule. The followers of Amon, with the growing support of the increasingly dissatisfied populace, plot with the priests to end Akhnaton's rule.

Nefertiti is ashamed and bitter that she has not given birth to a son, but Akhnaton comforts her by telling her that their daughters will marry good men who will rule. One of these men, Tutankhaton, listens with admiration as Horemheb discusses techniques of leadership. Nezzemut, Nefertiti's sister, pretends interest in Horemheb's exploits, and attempts to seduce him. When Queen Tyi arrives, ill and near death, she asks Horemheb to be an ally to Akhnaton. As Tyi dies, she warns Akhnaton to stop dreaming and to begin ruling.

One year later, Egypt is besieged, and Akhnaton refuses to fight back. Horemheb advises Akhnaton to take action, but he refuses, and orders the name of Amon erased from all monuments, and even from his father's grave, despite Horemheb's cautions against such sacrilege.

Act 3
Three years later, Akhnaton has retreated even further into his world of dreams and religious visions. He refuses Horemheb's request for troops to defend Egypt, and insists on negotiation. Nezzemut persuades Horemheb that Akhnaton is mad, and tells him that he will have to choose between friendship and his country.

After surveying the ruin into which Egypt has fallen and after learning that two more cities have fallen to enemies, Horemheb agrees to help depose Akhnaton. At the home of the High Priest of Amon, Horemheb agrees that Akhnaton must be replaced by Tutankhaton, who will be known as Tutankhamen, and whom Horemheb will join as adviser. After giving assurances to Horemheb that Akhnaton will be permitted to live in the City of the Horizon, the High Priest and Nezzemut plot to end the life of the already-ill king.

Horemheb announces to Akhnaton that he will no longer allow Egypt to be ravaged without retaliating. Nezzemut gives Nefertiti a strong poison to administer unknowingly to Akhnaton. When the horrified Nefertiti learns what she has been tricked into doing, she also drinks the poison.

Epilogue
Nezzemut has managed to do away with Tutankhamen, and now Horemheb reigns as King and she as Queen.

Akibombo, Mr.   One of the many students who lived in Mrs. NICOLETIS' youth hostel, this exceedingly civilized West African student finds English food as upsetting to his stomach as English customs and behavior are upsetting to his mind in HICKORY DICKORY DOCK.

Albert   An auto mechanic in THE HOLLOW, he keeps Henrietta SAVERNAKE's car running in top condition.

Alcadi   A young, handsome and competent airplane pilot in DESTINATION UNKNOWN who holds responsibility for flying the passengers safely to the Brain Trust complex.

Aldin, Mary   While life has forced her into the demeaning role of acting as a paid companion to Lady TRESSILIAN, she is a highly intelligent woman whom her employer describes as having "a really first-class brain" in TOWARDS ZERO.

Aldini, Carlo   He starred as Tommy BERESFORD in the first film adaptation of a Christie novel, THE SECRET ADVERSARY, which was filmed in 1928 as a German-made silent film entitled DIE ABENTEUER G.m.b.H.

Alfred   Recruited by Bundle BRENT to help her learn more about the members of the Seven Dials Club, he is a former footman at Chimneys in THE SEVEN DIALS MYSTERY. Mr. MOSGOROVSKY hired him away from Chimneys by giving Alfred a one-hundred-pound bonus and tripling his salary.

Alfredge, Madame   The sharp-tongued proprietor of a clothing shop in THE HOLLOW, she hires the chic but impoverished Midge HARDCASTLE to draw more socially prominent customers.

Ali, Achmed   An Egyptian student living in Mrs. NICOLETIS' youth hostel in HICKORY DICKORY DOCK, he is unpredictable and aggressive. He also owns a large collection of pornography.

Ali, Prince   When the priceless ruby which he has brought to London to be reset is stolen, this Middle Eastern prince turns to Hercule POIROT to find the gem in "THE THEFT OF THE ROYAL RUBY." His embarrassment is in admitting that a woman whom he met on the journey may be the thief. (See also "ADVENTURE OF THE CHRISTMAS PUDDING, THE.")

Alibi   Film released by Twickenham Film Studios in 1931. The movie is based on the 1926 novel, THE MURDER OF ROGER ACKROYD.

CAST
The cast consists of Austin Trevor as Hercule POIROT, as well as Elizabeth Allan, Franklin Dyall, Claire Greet, Mary Jerrold and J.H. Roberts.

PLOT SYNOPSIS
See THE MURDER OF ROGER ACKROYD.

CHANGES FROM THE ORIGINAL TEXT
The film retains the plot of the original, but makes changes in characters. Hercule Poirot became a slender, clean-shaven sleuth who is more than twenty years younger than his literary image. The character of Caroline Sheppard, the doctor's sister, is omitted from the film and replaced by a younger, more romantic character.

PRODUCTION NOTES
This was the first of three films to star Austin Trevor as Hercule Poirot, as well as the first of many which displeased the author in its many deviations from her original vision.

Alice   Completely devoted to Katherine GREY, she is a housemaid in THE MYSTERY OF THE BLUE TRAIN.

Ali Yusef   A thief and expert in jewels, he is caught stealing artifacts from the Tell Yarimjah expedition in Iraq and arrested in MURDER IN MESOPOTAMIA.

Ali Yusef, Prince, Hereditary Sheik of Ramat
A progressive, twenty-five-year-old political leader married to an English woman, he is assassinated by opponents of his attempts to democratize his sheikdom in CAT AMONG THE PIGEONS.

Allaby, Mr.   Fond of dogs, this widower hires Joyce LAMBERT to be his children's governess after viewing her great affection for her own dog in "NEXT TO A DOG."

Allen, Barbara   Twenty-seven years old and dreamy in appearance, she is engaged to a Member of Parliament, and desperately tries to keep secret that years before she had given birth to a daughter who died in infancy. She dies of a bullet wound in "MURDER IN THE MEWS" (2).

Allenson, Captain Jimmy   Handsome, thirty years of age and popular with women, he is shot while embracing Moira SCOTT in "THE SHADOW ON THE GLASS."

Allerton, Major   Possessed of a superficial charm, he easily attracts women, and almost makes a fatal error by dallying with Judith HASTINGS in CURTAIN, an action which angers her father nearly to the point of murder.

Allerton, Mrs.   A widow who dotes on her son in DEATH ON THE NILE (2), she develops a friendship with Hercule POIROT, and provides him with information regarding the murder on board ship.

Allerton, Tim   He and his widowed mother claim in DEATH ON THE NILE (2) that he is a writer, yet no one has ever seen his work. After being cleared of suspicion, he proposes marriage to Rosalie OTTERBOURNE.

Alloway, Lord   About to become the next Prime Minister of England, he turns to Hercule POIROT for help when an enemy agent blackmails him because of a past scandal in "THE SUBMARINE PLANS."

Alphabet Murders, The   Film released in 1966 by Metro-Goldwyn-Mayer. The movie is based on the 1936 novel, THE A.B.C. MURDERS by Agatha Christie.

CAST
The cast consists of Tony RANDALL as Hercule POIROT and Robert MORLEY as Captain Arthur HASTINGS, as well as Maurice Denham, Anita Ekberg, Clive Morton, Guy Rolfe and James Villiers.

CHANGES FROM THE ORIGINAL TEXT
The adaptation, written by David Pursall and Jack Seddon, added elements of comedy to the original text, partly in the form of slapstick comedy which resulted from incidents involving the accident-prone Hastings/Morley. The basic plot and setting reflect the original work (see A.B.C. MURDERS, THE), but

the characters of Poirot and Hastings border on caricature at times in the film, as their mannerisms are exaggerated.

The title of the novel was changed due to the fear that the public might be reluctant to attend showings of the movie in the chain of ABC cinemas, which were popular in England.

PRODUCTION NOTES
Production on the film was nearly halted when Agatha Christie objected to the first script, which added substantial violence to the story and included a bedroom scene for Poirot. The author only agreed to allow production to continue after both the violence and the love scene were removed from the script, and the original choice for Poirot, hefty comedian Zero Mostel, was replaced by Tony Randall.

Altamount, Lord Edward   A highly respected former State official in PASSENGER TO FRANKFURT, he retains intimate knowledge of English politicians and government officials.

Alton   Tall, fair and extremely handsome, he is a butler in LORD EDGWARE DIES who steals one hundred pounds in francs from his late employer, then disappears.

Alverstroke, Lord   Despite being very old, nearly blind and deaf, the former Lord Chief Justice remains a man to be feared for his adherence to the law in DESTINATION UNKNOWN.

Amalfi   See LEATHERN, SAMUEL.

Amalfi, Maria   See LEATHERN, EVE.

"Ambassador's Boots, The"   Mystery short story.

The plot focuses on a case of mistaken luggage in a switch of kit bags that may or may not have been deliberate. This story is another in the Tommy and Tuppence BERESFORD series, in which the author parodies popular fictional detectives of her day.

PUBLISHING AND DRAMATIZATION HISTORY
The story appeared in the short story collection, PARTNERS IN CRIME, published in 1929 by William

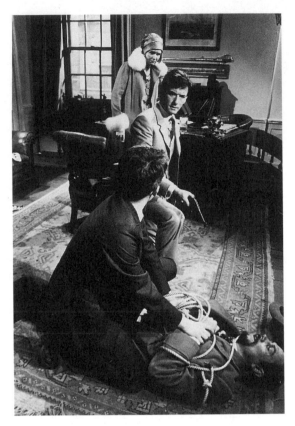

Force is called for when Tommy Beresford (James Warwick) meets resistance in "The Ambassador's Boots." (Photo courtesy of London Weekend Television)

Collins Sons and Co., Ltd., in London and by Dodd, Mead and Co. in New York.

The story was adapted for television in 1984 by London Weekend Television Productions in England, and also shown on the Public Broadcasting Service in the U.S.

CHARACTERS
Albert BATT, Tommy Beresford, Tuppence Beresford, Cicely MARCH, RICHARDS, Ralph WESTERHAM, Randolph WILMOTT

PLOT SYNOPSIS
The United States Ambassador to the Court of St. James contacts the International Detective Agency

for help in locating his kit bag, which apparently was switched by mistake with that of an American senator. After an imposter posing as the senator's valet arrives and exchanges kit bags with him, the ambassador becomes suspicious. Tommy uses the cover name of Theodore Blunt, founder of the International Detective Agency, and agrees to take the case.

CRIME NOTES
In this story, Tuppence imitates the style and mannerisms of the fictional detective created by H.C. Bailey (1878–1961), Dr. Reggie Fortune, a surgeon and consultant to Scotland Yard, who loves to live and eat well.

Amberiotis, Mr.   A blackmailer in ONE, TWO, BUCKLE MY SHOE, he had an earlier career as a spy in Germany and France. The police believe that he shot his dentist, although he becomes the second murder victim after being administered a drug overdose.

Amery, Blanche   A twenty-four-year-old aristocrat in "SWAN SONG" who unwittingly discovers the true identity of a mysterious ballerina.

Ames, Mr.   The real estate agent in "PHILOMEL COTTAGE," he becomes suspicious of his new client when he is given only two thousand pounds for the purchase of the cottage instead of the promised three thousand pounds.

Ames, Dr. Robert   A staff doctor on the Menher-Ra expedition in "THE ADVENTURE OF THE EGYPTIAN TOMB," he once saved a dissolute young man from drowning.

Amory, Barbara   The extremely modern, twenty-one-year-old daughter of the murder victim in BLACK COFFEE, she believes that "a girl simply can't have too much red on her lips."

Amory, Miss Caroline   An elderly lady "of the old school" in BLACK COFFEE, she is the fussy maiden aunt of Richard and Barbara AMORY, and the sister of the murder victim.

Amory, Sir Claud   A clean-shaven, ascetic-looking man of sixty who is also a leading research scientist in BLACK COFFEE, he has invented a substance to increase mankind's destructive capabilities in war. He dies of poisoning after his secret formula is stolen.

Amory, Lucia   The beautiful, twenty-five-year-old, half-Italian wife of Richard Amory in BLACK COFFEE, she fears her husband will learn that she is the daughter of the infamous international spy, Selma Goetz.

Amphrey, Miss   A successful headmistress in TOWARDS ZERO, she professes a belief in modern educational theories of self-determination yet, based on the result of a word association test, she coerces young Sylvia BATTLE to confess to a crime that she did not commit. This infuriates Superintendent BATTLE, but it also stimulates a new approach to an exasperating case.

Anastasia, Grand Duchess   Known familiarly as Alexa, she is a noblewoman of Catonia and the niece of Prince OSRIC. In "THE GIRL IN THE TRAIN," she is expected to marry Prince KARL, her cousin. Alexa falls in love with George ROWLAND, whom she finally marries only after Lady Elizabeth GAIGH intercedes.

Anchoukoff, Boris   A fanatically devoted butler in THE SECRET OF CHIMNEYS who vows to put his own life on the line for his master, Prince Michael OBOLOVITCH of Herzoslovakia. After the prince is murdered, the valet vows a particularly vicious revenge if he should find the murderer. He then obtains a new master, Anthony CADE, to whom he shows the same intense devotion.

Andersen, Dr.   A charismatic evangelist in "THE FLOCK OF GERYON" who preaches his own brand of religion to a following mainly of lonely, unattached women, the handsome "Great Shepherd" mesmerizes converts with his good looks and promises. As leader of the Flock of the Shepherd, the "Great Shepherd" charms his followers to make bequests to the religion, after which they frequently die of fatal illnesses.

Andersen, Thelma   Hired by an accomplice of Hercule POIROT to impersonate the companion of a well-known Argentine gigolo and dancer in "THE AUGEAN STABLES."

Anderson, Colonel   Credited as a man of action, he is a pessimistic chief constable whose perseverance is valuable in THE A.B.C. MURDERS.

Anderson, Esther   See WALTERS, ESTHER.

Anderson, Greta   Sensuous and earthy, she makes herself invaluable to her employers in ENDLESS NIGHT and provokes the observation that she looked like "a super Valkyrie with shining golden hair."

Andras, Count   Elegant, slender and young, he is a diplomat stationed in the Hungarian Embassy in London in THE SEVEN DIALS MYSTERY. Also known as "No. 5," he leads a secret life that places him in danger.

Andre   A subversive in THEY CAME TO BAGHDAD, he poses as a French archaeological assistant to locate secret information hidden in the Expedition House.

Andrenyi, Countess Helena Maria   A beautiful aristocrat with humble beginnings, she is a prime murder suspect in MURDER ON THE ORIENT EXPRESS whose monogrammed handkerchief is found at the murder site with her.

Andrenyi, Count Rudolph   A Hungarian nobleman and diplomat in MURDER ON THE ORIENT EXPRESS who attempts to protect his wife from suspicion of murder by tampering with her passport.

Andrew   Despite his love of poetry and plans to become a poet, the fifteen-year-old grandson of Tommy and Tuppence BERESFORD takes an active interest in solving crime in POSTERN OF FATE.

Andrews, Squadron Leader   Once a member of the Royal Air Force, he is experienced in flying secret missions of the sort for which he is retained in PASSENGER TO FRANKFURT.

Andrews, Betsy   The cook of murder victim Jonathan WHALLEY in THE BIG FOUR.

And Then There Were None   Mystery novel.

The novel is an example of the closed-society murder mystery. The plot centers on ten people from various social levels who are lured to a mansion on an island and methodically killed. The murders follow the order in which ten little boys die in a nursery rhyme, a framed copy of which appears above the mantelpiece of every bedroom in the mansion.

PUBLISHING AND DRAMATIZATION HISTORY

The novel was first published under the title of *Ten Little Niggers* by Collins in London in 1939, and under the title *And Then There Were None* by Dodd, Mead and Company in New York in 1940.

The novel was adapted for the stage in 1943 by the author, who decided that the stage demanded a more romantic ending. She rewrote the ending so that two characters survive the experience to create a future together. The stage adaptation, titled *Ten Little Niggers*, opened in London at the St. James Theatre on November 17, 1943, and the American stage version, retitled *Ten Little Indians*, opened at the Broadhurst Theatre in New York City on June 27, 1944.

The five adaptations which appeared after the stage version retained the happier ending of the play, rather than the original of the novel. The first feature film version of the novel was produced in the U.S. by Twentieth Century Fox, and released in 1945 under the title *And Then There Were None*. In 1965, the film was remade in England by Seven Arts Films and released in England and the U.S. as *Ten Little Indians*. In this version, the setting was moved to a remote mountaintop castle in the Austrian Alps. Avco-Embassy, Inc., produced a fourth version of the novel in 1975, titled *Ten Little Indians*, which moved the setting to a remote hotel in the Iranian desert. In 1989, in the third film of the novel to be titled *Ten Little Indians*, Breton Films moved the locale to an African safari.

In addition to these feature films, the BBC produced a television version of the stage adaptation, which aired as a live drama on August 20, 1949, under the title of *Ten Little Niggers*.

CHARACTERS

Dr. Edward George ARMSTRONG, William Henry BLORE, Emily Caroline BRENT, Vera Elizabeth CLAYTHORNE, Sir Thomas LEGGE, Captain Philip LOMBARD, General John MACARTHUR, Inspector

MAINE, Anthony James MARSTON, Fred NARRACOTT, Ethel ROGERS, Thomas ROGERS, Mr. Justice Laurence John WARGRAVE

PLOT SYNOPSIS
Chapter 1
The opening chapter is divided into eight distinct parts, each devoted to one of the eight people headed to Indian Island after being invited by the mysterious and elusive U.N. Owen. The reader learns each character's reason for accepting the invitation to Indian Island, and details are provided regarding their personalities.

Chapter 2
The guests arrive at the Oakbridge Train Station, then board the boat to Indian Island. All seem to be surprised at the makeup of the group. When they arrive at the house, the butler informs them that their mysterious host, U.N. Owen, will not arrive until the following day. The guests are shown to their rooms, where each sees a framed nursery rhyme above the mantel, the text of which stirs shivers in several of the people. That evening, individual personalities emerge, as General MacArthur petulantly complains that the trip is not what he had expected, Philip Lombard paces like a panther and Emily Brent quotes the Bible in regard to the wicked who "shall be returned unto Hell."

Chapters 3–4
The reasons for which all have been summoned to Indian Island are revealed. During dinner, a loud voice booms out and charges each guest, as well as the cook and the butler, with having been responsible for the deaths of others. After investigating, they learn that the voice was recorded, but they do not know who placed the record on the turntable. The guests discuss the charges, and all except Emily Brent offer explanations in their own defense. Anthony Marston chokes on his drink and falls off his chair.

Chapters 5–6
The guests realize that Anthony Marston is dead, poisoned by cyanide and thought to be a suicide. As the guests go to their rooms to sleep, they each remember the incidents of which they have been charged. At the same time, the butler counts the Indian statues on the mantelpiece of the main room,

and finds only nine. The next morning, the guests learn that the cook, Mrs. Rogers, has died in the night, and another statue has disappeared. As they wait for Fred Narracott to bring the motorboat, the remaining guests become accusatory and imply each other's guilt.

Chapters 7–8
Anxiety grows among the guests as they contemplate Anthony Marston's death and observe that the two deaths relate to the poems appearing in each room. They search the island and the house, believing that a murderer is hiding somewhere nearby. General MacArthur warns the others that no one will leave the island alive. After searching every foot of the island and every part of the house, they conclude that they are alone on the island.

Chapters 9–10
The guests eat lunch without MacArthur, then begin to worry as they see a darkening sky and hear someone running. They find the general dead from a blow to the head, and only seven statues remain. Judge Wargrave suggests that none of the murders required much force, and that even the women are suspects. They divide into pairs and discuss their suspicions. As they sit down to tea, the butler announces that the bathroom curtain is missing. After tea, Lombard and Blore watch as Vera and Emily enter their rooms and wait until they lock their doors and call out that they are safe.

Chapters 11–12
In the morning, the butler is missing and the mantel contains only six statues. They find Rogers in a washhouse across the yard with a meat cleaver wound on his head. They remind each other that the next part of the poem deals with a hive, and wonder if there are bees nearby. When Emily Brent is found dead of an apparent bee sting, someone suggests that a hypodermic needle might have made the same wound. They gather Dr. Armstrong's medical supplies and Philip Lombard's revolver, and lock them in a safe place. As they do so, they notice that the sixth statue is missing.

Chapters 13–14
After they go to their rooms, someone tries to strangle Vera with seaweed, and the judge disappears. He is later found shot, wearing a wig made of grey yarn.

Only Blore, Armstrong, Lombard and Vera remain. They go to bed, but lie awake and review everything which has transpired. Vera notices a black hook in her room which disturbs her. Dr. Armstrong disappears during the night, and Lombard searches futilely for him. They learn that only three statues remain.

Chapters 15–16
Lombard, Blore and Vera try to signal for help from the beach. When Blore wants to return to the house, Lombard offers him the revolver, and they hear a shot soon after. Returning to the beach, Vera and Lombard sit on the beach and look into the sea, where they spot a dead Dr. Armstrong. A panicked Vera takes Lombard's revolver and shoots him through the heart. Feeling safe, Vera returns to the house, where she finds a noose and chair in her room, corresponding to the final death in the poem. She hangs herself.

Epilogue
Scotland Yard investigators discuss the case, but cannot determine the identity of the murderer. Months later, Scotland Yard receives a bottle that had been found in the ocean. It contains a letter written by the murderer, who was one of the guests, and reveals the means of committing all of the murders.

CRIME NOTES
The novel is named for and constructed according to a popular Victorian music hall show song written by Frank Green in England in 1869. It was an adaptation of the American comic song, *Ten Little Indians*, written by Septimus Winner and published in 1868. The song was very well-known to children and adults in England. The author includes the complete song in Chapter 2 of the novel. The original title was deemed offensive by American publisher, Dodd, Mead and Company, who changed it to *And Then There Were None.*

Angelica   See SHAPLAND, ANN.

Angelique, Sister Marie   A Belgian refugee who holds the secret to the Sixth Sign, which she refuses to reveal, in "THE HOUND OF DEATH." She goes with it to her grave.

Angell, Henry   A forty-eight-year-old valet-attendant, possessed of a correct manner but a shifty eye, in THE UNEXPECTED GUEST, he attempts to supplement his severance pay with blackmail money after his employer is murdered.

Angkatell, David   An Oxford intellectual and heir to a fortune in THE HOLLOW whose future is more impressive than his present.

Angkatell, Edward   A wealthy landowner loves his cousin in vain, then realizes true love with another woman following a failed suicide attempt in THE HOLLOW.

Angkatell, Sir Henry   A fearful man who looks years older than his age, he hosts the party during which a murder occurs in THE HOLLOW.

Angkatell, Lady Lucy   An elderly noblewoman who charmed others even as she annoyed them in THE HOLLOW. Even Hercule POIROT was attracted to her and conceded that "she will always have magic."

Angus   Witness to the revising of a will who provided a murder suspect with information about arsenic in DUMB WITNESS.

Annesley, Gerard   Of a despairing appearance, he was usually ignored, and failed to hear his wife being murdered in an adjacent room in "THE BIRD WITH THE BROKEN WING."

Annesley, Mabelle   Ethereal in appearance, she evokes the sympathy of all who meet her in "THE BIRD WITH THE BROKEN WING." She reaches out for happiness in an affair but is soon murdered, strangled with a string from her ukulele.

Annette   Her beauty dazzles Tommy BERESFORD, for whom she risks her life, when she helps him to escape from a Bolshevist hideout in Soho, in THE SECRET ADVERSARY. Her heavily accented English hides an assumed identity, Jane FINN, which has sent her into hiding and which may cause her death.

Annie   She is Mrs. TODD's parlourmaid in "THE ADVENTURE OF THE CLAPHAM COOK" who is convinced that the missing cook was abducted by "white slavers."

Annis, Francesca A British actress, she played the role of Tuppence BERESFORD in the nine-part series of Tommy and Tuppence stories produced for television in 1983 by London Weekend Television Productions in England.

Ansell, Mr. The nervous solicitor in A POCKET FULL OF RYE who is eager to answer all questions regarding the will of Adele FORTESQUE.

Anthony, Mrs. See MERROWDENE, MARGARET.

Antoine, Monsieur See LEECH, ANDREW.

Anstruth, Mrs. The aunt of Bridget CONWAY in MURDER IS EASY.

Anstruther, Mr. One of the few people to whom Sister Marie ANGELIQUE revealed the secrets of the Hound of Death and the Sixth Sign in "THE HOUND OF DEATH."

Antrobus, Dr. An expert at disguise, also variously named CONSTANTINE or Dr. Claudius, he is an entertainer who specializes in soul transference in "THE CASE OF THE RICH WOMAN."

Appleby, Colonel A strong supporter of the police in THE MOVING FINGER who believes he knows who wrote the anonymous letters.

Appledore An excellent servant who is willing to work for very low wages in N OR M?

"Apples of the Hesperides, The" Mystery short story.

A priceless Borgia goblet disappears before the new owner receives it and, despite arrests, the goblet is not recovered until ten years later, when Hercule POIROT takes on the case.

PUBLISHING AND DRAMATIZATION
HISTORY
The story appeared in the short story collection, THE LABOURS OF HERCULES, published in 1947 by William Collins Sons and Co., Ltd., in London, and by Dodd, Mead and Company in New York.

The story has not been adapted for stage or screen.

CHARACTERS
ATLAS, Patrick CASEY, DUBLAY, GEORGE/GEORGES, Hercule Poirot, Emery POWER, RICOVETTI, Reuben ROSENTHAL, Marchese di SAN VERATRINO, Inspector WAGSTAFFE

PLOT SYNOPSIS
The theft of a priceless gold goblet made originally for Pope Alexander VI (Rodrigo Borgia), essentially an art object in the form of an apple tree design with emerald apples, results in two arrests, but the goblet is not recovered. After ten years, the owner of the goblet hears rumors that a ruthless art collector has the goblet, and he contacts Hercule Poirot to locate it.

CRIME NOTES
The story is a modern retelling of the eleventh labor of the Greek mythological figure Hercules, who was required to obtain the golden apples which had been given as a wedding present to Hera.

Appointment With Death Mystery novel.

The story takes place amid the ancient ruins of Petra and concerns the Boynton family, which is tyrannized by a cruel, overbearing matriarch. Despite their desire to break free of her control and to live their own lives, these adult children and their spouses are psychologically unable to take the needed steps. When Mrs. BOYNTON is murdered, the family feels freed, and all members ask that Hercule POIROT not pursue the case.

PUBLISHING AND DRAMATIZATION
HISTORY
The novel was first published by Collins in London in 1938, and by Dodd, Mead and Company in New York in 1938.

The novel was adapted by Agatha Christie for the stage, and the play opened at the Picadilly Theatre in London on March 31, 1945.

In 1988, EMI Pictures filmed the novel as a feature film, starring Peter Ustinov as Hercule Poirot.

CHARACTERS
ABDUL, Mrs. Boynton, Carol BOYNTON, Ginerva (Jinny) BOYNTON, Lennox BOYNTON, Nadine BOYNTON, Raymond BOYNTON, Colonel CARBURY, Jefferson COPE, Dr. Theodore GERARD, Sarah KING,

MAHMOUD, Miss Amabel PIERCE, Hercule Poirot, Lady WESTHOLME

PLOT SYNOPSIS
Part I: Chapter 1
The novel begins in Jerusalem, where Hercule Poirot hears a voice from the adjacent hotel window declare, "You do see, don't you, that she's got to be killed?" The words sound like a literary collaboration, yet the memory of the voice lingers in Poirot's mind.

Chapters 2–5
A doctor and psychologist respectively, Sarah King and Theodore Gerard, are on a tour of the Middle East when they meet in the hotel lobby. Their attention is riveted on the Boynton family, an American entourage with a Buddha-like matriarch at its center. While Sarah King's interest is piqued by the youngest son, Raymond, whom she intends to rescue from domination by his mother, Gerard observes the destructive pattern of the entire family and the evil malignancy of its matriarch. He learns more about the family history from another American on the tour, Jefferson Cope.

Chapters 6–9
Sarah King speaks with Carol Boynton and learns that the domineering Mrs. Boynton is a former prison wardress and stepmother to all but Ginerva, and she convinces Carol to meet her later to talk. The young woman keeps the appointment and reveals her strange family life. The two agree to meet the following day, but Carol does not appear, so Sarah speaks to her sister-in-law, Nadine, and learns that old Mrs. Boynton has forbidden all family members to speak to Sarah or to any other outsiders. As the family leaves the tour, Sarah tries one more time and fails to break through their shell.

Chapters 10–12
Booked for an excursion to Petra with an officious female politician, a twittering former governess and Dr. Gerard, Sarah tries to remove the memory of the Boyntons from her mind but encounters them again in Petra. After a day of joint exploration, Mrs. Boynton surprises the family by telling them to explore on their own, a move which permits Raymond to tell Sarah that he loves her. He vows to break free of

his stepmother's hold. By nightfall, Mrs. BOYNTON is dead.

Part II: Chapters 1–3
Hercule Poirot meets in Amman with Colonel Carbury, the man in charge of law enforcement in the region. When the conversation turns to crime, Carbury tells Poirot about a recent death which he believes is murder, although the official conclusion is death by natural causes. Poirot becomes especially interested when he learns that the victim is Mrs. Boynton. Dr. Gerard is called to give his expert views on the death, leading Poirot to recall the words heard earlier through his hotel window. He agrees to uncover the truth, and promises Colonel Carbury a solution in twenty-four hours.

Chapters 4–9
Poirot questions all the members of the traveling party individually to obtain information regarding their activities surrounding the time of the murder. They are questioned in the following order: Sarah King, Lady Westholme, Miss Pierce, Lennox Boynton, Mrs. Lennox (Nadine) Boynton, Carol Boynton, Raymond Boynton.

Chapter 10
Colonel Carbury presses Poirot for a solution and asks him to provide a list of significant facts, just like "the detective does in books."

Chapters 11–13
Poirot consults Drs. Gerard and King to obtain a clear psychological profile of the victim. As they speak, Ginerva Boynton wanders near, and Dr. Gerard admits his attraction to her. Nadine and Lennox discuss their new freedom and plan with other family members to live their lives in peace.

Chapters 14–17
Poirot learns from Miss Pierce that a key piece of syringe was discarded the morning after the murder by one character, and retrieved by another. After Poirot realizes the truth, he calls together the travelers and the family. He places the facts of the case before them and forces the murderer to admit guilt.

Epilogue
The fate of the Boynton family members five years later is revealed.

CRIME NOTES
Mrs. Boynton is murdered by an injection of digitoxin, obtained from digitalis purpurea (foxglove), a substance that is six to ten times the strength of digitalis taken for heart ailments.

Appointment with Death   Film released in 1988 by EMI Productions. The movie is based on the 1938 novel, APPOINTMENT wITH DEATH.

CAST
The cast includes Peter Ustinov as Hercule POIROT, as well as Lauren Bacall, Carrie Fisher, John Gielgud and Piper Laurie.

CHANGES FROM THE ORIGINAL TEXT
The plot and setting closely resemble the original text, but the character of Hercule Poirot is different from that in the novel. Peter Ustinov is a larger-sized version of Poirot, with a full head of hair. Further, Ustinov chose to play the detective as less methodical and analytical in manner than he is in the novel.

PRODUCTION NOTES
The script followed the novel, not the 1945 stage version written by the author, who omitted Poirot and made Colonel CARBURY the chief investigator.

Arbuthnot, Colonel   The only pipe smoker on the Calais Coach, he is implicated in the crime by the pipe cleaner left at the murder site in MURDER ON THE ORIENT EXPRESS (1).

Arbuthnot, Dr. George   A fast-thinking physician in WHY DIDN'T THEY ASK EVANS?, he agrees to sneak a young, adventurous aristocrat into the home of Sylvia BASSINGTON-FFRENCH.

"Arcadian Deer, The"   Mystery short story.
   In this touching romance, Hercule POIROT helps to uncover the mystery of the missing lady's maid.

PUBLISHING AND DRAMATIZATION HISTORY
The story appeared in the short story collection, THE TWELVE LABOURS OF HERCULES, published in 1947 by William Collins Sons and Co., Ltd., in London, and Dodd, Mead and Company in New York.

The story has not been adapted for stage or screen.

CHARACTERS
NITA, Hercule Poirot, Mademoiselle Katrina SAMOUSHENKA, Ted WILLIAMSON

PLOT SYNOPSIS
A young, handsome garage mechanic meets a beautiful young woman, and the two fall in love. She is lady's maid to a dancer and must leave soon, but promises to return in a month. When the young man goes to the house a month later, he learns that the maid has been dismissed, although her employer is a guest there. When he asks Hercule Poirot to investigate, they learn a startling fact about the mechanic's ladylove.

CRIME NOTES
The story is a modern version of the fourth labor of the Greek mythological hero, Hercules, whose task was to capture the golden-horned hind that lived in Arcadia.

Archdale, Betty   A parlourmaid with a habit of eavesdropping, she overhears threats of violence that endanger her in SPARKLING CYANIDE.

Archer, Mrs.   See DAVIS, JESSE.

Arden, Enoch   See TRENTON, CHARLES.

Arden, Linda   See HUBBARD, CAROLINE MARTHA.

Ardingly, David   A quick-witted young man in THE PALE HORSE who seeks liaisons only with girls who seem half-witted.

Ardley, Beatrice   One of the young girls at the party when murder occurs in HALLOWE'EN PARTY.

Arguileros, Karl   A former actor who has a swastika brand on his foot and uses the assumed name of Franz JOSEPH to perpetuate the myth that he is Adolf Hitler's son and the leader of the Youth Movement in PASSENGER TO FRANKFURT. Colonel PIKEAWAY considers him to be a fraud despite his arrogance.

Argyle, Christina (Tina) An apparently meek librarian of mixed racial parentage, she is a graceful and unlikely suspect in ORDEAL BY INNOCENCE when her adoptive mother is murdered.

Argyle, Hester Resentful of her overly competent adoptive mother, she ran away to experience freedom and had an unhappy affair with a married man. Her return home is marred by murder, and she becomes a suspect whose innocence is established only through the intervention of a stranger in ORDEAL BY INNOCENCE.

Argyle, Jack (Jacko) Always short of money and in trouble, he is convicted of murdering his adoptive mother after having argued with her over money in ORDEAL BY INNOCENCE. Although given a life sentence, his alibi is proved to be true after his death in prison from pneumonia.

Argyle, Leo A quiet, acquiescent man who married for love, he retreats into his own world as his wife ignores him and gives increasing amounts of attention to their five adopted children in ORDEAL BY INNOCENCE. Ever-faithful to his wife, he dismisses the possibility of either an affair or a divorce, even after falling in love with his secretary.

Argyle, Mary See DURRANT, MARY (1).

Argyle, Michael (Micky) Tormented by the knowledge that his real mother had sold him as a toddler to his adoptive parents for a hundred pounds, and despite the comfort of his surroundings, he wished throughout his life for his former noisy, dirty home in ORDEAL BY INNOCENCE.

Argyle, Rachel A woman obsessed by not being able to conceive children, she ran a wartime nursery, and acquired five children through various legal and illegal means to satisfy her need to nurture in ORDEAL BY INNOCENCE. Overindulgent, she attempts to chart her children's every move, but one of them murders her.

Aristides, Mr. An enormously wealthy megalomaniac who claims to have placed the services of the world's greatest young brains on his retainer in DESTINATION UNKNOWN.

Aristopoulos He is considered a genius in the art of making paste replicas of valuable jewels in "THE ORACLE AT DELPHI."

Armstrong, Dr. Edward George Physician to numerous wealthy women, he temporarily escaped detection in the death of a patient who died when he operated on her while drunk in AND THEN THERE WERE NONE.

Arrichet, Francoise An old servant at Villa Genevieve in MURDER ON THE LINKS who views the English with distrust.

Arundell, Charles The son of an acquitted murderess, he threatened his aunt when she refused to lend him money, and might be guilty of her murder in DUMB WITNESS.

Arundell, Emily She suspected that someone was trying to murder her, but her letter to Hercule POIROT arrived too late to save her life in DUMB WITNESS.

Arundell, Theresa Extravagant and impatient, she wanted to have the best of everything, but did not expect to work for it in DUMB WITNESS.

Ascanio, Signor Of a furtive appearance, he is suspected of murder after he visits the victim the night prior to its commission, in "THE ADVENTURE OF THE ITALIAN NOBLEMAN."

Ascher, Alice A tobacco shopkeeper who dies from a blow to the head, the first victim in THE A.B.C. MURDERS.

Ascher, Franz Suspected of his wife's murder in THE A.B.C. MURDERS, he was verbally abusive to his wife, but claims to have been drinking at a pub when she was killed.

Ashby, Joan An impish-looking guest in "THE SECOND GONG," she is on her visit to Lytcham Close, and highly amused by its routines.

Ashe, Old The gardener at Little Paddocks in A MURDER IS ANNOUNCED, he tells the police where to find the imposter Emma STAMFORDIS.

Ashfield The MILLER family residence in Torquay on the southern coast of England, and the author's beloved childhood home.

Ashley, Diana A seductive woman who uses her considerable physical charms to enthrall the men around her in "THE IDOL HOUSE OF ASTARTE."

Askew, Thomas The amiable but indiscreet landlord in WHY DIDN'T THEY ASK EVANS?

Astor, Anthony See WILLS, MURIEL.

Astwell, Lady Nancy Despite her lack of formal education, she has a highly developed intuition regarding her husband's murderer in "THE UNDER DOG."

Astwell, Sir Reuben His ruthless reputation created numerous enemies and many murder suspects in "THE UNDER DOG."

Astwell, Victor A violent temper marks him as a murder suspect in "THE UNDER DOG."

At Bertram's Hotel Mystery novel.

The novel concerns unusual occurrences in a restored London hotel which continues to court a pre-World War II clientele to mix with guests who exhibit changing contemporary values. The plot centers on the efforts of Miss Jane MARPLE to uncover a gang of criminals who are using Bertram's as their home base and endangering the lives of innocent guests.

PUBLISHING AND DRAMATIZATION HISTORY
The novel was published in 1965 by William Collins Sons and Co., Ltd., in London, and in 1966 by Dodd, Mead and Company in New York.

The novel was adapted for television in 1987 by the BBC, and was shown on the Public Broadcasting Service in the U.S.

CHARACTERS
The Honourable Elvira BLAKE, Mrs. CARPENTER, Chief Inspector Fred DAVY, Michael (Mickey) GORMAN, Miss GORRINGE, Sir Ronald GRAVES, Lady Selina HAZY, Robert HOFFMAN, Mr. HUMFRIES, Colonel Derek LUSCOMBE, Ladislaus MALINOWSKI, Miss Jane Marple, Contessa MARTINELLI, Mildred MELFORD, Canon PENNYFEATHER, Mr. ROBINSON, Lady Bess SEDGWICK, Rose SHELDON, Emma WHEELING, Raymond WEST

PLOT SYNOPSIS
Chapters 1–3
Miss Marple's nephew, novelist Raymond West, treats her to a week at the quaint and old-fashioned Bertram's Hotel in London. She marvels at the manner in which the establishment has managed to maintain prewar traditions yet integrate newer amenities and also draw a contemporary crowd. As she reviews the guests, Miss Marple sees Lady Bess Sedgwick arrive and indulges "in a frankly avid stare." Lady Bess is well known for her courageous and foolhardy deeds, as well as for her passionate affairs. Unknown to Lady Bess, the daughter whom she rarely sees, Elvira Blake, arrives at Bertram's.

Chapters 4–6
Scotland Yard is faced with a wave of very sophisticated crimes in London; Yard officials believe this indicates that the gang has a centrally located headquarters. Despite careful investigative work, no important information has turned up. The only lead is that the latest crime has implicated a court justice, who is presently staying at Bertram's Hotel. The various hidden relationships between the guests, as well as between some guests and hotel personnel, are revealed. While she eats lunch, Miss Marple overhears a heated conversation between Lady Bess and international racing car driver, Ladislaus Malinowski.

Chapters 7–9
The absentminded Canon Pennyfeather learns that he has mistaken the date and arrived a day late for his plane to Lucerne. As he returns to the hotel, someone attacks him in his room, and he disappears for a few days. The same night Pennyfeather disappears, the Irish Mail train is robbed of a great deal of money.

Chapters 10–12
Elvira Blake meets with the attorneys who oversee her trust fund to discuss her financial future and to learn more about her elusive mother. She startles the attorneys by asking who will inherit her fortune, should she die. Quite by accident, Miss Marple

discovers that Elvira is also involved with the racing car driver. At the same time, Canon Pennyfeather's housekeeper tries to locate him. She calls the hotel and the police, then appeals to the archdeacon to help her to locate the canon.

Chapters 13–15
The authorities review the case of Canon Pennyfeather, intrigued that he is a guest at Bertram's Hotel. They decide to question the manager about the missing man and request permission to speak with the chambermaid. They meet Mr. Humfries, whose manner makes them suspicious, and they decide to question several guests. While having tea, Chief Inspector Davy recognizes Miss Marple, and learns that she has observed a great deal about Canon Pennyfeather.

Chapters 16–18
Canon Pennyfeather awakens in a private home, unaware of what has happened to him. The authorities continue to search for him, as disturbing news comes from a witness who claims to have seen the canon in the vicinity of the mail train at the time of the robbery. Detectives from Scotland Yard speak with Mr. Robinson, viewed as being the top brain behind the international financiers of Europe, to learn who really owns Bertram's Hotel. Afterward, they learn that the canon has been located.

Chapters 19–21
Inspector Davy meets with Mr. Hoffman, identified as the owner of Bertram's, and tries to determine how he might be linked to the recent robberies. Hoffman is evasive, but he does admit that Lady Bess Sedgwick is a shareholder. When he returns to the hotel, Davy sees a car with a familiar license plate parked in front. He speaks with Mickey Gorman, then meets Miss Marple in the lounge. She tells him of her fears for Elvira, and reveals that she suspects that all is not right in the hotel. Even as Davy reassures Miss Marple that there will be no murders at the hotel, they hear shouts from outside and learn that Mickey has been shot dead. Davy questions Elvira, and learns that she was the target of the gunshot and that Mickey had jumped in the way to save her.

Chapters 22–24
Davy interviews Elvira's best friend to learn more about earlier attempts on her life, as well as other information that might link Elvira to the robberies. He next speaks with the law firm which represents Elvira's trust to learn more about her financial standing. Information obtained leads them to question Malinowski about his relationship to both Lady Bess and Elvira, but the racing car driver says little.

Chapters 25–27
Inspector Davy asks Miss Marple to return to Bertram's, at the same time that he summons Canon Pennyfeather back. He asks them to recreate the night that she saw the canon leave the hotel, and Miss Marple concludes that an imposter had left the canon's room. Inspector Davy and Miss Marple then meet with Lady Bess, and learn that Mickey Gorman had threatened to blackmail her. Davy explains that Bertram's Hotel is the headquarters of a crime syndicate and reveals what the police have learned about their operations, then makes a startling revelation regarding the leaders.

CRIME NOTES
The murder in this novel is the result of a gunshot wound.

"At The 'Bells and Motley'" Mystery short story.
The story features Mr. SATTERTHWAITE, who helps a young woman to clear her fiancé, who has been charged with murdering his former employer.

PUBLISHING AND DRAMATIZATION HISTORY
The story appeared in the short story collection, THE MYSTERIOUS MR. QUIN, published in 1930 by William Collins Sons and Co., Ltd., in London, and by Dodd, Mead and Company in New York.
The story has not been adapted for stage or screen.

CHARACTERS
Mr. Cyrus BRADBURN, Stephen GRANT, Captain HARTWELL, William JONES, Eleanor LE COUTEAU, John MATHIAS, Mr. Harley QUIN, Mr. Satterthwaite, Mrs. ST. CLAIR

PLOT SYNOPSIS
Mr. Satterthwaite's car breaks down near a small town, and he is forced to spend the night at the local inn, the Bells and Motley, which has only one other guest, the mysterious Mr. Quin. The innkeeper tells the two men that his daughter's fiancé has been accused of foul play in the disappearance of his

former employer, Captain Hartwell, but the two men become suspicious when the innkeeper also tells them that the widow quickly sold the home and furnishings soon after her husband's death, and left town.

CRIME NOTES
As in most of the stories that feature Mr. Harley Quin, he acts only as a light to focus attention on the vital facts Mr. Satterthwaite uses to solve the crime.

Atkinson, Colonel Nicknamed "Moustachio-Monty," this garrulous ex-military officer helps in the murder investigation in POSTERN OF FATE.

Atlas A heavy-drinking reporter for the *Dublin Sun* who takes a racing tip from Hercule POIROT in "THE APPLES OF THE HESPERIDES."

"Augean Stables, The" Mystery short story.

Scandal threatens to destroy the reputation of a prime minister and his wife, but Hercule POIROT turns the tables on the muckrakers and destroys their credibility.

PUBLISHING AND DRAMATIZATION HISTORY
The story appeared in the short story collection, THE LABOURS OF HERCULES, published in 1947 by William Collins Sons and Co., Ltd., in London and by Dodd, Mead and Company in New York.

The story has not been adapted for stage or screen.

CHARACTERS
Miss Thelma ANDERSEN, Dagmar FERRIER, Edward FERRIER, John HAMMETT, Percy PERRY, Hercule Poirot

PLOT SYNOPSIS
A muckraking newspaper threatens to print a story about former Prime Minister John Hammett, father-in-law of present Prime Minister Edward Ferrier, claiming that he embezzled party funds while in office. Afraid that his own political career will be harmed, Ferrier contacts Hercule Poirot for help and advice in cleaning up the dirty political situation. The detective creates his own scandal, and reverses the political tide.

CRIME NOTES
This story is a modern telling of the sixth labor of the Greek mythological figure, Hercules, who accepted a challenge from King Augeas that he could clean the King's filth-ridden stables in only one day, in return for one-tenth of the herd.

Austin, Celia An apparent kleptomaniac in HICKORY DICKORY DOCK, her death from morphine tartrate poisoning was linked to her work in a hospital dispensary.

Autobiography, An Non-fiction work.

The book is an intimate portrait of the author, full of remembered detail and characterized by the same charm that pervades her fiction.

PUBLISHING AND DRAMATIZATION HISTORY
The book was published in 1977 by William Collins Sons and Co., Ltd., in London, and by Dodd, Mead and Company in New York.

The book has not been adapted for stage or screen.

CONTENT
The work covers the author's life from birth to 1965, eleven years before her death in 1976. In this work, the author indicates that she stopped writing about herself on October 11, 1965, when she reached seventy-five years, because "as far as life is concerned, that is all there is to say."

An Autobiography is not an in-depth analysis of the author's life and work. Rather, it presents a long and loving look backward to the idyllic childhood that formed her imaginative powers and to the family that nurtured her. The remaining two-thirds of the book contain her thoughts about travel, marriage and the important relationships in her life, as well as anecdotes regarding her involvement in archaeological digs, the world wars and life in general. She omits any mention of her famous disappearance in 1926, and gives surprisingly little attention to her career, aside from discussions of people and places related to the works.

Averbury, Claud Given the alias of Claud LEASON by his first wife, he must deal with the exposure of his second wife's identity in "THE AFFAIR AT THE BUNGALOW."

B

Babbington, Reverend Stephen A kindly husband and father of four, his murder puzzles the other cocktail party guests in THREE-ACT TRAGEDY.

Bacon, Inspector A member of Scotland Yard, he works with Detective Inspector Dermot CRADDOCK on the case in 4.50 FROM PADDINGTON.

Badcock, Arthur An unlikely looking romantic figure whose real name is Alfred BEADLE, he was formerly married to a movie star in THE MIRROR CRACK'D FROM SIDE TO SIDE.

Badcock, Heather Garrulous yet well-meaning, she is poisoned at the dinner party honoring a well-known actress whom she had infected with German measles years before in THE MIRROR CRACK'D FROM SIDE TO SIDE.

Badgworth, Inspector A train traveler in "INGOTS OF GOLD," he knows an inordinate amount of information about the shipwrecked *Otranto*.

Badgworthy, Chief Inspector Proud and independent, he spearheads the investigation into the murder of Prince Michael OBOLOVITCH in THE SECRET OF CHIMNEYS.

Bailey, Donovan Now married to another woman, he and his former rival discover a dead body in the apartment of their former object of affection in "THE THIRD-FLOOR FLAT."

Bain, Mary Exotic in appearance and behavior, she wastes no time in trying to seduce the widower in THE MIRROR CRACK'D FROM SIDE TO SIDE.

Baker, Mr. and Mrs. A pleasant couple who served at Crabtree Manor, they play a central role as witnesses in "THE CASE OF THE MISSING WILL."

Baker, Mrs. Calvin The coldly efficient liaison officer for Mr. ARISTIDES' Brain Trust in DESTINATION UNKNOWN.

Baker, Cherry Young, modern and newly married, she becomes housekeeper-cook for Miss MARPLE in THE MIRROR CRACK'D FROM SIDE TO SIDE; she and her husband move into Miss Marple's house in NEMESIS.

Baker, David A preening peacock whose velvet waistcoat and shoulder-length curls belong to another century, he is a painter who becomes a suspect in THIRD GIRL.

Baker, Jim His hobby of assembling model airplanes causes his wife, CHERRY, to feel ignored in THE MIRROR CRACK'D FROM SIDE TO SIDE.

Baker, Richard (Owl) An archaeologist who accidentally becomes embroiled in intrigue, he wins the girl whom he rescues on his way to the dig in THEY CAME TO BAGHDAD.

Baldock, Mr. (Baldy) A curmudgeonly bachelor scholar in THE BURDEN, Baldy is a willing listener and a stable force throughout the novel for the two daughters of family friends. He wisely advises Laura FRANKLIN to stop sacrificing so much for her younger sister.

Baldwin, Superintendent His large and comfortable exterior masks a shrewd police mind in DEAD MAN'S FOLLY.

Ball, Mr. A slow-thinking innkeeper in THE A.B.C. MURDERS who smells strongly of beer.

Balsano, Giuseppe Drawn innocently into the circle of murder in SPARKLING CYANIDE, he is the waiter who serves at both the party at which a woman dies, and the one a year later on the anniversary of her death.

Banks, Miss The owner of a scrupulously clean, self-contained apartment which the newlyweds in UNFINISHED PORTRAIT decide against taking because they fear that their landlady will be a "tartar."

Banks, Gregory Possessed of a strong guilt complex for nearly killing a customer years earlier, this chemist seeks to punish himself by confessing to other murders in AFTER THE FUNERAL.

Banks, Susan Abernethie She inherits her uncle's strong will and determination but not his position as head of the family in AFTER THE FUNERAL.

Bantry, Colonel Arthur A typical country squire, he is the master of Gossington Hall in ST. MARY MEAD and a close friend of both Miss MARPLE and Chief Constable MELCHETT. He appears in THE THIRTEEN PROBLEMS and SLEEPING MURDER, and he is host to a body in THE BODY IN THE LIBRARY.

Bantry, Dolly Miss MARPLE's closest friend in St. Mary Mead and mistress of Gossington Hall. She shares with Miss MARPLE a fondness for gardening and detection, although her mysteries are all fiction until a body is discovered in her library. She appears with her husband in THE THIRTEEN PROBLEMS, SLEEPING MURDER and THE BODY IN THE LIBRARY, and as a widow in THE MIRROR CRACK'D FROM SIDE TO SIDE.

Barker, Sister A nurse in NEMESIS, she is abrupt and gives the appearance of disinterest in her patients.

Barley, Harley A scarecrow in Home Farm fields, he resembles Mr. Harley QUIN in "THE HARLEQUIN TEA SET."

Barling, Gregory A financial investor in "THE SECOND GONG," he loses money for a couple; the husband specifies in his will that his wife can inherit his estate only if she marries Barling.

Barnaby, Sir George A perpetually fussy man with annoying idiosyncrasies, he plays bridge with neighbors while his wife is murdered in "THE SIGN IN THE SKY."

Barnaby, Lady Vivien Married to a rich, elderly husband, she has an affair and is murdered in "THE SIGN IN THE SKY."

Barnard, Major One of the last to see the murdered man alive in "THE SUNNINGDALE MYSTERY."

Barnard, Mr. Grief-stricken by his daughter's murder in THE A.B.C. MURDERS, he can find no motive for the act.

Barnard, Mrs. Of Welsh origin, she falls into a state of shock upon learning of her daughter's death in THE A.B.C. MURDERS.

Barnard, Elizabeth (Betty) This twenty-three-year-old waitress was the second victim in THE A.B.C. MURDERS; her wandering eye and clandestine dating may have given her fiancé a motive for murder.

Barnard, Megan Sister of one of the victims in THE A.B.C. MURDERS, she actively joins in the search for her sister's killer.

Barnes, Mrs. This landlady's forbidding appearance hides a caring nature in "NEXT TO A DOG."

Barnes, George He operates a ferry with his brother in TOWARDS ZERO and informs police of a visitor to the victim on the night of the murder.

Barnes, Reginald An insignificant-appearing man also known as Albert Chapman, he is a member of British Intelligence whose code name is QX912 in ONE, TWO, BUCKLE MY SHOE.

Barnett, Inspector Military in bearing and discreet, he investigates the crime in "THE DREAM."

Barraclough, Raymond Suave and debonair, his affair with a married woman leads to blackmail and scandal in DEATH IN THE CLOUDS.

Barre, Monsieur A voice teacher at a French finishing school in UNFINISHED PORTRAIT.

Barrett, Jane An elderly and devoted maid who was drugged to prevent her from hearing the summons bell on the night of her mistress's murder in TOWARDS ZERO.

Barron, Barbara See STRANLEIGH, LADY.

Barron, Beatrice The ship on which she is traveling sinks, and she loses her memory and believes her name to be Alice Clayton in "THE VOICE IN THE DARK."

Barron, Dr. Louis A brilliant and dedicated bacteriologist, his concern is with furthering research for its own sake and not for the sake of humanity in DESTINATION UNKNOWN.

Barrow, Miss One of two private investigators hired by a millionaire to protect Miss MARPLE as she carries out his posthumous instructions in NEMESIS.

Barry, Major He has an eye for women, but this retired military man's repertoire of stories is unimaginative in EVIL UNDER THE SUN.

Bartlett, Mrs. A pleasant-faced, middle-aged woman in THE BODY IN THE LIBRARY who is in love with her boarder.

Bartlett, George The last to see one of the murder victims alive in THE BODY IN THE LIBRARY, he must explain why she was found dead in his luxury automobile.

Barton, Emily The last of the five Barton daughters, her delicate features mask years of disappointment and of being used by her family in THE MOVING FINGER.

Barton, George When his wife's apparent suicide is revealed to be murder, he plans to catch the murderer by reenacting the dinner party at which she was poisoned in SPARKLING CYANIDE, but the plan backfires.

Barton, Lady Laura Wealthy and well-connected, she is the last to be suspected of robbery until her kleptomania is discovered in "THE AFFAIR OF THE PINK PEARL."

Barton, Mary After assuming her late cousin's identity, she goes to Australia to inherit a fortune in "THE COMPANION."

Barton, Rosemary Beautiful but inconsiderate of others' feelings, she has too many lovers, knows too many secrets and makes too many enemies to remain alive in SPARKLING CYANIDE.

Bassington-ffrench, Henry A morphine addict, his reclusive ways convince others to deem his death a suicide in WHY DIDN'T THEY ASK EVANS?

Bassington-ffrench, Roger The black sheep of the family, he avoids work and schemes to acquire a large amount of money in WHY DIDN'T THEY ASK EVANS?

Bassington-ffrench, Sylvia Cool and controlled on the surface, her eyes betray her anxiety in WHY DIDN'T THEY ASK EVANS?

Bassington-ffrench, Tommy The victim of several near-fatal accidents, he is heir to the family estate in WHY DIDN'T THEY ASK EVANS?

Batani An old native woman who cares for a seriously injured woman in THE MAN IN THE BROWN SUIT.

Bateman, Rupert (Pongo) An intensely earnest young man entrusted with hiding the alarm clocks under the suspect's bed in THE SEVEN DIALS MYSTERY.

Bates, Annie When her instincts tell her that POIROT is going to be poisoned, she warns him and earns a reward in "THE ADVENTURE OF THE CHRISTMAS PUDDING."

Bateson, Leonard (Len) Warm-hearted, generous and kind, he is a seemingly dull-witted medical student in HICKORY DICKORY DOCK who becomes a suspect when the police discover that his father is confined to a mental institution.

Batt, Albert His career spans the five books in which Tommy and Tuppence BERESFORD appear, starting as a fifteen-year-old elevator operator and maturing into their loyal butler. Throughout THE SECRET ADVERSARY, PARTNERS IN CRIME, N OR M?, BY THE PRICKING OF MY THUMBS and POSTERN OF FATE, he follows his intuition to uncover important clues to help the detectives.

Batt, Elsie A parlourmaid whose specific information points to the murderer in CARDS ON THE TABLE.

Battersby, Miss This retired yet formidable seventy-year-old headmistress provides remarkable insight regarding one student in THIRD GIRL.

Battle, Superintendent A member of Scotland Yard, his powerful physique and impassive expression mislead new acquaintances into underestimating the determined lawman, who is usually assigned the most volatile political cases. Passing references are made in THE SECRET OF CHIMNEYS, THE SEVEN DIALS MYSTERY, CARDS ON THE TABLE and MURDER IS EASY to his family, which includes a wife and five children and a nephew who also works in the Yard. In TOWARDS ZERO, his daughter Sylvia BATTLE becomes involved in the action that points the superintendent towards the solution.

Battle, Sylvia Desiring to halt the interrogations, Superintendent BATTLE's youngest daughter falsely confesses to stealing at boarding school in TOWARDS ZERO.

Bauer, Carl A Russian spy, also known as Dr. Charles BOWER, whose assignment is to uncover the truth about a presumed double agent in "THE ADVENTURE OF THE SINISTER STRANGER."

Bauer, John As the new footman at Chimneys, he seems to be the perfect servant in THE SEVEN DIALS MYSTERY.

Bauerstein, Dr. An expert on poisons, he is a German spy who stays in St. Mary Mead under the cover of recuperating from a nervous breakdown in THE MYSTERIOUS AFFAIR AT STYLES.

Bault, Felicie A French peasant who suffers from multiple personality disorder in "THE FOURTH MAN," she chokes herself to death after her close female friend Annette RAVEL dies of consumption.

Beadle, Alfred See BADCOCK, ARTHUR.

Beadon, Badger A contradiction to his station in life and his expensive education, he helps in the murder investigation in WHY DIDN'T THEY ASK EVANS?

Beatrice She is a slatternly maid who is also careless in her duties in THE SITTAFORD MYSTERY.

Beauge, Madame A dressmaker in UNFINISHED PORTRAIT, she permits her daughter to leave France as governess to an English child.

Beauge, Jeanne She is the French governess in UNFINISHED PORTRAIT whom the English servants mock for sending her pay home.

Beck, Colonel The Chief of Special Branch at Scotland Yard who heads the murder investigation in THE CLOCKS.

Beddingfeld, Anne An adventurous young woman who calls herself "Anna the Adventuress," she becomes involved in danger in South America in THE MAN IN THE BROWN SUIT.

Belcher, Major E. A. A longtime friend of Archibald CHRISTIE from their days at Clifton School, he was the model for Sir Eustace PEDLER in THE MAN IN THE BROWN SUIT.

Bell, Miss The murder victim's typist in A POCKET FULL OF RYE who mistakes his dying agony for a seizure.

Bell, Sergeant Described as looking "like an eager greyhound," he is an enthusiastic Scotland Yard investigator in HICKORY DICKORY DOCK.

Bellever, Juliet (Jolly) Her harsh appearance masks the personality of a faithful nurse and devoted friend in THEY DO IT WITH MIRRORS.

Belling, Mrs. J. The "fat and excitable" proprietor of a public house who claims to have secret information in THE SITTAFORD MYSTERY.

Beltane, The Honorable Eustace Acquires the title of viscount after his nephew's death in "THE AFFAIR AT THE VICTORY BALL."

Ben The cook-housekeeper's son who has been in jail twice already, he leaves the country after the death of his mother's employer in "SING A SONG OF SIXPENCE."

Bence, Margot A celebrity photographer, she was sold by her natural mother to a film star at the age of five, then emotionally abandoned by the actress at the age of nine, in THE MIRROR CRACK'D FROM SIDE TO SIDE.

Benfield, Charlotte A sixteen-year-old shop assistant who is murdered in HALLOWE'EN PARTY; two men come under suspicion for the killing but no evidence is found.

Bennet, Alice This neat, middle-aged personal maid discovers her employer's body in LORD EDGWARE DIES.

Bennett, Miss (1) Viewed as "poor" Miss Bennett in UNFINISHED PORTRAIT, she is a seamstress who asserts that she is the illegitimate daughter of an unnamed but highly placed nobleman.

Bennett, Miss (2) A gray-haired, sensible former hospital nurse in THE UNEXPECTED GUEST, she is the alert, brisk housekeeper-secretary who is devoted to the murder victim, Richard WARWICK.

Bennington, Mrs. A friend of the Goodman family in ENDLESS NIGHT, she accidentally meets Ellie Goodman ROGERS at the Acropolis.

Benson, Mrs. Described as a difficult woman, she dies from eating hat paint that she mistakes for Syrup of Figs in CARDS ON THE TABLE.

Bent, Clifford The leader of the Youth Movement in PASSENGER TO FRANKFURT, he is the son of a wealthy oil magnate.

Bent, Sydney The settled, pragmatic, wealthy maternal uncle of the protagonist of GIANT'S BREAD, he becomes wealthier by manufacturing explosives during World War II.

Bentham, Alice Described by Superintendent BATTLE as "the pop-eyed one," the housemaid is an observant witness in TOWARDS ZERO.

Bentham, Mildred She is an elderly traveler who refuses to let her aches and pains prevent her from enjoying life in NEMESIS.

Bentley, James A repulsive man, he is convicted of murder and sentenced to hang, but a Scotland Yard superintendent is convinced of his innocence and tries to save him in MRS. McGINTY'S DEAD.

Bercy, Sir Ambrose He hides a fiery personality beneath his distinguished exterior in "THE HERB OF DEATH."

Beresford, Betty The adopted daughter of Tommy and Tuppence BERESFORD, she becomes a research anthropologist in Africa and is referred to in N OR M? and POSTERN OF FATE.

Beresford, Deborah One of Tommy and Tuppence BERESFORD's twins, she appears in N OR M?, BY THE PRICKING OF MY THUMBS and POSTERN OF FATE. She is a code-breaker for British Intelligence during World War II and returns with her three children to live with her parents after her husband's death.

Beresford, Derek Twin brother of Deborah BERESFORD and the son of Tommy and Tuppence BERESFORD, he serves in the Royal Air Force during World War II, and appears in N OR M?

Beresford, Prudence Cowley (Tuppence) The fifth daughter of an archdeacon, she is a lively and intelligent woman who works in a hospital during World War I. Out of a job after the war, she meets her childhood friend, Tommy BERESFORD, with whom she first forms Young Adventurers Ltd., followed by the International Detective Agency. Her strong intuition places her in danger but also helps her to sort out clues, and she is rarely modest about her success. In addition, she displays a lack of common sense as she rushes headlong into situations, often acting without thinking. She marries Tommy at the end of THE SECRET ADVERSARY, becoming the mother of three children as she ages during the course of PARTNERS IN CRIME, N OR M? and BY THE PRICKING OF MY THUMBS, until she finally appears as a grandmother living in retirement at The Laurels with Tommy in POSTERN OF FATE.

Beresford, Lieutenant Thomas (Tommy) Orphaned when young, Tommy is an unimaginative, ordinary but charming young man with bright red hair who serves in World War I, in which he is wounded twice. He meets his childhood friend, Tuppence COWLEY, after he is released from service and, because both are without jobs, they decide to start Young Adventurers Ltd. and pledge to accept all assignments. Their new adventures lead them into investigative work and they establish the International Detective Agency, dedicating their energies to solving crimes. Tommy marries Tuppence at the end of their first adventure in THE SECRET ADVERSARY, and the two later adopt a daughter, Betty BERESFORD, and have a set of twins, Deborah and Derek BERESFORD, as they grow old gracefully in the course of four subsequent books: PARTNERS IN CRIME, N OR M?, BY THE PRICKING OF MY THUMBS and POSTERN OF FATE, where they are seen as retired grandparents who still love a good mystery. To the end, Tommy remains the slower thinker whose reticence to act quickly serves as the perfect foil to Tuppence's impetuous nature.

Beresford, Sir William   Tommy BERESFORD's uncle, he took in the young orphan and made him heir to a fortune. Despite his stated misogyny, he is charmed by Tuppence's spirit in THE SECRET ADVERSARY, and Tommy remains his heir.

Bernard, Dr. Ralph   The elderly, stooping physician who pronounces the victim dead of an internal hemorrhage in "THE TRAGEDY AT MARSDEN MANOR," he is considered by HASTINGS to be "an old ass."

Beroldy, Jeanne   See DAUBREUIL, MADAME.

Bessner, Dr. Carl   An unlikely romantic figure, this vacationing German doctor in DEATH ON THE NILE (2) unwittingly reveals the murderer to investigators, and wins the hand of a lovely young woman.

Best, Grace   A member of Simeon LEE's household staff, she is the second housemaid in HERCULE POIROT'S CHRISTMAS.

Betterton, Olive   She dies in a plane crash only a short time after her husband of six months disappears in DESTINATION UNKNOWN.

Betterton, Thomas Charles (Tom)   Twice widowed, he poisons Elsa MANNHEIM, the scientific colleague whom he marries in order to steal her work on fission, and loses his second wife, Olive BETTERTON, in a plane crash in DESTINATION UNKNOWN. Greed leads him to join Mr. ARISTIDES' Brain Trust, but he balks at the restraints of the organization, and tries to escape.

Betts-Hamilton, Mr.   An extremely quiet man, he rarely speaks in "THE AFFAIR OF THE PINK PEARL," preferring to let his wife communicate for them both.

Betts-Hamilton, Mrs.   Staying with the KINGSTON BRUCES, this effusive woman discovers that her pendant is missing a pink pearl in "THE AFFAIR OF THE PINK PEARL."

Bex, Monsieur Lucien   Familiar with Hercule POIROT from a previous case, the Commissary of Police welcomes the detective in MURDER ON THE LINKS.

Big Charlotte   See VON WALDSAUSEN, THE GRAFIN CHARLOTTE.

Big Four, The   Mystery novel.
The novel contains two surprises, in the forms of a hitherto unknown Achille POIROT and a romantic interest for Hercule POIROT. The plot centers on efforts to expose the identity of Number 4, a master of disguise and a member of a ruthless international organization named "The Big Four."

PUBLISHING AND DRAMATIZATION HISTORY
The novel was published in 1927 by Collins in London, and by Dodd, Mead and Company in New York.
The novel has not been adapted for stage or screen.

CHARACTERS
Joseph AARONS, Betsy ANDREWS, Colonel APPLEBY, Sydney CROWTHER, Claud DARRELL, Monsieur DESJARDEAUX, Robert GRANT, Mr. and Mrs. HALLIDAY, Captain Arthur HASTINGS, John INGLES, Chief Inspector James JAPP, Captain KENT, LI CHANG YEN, Miss MARTIN, Mr. MAYERLING, Mr. MCNEIL, Inspector MEADOWS, Flossie MONRO, Madame OLIVIER,

Mabel PALMER, Mr. PAYNTER, Mrs. PEARSON, Achille Poirot, Hercule Poirot, Dr. RIDGEWAY, Countess Vera ROSSAKOFF, Abe RYLAND, Dr. TEEVES, Mr. and Mrs. TEMPLETON, Jonathan WHALLEY, Gilmour WILSON

PLOT SYNOPSIS
Chapters 1–2
Hercule Poirot is about to leave for South America on an assignment from a wealthy American soap manufacturer when he is surprised by a visit from Captain Hastings, who has lived in South America for more than a decade. As the two speak, a man arrives at Poirot's door and collapses. The detective sends for the doctor, then learns from the visitor the name of the leader of "the Big Four," before rushing out to catch the train. En route, Poirot realizes that his trip was meant to get him out of the way, and he returns home to find the visitor dead. Poirot calls Chief Inspector James Japp, who identifies the dead man as a former secret service agent named Mayerling, who disappeared in Russia five years earlier. They determine that he had been gagged and forced to inhale prussic acid. They also observe that the clock on Poirot's mantelpiece has stopped at "4," a clue that Number 4, "the Destroyer," killed him.

Chapters 3–4
Poirot and Hastings consult with retired civil servant John Ingles, who gives them information about the Big Four. He tells them about a letter written by Jonathan Whalley, expressing fear of the organization, which motivates Poirot to visit the frightened man. When he and Hastings arrive in Dartmoor, they find Whalley dead and his manservant Robert accused of murder. After a quick examination of the premises, during which he finds a frozen leg of mutton, Poirot questions Robert and learns that a man posing as a butcher is most likely the killer.

Chapters 5–7
Poirot, Hastings and Japp pursue all leads, and learn that Mr. Halliday, an authority on the Big Four, has disappeared. They attempt to meet with Madame Olivier, the last person to meet with Halliday, and nearly suffer a fatal accident. Finally, the Countess Rossakoff helps them to find the missing man, but threats from the Big Four prevent him from talking. A summons from Madame Olivier turns into a trap, but Poirot cleverly fools her into releasing them.

Chapters 8–10
A message arrives from Abe Ryland, expressing his disappointment that Poirot has not arrived in South America. A suspicious Poirot learns that Ryland is looking for a secretary, and he suggests that Hastings apply for the job and obtain inside information. Once hired, Hastings learns that Ryland's other secretary has been cautioned to open all mail except the blue envelopes which carry a little "4" in the corner. When such a letter is accidentally opened, Hastings deciphers the code and relays the message to Poirot. After a close call for Hastings, the detectives review related cases which Japp has reported. A Mr. Paynter, who had complained of chest pains, is later found dead, his face burned beyond recognition. The only clue lies in the words "Yellow Jasmine," found written on a newspaper, which may mean that the doctor injected him with strychnine. Japp also tells Poirot about an odd case in which a chess player died of an apparent heart attack. Poirot discovers that the man was electrocuted by running current through a bishop game piece, which was significantly heavier than the other.

Chapters 12–13
The two detectives receive a wire from Hastings's ranch manager in Argentina, stating that Mrs. Hastings has been kidnapped by the Big Four. Hastings is instructed to write Poirot a note to lure him, but he encodes within it a warning to his friend of danger. In the ensuing melee, Hastings is overcome by gas, but Poirot comes prepared with a muffler and a respirator. When Hastings regains consciousness, Poirot reveals that he had placed Mrs. Hastings into protective custody months before, and that she has not been in danger.

Chapters 14–15
Aware that the elusive Number 4 has taken on a range of roles, Poirot contacts Joseph Aarons, and obtains a list of character actors who have left the stage within the previous three years. He focuses his attention on Claud Darrell, who has been to both America and China, and advertises for contact from anyone who knows Darrell. The sole individual with information dies in a hit-and-run accident. Soon after, Poirot and Hastings are lured to the house of a man supposedly poisoned, but their captor is none other than Number 4, who is Claud Darrell. They escape, but disaster strikes when they return home.

Poirot lights a fire in the fireplace, and an explosion occurs. The doctor is called, but he reports that Poirot is dead.

Chapters 16–17
Hastings attends Poirot's funeral, and he is later warned to leave the Big Four alone. When he returns home, he is given a posthumous letter from Poirot, instructing him to return to South America. Hastings begins the return trip, but his boat is stopped and taken to a spa on the coast of Belgium, where he finds Poirot alive. Poirot and Hastings go to a resort in the Italian Tyrol, where Madame Olivier, Abe Ryland and Claud Darrell are expected. The detectives are joined at their table by a man who has the odd mannerism of playing with bread crumbs, a habit which the hit-and-run victim had described as unique to Claud Darrell. The Big Four capture Poirot and Hastings, and take them to their hideaway, where Countess Rossakoff is left to guard them. She looks closely at Poirot, then reaches out and pulls off his moustache, under which there is a scar. Hastings reveals that this is Achille, Hercule's twin brother. Poirot convinces Vera to help them escape only moments before the hideaway blows up. Poirot then reveals that he had masqueraded as Achille, in order to make the Big Four believe that he was still controlling everything from outside. At the end of the novel, Hercule returns, and Achille Poirot is sent back "to the land of myth."

CRIME NOTES
Of the murder victims in this novel, one is electrocuted, a second is forced to inhale prussic acid, a third is killed in a hit-and-run automobile accident, a fourth ingests strychnine and a fifth is hit on the head before his throat is cut.

Biggs, Abraham   See GRANT, ROBERT.

Biggs, Alfred   He is unable to keep the names of the dentists' patients straight, but Biggs' interest in detective fiction enables Hercule POIROT to determine the victim's time of death in ONE, TWO, BUCKLE MY SHOE.

Bill   An inarticulate workman who is embarrassed to be seen offering evidence to the police in "THREE BLIND MICE."

Billingsley, Mr.   A close-mouthed solicitor in A POCKET FULL OF RYE, he eventually reveals the terms of the murdered man's will.

Bimbo   Well-tanned and good company, he is a charming companion to the wealthy Lady STRANLEIGH in "THE VOICE IN THE DARK," and seems destined to become her fifth husband.

Bindler, Horace   Taken by Miss MARPLE's nephew, Raymond WEST, to view Greenshaw's Folly, he would love to add the structure's photograph to his already-full collection of monstrosities in "GREENSHAW'S FOLLY."

Binion, Dr.   A dental surgeon who sometimes masqueraded as his friend, Commander HAYDOCK, in N OR M?

Binns, Edith   The sharp-eyed maid in THE PALE HORSE whose description of her late mistress' symptoms leads Ariadne OLIVER to identify the means of murder.

Birch, Hugo   An irascible man in his sixties in SPIDER'S WEB, he is a proper, old-school type who becomes mixed up in murder, in spite of himself.

"Bird with the Broken Wing, The"   Mystery short story.
     The plot centers on the apparent suicide of a sad and ethereal woman which becomes a case of murder.

PUBLISHING AND DRAMATIZATION HISTORY
The story appeared in the short story collection, THE MYSTERIOUS MR. QUIN, published in 1930 by William Collins Sons and Co., Ltd., in London, and by Dodd, Mead and Company in New York.
     The story has not been adapted for stage or screen.

CHARACTERS
Gerard ANNESLEY, Mabelle ANNESLEY, Doris COLES, Mrs. GRAHAM, Roger GRAHAM, David KEELEY, Madge KEELEY, Harley QUIN, Mr. SATTERTHWAITE

PLOT SYNOPSIS

Faced with two competing social commitments, Mr. Satterthwaite attends a houseparty, and sends his regrets in response to a dinner invitation to Laidell. As he and the other guests play games after dinner, the fun becomes serious when the names "Quin" and "Laidell" are spelled out in a game of table turning. Mr. Satterthwaite goes to Laidell, and the next morning a young female houseguest is found dead, apparently by suicide. He realizes that a murder has occurred after he receives an unexpected message from Mr. Harley Quin.

CRIME NOTES

As with many of the Harlequin stories, Mr. Quin's presence is felt rather than seen.

Birell, Louise

Birell, Louise   Also known under the names of Louise CHARPENTIER and Louise CARPENTER, she contacts an old lover and suggests that they meet again, but dies after falling from a window before having any impact on the plot in THIRD GIRL.

Black, Captain

Black, Captain   Deeply bronzed and handsome, he locates a former love but becomes a suspect when her husband is murdered in "THE TRAGEDY AT MARSDON MANOR."

Black Coffee

Black Coffee   Mystery play.

The author's first original mystery play, the plot of *Black Coffee* centers on Hercule POIROT's attempts to solve a murder and to locate the secret formula for a substance that can increase by a hundredfold the human destruction wrought by war.

PUBLISHING AND DRAMATIZATION HISTORY

The play was written for production in 1930, and opened at the Embassy Theatre in London on December 8, 1930. A film version was produced in 1931 by Twickenham Studios in England, and it starred Austin Trevor as a clean-shaven Hercule POIROT.

CHARACTERS

Barbara AMORY, Miss Caroline AMORY, Sir Claud AMORY, Lucia AMORY, Richard AMORY, Dr. CARELLI, Dr. GRAHAM, Captain Arthur HASTINGS, Inspector James JAPP, JOHNSON (2), Hercule Poirot, Edward RAYNOR, TREDWELL (4)

PLOT SYNOPSIS

Act 1

The sudden appearance in the Amory household of Dr. Carelli has an unsettling effect on Lucia Amory, the half-Italian wife of Richard Amory. Barbara Amory and Miss Caroline Amory sort through a box of old dispensary medications to find something to calm Lucia, and find a variety of tubes containing potentially lethal substances "which could kill, roughly, twelve strong men." While the others are otherwise occupied, Lucia takes tablets from a tube of hyoscine hydrobromide, a potent poison that produces a painless death. Raynor watches as Lucia drops the pills into her coffee, but the cups are mixed up as the coffee cups are handed out. Somewhat dizzy, Lucia asks Richard to open the French windows as Sir Claud enters the room. He states that the doors and windows have been locked at his command, and announces that Hercule Poirot will soon arrive to investigate the theft of the secret formula. He drinks coffee and complains of its bitter taste. Sir Claud seeks to give the thief a chance to return the formula before Poirot searches everyone, so he shuts off the lights and instructs the thief to leave the envelope on the table in the dark. When the lights go on, a long white envelope is found on the table next to Sir Claud, who is now dead. Poirot appears as planned. While other family members tell the detective that he is no longer needed, Lucia begs him to stay.

Act 2

Early the next morning, Poirot asks Richard Amory to relate the events of the preceding evening. When Richard tells the detective that the formula and its monetary value hold no interest for him, Poirot reminds him that one person is guilty of stealing the formula, and four people must be proved innocent. Lucia speaks with Poirot, and she now tells him that she was wrong to ask him to stay. When Dr. Graham announces the autopsy results, showing that Sir Claud was poisoned with hyoscine, an inquest is scheduled, and Poirot must investigate the murder. Despite Richard's efforts to the contrary, Poirot interviews Miss Caroline Amory and learns a great deal about the events of the previous evening. She is a keenly observant woman, and she relates details which others either choose to omit or fail to remember. Poirot speaks once again with Lucia, telling her

Austin Trevor as Hercule Poirot in *Black Coffee* **plays the gallant to Adrienne Allen as Dino Galliene and Richard Cooper look on in the 1931 movie.**   (Photo courtesy of the National Film Archive)

that she should confess to "Papa" Poirot. After tricking her into believing that he has a photograph of her which proves that she is the daughter of a famous and beautiful female spy, Poirot receives her cooperation. She reveals her connection to Dr. Carelli, and admits putting hyoscine in her coffee cup just as Inspector Japp arrives.

Act 3
Barbara Amory flirts openly with Hastings and persuades him to give up his post in the library, where Poirot had instructed him to stand guard. After Hastings leaves, Miss Amory enters, and is caught by Carelli as she searches for something in the back of

the settee. He firmly makes her leave the room, because he has a private call to make to "Miguel." As he waits for the return call, Raynor enters and searches the vase, observed by a partially hidden Carelli, who steps out and startles the secretary. As Carelli attempts to leave the room, Poirot restrains him, until Japp appears and identifies the "doctor" as Tonio, a well-known criminal. Japp calls the family together and announces that Sir Claud was poisoned; then he and Poirot speak alone with Richard. Poirot sets a trap for the murderer, using the hidden formula as the bait. As Japp lies in wait, Poirot pretends to drink poisoned whiskey with the murderer, who arrogantly relates the details of the crime.

CRIME NOTES
The sole murder in this play occurs as the result of poisoning by hyoscine hydrobromide.

Blackett, Mrs.   A well-organized woman, she provides Miss MARPLE with valuable information regarding her cousin's daughter, Nora BROAD, in NEMESIS.

Blacklock, Dr.   An obstinate physician who resolutely adheres to old ideas and methods of treatment, he allows no disagreement regarding his opinions in A MURDER IS ANNOUNCED.

Blacklock, Charlotte (Lotty)   A physician's elderly daughter who impersonates her deceased sister in order to obtain an inheritance in A MURDER IS ANNOUNCED.

Blacklock, Letitia (Letty, Blackie)   A highly efficient secretary and confidante to her wealthy employer, she becomes his heiress but dies before enjoying her inheritance in A MURDER IS ANNOUNCED.

Blair, Suzanne   A young woman in THE MAN IN THE BROWN SUIT who becomes involved in an unlikely adventure when a film container filled with diamonds is dropped onto her bed.

Blairgowrie, Duke of   Married to the daughter of a Chicago pork butcher, this haughty and imposing nobleman attempts to lure Tommy BERESFORD to his death, but dies himself when he is electrocuted by his intended weapon against Tommy in "BLINDMAN'S BLUFF."

Blake, Miss   A junior school mistress at Meadowbank School in CAT AMONG THE PIGEONS, she returns from an unhappy holiday in the Middle East to start the new school term.

Blake, Basil   The object of gossip in ST. MARY MEAD because of his wild lifestyle and outrageous clothes, he is nearly framed for murder in THE BODY IN THE LIBRARY.

Blake, The Honourable Elvira   A young heiress in AT BERTRAM'S HOTEL who will inherit a trust fund when she turns twenty-one, she is having an affair with the same racing car driver as her mother.

Blake, Meredith   A quiet, sensitive, unassuming man with an interest in herbals, he is nearly framed when hemlock stolen from his laboratory is used to commit a murder in FIVE LITTLE PIGS.

Blake, Philip   Described by Hercule POIROT as looking "rather like a contented pig," he is in love with his best friend's sister, who he believes may have murdered her brother in FIVE LITTLE PIGS.

Blake, Susan   A shallow, self-centered young woman, she nonetheless convinces Hercule POIROT to smooth suntan lotion on her shoulder in "TRIANGLE AT RHODES."

Blanche, Angele   An imposter who is impersonating her dead sister as a French teacher at an expensive school for girls, her plans to vacation on the Riviera are cut short by murder in CAT AMONG THE PIGEONS.

Bland, Detective Inspector   The mild-mannered Chief Constable of the county earns the respect of Hercule POIROT with his meticulous examination of the case in DEAD MAN'S FOLLY.

Bland, Josiah   A corrupt member of the construction trade whose company's workmanship is shoddy, he lives near the murder victim in THE CLOCKS.

Bland, Valerie   An impersonator who has assumed the name of her husband's first wife, she collects the late woman's inheritance in THE CLOCKS.

Blatt, Horace   An expansive and outgoing man in EVIL UNDER THE SUN, he is suspected of smuggling heroin.

Bleibner, Mr. (1)   An American explorer and codiscoverer of the tomb of Men-her-Ra, he may have died from the Curse of the Mummy's Tomb in "THE ADVENTURE OF THE EGYPTIAN TOMB."

Bleibner, Mr. (2)   A tall, dyspeptic-looking American businessman in GIANT'S BREAD, he hires the amnesiac Vernon DEYRE as his chauffeur.

Bleibner, Rupert   Convinced that he is suffering from leprosy, this dissolute young man commits suicide after having named the man who convinced him of his affliction as his heir in "THE ADVENTURE OF THE EGYPTIAN TOMB."

Bletchley, Major An officer of the old school, he is shocked by the modern military and contends that democracy has weakened the strength of the nation in N OR M?

Bligh, Gertrude (Nellie) Posing as Mrs. JOHNSON, she is paid to watch Lady STARKE and to make arrangements to move her to another rest home in the event her behavior becomes more peculiar in BY THE PRICKING OF MY THUMBS.

"Blindman's Bluff" Mystery short story.

A troubled nobleman approaches Tommy and Tuppence BERESFORD as they lunch at a chic restaurant, and asks them to help him find his missing daughter.

PUBLISHING AND DRAMATIZATION HISTORY
The story appeared in the short story collection, PARTNERS IN CRIME, published in 1929 by William Collins Sons and Company, Ltd., in London, and by Dodd, Mead and Company in New York.

The story has not been adapted for stage or screen.

CHARACTERS
Tommy BERESFORD, Tuppence BERESFORD, Duke of BLAIRGOWRIE, Captain HARPER

PLOT SYNOPSIS
An apparently distraught father asks the Beresfords for help in locating his daughter, a request to which the pair immediately agrees. Tommy, using the name of the former owner of the International Detective Agency, Theodore BLUNT, leaves with the presumed nobleman and his aide to learn more about the case, and walks into a trap from which Tuppence has to spring him.

CRIME NOTES
Tommy Beresford role-plays in this story as the blind detective Thornley Colton, created by Clinton Holland Stagg (1890–1916), and he casts Tuppence into the role of Colton's secretary, who acts as his eyes.

Blondin, Monsieur Gaston The condescending proprietor of an exclusive restaurant, his reputation was once saved by Hercule POIROT, and he shows his appreciation in DEATH ON THE NILE (2).

Blood Will Tell See MRS. MCGINTY'S DEAD.

"Blood-Stained Pavement, The" Mystery short story.

Another of the stories related to the Tuesday Club, the plot centers on the drowning death of a frumpy wife who may or may not have been murdered.

PUBLISHING AND DRAMATIZATION HISTORY
The story appeared in the short story collection, THE THIRTEEN PROBLEMS, published in 1932 by William Collins Sons and Company, Ltd., in London, and, under the title, THE TUESDAY CLUB MURDERS, by Dodd, Mead and Company in New York.

The story has not been adapted for stage or screen.

CHARACTERS
Captain Denis DACRE, Mrs. Margery DACRE, Miss Carol HARDING, Joyce LEMPIERE, Miss Jane MARPLE, Raymond WEST

PLOT SYNOPSIS
Joyce Lempiere tells of an incident that occurred five years before when she was vacationing at a small inn on the Cornish coast. She was painting a picture of the front of the inn, including the realistic details of wet bathing suits drying on the balcony of Denis and Margery Dacre, when she realized that she had included bloodstains on the pavement. She walked over to the site on the pavement, and found only water from the wet suits above. A few days later, she learned that Margery Dacre had drowned. Miss Marple rightly assumes that the story holds great importance.

CRIME NOTES
The teller of the tale in this story appears in future novels and stories as Miss Marple's niece-in-law, after she married Miss Marple's writer nephew Raymond West.

Blore, William Henry A former member of British Intelligence who may have caused a man's death, he is the eighth victim of the Island murders in AND THEN THERE WERE NONE.

"Blue Geranium, The" Mystery short story.

The death of a neurotic woman who had been warned that the "Blue Geranium means death" takes on sinister overtones to Miss MARPLE.

PUBLISHING AND DRAMATIZATION
HISTORY
The story appeared in the short story collection, THE THIRTEEN PROBLEMS, published in 1932 by William Collins Sons and Company, Ltd., in London, and, under the title, THE TUESDAY CLUB MURDERS, by Dodd, Mead and Company in New York.

The story has not been adapted for stage or screen.

CHARACTERS
Colonel Arthur BANTRY, Dolly BANTRY, Sir Henry CLITHERING, Nurse COPLING, Jane HELIER, Dr. LLOYD, Miss Marple, George PRITCHARD, Mary PRITCHARD, ZARIDA

PLOT SYNOPSIS
The Tuesday Night Club hears the strange story of a semi-invalid woman who has been warned by one of the several fortune-tellers she consults to beware of blue geraniums. On the night of the full moon, a geranium in her wallpaper turns blue and she becomes upset. This occurs twice more, and the strain seems to cause the woman's death, but Miss Marple knows better.

CRIME NOTES
This story marks the reunion of the Tuesday Night Club members after a one-year hiatus.

Blundell, Caleb (Pop) His attempt at self-aggrandizement is revealed in "THE PEARL OF PRICE" when he brags that his daughter's nearly worthless earrings are worth eighty thousand dollars.

Blundell, Carol Fooled by her father into believing that her pearl earrings are worth eighty thousand dollars, she asks PARKER PYNE to help her when she loses one in "THE PEARL OF PRICE."

Blunt, Alistair Described as "so essentially British" for his apparent lack of emotion, he heads the most powerful banking organization in England, and can make or break government policy in ONE, TWO, BUCKLE MY SHOE.

Blunt, Major Hector An old friend of Roger ACKROYD and a renowned big game hunter, his painful shyness nearly prevents him from asking his late friend's niece to marry him in THE MURDER OF ROGER ACKROYD.

Blunt, Admiral Philip A highly placed Cabinet member, he maintains a policy of isolationism in regard to Russia in PASSENGER TO FRANKFURT.

Blunt, Theodore The former manager of the International Detective Agency who had been highly involved with international Communist spies, his identity is assumed by Tommy BERESFORD in PARTNERS IN CRIME.

Bodlicott, Henry (Chuck) The replacement gardener for Tommy and Tuppence BERESFORD when his predecessor is murdered, he devotes himself to helping them solve a crime in POSTERN OF FATE.

Bodlicott, Isaac Known by all of the townspeople, he is the handyman in POSTERN OF FATE whose curiosity results in his death.

Body in the Library, The Mystery novel.

The novel contains many of the residents of ST. MARY MEAD who appeared in the first full-length Miss MARPLE mystery, MURDER AT THE VICARAGE, published twelve years earlier. The plot centers on the discovery of the dead body of a hotel dancer in the library of Gossington Hall, the home of Colonel and Dolly BANTRY.

PUBLISHING AND DRAMATIZATION
HISTORY
The novel was published in 1942 by William Collins Sons and Company, Ltd., in London, and by Dodd, Mead and Company in New York.

The novel was adapted for television in 1985 by the BBC, and was shown on the Public Broadcasting Service in the U.S.

CHARACTERS

Colonel Arthur BANTRY, Dolly BANTRY, Mrs. BARTLETT, George BARTLETT, Basil BLAKE, Peter CARMODY, Griselda CLEMENT, Leonard CLEMENT, Sir Henry CLITHERING, Mark GASKELL, Superintendent HARPER, Miss HARTNELL, Dr. HAYDOCK, Adelaide JEFFERSON, Conway JEFFERSON, Ruby KEENE, Dinah LEE, Hugh MACLEAN, Miss Jane Marple, Colonel MELCHETT, Dr. METCALF, Constable PALK, Martha PRICE RIDLEY, Pamela REEVES, Inspector SLACK, Raymond STARR, Josephine TURNER, Caroline WETHERBY

PLOT SYNOPSIS

Chapters 1–4

Colonel and Dolly Bantry are awakened early by their maid, who tells them that there is a body in their library. They call the authorities to report the murder, and Dolly Bantry sends a car for her friend, Miss Marple. The police ask Colonel Bantry if he had been having an affair with the dead woman. The coroner places the time of death at between 10 P.M. and midnight. The police then match the dead woman's description with a list of missing persons, and determine that she is Ruby Keene, a dance hostess who worked at the Majestic Hotel. The identification is confirmed by her cousin, who also works at the Majestic.

Chapters 5–8

The police question Josephine Turner and learn that Mr. Conway Jefferson, an invalid of advanced age and an old friend of Miss Marple, had called the police to report Ruby missing. When police question the manager of the Majestic Hotel, they learn that Mr. Jefferson had paid a lot of attention to the dead woman, but his daughter-in-law did not like this association. Police also question others with whom Ruby had been friendly, and they learn that Conway Jefferson had grown fond of Ruby and planned to adopt her.

Chapters 9–12

The police inspect Ruby's room and find letters from a girl named Lil. They also question Raymond Starr, a good-looking fortune hunter who considers the dead woman to have been a pleasant but stupid girl. The police receive another call while at the Majestic, and learn that a burned car with a charred body inside has been found near the quarry. They later learn that the victim is a Girl Guide named Pamela Reeves.

Chapters 13–15

An investigation reveals that the girl in the car had been strangled before the car was set on fire. The car belonged to George Bartlett, but he had not reported it as missing until the next morning. At the same time, Miss Marple learns that Conway Jefferson's son-in-law and daughter-in-law hated Ruby because she was threatening their inheritance. Miss Marple's sharp eyes also notice that the dress worn by Ruby was inappropriately shabby for going on a date.

Chapters 16–19

Miss Marple knows who killed Ruby, but refuses to tell anyone yet. She also determines that Ruby had been murdered elsewhere, and taken to the Bantry's library. Even though Miss Marple knows that Basil Blake is not the killer, the police arrest him. They also question Conway Jefferson's butler, who relates an incident in which a picture of a young man fell from Ruby's purse and Jefferson had demanded to know who it was.

Chapters 20–22

Miss Marple determines that the body in the library was not that of Ruby Keene, but was in fact Pamela Reeves in disguise. Lured into being transformed for a promised screen test, Pamela had been made up, and her hair had been bleached. The real Ruby Keene had been knocked out, placed in the car, and set on fire. Miss Marple identifies the motive and the murderer, solving the crime ahead of the authorities.

CRIME NOTES

Pamela Reeves was strangled, while Ruby Keene was hit in the head and then burned.

Boehmer, Captain Frederick Agatha Christie's maternal grandfather, he was an officer in the Argyll Highlanders, and nearly twenty years older than her maternal grandmother. He died at the age of forty-seven, leaving a widow and four young children, one of whom was Christie's mother, Clarissa (Clara).

Boehmer, Mary Ann West (Grannie B.) Agatha Christie's maternal grandmother, who was married at the age of sixteen to an officer in the Argyll

Highlanders, and became a widow with four small children at the age of twenty-seven. She agreed to allow her daughter Clarissa (Clara), Christie's mother, to be adopted by her sister Margaret and Margaret's wealthy American husband, Nathaniel Frary Miller.

Bolford, Mr.   A man with his feet firmly planted in the past, this partner in a tailoring firm chose to cater to a largely male clientele, with only occasional attention to "certain favoured members of the feminine sex" in THEY CAME TO BAGHDAD.

Bollard, Mr.   His jewelry store had long served England's aristocracy, so he knew that eccentricity and even larceny were to be expected among the rich in AT BERTRAM'S HOTEL.

Bond, James   Despite his shy, retiring ways, he becomes an unlikely hero when he discovers a jewel thief in "THE RAJAH'S EMERALD."

Bond, Sergeant Percy   An otherwise stalwart law officer in CAT AMONG THE PIGEONS, he hesitates to question teachers, of whom he has retained a mortal fear since childhood.

Bones, Billy   See OSSINGTON, SIR WILLIAM.

Bonnington, Henry   A man of very particular tastes in food, he invites Hercule POIROT to dinner at his favorite restaurant, where he acquaints the detective with the case in "FOUR-AND-TWENTY BLACKBIRDS."

Boomerang Clue, The   See WHY DIDN'T THEY ASK EVANS?

Borrow, Richard (Dick)   A dedicated East-End parson, his intensity inspires a millionaire to give all of his money to the parson's mission in "THE CALL OF THE WINGS."

Boscombe, Mr.   A shrewd art gallery owner in THIRD GIRL, he is also a wise salesman who impresses Hercule POIROT by allowing the art to speak for itself.

Boscowan, Emma   The widow of a painter and herself a sculptress in BY THE PRICKING OF MY THUMBS, she provides vital information regarding a significant painting.

Bosner, Frederick   A former German spy who escapes from a train wreck with a badly damaged face, he seizes the opportunity to create a new life as archaeologist Dr. Eric LEIDNER in MURDER IN MESOPOTAMIA.

Bott, Police Constable   His enthusiasm for being a policeman shows as he walks his beat in HICKORY DICKORY DOCK, but he fails to identify a character's death as murder.

Bouc, Monsieur   A longtime friend of Hercule POIROT, he is the director of La Compagnie Internationale des Wagons Lits, whose bias against Italians prompts him to identify one man as the murderer in MURDER ON THE ORIENT EXPRESS (1).

Bourget, Louise   A lady's maid who tries to blackmail the man who killed her mistress, she is murdered in DEATH ON THE NILE (2).

Bourne, Ursula   A parlourmaid secretly married to Roger ACKROYD's stepson, she is dismissed from her job when her master is murdered in THE MURDER OF ROGER ACKROYD.

Bower, Dr. Charles   See BAUER, CARL.

Bower, John   See BAUER, JOHN.

Bowers, Miss   The nurse to a wealthy woman whose chief illness appears to be kleptomania in DEATH ON THE NILE (2).

Boyd Carrington, Sir William (Bill)   His boring habits and stuffy ways impress Captain HASTINGS as much as they exasperate Hercule POIROT in CURTAIN.

Boyle, Mrs.   A large, aggressive woman, she is unconcerned about making enemies, but one strangles her to death during a snowstorm in "THREE BLIND MICE."

Boynton, Mrs.   Described as "a distorted old Buddha" with eyes that emit "a wave of evil," she is a former prison wardress who now treats her family as prisoners in APPOINTMENT WITH DEATH. She is murdered while she and her family travel through Petra.

Boynton, Carol The nervous stepdaughter of a former prison wardress, she is emotionally incapable of breaking out of her restricted life in APPOINTMENT WITH DEATH.

Boynton, Ginerva (Jinny) The natural daughter of a former prison wardress who terrifies her stepchildren, she is an ethereal contrast to her mother in APPOINTMENT WITH DEATH.

Boynton, Lennox The stepson of a former prison wardress, he becomes another puppet of his stepmother, who "was quite aware of the power of sex." She chooses a weak-willed but lovely girl to be his wife, and commands that they live in her home in APPOINTMENT WITH DEATH.

Boynton, Nadine Married to Lennox BOYNTON, she is earning a nursing degree at her mother-in-law's command, but she tries to pry her husband loose from his mother's clutches by threatening to run away with another man in APPOINTMENT WITH DEATH.

Boynton, Raymond (Ray) His deep hatred of his controlling stepmother leads him to ponder murdering her, an act which he equates with killing a mad dog in APPOINTMENT WITH DEATH.

Brabazon, Archdeacon A guilt-ridden member of the clergy, he believes that he caused a young woman's death by pressuring her to break off her engagement to a scoundrel in NEMESIS.

Bradburn, Cyrus G. Apparently an American millionaire to all appearances, he pays a premium price for a mansion filled with valuable antiques in "AT THE BELLS 'AND MOTLEY.' "

Bradbury-Scott, Anthea Described by Miss MARPLE as "a mature Ophelia," she is one of three peculiar sisters who might be guilty of murder in NEMESIS.

Bradbury-Scott, Clotilde A woman who is fiercely protective of her ward, she is well-educated and dangerous, but Miss MARPLE rules her out as a murderer in NEMESIS.

Bradley, C.R. Viewed by the police as a cunning confidence man, he is a disbarred lawyer who is easily capable of evading the law in THE PALE HORSE.

Brandon, Eileen Currently a waitress at an espresso bar in THE PALE HORSE, she left her former job of taking customer surveys because she found that job "unsavoury."

Breck, Dr. Alan A physicist with the Harwell Atomic Institute, he is given uranium specimens to analyze by an explorer who is later killed in THEY CAME TO BAGHDAD.

Brent, Clement Edward Alistair Fond of doing absolutely nothing, he is master of Chimneys and the father of three lively young women—Daisy, Dulcie and Eileen. As the Ninth Marquis of Caterham and a Lord, he is expected to be a politician, but nothing bores him more. He appears in THE SECRET OF CHIMNEYS and THE SEVEN DIALS MYSTERY.

Brent, Daisy The middle daughter of Lord Caterham, she is a lively twelve-year-old who answers to the name of Guggle in THE SECRET OF CHIMNEYS.

Brent, Diana One of the schoolgirls at the party in HALLOWE'EN PARTY where a murder occurs.

Brent, Dulcie The youngest daughter of Lord CATERHAM, she is a high-spirited ten-year-old who prefers to be known as Winkle in THE SECRET OF CHIMNEYS.

Brent, Edna Possessed of a breathy and slightly nasal voice, she has the misfortune of being confined by a broken shoe heel to the typing service office on the morning of the murder, and becomes the second murder victim in THE CLOCKS.

Brent, Lady Eileen (Bundle) The eldest of Lord CATERHAM's daughters, she is an adventurous and intelligent young woman with a full social life and a penchant for driving at dangerously high speeds. She claims to be a "red hot Socialist" and also proves to have an interest in detection in THE SECRET OF CHIMNEYS and THE SEVEN DIALS MYSTERY.

Brent, Emily Caroline Her deliberately created aura of respectability covers the possibility that she may be a murderer in AND THEN THERE WERE NONE, and she becomes the fifth island victim.

Brent, Gladys The victim's maid in "THE TAPE-MEASURE MURDER," she was on her day off when Mrs. SPENLOW was murdered.

Brent, Marcia, Marchioness of Caterham The widow of Lord CATERHAM's brother Henry and aunt of Bundle, Guggle and Winkle, she is a majestically proportioned woman who freely offers her unwanted advice to her nieces in THE SEVEN DIALS MYSTERY.

Breon, Edouard When he agrees to take the place of the male lead in a local production of *Tosca,* this retired French opera star becomes the target of a murderer with a long memory in "SWAN SONG."

Brett, Dr. His observation of the placement of the gun turns a verdict of suicide into the charge of murder in MURDER IN THE MEWS.

Brewis, Amanda A well-organized, pleasant-faced secretary and housekeeper in DEAD MAN'S FOLLY, she is in love with her employer, and sees through his wife's pretense of vapidity.

Brewster, Emily Deep-voiced, hearty and athletic, she successfully obscures her good heart from all but Hercule POIROT in EVIL UNDER THE SUN.

Brewster, Jim He is a beetle-browed member of the Youth Movement in PASSENGER TO FRANKFURT who continually looks suspicious.

Brewster, Lola An actress with fiery red hair and an equally fiery temper, she has a habit of threatening to shoot people in THE MIRROR CRACK'D FROM SIDE TO SIDE.

Brice-Woodworth, Patricia Cool and competent, she is present at an anniversary dinner and takes control when the host is poisoned in SPARKLING CYANIDE.

Bridget A high-spirited fifteen-year-old, she joins two friends to stage a murder as a Boxing Day surprise in "THE THEFT OF THE ROYAL RUBY."

Brill, Inspector A highly experienced police officer with military bearing in SAD CYPRESS, he is a meticulous, competent investigator whose finding of a printed label nearly breaks the case.

Bristow, Frank An artist in "THE DEAD HARLEQUIN," he disdains the trappings of the rich, and his painting, "The Dead Harlequin," contains a figure strongly resembling Mr. Harley QUIN.

Broad, Nora A young woman with a reputation as a disreputable "goodtime girl" with loose morals in NEMESIS, her disappearance becomes a source of gossip, but not concern.

Broadribb, James The shrewd senior partner of the law firm representing the wealthy and deceased Mr. RAFIEL, he treats Miss MARPLE with courtesy and the caution of a man who knows the potentially deceptive quality of appearances in NEMESIS.

Brown, Mr. A sinister and elusive figure who was responsible for most of the peace movement propaganda during World War I, he remains a dangerous figure whose true identity is known only to a select few in THE SECRET ADVERSARY.

Brown, Geraldine Mary Alexandra Confined to her room by a broken leg, she uses binoculars to spy on her neighbors across the street, and obtains valuable information for the police in THE CLOCKS.

Brown, John See CRACKENTHORPE, CEDRIC.

Brown, Laurence A conscientious objector during World War I, he considers himself to be highly strung and overly sensitive. He is accused along with his late employer's wife of having murdered her husband, even though he claims that "the very idea is a *nightmare* to me." Despite his nervous exterior, another female member of the household in CROOKED HOUSE finds him very attractive and claims that "Laurence has got sex appeal, all right."

Browne, Anthony   A man with a disreputable past and a not quite savory present in SPARKLING CYANIDE, his real name is Tony Morelli.

Brunston, Mrs.   A fat, good-natured cook in THE BURDEN, she acts as a kind, nonjudgmental confidante to Laura FRANKLIN.

Brun, Mademoiselle Genevieve   See MORY, ANGELE.

Bryant, Dr. Roger James   An "ear-and-throat" medical specialist, his hobby of playing the flute makes him a suspect in the poisoned-dart murder of a fellow airplane passenger in DEATH IN THE CLOUDS.

Buckle, Mrs.   Her information regarding the four wigs owned by a murdered woman leads Mrs. Ariadne OLIVER to the right conclusions in ELEPHANTS CAN REMEMBER.

Buckley, Reverend Giles   A cleric in PERIL AT END HOUSE whose daughter is murdered, he turns to platitudes rather than action during the investigation.

Buckley, Jean   Unlike her husband, Reverend Giles BUCKLEY, she takes action when she learns of her daughter's death and provides evidence to help the investigation in PERIL AT END HOUSE.

Buckley, Magdala (Maggie)   Engaged to a pilot who is missing in action, she is mistakenly murdered while wearing her cousin's lacquer-red Chinese shawl in PERIL AT END HOUSE.

Buckley, Nick   Named after her grandfather, she inherits the family home, End House, after her brother's death, and attempts are later made on her life. She is a "heaven-sent little liar" to one friend and a "scatterbrain" and a "feather-head" to Hercule POIROT, yet she survives five attempts to murder her in PERIL AT END HOUSE.

Bullard, Louise   The parlourmaid in "THE SIGN IN THE SKY," her evidence regarding a figure formed in the sky by white smoke from a train leads to a man's acquittal.

Bulmer, Sir Edwin   Known as the "forlorn hope man" in SAD CYPRESS, he is counsellor for the defense in a murder trial in which the defendant is expected to be found guilty.

Bulstrode, Honoria   The formidable headmistress of Meadowbank School in CAT AMONG THE PIGEONS, she runs her school and faculty capably and efficiently, until the months before her retirement, when murder stalks her teachers.

Bunner, Dora (Bunny)   A "painstaking but never competent" individual in A MURDER IS ANNOUNCED, she is poisoned after learning the secret of an impersonator.

Burch, Bessie   A usually pleasant young country woman whose aunt is murdered in MRS. McGINTY'S DEAD, she has an innate distrust of foreigners which impedes Hercule POIROT's questioning of her.

Burch, Joe   A painter and husband of Bessie BURCH, his eagerness to cooperate makes Hercule POIROT suspicious in MRS. McGINTY'S DEAD.

Burden, The   Non-mystery novel.
The last of the romance novels written by Christie as Mary WESTMACOTT, *The Burden* explores the consequences of sacrificial love. An elder sister lavishes love on her younger sister and gives up her own life, but learns that no one can completely shield others from unhappiness.

PUBLISHING AND DRAMATIZATION HISTORY
The Burden was first published by Heinemann in 1956 in London and by Dell in 1963 in New York.
The novel has not been adapted for stage or screen.

CHARACTERS
Mr. BALDOCK, ETHEL, Lady Muriel FAIRBOROUGH, Angela FRANKLIN, Arthur FRANKLIN, Charles FRANKLIN, Laura FRANKLIN, Shirley FRANKLIN, Henry GLYN-EDWARDS, Dr. GRAVES, Reverend Eustace HENSON, Mr. HORDER, Llewellyn KNOX, Susan LONSDALE, Mrs. ROUSE, Miss WEEKES, Sir Richard WILDING

PLOT SUMMARY
Prologue
At the christening of their third child, Shirley, the Franklins think of their dead son, Charles, and question why their daughter Laura had not died instead. At the christening, Laura thinks of dropping her infant sister onto the stone floor. She decides against doing so, and the christening ends without incident.

Part 1: Laura—1929
Part 1 provides background to ten-year-old Laura's feelings at the christening. Her parents obviously prefered their high-spirited son Charles over their quiet, well-behaved daughter. When he died, the Franklins were devastated, and Laura hoped that they would now give her their attention and love. She is shocked to learn, after they return from a recuperative cruise, that her mother is pregnant. After the baby is born, Laura begins to plan the baby's death. A house fire provides the perfect opportunity, but Laura exerts supreme effort to save her baby sister, whose happiness becomes her paramount concern from that moment on.

Part 2: Shirley—1946
Seventeen years pass; Laura has been solely responsible for Shirley's well-being since their parents' death in a plane crash 14 years earlier. She has efficiently arranged Shirley's and her lives, but Mr. Baldock warns Laura that she has given up her own life.

Shirley meets charming but insolvent Henry Glyn-Edwards, who asks to marry her. When Laura demands that they wait a year, Henry accuses her of restricting Shirley's life, so she acquiesces.

Henry loses one job after another, and spends money freely. He is also unfaithful to Shirley with several women, one of whom confronts her and tells her that Henry wants a divorce. Shirley decides to leave Henry, but he develops polio and becomes an invalid. With nowhere else to turn, the couple move in with Laura and Henry dies soon after.

Part 3: Llewellyn—1956
Religious leader and evangelist Dr. Llewellyn Knox has gone to an island to recuperate from a nervous breakdown. He meets Shirley, now married to Sir Richard Wilding. He realizes that she is deeply unhappy with her life, despite all of Wilding's efforts. In conversation with Wilding, Knox reveals an early vision which led him to become a missionary and

evangelist and which also revealed a dark-haired, tragic woman.

Part 4: As It Was in the Beginning—1956
Knox informs Laura of her sister's death and realizes that Laura is the woman of his vision. They meet for dinner, and Laura admits that she killed Henry by giving him a double dose of sleeping tablets to free Shirley. Knox tells Laura that she cannot control fate, and he admits that Shirley committed suicide.

At the end, Laura accepts the burden of Llewellyn's solicitous love, finally learning to take as well as to give.

Burgess, William A manservant with pale, shifty eyes in "THE MYSTERY OF THE SPANISH CHEST," he becomes a murder suspect.

Burgoyne A manservant in "THE MYSTERY OF THE BAGHDAD CHEST," his observation of a stain on the rug and the location of a body in a trunk provide important clues for Hercule POIROT.

Burnaby, Major John Edward As a youth, he and the murdered man had been fearless big game hunters, mountain climbers and explorers, and they had remained friends as they grew old in THE SITTAFORD MYSTERY. He learns of his old friend's death during a seance at which he scoffs, but the murdered body is found soon afterward.

Burnaby, Mr. A good source of information in DEATH ON THE NILE (2), he is the landlord of the Three Crowns pub.

Burns, Charlie A shipping clerk in "THE FACE OF HELEN," he overcomes a rival to win love by remaining pleasant and good-tempered.

Burrows, Godfrey His sleek good looks and mannequinlike smile hide the background of this aristocrat's secretary in "DEAD MAN'S MIRROR."

Burshaw, Miss A gray-haired, fussy schoolmistress in "THE GIRDLE OF HIPPOLYTA," she is distressed to learn that she has lost one of her students.

Burt, Dr. As attending physician for a family suddenly taken ill, he discovers arsenic in the chocolates and ricin in the sandwiches in "THE HOUSE OF THE LURKING DEATH."

Burt, Mr. A member of the United States Secret Service, he shadows Elsa HARDT in "THE ADVENTURE OF THE CHEAP FLAT."

Burt, James A clever but brutish veterinarian in THE ROSE AND THE YEW TREE, he is prone to drink and to ugly, domineering behavior.

Burt, Mrs. Milly A pretty, gentle woman of twenty-eight in THE ROSE AND THE YEW TREE, she is physically and mentally abused by her brutish husband.

Burton, Jerry and Joanna When this sister and brother move to a quiet country village where Jerry can recuperate from war wounds, they are shocked to receive a vicious letter which claims that they are lovers. Murder soon follows, and then true love for both of them in THE MOVING FINGER.

Burton-Cox, Mrs. Twice widowed, she is a formidable, officious woman who delights in throwing her considerable weight around in ELEPHANTS CAN REMEMBER.

Burton-Cox, Desmond The adopted son of an obnoxious, controlling woman who dominates him in ELEPHANTS CAN REMEMBER, he is kept from the fact that his natural mother left him a fortune which becomes his when he turns twenty-five.

Bury, Dr. A condescending army doctor in GIANT'S BREAD, his patients frequently die.

Bury, Colonel Ned An elderly former soldier in "DEAD MAN'S MIRROR," he has suffered for decades from unrequited love for a woman whom he follows around "like a dog," yet he remains content to spend time with her family.

Butler, Judith The mother of a twelve-year-old daughter in HALLOWE'EN PARTY, she has the appearance of a Rhine maiden, with pale skin, long blond hair and sea-green eyes.

Butler, Miranda A friend of the murder victim in HALLOWE'EN PARTY, she is a perceptive twelve-year-old girl, elflike in appearance and possessed of an analytic mind admired by Hercule POIROT.

Butt, Johnnie The town paperboy in A MURDER IS ANNOUNCED, he delivers the *Gazette*, which carries the fateful announcement.

By the Pricking of My Thumbs Mystery novel.

The novel marks the return of Tommy and Tuppence BERESFORD after nearly three decades of silence. Unlike the author's other recurring characters, the detectives have aged in accordance with time. Thus, Tommy is now over seventy, and Tuppence is sixty-six. The plot centers on a painting given to Tommy's Aunt Ada only days before her death, and the terrible secret of the house in the painting.

PUBLICATION AND DRAMATIZATION HISTORY
The novel was published in 1968 by William Collins Sons and Company, Ltd., in London, and by Dodd, Mead and Company in New York.

The novel has not been dramatized for stage or screen.

CHARACTERS
Albert BATT, Tommy Beresford, Tuppence Beresford, Gertrude (Nellie) BLIGH, Emily BOSCOWAN, Mr. COPLEIGH, Mrs. COPLEIGH, Mr. ECCLES, Ada FANSHAWE, Mrs. LANCASTER, Dr. MURRAY, Nurse O'KEEFE, Miss PACKARD, Sir Josiah PENN, Alice PERRY, Amos PERRY, ROBERT (2), Ivor SMITH, Sir Philip STARKE, the VICAR

PLOT SYNOPSIS
Book 1: Chapters 1–2
Tommy and Tuppence BERESFORD visit elderly Aunt Ada at the Sunny Ridge Nursing Home, where Tuppence is told to leave because Aunt Ada thinks that Tommy is cheating on his "real" wife with Tuppence. As she wanders through the public rooms, Tuppence meets Mrs. Lancaster, who claims that she is being poisoned; then she asks Tuppence if it is her child buried behind the fireplace.

Chapters 3–5
Aunt Ada dies three weeks later, and the Beresfords return to Sunny Ridge to collect her possessions.

They see a painting in her room which was not there three weeks earlier. The nurse tells them that it was a gift from Mrs. Lancaster, who has since been removed from the nursing home. The scene in the painting looks vaguely familiar to Tuppence, and she decides to locate Mrs. Lancaster on the pretext of requesting permission to keep the painting. Letters to her forwarding address remain unanswered, as do letters forwarded through the elderly woman's bank. As she remembers their conversation regarding the child and the fireplace, Tuppence recalls the line from *Macbeth*, "By the pricking of my thumbs/ Something evil this way comes."

Chapter 6

Tuppence tries to remember why the scene in the painting is familiar. She concludes that she has passed that house while riding a train, but cannot remember which train. When her faithful Albert requests a few days off to help his wife because their youngest child has the measles, Tuppence remembers that she had seen the house while on a train to see her goddaughter receive an award at a ceremony that the child's mother couldn't attend because the other children in the family had the measles.

Book 2: Chapters 7–9

Tuppence finds the house and speaks to the present tenant, Mrs. Perry, who tells her that the house is actually two houses joined. An actress used to live in the house. While Tuppence is at the house, a bird becomes trapped in the chimney of the house on the other side. When they free the bird, they find a child's doll in the fireplace. Afterwards, Tuppence visits the local vicar, who tells her that the house used to be named Waterside. He also informs her that someone else had inquired about a dead child whose last name was Waters. He had looked up the name in the registry but found nothing, but he promises to examine all of the headstones for her. After finding a place to stay in the village, Tuppence learns that the house is considered haunted, and that a ballerina had killed her illegitimate child there, soon after which there had been three mysterious deaths of children in the area. She decides to look in the church cemetery. She finds the stone of Lily Waters only moments before someone knocks her out with a blow to the head.

Book 3: Chapters 10–11

Tommy becomes worried when Tuppence does not return home as planned, but he is distracted by the decision to have the painting appraised by an expert and a call from Aunt Ada's doctor. At the gallery, Robert tells him that the painting is by the late William Boscowan, and worth a little money. He gives Tommy Boscowan's widow's address. Tommy then visits Dr. Murray, who tells him that seven mysterious deaths have occurred in the last two years at Sunny Ridge, most recently a morphine overdose death of a relatively healthy patient.

Chapters 12–13

Tommy visits Mrs. Lancaster's attorney, Mr. Eccles, but learns nothing. A visit to Ivor Smith, a Secret Service friend, reveals that Eccles is under suspicion for criminal activities, though no evidence connects him directly. When Tommy visits the painter's widow, he learns the location of the house in the painting, and he is given the surprising news that the boat in the painting was added by someone other than the artist. Meanwhile, Tuppence awakens in the Market Basing Royal Hospital. She gives the staff her maiden name, thinking that she is still a nurse during World War II. Their daughter, Deborah, calls Tommy after reading in the newspaper about a Prudence Cowley in the hospital who does not know her address. Before retrieving Tuppence, Tommy and Albert search Aunt Ada's desk. They find a secret compartment containing a letter to her lawyers which states that Mrs. Lancaster had recognized a criminal at Sunny Ridge, and she asks her lawyers or Tommy to investigate.

Book 4: Chapters 14–15

Tommy signs Tuppence out of the hospital, and they update each other on what they have learned, trying to figure out why Tuppence was coshed on the head. They open the doll that Tuppence found in the fireplace chimney, and find diamonds inside. Ivor Smith visits them and tells the pair that the coffin of the presumed dead child, Lily Waters, has been opened and found to contain jewels, gold and other loot from a burglary near St. Albans.

Chapters 16–17

Tommy and Tuppence learn that the house, once called Lady Mead, was once a hideaway for criminals. During a visit to the vicar, Tuppence identifies her attacker and realizes that Mrs. Lancaster is in the area. When she returns to Waterside, Tuppence finds the Perrys gone, but Mrs. Lancaster who had been secreted there lets her in and shows her the secret room in which she hid. Tuppence also learns of a web of murder and blackmail which has extended for years, and she barely escapes with her life after all the dark secrets have been revealed.

CRIME NOTE

The title of the novel is taken from a line in William Shakespeare's *Macbeth* (Act IV, Scene 1), spoken by three witches as they await the arrival of Macbeth, now king and responsible for the deaths of two men.

The means of murder in this novel is through an overdose of morphine.

C

Cabot, Mr. and Mrs. Elmer Clever imperson-
ators in AT BERTRAM'S HOTEL, they almost escape
with three thousand pounds from a train robbery.

Cade, Anthony Possessed of a long line of
aliases, he is a charming adventurer who loves danger
and worries little about the law in THE SECRET OF
CHIMNEYS.

Cadwallader, Sergeant A youngish man of "a
Welsh and poetical type" in THE UNEXPECTED
GUEST, he is a local law enforcement officer with a
soft, musical voice who quotes Keats.

Calder, Alice The pretty and resourceful twenty-
five-year-old wife of the Hereditary Sheik of Ramat
in CAT AMONG THE PIGEONS, her husband manages
to smuggle her out of the country before he is assassinated.

Calgary, Dr. Arthur The only man who could
have verified Jacko ARGYLE's alibi and saved his life in
ORDEAL BY INNOCENCE, he is prevented from acting
when a bus hits him and he develops amnesia. The
geophysicist has returned from the Antarctic too late
to prevent the miscarriage of justice, but he vows to
clear Jacko's name and locate the real murderer.

Callaway, Michael A young, wild-looking artist
in ABSENT IN THE SPRING, he seriously proposes rape
as a solution for the uptight behavior of the main
character, Joan SCUDAMORE.

"Call of the Wings, The" Mystery short story.
   The haunting music of a flute seems to move a
millionaire into giving up his wealth and turning toward the spiritual.

PUBLISHING AND DRAMATIZATION
HISTORY
The story appeared in the short story collection, THE
HOUND OF DEATH, published in 1933 by William
Collins Sons and Company, Ltd., in London, and by
Dodd, Mead and Company in New York.
   The story has not been adapted for stage or
screen.

CHARACTERS
Richard BORROW, Silas HAMER, Bernard SELDON

PLOT SYNOPSIS
As wealthy Silas Hamer walks home after dinner with
a successful nerve specialist and others, he sees a man
run over by a bus, but ignores him. Later in the
walk, he hears a haunting melody played on the
flute, and feels as if a new power were invading his
body and lightening it. Soon after, he gives away all
his money and dies while trying to save another
man's life.

Campion, Lord Edward A famous sportsman
in "THE RAJAH'S EMERALD," he favors old, comfortable clothes and a low-profile lifestyle, despite his
wealth.

Capel, Derek Fearful of the results of an exhumation, he shoots himself to death in "THE COMING
OF MR. QUIN," rather than face the consequences.

Capelli, Bianca Described as having the "laugh
of a child, the digestion of an ostrich and the temper
of a fiend," she is considered to be the greatest so-
prano of her day in "SWAN SONG."

Capstick, Nurse The efficient and soothing
nurse in THE A.B.C. MURDERS, she tends to the dying
Lady Charlotte CLARKE.

"Capture of Cerberus, The" Mystery short story.

The reappearance of a woman who was Hercule POIROT's grand passion after nearly two decades leads him into the criminal underworld and to a nightclub named Hell.

PUBLISHING AND DRAMATIZATION HISTORY

The story appeared in the short story collection, THE LABOURS OF HERCULES, published in 1947 by William Collins Sons and Company, Ltd., in London, and by Dodd, Mead and Company in New York.

The story has not been adapted for stage or screen.

CHARACTERS

Dr. Alice CUNNINGHAM, Chief Inspector James JAPP, Miss LEMON, Hercule Poirot, Countess Vera ROSSAKOFF, Detective Inspector Charles STEVENS, Paul VARESCO

PLOT SYNOPSIS

Hercule Poirot passes his long-lost love the countess while the two are on London "tube" escalators going in opposite directions, and he has time only to ask where he can find her. Her brief reply, "In Hell," seems facetious until the remarkable Miss Lemon explains that Hell is the hottest new London nightclub, and the countess is its proprietor. Poirot's visit to the decadent club not only interests the object of his affections, but makes several underworld figures very nervous. He contacts his old friend, Chief Inspector James Japp, after noticing a young Scotland Yard detective casually impersonating a member of the idle rich among the nightclub crowd; he learns that the Yard is watching the site for large-scale drug transactions believed to involve the exchange of stolen jewels for drugs. To solve the crime, however, Poirot must learn the identity of the countess's silent partner in Hell.

CRIME NOTES

This story is a retelling of the last labor of the Greek mythological figure, Hercules, who was required to descend into Hades and bring back the three-headed dog, Cerberus, who guarded the entrance to the underworld.

Carbury, Colonel A man with a tidy mind who neatly dockets facts and sorts impressions in APPOINTMENT WITH DEATH, his disheveled appearance belies his inner calm.

Cardew Trench, Mrs. Overly talkative and nosy, she is a hoarse-voiced Englishwoman who alienates other hotel guests in THEY CAME TO BAGHDAD.

Cardiff, Peter A painter in THIRD GIRL, he sports oily, black hair and greasy, black, leather clothes and boots. Mrs. Ariadne OLIVER views him as "the dirtiest-looking young man she's ever seen."

Cardner, Mary A pleasant, plump butcher's daughter in GIANT'S BREAD, she volunteers for the Red Cross and works with the district nurse in World War II.

Cards on the Table Mystery novel.

Considered the best of Christie's closed door murders, *Cards on the Table* marks the first appearance of Mrs. Ariadne OLIVER in a novel. The plot centers on an evening of bridge with four successful murderers and four crime experts. Their host is killed, and Hercule POIROT must discover the murderer.

PUBLISHING AND DRAMATIZATION HISTORY

Cards on the Table was first published by William Collins Sons and Company, Ltd., in 1936 in London, and by Dodd, Mead and Company in 1937.

The novel was adapted for the stage, and the play opened at the Vaudeville Theatre, London, on December 9, 1981. The stage version eliminates Hercule Poirot and Colonel RACE from the action.

CHARACTERS

Superintendent BATTLE, Mrs. BENSON, Mrs. CRADDOCK, Charles CRADDOCK, Rhoda DAWES, Major John DESPARD, Gerald HEMMINGWAY, Mrs. LORRIMER, Mrs. LUXMORE, Anne MEREDITH, Sergeant O'CONNOR, Mrs. Ariadne Oliver, Hercule Poirot, Colonel Johnny Race, Dr. ROBERTS, Mr. SHAITANA

PLOT SYNOPSIS

Chapters 1–3

At an exhibition of snuffboxes, Poirot is invited to dinner by Mr. Shaitana, who promises Poirot four companions who have committed murder and escaped detection.

Poirot is joined at dinner by crime experts Mrs. Ariadne Oliver, Superintendent Battle and Colonel Race. Also present are Dr. Roberts, Mrs. Lorrimer, Anne Meredith and Major Despard. Conversation at dinner focuses on murder.

Chapters 4–8
The four crime experts question Dr. Roberts, Mrs. Lorrimer, Anne Meredith and Major Despard one at a time. They solicit their opinions of the others as possible murderers and as bridge players. After completing their interrogations, the crime experts conclude that more information is needed, and Colonel Race reminds them that all information must be turned over to the authorities.

Chapters 9–10
Superintendent Battle visits Dr. Roberts's office and learns of a patient's mysterious death and a possible marital scandal.

Poirot also visits Dr. Roberts, and asks him to describe how the suspects played their hands on the evening of the murder. He also asks Roberts to describe the contents of the room in which they played.

Chapter 11
Mrs. Lorrimer reminds Poirot that she does not have to answer his questions, but she agrees to reconstruct the bridge hands played. Her responses make Poirot suspicious.

Chapters 12–14
The focus turns to Anne Meredith. Mrs. Oliver disarms Anne with her apparent concern, and vows to clear her. As their interview ends, Major Despard suddenly appears.

Major Despards warns Anne that Superintendent Battle is on his way, and offers assistance. He is impressed by the spirit of Anne's roommate, Rhoda Dawes, and both girls find him attractive.

Superintendent Battle speaks with several people in Devonshire before questioning Anne. He asks Anne for background information and the names of her employers. Her roommate asks why Anne left out one particular name.

Chapters 15–16
The investigators delve more deeply not only into the character of the late Mr. Shaitana but also into the pasts of the suspects. Poirot questions Despard about the bridge hands and the contents of Shaitana's flat. Despard tells Poirot that Shaitana was a blackmailer who frightened women, but he refuses to be specific.

Scotland Yard sends Sergeant O'CONNOR to question the former parlourmaid of Dr. Roberts's late patient. The disguised lawman pretends to have worked for the victim, and learns that the Craddocks fought about the doctor.

Chapters 17–19
Rhoda visits Mrs. Oliver and tells her that Anne had worked for a woman who died of accidental poisoning. Mrs. Oliver cautions Rhoda to take care of herself.

Anne sees Rhoda enter Mrs. Oliver's apartment complex but is distracted by Mrs. Lorrimer, who invites her to tea. She later demands that Rhoda tell her the reason for the visit.

Later, when the four crime experts meet, Mrs. Oliver triumphantly produces information about Anne.

Chapters 20–21
Poirot turns his attention to Major Despard. He interviews Mrs. Luxmore and learns that Despard shot her husband to death.

He later receives a visit from Despard, who claims that Mrs. Luxmore's story is a lie.

Chapters 22–23
The web of suspicion around Anne Meredith appears to tighten. Superintendent Battle speaks to the police inspector who handled the case of the poisoning death of Anne's employer. He leaves, certain that Anne murdered her employer.

Poirot has purchased nineteen pairs of silk stockings, and he summons Anne and Rhoda on the pretext of testing Anne's memory, but sets a trap for Anne with the stockings.

Chapters 24–28
Poirot and Battle meet and eliminate Major Despard, Anne Meredith and Dr. Roberts as suspects, and Mrs. Lorrimer looms as the prime suspect. She calls and asks Poirot to visit her.

Poirot tells Mrs. Lorrimer that she was the most likely one to carry out a successful murder, but that killing Shaitana is not her type of crime. She insists that she did commit the murder. After further questioning by Poirot, Mrs. Lorrimer recounts what she saw, but promises to deny everything that she has said.

The following morning, the police report that Mrs. Lorrimer has committed suicide and left notes of apology for the three suspects, but Poirot suspects foul play.

Chapters 29–30
After Mrs. Lorrimer's death, the investigators determine that they have been following the wrong leads. Poirot and Battle rush to stop Anne from killing Rhoda, the only person who could betray her secret. As they arrive, Anne pushes Rhoda into the river, and Despard dives in to save her.

Poirot shocks the police and Mrs. Oliver by exposing the true murderer.

Chapter 31—Cards on the Table
Poirot explains how he uncovered the real murderer and identifies the bridge clues that led to the correct conclusion.

CRIME NOTES
Poirot revealed the plot for *Cards on the Table* in Chapter 3 of THE A.B.C. MURDERS, published in 1935, when he described for HASTINGS the crime he would order, if given the choice—"A crime with no complications. A crime of quiet domestic life."

The means of murder in *Cards on the Table* include a sharp, bejeweled stiletto, a deadly injection of the anesthetic Evipan, and a near-fatal murder attempt by drowning. Murders committed by the suspects before the novel opens utilize methods ranging from death by hat paint poisoning, to fatal gunshot, anthrax contamination of a shaving brush and a lethal injection of typhoid bacteria.

Carelli, Dr.   A very dark man with a small moustache in BLACK COFFEE, he is an Italian-born physician who exerts a strong power over Lucia AMORY, daughter-in-law of the murder victim.

Carey, Richard   An architect at an archaeological dig in MURDER IN MESOPOTAMIA, he is torn between his libido and loyalty, as he tries to resist the seductive wife of the dig leader.

Carfax, Colonel Maurice   An old friend of Lord LISTERDALE, he is given his power of attorney when the lord disappears in "THE LISTERDALE MYSTERY" (2).

Cargill, Rupert   A middle-aged doctor with an invalid wife in ABSENT IN THE SPRING, he falls in love with a young, unmarried assistant who gives him up to avoid ruining his career.

Caribbean Mystery, A   Mystery novel.
The novel offers the only instance in which Miss MARPLE applies her detecting skills outside England. The plot centers on a murder that occurs soon after the victim had offered to show Miss Marple the picture of a murderer while the two relaxed at the Golden Palm Hotel.

PUBLISHING AND DRAMATIZATION
HISTORY
The novel was published in 1964 by William Collins Sons and Company in London, and in 1965 by Dodd, Mead and Company in New York.

The novel was adapted for television in the U.S. in 1983 by Warner Brothers Studios, and starred Helen Hayes as Miss Marple. The novel was also adapted for television in 1989 by the BBC, starring Joan Hickson as Miss Marple, and was shown on the Public Broadcasting Service in the U.S.

CHARACTERS
Senora de CASPEARO, Gregory DYSON, Lucky DYSON, Big Jim ELLIS, Dr. GRAHAM, Colonel Edward HILLINGDON, Evelyn HILLINGDON, Arthur JACKSON, Victoria JOHNSON, Molly KENDAL, Tim KENDAL, Miss Jane Marple, Major PALGRAVE, Canon Jeremy PRESCOTT, Joan PRESCOTT, Jason RAFIEL, Esther WALTERS, Raymond WEST

PLOT SYNOPSIS
Chapters 1–2
The novel opens with Miss Marple on vacation on the island of St. Honore in the Caribbean, compliments of her nephew Raymond West and his wife Joan. Miss Marple meets the other guests, including the very rich Mr. Jason Rafiel and the extremely boring Major Palgrave. As she sits facing Palgrave and listens politely to stories of his exploits in Kenya, her interest is piqued when he asks her if she would like to see the photograph of a murderer. His manner suddenly changes as he stares at something over Miss

Marple's right shoulder, then quickly changes the subject.

Chapters 3–6
Major Palgrave dies in his sleep that night, and the suspicious Miss Marple believes that the snapshot he carried is the reason. She calls Dr. Graham, complaining of a knee problem, and lies to him that Palgrave had accidentally pocketed a picture of her nephew the day before. Dr. Graham promises to retrieve the photograph, but it has disappeared. The dead man is believed to have had high blood pressure because Serenite tablets are found in his room, and his death is determined to be an overdose. Victoria Johnson, the hotel maid, suspects foul play.

Chapters 7–9
Mr. Rafiel tells Miss Marple that he knows that Palgrave did not have high blood pressure because the man told him so as they drank together. The maid tells Dr. Graham that she did not see the Serenite tablets in Palgrave's room before the death. The personalities of the other vacationers are revealed through their actions. Miss Marple questions guests and learns important details about their pasts, and she also admits her lie to Dr. Graham.

Chapters 10–13
Dr. Graham contacts the authorities, telling them that Palgrave may have been murdered, and they decide to perform an autopsy. Meanwhile, the guests begin to act unusually; two of the husbands make advances to other men's wives, and Molly admits to blackouts and claims that everyone hates her. Victoria Johnson returns the Serenite tablets to their owner, and she is found stabbed to death hours later.

Chapters 14–18
The authorities question the guests about the maid's death, and the cook tells of seeing Molly run through the kitchen with a knife hours before. Mr. Rafiel informs Miss Marple that the autopsy results prove that Palgrave was murdered with poison. Esther Walters joins them and tells them that the mysterious photograph of which Palgrave spoke depicted a woman, while another guest states that the death of Gregory Dyson's first wife raised suspicion.

Chapters 19–21
Miss Marple sees Arthur Jackson sneak into Mr. Ra-

fiel's cottage and rifle through papers in the desk. Later, Molly attempts suicide with sleeping pills, and Miss Marple agrees to stay with her until she regains consciousness. She is startled when Arthur Jackson quietly enters the cottage and begins searching through Molly's cosmetics, with particular attention to her face cream, but his excuse is that Esther had lent Molly a lipstick which he had come to reclaim. When he leaves, Miss Marple puts the jar of face cream into her pocket.

Chapters 22–25
Miss Marple questions Dr. Graham about Molly's recovery, and he tells her that Molly swallowed a smaller number of pills than was first suspected. Molly sneaks out of her cottage, and Tim looks for her, only to find Lucky Dyson dead, face down in the creek. When Molly is found and returned, she has a narrow escape when she is offered a drink that turns out to contain poison. Miss Marple stops her from drinking it, and reveals that Molly's blackouts and delusions have been the result of belladonna placed in her face cream. As her skin absorbed the drug, Molly became increasingly paranoid and unstable. The end of the novel reveals that the killer had mistaken Lucky for Molly, the real target, and that Major Palgrave was killed to prevent his revealing the killer's identity.

CRIME NOTES
The novel initiates a relationship between Miss Marple and the wealthy and irritable Mr. Jason Rafiel, who after death will call upon the detective for help in NEMESIS.

Carlile, Charlie The confidential secretary to Lord MAYFIELD in "THE INCREDIBLE THEFT," he seems to be afraid of the French maid's advances.

Carlisle, Elinor Katherine A proud and controlled woman in SAD CYPRESS, she is accused of murdering her former fiancé's new love.

Carlo The sentry and a member of the Comrades of the Red Hand, he is outsmarted in THE SECRET OF CHIMNEYS.

Carlton, Mrs. A member of the household staff in HALLOWE'EN PARTY.

Carlton-Smith, Naomi   An artist who sketches Mr. Harley QUIN in "THE WORLD'S END," she contemplates suicide when her fiancé is accused of a jewel theft.

Carmichael, Lady (1)   A benevolent gossip in "THE HORSES OF DIOMEDES," she provides her old friend POIROT with valuable information.

Carmichael, Lady (2)   Believed by some to have occult powers, she is a widow in "THE STRANGE CASE OF SIR ANDREW CARMICHAEL" whose throat is attacked by a cat's claws as she sleeps, and who later dies of shock when her stepson recovers from a malady that would have left her a very rich woman had he died.

Carmichael, Sir Arthur   An unusual character in "THE STRANGE CASE OF SIR ARTHUR CARMICHAEL," his body survives the murder attempt by his stepmother, but his spirit is murdered and replaced by that of a Persian cat. He is restored to wholeness after falling into a pond of icy water.

Carmichael, Henry (Fakir)   A member of British Intelligence with linguistic fluency in six Middle Eastern languages and numerous mountain dialects, he is killed while trying to bring word to his supervisor regarding a secret weapon in THEY CAME TO BAGHDAD.

Carmichael, William   The uncle of Jim FANTHORP in DEATH ON THE NILE (2), he is a senior attorney in the law firm that represents the business interests of heiress Linnet DOYLE.

Carnaby, Amy (1)   To provide more for her invalid sister than she could on her salary as a lady's companion, she devises a cunning scheme to ransom dogs in "THE NEMEAN LION."

Carnaby, Amy (2)   A woman of "great determination and courage," she tries to save her friend from being harmed by a charismatic cult leader in "THE FLOCK OF GERYON."

Carnaby, Emily   Too ill to work, she is supported by her sister, who visits often her and her Pekinese Augustus in "THE NEMEAN LION."

Carpenter, Mrs.   Nicknamed "The Carpenter," she is a fussy, middle-aged lady's companion in AT BERTRAM'S HOTEL.

Carpenter, Adelaide   Described as "a big soft white purry person," she is the traveling companion to the murdered young woman in "THE HERB OF DEATH."

Carpenter, Dickie   The subject of legend in "THE GIPSY," he dies during an operation on his leg, which was smashed by debris from a torpedo, and his spirit remains restless.

Carpenter, Eve   A former employer of the first murder victim in MRS. McGINTY'S DEAD, her perfume is perceived in the room with the second corpse, and she tries desperately to refrain from saying or doing anything to hurt her husband's political aspirations.

Carpenter, Guy   A man of great political ambitions in MRS. McGINTY'S DEAD, he strives to keep both his past and his wife's past hidden.

Carpenter, Louise   See BIRELL, LOUISE.

Carr, Lady Esther   See KING, MURIEL.

Carr, Sister   Plump and good-tempered, she is a popular army hospital nurse in GIANT'S BREAD, but her lack of punctuality makes everything go wrong.

Carrege, Monsieur   The examining magistrate in the murder case in THE MYSTERY OF THE BLUE TRAIN.

Carrington, Lady Adeline   See CLAPPERTON, ADELINE.

Carrington, The Honourable Flossie   The daughter of a wealthy man and the wife of a scoundrel, she is murdered and her jewels stolen while she travels on a train in "THE PLYMOUTH EXPRESS."

Carrington, Air Marshal Sir George   A military man "of the old school" in "THE INCREDIBLE THEFT," he visits a government official's country retreat to review secret military plans.

Carrington, Lady Julia A nervous, abrupt woman whose life centers on playing bridge, she views her son with a disapproving eye in "THE INCREDIBLE THEFT."

Carrington, Reggie A spendthrift lady's man in "THE INCREDIBLE THEFT," he may have had a hand in a crime.

Carrington, The Honourable Rupert A man with an unsavory reputation in "THE PLYMOUTH EXPRESS," he may have married his wife for her money, while others suspect that he would have no qualms killing her for her jewels.

Carruthers, Miss An unattractive woman with horsy features and the habit of wearing masculine-appearing coats and skirts, she is a murder suspect in "MISS MARPLE TELLS A STORY."

Carruthers, Nurse A self-satisfied but professional, caring nurse, she knows that her late patient's companion lied about the will in DUMB WITNESS.

Carslake, Captain A Conservative politician in THE ROSE AND THE YEW TREE who leads a busy life as an Air Raid Warden and an officer in the Home Guard.

Carslake, Alan A caring brother in "IN A GLASS DARKLY," he provides shelter to his sister when she leaves her abusive, jealous husband.

Carslake, Sylvia Her innocent friendship with a childhood friend in "IN A GLASS DARKLY" drives her husband to jealous rages that frighten her into running back to her childhood home.

Carson Employed as a butler in ENDLESS NIGHT, he is really a security agent hired by a law firm to protect a recently married heiress.

Carstairs, Alan A Canadian naturalist, explorer and big game hunter in WHY DIDN'T THEY ASK EVANS?, his desire to prove that a friend's supposed suicide was really murder leads to his own murder.

Carstairs, Dr. Edward A psychologist in "THE STRANGE CASE OF SIR ARTHUR CARMICHAEL," he discovers that the attempt to murder a man has left the body alive and inhabited by the spirit of a cat.

Carstairs, The Honourable Julia A slightly deaf, very old woman who lives in a nursing home in ELEPHANTS CAN REMEMBER, she remembers clearly the details of a tragedy.

Carter, Colonel A mah-jongg partner of Caroline and Dr. James SHEPPARD in MURDER IS EASY.

Carter, Detective Sergeant Really a criminal in disguise, he is a member of the gang of thieves who rob a man of his silver and other valuables in "MR. EASTWOOD'S ADVENTURE."

Carter, A. Chief of British Intelligence, he takes a great interest in Tommy and Tuppence BERESFORD and sends them on numerous adventures in THE SECRET ADVERSARY, PARTNERS IN CRIME and N OR M? Described as being tall "with a lean, hawklike face and a tired manner," his true identity as Lord EASTERFIELD remains a secret until N OR M? when Tommy finally recognizes him from encounters during World War I.

Carter, Frank A social misfit in ONE, TWO, BUCKLE MY SHOE, he takes a job as gardener to a powerful investment banker and is later accused of murder.

Carter, Harry A coarse, heavy drinking pub owner in MURDER IS EASY, he verbally abuses others, and later drowns.

Carter, Lucy A barmaid in her father's pub in MURDER IS EASY, she has the misfortune to have gone riding with the chauffeur on the night that he is killed.

Carter, Stephen A taciturn man of the upper classes, he is discovered to have poison in his pocket after a fellow dinner guest collapses in "YELLOW IRIS."

Carton, L.B. With his wife he framed two other men for a diamond mine robbery but is murdered in THE MAN IN THE BROWN SUIT.

Cartwright, Dr.   As the local physician in Market Basing, he is called in by the owner of Chimneys to verify the deaths of victims in THE SECRET OF CHIMNEYS and THE SEVEN DIALS MYSTERY.

Cartwright, Sir Charles   A well-known stage actor who remains off the stage for two years following a nervous breakdown in THREE-ACT TRAGEDY, his real name is Charles MUGG, and he had once thought of changing his name to Ludovic Castiglione.

Carver, Dr.   An archaeologist in "THE PEARL OF PRICE," he plots to obtain a pair of worthless pearl earrings which he is led to believe are exceedingly valuable.

Cary, Frances   Sometimes an artists' model in THIRD GIRL, she plans a financial swindle with her boyfriend.

"Case of the Caretaker, The"   Mystery short story.

The village doctor treats Miss MARPLE for influenza and realizes that her spirit also needs healing, so he gives her a manuscript written about a village mystery, and asks her to find a solution.

PUBLISHING AND DRAMATIZATION
HISTORY
The story appeared in the short story collection, THREE BLIND MICE AND OTHER STORIES, published in 1950 by Dodd, Mead and Company in New York and later reprinted in MISS MARPLE'S FINAL CASES by William Collins Sons and Company, Ltd., in London in 1979.

The story has not been adapted for stage or screen.

CHARACTERS
Dr. HAYDOCK, Harry LAXTON, Louise LAXTON, Miss Marple, Mr. MURGATROYD, Mrs. MURGATROYD

PLOT SYNOPSIS
The story told in Dr. Haydock's manuscript is a tragedy regarding a couple who lived in the village. When Louise Laxton is riding one day, the caretaker's wife calls out and startles the horse, which throws its rider to her death. Miss Marple sees the

implications beyond the obvious. She solves the mystery and regains her zest for life.

"Case of the City Clerk, The"   Mystery short story.

A solid, dull city clerk yearns for excitement, but he may find more than he expects in this story of international intrigue.

PUBLISHING AND DRAMATIZATION
HISTORY
The story appeared in the short story collection, PARKER PYNE INVESTIGATES, published in 1934 by William Collins Sons and Company, Ltd., in London, and, under the title, *Mr. Parker Pyne, Detective,* by Dodd, Mead and Company in New York.

The story has not been adapted for stage or screen.

CHARACTERS
Mr. BONNINGTON, Mr. PARKER PYNE, Mr. ROBERTS, Mrs. ROBERTS

PLOT SYNOPSIS
Steady, hardworking Mr. Roberts craves excitement in his ordinary life and, when his wife and children leave for a holiday, he is given his chance—as a courier to Geneva for Mr. Parker Pyne. Espionage, royal jewels, secret plans and the thrill of danger make him feel as if he were living the life of the hero in one of his favorite novels.

"Case of the Discontented Husband, The"
Mystery short story.

The plot relies upon the cliché that "turnabout is fair play." A husband tries to win back his wife by making her think that he has fallen in love with another woman.

PUBLISHING AND DRAMATIZATION
HISTORY
The story appeared in the short story collection, PARKER PYNE INVESTIGATES, published in 1934 by William Collins Sons and Company, Ltd., in London, and, under the title, *Mr. Parker Pyne, Detective,* published by Dodd, Mead and Company in New York.

The story has not been adapted for stage or screen.

CHARACTERS
Miss Madeleine DE SARA, Sinclair JORDAN, Mr. PARKER PYNE, Mrs. Iris WADE, Mr. Reginald WADE

PLOT SYNOPSIS
When his wife leaves him for a young artist, Mr. Reginald Wade asks for a six-month grace period before she sues for divorce. He contacts Mr. Parker Pyne for help in winning her back, and they decide that an attractive member of the office staff should pose as Mr. Wade's love interest to make Mrs. Wade jealous. The plan works very well, and the errant wife decides that she wants her husband back, but he has already fallen in love with his partner in the deception.

"Case of the Discontented Soldier, The"
Mystery short story.

Civilian life proves too dull for an ex-soldier, whose search for adventure soon has him in the midst of danger and excitement.

PUBLISHING AND DRAMATIZATION HISTORY
The story appeared in the short story collection, PARKER PYNE INVESTIGATES, published in 1934 by William Collins Sons and Company, Ltd., in London, and, under the title, *Mr. Parker Pyne, Detective*, by Dodd, Mead and Company in New York.

The story was adapted for television in 1982 by Thames Television in England.

CHARACTERS
Miss Freda CLEGG, Miss Madeleine DE SARA, Mr. PARKER PYNE, Major WILBRAHAM

PLOT SYNOPSIS
Major Wilbrahams contacts Mr. Parker Pyne to help him escape his boredom soon after an attractive woman, Freda Clegg, has also contacted the detective. Parker Pyne's assistant arranges for the two to meet in a planned incident which will require that the major rescue Freda from attackers. The couple join forces, leave for Africa to search for buried treasure, and eventually marry.

"Case of the Distressed Lady, The"   Mystery
short story.

A young woman's desire to return a valuable dia-

In "The Case of the Discontented Soldier," Major John Wilbraham, played by William Gaunt, has finally found the adventure his life has lacked. (Photo courtesy of Thames Television)

mond that she had stolen from her friend, pawned, and replaced with a replica turns into a difficult task when Mr. PARKER PYNE discovers the truth about the diamond.

PUBLISHING AND DRAMATIZATION HISTORY
The story appeared in the short story collection, PARKER PYNE INVESTIGATES, published in 1934 by William Collins Sons and Company in London, and, under the title, *Mr. Parker Pyne, Detective*, by Dodd, Mead and Company in New York.

The story has not been adapted for stage or screen.

CHARACTERS

Madeleine DE SARA, Lady DORTHEIMER, Claude LUTTREL, Mr. Parker Pyne, Mrs. Daphne ST. JOHN

PLOT SYNOPSIS

Mrs. St. John visits Mr. Parker Pyne to obtain his help in returning the diamond ring she stole from Lady Dortheimer and replaced with a replica in order to pay off her gambling debts. She redeems the ring from the pawnshop and wants to unobtrusively place the ring in the rightful owner's hands, but Parker Pyne's discovery seems to make that impossible.

"Case of the Middle-aged Wife, The" Mystery short story.

A middle-aged woman whose husband seems to be having an affair with his secretary responds to an advertisement which suggests that there is a remedy for unhappiness, and finds her life revitalized.

PUBLISHING AND DRAMATIZATION HISTORY

The story appeared in the short story collection, PARKER PYNE INVESTIGATES, published in 1934 by William Collins Sons and Company, Ltd., in London, and, under the title, *Mr. Parker Pyne, Detective*, by Dodd, Mead and Company in New York.

The story was adapted for television in 1982 by Thames Television in England.

Romance—in the form of Claude Luttrell, played by Rupert Frazer—is Parker Pyne's prescription to provide a cure for Maria Packington, played by Gwen Watford, in "The Case of the Middle-aged Wife." (Photo courtesy of Thames Television)

Heavily disguised, Tommy and Tuppence Beresford (James Warwick and Francesca Annis) pursue "The Case of the Missing Lady." (Photo courtesy of London Weekend Television)

CHARACTERS

Claude LUTTREL, George PACKINGTON, Maria PACKINGTON, Mr. PARKER PYNE

PLOT SYNOPSIS

Eager to recapture her husband's heart, Maria Packington consults Mr. Parker Pyne, whose advertisement promises solutions to unhappiness. Upon his recommendation, she undergoes a makeover in appearance and begins to be seen at fashionable restaurants and clubs with a young man who is really Parker Pyne's assistant, Claude Luttrel. After seeing her in this new light, Maria's husband returns to her.

"Case of the Missing Lady, The" Mystery short story.

A famous explorer asks Tommy and Tuppence BERESFORD for assistance in locating his missing fiancée, but the pair of sleuths keep a secret from their client.

PUBLISHING AND DRAMATIZATION HISTORY

The story appeared in the short story collection, PARTNERS IN CRIME, published in 1929 by William Collins Sons and Company, Ltd., in London, and by Dodd, Mead and Company in New York.

The story was adapted for television in 1984 by London Weekend Television in England, and was also shown on the Public Broadcasting Service in the U.S.

CHARACTERS

Tommy Beresford, Tuppence Beresford, Lady Susan CLONRAY, The Honourable Hermione CRANE, Dr. HORRISTON, Mr. Gabriel STAVANSSON

PLOT SYNOPSIS

The Beresfords agree to search for Mr. Gabriel Stavansson's missing fiancée after he tells them that he has returned after two years in the Arctic, and no one in her family will help him to locate her. The trail leads the married sleuths to a nursing home in an outlying village, where they discover a secret that would destroy Stavansson's love for his fiancée, were it to be revealed.

CRIME NOTES

In this story, Tommy takes on the characteristics and mannerisms of the great Sherlock Holmes, even to the point of playing the violin, to the chagrin of his ever-patient Tuppence.

"Case of the Missing Will, The" Mystery short story.

A young woman appeals to Hercule POIROT for his help in uncovering her uncle's hidden legacy to her.

PUBLISHING AND DRAMATIZATION HISTORY

The story appeared in the short story collection, POIROT INVESTIGATES, published in 1924 by John

Chief Inspector Japp (Philip Jackson) and Felicity Lemon (Pauline Moran) take a friendly boat ride in "The Case of the Missing Will." (Photo courtesy of London Weekend Television)

Lane, Publishers in London, and in 1925 by Dodd, Mead and Company in New York.

The story was adapted for television in 1993 by London Weekend Television in England, and was also shown on the Public Broadcasting Service in the U.S.

CHARACTERS

Mr. and Mrs. BAKER, Andrew MARSH, Miss Violet MARSH, Hercule Poirot

PLOT SYNOPSIS

The orphaned Violet Marsh has been granted only a one-year trust by her late uncle who raised her but who disapproved of her independent mind and career. Because the will refers to the one-year period as a "test of her wits," Violet recognizes that her uncle had placed a challenge in the will for her to locate the true will, which will provide her with the full title to her inheritance.

"Case of the Perfect Maid, The" Mystery short story.

The disappearance of jewelry leads two old women to wrongly accuse their maid of theft, and Miss MARPLE must step in to clear the maid's reputation.

PUBLISHING AND DRAMATIZATION
HISTORY
The story appeared in the short story collection, THREE BLIND MICE AND OTHER STORIES, published in 1950 by Dodd, Mead and Company in New York.

The story has not been adapted for stage or screen.

CHARACTERS
EDNA (1), GLADYS, Miss Jane Marple, Emily SKINNER, Lavinia SKINNER, Inspector SLACK

PLOT SYNOPSIS
Times have changed in St. Mary Mead, good servants are hard to find, and the Old Hall has been split into four flats. Two sisters who live in one of those flats claim that a piece of jewelry is missing. They blame their maid, Gladys, whom they immediately dismiss. They hire another maid who soon disappears with all of the jewelry from the four flats; following which, the sisters move away. Miss Marple intervenes to guide the inspector in charge of the case in the right direction, and to make certain that he clears Gladys of suspicion and he charges the real thieves with the crime.

CRIME NOTES
This story concerns the impact of modernity upon Miss Marple, in which new faces and new customs make life unpredictable in St. Mary Mead.

"Case of the Rich Woman, The" Mystery short story.

The story illustrates once again the lesson that money does not buy happiness.

PUBLISHING AND DRAMATIZATION
HISTORY
The story appeared in the short story collection, PARKER PYNE INVESTIGATES, published in 1934 by William Collins Sons and Company, Ltd., in London, and, under the title, *Mr. Parker Pyne, Detective*, by Dodd, Mead and Company in New York.

The story has not been adapted for stage or screen.

CHARACTERS
Doctor CONSTANTINE, Hannah MOORHOUSE, Mr. PARKER PYNE, Mrs. Amelia RYMER, Joe WELSH

PLOT SYNOPSIS
Wealthy widow Mrs. Amelia Rymer consults Mr. Parker Pyne because she is lonely and unhappy. He arranges for her to meet an Oriental doctor, who uses "Eastern Magic" to make her fall asleep only to reawaken as a penniless farm worker, Hannah Moorhouse. In her new persona, the formerly wealthy woman finds love and happiness.

Casey, Mrs. The landlady of the house in which Mrs. LYON is murdered in "THREE BLIND MICE."

Casey, Patrick An expert cat burglar in "THE APPLES OF THE HESPERIDES," he is rumored to have stolen the Borgia goblet.

Caspar, Mr. A fellow traveler on the tour of famous houses and gardens with Miss MARPLE, who preceives her behavior as excitable and dangerous in NEMESIS.

Caspearo, Senora de Outspoken and emotional, she rails against the lack of appeal of men older than thirty-five in A CARIBBEAN MYSTERY, but her dramatics may mask a complex mind.

Cassell, Dr. A physician in Market Basing, he tells a worried young woman in THE SEVEN DIALS MYSTERY that the man she thought she had run down with her car was actually shot.

Cassetti See RATCHETT, SAMUEL EDWARD.

Casson, Mrs. Involved in psychic research, she brings a medium to the village to help solve a mystery in "THE VOICE IN THE DARK."

Castiglione, Ludovic See CARTWRIGHT, SIR CHARLES.

Castle, Mrs. A middle-aged harridan with a large bosom and violently colored red hair, she is the owner of the hotel in EVIL UNDER THE SUN where murder occurs.

Castleton, Harry See DUGUESCLIN, QUENTIN.

Cat Among the Pigeons Mystery novel.
The novel blends international intrigue with the

standard elements of the murder mystery as it moves from an anti-government plot in a small Middle Eastern country to the comforting discipline of an English school for girls. The plot centers on the effect smuggled diamonds have on the safety and well-being of both students and staff of the Meadowbank School.

PUBLISHING AND DRAMATIZATION HISTORY

The novel was published in 1959 by William Collins Sons and Company, Ltd., in London, and in 1960 by Dodd, Mead and Company in New York.

The novel has not been adapted for stage or screen.

CHARACTERS

Prince ALI YUSEF, Miss BLAKE, Mlle. Angele BLANCHE, Sergeant Percy BOND, Miss BULSTRODE, Alice CALDER, Miss CHADWICK, John EDMUNDSON, GEORGES, Adam/Ronnie GOODMAN, Miss JOHNSON (2), Detective Inspector KELSEY, Derek O'CONNOR, Colonel PIKEAWAY, Hercule POIROT, Denis RATHBONE, Bob RAWLINSON, Eileen RICH, Mr. ROBINSON, Miss ROWAN, Princess SHAISTA, Ann SHAPLAND, Miss Grace SPRINGER, Jennifer SUTCLIFFE, Joan SUTCLIFFE, Mrs. UPJOHN, Julia UPJOHN, Miss VANSITTART

PLOT SYNOPSIS

Prologue

The summer term opens at the exclusive Meadowbank School; the character of their students and their school is revealed in expensive cars and the concerns of both parents and girls.

Chapters 1–3

The story shifts to two months earlier, at the Royal Palace in Ramat. Threatened by government unrest, Prince Ali Yusef and his private pilot, Bob Rawlinson, plan their escape, and the prince entrusts Rawlinson with a bag which contains three-quarters of a million dollars in jewels. Fearful of being detained, Rawlinson stops to see his sister Joan Sutcliffe, but she is not home, so he writes a note and hides the jewels among her possessions. A few days later, the plane in which the prince and Rawlinson left the country amidst rioting is reported missing, but wreckage of a plane containing two unidentified bodies has been found. Concerned members of British Intelligence

assign an agent, Ronnie Goodman, to act as a gardener at Meadowbank School to protect the late prince's nearest relative, Princess Shaista, who will be attending the school. At the same time, they try to locate the jewels.

Chapters 4–8

Derek O'Connor is sent by Intelligence to inform Mrs. Sutcliffe of her brother's death and to question her. She knows nothing about the jewels, and they find nothing among her belongings when she unpacks. Her house is later burglarized, but the thief goes away empty-handed. Jennifer Sutcliffe enters Meadowbank School, and the usual confusion reigns at the opening of a school term. The headmistress considers possible successors, for she plans to retire in two years, and various contenders are mentioned. The ordinary tenor of the school atmosphere is disrupted when Miss Springer, the games mistress, is found shot to death in the sports pavilion. Police investigators find only the victim's fingerprints on the flashlight.

Chapters 9–11

Detective Kelsey questions all the staff members, and learns that several had felt uneasy in the previous weeks. Eileen Rich expresses the feeling that there is someone among them who does not belong, "a cat among the pigeons." Princess Shaista insists on talking to the detectives. She tells them that the Communists are after her and that they killed Miss Springer. When the detectives question the gardener, they learn that he is an undercover agent sent to protect the princess, and all agree that the time has come to tell Miss Bulstrode about him.

Chapters 12–13

Miss Bulstrode tells the investigators that Mrs. Upjohn, a member of British Intelligence during World War II, had been startled when she recognized someone among the crowd on the opening day of school, but had not named the individual. The authorities try to reach Mrs. Upjohn, but she is traveling by bus to Anatolia. Meanwhile, Miss Bulstrode uses her influence to make the newspapers downplay the murder so that the authorities can continue their investigation. Princess Shaista's uncle sends a car to pick her up for a day away from the school, but the arrival of a second car alerts authorities to the fact that the princess has been kidnapped.

Chapters 14–16

Miss Chadwick sees a light in the sports pavilion at night, and goes alone to investigate. She finds another teacher, Miss Vansittart, dead, having been hit on the back of the head while standing in front of the princess's locker. The school receives a ransom note for Princess Shaista. The newspapers announce the second murder, motivating Mrs. Sutcliffe to remove Jennifer from the school.

Chapters 17–19

Left with Jennifer's tennis racket, Julia feels that something in the handle has made it unbalanced. After prying the handle open, she finds the jewels, held in place by modeling clay. She quickly removes the jewels, hides them and retapes the handle. The next day, Julia goes to London to speak with Hercule Poirot, a friend of her mother's friend, Mrs. Summerhayes. She convinces him to return to Meadowbank with her. Poirot first confers with the authorities, then returns to the school, where he asks the art teacher to make sketches of several teachers but to change their eyebrows and hair. Two of the teachers appear completely different in the sketches.

Chapters 20–22

Poirot visits Mrs. Sutcliffe and Jennifer, and asks them to review the modified sketches, but they find nothing familiar about the pictures. As the school's reputation suffers, Miss Bulstrode continues to plan for her succession, but her offer to Eileen Rich is set aside for a time. At the same time, Angele Blanche attempts to blackmail someone at the school, because she has learned something damaging concerning Miss Springer's death. When she returns to her room, Angele is killed by a blow to the head.

Chapters 23–25

The authorities learn that the real Princess Shaista is safely in the Swiss Alps, and that a different girl has been impersonating her at Meadowbank. The false princess left in the wrong limousine to escape detection. Through meticulous detection, Poirot learns that the person who killed Miss Springer had been looking for Jennifer's tennis racket, but the girls had switched rackets several days before. When Mrs. Upjohn is located and returns to the school, she identifies school secretary Ann Shapland as a former member of Intelligence whose specialty had been killing. Questioning reveals that Miss Springer and

Miss Vansittart were killed by two different people, for two radically different reasons. At the end, the jewels are returned to Prince Ali Yusef's widow and his child.

CRIME NOTES

The first murder in the novel results from a gunshot wound, while two other murders result from a blow to the head with a sandbag.

Caterham, Lord   See BRENT, ALISTAIR EDWARD, NINTH MARQUIS OF CATERHAM.

Cauldfield, Richard   Middle-aged and slightly pompous, this former British military officer in A DAUGHTER'S A DAUGHTER yearned only for a quiet married life with a garden to tend. He thought that Ann PRENTICE was the perfect wife, but she gave him up to please her daughter. On the rebound, he marries a much younger woman whom he does not love.

Caux, Monsieur   He is the Commissary of Police in charge of the murder investigation in THE MYSTERY OF THE BLUE TRAIN.

Cavendish, John   A forty-five-year-old childhood friend of Captain HASTINGS, he lives with his stepmother, wife and brother at the family home, Styles Court, in THE MYSTERIOUS AFFAIR AT STYLES. He invites Hastings to convalesce from war wounds at his home. When Cavendish's stepmother is murdered, he asks Hastings to help, and Hastings asks another old friend to assist, a Belgian refugee named Hercule POIROT, who has been living with other refugees in town.

Cavendish, Lawrence   At forty years of age, five years younger than his brother John, he has spent his inheritance and lives on the kindness of his family in THE MYSTERIOUS AFFAIR AT STYLES.

Cavendish, Mary   Married to John CAVENDISH, she unwittingly inspires romantic thoughts in Captain HASTINGS in THE MYSTERIOUS AFFAIR AT STYLES. Her friendship with an apparently respectable medical expert on poisons becomes dangerous to her marriage when he is discovered to be a German spy. Nonetheless, her spirit prevails and she reappears in

"THE ADVENTURE OF 'THE WESTERN STAR' " as having recommended that another character seek out Hercule POIROT.

Cawthorn, The Honourable Virginia   See REVEL, VIRGINIA.

Cayley, Alfred   A hypochondriacal husband who delights in his role as invalid, he makes his wife a veritable slave to his misery in N OR M?

Cayley, Elisabeth   Married to Alfred CAYLEY in N OR M?, she appears to have dedicated her life to ensuring his comfort, but the strain shows in her face.

Cayman, Amelia   Described by young Lady Frankie DERWENT as being "a painted-up raddled bitch" in WHY DIDN'T THEY ASK EVANS?, she also proves herself to be dishonest by falsely identifying a man's body as that of her brother.

Cayman, Leo   The likable bigamist in WHY DIDN'T THEY ASK EVANS?, he is married to Amelia CAYMAN and, under the name of Edgar TEMPLETON, to Rose Emily TEMPLETON.

Cazalet, Dr.   A cheerful, benevolent physician with a Harley Street practice in "THE UNDER DOG," he is called in by Hercule POIROT to hypnotize a key witness.

Celestine   A personal French maid in "THE JEWEL ROBBERY AT THE GRAND METROPOLITAN," she is fortunate that Hercule POIROT steps in to clear her name when her mistress accuses her of stealing a pearl necklace.

Celia   The name given by the narrator of UNFINISHED PORTRAIT to the unnamed character whom he saves. Her life and experiences closely parallel those of Agatha Christie. She is a dreamy, imaginative child who grows to be a tender, trusting adult. Throughout her life, in times of stress she experiences recurring nightmares of The Gun Man, a man who has stumps instead of hands. The reader learns about her through the story that she relates to a man whom she meets on an island where she intends to take her life ten years after her husband leaves her. Only after she tells her story to the former portrait painter, who

has only a stump instead of his painting hand, is she ready to face life and to look for happiness.

Chadwick, Miss   To all appearances an ordinary woman of no particular distinction in CAT AMONG THE PIGEONS, she is a teacher called "Faithful Chaddy" by those who know her; she proves her loyalty by sacrificing her life for another.

Challenger, Commander George   With his physician uncle, he supplies cocaine to several friends, including the woman he loves, in PERIL AT END HOUSE.

Chandler, Admiral Charles   Pride runs in the Chandler family, which traces its service in the British navy to the sixteenth century, but insanity is another family trait which the admiral expects to pass on to his son in "THE CRETAN BULL."

Chandler, Hugh   A handsome, athletically built young man in "THE CRETAN BULL," he leaves the navy and breaks off his engagement when circumstances make him believe that he is suffering from the family trait of insanity.

Chantry, Commander Tony   A bored husband in "TRIANGLE AT RHODES," he falls in love with another woman after six months of marriage.

Chantry, Valentine   Flamboyant, flirtatious and fickle, she has just married her sixth husband, and seems already to be hunting for her seventh when she dies of poisoning in "TRIANGLE AT RHODES."

Chapman, Albert   See BARNES, REGINALD and BLUNT, ALISTAIR.

Chapman, Nigel   A spoiled child in an adult's body, he is a student of medieval history also known under the name of Nigel STANLEY in HICKORY DICKORY DOCK.

Chappell, Anthony (Tony)   A desperate, grieving lover in "YELLOW IRIS," he seriously contemplates poisoning himself, but Hercule POIROT intervenes.

Charles   The highly visible and efficient headwaiter in SPARKLING CYANIDE, he poured the wine at a party where poison ended the life of the guest of honor.

Charlton, Mr.   An old-fashioned solicitor in HERCULE POIROT'S CHRISTMAS, his experience of reading wills to heirs leaves him reluctant to take on the task.

Charnley, Lady Alix   A widow in "THE DEAD HARLEQUIN," she has lived in torment for fourteen years under the false belief that guilt over a sexual indiscretion caused her husband to commit suicide one month after they married.

Charnley, Hugo   Obsessed with acquiring the family title and estate, he loses all feelings of brotherly love in "THE DEAD HARLEQUIN."

Charnley, Lord Reggie   A close friend could not believe that this usually socially correct man would have the "damned bad taste" to commit suicide just as guests were arriving at a party to celebrate his recent marriage, and he was right. The truth of what actually happened in THE DEAD HARLEQUIN is not revealed until fourteen years later.

Charpentier, Louise   See BIRELL, LOUISE.

Charteris, Mrs. Bigham   Lean and leathery, with something of the appearance of a black crow, she is a widow and one of "the three old ladies of St. Loo Castle" in THE ROSE AND THE YEW TREE.

Charteris, Isabella   Tall and thin, she has a long, narrow face with a high forehead and straight, ash-blond hair which make her look like an enchanted maiden in THE ROSE AND THE YEW TREE.

Chatterton, Lady Abbie   Admired by Hercule POIROT as an intelligent, beautiful and vivacious woman, she arranges a party in "THE MYSTERY OF THE SPANISH CHEST" in order to introduce the detective to a friend in distress who wishes to consult him.

Chatterton, Lady Alice   An enthusiastic admirer of Hercule POIROT in "THE MYSTERY OF THE BAGHDAD CHEST," she was impressed with his detection skills in an earlier case, and now she hopes that he can help her friend.

Checkheaton, Lady Matilda   Conservative, opinionated and strong-willed, she enjoys a good mystery and assiduously pries confidential details from her many powerful friends. She is also adamant about retaining her freedom of movement, and lectures her doctor in PASSENGER TO FRANKFURT that she does not want "to look absolutely a crock or bedridden or something."

Chelles, Monsieur   See VICTOR, KING.

Chester, Adela   A manipulative mother in "PROBLEM AT POLLENSA BAY," she seeks to manage everything for her son, including his love life.

Chester, Basil   Although he may sometimes resent his mother's constant meddling in his life in "PROBLEM AT POLLENSA BAY," Adela CHESTER's son also thrives on it, until her attention turns to his choice of female companionship.

Chetwynd, George   A rich American in GIANT'S BREAD, he is an older, stable businessman who marries a young widow who does not love him.

Chetwynd, Gordon   A man in PASSENGER TO FRANKFURT with the reputation of being mean, he is said to have made many enemies during his career.

Chevenix-Gore, Sir Gervase Francis Xavier   An egoist in "DEAD MAN'S MIRROR" who seeks to preserve the purity of the family bloodline as well as the family fortune, he hopes to force a marriage between his daughter and his nephew. He is found dead in a locked room before this plan can be carried out.

Chevenix-Gore, Ruth   A beautiful young woman in "DEAD MAN'S MIRROR," her black hair, fine features and beautiful coloring impress even the worldly Hercule POIROT, who must investigate the murder of her adoptive father.

Chevenix-Gore, Lady Vanda Elizabeth   A wealthy and attractive elderly noblewoman in "DEAD MAN'S MIRROR," she believes herself to have been both Queen Hatshepsut and a princess of Atlantis in earlier lives.

Chichester, Reverend Edward   See MINKS, ARTHUR.

Chilcott, Mary   An old friend of the poisoned woman in "THE HOUSE OF THE LURKING DEATH," she maintains an exterior calm that belies her internal anxiety as she makes necessary funeral arrangements and attempts to continue life as usual.

"Chocolate Box, The"   Mystery short story.

This story offers a rare admission by Hercule POIROT of how he made a fool of himself by ignoring an obvious clue.

PUBLISHING AND DRAMATIZATION
HISTORY
The story appeared in the short story collection, POIROT INVESTIGATES, published in 1924 by John Lane, Publishers in London, and in 1925 by Dodd, Mead and Company in New York.

The story was adapted for television in 1993 by London Weekend Television in England, and was also shown on the Public Broadcasting Service in the U.S.

CHARACTERS
Madame DEROULARD, Paul DEROULARD, M. DE SAINT ALARD, FELICIE, Captain HASTINGS, Virginie MESNARD, Hercule Poirot, Mr. John WILSON

PLOT SYNOPSIS
Captain Hastings asks Poirot to reveal if he has ever failed in an investigation, and the great detective relates this story, in which he focused solely on the means of death and ignored the obvious clues that pointed to the murderer. The death of Paul Deroulard was diagnosed as heart failure, but his late wife's cousin thought it was murder, and she contacted Poirot to help her to prove that. He discovered that the murderer had poisoned the chocolates, but he failed to observe the significance of the mismatched colors of the chocolate box and lid.

CRIME NOTES
The substance used to commit murder is the medication Trinitrin, actually nitroglycerin tablets taken in excess.

Christie, Colonel Archibald   Agatha Christie's first husband and the father of her only child, Rosa-

lind, he was a handsome, dashing officer in the Royal Flying Corps when they first met. After their wartime marriage, he went off to fight in World War I, while the new bride volunteered to work first as a nurse in a local hospital and then at a pharmacy as a dispenser. When the war ended, Colonel Christie joined a London business firm and became an avid golfer, much to his wife's disappointment. After several years, he took the opportunity to travel around the world for a year on the British Empire Mission, and he took Agatha with him. When they returned, Colonel Christie found another job in finance and agreed to move to a home in the country, as long as it was near a golf course. He become so intensely involved in the game that his wife said in AN AUTOBIOGRAPHY that "he was taking the game so seriously now that it might have been a religion." He was also a man who could not stand when people were ill or unhappy, because it spoiled everything for him. Thus, when his wife's mother passed away, he suggested that they go away for a holiday to Spain to make her feel better. When she refused, he went to live at his club in London, while Agatha went alone to the family home at Ashfield to clean out her family belongings. When they met again, over a month later, Colonel Christie told his wife that he had fallen in love with another woman and wanted a divorce. The Christies were divorced in 1928. Colonel Christie died in 1962.

"Christmas Tragedy, A"   Mystery short story.

Miss MARPLE tells the members of the Tuesday Night Club the story of a man who thought that he committed the perfect murder, until Miss Marple stepped in.

PUBLISHING AND DRAMATIZATION
HISTORY
The story appeared in the short story collection, THE THIRTEEN PROBLEMS, published in 1932 by William Collins and Sons, Ltd., in London, and, under the title, *The Tuesday Club Murders,* by Dodd, Mead and Company in New York.

The story has not been adapted for stage or screen.

CHARACTERS
Colonel BANTRY, Dolly BANTRY, Miss Jane Marple, Gladys SANDERS, Jack SANDERS

PLOT SYNOPSIS
The tragedy in this story had occurred some years before, during a Christmas Miss Marple spent at a spa. She met a married couple there, and became convinced that the husband intended to kill his wife, but even the sharp-eyed detective was unable to prevent the murder. Despite the killer's seemingly perfect alibi, Miss Marple's observant eyes saw the clues that solved the case.

CRIME NOTES
The crude murder weapon in this story is a sandbag.

Christow, Gerda The submissive appearance of this wife and mother of two in THE HOLLOW masks a strong, nearly fanatical personality who might do anything to keep from losing the husband she worships to another woman—even commit murder. Those who know Gerda well realize that she is a very clever woman.

Christow, Dr. John While his rich patients thought him a genius, and his efforts to find a cure for a rare disease were laudable, the husband and father of two in THE HOLLOW rated low in regard to character. Few who knew that he was carrying on simultaneous affairs with a former fiancée and a more recent female acquaintance were surprised when he was found shot to death near the swimming pool.

Christow, Zena The nine-year-old daughter of Dr. John and Gerda CHRISTOW in THE HOLLOW, she reads cards and predicts her father's death.

Chudleigh, Rose A cook in WHY DIDN'T THEY ASK EVANS?, she witnessed the signing of the forged will.

Church, Miss An aunt of Amy Gibbs in MURDER IS EASY, she does not believe that her niece accidentally swallowed oxalic acid instead of cough syrup.

Clancy, Daniel A detective story writer who is present when murder occurs in DEATH IN THE CLOUDS, he becomes a prime suspect for the police.

Clapperton, Adeline An unpleasant woman in "PROBLEM AT SEA," she repeatedly reminds her present husband that she was the wealthy widow of Lord CARRINGTON before her present marriage. Her body is discovered stabbed to death with a native knife.

Clapperton, Colonel John Married for money to the former Lady CARRINGTON, he can never forget that he is a former music hall entertainer with a dubious war record in "PROBLEM AT SEA."

Clark, Sergeant A highly observant local law enforcement officer in THE HOLLOW, he learns that the wife was not the only person with a gun on the day of the murder.

Clark, Dr. Campbell Possessed of a keen knowledge of the unconscious mind, he is viewed by other characters in "THE FOURTH MAN" as an expert regarding mental difficulties and the relationship between mind and body.

Clark, Milly The stout and cheerful companion of the murder victim in "THE TUESDAY NIGHT CLUB."

Clarke, Sir Carmichael A collector of Chinese art who lives near Devon, he becomes the third victim in THE A.B.C. MURDERS when he is killed with a blow to the head during his evening walk.

Clarke, Lady Charlotte The ailing wife of the third victim in THE A.B.C. MURDERS, she sends for Hercule POIROT to investigate her husband's murder.

Clarke, Franklin The brother of the third victim in THE A.B.C. MURDERS, he benefits by his brother's death, and would benefit even more financially if his sister-in-law died. Yet his suggestions to aid Hercule POIROT in the investigation and his own efforts seemed sincere.

Claythorne, Vera Elizabeth One of the prisoners on Indian Island in AND THEN THERE WERE NONE, she is a former games mistress who had been accused in the past of the murder of a young boy. Although she realizes, early on, the importance of the rhyme that hangs in all of the guest rooms, she is ineffective in avoiding her fate, and she fulfills the final verse of the rhyme.

Clayton, Arnold His murdered body is discovered in a Spanish chest in "THE MYSTERY OF THE SPANISH CHEST."

Clayton, Elsie Possessed of a shy, retiring nature, she is highly attractive to a young man whom she meets while on vacation with her mother in Herzoslovakia in "THE STYMPHALEAN BIRDS." This leads Hercule POIROT to observe that her act of innocence is very seductive because she appeals "not to sex, but to chivalry."

Clayton, Margharita The type of woman whom Hercule POIROT considers to be most dangerous, she holds an irresistible allure for men, the power of which she is not aware. When her husband is murdered in "THE MYSTERY OF THE SPANISH CHEST," she asks Poirot to clear the name of the man suspected of the murder.

Cleat, Mrs. The village witch in THE MOVING FINGER.

Clegg, Emmeline One of the many women who have become entranced by the cult leader of the Flock of the Great Shepherd in "THE FLOCK OF GERYON." Even though she knows that three women have died after making wills in favor of the cult, she also bequeaths her estate to the group, despite warnings from her best friend, who finally consults Hercule POIROT.

Clegg, Freda Bored and lonely, she responds to Mr. PARKER PYNE's advertisement and finds adventure and love in PARKER PYNE INVESTIGATES.

Clegg, Joe Married to the widow of an accused murderer in ORDEAL BY INNOCENCE, he refuses to agree with the possibility that the English court could be mistaken in its verdict.

Clegg, Maureen Married secretly to Jacko ARGYLE in ORDEAL BY INNOCENCE, she attempts to divorce him to marry Joe CLEGG after Jacko is imprisoned for murder.

Clement, Father See GABRIEL, JOHN.

Clement, Dennis The sixteen-year-old nephew of the vicar of ST. MARY MEAD, he has an interest in murder and detection and chivalrously defends the strange actions of a young woman in MURDER AT THE VICARAGE.

Clement, Griselda Twenty years younger than her husband, the vicar of ST. MARY MEAD, she is a pretty and lively woman who eventually becomes the mother of two sons. Throughout her appearances in MURDER AT THE VICARAGE, THE BODY IN THE LIBRARY and 4.50 FROM PADDINGTON, she becomes a close friend of Miss MARPLE, and continues to live at the vicarage even after her husband passes away.

Clement, Leonard (Len) The vicar of ST. MARY MEAD, his home is next door to Miss Marple's and he is her close confidant. He is viewed as a confirmed bachelor and shocks his parishioners when he marries Griselda, twenty years younger than he and bubbling over with life. He becomes the father of two sons and eventually dies in St. Mary Mead, leaving Griselda a widow. The vicar appears in MURDER AT THE VICARAGE and THE BODY IN THE LIBRARY.

"Clergyman's Daughter, The" Mystery short story.

The International Detective Agency comes to the rescue of a clergyman's daughter, but the true solution lies in a companion story, "THE RED HOUSE."

PUBLISHING AND DRAMATIZATION
HISTORY
The story appeared in the short story collection, PARTNERS IN CRIME, published in 1929 by William Collins Sons and Company, Ltd., in London, and by Dodd, Mead and Company in New York.

The story was combined with "The Red House" and adapted for television in 1984 by London Weekend Television. It was also shown on the Public Broadcasting Service in the U.S.

CHARACTERS
ALBERT, Tommy BERESFORD, Tuppence BERESFORD, Theodore BLUNT, Monica DEANE, Miss SHERINGHAM

PLOT SYNOPSIS
A young woman arrives at their detective agency to ask Tommy and Tuppence, calling themselves Theodore BLUNT and Miss SHERINGHAM, respectively, for help in locating the source of strange happenings in

A vicar's daughter herself, Tuppence Beresford (Francesca Annis) joins Tommy (James Warwick) to solve the problem of "The Clergyman's Daughter." (Photo courtesy of London Weekend Television)

the house she has recently inherited. She wants to keep the house, but a self-styled psychic researcher has approached her with an offer, and the money is tempting, for she wants to marry. The detectives confidently promise to help, and Monica Deane is reassured.

CRIME NOTES
In this story, Tuppence assumes the personality of another fictional detective, the garrulous and self-centered Roger Sheringham, who was created by Anthony Berkley Cox (1893–1970). Cox also founded the Detection Club, of which Agatha Christie was a member.

Cleveland, Jane Hired in "JANE IN SEARCH OF A JOB" to impersonate a duchess whose life is in danger from assassins, she is also known as MONTRESOR, a reporter from New York.

Cleveland, Mortimer He is a psychic investigator whose sensitivity to atmosphere alerts him to danger in "S.O.S." and whose combination of intuition and scientific procedure helps him to prevent a murder.

Cleves, Diana A decidedly unsentimental girl in "THE SECOND GONG," she pleads modernity when questioned by Hercule POIROT as to why she has shown little grief over the death of her adoptive father. In love with one man, loved by another, and flirting with a third, she can claim her inheritance only if she marries the man decreed by the will.

Clithering, Sir Henry A close friend of Miss Jane MARPLE, he is a former Scotland Yard Commissioner and a present member of the Tuesday Night Club who holds Miss Marple and her investigative capabilities in high regard. He is unlike the younger generation of law enforcement officers in his belief that older women can be valuable in an investigation, because they are the eyes and ears of the village and "unlike the famous adage, they speak all evil." He appears in THE THIRTEEN PROBLEMS, THE BODY IN THE LIBRARY and A MURDER IS ANNOUNCED.

Cloade, Frances The daughter of a notoriously dishonest nobleman, she turns to blackmail in TAKEN AT THE FLOOD to obtain money for her husband's business.

Cloade, Gordon Viewed as the benevolent uncle by his family before his marriage in TAKEN AT THE FLOOD, he dies when his house is bombed, and his brothers and sister vie for the estate.

Cloade, Jeremy A solicitor with a very solid firm in TAKEN AT THE FLOOD, he mourns the death of his brother.

Cloade, Katherine (Kathie) Her combination of well-bred background with incongruous behavior in working to find some way to deprive her brother's widow of any part of the estate in TAKEN AT THE

FLOOD is reflected in the incongruity of her clothing, which Hercule POIROT's valet, George, notices.

Cloade, Dr. Lionel Married to Katherine CLOADE, he is the physician in TAKEN AT THE FLOOD who examines the body of the mysterious stranger and provides testimony regarding the cause and time of death at the inquest.

Cloade, Rosaleen As the widow of Gordon CLOADE in TAKEN AT THE FLOOD, she will inherit his estate unless her sister-in-law successfully proves the marriage to be illegal or she is unmasked as Eileen CORRIGAN.

Cloade, Rowland (Rowley) A young man who already bears the guilt for another man's suicide in TAKEN AT THE FLOOD, he is stopped in time by Hercule POIROT when he attempts to strangle his fiancée, Lynn MARCHMONT, after she breaks off their engagement.

Clocks, The Mystery novel.

The novel blends espionage with a good old-fashioned murder mystery. The plot centers on the murder of a man whose body is found in the home of a blind woman, who is herself surprised by the four clocks apparently left by the murderer.

PUBLISHING AND DRAMATIZATION HISTORY
The novel was published in 1963 by William Collins and Sons, Ltd., in London, and in 1964 by Dodd, Mead and Company in New York.

The novel has not been adapted for stage or screen.

CHARACTERS
Colonel BECK, Josiah BLAND, Valerie BLAND, Edna BRENT, Mr. R.H. CURRY, Detective Inspector Dick HARDCASTLE, Mrs. HEMMINGS, Colin LAMB, Mrs. LAWTON, Miss MARTINDALE, Mrs. McNAUGHTON, Angus McNAUGHTON, Millicent PEBMARSH, Hercule POIROT, Professor PURDY, Mrs. RAMSEY, Ted RAMSEY, Dr. RIGG, Merlina RIVAL, Edith WATEROUSE, James WATERHOUSE, Sheila WEBB

PLOT SYNOPSIS
Chapters 1–3
Sheila Webb of the Cavendish Secretarial Bureau is sent to the home of Millicent Pebmarsh, with orders

to let herself into the house should the client not be home. When she enters, she finds a dead man behind the couch. She runs swiftly out of the front door and into the arms of a Special Branch investigator, Colin Lamb. He reenters the house with Sheila and calls Detective Inspector Dick Hardcastle at Scotland Yard. When Miss Pebmarsh returns, she claims that the travel clock, the Dresden china clock, the French gilt Ormolu and the silver clock are not hers. All four clocks have been stopped at 4:13.

Chapters 4–6
Together, Lamb and Hardcastle visit the secretarial bureau to speak with Miss Martindale, who tells them that the call for a stenographer came at three o'clock. She does not recognize the business card found on the dead man, which lists his name as R.H. Curry and his profession as insurance salesman. The men learn nothing from questioning Miss Pebmarsh's housekeeper, who claims that the clocks were not in the house when she was there from ten o'clock to noon. Lamb reveals that he happened to be in the area because he is following up on an espionage case in which a man killed in a hit-and-run accident had a scrap of paper in his wallet with a crescent and the number "61" on it. At the police station the next morning, Lamb learns that the business card is a fake.

Chapters 7–10
Detective Inspector Hardcastle and Sergeant Lamb question residents of the neighborhood and show them a snapshot of the dead man. Miss Waterhouse, Mrs. Hemmings and Mr. and Mrs. Bland claim not to have seen anything. Mrs. McNaughton unconvincingly claims to have seen the man. They have better luck when they visit the Ramsey home, for the young Ramsey sons show them a way through Miss Pebmarsh's fence and into Mrs. Hemmings' garden. There, Lamb finds a piece of glass and a coin which could prove valuable.

Chapters 11–15
Hardcastle questions Sheila's aunt and learns that Sheila's unmarried mother gave her up at birth, but that her mother is still alive. When Lamb speaks with Colonel Beck about the case, he receives a stern warning to be wary of Sheila. Lamb then meets with his old friend, Hercule Poirot, who advises him to engage the neighbors and Sheila in friendly conversation to draw them out. The inquest is held, and the

coroner testifies that "R.H. Curry" was first given chloral hydrate in alcohol, then stabbed to death.

Chapters 16–20

The murder weapon is found in a neighbor's yard, and the detectives speculate that Miss Pebmarsh, even though blind, might have committed the murder because the man was drugged. They learn that a secretary from the Cavendish Secretarial Bureau has been strangled shortly after attempting to contact Hardcastle. After interviewing Miss Pebmarsh, her neighbors and Sheila Webb at her new assignment, the detectives have no further information. Lamb learns that he is being sent to shadow Mr. Ramsey in Rumania.

Chapters 21–25

Merlina Rival appears and identifies the dead man as her husband, who disappeared fifteen years earlier. When Poirot is told this, he cautions Lamb to ask further questions. Returning to the crescent, Lamb speaks with Mrs. Ramsey, who knows of her husband's espionage. She claims that he had asked her to join him in Moscow, but she wishes to raise her sons in England. After interviewing others, he notices a blond child peering out of the window of number 77. She tells him that she saw a laundry enter Miss Pebmarsh's home on the day of the murder.

Chapters 26–29

Merlina Rival has a few drinks at the Peacock Arms, then finds Hardcastle waiting for her when she returns home. She claimed that the dead man had received the scar behind his left ear over fifteen years ago, but the police surgeon says that the scar is only five or six years old. After the detective leaves, Mrs. Rival makes a call. She is later found stabbed to death at Victoria Station. Poirot calls a meeting with the detectives and reveals the murderer. Several startling revelations occur, as the detectives learn that the clocks were added simply to make the murder look more complicated, the blind Miss Pebmarsh is a spy, and the real reason for the murder involved an inheritance and Mrs. Bland. In the end, Colin and Sheila are headed for the altar.

CRIME NOTES

The first murder in this novel is due to poison with chloral hydrate and stabbing, and the second murder is due to strangulation.

Clode, Christobel Until her death, she lived with her grandfather, Simon CLODE, from the time her father died in World War I. She tried to contact her late mother through participation in seances run by Eurydice SPRAGG in "MOTIVE VERSUS OPPORTUNITY."

Clode, George A suspicious nephew of Simon CLODE in "MOTIVE VERSUS OPPORTUNITY," he hires a man to obtain information about the woman who has so great an influence over his uncle.

Clode, Mary A quiet, shy girl, she is Simon CLODE's niece in "MOTIVE VERSUS OPPORTUNITY." She is at risk of being written out of her uncle's will.

Clode, Simon A very wealthy man in "MOTIVE VERSUS OPPORTUNITY," his entire fortune may fall into the hands of an unscrupulous woman who claims to be able to communicate with the dead.

Clonray, Lady Susan She keeps her niece's secret in "THE CASE OF THE MISSING LADY," telling no one that she is at a weight-loss spa, rather than on vacation.

Cobb, Mr. An art gallery director in "THE DEAD HARLEQUIN," he recognizes Mr. SATTERTHWAITE's knowledge of the art world.

Cocker, Mrs. A normally level-headed cook and housekeeper in SLEEPING MURDER, she nearly dies when she is accidentally given poisoned brandy to revive her after she discovers a skeleton.

Cocker, Doris The housemaid who waited on the table of a man who died of poisoning in THREE-ACT TRAGEDY, she fell under strong suspicion until the investigator realized that she had been absent during the previous murder.

Codders See LOMAX, THE HONOURABLE GEORGE.

Codson, Anthony A man who lives what Mr. SATTERTHWAITE labels "an animal's life," the prediction that he had only six months to live drives him to attempt suicide twice in "THE MAN FROM THE SEA," but Mr. SATTERTHWAITE interrupts his second attempt.

Coggins   A brutal hoodlum in "THE ADVENTURE OF THE SINISTER STRANGER," he tortures Tommy BERESFORD, who refuses to reveal the location of the Russian letter.

Coghan, Mr.   He helps Hercule POIROT complete the case in "THE CASE OF THE MISSING WILL" by showing the secret hiding in the fireplace.

Cohen, Sir Herman   See SALMON, SIR JOSEPH.

Coldwell, Susan   A guest and family friend of the suicide victim in "DEAD MAN'S MIRROR."

Cole, Miss   Manager of the Mitre Hotel in "THE UNDER DOG," she provides Hercule POIROT with information regarding Captain NAYLOR.

Cole, Mr. (Detective Inspector)   An undercover police officer who infiltrates the Flock of the Great Shepherd in "THE FLOCK OF GERYON," he plays the convincing part of a zealot as he tells other members about visions of ancient religious rites and sacrificial offerings.

Cole, Elizabeth   After her sister murders their father, Matthew LITCHFIELD, in CURTAIN, she experiences deep guilt and withdraws from life. Captain HASTINGS empathizes with her, and his growing affection becomes apparent to Hercule POIROT, who urges Hastings to rescue Elizabeth and to create a future with her.

Coleman, Bill   His behavior on the expedition at Tell Yarimjah in MURDER IN MESOPOTAMIA led others to view this British archaeologist as an unintelligent boor.

Coleman, Monkey   See DRAKE, VICTOR.

Coles, Dr.   The physician who attends Miss MARPLE at the Keston Spa Hydro in "A CHRISTMAS TRAGEDY."

Coles, Doris   She becomes valuable to Mr. SATTERTHWAITE in helping to solve the unusual murder in "THE BIRD WITH THE BROKEN WING."

Colgate, Inspector   A rugged looking police inspector in EVIL UNDER THE SUN, his unhurried approach to investigating the murder impresses Hercule POIROT.

Collins, Miss   An efficient housekeeper and invaluable secretary-companion to Mrs. WAVERLY, she becomes a suspect to Hercule POIROT when he investigates the kidnapping of a young child in "THE ADVENTURE OF JOHNNIE WAVERLY," because so little is known about this obviously intelligent young woman.

Collins, Beryl   The calm, controlled secretary and receptionist of the murdered physician in THE HOLLOW, she refuses to accept the suggestion of the police inspector that the man's wife committed the murder.

Collodon, Miss   A mature woman of between sixty and sixty-five years of age, she serves as a researcher for Tommy BERESFORD in POSTERN OF FATE.

"Colonel"   See PEDLER, SIR EUSTACE.

Combeau, Pierre   A longtime friend of Hercule POIROT who appears in THE BIG FOUR, he has worked with the detective in the past and is fully familiar with his methods.

Come, Tell Me How You Live   Non-fiction work.

The book was written during World War II and published under the author's married name of Agatha Christie Mallowan to refrain from confusing fans of her mystery novels.

PUBLISHING AND DRAMATIZATION
HISTORY
The book was published in 1946 by William Collins Sons and Company, Ltd., in London, and by Dodd, Mead and Company in New York.

The book has not been adapted for stage or screen.

CONTENT
The work is a charming account of the author's experiences on archaeological digs in the Middle East from 1935 to 1938 with her husband, archaeologist Sir Max Mallowan. In Syria and Iraq she carefully

kept journals of daily occurrences and of the people whom she met. Included are the eccentricities and kind acts of those on the dig, as well as Middle Eastern workmen, desert sheikhs, Turkish associates and women who appealed to the author for her nursing knowledge. She recounts incidents as they occurred, and provides lively, colorful accounts of life at the dig without making judgments.

"Coming of Mr. Quin, The" Mystery short story.

This is the first story to feature Mr. Harley QUIN, whose tale about the tragic lives of the former occupants of Royston Hall have a dramatic effect on its present inhabitants.

PUBLISHING AND DRAMATIZATION HISTORY

The story appeared in the short story collection, THE MYSTERIOUS MR. QUIN. published in 1930 by William Collins Sons and Company, Ltd., in London, and by Dodd, Mead and Company in New York.

The story was the basis for the first film version in English of a work by Christie. Released in 1928, the film was retitled *The Passing of Mr. Quinn [sic]*, and the plot was changed drastically to become a story in which an investigation is launched to save an abused wife whose husband has been having an affair. The movie was only moderately successful at the box office.

CHARACTERS

Derek CAPEL, Laura CONWAY, Sir Richard CONWAY, Alec PORTAL, Eleanor PORTAL, Mr. Harley QUIN, Mr. SATTERTHWAITE

PLOT SYNOPSIS

On a dark evening, Mr. Harley Quin appears at the door of Royston Hall with the story that his car has broken down. As the gathered guests speak about the suicide ten years before of the former owner of the hall, the stranger says that he knew Derek Capel well. The facts of the case are discussed, and the role played by a married woman whose husband was poisoned is examined, as a woman secretly listens on the landing above. The sage observations by Mr. Quin and added comments by Mr. Satterthwaite change the views of the group regarding the tragedy, and they save the life of a woman.

CRIME NOTES

As in all of his appearances, Mr. Harley Quin appears mysteriously and serves as a catalyst to uncovering truth.

"Companion, The" Mystery short story.

At yet another meeting of the Tuesday Night Club, Dr. LLOYD relates the story of a mysterious drowning in Las Palmas which he had heard of some years before.

PUBLISHING AND DRAMATIZATION HISTORY

The story appeared in the short story collection, THIRTEEN PROBLEMS, published in 1932 by William Collins Sons and Company, Ltd., in London, and in 1933, under the title, *The Tuesday Club Murders*, by Dodd, Mead and Company in New York.

The story has not been adapted for stage or screen.

CHARACTERS

Colonel Arthur BANTRY, Dolly BANTRY, Mary BARTON, Sir Henry CLITHERING, Miss Amy DURANT, Jane HELIER, Dr. Lloyd, Miss Jane MARPLE

PLOT SYNOPSIS

Dr. Lloyd relates the story of an Englishwoman and her companion who were vacationing in Las Palmas. When the two went swimming, the companion, Amy Durant, drowned and a witness on shore insisted that the drowning was deliberate. A few months later, Mary Barton was reported drowned, but her body was never found. Miss Marple reviews the facts and presents Dr. Lloyd and the club with a very logical solution.

CRIME NOTES

The sole murder in the story occurs as the result of drowning.

Conneau, George See RENAULD, PAUL T.

Connell, Marjorie A young secretary in UNFINISHED PORTRAIT, her affair and subsequent marriage to the main character's husband closely mirror the real-life actions of Teresa NEELE, the woman for whom Colonel CHRISTIE left the author.

Conrad, Mrs. Well-known in London society and an attractive woman, she charms Captain HAS-TINGS, but Hercule POIROT reveals in "THE SUBMA-RINE PLANS" that she is associated with blackmailers.

Constantine, Dr. A Greek physician on board the Orient Express, he examines the murder victim in MURDER ON THE ORIENT EXPRESS and determines that the dagger wounds have been made by at least two people.

Constantine, Dr. Claudius See ANTROBUS, DR.

Constantine, Dimitri A wealthy man in END-LESS NIGHT, he protests the cost of the new house being designed by the rude but talented architect, Rudolf SANTONIX.

Conway, Bridget A painful love affair has hardened her heart and she considers marrying simply for convenience, until she meets a persistent investigator who falls immediately in love with her in MURDER IS EASY. She throws herself entirely into the investigation, and grows to love Luke FITZWILLIAM as they work to identify the murderer.

Conway, Sir George Possessed of valuable information for Hercule POIROT in "THE AUGEAN STA-BLES," he is unable to express himself because he is only comfortable with trite and meaningless phrases.

Cooke, Miss One of two female bodyguards secretly assigned to guard Miss MARPLE on a tour of famous houses and gardens in NEMESIS, she captures the killer.

Coombe, Alicia A dressmaker to wealthy women, she has an unusual problem in "THE DRESS-MAKER'S DOLL." The life-sized doll that adorns her couch is so realistic that it seems to pulse with life, haunting her shop. The doll changes its position on the couch when no one is around, moving from place to place. Alicia finally throws the doll out of a window.

Coote, Lady Maria A lonely woman in THE SEVEN DIALS MYSTERY, she longs for the old days, before her husband became a successful business-man. To ease her loneliness, she rents Chimneys and invites numerous young people to stay as guests. She also enjoys playing bridge, and is known to cheat.

Coote, Sir Oswald A wealthy businessman in THE SEVEN DIALS MYSTERY, he rises from being the owner of a bicycle shop to buying a factory and then becomes a steel magnate. He is granted a peerage and then becomes one of the wealthiest men in England.

Cope, Jefferson Described by a physician in AP-POINTMENT WITH DEATH as believing in good rather than evil, he has loved Nadine BOYNTON since she was studying to be a nurse, and fails to see the less sympathetic side of her nature.

Copleigh, George and Liz Owners of the guest house in Sutton Chancellor in BY THE PRICKING OF MY THUMBS, they offer little information, aside from hearsay and imagination, when questioned about the town.

Copling, Nurse The nurse to invalid Mrs. PRITCHARD, she consults stargazers and fortune-tellers in "THE BLUE GERANIUM." Copling falls in love with her patient's husband and disguises herself as the fortune-teller ZARIDA.

Cork, Edmund The author's literary agent with the Hughes Massie agency, as well as her personal friend for over forty years.

Cornelly, Lord A rich, eccentric nobleman, he searches the world over for honest men to represent his company in TOWARDS ZERO. When he hires Andrew MacWHIRTER, he tells him that he will not ask his men to tell lies for him, nor does he expect them to tell him lies.

Corner, Sir Montague A man whose personality thrives on affectation, he plays the role of the connoisseur and collector of artifacts in LORD EDG-WARE DIES, and fails to discern that the young woman offering opinions on Greek art at his dinner party is an imposter.

Cornish, Inspector A member of Scotland Yard in THE MIRROR CRACK'D FROM SIDE TO SIDE who works with Detective Inspector CRADDOCK.

"Cornish Mystery, The" Mystery short story.
Hercule POIROT and Captain HASTINGS meet with a woman who is convinced that her gastritis is the

result of her husband's slow poisoning of her, but she dies before the detectives can act on the case.

PUBLISHING AND DRAMATIZATION
HISTORY
The story appeared in the short story collection THE UNDER DOG AND OTHER STORIES, published in 1951 by Dodd, Mead and Company in New York.

The story was adapted for television in 1990 by London Weekend Television in England, and was also shown on the Public Broadcasting Service in the U.S.

CHARACTERS
Dr. ABRAMS, Captain HASTINGS, Miss MARKS, Mrs. PENGELLY, Edward PENGELLY, Hercule Poirot, Jacob RADNOR

PLOT SYNOPSIS
His client dies before the case can begin, but Hercule Poirot feels an obligation to solve the mystery of the murder nonetheless. The attending physician cites gastritis as the cause of death, and no suspicion arises in the village until the victim's dentist husband marries his assistant soon after Mrs. Pengelly's demise. The body is exhumed and found to contain a high level of poison, but Poirot proves that the killer was not whom everyone expects.

CRIME NOTES
The poison in this story is arsenic, found in the gardener's weed killer.

Cornworthy, Hugo   The secretary to eccentric millionaire Benedict FARLEY in "THE DREAM."

Corrigan, Eileen   Forced to impersonate his dead sister by a man who knows the secret of her earlier marriage, she will inherit money that she must share with her blackmailer in TAKEN AT THE FLOOD.

Corrigan, Dr. Jim   A police surgeon who also conducts research into physical predeterminants of criminal behavior in THE PALE HORSE, he locates the crucial list of names on Father GORMAN's body when he conducts a preliminary medical examination.

Corrigan, Katherine (Ginger)   An amateur detective, she collaborates with Mark EASTERBROOK and assumes his last name as his wife to solve the mystery in THE PALE HORSE.

Cortman, Mildred Jean   In her several roles in PASSENGER TO FRANKFURT, she is, first, Sam CORTMAN's wife, a beautiful and felinelike woman; as JUANITA, she serves as a member of the radical Youth Movement; as Miss ELLIS, she poses as a nurse to Robert SHOREHAM.

Cortman, Sam   The American ambassador to the Court of St. James, he is shot to death by a masked group on the steps of the American Embassy in PASSENGER TO FRANKFURT.

Cosden, Anthony   A dispirited man with only six months to live, he returns to die at the site of his greatest happiness, in "THE MAN FROM THE SEA."

Costello, Oliver   Involved in drug distribution, he is "a nasty bit of goods" in SPIDER'S WEB who is murdered when he tries to steal something from the home of his wife's very respectable first husband.

Courtenay, Coco   A popular actress who dresses as Columbine for the Victory Ball, she quarrels with the man who takes away her cocaine in "THE AFFAIR AT THE VICTORY BALL," and is found dead of an overdose the next day.

Cowan, Mr.   Business manager to the opera star, Madame NAZORKOFF, in "SWAN SONG," he calmly endures her temperamental outbursts.

Cowley, Prudence   See BERESFORD, TUPPENCE.

Crabtree, Mrs.   The patient of a murdered doctor in THE HOLLOW, she suffers from Ridgeway's disease, having earned the doctor's respect because she is "a fighter" whom he tried hard to cure with hormone injections. After the doctor's death, the woman he had loved continues to encourage Mrs. CRABTREE.

Crabtree, Emily   Often in disagreement with her husband's aunt, Lily CRABTREE, her argument at lunch on the day that Lily died becomes particularly significant in "SING A SONG OF SIXPENCE."

Crabtree, Lily   A wealthy and often irritable unmarried elderly woman, she is killed by a powerful blow to her head in "SING A SONG OF SIXPENCE." She leaves her family an estate of eighty thousand pounds.

Crabtree, William   A somewhat retiring man in "SING A SONG OF SIXPENCE," he is the husband of Emily CRABTREE, and claims to have been working on his stamp collection at the time that his aunt, Lily CRABTREE, was attacked.

Crackenthorpe, Alfred   One of seven Crackenthorpe brothers and sisters, he is the small-time crook in 4.50 FROM PADDINGTON of whom his siblings are ashamed. He is poisoned with arsenic, but the blame is first assigned to poisonous mushrooms.

Crackenthorpe, Lady Alice   She married Harold CRACKENTHORPE to escape poverty, and now has become a woman who shows no emotion in 4.50 FROM PADDINGTON.

Crackenthorpe, Cedric   Heir to a family estate, he is a painter in 4.50 FROM PADDINGTON who returns to England only because a death has occurred. He is judged by Miss MARPLE to be a man who works hard to shock people.

Crackenthorpe, Emma   One of the seven children of Luther CRACKENTHORPE in 4.50 FROM PADDINGTON, she strikes Miss MARPLE as a woman who instinctively knows how to make the men in her life happy, and a doctor is very interested in her.

Crackenthorpe, Harold   One of Luther CRACKENTHORPE's seven children in 4.50 FROM PADDINGTON, he lives the life of the financially successful businessman but really he is deep in debt. Dissatisfied by his childless marriage and a man who would do anything to avoid scandal, he dies of aconite poisoning.

Crackenthorpe, Luther   A stingy and bitter old man in 4.50 FROM PADDINGTON, he plays the role of the invalid while bullying his seven children. He had been a disappointment to his own father for refusing to become involved in the family business, and he often makes the pronouncement that none of his sons have any merit. Despite his invalid status, he propositions his young female companion.

Crackenthorpe, Martine   Born Martine DU-BOIS, she may or may not be the legal wife of a man who was reported missing in action at Dunkirk, though a letter bearing her signature claims that she married Edmund CRACKENTHORPE and is the mother of his son. The rest of the Crackenthorpe family in 4.50 FROM PADDINGTON disbelieves her claim.

"Crackler, The"   Mystery short story.

Scotland Yard asks the assistance of Tommy and Tuppence BERESFORD in uncovering a counterfeiting ring, and they have a wonderful time mixing with high society.

PUBLISHING AND DRAMATIZATION HISTORY
The story appeared in the short story collection, PARTNERS IN CRIME, published in 1929 by William

Counterfeit money and high-speed action are the rule for Tommy and Tuppence Beresford (James Warwick and Francesca Annis) in "The Crackler." (Photo courtesy of London Weekend Television)

Collins Sons and Company, Ltd., in London, and by Dodd, Mead and Company in New York.

The story was adapted for television in 1984 by London Weekend Television in England, and was also shown on the Public Broadcasting Service in the U.S.

CHARACTERS
Tommy Beresford, Tuppence Beresford, Jimmy FAULKENER (1), M. HEROULDE, Inspector MARRIOT, Hank RYDER, Lawrence ST. VINCENT

PLOT SYNOPSIS
Tommy and Tuppence eagerly accept Scotland Yard's request for help in breaking up a counterfeiting ring, especially because the money is being passed among the monied nightclub set and they stand to have fun. They are almost captured by the counterfeiters, but Tommy's quick thinking saves their lives and leads the police to the counterfeiters.

CRIME NOTES
In this story, both Beresfords assume the roles of the "Busies" in their version of an adventure team that mimics one created by Edgar Wallace (1875–1932).

Craddock, Mrs. Married to Charles CRADDOCK in CARDS ON THE TABLE, she is known to like the company of many men beyond her husband. Her husband is suspicious of her relationship with Dr. ROBERTS, but she dies of an infection in Egypt before her husband can do anything about it.

Craddock, Charles Suspicious that his wife is involved with Dr. ROBERTS, he intends to report the doctor to the General Medical Council in CARDS ON THE TABLE, but dies of anthrax transferred from his shaving brush.

Craddock, Chief Inspector Dermot Eric A longtime acquaintance of Miss MARPLE and the nephew of her close friend, Sir Henry CLITHERING, he appears in A MURDER IS ANNOUNCED, "SANCTUARY," 4.50 FROM PADDINGTON and THE MIRROR CRACK'D FROM SIDE TO SIDE, rising from a Detective Inspector in Middleshire to the highest-ranking officer at Scotland Yard.

Craig, Dr. Donald In love with Hester ARGYLE even though he suspects that she may have murdered her mother in ORDEAL BY INNOCENCE, he wants to be certain so that can he can "look after her" if she is guilty.

Crale, Amyas A famous painter, well known for his many love affairs, he died of hemlock poisoning believed to have been administered by his wife sixteen years before FIVE LITTLE PIGS begins.

Crale, Carla See LEMARCHANT, CARLA.

Crale, Caroline The wife of the painter, Amyas CRALE, she was convicted of having poisoned him sixteen years before FIVE LITTLE PIGS begins, but her daughter Carla LEMARCHANT believes her to be innocent, and retains Hercule POIROT to clear Caroline's name.

Cram, Gladys A high-spirited, noisy woman in MURDER AT THE VICARAGE, she serves as secretary to Dr. STONE.

Crane, The Honourable Hermione A young widow in "THE CASE OF THE MISSING LADY," she pretends to have disappeared while she is at a weight-loss spa.

Crawford, Mr. An attorney in ENDLESS NIGHT who consults with the American attorney for Ellie ROGER.

Crawford, Joanna While on a tour with her aunt in NEMESIS, she and fellow traveler Emlyn PRICE see a figure push the boulder that crushes Elizabeth TEMPLE.

Crawley, Charles A tall, dark-complected man with a scar running down the left side of his face, his fiancée leaves him after the narrator of "IN A GLASS DARKLY" has a vision of her being strangled by a man with such a scar.

Craven, Nurse An opportunist in CURTAIN, she provides care for a patient who is completely healthy. At the same time, she manipulates Sir William Boyd CARRINGTON in an effort to win his affections, even though she is presently involved with Major AL-LERTON.

Craven, Hilary Depressed after the death of her daughter and a recent divorce, she contemplates suicide, but is prevented from acting when a member of the Special Intelligence Unit intervenes in DESTINATION UNKNOWN. He suggests that if she wants to die, she should aid the British government and take part in a mission that would provide a more certain means of death than her attempts could offer. Hilary is asked to impersonate Olive BETTERTON and find a means of penetrating the Brain Trust in order to guide Intelligence to the site.

Cray, Veronica A patient woman who has waited fifteen years to win back the love of Dr. John CHRISTOW, to whom she had once been engaged, this glamorous movie star had been rejected by him years before but lies to Hercule POIROT in her account in THE HOLLOW.

Cregan, Pam An eighteen-year-old girl in "PROBLEM AT SEA," she exerts a great effort to make Colonel CLAPPERTON defy his wife's restrictions.

Cresswell, Mrs. As second wife to the brother-in-law of a wealthy woman, she has no claim on the estate in "GREENSHAW'S FOLLY." However, she agrees to work for Miss GREENSHAW for only room and board because the old woman promises her that her payment will come in the will, when Mrs. Cresswell can expect to inherit the entire estate. She is an incongruous figure as a housekeeper, with her elaborately coiffed head of curls and her rustling black rayon dress.

"Cretan Bull, The" Mystery short story.

Hercule POIROT is consulted by a young woman who asks him to determine why her fiancé broke off their engagement.

PUBLISHING AND DRAMATIZATION HISTORY

The story appeared in the short story collection, THE LABOURS OF HERCULES, published in 1947 by William Collins Sons and Company, Ltd., in London, and by Dodd, Mead and Company in New York.

The story has not been adapted for stage or screen.

CHARACTERS

Admiral Sir Charles CHANDLER, Hugh CHANDLER, Colonel George FROBISHER, Diana MABERLY, Hercule Poirot

PLOT SYNOPSIS

A young man who experiences blackouts, wakes up with blood-stained weapons close at hand, and hears stories of animals killed nearby could easily be convinced that he is insane. Faced with the possibility, Hugh Chandler chooses to break off his engagement rather than to subject his future wife to the pain of being married to a madman. When Hercule Poirot intervenes, not only is Hugh proved to be sane, but a twist of fate prevents him from inheriting the Chandler family insanity.

CRIME NOTES

The story features use of the exotic substance, datura, which slowly drives Hugh Chandler insane.

Crispin, Angus A member of British Intelligence who poses as the gardener HORSHAM, he is sent to protect Tommy and Tuppence BERESFORD in POSTERN OF FATE. He succeeds in foiling a third attempt on Tuppence's life.

Crockett An elderly servant in "THE CLERGYMAN'S DAUGHTER" and "THE RED HOUSE," she is unpleasant and "gives herself airs" because her sister married above their station.

Croft, Bert A lodger in PERIL AT END HOUSE, he and his wife Milly play up his Australian background and make Hercule POIROT suspicious of his motives. The suspicion deepens when POIROT learns that Bert has suggested to his landlady that she make a will just before she is to undergo a minor surgical procedure.

Croft, Milly Married to Bert CROFT and a woman of apparently Australian background who is confined to a wheelchair in PERIL AT END HOUSE, she is, nonetheless, well known to Inspector JAPP as a forger.

Crofton Lee, Sir Rupert An accomplished traveler in THEY CAME TO BAGHDAD, he is well-known for his theatrical self-promotion. His death occurs because he has located a site in China where a secret weapon is being constructed, but he manages to get the information into the right hands before he dies.

Croker See LAVINGTON, MR.

Crome, Inspector Officially in charge of the investigation in THE A.B.C. MURDERS, he is a young Scotland Yard inspector about whose capabilities Hercule POIROT and Captain HASTINGS disagree.

Cronshaw, Lord Cronch Dressed in a harlequin costume for the Victory Ball in "THE AFFAIR AT THE VICTORY BALL," he is stabbed to death after an argument with his fiancée, Coco COURTENAY.

Crooked House, The Mystery novel.

This novel was one of Agatha Christie's two personal favorites among her many works, and she noted in AN AUTOBIOGRAPHY that it had been a pure pleasure to write. Her fondness lay in its subject matter, specifically the way in which the lives of family members intertwine and determine events. The title of the novel is derived from the nursery rhyme which begins with the line "There was a crooked man . . ." and which ends with the line "and they all lived together in a crooked little house." The murdered patriarch of the family is an aged little man who, over the course of decades, has commissioned numerous additions to his house to produce an erratically created structure.

PUBLISHING AND DRAMATIZATION HISTORY

The novel was first published by William Collins Sons and Company, Ltd., in London, in 1949 and by Dodd, Mead and Company in New York.

The novel has not been adapted for stage or screen.

CHARACTERS

Mr. AGRODOPOLOUS, Lawrence BROWN, Miss Edith DE HAVILAND, Mr. GAITSKILL, Dr. GRAY, Assistant Commissioner Sir Arthur HAYWARD, Charles HAYWARD, Mr. JOHNSON, Detective Sergeant LAMB, Aristide LEONIDES, Brenda LEONIDES, Clemency LEONIDES, Eustace LEONIDES, Josephine LEONIDES, Magda LEONIDES, Philip LEONIDES, Roger LEONIDES, Sophia LEONIDES, Janet (Nannie) ROWE, Chief Inspector TAVENER, Magda WEST, Janet WOOLMAR

PLOT SYNOPSIS
Chapters 1–2

Charles Hayward and Sophia Leonides are English nationals stationed in Egypt during World War II. As the two prepare to separate in the waning days of the war, they vow to meet again in England as soon as they can, but they do not meet until Charles sees an obituary for Sophia's eighty-five-year-old grandfather, Aristide Leonides, and calls her. Because of the mysterious circumstances surrounding the death, she suggests that Charles wait to receive an unbiased report of the incident from his father, an assistant commissioner at Scotland Yard.

Chapters 3–10

At Scotland Yard, Charles learns of Aristide Leonides' shadowy past, and murder is confirmed. At his father's urging, Charles infiltrates the Leonides house with Sophia's approval. With Chief Inspector Tavener, he questions the numerous odd inhabitants of the Leonides house. The police and family also discover Aristide's unsigned final will in the wall safe, thus raising concerns among family members that the late millionaire's much younger second wife will inherit his vast estate. At the same time, Charles learns that Roger Leonides had been embezzling funds from one of the family businesses.

Chapters 11–12

At Scotland Yard, Roger admits that his business was foundering. He produces a letter which proves that his father had intended to bail him out. Unsettled by the possibility that any one of the Leonides clan could be the murderer, Charles asks his father for guidance in spotting a murderer.

Chapters 13–16

Charles returns to the crooked house to gather more information and to determine what Josephine Leonides knows. She plays exasperating guessing games with him. Charles soon finds himself drawn by Sophia into a family meeting regarding Roger's financial troubles. After the meeting ends, Charles speaks to a family member and learns of the dark undercurrents that have existed for a long time, as well as of a sudden decision by Magda Leonides to immediately send her youngest child to boarding school in Switzerland. While at the house, Charles unsettles a few suspects with his questions.

Chapters 17–20
A secret will is discovered that makes Sophia the main beneficiary of Aristide's estate and also places suspicion on her. As the terms of the will are revealed, an attempt is made on Josephine's life. Charles returns to investigate the attack, and locates a packet of incriminating love letters that seem to clinch the case.

Chapters 21–26
The police make an arrest but remain unsatisfied, a concern further justified by the poisoning death of another character. After a series of surprises, the real murderer is identified, thus clearing the way for Sophia and Charles to marry.

CRIME NOTES
The author was criticized for her choice of murderer and her publishers wanted her to change the ending, but she held her ground.

Two different poisons are used to murder characters in this novel. Aristide Leonides dies when physostigmine, better known as eserine, from his eyedrops is substituted for the insulin he injects to control his diabetes. Later in the novel, digitalin tablets are added to cocoa to kill Janet (Nannie) Rowe.

Crosbie, Captain   A police agent described by a female acquaintance in THEY CAME TO BAGHDAD as having "protuberant eyes," may be highly interested in a pretty girl, but he is also alert, and aids in capturing a group of subversives.

Crossfield, Superintendent   He heads the investigation into the murder of Sir Bartholomew STRANGE in THREE-ACT TRAGEDY and refuses to let mere civilians get the better of him and his men in the gathering of clues.

Crossfield, George   An inept investor with an active gambling habit, he loses substantial amounts of money in AFTER THE FUNERAL, so he is one relative who really needs the inheritance to cover his debts.

Crotchet, Mr.   See SIMPSON, MR.

Crowther, Sydney   The Secretary of State for Home Affairs in THE BIG FOUR, he enjoys so close a relationship with Hercule POIROT that he is designated the executor of the detective's will.

Crump, Mr.   A man who is hitched to the tail of a star cook in A POCKET FULL OF RYE, this alcoholic butler keeps his job only because Mrs. Crump is a talented chef.

Cunningham, Dr. Alice   Engaged to Niki ROSSAKOFF, son of the love of Hercule POIROT's life, the Countess Vera ROSSAKOFF, this psychologist spends a great deal of time at the nightclub Hell in "THE CAPTURE OF CERBERUS," purportedly as a student of human behavior, observing the patrons and recording their actions. The worldly POIROT carefully observes her and provides her with an unfavorable critique of her clothing and makeup choices.

Curry, Inspector   As head of the investigation into the murder of Christian GULBRANDSEN, he is a competent and diligent police officer who prefers to maintain a low public profile in THEY DO IT WITH MIRRORS.

Curry, R.H.   See DUGUESCLIN, QUENTIN.

Curtain   Mystery novel.

The novel recounts the last case of Hercule POIROT, who dies at the end. Not published until 1975, the novel was actually written early in World War II, during the London Blitz. Agatha Christie feared that she would not survive the bombing raids, so she wrote this novel and SLEEPING MURDER at this time, insured both novels heavily and placed them in bank vaults, where they remained until publication. They were in safekeeping should she run out of ideas.

PUBLISHING AND DRAMATIZATION HISTORY
Curtain was published in 1975 by William Collins Sons and Company, Ltd., in London, and by Dodd, Mead and Company in New York.

The novel has not been adapted for stage or screen.

CHARACTERS
Major ALLERTON, Sir William BOYD-CARRINGTON, Elizabeth COLE, Nurse CRAVEN, CURTISS, Barbara FRANKLIN, Dr. John FRANKLIN, GEORGE, Captain Arthur HASTINGS, Judith HASTINGS, Colonel George (Toby) LUTTRELL, Daisy LUTTRELL, Stephen NORTON, Hercule Poirot

PLOT SYNOPSIS
Chapter 1
Recently widowed Captain Arthur Hastings has returned to England from Argentina at the invitation of his longtime friend, Hercule Poirot, who has organized a reunion of sorts at Styles, the site of their first meeting. The famed detective has arranged for Hastings' daughter, Judith, and her employer also to stay at Styles, a former family estate now turned guesthouse.

Chapters 2–4
Upon arrival, Hastings finds a frail and wheelchair-bound Poirot, who claims that he must "be attended to like a baby," yet he reveals that he is at Styles to hunt down a murderer. After discussing five apparently unrelated murder cases in which no murderer was identified, Poirot states that a murder will occur soon, and that he knows the identity of the murderer, whom he calls "X" and refuses to reveal.

At dinner, Hastings examines his companions intently in the effort to determine the murderer's identity, but he is unsuccessful. Judith Hastings shocks him with her views regarding murder, in words which remind her father of one of Poirot's earlier case descriptions.

Chapters 5–7
After a meeting with the bedridden and neglected Mrs. Franklin, Hastings speaks with Poirot, who rebuffs all requests for clues regarding the murderer. The two part, and Hastings plays bridge with the other guests in the hope of learning the murderer's identity. The following day, Hastings speaks with Dr. Franklin, his daughter's employer, and others in an attempt to ferret out the murderer, but he remains unsuccessful.

Chapters 8–11
Hastings speaks with all the guests and learns that each is related to one of the five unsolved murder cases that Poirot discussed earlier. When the guest-house hostess, Mrs. Luttrell, is accidentally shot by her husband, Poirot declares this to be "another X case," but one in which the intended victim survives. Hastings turns his scrutiny to Major Allerton, a task which is complicated by Judith's apparent attraction to this man with a very unsavory past.

Chapters 12–14
The search for the murderer is put aside when Hastings becomes concerned over his daughter's relationship with Allerton. He fears that she will be disgraced and commit suicide, as did an earlier girlfriend of the major. Desperation leads Hastings to contemplate murder, and he goes so far as to dissolve a lethal dose of sleeping pills in whiskey with the goal of poisoning Allerton, but no opportunity occurs. Instead, the invalid Mrs. Franklin dies of poisoning, although the official cause of death is suicide.

Chapters 15–19
Poirot has another heart attack, and decides to consult Dr. Franklin, who later tells Hastings that Poirot is "for it, all right" and only has a short time to live. At the same time, Poirot is heartened that the case is nearly solved when he learns that Stephen Norton has seen something incriminating through his binoculars. Before Norton can tell his story, he is found shot through the center of his forehead, an apparent suicide. The same day, Poirot dies from an apparent heart attack, which could have been prevented had he placed his amyl nitrite ampules near his bed. In his grief, Hastings locates Poirot's valet George and learns that the detective had deliberately sent him away for a time.

Postscript
Four months after the death, Hastings reads a manuscript written by Poirot, and given to him by Poirot's lawyers. In it, the detective reveals the identity of the murderer, and tells Hastings that he had moved the amyl nitrite ampules away from beside his bed, preferring to leave himself in the hands of the "*bon Dieu.*"

CRIME NOTES
On August 6, 1975, *The New York Times* published a front-page obituary of Hercule Poirot with a photograph to mark his death in the newly published *Curtain*.

The means of murder in *Curtain* include a gunshot wound and a fatal ingestion of the poison physostigmine sulphate.

Curtain, Miss   Tall and thin, with "a face like a dreaming duchess," she is the chief of hospital wardmaids in GIANT'S BREAD.

Curtis, Amelia   A day-servant who gossips extensively in THE SITTAFORD MYSTERY. A reporter and the fiancée of the man accused of murder pose as cousins and rent rooms in the house in which she works, and she speculates as to the true nature of their relationship.

Curtis, Sir Ralph   See ALLOWAY, LORD.

Curtis, Inspector   The big, soldierlike police inspector in "THE LOVE DETECTIVE."

Curtis, Mr.   Formerly a gardener at Sittaford House and now married to Amelia CURTIS, he is a pipe-smoking, misogynist philosopher in THE SITTAFORD MYSTERY who expresses the thought that women talk too much, and that they frequently "don't know the truth of what they are talking about."

Curtis, Mrs.   An officious and incompetent Red Cross commandant in GIANT'S BREAD.

Curtiss   Manservant to Hercule POIROT in the detective's final appearance in CURTAIN, he replaces the faithful GEORGE, who must leave to care for his ill father. Despite George's assessment that Curtiss is "hardly the class M. Poirot would have liked," the physically strong man has the sad task of carrying the ailing detective to the garden and back each day.

Curtiss, Major   Present at the card party on the night that Arnold CLAYTON is murdered in "THE MYSTERY OF THE BAGHDAD CHEST," he appears to be the model of control, but beneath the surface seethe unexplored passions.

Cust, Alexander Bonaparte   Named so grandly by his late mother, who hoped to inspire him to great deeds in his life, the grown man views his names as "ridiculous" and himself as insignificant. He is seen washing blood off his sleeve in THE A.B.C. MURDERS and, once other clues are revealed, he becomes a likely suspect in the murders.

Cyril   The carefree brother of the main character in UNFINISHED PORTRAIT, his behavior and description mirror those of the author's brother, Louis (Monty) MILLER.

Czarnova, Countess   See VAUCHER, JEANNE.

D

Dacre, Major A penniless, low-ranking, young, military officer in GIANT'S BREAD.

Dacre, Denis See DAVIS, DENIS.

Dacre, Joan A young, poorly dressed, insignificant-looking woman in "THE BLOOD-STAINED PAVEMENT," she is married to the bigamous Denis DACRE, and resembles his first wife.

Dacre, Margery The first wife of the bigamous Denis DACRE in "THE BLOOD-STAINED PAVEMENT," she dies in a suspicious drowning accident.

Dacres, Mr. A lawyer in THE SITTAFORD MYSTERY, he represents the legal interests of Emily TREFUSIS and serves as the defense lawyer for accused murderer James PEARSON. He admits that Pearson had asked his murdered uncle for money but believes Pearson is innocent.

Dacres, Cynthia A violent-tempered woman with "greenish-bronze hair" in THREE-ACT TRAGEDY, she is an elegant dressmaker whose business has recently suffered setbacks. She is present during two murders, and becomes a suspect.

Dacres, Captain Freddie Married to the successful, ambitious Cynthia DACRES in THREE-ACT TRAGEDY, he spends his life on the race course.

Dakin, Mr. His lethargic behavior and seeming indifference to life mask a shrewd and perceptive and knowledgeable mind. These characteristics heighten his effectiveness as an Intelligence supervisor in THEY CAME TO BAGHDAD, although agents who work with him doubt him at first.

Dale, Sylvia Loyal to the man she loves in "THE SIGN IN THE SKY," she uses all of her resources to have him acquitted of murder.

Dalehouse, Harry Accustomed to the rigid schedule of meals at Lytcham Close in "THE SECOND GONG," the nephew of Sir Hubert Lytcham ROCHE is surprised when the dinner schedule is changed to accommodate a guest whose train is late. The guest is Hercule POIROT.

Dane Calthrop, Reverend Caleb The elderly local vicar of Much Deeping, his scholarly mind finds great pleasure in identifying appropriate Latin quotations for each occasion of note. He appears in both THE PALE HORSE and THE MOVING FINGER.

Dane Calthrop, Maud Married to the Reverend Caleb DANE CALTHORP, she appears in THE PALE HORSE and THE MOVING FINGER, and functions as the organizing principle in her husband's life.

Danemead A small but charming, Georgian-style cottage in which Miss Marple resides on the High Street in ST. MARY MEAD.

Daniels, Captain A talented linguist in "THE KIDNAPPED PRIME MINISTER" who speaks seven languages, his skill makes Hercule POIROT suspicious. He is officially employed as the secretary to the Prime Minister, but he also spies for the Germans.

Darnley, Rosamund A fashionable business woman in EVIL UNDER THE SUN, she runs a dressmaking company named Rose Mond Ltd. Unable to bear seeing her longtime friend, Kenneth MARSHALL, suffer in an unhappy marriage, she advises him to leave his wife, Arlena, for the sake of his young daughter. When the wife dies, Rosamund joins her old friend and his daughter to create a new life in the country.

Darrell, Claud A master of disguise who assumes a variety of personalities in THE BIG FOUR, he changes his looks to appear as the footman JAMES at the country home of Abe RYLAND, the Russian chess champion, Dr. SAVARONOFF, the doctor who administers the injection to Mr. PAYNTER on the night Paynter died, and the phony son of the equally phony Mr. TEMPLETON. He is believed to have died in an explosion.

Darrell, Richard The head of the firm, Hobson, Jekyll and Lucas, which goes bankrupt in "MAGNOLIA BLOSSOM" because of his illegal maneuvering.

Darrell, Theodora Married to Richard DARRELL and having an affair with another man in "MAGNOLIA BLOSSOM," she leaves both men, and determines to do penance alone for her sin.

Dashwood, Everett An enthusiastic young reporter who will do anything to get a story in "THE AUGEAN STABLES," he learns of a scandal being created by another newspaper, and asks Hercule POIROT to help him discredit the rival paper.

Da Silva, Mrs. See HOBHOUSE, VALERIE.

Daubreuil, Madame A woman with an extremely shady past in MURDER ON THE LINKS. She is really Jeanne BEROLDY, who plotted with her lover George CONNEAU to kill her husband, then was forced to stand trial when Conneau disappeared. Acquitted of the crime, she changed her name and moved to the south coast of France, where rumors contend that she had once been the mistress of the murdered Paul RENAULD. She fascinates Captain HASTINGS with her femininity and charm, which remain seductive, despite her age.

Daubreuil, Marthe The twenty-two-year-old daughter of Madame DAUBREUIL and her late husband in MURDER ON THE LINKS, she captivates Captain HASTINGS with her innocent beauty and elicits the sympathy of Hercule POIROT with her "anxious eyes."

Daubreuil, Raoul Engaged to Madame SIMONE in "THE LAST SEANCE," he demands that she not hold a seance because of her ill health.

A Daughter's a Daughter Non-mystery novel.
The fifth of the non-mystery novels published as Mary WESTMACOTT, this novel wryly and sympathetically portrays a mother-daughter relationship, and questions the wisdom of sacrificial love.

PUBLISHING AND DRAMATIZATION HISTORY
A Daughter's a Daughter was first published by Heinemann in London in 1952, and by Dell in New York as a paperback in 1963. The first hardcover version in the U.S. was published by Arbor House in 1972.

The novel has not been adapted for stage or screen.

CHARACTERS
Richard CAULDFIELD, EDITH, Geoffrey FANE, Jennifer GRAHAM, James GRANT, Gerald LLOYD, Mrs. MASSINGHAM, Ann PRENTICE, Sarah PRENTICE, Lawrence STEENE, Dame Laura WHITSTABLE

PLOT SYNOPSIS
Book 1
The novel opens as forty-one-year-old widow Ann Prentice forlornly watches the train bearing her nineteen-year-old daughter, Sarah, away for a three-week vacation in Switzerland. Their symbiotic relationship has developed over the sixteen years during which Ann has raised Sarah alone. Although Ann feels her daughter's absence acutely, she also recognizes that Sarah is now a young woman, and they must both become more independent of each other.

Psychologist Dame Laura Whitstable, Ann's friend and Sarah's godmother, urges Ann to begin life again, and warns that Sarah has too much influence in Ann's life. Ann protests, but Dame Laura's words run through her mind when she meets Richard Cauldfield, a former British army officer whose wife had died years before in childbirth. The two are agreeably companionable and, although neither is passionately in love, they decide to marry after only a few days of acquaintance. When Sarah returns, she resumes her dominance over Ann, makes every effort to impede her mother's remarriage, and succeeds.

Book 2

Two years pass, during which Ann undergoes dramatic changes. Her hair is fashionably styled, her makeup is artificial, and she lives in a frenetic social whirl. Sarah has become emotionally distant, in her own social orbit with the wealthy, dissipated playboy Lawrence Steene. When she receives a letter from former boyfriend Gerald Lloyd, who has failed in every business venture to date, Sarah yearns to renew their acquaintance. Ann receives a call from Richard Cauldfield, and is surprised by his recent marriage to a young, wealthy and attractive woman who confesses that she has been jealous of Ann. Despite the careful social veneer, Ann and Richard sense each other's regrets. After the couple leaves, Sarah asks Ann's advice regarding Lawrence Steene's marriage proposal, hoping for disapproval, but finds that Ann refuses to spare the time. Feeling alone and frightened, Sarah turns to her housekeeper Edith, who bluntly reminds her to consider marriage more seriously.

Book 3

Another year passes, during which Ann has become increasingly brittle and afraid of growing old alone. Sarah has married Steene; Dame Laura tells Ann that Sarah drinks too much and is rumored to be a cocaine addict. Gerald Lloyd, now heir to 110,000 pounds, reappears and tries to convince Sarah to leave her husband and go with him to Canada to start again. Her indecisiveness sets off a major confrontation with Ann, who finally admits to Sarah that the loss of Richard has made her bitter and hateful. The two part angrily.

Ann sinks into a deep depression, and Sarah enters a nursing home to break her addiction before leaving with Gerry for Canada. At the end of the novel, Ann and Sarah reconcile as the plane for Canada is about to leave. At the end of the novel, Ann is once again her former placid self, lonely in her home with only Edith for company.

Davenheim, Mr. A respectable banker and financier in "THE DISAPPEARANCE OF MR. DAVENHEIM," he serves three months in prison for working as a pickpocket under the name of Billy KELLET. He hides this fact from his partners in the firm by claiming to have gone to South America on business in those three months.

Daventry, Mr. A thirty-five-year-old assistant to the Administrator of St. Honore in A CARIBBEAN MYSTERY, he is consulted by the hotel doctor in the murder of Major PALGRAVE.

Daventry, Vera (Socks) A young, exuberant woman, she is welcomed at Chimneys by her hosts in THE SEVEN DIALS MYSTERY because of her liveliness.

David, Lucy A witness to Simon CLODE's new will in "MOTIVE VERSUS OPPORTUNITY," she is the cook, and about thirty years of age.

Davidson, Mrs. Married to Chris DAVIDSON, she wears the Pierette costume while he dresses as Pierot in "THE AFFAIR AT THE VICTORY BALL," and she is among the guests who discover the body of the murder victim.

Davidson, Chris Tall, dark and handsome, he is a drug supplier in "THE AFFAIR AT THE VICTORY BALL" who counts several cocaine addicts among his friends.

Davis One of two stewards on the plane in "DEATH IN THE CLOUDS," he becomes a suspect in murder.

Davis, Mr. See BLORE, WILLIAM HENRY.

Davis, Carol The only legitimate wife of the bigamous Denis DAVIS, she has called herself Carol HARDING as her husband's partner in a swindle, and appears in "THE BLOOD STAINED PAVEMENT."

Davis, Denis A bigamist whose only legitimate marriage is to Carol DAVIS, he uses the name Denis DACRE to marry two other women in "THE BLOODSTAINED PAVEMENT."

Davis, Giles Proprietor, along with his wife Molly, of the Monkswell Manor boarding house, he is a gloomy man in "THREE BLIND MICE" who fears that his wife is having an affair with Christopher WREN, the man whom he claims is a murderer.

Davis, Jesse Once married, she has resumed her maiden name and works for Zachariah Osborne's Customer's Reactions Classified in THE PALE HORSE.

When dying, she supplies Father GORMAN with a list of names that provides a clue to the mystery.

Davis, Molly   An attractive, twenty-two-year-old bride, she is married to Giles DAVIS and runs a boarding house with him in "THREE BLIND MICE."

Davy, Chief Inspector Fred   Referred to behind his back as "Father" at Scotland Yard, he is a large, placid man with a pleasingly deep voice. When he is called to look into the disappearance of a cleric in AT BERTRAM'S HOTEL, he becomes suspicious and uses all of his resources to uncover the secret of the hotel.

Dawes, Rhoda   See DESPARD, RHODA DAWES.

Dawlish, Lord   An extremely wealthy nobleman in DEATH ON THE NILE (2), he embraced Communism while a student at Oxford, and now travels under the name of Mr. FERGUSON.

Deacon, Phillis   The matchmaking wife of a baronet in GIANT'S BREAD.

"Dead Harlequin, The"   Mystery short story.
   The purchase of a painting by an up-and-coming artist sets this mystery into motion for Mr. SATTERTHWAITE.

PUBLISHING AND DRAMATIZATION HISTORY
The story appeared in the short story collection, THE MYSTERIOUS MR. QUIN, published in 1930 by William Collins Sons and Company, Ltd., in London, and by Dodd, Mead and Company in New York.
   The story has not been adapted for stage or screen.

CHARACTERS
Frank BRISTOW, Alix CHARNLEY, Hugo CHARNLEY, Lord Reggie CHARNLEY, Monica FORD, Aspasia GLEN, Colonel MONCKTON

PLOT SYNOPSIS
Mr. Satterthwaite finds a painting of a harlequin figure peering through a window at a similar figure dead on the floor, and purchases it because the face in the portrait is that of his friend Mr. Harley Quin.

The site of the painting is the gloomy family home of the Charnleys, where a suicide occurred fourteen years earlier. The painting draws together several of the people involved in the suicide and, with the help of Mr. Quin, they reach a very different conclusion concerning the tragedy.

CRIME NOTES
The appearance of Mr. Harley Quin in this story is more strongly linked to the supernatural than in other stories.

Dead Man's Folly   Mystery novel.
   The novel pairs the incomparable Mrs. Ariadne OLIVER with the fastidious Hercule POIROT in providing a solution to the murders. The plot centers on a murder hunt, organized as part of a charity function, which results in an all-too-real murder.

PUBLISHING AND DRAMATIZATION HISTORY
The novel was published in 1956 by William Collins Sons and Company, Ltd., in London, and by Dodd, Mead and Company in New York.
   The novel was adapted for television by Warner Brothers Television in 1986 and starred Peter Ustinov as Hercule Poirot and Jean Stapleton as Ariadne Oliver.

CHARACTERS
Superintendent BALDWIN, Miss Amanda BREWIS, Detective-Inspector BLAND, ELSA, Amy FOLLIAT, James FOLLIAT, Marilyn GALE, Robert HOSKINS, Alec LEGGE, Peggy LEGGE, Felicity LEMON, Mrs. Connie MASTERTON, Major MERALL, MERDELL, Mrs. Ariadne Oliver, Hercule Poirot, Etienne de SOUSA, Sir George STUBBS, Lady Hattie STUBBS, Marilyn TUCKER, Marlene TUCKER, Captain Jim WARBURTON, Michael WEYMAN

PLOT SYNOPSIS
Chapters 1–2
Hercule Poirot receives a phone call from Mrs. Ariadne Oliver, asking him to meet her at Nasse House. The urgency of her voice leads Poirot to believe that a murder has occurred. When he arrives, he learns that she is setting up a novelty murder for her charity murder hunt, and something feels wrong. Poirot meets Mrs. Amy Folliat.

Chapters 3–4

Mrs. Folliat shows Poirot around the house, and several of the other characters are introduced. Alec Legge expresses her hatred for Lady Stubbs, who appears to be vain and selfish. When Mrs. Oliver shows Poirot the setup for the murders, he tells her that everything seems normal. Mrs. Folliat regales the company with the tragedies she has suffered, and reminds everyone that Nasse once belonged to her.

Chapters 5–6

Poirot speaks with the old man who runs the ferries to the mainland in order to obtain information about the deaths of Mrs. Folliat's sons years before. Later, the group has dinner, then goes to bed without event. In the morning, Lady Stubbs expresses chagrin over the letter from her scoundrel of a cousin, Etienne, who plans to visit. Mrs. Masterton tells Poirot that Sir George Stubbs' secretary, Miss Brewis, dislikes Lady Stubbs and often looks as if she wants to murder her. The members of the group meet the mock murder victim, Marlene Tucker. As the murder party begins, Etienne de Sousa arrives, and he later joins Poirot in searching for Lady Stubbs. Instead, they find Marlene Tucker murdered.

Chapters 7–10

Inspector Bland arrives to investigate the murder. He wants to know why Marlene was chosen as the mock victim, and who made that choice. No one has the answer. Mrs. Oliver is very upset about the murder, and she tells Bland about the arrival of de Sousa. The investigator fears that Lady Stubbs is in danger; he questions de Sousa and speaks with Sir George, who tells Bland that his wife had said that de Sousa kills people. While Bland tries to narrow the list of suspects, and questions all of the guests, Lady Stubbs disappears.

Chapters 11–13

Poirot speaks with Mrs. Folliat, who suggests that Hattie is not accountable for her actions and that, in a fit of rage, people like her might even kill. Poirot and Bland compare the statements taken from the guests, and find that many are conflicting. His assurances to Sir George Stubbs aside, Poirot believes that the missing Lady Stubbs is dead. Mrs. Masterton asserts that there is someone evil on the island, and suggests that they release bloodhounds. Meanwhile, Poirot finds at the scene of Marlene's murder a gold charm that matches the missing link on Peggy Legge's bracelet. She seems nervous and is unhappily married.

Chapters 14–16

Bland tells de Sousa to stay for the inquest, and he continues to search for Lady Stubbs' body. Poirot searches the grounds of Nasse House but finds nothing, yet he feels that something is missing. Major Merall joins the investigation and, with Bland, tries to learn why de Sousa came to visit Lady Stubbs. As they try to eliminate everyone who is not a suspect in the murder, they learn that the old ferryman, Merdell, has died. The death is ruled accidental. As the mystery surrounding Lady Stubbs deepens, Poirot begins to suspect even Mrs. Oliver.

Chapters 17–20

On a visit to the Tucker residence, Poirot learns that the dead Mr. Merdell is the grandfather of the murdered Marlene Tucker. He also learns that Marlene used to spy on people, then accept gifts to keep quiet about their secrets. After asking a few more questions, Poirot tells the police investigators that he knows the location of Lady Stubbs, and he names her murderer. The novel closes with the revelation that Sir George Stubbs is really James Folliat, thought lost in the war. Poirot reveals that there are two murderers in this case, the individual who killed Marlene and another who killed Lady Stubbs and Merdell.

CRIME NOTES

The first murder victim is strangled while the two later victims are drowned.

"Dead Man's Mirror"   Mystery short story.

The story contains a locked-room murder which all but Hercule POIROT believe to be suicide.

PUBLISHING AND DRAMATIZATION HISTORY

The story appeared in the short story collection, MURDER IN THE MEWS, published in 1937 by William Collins Sons and Company, Ltd., in London, and, under the title, *Dead Man's Mirror and Other Stories,* by Dodd, Mead and Company in New York.

The story was adapted for television in 1993 by London Weekend Television in Britain, and was also shown on the Public Broadcasting Service in the U.S.

CHARACTERS

Godfrey BURROWS, Colonel Ned BURY, Gervase CHEVENIX-GORE, Ruth CHEVENIX-GORE, Lady Vanda Elizabeth CHEVENIX-GORE, Susan COLDWELL, Ogilvie FORBES, Captain LAKE, Miss LINGARD, Hercule Poirot, Chief Constable Major RIDDLE, SNELL, Hugo TRENT

PLOT SYNOPSIS

Gervase Chevenix-Gore writes to Hercule Poirot, asking him to visit his estate to discuss a problem of fraud. When Poirot arrives, he learns that the man has been found in his locked study, an apparent suicide victim. After questioning everyone in the house, Poirot and the Chief Constable become suspicious, and this feeling is increased further when they learn of the provisions of the dead man's will.

CRIME NOTES

The story provides a variation on the locked-room theme, and adds a shattered mirror to complicate the situation.

Dead Man's Mirror and Other Stories See MURDER IN THE MEWS.

Deane, Molly A charming and beautiful girl in "WASPS' NEST," she remains in love with her former fiancé although she is currently engaged to John HARRISON.

Deane, Monica The daughter of a clergyman, she recently inherited the Red House from her aunt. When she and her mother are bothered by a poltergeist as they try to turn their recently inherited home into a guesthouse, they turn to Tommy and Tuppence BERESFORD for help in "THE CLERGYMAN'S DAUGHTER."

"Death by Drowning" Mystery short story.

The drowning death of an unmarried pregnant woman is murder, and Miss MARPLE believes that the police have accused the wrong man.

PUBLISHING AND DRAMATIZATION HISTORY

The story appeared in the short story collection, THE THIRTEEN PROBLEMS, published in 1932 by William Collins Sons and Company, Ltd., in London, and,

under the title, *The Tuesday Club Murders,* by Dodd, Mead and Company in New York.

The story has not been adapted for stage or screen.

CHARACTERS

Sir Henry CLITHERING, Joe ELLIS, Rose EMMOTT, Tom EMMOTT, Miss Marple, Rex SANDFORD

PLOT SYNOPSIS

Miss Marple asks Sir Henry Clithering to help her to solve the case of the drowning death of young, unmarried mother-to-be, Rose Emmott. Even though the evidence points to one man in the case, Miss Marple's intuition and observations make her certain another man murdered the girl, and she sets out to prove it.

CRIME NOTES

The story is out of the ordinary because Miss Marple asks an acquaintance to help in the investigation.

Death Comes As the End Mystery novel.

The novel presents a picture of life and murder in a civilization of four thousand years ago. The plot centers on the murders that occur in the family of a wealthy priest-landowner in Egypt, approximately 2000 B.C.

PUBLISHING AND DRAMATIZATION HISTORY

The novel was published in 1945 by William Collins Sons and Company in London, and in 1944 by Dodd, Mead and Company in New York.

The novel has not been adapted for stage or screen.

CHARACTERS

ESA, HENET, HORI, IMHOTEP, IPY, KAIT, KAMENI, KHAY, Divine Father MERSU, MONTU, NOFRET, RENISENB, SATIPY, SOBEK, TETI, YAHMOSE

PLOT SYNOPSIS
Chapters 1–2
The opening chapters offer an overview of the members of Imhotep's family and their concerns as they await his arrival. The widow Renisenb returns home with her son, Teti, and claims that nothing has changed since the marriage, but her father's chief

scribe tells her that she is wrong, and that an evil is attacking the world. The anxieties of her siblings and their spouses show that Hori is correct, and that great unrest exists in the family.

Chapters 3–6
The family unrest increases after Imhotep returns with a young concubine, who seems to have substantial influence over him. Esa, Imhotep's mother, suggests that he take Nofret with him when he travels north because of the bitter family feelings, but Imhotep refuses. Other family members express their hatred for Nofret and suggest that she is turning the family patriarch against his own children. When Imhotep travels north and leaves Nofret behind, his scribe and children try to scare her by continually speaking about death.

Chapters 7–9
Renisenb offers Nofret her friendship, but the concubine refuses and calls Renisenb stupid. Nofret makes additional enemies in the family by arguing, and by hitting Kait's children. Anger is fanned and revenge is suggested when the family receives a letter in which Imhotep states that he will no longer support Sobek or Ipy. Renisenb is the only family member who seeks to warn Nofret of her danger, but her warning comes too late, because Nofret is found dead at the edge of a cliff with a frightened Satipy nearby.

Chapters 10–12
The family informs Imhotep of Nofret's death, portraying it as an accident. Although the others feel that everything is back to normal now that Nofret is dead, Renisenb and Hori feel increasingly sure that she was murdered. Once the funeral is over, Satipy acts even more strangely. She falls off a cliff and plunges to her death, shouting "Nofret!" just before she dies. Renisenb is now convinced that Satipy murdered Nofret.

Chapters 13–16
Henet finds some of Nofret's jewelry and shows it to Esa, who returns the jewelry to Imhotep. He cannot decide to whom he will give the jewelry, as he has become increasingly sure that his concubine was murdered. Imhotep comforts his son Yahmose, Satipy's widower, telling him to drink and forget his wife's death, but Yahmose experiences a painful

stomach spasm and suspects that the wine is poisoned. Although Yahmose does not die, he is greatly weakened by the poison. The report of a slave boy that a woman who looked like Nofret had been near the wine terrifies the family into believing that the concubine has returned to persecute them. The fear seems confirmed when Renisenb finds the necklace which the slave boy saw the woman wearing, and it turns out to be Nofret's. Imhotep holds a ceremony over her tomb.

Chapters 17–19
Esa suspects Henet and confronts her, but the housekeeper simply smiles in a suspicious manner and alludes obliquely to Sobek's death. At the same time, Ipy seems sure that Yahmose will die, a view with which the greatly weakened Yahmose concurs. Henet disagrees, stating only that Yahmose will not be the next to die. As romance blossoms for Kameni and Renisenb, tragedy again strikes the family when Ipy is found drowned face down in water. The latest death unnerves Imhotep, who believes that they are all doomed. He refuses Kameni's request to marry Renisenb, stating that the time is wrong for a wedding.

Chapters 20–23
Fearful of being the next to be murdered, Esa takes special precautions with her food and physical safety, but the murderer places poison in her pot of sweet-smelling unguent. The other members of the household believe that Esa has died of old age or as the result of a magic spell, yet they all begin to regard each other with suspicion. Left alone when the others go up to the tomb, Henet rummages in the linen closet, chuckling to herself that she is now the mistress of the house. The killer sneaks up on her and suffocates her by throwing a linen sack over her head. Soon after, an attempt is made on Renisenb's life, but she survives and decides to marry Hori.

CRIME NOTES
The author provides an opening note to explain the motivation for the choice of setting and to explain that the story and chapter titles are keyed to the agricultural calendar of the time. Among the murders in this novel, one person is killed by an arrow, two fall off a cliff, one drowns, another is suffocated with linen and two are poisoned.

Death in the Air   See DEATH IN THE CLOUDS.

Death in the Clouds   Mystery novel.

The novel is a variation on the sealed-room mystery, because the murder occurs in the cabin of a passenger airplane in flight, and the murderer can only be one of the two stewards or eleven passengers, who include Hercule POIROT. The plot centers on Poirot's efforts to identify the murderer, as he works with both Scotland Yard and the Sûreté, and to discover why the murder victim had two coffee spoons on her meal tray.

PUBLISHING AND DRAMATIZATION
HISTORY
The novel was published in 1935 by William Collins Sons and Company, Ltd., in London, and, under the title, *Death in the Air,* by Dodd, Mead and Company in New York.

The novel was adapted for television in 1992 by London Weekend Television in Britain, and was also shown on the Public Broadcasting Service in the U.S.

CHARACTERS
Raymond BARRACLOUGH, Doctor Roger James BRYANT, Daniel CLANCY, DAVIS, Lord DAWLISH, Armand DUPONT, Jean DUPONT, Monsieur FOURNIER, Norman GALE, Madame GISELLE, Elise GRANDIER, Jane GREY, Lady Cicely HORBURY, Lord Stephen HORBURY, Chief Inspector James JAPP, The Honourable Venetia Anne KERR, Andrew LEECH, Henry Charles MITCHELL, Ruth MITCHELL, Anne MORISOT, Jules PERROT, Hercule Poirot, Miss ROSS, James Bell RYDER, Maitre Alexandre THIBAULT, Dr. James WHISTLER, Detective Sergeant WILSON, Henry WINTERSPOON, Monsieur ZEROPOULOS

PLOT SYNOPSIS
Chapters 1–3
The passengers on the *Prometheus,* an airplane en route from Paris to London, are preoccupied with their own concerns and notice little of the others on board. Even Hercule Poirot is more interested in the attraction between Jane Grey and Norman Gale than in the passenger in seat number 2, Madame Giselle. When she is discovered to be dead, they blame her death on a wasp that was recently killed in the cabin, but Poirot finds a poisoned dart of the type used by

South American Indians. All the passengers are questioned, and mystery writer Daniel Clancy admits to owning a blowpipe as research for a book in progress, but this blowpipe is not on the plane.

Chapters 4–6
An inquest reveals that the victim was an extremely wealthy woman and a moneylender. The blowpipe in question has been found hidden under Poirot's seat, and the court first presents a verdict of willful murder against the detective, but the coroner does not accept it, so it is amended to death by poison by a person unknown. As he delves into the victim's life, Poirot learns that Madame Giselle was ruthless in her business dealings, and that she threatened scandal to make people repay their debts. Her estate is left to her daughter, Anne Morisot.

Chapters 7–10
Poirot, Japp of Scotland Yard and Fournier of the Sûreté discuss which passenger would have access to poisoned darts and snake venom, as Poirot tries to remember who left their seats on the plane. As Poirot examines the passengers' belongings, he notes that Lady Horbury carries a bottle marked "Boracic Acid" that really contains cocaine. Fournier flies back to Paris, accompanied by Poirot, and the two question the victim's maid, Elise Grandier, who had been instructed by her mistress to burn all papers should Madame Giselle meet with an accident. Elise reveals that the victim had not seen her now-grown daughter since she was a baby. She gives Poirot a notebook which she had not been instructed to burn.

Chapters 11–14
Poirot and Fournier meet with the Chief of the Detective Force, who tells them that an antique dealer named Zeropoulos had reported the sale of a blowpipe and darts three days earlier, but the darts had not red silk, but black and yellow silk on them. At the airline office, the reservations clerk admits that he was paid five thousand francs by an American named Silas Harper to delay Madame Giselle's departure, and to place her on a later flight and himself in seat number 1-S. Poirot observes that there was no one sitting in that seat, and the flight list has no one by that name. The reader learns that Lady Horbury has a gambling addiction, and her husband accuses her of borrowing from the victim to cover gambling debts. At the same time, Jane Grey has become

annoyed with the attention from the case, and rejects a dinner offer from Jean Dupont but accepts one from Norman Gale. While at dinner, they see the mystery writer, Clancy, who talks to himself about a woman who has to be silenced. When they follow him home, they encounter Poirot.

Chapters 15–17
Poirot questions Clancy, learns about his next book and asks him where he purchased the blowpipe. The detective also wants to draw out Lady Horbury by having Norman pretend to be a blackmailer. While these plans are formulated, Poirot questions the two airplane stewards to learn if they noticed anything out of the ordinary, and only Davis notes that the presence of two spoons in the victim's saucer was unusual.

Chapters 18–20
The investigators uncover the ways in which various passengers were associated with the victim. He does not believe James Ryder's claim that he had never had dealings with Madame Giselle. His blackmail charade involving Norman makes Lady Horbury reveal that she had approached the victim for money, but Poirot believes her when she swears that she is innocent of murder. When Japp questions Dr. Bryant about snake venom, he learns that the doctor has a friend involved in tropical research which uses dried snake venom, but the specific snake venom used in the murder is not among his specimens.

Chapters 21–24
Poirot makes a list of how Madame Giselle's death affects or does not affect the lives of the other passengers, and he feels that information is lacking. Finished with Norman as a blackmailer, Poirot asks Jane Grey to pose as his secretary to speak with the Duponts. After learning nothing helpful, Poirot meets with Fournier, who suggests that the killer wanted the blowpipe to be found in order to mask a more ordinary object. They learn that the victim's daughter has arrived to claim her inheritance. While having dinner with Jane Grey, Poirot remembers that he has seen Anne Morisot before, working as Lady Horbury's personal maid.

Chapters 25–26
Soon after their meeting, Anne Morisot is found dead on a boat train to Boulogne, a glass of prussic acid in her hand. Poirot confronts the killer at din-

ner, and reveals that the man had impersonated a steward on the airplane in order to come close enough to the victim to use a spoon to press a dart dipped in snake venom into her neck. He had then gone to the bathroom and removed the disguise. After the flight, he met with Anne Morisot, whom he had known for nearly a year, and convinced her to marry him. They made wills in which each left everything they owned to the other, and he counseled her to hide her employment background when she claimed the inheritance.

CRIME NOTES
The first murder in this novel occurs when a dart coated with venom from the South African boomslang snake is injected into the victim. The second murder victim is forced to drink prussic acid.

"Death on the Nile" (1)   Mystery short story.
The story concerns the fears of one wealthy British woman on a Nile charter boat who believes that her husband is poisoning her.

PUBLISHING AND DRAMATIZATION HISTORY
The story appeared in the short story collection, PARKER PYNE INVESTIGATES, published in 1934 by William Collins Sons and Company, Ltd., in London, and, under the title, *Mr. Parker Pyne, Detective*, by Dodd, Mead and Company in New York.

The story has not been adapted for stage or screen.

CHARACTERS
Lady Ariadne GRAYLE, Sir George GRAYLE, Pamela GRAYLE, Elsie MACNAUGHTON, Mr. PARKER PYNE, Basil WEST

PLOT SYNOPSIS
The plot concerns the wealthy Sir George and Lady Ariadne Grayle and their entourage, who are steaming up the Nile River on a pleasure charter. Lady Grayle has a nurse in attendance, although the nurse confides in Mr. Parker Pyne that the illness does not require a nurse. During the voyage, Lady Grayle speaks with Parker Pyne and tells him that she suspects that her husband is trying to poison her because she feels ill only when he is with her. Despite

the disbelief of others, Lady Grayle dies, and Parker Pyne unmasks the murderer.

CRIME NOTES
The story was published in 1934, three years before Agatha Christie wrote a full-length novel published under the same name.

Death on the Nile (2)   Mystery novel.
The novel uses the exotic locale of the Nile in Egypt as the setting for murder. The plot centers on the death of a newly married heiress on a river steamer carrying travelers up the Nile.

PUBLISHING AND DRAMATIZATION HISTORY
The novel was published in 1937 by William Collins Sons and Company, Ltd., in London, and in 1938 by Dodd, Mead and Company in New York.

The novel was adapted by the author for the stage in 1946 as *Murder on the Nile*, and it opened at the Ambassadors Theatre in London on March 19, 1946. The play was renamed *Hidden Horizon* and opened at the Plymouth Theatre in New York on September 19, 1946.

The film version, entitled *Death on the Nile*, was produced by EMI in 1978 and starred Peter Ustinov as Hercule POIROT. The all-star cast and attention to glamour in period and location made it a big-budget production.

CHARACTERS
Mrs. ALLERTON, Tim ALLERTON, Dr. Carl BESSNER, Monsieur Gaston BLONDIN, Louise BOURGET, Miss BOWERS, Mr. BURNABY, Jacqueline (Jackie) DE BELLEFORT, Linnet Ridgeway DOYLE, Simon DOYLE, James FANTHORP, Mr. FERGUSON, Mr. FLEETWOOD, JULES, MARIE, Rosalie OTTERBOURNE, Salome OTTERBOURNE, Andrew PENNINGTON, Hercule Poirot, Colonel Johnny RACE, Signor Guido RICHETTI, Cornelia Ruth ROBSON, Sterndale ROCKFORD, The Honourable Joanna SOUTHWOOD, Mrs. Marie VAN SCHUYLER, Charles WINDLESHAM

PLOT SYNOPSIS
Part I—England: Chapters 1–5
The opening chapters provide the background of the young heiress, Linnet Ridgeway, who is engaged to Lord Charles Windlesham when she meets Simon Doyle, the fiancé of her best friend, Jackie De Bellefort. For the sake of friendship, Linnet agrees to provide Simon with a job as a land agent so that the young couple can marry.

Chapters 6–7
Hercule Poirot meets M. Blondin at the Chez Ma Tante restaurant to tell him about his upcoming trip to Egypt. In passing, he observes and accidentally eavesdrops on a young couple, obviously very much in love, who spoke of the right job for Simon and a honeymoon in Egypt. He will later learn their names, Jackie De Bellefort and Simon Doyle. Only days later, Linnet tells her fiancé that she is unsure that she wants to marry him, and she admits to herself, as she hires Doyle, that she is attracted to him. She soon marries him.

Chapters 8–12
The many intricate relationships of characters in this novel are revealed. Mrs. Allerton and her son Tim, Cornelia Robson, Andrew Pennington, Jim Fanthorp, Rosalie Otterbourne and her mother Mrs. Salome Otterbourne all complete preparations for their journey to Egypt.

Part II—Egypt: Chapters 1–2
The travelers stay temporarily at the Cataract Hotel in Assuan, where Poirot strikes up a conversation with Rosalie Otterbourne. The detective sees Jackie De Bellefort sitting on a bench overlooking the Nile and recognizes her from Chez Ma Tante. At the same time, Tim Allerton introduces himself to Linnet Doyle as the cousin of Joanna Southwood, her longtime friend, and she, in turn, introduces him to Andrew Pennington, her American trustee.

Chapters 3–5
Linnet later speaks with Poirot and asks his help in dealing with Jackie, who has been following the Doyles on their honeymoon. After first pointing out that a person must accept the consequences of her behavior, he agrees to reason with Jackie. The jilted young woman is adamant in her desire for revenge and refuses to listen to Poirot. An undaunted Poirot speaks with Simon Doyle regarding the young woman's vendetta and concludes that she will not be able to afford to follow them much longer.

Chapters 6–10
The travelers have lunch, then board a bus that takes them to the *Karnak*, a small river steamboat.

Andrew Pennington approaches Linnet with important business papers and appears annoyed when she reads each paper carefully before signing. The passengers tour temples along the Nile, and Linnet and Simon narrowly miss being killed when a boulder falls from a cliff and lands near them. They blame Jackie at first, but they learn later that she had not yet come ashore.

Chapters 11–12
That evening, Jackie continues to antagonize the honeymoon couple. She drinks too much and argues with Simon, then pulls out her pistol and shoots him. Immediately remorseful, she drops the pistol and runs out of the room. Dr. Bessner treats Simon's leg injury, and Jackie is given a morphine sedative, which makes her sleep all night. The gun disappears. Colonel Race informs Poirot the next morning that Linnet Doyle was murdered in the night with the missing pistol, and she has written a "J" on the wall in blood, an act which the doctor claims is impossible because Linnet died instantly. The bullet is found and matches Jackie's pistol.

Chapters 13–16
Race and Poirot interview all the passengers, starting with Linnet's personal maid, Louise, who tells them that Linnet had recently received a threat from a ship employee, Fleetwood, because she had revealed to her former maid, Marie, that he was a married man with children. The investigators also learn that the heiress had a string of pearls worth fifty thousand dollars that is now missing from her dresser. Interviews with the other travelers reveal that several heard what seemed to be the sound of a champagne cork popping, followed by a splash. A check of the water yields a velvet shawl, a pink-stained man's handerkerchief and a gun with two bullets fired. Mrs. Van Schuyler had misplaced the shawl the night before.

Chapters 17–22
As Poirot delves more deeply into the case, he uncovers the travelers' secrets. Andrew Pennington lied about his whereabouts during the time that the boulder fell. Rosalie Otterbourne was on the deck on the night of Linnet's murder, throwing her mother's liquor bottles overboard. Mrs. Van Schuyler, a kleptomaniac, stole the pearls. When they check the cabins, Race and Poirot find that Pennington, Richetti and

Rosalie all have pistols. They also find Louise dead in her cabin, stabbed through the heart and clutching the corner of a thousand-pound note, which leads them to conclude she had been blackmailing the killer.

Chapters 23–26
Mrs. Otterbourne tells Race and Poirot that she saw Louise's killer, but she is shot just as she is about to reveal the name. The killer disappears, leaving Pennington's Colt revolver on the deck. Under questioning, Jim Fanthorp admits that his uncle had sent him to keep an eye on Linnet's business interests because they suspected that Pennington was siphoning off funds. Poirot also reveals that Tim Allerton and Joanna Southwood had stolen the real pearls and replaced them with imitations for Mrs. Van Schuyler, duplicating a scam they had enacted several times before.

Chapters 27–30
Poirot remembers that he slept heavily on the night of the murder, and realizes that he was drugged. After consulting with Dr. Bessner, he learns that the scorch marks on Linnet's scalp mean that the shot was not fired through the shawl. By careful use of his "gray cells," Poirot identifies the murderers and the reasons for each of the murders. Yet at the end of the novel, no one is left to bring to trial, because the prospect of jail has led to a murder-suicide.

CRIME NOTES
Two of the victims in this novel die of gunshot wounds and a third victim is stabbed.

Debanham, Mary Hermione An emotionally cold woman in MURDER ON THE ORIENT EXPRESS (1), she has served as governess to Helena GOLDENBERG and as private secretary to Sonia ARMSTRONG.

De Bathe, Colonel See EUSTACE, MAJOR.

De Bellefort, Jacqueline (Jackie) The woman scorned in DEATH ON THE NILE (2), her best friend is now married to her former fiancé. She follows the newly married couple on their honeymoon, annoying them whenever possible, and comes very close to becoming a suspect in the murder of Linnet DOYLE.

Debrugh, Major Johnnie Financially well-off, this red-faced, middle-aged, military man asks young

CELIA to marry him in UNFINISHED PORTRAIT, and attempts to dazzle her with expensive gifts.

De Castina, Mrs.　See GRUNBERG, ANITA.

De Haviland, Edith Elfrida　The sister-in-law of the wealthy Aristide LEONIDES, she helps him to raise his seven children after her sister dies in CROOKED HOUSE. After many years, she remains hostile toward him.

Delafontaine, Henry　A diffident man in "HOW DOES YOUR GARDEN GROW?", he does not interfere with his wife and often complies with her demands simply to keep the peace.

Delafontaine, Mary　A domineering wife, she is a tall woman with an authoritative voice who exerts equal control over her husband and her garden in "HOW DOES YOUR GARDEN GROW?" She inherits her aunt's estate.

Delahaye, Sir Rowland (Roly)　A distinguished, highly respectable and charming man in his late fifties in SPIDER'S WEB, he reluctantly helps his former war comrade to dispose of a body.

Delangua, Paul　A philanderer, his host, Sir James DWIGHTON, discovers him in an embarrassing situation with Lady Laura DWIGHTON in "THREE BLIND MICE." His later confession that he murdered Sir James is not taken seriously because others think he is protecting Lady Laura.

De la Roche, Comte Armaud　A fraudulent count in THE MYSTERY OF THE BLUE TRAIN, he uses charm and his fake noble title to seduce women, and their letters to blackmail them. He has a particularly strong hold over Ruth KETTERING because of their affair years before, and he convinces her to give him the Heart of Fire rubies.

De la Rochefour, Count Armand　A fortune-hunting noble in "THE PLYMOUTH EXPRESS," he wrote to the Honorable Flossie CARRINGTON and planned a rendezvous shortly before her murder.

Demetrius the Black Browed　The head of a gang of Greek jewel thieves in "THE ORACLE AT DEL-PHI," he uses the identity of Mr. PARKER PYNE to deceive a potential victim.

Demiroff, Olga　A Russian prostitute also known as Olga VASSILOVNA in THE MYSTERY OF THE BLUE TRAIN, she lives in Paris and hides the Heart of Fire rubies for Count DE LA ROCHE.

Denby, Mr.　Financial overseer of Styles Court in THE MYSTERIOUS AFFAIR AT STYLES, his work with Alfred INGLETHORPE on the night of the murder provides the old man with an alibi.

Denman, Mr.　A handsome, older man, he is calm and controlled most of the time, but his sometimes odd behavior in "THE THUMB MARK OF ST. PETER" worries his son Geoffrey DENMAN.

Denman, Anna　Once known as Anna KHARSANOVA, a great Russian ballerina, she gave up her career to marry John DENMAN and to live in the English countryside in "HARLEQUIN'S LANE."

Denman, Geoffrey　A violent man who bullied his wife, Mabel DENMAN, and who dies suddenly in "THE THUMB MARK OF ST. PETER," he becomes concerned about his elderly father's sometimes odd behavior, and angers the older man by suggesting that he move into a nursing home.

Denman, John　An unimaginative Englishman married to a Russian prima ballerina in "HARLEQUIN'S LANE," his cool, aloof personality is in marked contrast to that of the fiery artist.

Denman, Mabel　A melodramatic woman, she calls upon her Aunt Jane MARPLE when her husband dies suddenly in "THE THUMB MARK OF ST. PETER," and the police consider her a suspect.

Denman, Mary　A tyrannical nursemaid in UNFINISHED PORTRAIT, she gladly stays with the financially strapped family but leaves when they become financially sound and move to the country.

Depleach, Sir Montague　A well-respected lawyer, he is used to winning his cases, often through a well-orchestrated series of dramatic moves that range from an urbane and charming manner to an aggressive defender out for blood. In FIVE LITTLE PIGS, his own client, Caroline CRALE, defeats him as she refuses to assist in her own defense.

Dering, Martin A good-looking man, attractive to women, and a moderately successful author in THE SITTAFORD MYSTERY, he claims to have been absent from dinner on the night that his wife's uncle, Captain TREVELYN, was murdered.

Dering, Sylvia The wife of Martin DERING and niece of the murdered Captain TREVELYN in THE SITTAFORD MYSTERY, she has an unpleasant whining sound to her voice.

Dermot Young, dashing and insistent, he captivates the naïve heroine in UNFINISHED PORTRAIT and marries her. Despite his vigor for life, he is emotionally distant and cannot stand illness or weakness in anyone. He begins an affair while his wife grieves for her mother's death, and leaves her to marry a young secretary, as did the author's first husband, Colonel Archibald CHRISTIE.

Deroulard, Madame An aged and ill mother in "THE CHOCOLATE BOX," she is torn between love for her son and the desire to protect others from him.

Deroulard, Monsieur Le Baron Paul A successful politician in "THE CHOCOLATE BOX," he was expected to rise from his current position as French Deputy to Prime Minister, but death cut his career short. Although the authorities thought his death was due to natural causes, Hercule POIROT discovers that Paul's passion for chocolate made murder convenient.

De Rushbridger, Margaret Committed to the sanitorium under mysterious circumstances in THREE-ACT TRAGEDY, she contacts Hercule POIROT to arrange a meeting, but is murdered after eating poisoned chocolates before Poirot can learn her secrets.

Derwent, Lady Frances (Frankie) The wealthy daughter of Lord MARCHINGTON enjoys the benefits of a liberal clothing allowance, servants and abundant credit, but she also wants meaning and purpose in her life. She finds a purpose in WHY DIDN'T THEY ASK EVANS? when she joins Robert (Bobby) JONES in the investigation.

De Sara, Madeleine Her ancestry may be good, hard-working, English stock, but the former Maggie SAYERS has become the "Queen of the Vamps" in PARKER PYNE INVESTIGATES and "PROBLEM AT POLLENSA BAY." Working for Mr. PARKER PYNE, she takes on numerous disguises, including that of Delores RAMONE, SANCHIA and the Grand Duchess OLGA, all of them dangerously attractive women who are irresistible to men.

Desjardeaux, Monsieur The tall, thin, bearded French Premier in THE BIG FOUR, he is astounded by Hercule POIROT's identification of Madame OLIVIER as a member of the gang.

Despard, Colonel John Hugh Married to the former Rhoda DAWES, he saves her from drowning in CARDS ON THE TABLE and makes a loving marriage with her in THE PALE HORSE. As a major, he was a suspect in the murder of Mr. SHAITANA in *Cards on the Table*. He rose to the rank of colonel and eventually retired to the country.

Despard, Rhoda Dawes The roommate of Ann MEREDITH and a suspect in the murder of Mr. SHAITANA in CARDS ON THE TABLE, she is nearly murdered by her roommate. She is saved by the man who becomes her husband, Colonel John Hugh DESPARD, and they retire to Much Deeping, where they once again encounter adventure in THE PALE HOUSE.

Dessin, Armand The Paris Prefecture in DEATH IN THE CLOUDS who aids in the murder investigation.

Destination Unknown Mystery novel.

Set in exotic Casablanca, the novel reflects the true-life, 1950s espionage case of Bruno Pontecorvo and Klaus Emil Fuchs, two physicists who turned against their own countries to work for Communist Russia. The plot centers on the mysterious disappearance of several promising young scientists, and their involvement with a secret scientific complex run by a megalomaniac.

PUBLISHING AND DRAMATIZATION HISTORY

The novel was published in 1954 by William Collins Sons and Company, Ltd., in London, and, under the title, *So Many Steps to Death*, in 1955 by Dodd, Mead and Company in New York.

The novel has not been adapted for stage or screen.

CHARACTERS

ALCADI, Mr. ARISTIDES, Mrs. Calvin BAKER, Dr. Louis BARRON, Olive BETTERTON, Thomas BETTERTON, Hilary CRAVEN, Herr DIRECTOR, Torquil ERICSSON, R. EVANS, Major Boris Andrei Pavlov GLYDR, Walter GRIFFITHS, Janet HETHERINGTON, Miss JENNSON, Mr. JESSOP, Mademoiselle LA ROCHE, Henri LAURIER, Monsieur LEBLANC, Dr. Mark LUCAS, Professor MANNHEIM, MOHAMMED, Bianca MURCHISON, Dr. Simon MURCHISON, Helga NEEDHEIM, Andrew PETERS, Dr. RUBEC, Carol SPEEDER, Paul VAN HEIDEM, Colonel WHARTON

PLOT SYNOPSIS

Chapters 1–3

Mr. Jessop and Colonel Wharton attempt to find scientist Thomas Betterton, who has disappeared, but questioning of his wife and associates brings no results. When Olive Betterton goes to Morocco for a vacation, Jessop follows her, but his surveillance is cut short when her plane crashes and she is badly injured. Jessop observes a young woman, similar in appearance to Olive, enter several drug stores and purchase sleeping pills. Surmising that Hilary Craven plans to commit suicide, he stops her and offers her another way to endanger her life while helping out her country. He asks her to assume the identity of Olive Betterton and to become a spy.

Chapters 4–7

Hilary goes to the hospital to meet Olive, who tells her to inform Tom that "Boris is dangerous." When Hilary asks her how to contact Tom, Olive says, "Snow, snow, beautiful snow. You slip on a lump and over you go," then dies. For a few days, Hilary learns everything that she can about the woman whom she will impersonate. With her face bandaged, Hilary becomes Mrs. Thomas Betterton and begins her journey to Casablanca. On the way, she meets Henri Laurier, who gives her his card and tells her to call

him at the Grand Hotel. When they meet again in Fez, he asks her about the weather, and she sparks recognition in him when she recites Olive's lines about the snow.

Chapters 8–12

Hilary boards a plane for Marrakesh, but the plane lands in a deserted area where the passengers are made to disembark before being ushered into a waiting station wagon. They watch as bodies are arranged on the plane, which is then blown up. Hilary's fellow travelers are scientists who all seem to think that they can rule the world through science. After driving around for a few days, they board another plane which takes them to an unknown destination. Upon their arrival, Hilary is taken to Tom Betterton, whose appearance has been altered by plastic surgery. He knows that she is an imposter, but cautions her to play along until later.

Chapters 13–17

Hilary has dinner with Tom; then they go to the rooftop, where he tells her that he wants to escape because he is disillusioned and his creativity is being stifled. Meanwhile, Jessop attempts to determine if the plane crash was real or faked, and offers a reward for information. When a Berber brings some pearls found a half-mile from the plane crash, Jessop realizes that Hilary is still alive. At the complex, Hilary attracts the attention of Andrew Peters, who confides in Hilary that he is also dissatisfied and wants to leave. She agrees, but insists that Tom must leave with them. As if aware of growing dissatisfaction among the scientists, the director of the complex gives a spirited speech about youth and the future of mankind. Later, Mr. Aristides, the master of the complex, asks to meet with Hilary.

Chapters 18–20

Aristides informs Hilary that he buys scientific brains, and that his aim is not political but financial. He plans to assemble a huge pool of scientists and send them out for hire to nations. He will subject them to leukotomies, which will make them docile and happy in their jobs. Soon after, British Intelligence locates the site, and a combined force of British, French and American diplomats join with Intelligence agents in entering the compound. They dine with Aristides, then Jessop accuses him of detaining people against their will, but Aristides denies all but financial involvement in the complex.

Chapters 21–22
Tom tries to convince Hilary to let him slip away to start a new life, but Peters prevents him from doing so and reveals himself as Boris Glydr, the cousin of Tom's first wife, Elsa. He charges that Tom married and then murdered Elsa only to obtain scientific data regarding ZE Fission, and he wants revenge. As the novel ends, the evil scheme is destroyed, and Major Glydr and Hilary appear to be headed toward a future together.

CRIME NOTES
The only murder in this novel occurs before it opens, the result of poison.

De Toredo, Senora Angelica   See SHAPLAND, ANN.

Devereaux, Ronny   A secret agent identified as Number Two, his last words in THE SEVEN DIALS MYSTERY are heard by Lady Eileen (Bundle) BRENT, who first believes that she has run him over with her car but later learns that he was shot.

Deveril   The butler in the home of the murdered Sir Carmichael CLARKE in THE A.B.C. MURDERS.

Deyre, Myra   The attractive but possessive mother of the main character of GIANT'S BREAD, she is prone to hysterics and tantrums, and plays on her son's sympathy after her husband leaves her.

Deyre, Vernon   A composer in GIANT'S BREAD, he has only his imaginary companions for company as a young boy. The sound of music frightens and depresses him until he becomes overwhelmed at the age of twenty by the desire to create music. He dedicates his life to composing music.

Deyre, Walter   A philandering husband in GIANT'S BREAD who married for the money to keep his ancestral home rather than for love, he is killed in the Boer War.

Die Abenteur G.m.b.H.   Film released by Fox Film Corporation in Germany in 1928. The movie is based on the author's second novel, THE SECRET ADVERSARY.

CAST
The cast consists of Carlo ALDINI as Tommy BERESFORD and Eve Gray as Tuppence BERESFORD, as well as Hilda Bayley, Shayle Gardner and Mikhail Rasumny, a Russian character actor who appeared in numerous Hollywood films of the 1940s and 1950s.

PLOT SYNOPSIS
See THE SECRET ADVERSARY.

CHANGES FROM ORIGINAL TEXT
The most notable change is in the title, because the German *Die Abenteur G.m.b.H.* translates as Adventure, Ltd. When the film was shown in other European countries, the title of the novel was used. The plot remains close to that of the original.

PRODUCTION NOTES
The movie is the first filmed version of any work by Agatha Christie.

Deverill, Christine   See REDFERN, CHRISTINE.

Digby, Captain   Having served with Lord CRONSHAW, he has the misfortune of being the first to discover his friend's body in "THE AFFAIR AT THE VICTORY BALL."

Digby, Mr.   The butler at Lytcham Close in "THE SECOND GONG," he sounds the dinner gong and also identifies the person who picked the daisies for the table.

Digby, Sir Stanley   Dubbed "a good-natured, tubby little chap" in THE SEVEN DIALS MYSTERY, he is the Air Minister who seeks to obtain a scientist's secret metal formula.

Dinsmead, Mr.   A genial and talkative man who readily confides in a stranger in "S.O.S.," he is the father of Magdalen and Johnnie DINSMEAD, as well as the husband of Maggie DINSMEAD.

Dinsmead, Charlotte   A foundling in "S.O.S.," her real father leaves her sixty thousand pounds long after she is adopted by Mr. and Mrs. DINSMEAD.

Carlo Aldini and Eve Gray play Tommy and Tuppence Beresford in the 1928 *Die Abenteur G.m.b.H.*, a German film version of *The Secret Adversary.*   (Photo courtesy of The Museum of Modern Art, Film Stills Archive)

Now a young woman, she may have traced an "SOS" in the dust on the dressing table of psychic investigator Mortimer CLEVELAND.

Dinsmead, Johnnie   A young man who enjoys conducting chemical experiments in "S.O.S.," he remains undisturbed by the arrival of a psychic investigator at the Dinsmead house and provides information which helps to solve the mystery.

Dinsmead, Magdalen   Falsely identified by her father as a foundling in "S.O.S.," she is actually his natural daughter and claims to have traced a cry for help in the dust of the investigator's dressing table.

Dinsmead, Maggie   A thoroughly disconcerting woman in "S.O.S.," she is a high-strung, shrieking, hysterical woman who often throws and smashes objects.

Director, Herr   A man who formerly ran revivalist meetings and whose presence transfixes his followers, he is hired by Mr. ARISTIDES to head the Brain Trust complex in the Atlas Mountains in DESTINATION UNKNOWN.

Disappearance of Agatha Christie, The   The author includes no mention of the event in AN AUTOBIOGRAPHY, but her disappearance on December 3, 1926, caused a major stir in Britain, where she was a well-known and best-selling mystery author. Despite attempts in fiction to explain the disappearance (see AGATHA), neither the author nor her family have ever provided an explanation nor chosen to discuss the event.

Certain facts of the disappearance are clear from newspaper accounts of the time. The year 1926 was a difficult one for the author, whose beloved mother had died, after which her first husband, Colonel Archibald CHRISTIE, announced that he was leaving her for another woman, whose name was Nancy NEELE. On the morning of December 3, 1926, Colonel Christie had argued with the author, then packed a bag and left to spend the weekend with his new love. That same evening, the author drove away from her home in a car that was later found abandoned near a lake, with its lights still on and the author's fur coat, suitcase with clothing and expired driver's license in the car.

The newspapers followed the case on a minute-by-minute basis, reporting every comment, clue and false lead, as the police and thousands of volunteers scoured the countryside for the body. The lake was dredged, aircraft flew low over the area's fields, and bloodhounds were used to go carefully over the ground. On Saturday, December 4, 1926, fifteen thousand volunteers searched the area.

Theories abounded, from suicide to murder by Colonel Christie, but several columnists dismissed the disappearance as a publicity stunt. Colonel Christie told a newspaper reporter that his wife had often said she could disappear at will and no one would be able to find her.

During the week following, police learned of a "Mrs. Neele" staying at an elegant spa resort, the Hydropathic Hotel in Harrogate. She had arrived by taxi on December 4, 1926, carrying only a small suitcase, and had told other guests that she was a bereaved mother recently arrived from Cape Town. Employees and guests reported that "Mrs. Neele" had danced the Charleston one evening and that she appeared to have quite a lot of money with her, with which she bought numerous new clothes. For reasons unknown, she also placed an advertisement in the personal column of *The Times,* in which she asked "Friends and relatives of Teresa Neele, late of South Africa, please communicate.—Write Box R 702, *The Times,* EC4."

A young reporter, later to become the Baron Ritchie-Calder, was the first person to confront the author at the hotel. He reported that he walked up to her and addressed her as "Mrs. Christie," and she acknowledged her name. He also reported that, when he asked the author how she had reached Harrogate, she responded that she had suffered amnesia, then she went quickly up to her room. When Colonel Christie arrived later in the day, she stated clearly to other guests that her brother had just arrived.

In later weeks, doctors consulted in the case issued statements certifying that the author had suffered "an unquestionable loss of memory," and noted that her recovery required that she be spared further anxiety. The press found the memory-loss explanation difficult to believe, because, while at Harrogate, the author had written to Harrod's to ask about a diamond ring she had lost there in the week preceding the disappearance. She described the ring precisely, and asked the department store to send the ring to Mrs. Theresa Neele at the Hydro Hotel, should they find it. The ring was found and it was sent to and received by "Mrs. Theresa Neele" at the Hydro Hotel.

What really happened is known only by the author. She speaks in AN AUTOBIOGRAPHY of the emotional pain and turmoil that she suffered in 1926 without discussing the disappearance.

"Disappearance of Mr. Davenheim, The"
Mystery short story.

The plot centers on a clever man who hides in the one place where the police would never think to look.

PUBLISHING AND DRAMATIZATION HISTORY
The story appeared in the short story collection, POIROT INVESTIGATES, published in 1924 by John Lane in London, and in 1925 by Dodd, Mead and Company in New York.

The story was adapted for television in 1990 by London Weekend Television in England, and was also shown on the Public Broadcasting Service in the U.S.

CHARACTERS
Mr. DAVENHEIM, Mrs. DAVENHEIM, Captain HASTINGS, Inspector JAPP, Billy KELLETT, Mr. LOWEN, Hercule POIROT

Only a fast car will do for the villain's (Tony Matthews) getaway in "The Disappearance of Mr. Davenheim." (Photo courtesy of London Weekend Television)

PLOT SYNOPSIS
Mr. Davenheim, a wealthy financier, leaves his home to mail a letter, then fails to return. The story fills the newspapers and intrigues Hercule Poirot, who challenges Inspector Japp that he can solve the case without leaving his flat. Once he learns of an earlier disappearance by Davenheim and of the pickpocket who tried to pawn the missing man's diamond ring, Poirot is ready to give his solution, which differs substantially from that of the police.

CRIME NOTES
This story is one of many instances in which Poirot pointedly relied upon "the little gray cells" rather than the gathering of physical clues to solve a case.

Dittisham, Lady   See GREER, ELSA.

Dittisham, Lord   An attractive and imaginative man in FIVE LITTLE PIGS, he is the third husband of Elsa GREER, as well as a writer of "fantastical poetic dramas."

Dixon, Gladys   A maid who sees too much for her own good in THE MIRROR CRACK'D FROM SIDE TO SIDE, she is sent into hiding by Miss MARPLE, who fears for her life.

Dobbs, Mr.   A local gardener in "THE FOUR SUSPECTS," and one of the four suspects in the crime.

Dodge, Bernard   Close friend of the Prime Minister and a member of the War Cabinet in "THE KIDNAPPED PRIME MINISTER," he joins the leader of the House of Commons to ask Hercule POIROT to solve the kidnapping case.

Dodo   See MULLINS, IRIS.

Donaldson, Dr.   The young personal physician to Lady Matilda CHECKHEATON, he has a difficult time replacing his patient's recently retired longtime physician in PASSENGER TO FRANKFURT.

Donaldson, Dr. Rex   A young physician with little money but a great deal of intelligence and ambition in DUMB WITNESS, he lacks the personal touch.

Donovan, Sheila   See HOBHOUSE, VALERIE.

Dortheimer, Lady Naomi   Married to Sir Reuben DORTHEIMER, she eagerly listens to the handsome young man's compliments in "THE CASE OF THE DISTRESSED LADY."

Dortheimer, Sir Reuben   An extremely rich man in "THE CASE OF THE DISTRESSED LADY," he becomes infatuated with a female dancer.

"Double Clue"   Mystery short story.
   Hercule POIROT is called in by a wealthy jewelry collector to discover who broke into his safe and stole a priceless cache of medieval jewels.

PUBLISHING AND DRAMATIZATION HISTORY
The story appeared in the short story collection, DOUBLE SIN AND OTHER STORIES, published in 1961 by Dodd, Mead and Company in New York.
   The story was adapted for television in 1990 by London Weekend Television in England, and was also shown on the Public Broadcasting Service in the U.S.

CHARACTERS
Mr. Marcus HARDMAN, Captain HASTINGS, Mr. JOHNSTON, Bernard PARKER, Hercule Poirot, Countess Vera ROSSAKOFF

Jewel thief Countess Vera Rossakoff (Kika Markham) is the love of Hercule Poirot's (David Suchet) life in "Double Clue." (Photo courtesy of London Weekend Television)

PLOT SYNOPSIS

Discretion is important to collector Marcus Hardman when his safe is robbed during a dinner party of a priceless necklace made of emeralds and rubies. He invited four important guests, none of whom he wishes to confront personally, so he calls in Hercule Poirot. Upon examining the safe, Poirot finds a man's glove and a cigarette case marked with initials *B* and *P*, and the likely thief is Bernard Parker. The clever Poirot refuses to settle for the obvious and, after interviewing all of the guests and consulting a Russian dictionary, he identifies the thief, who gives up the necklace.

CRIME NOTES

The story marks the first time in which Hercule Poirot shows an attraction to a woman. He is very taken with Countess Rossakoff, of whom he says "Quelle femme!" She is "a remarkable woman" whom he hopes to meet again.

"Double Sin"   Mystery short story.

The story concerns the theft of a set of miniatures being taken by train to a prospective buyer.

PUBLISHING AND DRAMATIZATION HISTORY

The story appeared in the short story collection, DOUBLE SIN AND OTHER STORIES, published by Dodd, Mead and Company in New York.

The story was adapted for television in 1990 by London Weekend Television in England, and was also shown on the Public Broadcasting Service in the U.S.

CHARACTERS

Joseph AARONS, Mary DURRANT, Captain HASTINGS, Norton KANE, Miss Elizabeth PENN, Hercule POIROT, Mr. J. Baker WOOD

Hercule Poirot (David Suchet) moved into Whitehaven Mansions, shown here in "Double Sin," because its geometric symmetry appealed to his sense of order. (Photo courtesy of London Weekend Television)

PLOT SYNOPSIS

Traveling by motor coach to Charlock Bay to advise an old friend, Joseph Aarons, Hercule Poirot and Captain Hastings converse with Mary Durrant, who claims to be acting as an agent for her aunt, taking miniatures worth five hundred pounds to a prospective American buyer. When they reach the hotel, Mary frantically contacts them and tells them that the miniatures have been stolen from her case. Poirot promises to help, and he learns from the police that a woman had met the buyer earlier and sold him the miniatures. The finger of guilt points to the young man whose suitcase on the motor coach closely resembled Mary's, but Poirot realizes that a more clever crime has taken place.

CRIME NOTES

Once again, Captain Hastings chivalrously wants to help a young woman who is beautiful and who has, as Poirot teases, "Auburn hair—always the auburn hair!"

Double Sin and Other Stories   Mystery short story collection.

The book contains eight stories, most of which had already been published. Four stories feature Hercule POIROT, two feature Miss MARPLE and two present supernatural circumstances.

PUBLISHING AND DRAMATIZATION HISTORY

Double Sin and Other Stories was published in the United States by Dodd, Mead and Company in New York in 1961, but it was not published intact in Britain. "THE THEFT OF THE ROYAL RUBY" was simply a retitling of "THE ADVENTURE OF THE CHRISTMAS PUDDING," which appeared in the short story collection of the same name, as did "GREENSHAW'S FOLLY." "THE DRESSMAKER'S DOLL" and "THE LAST SEANCE" had appeared in the short story collection, THE HOUND OF DEATH.

"DOUBLE SIN," "WASP'S NEST," "The Last Seance" and "THE DOUBLE CLUE" have been adapted for television.

TITLES IN THE COLLECTION

Double Sin and Other Stories contains the following short stories: "Double Sin," "Wasp's Nest," "The Theft of the Royal Ruby," "The Dressmaker's Doll," "Greenshaw's Folly," "The Double Clue," "The Last Seance" and "SANCTUARY."

Dove, Mary   The highly efficient manager and housekeeper of Yewtree Lodge in A POCKET FULL OF RYE, she always maintains complete control of the situation.

Downes, Roger Emmanuel   A shrill-voiced, excitable instructor at a school for boys, he has a strong resemblance to the frog footman in *Alice in Wonderland*. He is also a very fortunate man because he was probably meant to be the fourth victim in THE A.B.C. MURDERS, but the movie theatre was too dark for an accurate strike by the killer.

Doyle, Linnet   A wealthy, pampered, beautiful woman in DEATH ON THE NILE (2), she is shot to death on the S.S. *Karnak* while on her honeymoon. She had always had everything she could ever want. When her friend Jackie DE BELLEFORTE asked Linnet to find a job for her fiancé, Linnet complied, and promptly fell in love with and married him.

Doyle, Simon   A handsome man in DEATH ON THE NILE (2) with broad shoulders and an appealing smile, he easily falls out of love with his fiancée and into love with the wealthy Linnet DOYLE within days. He becomes a widower while on his honeymoon when his wife is shot to death on board ship on the same night that he is shot in the leg.

Drage, Lady Cynthia   A friend of Mr. SATTERTHWAITE, she is a hard-faced, middle-aged woman in "THE SHADOW ON THE GLASS" who wears too much makeup. She makes her living by coaching women in social skills.

Dragomiroff, Princess Natalia   An elderly aristocrat in MURDER ON THE ORIENT EXPRESS, she has a "yellow toadlike face," and Hercule POIROT thinks she is the ugliest old woman he has ever seen. She wears a fortune in pearls and gems, and her monogrammed handkerchief is found at the murder scene.

Drake, Allen   A garrulous, cheerful man in TOWARDS ZERO, his outgoing nature is a marked contrast to the introverted, taciturn behavior of his partner, Thomas ROYDE.

Drake, Hugo   The hit-and-run victim in HAL-LOWE'EN PARTY.

Drake, Lucilla   The widow of a clergyman in SPARKLING CYANIDE, she wears black crepe mourning for twenty years after his death. She is also the aunt of the murdered Rosemary BARTON and mother of Victor DRAKE.

Drake, Rowena Arabella   A dynamic woman in HALLOWE'EN PARTY who has been a widow for two years, she overwhelms Hercule POIROT by her energy when they first meet. She organizes the party at which Joyce REYNOLDS is murdered.

Drake, Una   An adventurous young woman in "THE UNBREAKABLE ALIBI," she bets a young man that she can create an alibi which would allow her to be seen in two distant geographical locations at the same time. When her presence at both locations at precisely the same time is verified by witnesses, the young man consults Tommy and Tuppence BERESFORD to help him to win the bet by breaking her alibi.

Drake, Victor   A smooth-talking confidence man in SPARKLING CYANIDE, he also uses the names Monkey COLEMAN and Pedro MORALES. The son of a now-deceased clergyman, he has had varied careers as an actor, waiter, porter, circus propman and political candidate, all of which followed his exit from Oxford University after a check-forging incident. He is a cousin of the murdered Rosemary BARTON.

Draper, Mary   Perceived by Hercule POIROT as "a remorseless and unscrupulous woman," she is the aunt of Mary GERRARD in SAD CYPRESS. As a nurse under her maiden name of Mary RILEY in New Zealand, she received a legacy from a patient who died mysteriously. When she married and became Mary Draper, her wealthy husband died suddenly. She returns to England as Mary HOPKINS, after taking the name of a dead colleague, and manipulates her niece in the effort to obtain another fortune.

"Dream, The"   Mystery short story.
The story concerns an eccentric millionaire who asks Hercule POIROT to help him interpret his recurring dream of suicide.

A wealthy man's daughter (Joely Richardson) expresses relief to investigators when her father is murdered in "The Dream." (Photo courtesy of London Weekend Television)

PUBLISHING AND DRAMATIZATION HISTORY
The story appeared in the short story collection, THE REGATTA AND OTHER STORIES, published in 1939 by Dodd, Mead and Company in New York.

The story was adapted for television in 1989 by London Weekend Television in England, and was also shown on the Public Broadcasting Service in the U.S.

CHARACTERS
Inspector BARNETT, Hugo CORNWORTHY, Benedict FARLEY, Joanna FARLEY, Louise FARLEY, HOLMES, Hercule Poirot, Dr. STILLINGFLEET

PLOT SYNOPSIS

Eccentric millionaire Benedict Farley calls Hercule Poirot to his home to consult him regarding a nightly dream of suicide in which he shoots himself at exactly 3:28 P.M. When Poirot can suggest no interpretation, Farley dismisses him, asking first for the letter which summoned him. A week later, Dr. Stillingfleet calls Poirot and tells him that Farley committed suicide at the approximate time of his dream. During the investigation, Poirot ponders several incongruities between the dead man's habits and what he saw of him in their brief interview, and comes to the conclusion that a murder has occurred.

CRIME NOTES

Dr. Stillingfleet asks Poirot if he will ever commit a crime, then tells him that getting away with a crime would be far too easy for the detective, "definitely too unsporting."

"Dressmaker's Doll, The" Mystery short story.

A dressmaker's doll appears suddenly and seems to have a life of its own.

PUBLISHING AND DRAMATIZATION HISTORY

The story appeared in the short story collection, DOUBLE SIN AND OTHER STORIES, published in 1961 by Dodd, Mead and Company in New York.

The story has not been adapted for stage or screen.

CHARACTERS

Alicia COOMBE, Sybil FOX, Mrs. FELLOW-BROWN, Mrs. GROVE

PLOT SYNOPSIS

No one can remember when the puppet doll first appeared or where it came from, but the dressmakers and their workers feel its creepy presence. When the doll begins to move about from place to place when no one is around, everyone becomes frightened. At first, shop owner Alicia Coombe simply locks the room and gives it up to the doll, but the doll is found a few weeks later seated in another room. Overcome with fear, Alicia throws the doll out of the window to the ground below, where a child rescues it, claiming that it just wants love.

Driver, Inspector The Scotland Yard Inspector who interviews Anthony EASTWOOD when his valuable old enamels are stolen in "MR. EASTWOOD'S ADVENTURE."

Driver, Jenny A lively, petite woman who has flaming red hair, she is the proprietor of a hat shop and a good friend of Carlotta ADAMS in LORD EDGWARE DIES.

Drouet, Inspector A member of the Sûreté disguised as the waiter, Robert, in "THE ERYMANTHIAN BOAR," he dies when the villains discover his identity, murder him, and mutilate his face.

Drower, Mary The niece of Alice ASCHER, the first murder victim in THE A.B.C. MURDERS, she joins Hercule POIROT's "Special Legion" to find the murderer.

Dublay The mastermind of an international gang of thieves accused of stealing the Borgia goblet in "THE APPLES OF THE HESPERIDES."

Dubois, Martine A young woman who lost her fiancé at Dunkirk, she later married another man. After a letter bearing her name is sent to her late fiancé's sister, the body found in the sarcophagus in 4.50 FROM PADDINGTON is mistakenly identified as hers.

Dubois, Vivian A favorite among rich, married women with elderly husbands in A POCKET FULL OF RYE, he is a smooth-talking blackmailer who makes Adele FORTESCUE the beneficiary of his will.

Dubosc, Colonel One of a group of tourists in "THE PEARL OF PRICE," he dislikes Americans and feels that honesty is simply a convention.

Dubosc, Lieutenant A young French military officer in MURDER ON THE ORIENT EXPRESS (1), he escorts Hercule POIROT to the train in Syria.

Duguesclin, Quentin His dead body is discovered bearing business cards which identify him as "Mr. R.H. CURRY" in THE CLOCKS.

Duke, Mr. A former Chief Inspector of Scotland Yard in THE SITTAFORD MYSTERY, he believes in the supernatural, and attends the seance on the night that murder occurs.

Dumb Witness Mystery novel.

The novel concerns a murder to which the sole witness is a dog, the "dumb" witness of the title. The plot centers around the efforts of Hercule POIROT to expose the murderer of a woman whose letter requesting his help reaches him more than two months after her death.

PUBLISHING AND DRAMATIZATION HISTORY

The novel was published in 1937 by William Collins Sons and Company, Ltd., in London, and, under the title, *Poirot Loses a Client*, by Dodd, Mead and Company in New York.

The novel has not been adapted for stage or screen.

CHARACTERS

ANGUS, Emily ARUNDELL, Charles ARUNDELL, Theresa ARUNDELL, Nurse CARRUTHERS, Dr. Rex DONALDSON, ELLEN, Dr. GRAINGER, Captain Arthur HASTINGS, Wilhelmina (Minnie) LAWSON, Caroline PEABODY, Hercule Poirot, William PURVIS, Bella TANIOS, Dr. Jacob TANIOS, Isabel TRIPP, Julia TRIPP

PLOT SYNOPSIS

Chapters 1–3

The Arundell family gathers for Easter at the home of the unmarried Emily Arundell, and each member appears to want something from her. The family gathering is disturbed by Minnie Lawson's report that Emily's initials had appeared at a seance and that something was said about a will in the Boulle cabinet. One night, Emily gets up from her bed and stumbles down the stairs, falling in a heap at the bottom. Her nephew-in-law, Dr. Tanios, treats her and gives her a sleeping powder.

Chapters 4–6

The day after her fall, Emily writes two letters, one to her attorneys and the second to Hercule Poirot, who receives the letter more than 2 months later. Poirot decides to take the case. When he arrives in Market Basing to visit Emily at Little Green House, he learns that Emily died two months previously and

that her house is for rent, so he assumes the name of Parotti and rents the house.

Chapters 7–8

When Poirot and Hastings visit Little Green House, they learn that Emily left her entire estate to her companion, Miss Lawson, and nothing to her nieces and nephews. They also learn that she had a serious fall several weeks before her death, which confined her to bed for a week. The blame was placed on her terrier, Bob, and the black ball he left on the stairs. The maid tells the detectives that the letter was mailed late because it was found in a blotter when the maids were packing up Emily's belongings. She also tells them that Bob sometimes stayed out all night and that his ball was always put away in a drawer at night. The maid states that the dying Emily rambled about Bob and his ball and about a picture being ajar.

Chapters 9–12

As he inspects the house, on the pretense of being the new tenant, Poirot observes that a nail had been driven into the top of the stairs and varnished over. He also deduces that, since Bob did not return home until 5 A.M. on the night of the murder, Emily must have put the ball away for the night, and someone else took it out again. The Tripp sisters, described as vegetarians, Theosophists, British Israelites, Christian Scientists and spiritualists, as well as amateur photographers, tell him that they saw a halo around Emily's head on the night she was taken ill. They also inform him that Miss Lawson views her legacy as a "sacred trust."

Chapters 13–17

Poirot speaks with the victim's nieces and nephew and learns that they want their late aunt's money despite the stipulations in her will. Theresa asks the detective to help her to break the will and tells him that she is willing to be unscrupulous, if necessary. He interviews Miss Lawson, who tells him that Emily most likely wrote to him regarding money that had been stolen from the drawer. She also tells him that Charles had once told Emily that he would "bump her off" if she did not give him money. When Poirot speaks with Bella Tanios and her husband, he learns that Bella will follow Theresa's lead regarding the will. Dr. Tanios suggests that Emily was not of sound mind when she drew up the new will.

Chapters 18–21
Convinced that Emily's death is a murder, Poirot visits the victim's attorney, Mr. Purvis, who tells him that Emily probably would have changed her mind about the new will had she lived. She kept both locked in a drawer, and Poirot suggests that she might have intended to destroy one, but destroyed the wrong will. In casual conversation with the gardener, Poirot learns that the tin of arsenic used in killing weeds is nearly empty. During a visit to the local druggist, the detective learns that Dr. Tanios had some liver pills made up for Emily and that Mrs. Tanios had come in for chloral, a sleeping drug. Nurse Carruthers, who attended the dying woman, tells him that Emily asked repeatedly for her will, which she claimed to have placed in the drawer downstairs, but which Miss Lawson claimed was in the possession of Mr. Purvis. Despite the doctor's insistence that Emily died of liver atrophy, Poirot believes that she died of arsenic poisoning, and he requests an exhumation.

Chapters 22–24
Miss Lawson asks to speak with Poirot, who tells her about the nail and thread found after Emily's fall. She claims to have observed Theresa in her mirror bending over the stairs one night, wearing a dressing gown with a brooch with the initials "T.A." on it, which she often wore. Dr. Tanios approaches Poirot and tells him that his wife is acting as if she were headed for a nervous breakdown and has accused him of wanting to poison her. She has taken the children and moved to a hotel. Poirot speaks with Theresa, who tells him that Miss Lawson is mistaken about seeing her on the stairs. He then asks to see her brooch, which he puts on his lapel as he looks into a mirror.

Chapters 25–28
Poirot tells Hastings that the initials seen by Lawson in the mirror were reversed; they were really "A.T." Bella arrives at Little Green House and tells the detective that her husband killed Emily. When Dr. Tanios arrives, Miss Lawson turns him away. Poirot tells Bella to take her children to the Coniston Hotel and to tell no one of their plans.

Chapters 29–30
The murderer is identified, and Poirot reveals that Emily was poisoned by the administration over time of phosphorus, giving the appearance of liver atrophy. Before justice is served, the murderer commits suicide.

CRIME NOTES
The sole murder in this novel is due to poisoning with phosphorus, and the murderer commits suicide by ingesting an overdose of chloral hydrate.

Dundas, George A well-dressed young man with polished manners in "THE GOLDEN BALL," he uses an intriguing trick to effect a marriage proposal.

Dunlop, Sister A lazy, placid army hospital nurse in GIANT'S BREAD.

Dunn, Eliza A cook in "THE ADVENTURE OF THE CLAPHAM COOK," she is lured away from her employer with the offer of a house and a yearly income.

Dupont, Armand A French archaeologist in DEATH IN THE CLOUDS, he is accused of a blow-pipe murder because of the Kurdish pipes found in his luggage. Hercule POIROT finds Armand to be an unlikely murderer, stating that the archaeologist's mind remains focused on the activities of 5000 B.C., to the detriment of the present time.

Dupont, Jean Accused, along with his father, of murder in DEATH IN THE CLOUDS, he protests that the dead Madame Giselle MORISOT was too ugly to kill. He claims that he might be able to kill a beautiful woman who had made him jealous, but never one as ugly as Giselle.

Durand, Sir George A lawyer in "THE FOURTH MAN" whose every action evinces his profession.

Durrance, Mr. A former photographer whom Tuppence BERESFORD consults when she finds an old photograph album in her recently purchased home in POSTERN OF FATE.

Durrant, Amy A paid companion to her cousin, Mary BARTON, in "THE COMPANION," she drowns while vacationing at Grand Canary Island.

Durrant, Mary (1) A seemingly calm, woman in ORDEAL BY INNOCENCE, she is obsessed with her husband's needs, and subconsciously strives to keep him dependent.

Durrant, Mary (2)   A lively, lovely young woman with auburn hair to whom Captain HAS-TINGS is immediately attracted in "DOUBLE SIN," he claims that a case of expensive miniatures was stolen from her luggage.

Durrant, Philip   A former pilot in ORDEAL BY IN-NOCENCE, he is now paralyzed and confined to a wheelchair after being stricken with polio. Smoth-ered by his overly solicitous wife, he nonetheless launches his own investigation into the murder of his mother-in-law.

Dutch Pedro   A thief and blackmailer in THE SE-CRET OF CHIMNEYS, he gratefully turns the presumed love letters over to Jimmy MCGRATH, who saved his life.

Duval, Aristide   A.k.a.   CARTWRIGHT, SIR CHARLES.

Duveen, Bella   A former vaudeville performer in MURDER ON THE LINKS who was part of a duo with her twin sister, she is the future wife of Captain HAS-TINGS. She confesses to murder to save the man she loves, who then marries her and takes her away to South America.

Duveen, Dulcie   See HASTINGS, DULCIE DUVEEN.

Dwighton, Sir James   A parsimonious man in "THE LOVE DETECTIVES," he abuses his wife and dis-misses his butler without a character reference. When he is found dead in his library, his skull crushed by a bronze statuette, few of his acquaintances grieve.

Dwighton, Lady Laura   The unhappy wife of an abusive husband in "THE LOVE DETECTIVES," she looks like "a visitor from another world" because of her clothing and appearance.

Dyer   A man of unsavory reputation in "THE LOST MINE," he is known to be mixed up with Chinese gangsters.

Dymchurch, Detective Inspector   An impos-ter who contacts the International Detective Agency with a false warning of danger in "THE ADVENTURE OF THE SINISTER STRANGER."

Dyson, Greg   An American botanist in A CARIB-BEAN MYSTERY, he suffers from heart trouble and his medication is discovered in a dead man's room. He is in love with his wife and considers her to be his source of good luck, but he flirts constantly with other women. He and his wife visit St. Honore an-nually with Colonel Edward and Evelyn HILL-INGDON.

Dyson, Lucky   Before becoming the second wife of Greg DYSON in A CARIBBEAN MYSTERY, she had an affair with Colonel Edward HILLINGDON and con-vinced him to help her manipulate Dyson into mar-rying her. She drowns while on their annual excursion to St. Honore with the Hillingdons.

E

Eardsley, John See RAYBURN, HARRY.

Earl, William A young assistant gardener in THE MYSTERIOUS AFFAIR AT STYLES, he witnesses Emily INGLETHORPE's will the day before she is murdered.

Earlsfield, George The fourth victim in THE A.B.C. MURDERS, he is stabbed to death in a movie theater. Because someone whose last name begins with the letter "D" should have been the victim, investigators believe the killer has made a mistake.

Easterfield, Lord Despite his title, he began life as Gordon RAGG, and owes his wealth in MURDER IS EASY to his success as the publisher of a number of "nasty little weekly newspapers."

Easterbrook, Doreen See CORRIGAN, KATHERINE (GINGER).

Easterbrook, Mark A good friend of Mrs. Ariadne OLIVER who attends a church social event with her in THE PALE HORSE, he is writing a book on the topic of Mogul architecture. As the cousin of Rhoda DESPARD and the godson of Lady HESKETH-DUBOIS, he is very much linked to the society and the secrets of Much Deeping.

Eastley, Alexander A young boy in 4.50 FROM PADDINGTON who is protective of his father, he takes the initiative to issue a marriage proposal to a likeable young woman in his widower father's name.

Eastley, Bryan A still-young former fighter pilot and World War II hero, he is a widower in 4.50 FROM PADDINGTON who seems bewildered by civilian life. He is more of a sibling than a father to his son, Alexander EASTLEY.

Eastney, Phil A musical genius in "THE FACE OF HELEN" who works in a glass-blowing factory, he plots the murder of Gillian WEST after she rejects his advances.

Easton, Vincent The lover of Theodora DARRELL in "MAGNOLIA BLOSSOM," he plans to run away with her to grow oranges in the Transvaal, but does not realize that he possesses incriminating papers which implicate her husband in shady business deals.

Eastwood, Anthony A mystery writer in "MR. EASTWOOD'S ADVENTURE" who is currently at work on a story entitled "The Mystery of the Second Cucumber," he loses a valuable set of old enamels to the Patterson gang.

Easy To Kill See MURDER IS EASY.

Ebenthal, Bertha A German spy in "THE KIDNAPPED PRIME MINISTER," she poses as the aunt of the Prime Minister's secretary, and provides the setting for the crime.

Eberhard, Herr A brutish, nail-biting man with coarse manners in THE SEVEN DIALS MYSTERY, he develops a formula for strengthening and lightening steel, which the government wishes to obtain for use in the manufacture of aircraft.

Eccles, Mr. (1) He and his wife Pam ECCLES appear in Chipping Cleghorn in "SANCTUARY" to identify the man found dying in the local church and to obtain his personal items.

Eccles, Mr. (2) A cunning and cautious lawyer in BY THE PRICKING OF MY THUMBS, he presents a respectable image, but those who know him well view him as having one of the best criminal minds in the nation.

Eccles, Pam   An imposter, claiming to be William SANDBOURNE's sister in "SANCTUARY," she arrives in Chipping Cleghorn with her husband to collect the dead man's effects.

Eckstein, Professor   A self-effacing man, he is a top scientist in PASSENGER TO FRANKFURT whom Cabinet officials consult regarding the use of chemical weaponry.

Edge, Bella   Married to the village chemist in "THE CASE OF THE CARETAKER," she is a former romantic interest of the local scoundrel, Harry LAXTON.

Edge, Mr.   The village chemist in "THE CASE OF THE CARETAKER," he is not upset that his wife's old boyfriend still patronizes his shop.

Edgerton, Sir James Peel   Believed by most to be the next British Prime Minister in THE SECRET ADVERSARY, he is a highly observant and perceptive man who is especially interested in criminology.

Edgware, the Fifth Baron, Lord   See MARSH, RONALD.

Edgware, Lord   See MARSH, GEORGE.

Edith   A longtime family servant, she remains loyal to her mistress in A DAUGHTER'S A DAUGHTER despite extenuating circumstances.

Edmunds, Alfred   A managing clerk in a law firm in FIVE LITTLE PIGS, he is visited by Hercule POIROT in connection with a murder.

Edmundson, John   A close friend of Bob RAWLINSON and a secretary at the British Embassy at Ramat in CAT AMONG THE PIGEONS.

Edna (1)   Miss MARPLE's maid in "THE CASE OF THE PERFECT MAID," she confides in her employer about her concern over the recent dismissal of her cousin, Gladys HOLMES, on charges of theft.

Edna (2)   A dull-witted young girl in MRS. McGINTY'S DEAD who is a regular customer at Mrs. SWEETIMAN's combined candy store and post office, she becomes romantically involved with a married man.

Egerton, Richard   A tall, dark, distinguished lawyer in AT BERTRAM'S HOTEL, he is highly successful in his field, and well-versed in both law and in human nature. Also very blunt when giving advice, he is a partner in the firm that manages a trust for Elvira BLAKE.

Elephants Can Remember   Mystery novel.

The novel teams mystery writer Mrs. Ariadne OLIVER and detective Hercule POIROT to solve a decades-old mystery. The plot centers on the attempt to determine who killed whom in the murder-suicide of the Ravenscrofts, an attempt requested by the future mother-in-law of Mrs. OLIVER's goddaughter, Celia RAVENSCROFT.

PUBLISHING AND DRAMATIZATION HISTORY

The novel was published in 1972 by William Collins Sons and Company, Ltd., in London, and by Dodd, Mead and Company in New York.

The novel has not been adapted for stage or screen.

CHARACTERS

Mrs. BUCKLE, Mrs. BURTON-COX, Desmond BURTON-COX, The Honourable Julia CARSTAIRS, Kathleen FENN, Chief Superintendent GARROWAY, Mr. GOBY, Dorothea JARROW, Miss Felicity LEMON, Miss LIVINGSTONE, Mrs. MATCHAM, Mademoiselle Zellie MEAUHOURAT, Mrs. Ariadne Oliver, Hercule Poirot, Sir Alistair RAVENSCROFT, Celia Ravenscroft, Lady Margaret (Molly) RAVENSCROFT, Madame (Maddy) ROUSELLE, Miss SEDGWICK, Superintendent SPENCE, Dr. WILLOUGHBY, Fred WIZELL

PLOT SYNOPSIS
Chapters 1–2
Mrs. Ariadne Oliver is a guest at an elaborate luncheon when she is approached by an officious woman who first praises Mrs. Oliver's writing, then asks her to tell the truth about two deaths which occurred nearly two decades earlier. Mrs. Burton-

Cox reveals that her son is engaged to Celia Ravenscroft, Mrs. Oliver's goddaughter, whose parents died in what seemed to be a joint suicide pact. She wants to know who killed whom, but Mrs. Oliver claims to not know the details, and leaves the luncheon. The question haunts her, so she visits Hercule Poirot, who advises her to do nothing. Unable to put it out of her mind, Mrs. Oliver decides that she has to find people with the memory capacity of an elephant, because an elephant never forgets.

Book 1: Chapters 3–5
Mrs. Oliver visits Celia Ravenscroft, and mentions the conversation with Mrs. Burton-Cox. Celia observes that when the deaths occurred fifteen years earlier she was only twelve years old and, although she does not know what actually happened, she is now of age when she thinks about it constantly. At the same time, Poirot meets with members of Scotland Yard to discuss earlier cases that were solved long after the crimes had been committed. (See FIVE LITTLE PIGS; HALLOWE'EN PARTY.) They review the Ravenscroft case, and Poirot learns that there was no financial motive, nor one of hatred, sexual involvement or jealousy. They do know that Lady Ravenscroft had been in a nursing home.

Chapters 6–8
Mrs. Oliver visits a nursing home to speak with Julia Carstairs, an old friend of the Ravenscrofts, who tells her that Lady Ravenscroft had four wigs, one of which she always wore. She then visits her own old nanny, Mrs. Matcham, who remembers that a mentally unbalanced sister of one of the Ravenscrofts lived with them for a time, then left when she married a soldier. Another former Ravenscroft employee, Mrs. Buckle, who worked three days a week for them, tells Mrs. Oliver that she suspects that the gardener killed the Ravenscrofts.

Chapters 9–10
Mrs. Oliver has coffee with Poirot and recounts to him all that she has learned to date. He expresses the desire to meet with both Mrs. Burton-Cox and Celia. When he receives a letter from Desmond Burton-Cox, who is trying to get in touch with Mrs. Oliver, Poirot sets up an appointment with him. While speaking with the detective, Desmond reveals that he

is adopted, and suggests that Poirot contact two former au pairs who might know something.

Book 2: Chapters 11–13
Poirot consults with Chief Superintendent Garroway, who tells the detective that Lady Ravenscroft had a twin sister, Dorothea, who married and had two children, a girl and a boy. The girl knocked the boy into a pond where he drowned, after which their mother had a mental breakdown. Sometime later, Dorothea fell off a cliff and died at the Ravenscrofts' house, three weeks before they did. Poirot then meets with Celia and asks if Mrs. Burton-Cox might possibly know something about her adopted son Desmond's natural family that she has not told him. He asks Celia if her future mother-in-law knew the Ravenscrofts, but Celia does not think that she did. The detective then speaks with Mrs. Burton-Cox, who rushes off hurriedly, giving Poirot the impression that she does not want an official investigation.

Chapters 14–16
Poirot visits Dr. Willoughby, who tells him that Captain Ravenscroft had originally planned to marry Dorothea, but he transferred his affections to Molly and he married her instead. Dolly was bitterly jealous of her sister. In addition, he notes that Dolly had been suspected in the deaths of both her son and a neighbor's child in India, although no evidence was ever found. Mrs. Oliver visits a hair specialist, and learns that Molly had purchased two wigs, later sending her maid to purchase another two wigs only six weeks before the deaths. At the same time, Poirot receives information from Mr. Goby who reports that Mrs. Burton-Cox's first husband died, and her child of this marriage was killed soon afterward in an accident. She later adopted Desmond from Kathleen Fee, her late husband's mistress, after which she married Mr. Burton-Cox. When Kathleen died, she left a large sum of money to become Desmond's upon his reaching twenty-five years of age.

Chapters 17–20
Mrs. Oliver learns that Celia's brother was sent away from home to preparatory school, and that Celia had been sent to finishing school. Poirot visits the two au pairs who had worked for the Ravenscrofts; then he meets with Celia, Desmond and Mrs. Oliver to reveal the truth behind the Ravenscroft deaths and the role

the wigs played in keeping the truth secret for fifteen years.

CRIME NOTES
The two murders which occur in this novel remain hidden for fifteen years. The first murder victim is pushed off a cliff and the second victim is shot to death.

Elgin   The tactful and discreet butler in SPIDER'S WEB, his early return from a night out complicates the situation when murder occurs.

Elise   The French personal maid of a temperamental opera star in "SWAN SONG."

Elizabeth   The tall, gaunt woman who serves as Mrs. Harter's maid in "WHERE THERE'S A WILL," she possesses an "unbending exterior" to hide "a wealth of affection and tenderness for her mistress."

Ellen (1)   Really named Helen, she is a maid and cook for Amelia VINER who changes Helen's name to Ellen, a more fitting name for a servant in THE MYSTERY OF THE BLUE TRAIN.

Ellen (2)   Two months after her employer, Emily ARUNDELL, dies in DUMB WITNESS, this maidservant finds and mails the letter written by her employer to Hercule POIROT.

Ellen (3)   The housemaid in The White House in "THE MAN IN THE MIST," she becomes hysterical when murder occurs.

Ellen (4)   The housemaid in A POCKET FULL OF RYE whose mother warned her never to touch yew berries.

Elliot, Mrs.   Accompanied by the baker in MRS. McGINTY'S DEAD, she discovers the dead body of Mrs. McGINTY.

Elliot, James   A crook already under suspicion by the police, he kidnaps a young woman in "THE GIRDLE OF HIPPOLYTA," and smuggles a valuable stolen painting by Rubens into France.

Elliot, Lady Noreen   An aristocratic member of the group called the "Bright Young People" in "THE MANHOOD OF EDWARD ROBINSON," she adds excitement to her life by stealing jewelry, which she wears for a while and then returns.

Ellis   A maid in LORD EDGWARE DIES, her employer, Jane WILKINSON, trusts her so completely that she sends her to Paris to obtain a valuable box made of gold and decorated with rubies which form the initials "C.A."

Ellis, Miss (1)   See CORTMAN, MILDRED JEAN.

Ellis, Miss (2)   Secretary to Harold CRACKENTHORPE in 4.50 FROM PADDINGTON.

Ellis, Big Jim   In A CARIBBEAN MYSTERY he is the common-law husband of Victoria JOHNSON, and a suspect in murder.

Ellis, Joe   A somewhat dull-witted yet competent carpenter in "DEATH BY DROWNING," he is oblivious to the attraction which his landlady, Mrs. Bartlett, feels toward him. Instead, he is in love with and wants to marry Rose EMMOTT, who is pregnant by another man, who is later murdered.

Ellis, John   A recently hired butler at the home of Sir Bartholomew STRANGE, he disappears soon after his employer's murder in THREE-ACT TRAGEDY. Notes alluding to blackmail and secret information about his employer are discovered in the butler's room but is found no clue to his past. He is later discovered to be the disguised Sir Charles CARTWRIGHT.

Ellis, Lou   Blond and bosomy, she is a young woman who gets involved in a hair-pulling fight with Thomasina TUCKERTON in an espresso bar in THE PALE HORSE. Her opponent dies suddenly a week after the fight.

Ellsworthy, Mr.   A local antique dealer in MURDER IS EASY who is also an adherent of witchcraft. An unlikable and effete bachelor, he has "a womanish mouth, long black artistic hair and a mincing walk," and he is a suspect in the deaths of five Wychwood residents.

Elsa   Aa sunburned young Italian woman with red, curly hair in DEAD MAN'S FOLLY, she meets her husband James FOLLIAT in Italy after he deserts from the British Army. She joins him in plotting to take back his family estate.

Elsie   A devout Catholic, she is a housemaid who disapproves strongly of her mistress Madame SIMONE's seances in "THE LAST SEANCE." She discovers her employer's body after the last seance, and is puzzled by its greatly reduced appearance.

Elspeth   A stern-faced woman who supervises the dressmakers in "THE DRESSMAKER'S DOLL."

Emlyn, Miss   The experienced, elderly headmistress of a school for girls in HALLOWE'EN PARTY where Joyce REYNOLDS is murdered.

Emmott, David   A seemingly passive, young, American, assistant archaeologist in MURDER IN MESOPOTAMIA, he accurately judges the personalities of his fellow travelers, and marries the strong-willed Sheila REILLY.

Emmott, Rose   A young woman who is murdered in "DEATH BY DROWNING," she becomes pregnant, and is deserted by one man and loved by another who wishes to marry her.

Emmott, Tom   Proprietor of an inn named the Blue Boar in "DEATH BY DROWNING," he is certain that his daughter Rose became pregnant by Rex SANDFORD, whom he also believes responsible for her murder.

Enderby, Charles   A young reporter who tries to obtain an exclusive story about the murder of Captain TREVELYAN in THE SITTAFORD MYSTERY.

Endicott, Mr.   An elderly attorney who represents Sir Arthur STANLEY in HICKORY DICKORY DOCK.

Endless Night   Mystery novel.
   The title of the novel is drawn from the Romantic poet William Blake's *Auguries of Innocence,* of which a key line is "Some are born to Endless Night." The plot centers on the marriage of a working-class drifter to a young heiress, and the evil that a gipsy's curse exerts on them.

Hywel Bennett and Hayley Mills star in the **1971 film version of** *Endless Night.*   (Photo courtesy of The Museum of Modern Art, Film Stills Archive)

PUBLISHING AND DRAMATIZATION HISTORY
The novel was published in 1967 by William Collins Sons and Company, Ltd., in London, and in 1968 by Dodd, Mead and Company in New York.
   The film version, released in 1972 by United Artists, was entitled *Endless Night,* and starred Hayley Mills, Hywel Bennett, Britt Eklund, Per Oscarsson and George Sanders. The author was unhappy with the attempt to enliven the plot by infusing the movie with sexual scenes.

CHARACTERS
Greta ANDERSON, Dimitri CONSTANTINE, Claudia HARDCASTLE, Sergeant KEENE, Mrs. Esther LEE, Andrew P. LIPPINCOTT, Stanford LLOYD, Major PHILLPOT, Gervase PHILLPOT, Mrs. ROGERS, Ellie Guteman ROGERS, Michael ROGERS, Rudolf SANTONIX, Dr. SHAW, Cora VAN STUYVESANT

PLOT SYNOPSIS

Book 1: Chapters 1–3

Michael Rogers is a chauffeur who develops a strange attraction toward an estate named Gipsy's Acres, a place rumored to be cursed by gipsies who had been forced to leave it. The place and its contents are for sale, but Michael has little money. Mrs. Lee, an old gipsy woman who lives on the estate, reads his palm. She tells him that he must leave, for he is doomed if he stays. Putting the curse aside, he continues his work, one assignment being to drive the Constantines to the building site of their new home. While there, Michael meets and befriends the ailing architect, Rudolf Santonix, whom Michael hopes will one day build a house for him.

Chapters 4–6

After attending an auction at the mansion at Gipsy's Acres, Michael meets Ellie Guteman walking on the property. He tells her that he wants to buy the land but does not have the money. He passionately describes the wonderful house that Santonix is building for the Constantines. Together they meet Mrs. Lee, who gives Ellie the same dire warning she gave Michael. In the days that follow, Michael and Ellie meet for tea and to walk in the park. Michael learns that Ellie is a rich orphan whose guardian is her stepmother. He also learns about her close friend, Greta. Michael visits his mother, who expresses displeasure when he tells her about Ellie.

Chapters 7 8

Ellie and Michael plan to marry immediately, and they will have Santonix build them a dream house on Gipsy's Acres, which Ellie has bought for them. She reveals to Michael that she is the only heir to her father's vast fortune.

Book 2: Chapters 9–12

They marry and meet with Santonix in Greece to review plans for their new house. Ellie also informs Michael that she wants Greta to live with them. When Ellie runs into an old family friend in Athens, she realizes that she has to inform her family and lawyers about her marriage. A family meeting is called, and Andrew Lippincott, the family lawyer, is the first to meet the new couple and discuss their plans for their house. Greta joins Ellie in London, where she has found a new job after being fired by Ellie's family. After the family meeting, Ellie admits how lonely she

has been over the years because she really has no blood relatives. That is why she became so close to Greta, and now she feels genuinely loved by Michael. Michael admits that he is jealous of her closeness to Greta.

Chapters 13–15

Soon after Ellie and Michael move into their dream house, their dinner is interrupted by a rock that crashes through a window and sends a sliver of glass against Ellie's cheek. Ellie is frightened, and they tell Major Phillpot about the experience when he visits. Shortly after, they find a dead bird on a skewer with the following note attached: "Get out if you know what's good for you!" They meet Claudia Hardcastle, Rudolf Santonix's half-sister, at a dinner party at the Phillpots', and Ellie reveals that she has allergies and has to take "orange capsules" before going horseback riding. A few days later, while Michael and Ellie stroll through Gipsy's Acre, Ellie trips over a root and sprains her ankle. Greta is summoned to care for her, and takes over the household. Santonix warns Michael of Greta's power over Ellie.

Chapters 16–18

Michael's mother visits the couple and tells Michael that Ellie visited her before the wedding. Later, a nervous Ellie suspects that the new manservant hired through her family law firm might be a security man. As Ellie's birthday nears, Michael seeks a special gift for her. He accompanies Major Phillpot to an auction, where he buys her a papier-mâché table. Ellie had planned to go horseback riding all morning, then meet the two men for lunch at The George at Barrington, but she does not return from her ride; later, Michael and the Major find her dead at the edge of the woods. Dr. Shaw examines the body, and determines that she has been dead for three hours.

Book 3: Chapters 19–22

Mrs. Lee is conspicuous in her absence from the inquest, even though she had been summoned. All the evidence points to an accidental death due to a fall, but the judge adjourns the proceedings until Mrs. Lee can be located. The Major and Michael express suspicion that someone could have caused Ellie's fall, and Michael reveals that a stone was thrown through his window that morning to which a note was attached, reading "It was a woman who killed your wife." The police find a cigarette lighter with the letter "C" in diamonds on the property. Ellie's body is transported to New York for burial, where her principal beneficiary, Michael, has some business to conduct. While in America, Michael learns that Mrs. Lee's body has been found in a quarry. A few days later, Claudia Hardcastle dies after a fall from her horse, and Santonix dies of natural causes.

Chapters 23–24
Michael returns to Gipsy's Acres and thinks back over his checkered past. He returns to be with Greta, but their happiness is short-lived.

CRIME NOTES
Both the author and her husband claim in their respective autobiographies that the novel is among their favorites because of the "twisted" character who had a chance of turning to the good and instead chose evil. The book is dedicated to Nora Prichard, the paternal grandmother of the author's only grandson, Mathew. Mrs. Prichard first told the author about the field called Gipsy's Acres on the Welsh moors.

In the novel, one victim is murdered by being made to fall into a quarry, while two others are poisoned with cyanide.

Enrico   A Cuban cook in A CARIBBEAN MYSTERY, he sees a hotel guest carrying a knife in her hand moments before another guest is stabbed.

Entwhistle, Miss   The irritable, bullying but devoted sister of Mr. ENTWHISTLE, she tries to keep her brother from becoming involved in the affairs of the Abernethie family in AFTER THE FUNERAL.

Entwhistle, Mr.   An old friend of Richard ABERNETHIE, he is a lawyer who continues to manage the Abernethie estate even after retirement in AFTER THE FUNERAL. When one of the family suggests that his client was murdered, he contacts Hercule POIROT.

Ericsson, Torquil   A brilliant young Norwegian scientist who becomes a part of the Brain Trust in DESTINATION UNKNOWN, he believes scientific discovery is of more value than any individual human life, and asserts that scientists ought to rule the world with all others becoming their slaves.

Erskine, Major Richard Setoun   A married man in SLEEPING MURDER who falls in love with another woman, he remains with his wife for the sake of their children.

"Erymanthian Boar"   Mystery short story.
The adventure begins when Hercule POIROT receives a mysterious message from a French lawman, asking for help in capturing a dangerous criminal.

PUBLISHING AND DRAMATIZATION HISTORY
The story appeared in the short story collection THE LABOURS OF HERCULES published in 1947 by William Collins Sons and Company, Ltd., in London, and by Dodd, Mead and Company in New York.

The story has not been adapted for stage or screen.

CHARACTERS
Inspector DROUET, Madame GRANDIER, Inspector GUSTAVE, Commissionaire LEMENTEUIL, Dr. Karl LUTZ, MARRASCAUD, Hercule Poirot, Mr. SCHWARTZ

PLOT SYNOPSIS
Hercule Poirot plans a holiday in the Alps, but a hastily passed note from Commissionaire Lementeuil sends him to a mountain resort to trap a dangerous criminal. The Hotel Rochers Neige contains several guests, any of whom might be Marrascaud. A waiter at the hotel claims to be a police inspector working undercover, but he is found dead shortly after Poirot is attacked. Among the other guests are a medical doctor who poses as a psychoanalyst, and a mysterious woman whose melancholy behavior may be either a consequence of grief over a dead husband or a desire to seclude herself from the other guests. The detective unmasks the criminal and uses a novel means of alerting the police, even though the hotel is entirely cut off from the outside world.

CRIME NOTES
Transportation is not operating, there is no telegraph and the telephone is not working, but Hercule Poirot uses solar energy to call in the police by sending a "heliograph." The task in this story is a contemporary version of the fourth labor of Hercules, in which he captured the wild Erymanthian boar.

Lementeuil refers to Marrascaud as a "wild boar" in his note requesting help from Poirot.

Esa The matriarch of the family in DEATH COMES AS THE END, she warns her son IMHOTEP, when he brings home a concubine, that men become fools over women, who eventually age, and "death comes as the end."

Estair, Lord The leader of the House of Commons during World War I, he requests help from Hercule POIROT in "THE KIDNAPPED PRIME MINISTER" in locating the Prime Minister before England's morale is damaged.

Estcourt, Mervyn (Bugler) An old friend of Tommy and Tuppence BERESFORD, he meets his friends while he is dining with the well-known and beautiful actress Gilda GLEN in THE MAN IN THE MIST.

Ethel A parlourmaid in THE BURDEN.

Estravados, Pilar See LOPEZ, CONCHITA.

Eustace, Major A former military man in "MURDER IN THE MEWS" who had been stationed in India, where he met Barbara ALLEN, he is coarsely good-looking but dishonest and "Definitely not out of the top drawer." He has several assumed identities, including Colonel DE BATHE.

Evans A Secret Service agent in "THE MAN WHO WAS NO. 16," he assists Tommy BERESFORD in a break-in.

Evans, Dr. A scientist in DESTINATION UNKNOWN, he and his wife are bridge partners to Thomas and Olive BETTERTON.

Evans, Inspector A perceptive retired detective police inspector in "ACCIDENT" who prefers to gather his own evidence, he recognizes a woman involved in a current murder who was once acquitted of murdering her husband.

Evans, Albert An opportunist in A POCKET FULL OF RYE, he is really Lance FORTESCUE, who disguises

himself in order to court the maid and to convince her to mix poison into his father's marmalade. He makes the mistake of allowing himself to have his picture taken with the girl he tricks.

Evans, Charles (Chubby) Married to a wealthy woman in THE MYSTERY OF THE BLUE TRAIN, he is described by her daughter, Lenox TAMPLIN, as "an expensive luxury" who fully enjoys his pampered existence.

Evans, Doris A typist in "THE SUNNINGDALE MYSTERY," she is charged with murder by hatpin after resisting her companion's demand that she join him in a suicide pact, and running away.

Evans, Gladys See ROBERTS, GLADYS.

Evans, Rebecca Married to Captain TREVELYAN's valet in THE SITTAFORD MYSTERY, she is an excellent cook, but Trevelyan refuses to employ her or any other female servant in his house.

Evans, Robert Henry A retired sailor who serves as manservant to Captain TREVELYAN in THE SITTAFORD MYSTERY, he tries to convince his misogynist employer to allow his wife to cook in the house.

Everard, Mrs. See EBENTHAL, BERTHA.

Everett, Mr. An actor whom Hercule POIROT recruits to take the role of the late Mr. MALTRAVERS in "THE TRAGEDY AT MARSDON MANOR."

Eversleigh, Bill A member of the Seven Dials group, also known as Number 3, he appears in both THE SECRET OF CHIMNEYS and THE SEVEN DIALS MYSTERY. Although a homely man, he becomes engaged to the vivacious Bundle BRENT.

Eversleigh, Mrs. Violet A guest at the Trent home in "THE RED SIGNAL," she is very interested in the supernatural, especially in premonitions.

Evesham, Lady Laura Keene A superstitious woman in "THE COMING OF MR. QUIN," she wishes for a dark man to be the first to step over her doorstep on New Year's Day as a portent of good luck.

Evesham, Tom   Married to Lady Laura EVES-HAM, he tells his guests in "THE COMING OF MR. QUIN" of the suicide that occurred in his home while he and another man were present.

Evil Under the Sun   Mystery novel.

The novel takes place on a holiday resort island off the coast of Devon, and deals with a love triangle. The plot centers on several hidden connections between the characters that make identifying the murderer difficult.

PUBLISHING AND DRAMATIZATION HISTORY
The novel was published in 1941 by William Collins Sons and Company in London, and by Dodd, Mead and Company in New York.

The novel was adapted and filmed in 1981 by EMI and starred Peter Ustinov as Hercule POIROT.

CHARACTERS
Major BARRY, Mr. Horace BLATT, Emily BREWSTER, Mrs. CASTLE, Inspector COLGATE, Alice CORRIGAN, Edward CORRIGAN, Rosamund DARNLEY, Carrie GARDENER, Odell GARDENER, Chief Inspector JAPP, Reverend Stephen LANE, Arlena MARSHALL, Captain Kenneth MARSHALL, Linda MARSHALL, Gladys NAR-RACOTT, Dr. NEASDON, Sergeant PHILLIPS, Hercule Poirot, Christine REDFERN, Patrick REDFERN, Colonel WESTON

PLOT SYNOPSIS
Chapters 1–3
The first three chapters provide a general introduction to the Jolly Roger Hotel and the guests, including Hercule Poirot. As several of the guests debate the possibility of a body being found in the area, Poirot argues that a murder, or any crime for that matter, can occur anywhere. Stephen Lane adds his support for Poirot's views, while the other guests discuss Arlena Stuart Marshall, a beautiful guest with the reputation of being a homewrecker. Later, when Poirot and Rosamund Darnley discuss her childhood, the detective learns that her recent remorse is motivated by the reappearance in her life of Captain Kenneth Marshall, a childhood friend who is now married. The scene shifts to the rooms of various other characters, who reveal their secret hatred for others and their motives for vacationing at the Jolly Roger. Most significant is the conversation between Captain Marshall and Rosamund Darnley, in which she suggests that he divorce his wife. He is appalled, and states that no one ever finishes what they start anymore. Other characters converse, and the reader learns more about their personalities.

Chapters 4–5
Linda Marshall walks to the general store to buy candles. When she returns, Christine Redfern suggests that they go to Gull Cove, where Christine will sketch. They invite Rosamund to join them, but she "has other fish to fry." Poirot later encounters Arlena Stuart Marshall on the beach, and she asks him not to tell anyone of her whereabouts. Later, Patrick Redfern asks about Arlena, but it is apparent that no one has seen her, so he decides to take a boat ride with Miss Brewster. As they row, they happen upon a small cove, where they find Arlena's body. Miss Brewster rows back to shore to get the chief constable while Patrick stays with the body. Inspector Colgate determines the time of death to be between 10:45 and 11:40 A.M. Arlena was strangled quickly and with substantial force, suggesting that a man killed her. Colonel Weston, an investigator, solicits the help of Poirot, and the two discuss the general nature of Arlena and her relationships with the other guests. Kenneth Marshall is questioned regarding his whereabouts at the time of his wife's death, and the reader learns that he will inherit his wife's fortune.

Chapters 6–8
Weston, Poirot and Colgate eliminate suspects from the hotel register. They question Linda Marshall about her stepmother's character, and she states that the only person who might want to kill Arlena is Christine. Patrick is questioned and corroborates that he and Arlena were having an affair. Christine admits that she detested Arlena and states that the dead woman was a parasite who brought out the worst in people. She states that she overheard Arlena speaking with an unknown man who seemed to be blackmailing the deceased. The sleuths reason that this was the purpose for Arlena's covert actions and for her being at Pixey Cove, where she was found dead. During their search of Arlena's room, Colgate and

Poirot find a love letter written by someone with the initials "J.N." The chambermaid is questioned and corroborates Captain Marshall's claim that he was typing at the time of the murder, and she also states that Linda did not wake up at her usual early hour.

Chapters 9–10
Poirot, Colgate and Reverend Stephen Lane return to the scene of the crime and discover a box lunch with some sort of drug in the saltshaker. Mr. Horace Blatt is questioned about his whereabouts during the time of Arlena's murder; he states that he was sailing. He thinks that Captain Marshall knew about Arlena's affair with Patrick. A drug analysis determines that the substance in the saltshaker is heroin. The investigators try to identify whose pipe was found at the site of the murder. Poirot learns that Linda had been out of the hotel earlier than the chambermaid reported. He interviews Rosamund and Linda separately. Rosamund takes offense at his questions, while Linda panics when he mentions her trip to the general store for candles.

Chapter 11
New facts come to light about the victim and the guests. Inspector Colgate discovers that Arlene had withdrawn sizable, untraceable amounts of money from her personal account over the previous months. Further, Reverend Lane had recently been institutionalized because of an obsession with the devil. Poirot also reads two newspaper articles which discuss the deaths of two young women who lived within miles of the area in which Lane is the vicar. Another similarity in each death is that the husbands in both cases seem to have airtight alibis. Weston speaks to Poirot about turning the case over to Scotland Yard because narcotics are involved, but Poirot disagrees.

Chapter 12
Poirot assembles the guests for a picnic, but a chambermaid appears and exclaims that Linda Marshall is very sick. She has tried to commit suicide, and she has left a letter for Poirot in which she admits to murdering her stepmother. Poirot then addresses the group. He describes how several of the guests had the opportunity to murder Arlena and the motive. Recalling the air of eagerness with which the victim had headed for the cove on the morning of her death, Poirot concludes that she must have been headed to meet a lover. He sees that this case is connected with the earlier cases of which he had read.

Chapter 13
Poirot identifies the murderer and explains how time and people were manipulated to cover the killer's trail. Linda recovers, and she looks forward to a happy family life because her father is finally going to marry his childhood love, Rosamund.

CRIME NOTES
The murder victim in this novel is strangled.

Exe, Madame   Deeply aggrieved over her daughter's death, she exudes a depth of love for her late daughter that frightens Madame SIMONE in "THE LAST SEANCE."

Eyelesbarrow, Lucy   An attractive and highly in telligent woman who had taken first honors in mathematics at Oxford, she prefers to work in domestic service. Her highly efficient manner and intelligent mind make her a popular temporary employee, and in 4.50 FROM PADDINGTON, Miss MARPLE contacts her to find the body of the murdered woman.

F

"Face of Helen, The" Mystery short story.

Two men fight over the woman they both love, but Mr. SATTERTHWAITE must intervene to save her life from the lover who would rather see her dead than with another man.

PUBLISHING AND DRAMATIZATION HISTORY

The story appeared in the short story collection, THE MYSTERIOUS MR. QUIN, published in 1930 by William Collins Sons and Company in London, and by Dodd, Mead and Company in New York.

The story has not been adapted for stage or screen.

CHARACTERS

Charles BURNS, Philip EASTNEY, Mr. QUIN, Mr. SATTERTHWAITE, Gillian WEST

PLOT SYNOPSIS

During intermission at the opera, Mr. Satterthwaite unexpectedly meets the very mysterious Mr. Quin, and they witness two men fighting over a young woman. Mr. Satterthwaite escorts the woman home, and learns of the longtime rivalry between the two men and of her recent decision to marry one of them. The rejected suitor sends her a gift with the seemingly sentimental request that the young woman listen to a radio concert at a specified time in the evening. Mr. Satterthwaite fortuitously meets the young man on the evening of the concert and learns that the gift was a ploy to arrange the young woman's death.

CRIME NOTES

The means of attempted murder is an unspecified gas, which the author describes as nearly unknown but so deadly as to cause death with "one whiff."

Fairborough, Lady Muriel An eccentric aristocrat with a strong interest in astrology in THE BURDEN, she is the aunt of Henry GLYN-EDWARDS and, like others, is manipulated by him.

"Fairy in the Flat, A" Mystery short story.

This story moves Tommy and Tuppence BERESFORD from boredom to intrigue as they take over the International Detective Agency and take on the search for Number 16.

PUBLISHING AND DRAMATIZATION HISTORY

The story appeared in the short story collection, PARTNERS IN CRIME, published in 1929 by William Collins Sons and Company, Ltd., in London, and Dodd, Mead and Company in New York.

The story has not been adapted for stage or screen.

CHARACTERS

Tommy BERESFORD, Tuppence BERESFORD, Theodore BLUNT, Mr. CARTER

PLOT SYNOPSIS

The brief story serves as a prelude to adventure and exhibits the fulfillment of a wish made by Tommy and Tuppence Beresford. They are approached by a high-ranking member of British Intelligence who asks them to take over a detective agency, run formerly by double agent Theodore Blunt, who is now in prison, and to be on alert for anyone identified as Number 16 and for letters with the number 16 on the envelope.

CRIME NOTES

The title is drawn from Tuppence's wish for a fairy to rescue them from their boredom. As she expresses that wish, Tommy shows her a photograph of their apartment that contains a flash of light in which an imaginative person might very well see a winged fairy.

Fane, Eleanor   An elderly, meddling mother in SLEEPING MURDER, she attempts to dictate every aspect of her three sons' lives, even to the point of determining their love interests.

Fane, Geoffrey   A stuffy archaeology professor, he is the sometime suitor of Ann PRENTICE in A DAUGHTER'S A DAUGHTER.

Fane, Walter   A repressed young man in SLEEPING MURDER, he leaves England for Ceylon after being jilted by the woman he loves. Described by Miss MARPLE as the "type of young man whom women ignore and marry only because the man they love does not return their affection," he lives with his controlling widowed mother.

Fanny   The nurse of an American girl visiting France in UNFINISHED PORTRAIT.

Fanshaw, Ada   Opinionated and often ill-tempered, she is the eighty-three-year-old aunt of Tommy BERESFORD who inspires a variety of reactions among other characters in BY THE PRICKING OF MY THUMBS. Confined to the Sunny Ridge Nursing Home, Aunt Ada observes many secrets around the nursing home, which she details in a letter marked "Confidential," left in a secret drawer of the desk that Tommy and Tuppence BERESFORD inherit upon her death.

Fanthorpe, James Lechdale   Quiet but constantly alert, he is a lawyer sent to Egypt to safeguard the fortune of his client, Linnet DOYLE, and to keep another character under surveillance in DEATH ON THE NILE (2). His presence on the river steamboat intrigues Hercule POIROT, who determines that Fanthorpe is not the type of person who would normally take such a trip for pleasure alone.

Farley, Benedict   A parsimonious and sometimes mean-spirited man in "THE DREAM," he is an eccentric millionaire who appears to have committed suicide. He is known to favor a twenty-eight-year-old

patchwork dressing gown and to eat cabbage soup and caviar each night for dinner.

Farley, Joanna   The unhappy daughter of Benedict FARLEY and the primary heir to his estate in "THE DREAM," she is embittered when her father's intervention costs her former fiancé his job, and she openly expresses her hatred for her late father when questioned by Hercule POIROT.

Farley, Louise   The young second wife of the wealthy but eccentric Benedict FARLEY, she exhibits no grief at her husband's death, and supports the false story told by another character in "THE DREAM."

Farquhar, Esmee   Beautiful and young, she appeals to Hercule POIROT to uncover the true fate of the stolen Liberty Bonds in "THE MILLION DOLLAR BOND ROBBERY." Her great fear is that her fiancé, Philip Ridgeway, may be the thief.

Farr, Stephen   See GRANT, STEPHEN.

Farraday, Lady Alexandra Catherine (Sandra)   The highly intelligent, strong-willed wife of a Tory Member of Parliament to whom she is intensely devoted in SPARKLING CYANIDE, she becomes a suspect when her husband's mistress is murdered.

Farraday, Stephen   A Member of Parliament and the husband of Lady Alexandra FARRADAY in SPARKLING CYANIDE, he regrets his love affair with Rosemary BARTON, and fears her threats to expose the relationship.

Farrar, Julian   A handsome, thirty-six-year-old, former army major in THE UNEXPECTED GUEST, he is a Liberal candidate for Parliament, and has been having an affair with the murder victim's wife.

Farrell, Detective Inspector   A member of Scotland Yard in "JANE IN SEARCH OF A JOB," he is assigned to capture the "American girl bandit."

Fat Ikey   See ISAACSTEIN, HERMAN.

Faulkener, Jimmy (1)   A young man who innocently passes counterfeit bills among the society set in "THE CRACKLER."

Faulkener, Jimmy (2)   In competition with another man for the love of Patricia GARNETT, he discovers the dead woman in the apartment in THE THIRD-FLOOR FLAT.

Faulkner, Leslie   A young playwright in "THE AFFAIR AT THE BUNGALOW," he is framed by the scheming Jane HELIER.

Faussett, Dr.   The physician who determines how Amyas CRALE dies in FIVE LITTLE PIGS.

Felice   Accused of having stolen a bottle of heart medicine in "THE CHOCOLATE BOX," this housemaid eagerly cooperates with Hercule POIROT to clear her name.

Fellows-Brown, Mrs.   A somewhat rotund woman in "THE DRESSMAKER'S DOLL" who agonizes over her bulk, she patronizes Alicia COOMBE's shop because any clothing purchased there "really does minimize my behind." She is one of the customers frightened by the lifelike appearance of the dressmaker's doll.

Fenn, Ardwyck   A prominent figure in the film world in THE MIRROR CRACK'D FROM SIDE TO SIDE, he refuses to speculate as to who might have murdered a fading movie star.

Fenn, Kathleen   The natural mother of Desmond BURTON-COX, she gave him up for adoption to her lover's wife in ELEPHANTS CAN REMEMBER. Upon her death, after creating a successful career as an entertainer, she leaves a sizeable estate to her son.

Feodor, Count   See PAUL, PRINCE OF MAURANIA.

Ferguson, Dr.   A physician in HALLOWE'EN PARTY, he asserts that the victim died of natural causes.

Ferguson, Mr.   A radical and outspoken advocate of Communism in DEATH ON THE NILE (2), he is actually the wealthy, very well-connected Lord DAWLISH. He criticizes a young heiress for her useless luxuries and contemptuously refers to Hercule POIROT as just another of the "dressed-up, foppish good-for-nothings."

Ferrarez, Carmen   Born in Hampstead, England, but masquerading as a Spaniard, she is part of a gang that plots to steal a valuable collection of old enamels in "MR. EASTWOOD'S ADVENTURE."

Ferrars, Mrs.   A widow and the romantic interest of Roger ACKROYD, she commits suicide by swallowing an overdose of veronal in THE MURDER OF ROGER ACKROYD.

Ferrier, Dagmar   The daughter of a former British Prime Minister and the wife of the present Prime Minister in "THE AUGEAN STABLES," she nearly loses her spotless reputation when political rivals circulate photographs of her physical double in compromising situations.

Ferrier, Edward   The British Prime Minister in "THE AUGEAN STABLES," he is respected for being a solid but not brilliant or eloquent individual. Political pressures weigh heavily on him, and he turns to Hercule POIROT for assistance when he learns that a newspaper plans to expose an incident that will threaten national stability.

Ferrier, Lesley   A solicitors' clerk and suspected forger in HALLOWE'EN PARTY, he is knifed to death after having an affair with another man's wife.

Finch, Sally   An American student living in Mrs. NICOLETIS' youth hostel in HICKORY DICKORY DOCK, she proposes marriage to fellow student, Len BATESON.

"Finessing the King"/"The Gentleman Dressed in Newspaper"   Mystery short story.

The crime occurs in the first story, but Tommy and Tuppence BERESFORD solve it in the second.

PUBLISHING AND DRAMATIZATION HISTORY
The two stories appear in the short story collection, PARTNERS IN CRIME, published in 1929 by William Collins Sons and Company in London, and by Dodd, Mead and Company in New York.

The two stories were adapted for television in 1984 by London Weekend Television in England, and were also shown on the Public Broadcasting Service in the U.S.

In "Finessing the King," Tommy and Tuppence Beresford (James Warwick and Francesca Annis) learn that 'finessing' means murder. (Photo courtesy of London Weekend Television)

CHARACTERS
Tommy BERESFORD, Tuppence BERESFORD, Captain Bingo HALE, Inspector MARRIOT, Sir Arthur MERIVALE, Lady Vere MERIVALE

PLOT SYNOPSIS
A personal advertisement written in code attracts the attention of Tuppence Beresford, who deciphers it and then convinces her husband to attend the Three Arts Ball in costume. When a murder occurs at the ball, the two detectives join the police in tracking the killer, although the task is made difficult by the masks and costumes worn by all who attended the ball. The killer seems to have left behind a strong clue, but the fact that the case is too clear makes the detectives search more thoroughly to identify the true murderer, whose motive is unexpected.

CRIME NOTES
The Beresfords play the parts of earlier fictional detectives, Riordan and McCarty, created by Isabel Ostrander (1885–1924), in their approach to the case.

Finn, Jane   A passenger on the doomed ship the *Lusitania*, she inadvertently becomes involved in international intrigue when a British Intelligence agent entrusts her with a packet of valuable documents in THE SECRET ADVERSARY. She loses her memory, and enters medical care under the name of Janet VANDEMEYER.

Finney, Major   As the chief constable in ORDEAL BY INNOCENCE, he is convinced that Jacko ARGYLE is the murderer until facts presented by Dr. CALGARY convince him otherwise.

Fish, Hiram   An American in THE SECRET OF CHIMNEYS, his presence is used to deflect attention away from the highly political nature of the gathering at Chimneys. Despite his professed interest in rare books and paintings, Mr. Fish seems to have in-depth knowledge of neither.

Fitzroy, Mr.   An anemic-looking young man with "a frigid expression" in "THE SUBMARINE PLANS," he is secretary to the head of the Ministry of Defense, and becomes a suspect when vital plans disappear.

Fitzwilliam, Luke   Returning to England after years spent as a policeman in the Mayang Straits, he is intrigued by a fellow passenger's account of suspicious deaths in her village in MURDER IS EASY. He poses as a writer gathering material for a book on superstitions to prevent suspicion in the small village, and finds both the perpetrator and love as the result of his efforts.

Five Little Pigs   Mystery novel.
   The novel concerns a murder considered in retrospect, the first of five such murder mysteries written by the author. The plot centers on the attempt of Hercule POIROT to clear a young woman's late mother of a murder for which she was executed sixteen years earlier.

PUBLISHING AND DRAMATIZATION
HISTORY
The novel was published in 1943 by William Collins
Sons and Company in London, and, under the title,
Murder in Retrospect, by Dodd, Mead and Company
in New York.

The novel was adapted by Agatha Christie into the
play, *Go Back for Murder,* which was presented at the
Duchess Theatre in London on March 25, 1960.
Hercule Poirot was eliminated as a character in the
play.

CHARACTERS
Meredith BLAKE, Philip BLAKE, Caroline CRALE, Sir
Montague DEPLEACH, Lord DITTISHAM, Alfred ED-
MUNDS, Quentin FOGG, Elsa GREER, Inspector
HALE, Caleb JONATHAN, Carla LEMARCHANT,
George MAYHEW, Hercule Poirot, John RATTERY,
Angela WARREN, Cecilia WILLIAMS

PLOT SYNOPSIS
Chapter 1
Carla Lemarchant asks Hercule Poirot to investigate
a murder committed sixteen years earlier, in which
her mother, Caroline Crale, was convicted of poisoning her father, Amyas Crale. Carla is engaged to be
married, and fears that her future husband will always view her with suspicion unless she can prove
her mother innocent of the crime. Poirot agrees to
help her; he meets with Quentin Fogg, the Crown
Attorney in the case, to learn the complete details of
the trial.

Chapters 2–3
Poirot speaks with the lawyers who represented the
Crale family interests at the time of the murder and
learns that there was substantial evidence to implicate
Caroline Crale. Inspector Hale tells Poirot that he
believes that Mrs. Crale did not plan to poison her
husband, but that she did so nevertheless. The detective compiles a list of five suspects, his "five little
pigs," from his conversations with Hale, and decides
to determine where everyone was when the murder
occurred. He begins with Philip Blake, a friend of
Amyas, who expresses his view that Mrs. Crale is
guilty.

Chapters 4–6
Meredith Blake, Philip's brother, tells Poirot that
Amyas was having an affair with Elsa Greer, and he

had disapproved. Meredith blames himself for the
murder because the poison was stolen from his laboratory. When he accompanies Poirot to Handcross
Manor to look at Amyas' paintings, the detective
speaks with Lord Dittisham, Elsa's new husband, and
with Elsa about the past. He also interviews the former governess, Cecilia Williams, who states that she
was fond of Mrs. Crale, yet certain of her guilt. Angela Warren, Mrs. Crale's sister, is the only person
who expresses a belief in her innocence.

Chapters 7–9
Poirot asks that each of the five suspects provide him
with a written narrative of the events leading up to
the murder of Amyas Crale. Each provides a different
perspective on the day, and Meredith suggests that
Amyas might have committed suicide. Aside from his
suggestion and Angela's insistence that Mrs. Crale
was innocent, most of the accounts suggest to Carla
that her mother was guilty. In a final effort to obtain
the truth, Poirot calls the five suspects together.

Conclusion
The five suspects arrive and Poirot tries to refresh
their memories about the murder. He correctly identifies the person who really murdered Amyas, then
promises to do everything in his power to obtain a
pardon for Caroline Crale.

CRIME NOTES
The murder in this novel is the result of poisoning
by coniine, a potent extract of hemlock.

Flavelle, Hippolyte A manservant in THE MYS-
TERY OF THE BLUE TRAIN who seeks to protect his
master by lying about the day of his return.

Flavelle, Marie A cook and the wife of Hippolyte FLAVELLE in THE MYSTERY OF THE BLUE TRAIN
who lies about the day of her master's return to protect him.

Fleetwood, Mr. A ship's engineer in DEATH ON
THE NILE (2), he is angry with heiress, Linnet
DOYLE, for revealing to her former maid MARIE that
he is married and has three children.

Flemming, Mr. (1) A London solicitor and an
amateur anthropologist in THE MAN IN THE BROWN

SUIT, he invites the daughter of his late client, Professor BEDDINGFELD, to live with him and his wife.

Flemming, Mr. (2) An attorney in GIANT'S BREAD, he convinces the young heir of Abbots Puissant to leave the estate.

Flemming, Mrs. The wife of a London solicitor in THE MAN IN THE BROWN SUIT, she exudes generosity until called upon to act. When her husband invites a late client's daughter to live with them, Mrs. Flemming reluctantly offers the girl a position as governess.

Fletcher, Sergeant A member of local law enforcement in A MURDER IS ANNOUNCED, he aids Detective Inspector Dermot CRADDOCK in the investigation of murder.

Fletcher, Agnes A parlourmaid in ONE, TWO, BUCKLE MY SHOE who distrusts the police, she waits a long while to report that Frank CARTER had entered the victim's premises near the time of the murder.

Fletcher, Nat Appearing after the murder of Miss GREENSHAW, who had referred to him as her nephew despite the absence of any blood relationship, he provokes suspicion in "GREENSHAW'S FOLLY."

Floating Admiral, The Collaborative mystery novel.

The novel was written serially, with each member of the Detection Club, a prestigious organization of mystery writers, writing a chapter. It was published in the first year of the Detection Club's existence. In addition to Agatha Christie, the following mystery writers contributed to the book: G.K. Chesterton, Canon Victor L. Whitechurch, G.D.H. and M. Cole, Henry Wade, John Rhode, Milward Kennedy, Dorothy L. Sayers, Ronald A. Knox, Freeman Wills Crofts, Edgar Jepson, Clemence Dane and Anthony Berkeley.

PUBLISHING AND DRAMATIZATION
HISTORY
The book was published in 1932 by Doubleday, Doran and Company, Inc., in Garden City, New York.

CONTENT
The novel consists of twelve chapters, of which Agatha Christie wrote Chapter IV, entitled "Mainly Conversation." The overall plot takes place in southern England, where the corpse of Admiral Penistone is found in the vicar's boat, floating down the river Whyn. The established fictional detectives created by the contributors are not involved in the action. Instead, the investigator is a local police inspector, Inspector Rudge of the Whynmouth police. The "Introduction," written by Dorothy L. Sayers, sets forth the rules for each author. Each writer had to write the chapter "with a definite solution in view—that is, he must not introduce new complications merely 'to make it more difficult'." Writers had to also be ready to explain their clues "coherently and plausibly." Christie's eight-page chapter includes her usual tricks, and her solution proposed making the murderer a young man in drag. Writers who followed her subverted that solution by taking the plot into numerous other directions.

"Flock of Geryon, The" Mystery short story.

The story centers on a religious sect that entices new members to bequeath their property to the cult.

PUBLISHING AND DRAMATIZATION
HISTORY
The story appeared in the short story collection, THE LABOURS OF HERCULES, published in 1947 by William Collins Sons and Company, Ltd., in London, and by Dodd, Mead and Company in New York.

The story has not been adapted for stage or screen.

CHARACTERS
Dr. ANDERSEN, Amy CARNABY, Emmeline CLEGG, Mr. COLE, Inspector JAPP, Hercule POIROT

PLOT SYNOPSIS
The Flock of the Shepherd is a religious cult, led by the Great Shepherd, Dr. Andersen, which attracts lonely women who are entranced by the charismatic leader's combination of emotional rhetoric, a magnetic personality, and proffering of drugs. Amy Carnaby suspects Andersen of ulterior motives when her friend joins the cult and is induced to make out a will that leaves all her money to the Flock. She becomes alarmed when she learns that several women have

died of seemingly natural causes soon after making out their wills, so she contacts Hercule Poirot for help.

CRIME NOTES
The murderer makes intensified cultures of various bacteria, such as those that cause ulcerative colitis, typhoid, and pneumonia, and old tuberculin, which stimulates old tubercular lesions into activity, then injects these into his victims.

Florence   A formidable woman in THE MOVING FINGER, she was once the parlourmaid for Emily BARTON, but circumstances have forced her to operate a boardinghouse. Despite her contention that the Barton family caused her change in fortune, she remains fiercely protective of Emily.

Fogg, Quentin   Quiet and unemotional, he is the attorney in FIVE LITTLE PIGS whose persistence achieves remarkable results.

Folliat, Amy   A gardening enthusiast in DEAD MAN'S FOLLY who dresses in shabby tweeds, she lives in the gardener's cottage on the estate of Sir George STUBB. Despite her seemingly innocuous manner, Hercule POIROT perceives that she is capable of being ruthless under the right circumstances.

Folliat, James   A war deserter in Italy who was reported dead, he lives under the assumed name of Sir George STUBBS in DEAD MAN'S FOLLY. He becomes wealthy through the marriage his mother, Amy FOLLIAT, engineers with her mentally deficient but rich ward, Hattie, whom James soon replaces with his real wife, an Italian woman named Elsa who assumes the name of Lady Hattie STUBBS.

Folliott, Mrs. Richard   Anxious to preserve her social position in THE MURDER OF ROGER ACKROYD, she conceals the fact that Ursula BOURNE, the parlourmaid in the household, is her sister, and exhibits disapproval when Ursula marries Roger ACKROYD's stepson.

Forbes, General   Straitlaced and ill-tempered, he is an old army man in "PROBLEM AT SEA" who cannot accept that a former music hall entertainer has earned the right to be called "Colonel." To discharge his consternation, FORBES circles the ship's deck forty-eight times daily.

Forbes, Olgilvie   Present when an old friend and client is murdered, this shrewd lawyer was once a rival for the affections of the dead man's wife in "DEAD MAN'S MIRROR."

Ford, Monica   See GLEN, ASPASIA.

Forrester, Mrs.   A wealthy and neurotic woman in THE HOLLOW, she spends a fortune on her imaginary ills.

Fortescue, Adele   The glamorous young second wife of Rex FORTESCUE, she exudes sex appeal and broadcasts her love of men and money in A POCKET FULL OF RYE. She is a suspect in her husband's murder, but soon afterwards becomes a victim of cyanide.

Fortescue, Elaine   Young and athletic, she is the only daughter of Rex FORTESCUE, and appears bound for a life alone in A POCKET FULL OF RYE. She had once planned to marry Gerald WRIGHT, but her father denounced the relationship and claimed that Gerald was obsessed with Communistic ideas.

Fortescue, Jennifer   A former nurse whose real name is Ruby MACKENZIE, she had tended Percival FORTESCUE when he suffered from pneumonia, after which she married him in A POCKET FULL OF RYE. Her father-in-law feels that his son has married far beneath the social station of the family.

Fortescue, Lancelot   Forced to leave England after forging a check, he lived for a time in East Africa, where he met his wife, Patricia. As part of his plan to obtain the family fortune in A POCKET FULL OF RYE, he takes the name of Albert EVANS, and strikes up a romance with, parlourmaid Gladys MARTIN, who was formerly employed by Miss MARPLE.

Fortescue, Patricia   The twice-widowed daughter of an Irish peer in A POCKET FULL OF RYE, she marries Lancelot FORTESCUE in Kenya, and returns to England with him.

Fortescue, Percival (Val)   Nicknamed "Prim Percy," he is an anemic-looking, tightfisted man in his mid-thirties in A POCKET FULL OF RYE. The likely successor in his father's business, he frequently quarrels with Rex FORTESCUE over investments.

Fortescue, Rex   Twice married, first to Elvira, with whom he produced Lancelot, Percival and Elaine, and then to the much younger Adele, he is an unpleasant man in A POCKET FULL OF RYE who may have cheated a business partner and abandoned him him to die. When Fortescue dies of taxine poisoning, his jacket pocket is found to be filled with rye grain.

Foscarelli, Antonio   A former chauffeur in MURDER ON THE ORIENT EXPRESS (1), he is an Italian with an explosive temper who has become a naturalized America citizen. When questioned, he tells his interrogators more than they wish to know.

Foscatini, Count   A successful blackmailer who bears a false noble title, he becomes a murder victim in "THE ADVENTURE OF THE ITALIAN NOBLEMAN."

Fothergill, Sir Hugo   An old acquaintance of Ariadne OLIVER who is approached by her for information in ELEPHANTS CAN REMEMBER. Despite his numerous stories, his information is of little use.

"Four-and-Twenty Blackbirds"   Mystery short story.
   The change in a man's dining habits intrigues Hercule POIROT, who investigates further to uncover a crime.

PUBLISHING AND DRAMATIZATION HISTORY
The story appeared in the short story collection, THREE BLIND MICE AND OTHER STORIES, published in 1950 by Dodd, Mead and Company in New York.
   The story was adapted for television in 1989 by London Weekend Television in England, and was also shown on the Public Broadcasting Service in the U.S.

CHARACTERS
Henry BONNINGTON, Anthony GASCOIGNE, Henry GASCOIGNE, Dr. George LORIMER, MOLLY, Hercule Poirot

Hercule Poirot (David Suchet) reminds Captain Hastings (Hugh Fraser) once again to observe very carefully in "Four-and-Twenty Blackbirds." (Photo courtesy of London Weekend Television)

PLOT SYNOPSIS
Hercule Poirot is dining with a friend at the Gallant Endeavour when Molly, the waitress, relates a curious story to them. For ten years, an old, bearded man dined every Tuesday and Thursday evening, always ordering the same simple meal. She had been surprised the week before when he entered the restaurant on a Monday evening and ordered thick soup, suet pudding and blackberries, foods he had never ordered before in the whole ten years. This story intrigues the detective, who learns that the old man is dead, and that he had a twin brother.

CRIME NOTES
The sole murder in this story is as a result of being pushed down the stairs.

4.50 from Paddington   Mystery novel.
   The novel concerns the long-hidden secrets of a large family and the consequences of these secrets when murder occurs. The plot centers on the efforts of Miss MARPLE to identify a murderer whom her friend observed strangling a woman on a train.

PUBLISHING AND DRAMATIZATION HISTORY
The novel was published in 1957 by William Collins Sons and Company in London, and, under the title,

The paperback book for the 1961 movie version of *4.50 from Paddington,* **which was entitled** *Murder She Said.* (Photo courtesy of the R. Gregor collection)

What Mrs. McGillicuddy Saw!, by Dodd, Mead and Company in New York.

The novel was adapted for television in 1988 by the BBC and also shown on the Public Broadcasting System in the U.S. The feature film adapted from this novel, entitled *Murder She Said,* was released by MGM in 1962 and starred Margaret Rutherford as Miss Marple.

CHARACTERS

Inspector BACON, Alfred CRACKENTHORPE, Lady Alice CRACKENTHORPE, Cedric CRACKENTHORPE, Emma CRACKENTHORPE, Harold CRACKENTHORPE, Luther CRACKENTHORPE, Chief Inspector Dermot CRADDOCK, Armand DESSIN, Alexander EASTLEY, Bryan EASTLEY, Miss ELLIS, Lucy EYELESBARROW, Florence HILL, Madame JOLIET, Mrs. KIDDER, Miss Jane Marple, Elspeth McGILLICUDDY, Dr. MORRIS, Dr. QUIMPER, Lady STODDARD-WEST, James STOD-DARD-WEST, Anna STRAVINSKA, David WEST, Mr. WIMBOURNE

PLOT SYNOPSIS
Chapters 1–3
Mrs. McGillicuddy sees a woman being strangled on a passing train as she returns to her friend Jane Marple's home after a day of Christmas shopping. She tells the ticket collector, but he simply takes her name and address. She tells Miss Marple about what she saw, and the two friends search the next morning's newspapers but find no word of the murder. Miss Marple contacts a friend in law enforcement, but no recent murders have been reported. Undaunted, the elderly detective takes a train to pinpoint the scene of the crime, then uses maps and a railroad schedule to determine the most opportune place for the body to have been thrown from the train.

Chapters 4–7
After identifying Rutherford Hall, the ancestral home of the Crackenthorpe family, as the most likely site, Miss Marple contacts Lucy Eyelesbarrow, who once took care of her when she had pneumonia. She asks Lucy to obtain a position at Rutherford Hall to gather information, a plan to which Lucy agrees but which she can do for only three weeks. Lucy takes a position working for Luther Crackenthorpe and his daughter Emma. While playing golf one day, she finds some brownish fur on a twig, and a makeup compact nearby. When she takes these to Miss Marple, the two discuss the sheds, barns and bushes as possible hiding places for the body. On the pretext of searching for paint with Emma's schoolboy nephew and his friend, Lucy finds the body in a sarcophagus. After telling Miss Marple, she calls the police and tells Emma. No one can identify the body, and everyone agrees that the barn was freely open to everyone in the area, because the key always hangs outside the door.

Chapters 8–11
The local police believe that the dead girl came from France, based on an examination of her clothing, so they feel it necessary to call in Scotland Yard. When the family lawyer informs the Crackenthorpe family that the dead woman is probably a foreigner, Emma blurts out "Was she French?" Chief Inspector

Craddock questions the family members, then visits Miss Marple to provide her with an update on the investigation. The authorities send a photograph of the woman to Mrs. McGillicuddy, now in Ceylon, and she identifies her as the woman she saw strangled on the train. She cannot, however, provide a description of the man, aside from remembering that he was tall, dark and more than thirty years of age. Emma questions whether the dead woman might be her late brother Edmund's widow Martine, who had made contact with the family for the first time only a month before but canceled a scheduled visit.

Chapters 12–13
While the investigation continues, Lucy becomes the object of affection of the Crackenthorpe men. First, Luther advises her that young men are no good and have nothing to offer, then, Alfred offers her a job and asks her to marry him, and finally, Harold asserts that he could make better use of her obvious talents at a good salary in his firm. She puts off all three suitors.

Chapters 14–18
Craddock follows a lead to Paris to investigate the possibility that the dead woman might be a ballerina named Anna Stravinska. He interviews several people and learns that she left at about the same time that the dead woman was found. When he returns to England, Craddock speaks with Mr. Wimbourne in order to learn to what Edmund's son might be entitled. He questions Harold, Alfred and Cedric regarding their whereabouts on the day of the murder, but their responses are vague. Craddock also speaks with Dr. Quimper regarding Luther's gastritis attack at Christmas, and learns that he showed signs of arsenic poisoning.

Chapters 19–22
Harold and Alfred chastise Emma for telling the police about Martine, and Harold tells Dr. Quimper that he should not have advised Emma to do so. After dinner, everyone in the house except Lucy becomes ill, so she calls Dr. Quimper. He diagnoses arsenic poisoning, of which Alfred dies. When Luther learns that his son has died, he laughs and states that he will outwit them all. Bryan Eastley, widower of Luther's daughter, comments that everyone left in the family would have to die for his son, Alexander, to get his inheritance.

Chapters 23–25
During this time, Lady Stoddard-West, the mother of Alexander's schoolfriend, arrives and tells Emma that she is really Martine, the woman who had been married to and then widowed by Edmund Crackenthorpe. She had worked with the French Resistance, which was how she met her present husband. Meanwhile, Harold returns to his office and wonders why Alfred died and Luther lived. When he goes home that evening, he tells his wife about his concerns. He notices a small parcel on the hall table. The bottle within is from Dr. Quimper, and the label states "two tablets to be taken nightly." Harold takes them and dies. Dr. Quimper claims not to have sent the parcel. Lucy learns that Bryan had been on the 4.50 from Paddington, and observes that his fair hair could look dark in dim light.

Chapters 26–27
Mrs. McGillicuddy returns from Ceylon and accompanies Miss Marple to Rutherford Hall to join the family in celebrating Dr. Quimper's birthday. Miss Marple pretends to choke on a fish bone and one of the men present attempts to help her. As he stands in front of her, forceps in hand and peering down her throat, Mrs. McGillicuddy views him from behind and recognizes him as the man on the train. Miss Marple then reveals that the dead girl was Anna Stravinska and that the killer was married to her. He had poisoned the family members and killed her in an attempt to gain control of the Crackenthorpe family fortune.

CRIME NOTES
In this novel, one murder victim is strangled and two die of arsenic poisoning.

The introduction of Lucy Eyelesbarrow as a sidekick to Miss Marple was lauded by critics when the book came out, but Miss Marple did not work with her again.

Fournier, Monsieur A French Inspector from the Sûreté, he works with Hercule POIROT and Inspector JAPP to solve a murder in DEATH IN THE CLOUDS.

"Four Suspects, The" Mystery short story.

The story involves the murder of a retired counterspy by one of four trusted members of his household.

PUBLISHING AND DRAMATIZATION HISTORY

The story appeared in the short story collection, THE THIRTEEN PROBLEMS, published in 1932 by William Collins Sons and Company in London, and, under the title, *The Tuesday Club Murders,* by Dodd, Mead and Company in 1933 in New York.

The story has not been adapted for stage or screen.

CHARACTERS

Colonel BANTRY, Dolly BANTRY, Sir Henry CLITHER-ING, Mr. DOBBS, Miss MARPLE, Dr. ROSEN, Greta ROSEN, Mrs. Gertrud SCHWARTZ, Charles TEM-PLETON

PLOT SYNOPSIS

At a meeting of the Tuesday Night Club, Sir Henry Clithering tells the story of former counterspy Dr. Rosen, whose activities had helped to weaken the German secret society, the Schwarze Hand. He retired to a small English village, where he lived in obscurity with a secretary appointed by Scotland Yard, his longtime maid, his niece, and a local gardener. He had recently died of a broken neck after falling down a flight of stairs, and his four household members were all suspects. Given the details by Sir Henry, Miss Marple correctly names the murderer.

CRIME NOTES

The secret organization, the Schwarze Hand, is German for Black Hand.

"Fourth Man, The"   Mystery short story.

Four men who are traveling by train in the same first-class carriage discuss the strange case of a woman with four distinct personalities.

PUBLISHING AND DRAMATIZATION HISTORY

The story appeared in the short story collection, THE HOUND OF DEATH AND OTHER STORIES, published in 1933 by William Collins Sons and Company in London.

The story was adapted for television in 1982 by Thames Television in England.

As the mysterious French traveler, Raoul Letar-deau (played by John Nettles) in "The Fourth Man" provides fellow travelers with information about a girl with multiple personalities.   (Photo courtesy of Thames Television)

CHARACTERS

Felicie BAULT, Dr. Campbell CLARK, Sir George DURAND, Raoul LETARDEAN, Canon PARFITT, Annette RAVEL

PLOT SYNOPSIS

A discussion by three travelers—a lawyer, a cleric and a psychologist—turns to the famous case of Felicie Bault, a mentally limited French peasant who had developed four distinct personalities by the age of twenty-two. A fourth man in the carriage listens as they ponder the fragmented personalities, which ranged from the lazy and stupid Felicie to the intelligent and pleasant Felicie, the immoral third Felicie, and the ethereal Felicie. The fourth man joins them with firsthand information about the case. He claims that Felicie had been hypnotized and enslaved by a singer named Annette Ravel, whose influence on the peasant girl continued even after death.

Fowler, Mrs.   A witness in THE A.B.C. MURDERS, she accepts five pounds from Hercule POIROT to tell all that she knows about the murder of Alice ASCHER.

Fox, Sybil   Obsessed by the puppet doll in "THE DRESSMAKER'S DOLL," the fabric cutter insists that the doll was becoming too strong to deal with.

Frances, Nurse   Hired to care for the young protagonist in GIANT'S BREAD when he breaks his leg in a fall, she is the first adult to treat his childhood fears with dignity, and his first friend.

Francois   A butler in "THE CHOCOLATE BOX," he provides Hercule POIROT with an important clue when he informs the detective that the victim was extremely fond of chocolates.

Franklin, Angela and Arthur   Parents in THE BURDEN who shut out the love of their daughter after the death of their son, they fail to perceive the intensity of their daughter's desire to be loved. They die in a plane crash while returning from a vacation.

Franklin, Barbara (Babs)   The unhappy wife of a physician in CURTAIN, she is a frail, sickly woman who moved Captain HASTINGS to view her as "the madonna type." Criticized by others for feigning illness, she is murdered by someone who places a Calabar bean in her coffee.

Franklin, Charles   Viewed as the light of his family, he dies of polio early in THE BURDEN, thus setting the events of the novel into motion.

Franklin, Dr. John   A brilliant researcher in tropical diseases in CURTAIN, he contends that he would like to kill many people, and that he would have no guilt afterwards, especially since "about eighty percent of the human race *ought* to be eliminated." After his wife dies from Calabar bean poisoning, he marries his assistant and they leave for Africa.

Franklin, Laura   An intensely loving and solicitous child in THE BURDEN, she is ignored by her parents, who consider her inferior to their high-spirited son. After her brother dies from polio, she feels that her parents will now love her. After recuperating from their grief, they have another child. Laura prays for her infant sister Shirley to die but, when her prayers seem to be answered in the form of an extensive house fire, eleven-year-old Laura risks her life to save the baby. She then makes it her life's mission to guarantee Shirley's happiness. Only after Shirley dies can Laura seek her own happiness.

Franklin, Shirley   Conceived by her grief-stricken parents as a child to replace their dead son in THE BURDEN, she experiences first the jealousy and then the undying devotion of her older sister. After a first marriage to a selfish philanderer, she marries a wealthy adventurer who also tries to protect her. Unable to attain happiness, Shirley turns to drink, eventually taking her own life.

Fraser, Donald   The fiancé of murder victim Elizabeth BARNARD in THE A.B.C. MURDERS, he had threatened to kill her if she dated other men.

Freebody, Miss   See DEBANHAM, MARY HERMIONE.

French, Emily   The elderly murder victim in "WITNESS FOR THE PROSECUTION," she leaves all her money to Leonard VOLE, her friend and financial manager.

French, Irene   See HOBHOUSE, VALERIE.

Frobisher, Colonel George   Aware of the history of insanity in the family of Admiral Charles CHANDLER, he becomes concerned about the actions of young Hugh CHANDLER, but refrains from interfering in family matters in "THE CRETAN BULL."

"Fruitful Sunday, A"   Mystery short story.
   The plot centers on the adventures of a young office clerk whose Sunday afternoon drive and stop at a fruit stand result in a valuable surprise.

PUBLISHING AND DRAMATIZATION HISTORY

The story appeared in the short story collection, THE LISTERDALE MYSTERY (1), published in 1934 by William Collins Sons and Company, Ltd., in London.

The story has not been adapted for stage or screen.

CHARACTERS

Edward PALGROVE, Dorothy PRATT

PLOT SYNOPSIS

The story concerns Edward Palgrove, an office clerk who takes his girlfriend, Dorothy, out for a Sunday drive. They stop at a fruit stand and buy a box of cherries, then sit alongside the river and read the newspaper, learning about the theft of a valuable ruby necklace. As they eat the cherries, Dorothy finds a necklace underneath them in the box, which is identical to the one described in the article. The pair must then decide whether to keep it or to turn it over to the authorities.

Fullerton, Jeremy   Well-respected as a partner in the respectable old law firm of Fullerton, Harrison and Leadbetter in HALLOWE'EN PARTY, he misjudges the acuity of Hercule POIROT when the detective questions him about a murder.

Fullerton, Lavinia   While on a train journey to Scotland Yard to report the many suspicious deaths in her village, she meets retired policeman Luke FITZWILLIAM and provides him with clues to solve the case in MURDER IS EASY. He intervenes too late to save her life.

Funerals Are Fatal   See AFTER THE FUNERAL.

G

Gabriel, John An evil and ambitious politician in THE ROSE AND THE YEW TREE, he ruthlessly uses those around him to achieve his own aims, without concern for their suffering and pain. After the self-sacrificing death of a young woman, he reevaluates his life, and devotes himself to easing human misery, becoming the highly respected Father Clement.

Gaigh, Lady Elizabeth The daughter of a marquis in "THE GIRL IN THE TRAIN," she impersonates the Grand Duchess ANASTASIA in order to help her brother to elope with the real Anastasia. She eventually marries George ROWLAND because he is not only gallant but wealthy, and will allow her to continue her favorite activity, spending money. The match is approved by both families because her father has wanted a rich son-in-law, while George's family is impressed by her social position.

Gaitskill, Mr. A competent and respected elderly solicitor in CROOKED HOUSE, he is fooled when his client, Aristide LEONIDES, substitutes a different version for the original will. The cautious and precise solicitor feels particularly insulted because his long friendship with the client should have inspired trust.

Galbraith, Mr. An eighty-year-old man in SLEEPING MURDER who has recently suffered a stroke, he is the senior partner in a realty firm, and had served in India. He now tells the same stories repeatedly.

Gale, Margery Heir to the STRANLEIGH title, she is a young woman who loves one man, but is pursued by a distant relative who just happens to be next in line for the family title in "THE VOICE IN THE DARK."

Gale, Marilyn A celebrity in DEAD MAN'S FOLLY, she is scheduled to appear and participate in the murder hunt.

Gale, Norman Known in a previous life in South America as James RICHARDS, he is a dentist who is flying home on the *Prometheus* when Madame Giselle MORISOT is murdered in DEATH IN THE CLOUDS. Infatuated with fellow passenger Jane GREY, he agrees to help Hercule POIROT in the investigation and disguises himself as "John ROBINSON" to pretend to blackmail a suspect as a means of gaining information.

Ganett, Miss A neighbor of Caroline and Dr. James SHEPPARD in MURDER IS EASY, she is also a member of their mah-jongg group.

Gapp, Florence (Flossie) See RIVAL, MERLINA.

Garcia, Dr. Alan A distinguished and learned pathologist attached to the British Home Office in both SAD CYPRESS and "THE LERNEAN HYDRA," he enthusiastically describes the results of autopsies and exhumations.

Gardener, Carrie An annoyingly talkative American tourist in EVIL UNDER THE SUN, she bores everyone within earshot, including her apparently pliant husband.

Gardiner, John Secretary to Hugo LEMESURIER, he has an affair with his employer's wife that results in the birth of a son whom Hugo believes is his. After his employer's death, John marries the widow in "THE LEMESURIER INHERITANCE."

Gardner, Mrs. Her only son had been saved from prison by Mr. PARKER PYNE, so she gratefully agrees to carry out his plan to arrange happiness for the wealthy Amelia RYMER in "THE CASE OF THE RICH WOMAN."

Gardner, Jennifer The doting wife of the invalid Captain Robert GARDNER, she is a beautiful woman with an overpowering personality in THE SITTAFORD MYSTERY. She is estranged from her brother, Captain TREVELYAN, and openly hostile toward her husband's nurse.

Gardner, Captain Robert An invalid with no physical basis for the loss of the use of his limbs in THE SITTAFORD MYSTERY, he is incapacitated by his psychological disorder and basks in the adoration of both his wife and his nurse, while he peevishly courts their constant attention.

Garfield, Michael This attractive, mysterious, young architect in HALLOWE'EN PARTY irreverently calls Hercule POIROT "Senior Mustachios" and criticizes the famous detective's habit of wearing elegant yet painful footwear. Bequeathed property when a wealthy former client dies, he too loses his life soon afterwards.

Garfield, Ronald The weak, spineless nephew of the ailing Caroline PERCEHOUSE, he accedes to his aunt's every wish in the hope of becoming heir to her substantial fortune in THE SITTAFORD MYSTERY. He is unaware that she pities him and wishes that he would stand up to her.

Garnett, Patricia (Pat) Attractive and impulsive, she is close friends with two young men who are rivals for her affection in "THE THIRD-FLOOR FLAT." She becomes involved in a murder when she is locked out of her apartment and the two young men break into the wrong apartment while assisting her.

Garrod, Grace The niece of Simon CLODE, she fears being disinherited in "MOTIVE VERSUS OPPORTUNITY."

Garrod, Philip Anxious to guarantee that his wife, Grace GARROD, will receive her inheritance in "MOTIVE VERSUS OPPORTUNITY," he concocts a disappearing ink and fills her uncle's fountain pen with it. The pen is used to write a new will, but the ink fades soon after the will is written, and the late uncle's new will appears as only a blank sheet of paper.

Garroway, Chief Superintendent Head of the investigation into the presumed suicides of General and Lady RAVENSCROFT, he refuses to accept the official version of the deaths in ELEPHANTS CAN REMEMBER; he suspects murder instead.

Gascoigne, Henry An artist estranged from his twin brother, who had married and given up art, he is a diner of regular habits in "FOUR-AND-TWENTY BLACKBIRDS" whom the waitresses call "Old Father Time" because of his long white beard. On the Monday night before his death from a fall downstairs, he not only dines on a night other than his usual Tuesday and Thursday, but also orders a very rich meal unlike any he had ordered in the previous ten years.

Gaskell, Mark Boastful and unreliable, he is nonetheless a man who attracts women and who usually asserts his will with competitors in THE BODY IN THE LIBRARY. He keeps his second marriage a secret in order to inherit half of his late first wife's estate.

"Gate of Baghdad, The" Mystery short story.

A worried military officer is murdered before he reveals his concern to Mr. PARKER PYNE, who must now discover the murderer.

PUBLISHING AND DRAMATIZATION HISTORY

The story appeared in the short story collection, PARKER PYNE INVESTIGATES, published in 1934 by William Collins Sons and Company, Ltd., in London, and, under the title, *Mr. Parker Pyne, Detective*, in 1934 by Dodd, Mead and Company in New York.

The story has not been adapted for stage or screen.

CHARACTERS

Mr. HENSLEY, Flight Lieutenant LOFTUS, Flight Lieutenant O'ROURKE, Mr. and Mrs. PENTEMIAN, Signor POLI, Miss PRYCE, Netta PRYCE, Mr. Parker Pyne, Captain SMETHURST, Flight Lieutenant WILLIAMSON

PLOT SYNOPSIS

A murder occurs while a group of people on tour in the Middle East are traveling from Damascus to Baghdad. The party includes Mr. Parker Pyne, as well as RAF officers and several civilian tourists. Captain Smethurst tells Parker Pyne that he is worried, but he is murdered before he can go into detail. After investigating the group, Parker Pyne learns that the murder is related to the disappearance of a stock market embezzler, Samuel LONG.

CRIME NOTES

The sole murder results from a blow to the head.

Gaunt, Emma   A devoted housemaid who nurses her master, Simon CLODE, without complaint in "MOTIVE VERSUS OPPORTUNITY," she serves as a witness to the new will written in disappearing ink.

Gentleman Dressed in Newspaper, The   See FINESSING THE KING.

George   The talkative old gardener in "PHILOMEL COTTAGE" whose questions raise doubts in the mind of the newly married Alix King MARTIN.

George/Georges   He is the epitome of the English valet, a gentleman's gentleman who agreed to serve Hercule POIROT only after the great detective had been received at Buckingham Palace. Through twenty-one adventures, he hovers in the background, referred to as "George" in some adventures and as "Georges" in others, impeccable and imperturbable no matter how great the danger or the distress of his famous employer. George first appears in MURDER ON THE LINKS as a new foil for Poirot, whose friend, Captain HASTINGS, has long since departed for Argentina. He is frequently consulted by Poirot for background knowledge of the English aristocracy and to confirm the appropriateness of behavior peculiar to the English upper classes. In the rare instances when Poirot seeks an opinion from George, neither appears very comfortable, and the result is usually discreet throat-clearing with a laconic response from George and an assertion by Poirot that his valet does not possess an imagination. George is with Poirot until the final novel, CURTAIN, in which he barely manages to maintain his unemotional facade when

informed that his employer has died. (See also CATEGORICAL INDEX.)

George, Uncle   A white-haired old man in "MYSTERY OF THE BLUE JAR," he returns early from a trip to the Continent. He is also the owner of the blue jar that his nephew Jack, HARTINGTON, attempts to use in contacting the ghost of Mrs. TURNER.

Gerard, Ted   A handsome and charming young man in "THE TAPE-MEASURE MURDER," he recruits members for a religious organization named The Oxford Group.

Gerard, Dr. Theodore   An accidental witness to the dysfunctional BOYNTON family while on vacation in Jerusalem, this well-known and highly respected psychologist in APPOINTMENT WITH DEATH is close at hand when murder occurs. He falls under suspicion when an investigation reveals that a hypodermic needle and digitoxin are missing from his medical case.

Geronimo   An Italian-born servant in HICKORY DICKORY DOCK, his eavesdropping provides investigators with valuable information.

Gerrard, Bob   See GERRARD, EPHRAIM.

Gerrard, Ephraim   A caretaker on the Welman estate, he and his wife have been paid to raise Mary GERRARD as their own daughter in SAD CYPRESS. He begins to resent his foster daughter because her real mother provides the money for Mary to obtain a good education and to enjoy other lessons of refinement.

Gerrard, Mary   The offspring of a passionate love affair between Sir Lewis RYCROFT and Laura WELMAN, she is raised by the estate caretaker and his wife in SAD CYPRESS. Her real mother provides for her education and plans to secure Mary's future, but the young woman dies when she ingests fish paste sandwiches laced heavily with morphine.

Gertie   The real name of a longtime jewel thief in "THE VEILED LADY" who is well-known to Inspector JAPP, she assumes the name Lady Millicent Castle VAUGHN, and claims that she must gain access to a particular home to retrieve a letter which could destroy her engagement to the jealous Duke of Southshire. Despite her clever acting, Hercule POIROT unmasks her.

Giant's Bread   Non-mystery novel.

The first of the novels written as Mary WESTMACOTT, and the only one dedicated to the author's "truest friend," her mother Clara MILLER, Giant's Bread displays an extensive knowledge of music. The story centers on composer Vernon DEYRE, erroneously reported as killed in action in World War I, who assumes a new identity, and wins acclaim in the music world.

PUBLISHING AND DRAMATIZATION HISTORY
Giant's Bread was first published in 1930 by William Collins Sons and Company in London, and by Doubleday and Company in New York in 1930.

The novel has not been adapted for stage or screen.

CHARACTERS
George CHETWYND, Myra DEYRE, Vernon Deyre, Walter DEYRE, Mr. FLEMING, Nurse FRANCES, Mr. GREEN, Jane HARDING, KATIE, Mr. and Mrs. LEVINNE, Sebastian LEVINNE, Aunt NINA, Mrs. PASCAL, Miss ROBBINS, SUSAN, Uncle SYDNEY, Nell VEREKER, Josephine WAITE, WINNIE

PLOT SYNOPSIS
Book I–Abbots Puissants
The decaying Deyre family estate is the setting of arguments between Walter and Myra over Walter's philandering, while their young son Vernon listens. Vernon lives on the family estate, Abbots Puissants, for ten years and forms lifelong attachments to his cousin Josephine and a neighbor Sebastian. Book I ends as young Vernon yearns to keep Abbots Puissants in the family.

Book II–Nell
Nearly twenty-one years old, Vernon fears that he will lose his heavily mortgaged estate. He meets and falls in love with Nell Vereker, but her social-climbing mother aims for a rich match. Torn between Nell and his music, Vernon is influenced by the worldly Jane Harding, who forces him to confront his desires.

Book III–Jane
Vernon risks his future, severs family ties and throws himself into composing an opera. Jane encourages him, and obtains funding to produce the opera.

Jane consoles Vernon when Josephine runs off with a married sculptor and Nell contemplates marrying a rich American businessman, but he drinks heavily. When war is declared, Nell begs Vernon's forgiveness, and the two marry immediately.

Book IV–War
Vernon goes into combat and Nell becomes a hospital volunteer. She learns in a telegram that Vernon is dead; she inherits his family estate. Nell sells it to an unnamed buyer. She learns later that he is her former fiancé George Chetwynd, and they marry. When Vernon escapes from a prison camp and learns of Nell's remarriage, he tries to commit suicide, but loses his memory.

Book V–George Green
Four years later, Vernon is a chauffeur for a rich American acquaintance of George Chetwynd. They have lunch at Abbots Puissants on the same day as Jane Harding. Nell is shocked to see Vernon, who does not remember her, but Jane later jars Vernon's memory. He speaks with Nell, but leaves her alone when she hints that she is pregnant. Vernon goes to Russia with Jane, and studies the social concepts of the Machine Age and Collective Man. When they leave Russia, they meet Nell and George Chetwynd on the return ship, which rams an iceberg. Vernon is forced to choose who to save from drowning, Nell or Jane.

Gibbs, Amy   Impertinent and lacking moral sense, she is a maid who is fired by Lord EASTERFIELD because of her behavior in MURDER IS EASY. When she dies in her locked bedroom after swallowing red hat paint which looks similar to cough syrup, her death is ruled a suicide.

Gibson, Old Mother   She is an old and irascible woman in "MR. EASTWOOD'S ADVENTURE" who owns an antique glassware shop. The Patterson gang uses the rooms above her shop to swindle a collector of valuable miniature enamels.

Gilbey, Miss   As the stern headmistress of St. Anne's School in ABSENT IN THE SPRING, her

advocation of discipline makes a lasting impression on the main character's life.

Gilchrist, Miss A long-suffering housekeeper and companion to the constantly complaining Cora LANSQUENET, she is the stereotypical spinster in AFTER THE FUNERAL. A piece of wedding cake laced liberally with arsenic nearly kills her.

Gilchrist, Dr. Maurice The resident physician to movie star Marina GREGG, he fully understands the pressures under which his patient must function in THE MIRROR CRACK'D FROM SIDE TO SIDE. The doctor recognizes that Marina needs a psychologist more than a physician.

Giles, Dr. His capable appearance and commanding presence in "THE MARKET BASING MYSTERY" make it possible for the doctor to assume control when he is called in at the death of Walter PROTHERO.

Gilles, M. The Chief of the Detective Force of the Sûreté in Paris, he works with Hercule POIROT to investigate murder in DEATH IN THE CLOUDS.

Gilliat, Beryl The scheming second wife of Simon GILLIAT, she plots in "THE HARLEQUIN TEA SET" to gain an inheritance for her son. In the process, she must do away with her stepson, Timothy GILLIAT, the grandson of the man whose fortune she hopes to claim.

Gilliat, Lily Addison The victim of an automobile accident in Kenya, she is already dead when "THE HARLEQUIN TEA SET" begins, but her presence is felt throughout the story. Her son is in danger from the stepmother who seeks to claim a family fortune, and Lily's spirit must depend upon the intervention of Mr. SATTERTHWAITE to save him.

Gilliat, Roland (Roly) Born Roland EDEN, he is the stepson of Simon GILLIAT and the son of Lily Addison GILLIAT, and he assumes his stepfather's last name in "THE HARLEQUIN TEA SET." Beryl GILLIAT, his mother, strives to make him heir to Thomas ADDISON's fortune in place of his stepbrother, Timothy GILLIAT, and passes her son off as the actual grandson.

Gilliat, Simon A former World War II Squadron Leader in the Royal Air Force in "THE HARLEQUIN TEA SET" whose first wife, Lily Addison GILLIAT, died and left him with a son, Timothy GILLIAT. He is unaware of his second wife's determined scheming to obtain his former father-in-law's fortune for her son, Roland GILLIAT, and of her plot to make everyone believe that Roland is a blood member of the Gilliat family.

Gilliat, Timothy The son of Simon GILLIAT and the late Lily Addison GILLIAT, he has watched for years as his stepbrother has been identified as Simon's real son in "THE HARLEQUIN TEA SET." Despite the efforts of his stepmother, Beryl GILLIAT, to deny that he is the true heir to Thomas ADDISON's fortune, he carries the family trait of color blindness borne by Addison males.

Gince, Miss A fortyish frump with frizzy hair, a pince-nez, buck teeth and a simpering smile in THE MOVING FINGER, she is the victim of a poison-pen letter that accuses her of having an affair with her boss. To save her reputation from further harm, she leaves the law firm where she works as a clerk.

"Gipsy, The" Mystery short story.
A man who is deathly afraid of gipsies encounters a woman with second sight who foresees his demise.

PUBLISHING AND DRAMATIZATION HISTORY
The story appeared in the short story collection, THE HOUND OF DEATH AND OTHER STORIES, published in 1933 by William Collins Sons and Company in London.

The story has not been adapted for stage or screen.

CHARACTERS
Dickie CARPENTER, Mrs. Alistair HAWORTH-FERGUESSON, Esther LAWES, Rachel LAWES, Mr. MACFARLANE

PLOT SYNOPSIS
As a child, sailor Dickie Carpenter had been badly frightened by a gipsy, and he carries his fear into adulthood. Brokenhearted after Esther Lawes breaks off their engagement, he visits his friend, Macfarlane,

who is engaged to Esther's younger sister, Rachel. He tells Macfarlane about a dream in which the fair-haired Alistair Haworth-Ferguesson appears as a gipsy to warn him of danger. Soon after, he dies during surgery on his leg.

Giraud, Monsieur A proponent of scientific methodology and hard evidence in crime detection, this member of the Paris Sûreté clashes with the cerebral approach of Hercule POIROT when the two work together on the murder investigation in MURDER ON THE LINKS. As a man of action, Giraud views Poirot as quaint and old-fashioned, while the great detective views Giraud as nothing more than a "human foxhound." In the end, Giraud must yield to Poirot's expertise in solving the case.

"Girdle of Hippolyta, The" Mystery short story.

The plot centers on the missing pupil of an exclusive finishing school for girls in Paris, and a stolen painting by Rubens.

PUBLISHING AND DRAMATIZATION HISTORY
The story appears in the short story collection, THE LABOURS OF HERCULES, which was published by William Collins Sons and Company, Ltd., in London, in 1947 and by Dodd, Mead and Company in New York.

The story has not been adapted for stage or screen.

CHARACTERS
Miss BURSHAW, Detective Inspector HEARN, Chief Inspector JAPP, Winifred KING, Hercule POIROT, Miss Lavinia POPE, Alexander SIMPSON

PLOT SYNOPSIS
Two apparently unrelated crimes attract the attention of Hercule Poirot, and only he is able to determine their connection. Contacted by the owner of Simpson's Gallery regarding a stolen painting by Rubens, the detective prepares to leave for France to investigate the theft. At the same time, Chief Inspector Japp consults Poirot about the intriguing puzzle of an English schoolgirl who has been kidnapped while en route to a prestigious finishing school for girls in Paris. When the obviously drugged girl is

found along a road the following day, Poirot uncovers the clues which help him to locate the missing painting and to discover the reason for the kidnapping.

CRIME NOTES
In Greek mythology, the ninth labor of Hercules was to enter the land of the Amazons and to obtain the golden girdle of Hyppolita, the Queen of the Amazons. In this story, the stolen painting is Rubens' *The Girdle of Hyppolita*.

"Girl in the Train, The" Mystery short story.

The plot focuses on the adventures of a recently disinherited playboy who befriends a woman whom he believes to be a Grand Duchess, and becomes involved with German spies who seek plans to Portsmouth harbor.

PUBLISHING AND DRAMATIZATION HISTORY
The story appeared in the short story collection, THE LISTERDALE MYSTERY, published in 1934 by William Collins Sons and Company, Ltd., in London.

The story was adapted for television in 1982 by Thames Television in England, and was also shown on the Public Broadcasting Service in the U.S.

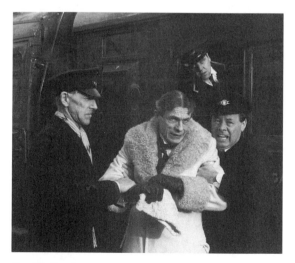

David Neal as Prince Osric in "The Girl in the Train" is accosted by porters as he tries to find his niece, the Grand Duchess. (Photo courtesy of Thames Television)

CHARACTERS
Grand Duchess ANASTASIA (Alexa), Lady Elizabeth GAIGH, Detective Inspector JARROLD, Prince KARL, Prince OSRIC, George ROWLAND

PLOT SYNOPSIS

After being disinherited by his uncle, a dejected George Rowland boards a train bound for a destination chosen only because it contains his last name. On the train, a young woman claiming to be the Grand Duchess Anastasia pleads for him to hide her, which he does. She hints at grave danger, and asks him to follow a mysterious, black-bearded man while she heads for safety. After an encounter with the police over the matter of German spies and espionage, George learns that the mysterious woman is actually the Lady Elizabeth GAIGH, who had posed as the Grand Duchess to allow her brother to elope with the real Anastasia. He proposes to Elizabeth, whose father is looking for a rich son-in-law, which George will easily become once his uncle learns that Elizabeth is a blue-blood.

Giselle, Madame   Unattractive in both appearance and personality, she is a moneylender also known as Marie Angelique MORISOT in DEATH IN THE CLOUDS who gathered damaging information about her clients to use for purposes of blackmail. When she dies on a Paris-to-England flight, during which she is shot with a poisoned dart dipped in boomslang snake venom, she leaves her daughter an estate worth over one hundred thousand pounds.

Giuseppe   Charming, handsome and passionate, he is an Italian butler employed by actress Marina GREGG and desired by all the female servants of nearby households in THE MIRROR CRACK'D FROM SIDE TO SIDE. He makes the fatal mistake of attempting blackmail, and is shot to death.

Gladys (1)   A young, pretty parlourmaid in UN-FINISHED PORTRAIT, she replaces an old retainer.

Gladys (Gladdie) (2)   Colonel PROTHEROE's kitchenmaid in MURDER AT THE VICARAGE, she resembles a shivering rabbit.

Gladys (3)   A maid in "THE CASE OF THE PERFECT MAID," she is falsely accused of theft.

Gladys (4)   A silly and curious maid in "THE LERNEAN HYDRA," she yields to Hercule POIROT's charming questions.

Gladys (5)   The third housemaid in the Astwell residence in "THE UNDER DOG," she humors Hercule POIROT when he asks to see the dress worn by her mistress on the night of the murder.

Glen, Aspasia   An extremely skilled impersonator in "THE DEAD HARLEQUIN," she works as a nursery governess under the name of Monica FORD and falsely claims that she was pregnant by the lord of the manor. She also disguises herself to be mistaken for the ghostly figures of "The Weeping Lady with the Silver Ewer" and "The Woman with the Scarf."

Glen, Gilda   A famous and beautiful English actress in "THE MAN IN THE MIST," she hides her common origins and marriage to a policeman, from whom she seeks a divorce. A veteran performer, she is aware of her personal magnetism and the effect her beauty has upon men, but she is unaware that an enemy wants her dead.

Gldyr, Major Boris Andrei Pavlov   A man of many faces and identities in DESTINATION UN-KNOWN, and the nephew of the brilliant scientist, Professor MANNHEIM, he seeks the truth about the disappearances of major scientists worldwide. An F.B.I agent, he poses as research chemist Andrew PETERS to infiltrate Mr. ARISTIDES' closely guarded Brain Trust, where he espouses an idealist view of the future. He later disguises himself as a Moroccan servant named Sidi to gain further information about the Brain Trust. His plans are endangered when he falls in love with Hilary CRAVEN.

Glyn-Edwards, Henry   A self-centered, charming philanderer in THE BURDEN, he makes his wife's life miserable by keeping them in debt and having numerous extramarital affairs. He contracts polio and becomes an invalid, then dies after receiving a double dose of sleeping potion.

Glynne, Lavinia Bradbury-Scott   One of three sisters in NEMESIS, she is perceived by Miss MARPLE as being normal and pleasant but not a happy woman.

Go Back for Murder   See FIVE LITTLE PIGS.

Goby, Mr.   A nondescript man who seems to fade into the woodwork and who assiduously avoids eye contact, he is the private investigator to whom Hercule POIROT turns for critical and difficult-to-obtain information in AFTER THE FUNERAL, THIRD GIRL and ELEPHANTS CAN REMEMBER. His services are also retained by millionaire Rufus VAN ALDIN in THE MYSTERY OF THE BLUE TRAIN.

Goedler, Belle   A widowed invalid who enjoys life immensely in A MURDER IS ANNOUNCED, she inherits a substantial fortune upon her husband's death, and lives in Scotland. The terms of her husband's will determine that his secretary, Letitia BLACKLOCK, will receive the estate upon Belle's death.

Goedler, Randall   A wealthy businessman in A MURDER IS ANNOUNCED, he leaves his money and home to his wife with the provision that his secretary, Letitia BLACKLOCK, will inherit the property after his wife's death.

Goedler, Sonia   Randall GOEDLER's sister and the mother of Pip and Emma in A MURDER IS ANNOUNCED, she would have inherited Little Paddocks had she not quarreled with her brother.

Gold, Douglas Cameron   Married to Marjorie GOLD but infatuated with another woman while on vacation in Rhodes in "TRIANGLE AT RHODES," he is framed for murder, and owes his life to Hercule POIROT, who clears him of the charge by solving the case.

Gold, Marjorie Emma   Meek in appearance and mild in manner, she plots to frame her husband for murder so that she can join her lover in TRIANGLE AT RHODES. Hercule POIROT sees through her deception, and recognizes the "cold-blooded devil" beneath the surface.

"Golden Ball, The"   Mystery short story.

The story focuses on the misadventures of a man fired by his rich uncle who meets and becomes engaged to a wealthy and beautiful socialite on the same day of his firing.

PUBLISHING AND DRAMATIZATION HISTORY
The story was first published in the short story collection, THE LISTERDALE MYSTERY, by Collins in London in 1934.

The story has not been adapted for stage or screen.

CHARACTERS
George DUNDAS, Ephraim LEADBETTER, Mary MONTRESOR, Bella WALLACE, Rube WALLACE

PLOT SYNOPSIS
After being fired by his wealthy uncle for taking a day off, George Dundas takes a stroll. The wealthy Mary Montresor stops her car, invites him to take a ride and proposes to him, despite her present engagement to a duke. The two take a ride into the country, where Mary hopes to find their dream house which, when they peek inside, is inhabited by what appear to be kidnappers. George shows courage and extricates them from the situation, thus gaining Mary's undying love, and guaranteeing marriage and a twenty-thousand-pound income yearly.

Golden Ball and Other Stories, The   Mystery short story collection.

The collection contains only two formerly unpublished stories. Of the remaining stories, five supernatural tales are reprinted from THE HOUND OF DEATH AND OTHER STORIES, and eight mysteries were originally published in THE LISTERDALE MYSTERY (1).

The collection contains an intriguing error which persists in reprints. As reprinted in this collection, the story "THE STRANGE CASE OF SIR ARTHUR CARMICHAEL" is mistakenly renamed "The Strange Case of Sir Andrew Carmichael" both in the table of contents and as the title of the story. Nonetheless, the character remains Sir Arthur in the text.

PUBLISHING AND DRAMATIZATION HISTORY
The Golden Ball and Other Stories was published in 1971 by Dodd, Mead & Company in New York.

"MAGNOLIA BLOSSOM" was adapted for television in 1982 by Thames Television in England, and was also shown on The Public Broadcasting Service in the U.S. See *The Hound of Death and Other Stories* and "*The Listerdale Mystery*" (1) for additional adaptations.

TITLES IN THE COLLECTION
The Golden Ball and Other Stories contains the following short stories: "THE LISTERDALE MYSTERY" (2), "THE GIRL IN THE TRAIN," "THE MANHOOD OF EDWARD ROBINSON," "A FRUITFUL SUNDAY," "THE GOLDEN BALL," "THE RAJAH'S EMERALD," "SWAN SONG" (see "*The Listerdale Mystery*" [1]; "THE HOUND OF DEATH," "THE GIPSY," "THE LAMP," "THE STRANGE CASE OF SIR ARTHUR CARMICHAEL," "THE CALL OF WINGS" (see "*The Hound of Death and Other Stories*"); "Magnolia Blossoms" and "NEXT TO A DOG."

Goodbody, Mrs. A highly sensitive psychic in HALLOWE'EN PARTY, she is the cleaning lady at Woodleigh Common and also a witch who dismisses black magic and other trappings of witchcraft as "tomfoolery." Instead, she accurately delineates the habits and characteristics of the Reynolds family for Hercule POIROT, and provides him with cryptic yet substantive information regarding the fate of other characters.

Goodman, Adam A former newspaper gardening columnist turned Special Branch agent in CAT AMONG THE PIGEONS, he poses as a gardener at the Meadowbank School to uncover a killer.

Gordon Leigh, The Honourable Hermione A wealthy young widow in "THE CASE OF THE MISSING LADY" whose worried fiancé, the explorer Gabriel STAVANSSON, consults Tommy and Tuppence BERESFORD when she disappears.

Goring, Edward A former World War II fighter pilot with the Royal Air Force, he uses a coffee shop called the Olive Branch as a front for a subversive organization in THEY CAME TO BAGHDAD. He takes advantage of Victoria JONES' infatuation for him to enlist her in his cause.

Gorman, Father The tall, elderly Presbyterian minister of St. Dominic's Church, he is hit on the head and killed while returning from the deathbed of the widow of a small-time crook in THE PALE HORSE. She gives him a list of names before she dies, and he puts these in his shoe, thus preventing his killers from taking what becomes an important clue in the mystery.

Gorman, Michael (Mickey) The first and only legal husband of the internationally known wealthy adventuress, Lady Bess SEDGWICK, who has married several times since, he is the commissionaire doorman in AT BERTRAM'S HOTEL. When they meet after years apart, he reminds her that their marriage was never legally dissolved, and teases that he should expose their marriage to the world and reveal that her other marriages have all been illegal. He later dies of a bullet wound.

Gorringe, Miss A keen observer of human nature, she is the respected receptionist in AT BERTRAM'S HOTEL who seems to have an unfailing ability to remember the needs and faces of her guests. She seeks to outwit Chief Inspector DAVY when he questions her, and coaches employees to cover up the disappearance of a hotel guest.

Gottlieb, Professor John A man in PASSENGER TO FRANKFURT who not only has the physical appearance of a monkey but also exhibits monkeylike gestures. Involved in espionage, he uses a letter of introduction from the President of the United States to meet Countess Renata ZERKOWSKI, and provides her with information regarding Project Benvo.

Grace A materialistic young woman in "THE RAJAH'S EMERALD," she "keeps company" with James BOND, a man of modest means whose style of dress and aspirations are a source of humor to her. When she attracts a wealthier suitor, she decides to vacation at a fashionable resort, and goads James to join her there. She stays at an expensive hotel while James can afford only a boardinghouse.

Grace, Inspector An inspector from Scotland Yard who works with Tommy and Tuppence BERESFORD to solve the mystery in "THE AMBASSADOR'S BOOTS."

Grace, Patience A thoroughly dissipated young woman in "THE HORSES OF DIOMEDES," she snorts cocaine, and urges others to use the drug. While under the influence of cocaine, she shoots her boyfriend.

Graham, Dr. (1)   A physician who resides at the Golden Palm Hotel, he meets Miss MARPLE when she vacations in A CARIBBEAN MYSTERY. He strikes up a conversation with her because he believes she is lonely. He later initiates an investigation into the death of another hotel guest, Major PALGROVE.

Graham, Dr. (2)   The personal physician to the Amory family in BLACK COFFEE, he is called in to examine the body when Sir Claud AMORY dies.

Graham, Jennifer   A horse-faced woman in A DAUGHTER'S A DAUGHTER, she whinnies when she laughs.

Graham, Ralph   A tea planter in Ceylon, he grows from a young and freckle-faced dance partner to a charming suitor in UNFINISHED PORTRAIT.

Graham, Roger   Engaged to Madge KEELEY, he becomes infatuated with the ethereal Mabelle ANNESLEY, for whom he wants to leave his fiancée in "THE BIRD WITH THE BROKEN WING." He realizes his error and decides to return to Madge.

Grainger, Dr.   A popular and robust physician to Emily ARUNDELL, he fails to diagnose murder by means of phosphorous in DUMB WITNESS due to the curry for supper and his diminished sense of smell after an illness.

Granby, Mrs.   Miss MARPLE's prime suspect in "MISS MARPLE TELLS A STORY," she may have murdered Mrs. RHODES while disguised as a man.

Grandier, Madame   A beautiful and melancholy widow in "THE ERYMANTHIAN BOAR," she returns yearly to the hotel Rochers Neige to commemorate her husband's death while climbing a nearby mountain. Nothing, not even being cut off from the outside world by the wreck of the funicular, can cut through her grief and shake her indifference to everything else.

Grandier, Elise   A personal maid in DEATH IN THE CLOUDS, her employer is murdered with a poisoned blowdart while they are on an airplane. Years before, she had been robbed of her life savings by a man who abandoned her when he learned that she was pregnant. Upon her employer's death, Elise gave Hercule POIROT a very important notebook.

Grange, Inspector   A Chief Inspector from Scotland Yard in THE HOLLOW, his instincts tell him that jealousy motivated the murder of Dr. John CHRISTOW.

Grannie   Paternal grandmother of the main character in UNFINISHED PORTRAIT, she professes a special knowledge of "the men" and their habits, which she tries to impart to her granddaughter. She has been married and widowed three times and, even in her eighties, she continues to flirt with and to receive gifts and letters from admirers. Her granddaughter ignores Grannie's advice to "never leave your husband alone," the same advice given to Agatha Christie by her own grandmother, with similar results.

Grant, General   A former colonial officer in "THE HORSES OF DIOMEDES," he pretends to have the gout but doesn't notice when Hercule POIROT determinedly stumbles and clutches his bandaged foot.

Grant, Mr.   An operative of British Intelligence and a friend of A. CARTER, he employs Tommy and Tuppence BERESFORD to spy for him in N OR M? His original plan to use only Tommy is quickly foiled when Tuppence intrudes on the case, leaving him to disguise himself as a fisherman and remain discreetly available should the Beresfords require his help.

Grant, Mrs.   Viewed by the main character of UNFINISHED PORTRAIT as "the loveliest thing she had ever seen," she is devoted to her son and does not interfere in his unsuitable engagement.

Grant, Bernard   A big, jolly man, he is an old friend of the main character's father in UNFINISHED PORTRAIT.

Grant, Ernestine   The second-floor flat tenant in "THE THIRD-FLOOR FLAT" who lives below Patricia GARNETT, she writes Patricia a note requesting a meeting on the morning that she is shot.

A moment of thought before murder for Mrs. Grant (Josie Lawrence) in "The Third Floor Flat." (Photo courtesy of London Weekend Television)

Grant, Gerda   A former actress and the first wife of Alison BLUNT in ONE, TWO, BUCKLE MY SHOE, she plays the additional roles of Sylvia CHAPMAN and Helen MONTRESSOR in the novel.

Grant, James   One of Ann PRENTICE's suitors in A DAUGHTER'S A DAUGHTER, he is a tall man of stiff military bearing who has been Ann's friend for twenty-five years.

Grant, Jim   A pleasant, good-tempered schoolboy when he first meets the main character of UNFINISHED PORTRAIT in France, he later becomes engaged to her, but realizes that they are incompatible.

Grant, Pam   An angelic-looking woman with fair features, she pretends to be the sister of Sheila GRANT and the daughter of General GRANT in "THE HORSES OF DIOMEDES."

Grant, Robert   An ex-convict in THE BIG FOUR who is also known as Abraham BIGGS, he is an unpleasant-looking man who is employed by Jonathan WHALLEY as a manservant.

Grant, Sheila   A convicted shoplifter named Sheila KELLY, she pretends to be the sister of Pam GRANT and the daughter of General GRANT in "THE HORSES OF DIOMEDES." Despite her hardboiled exterior, she draws the romantic interest of Dr. Michael STODDART, who treats her for cocaine poisoning and decides to reform her.

Grant, Stephen (1)   A young man in "AT THE 'BELLS AND MOTLEY,' " he had been hired to care for the horses of Captain Richard HARWELL at Ashley Grange. When Harwell disappears, Stephen is questioned but released because the authorities have no evidence.

Grant, Stephen (2)   Under the assumed name of Stephen FARR, he flies from South Africa to England to meet Simeon LEE, his natural father, in HERCULE POIROT'S CHRISTMAS. He resembles his halfbrothers strongly, and the police superintendent several times mistakes him for one of Simeon's legitimate sons. He becomes a suspect when Simeon is murdered. After being cleared of the crime, he becomes engaged to Conchita LOPEZ.

Graves, Constable   The police constable for the Sittaford area who joins Major BURNABY and Dr. WARREN when they break into a murder victim's bungalow in THE SITTAFORD MYSTERY.

Graves, Dr.   The physician who treats the poliostricken, philandering husband in THE BURDEN.

Graves, Inspector   A deep-voiced police inspector from London who specializes in anonymous-letter cases, he arrives in the village of Lymstock to investigate the series of poison-pen letters received by town inhabitants in THE MOVING FINGER. He amuses locals with his admiration for the letters.

Graves, Mr.   Count FOSCATINI's valet and butler at the flat in Regent's Court in "THE ADVENTURE OF THE ITALIAN NOBLEMAN."

Graves, Sergeant   A tactful young police constable in Warmsley Vale who hides his knowledge of French from his superior, he helps in a murder investigation in TAKEN AT THE FLOOD.

Graves, Sir Ronald   As the Assistant Commissioner of Scotland Yard in AT BERTRAM'S HOTEL, he is kept up to date on all crimes, and his mind absorbs every detail despite his habit of doodling during conferences. His one apprehension is that he must obtain clearance for Chief Inspector DAVY to speak with the mysterious Mr. ROBINSON, who is a key figure in international finance.

Gray, Dr.   The physician in CROOKED HOUSE who tends the ailing patriarch, Aristide LEONIDES.

Grayle, Lady Ariadne   An extremely wealthy woman in "DEATH ON THE NILE" (1), she consults Mr. PARKER PYNE because she believes that her husband is poisoning her. A difficult person, she complains constantly and seems to thrive on her own misery.

Grayle, Sir George   Married to Lady Ariadne GRAYLE, he is a quiet and easily manipulated man in "DEATH ON THE NILE" (1) whose wife has bullied him for ten years. He is suspected of slowly poisoning her, because her attacks of illness only take place when he is present.

Grayle, Pamela   The niece of Sir George and Lady Ariadne GRAYLE who support her financially in "DEATH ON THE NILE" (1). She has no patience with her aunt, but she affectionately calls her uncle "Nunks" and is having an affair with his secretary, Basil WEST.

Green, Cyril   A rather unstable witness in ORDEAL BY INNOCENCE, he first tells the police that Rachel ARGYLE was murdered by Russians who came down in their sputniks. He later describes the car he noticed near the murder site.

Green, George   An imaginary character in GIANT'S BREAD, the main character assumes this name when he has amnesia.

Greenholtz, Mr.   A partner in the firm of Greenholtz, Simons and Lederbetter in THEY CAME TO BAGHDAD, he fires Victoria JONES for doing an impression of his wife.

Greenshaw, Katherine Dorothy   The mistress of the estate in "GREENSHAW'S FOLLY," she avoids paying her housekeeper-companion for several years by promising to leave her the estate in her will. After she is murdered by an arrow shot through her neck, potential heirs learn that she fooled everyone by leaving her estate to the grandson of one of her grandfather's illegitimate children.

"Greenshaw's Folly"   Mystery short story.

The plot centers on a will which leads the presumed beneficiary to commit murder.

PUBLISHING AND DRAMATIZATION HISTORY
The story appeared in the short story collection, THE ADVENTURE OF THE CHRISTMAS PUDDING AND OTHER ENTREES, published in 1960 by William Collins Sons and Company, Ltd., in London.

The story has not been adapted for stage or screen.

CHARACTERS
Horace BINDLER, Mrs. CRESSWELL, Nat FLETCHER, Miss Katherine GREENSHAW, Miss Jane MARPLE, Louise OXLEY, Alfred POLLOCK, Inspector WELCH, Joan WEST, Raymond WEST.

PLOT SYNOPSIS
Raymond West and his friend, literary critic Horace Bindler, visit Greenshaw's Folly, an architectural monstrosity, out of curiosity. They coincidentally become witnesses to Miss Greenshaw's will, in which she presumably leaves her estate to her housekeeper, Mrs. Cresswell. When Miss Greenshaw is murdered by a shot from a bow and arrow a short time later, only days after engaging Joan West's niece to edit her grandfather's diaries, the suspicion falls on the gardener, who bears a strong resemblance to old Nathan Greenshaw. After old family alliances are examined, Miss Marple uncovers the true murderer and the real beneficiary of the will is revealed.

CRIME NOTES
The sole murder is the result of being shot by an arrow.

Greenway House   The house purchased by Sir Max MALLOWAN and Agatha Christie Mallowan, it overlooks the river Dart in Devon. The white, Georgian-styled house in Torquay was built in approximately the 1790s, and the author recounts in AN AUTOBIOGRAPHY that her mother used to call it "the most perfect of the various properties on the Dart." Mallowan writes in his memoirs that the house, centered on thirty-five acres, was a "little paradise." For her part, the author labeled Greenway "a dream house," and she was highly apprehensive when the British Admiralty requisitioned the house during World War II as quarters for U.S. Navy officers of the flotilla. Afterward, she praised the occupants, who had respected the beauty of the home and left no damage, aside from the addition of fourteen latrines lined up in the hallway, which the author had a difficult time getting the government to remove once the war was over.

Greer, Elsa   Once the mistress of artist Amyas CRALE, she has also been married three times, currently to Lord DITTISHAM. When her former lover dies from hemlock poisoning in FIVE LITTLE PIGS, his wife, Caroline CRALE, is the main suspect, for she believed that her husband was going to run away with Elsa. The deaths of both Crales drain Elsa emotionally, leaving Hercule POIROT to compare her eyes to "dead lakes."

Gregg   A first-class parlourmaid in UNFINISHED PORTRAIT, she returns to the household after the master dies, but is unable to adjust to an economical lifestyle.

Gregg, Betty   A free-spirited young woman who drinks, swears and wears risque clothes in "PROBLEM AT POLLENSA BAY," she is engaged to Basil CHESTER, whose mother does not approve.

Gregg, Ernie   A young delinquent who is an experienced lockpicker in THEY DO IT WITH MIRRORS, he is killed because he can identify the murderer of Christian GULBRANDSEN.

Gregg, Marina   She is a much-married, famous film star of about fifty in THE MIRROR CRACK'D FROM SIDE TO SIDE. At a party in her honor, she fails to recognize former spouses and the now-grown child whom she had adopted years before. Privately tortured by old losses, she finds life unbearable, and commits suicide.

Gregson, Garry   A writer of detective fiction in THE CLOCKS, he once employed a suspect in the case as a typist. His unpublished manuscript provides Hercule POIROT with a clue to solve the crime.

Greta   A haughty, blonde secretary to the wealthy, married Sir Joseph HOGGIN in "THE NEMEAN LIONS," she hopes to become the next Lady Hoggin.

Grey, Detective Sergeant   A member of the Berkshire police in "THE LERNEAN HYDRA," he discovers the makeup compact containing mysterious white powder which plays an integral role in the murder.

Grey, Mrs.   See GRUNBERG, ANITA.

Grey, Jane   A winner of the Irish Sweepstakes, the former hairdresser is on the flight in DEATH IN THE CLOUDS when Madame GISELLE is murdered. She is in love with Norman GALE, but she also attracts the attentions of Jean DUPONT, to whom she plays the role of secretary in order to help Hercule POIROT solve the case.

Grey, Katherine   A serene young woman in THE MYSTERY OF THE BLUE TRAIN, she serves as a companion to Miss Amelia VINER, an old woman who is dying of cancer in ST. MARY MEAD.

Grey, Mary   A saleslady in THE MOVING FINGER, she outfits Megan HUNTER and creates her new look.

Grey, Thora   A beautiful young woman glowing with health and vitality, she captivates Captain HASTINGS in THE A.B.C. MURDERS. Her employer, Sir Carmichael CLARKE, had planned to ask her to marry him upon his ill wife's death, but Sir Carmichael is murdered, and his wife fires Thora.

Grey, Thyrza   A mysterious woman living in the village of Much Deeping, she is involved with the occult in THE PALE HORSE. She disdains black masses, but has an in-depth knowledge of spiritualism, trances and magic, and she influences Mark EASTERBROOK to investigate a mystery.

Griffin, Dr. The doctor in the little village of Chipping Cleghorn in "SANCTUARY," he is called upon to treat the dying Walter ST. JOHN.

Griffin, Mrs. A ninety-three-year-old woman in POSTERN OF FATE, she recalls important events which help Tuppence BERESFORD to solve a six-decades-old mystery.

Griffith, Miss A coldly efficient woman and head typist for sixteen years at Consolidated Investments Trust, she treats all the other typists with disdain in A POCKET FULL OF RYE. She calls a doctor when company head Rex FORTESCUE becomes ill at work, and harbors a secret passion for the ne'er-do-well Lancelot FORTESCUE.

Griffith, Aimee The aggressively cheery, masculine sister of village doctor Owen GRIFFITH in THE MOVING FINGER who dominates her brother. Her intensely jealous unrequited love for Richard SYMMINGTON leads to her public humiliation.

Griffith, Dr. Owen An awkward, shy man with an overbearing and aggressive sister, he is the village doctor in THE MOVING FINGER. His melancholy personality takes a pleasant turn when he meets and falls in love with Joanna BURTON, whom he eventually marries.

Griffiths, Walter One of three people who are the last to see Thomas BETTERTON before he disappears in DESTINATION UNKNOWN.

Grosjean, Monsieur Le President The charming and diplomatic president of France in PASSENGER TO FRANKFURT, he calls a worldwide meeting regarding growing student unrest.

Grosvenor, Irene Expensively clothed and coiffed, she is the personal secretary to financier Rex FORTESCUE and goes to pieces when he collapses from poisoning in A POCKET FULL OF RYE. She suits the luxurious decor of the offices with her expensive appearance, which is only a facade; her voice loses its polish and reveals lower-class roots whenever she loses emotional control.

Groves, Mrs. The cleaning woman in "THE DRESSMAKER'S DOLL" who feels certain the doll is watching her.

Grunberg, Anita A young, beautiful actress who was born in South Africa of presumed Hungarian parentage, she is a master of disguise who appears in THE MAN IN THE BROWN SUIT as the Russian dancer NADINA, a shipboard traveler named Mrs. GREY, and Mrs. DE CASTINA. She is using the latter identity when she is found dead.

Gudgeon, Mr. A dedicated butler in service to Lady ANGKATELL, he not only cleans up the physical messes that she makes but protects her image as well in THE HOLLOW.

Gulbrandsen, Christian A trustee of the Gulbrandsen Institute in THEY DO IT WITH MIRRORS, he is killed at Stoneygates, a family estate which had become a home for delinquent boys.

Gun Man, The A shadowy figure with stumps instead of hands in UNFINISHED PORTRAIT, he appears in CELIA's nightmares when she is emotionally distressed. Young Agatha Christie also had nightmares in which the recurring figure of the Gun Man appeared.

Gustave A highly skilled waiter in "THE ERYMANTHIAN BOAR," he claims to be Police Inspector DROUET, but his main concern is that the high altitude and low boiling point prevent him from making a good cup of coffee.

Guteman, Ellie See ROGERS, ELLIE.

Guthrie, Alexander An old friend of Cora LANSQUENET, he is an art critic who often advised her regarding the value of her art purchases in AFTER THE FUNERAL. While he found most of her acquisitions relatively worthless, he is intrigued by the piece he sees after she is killed.

Gwenda A clerk in the Hollowquay post office in POSTERN OF FATE, she relates old local legends about Mary JORDAN for Tuppence BERESFORD.

H

Haggard, Blanche A former schoolmate of the main character in ABSENT IN THE SPRING, she lives a rootless lifestyle and remains unconcerned with what others may think about her five husbands and the two children she leaves behind. Her hints about infidelity and scandal are catalysts for Joan SCUDAMORE's introspection.

Hailsham-Brown, Clarissa A very attractive young woman with a penchant for fantasizing, she is the second wife of diplomat Henry HAILSHAM-BROWN and the loving stepmother of Pippa HAILSHAM-BROWN in SPIDER'S WEB. Fond of playing a game of "supposing," she finds herself with a real dead body in her drawing room, and no one who will believe how it really came to be there.

Hailsham-Brown, Henry Viewed by his friends as "a really nice fellow," he is a Foreign Service diplomat whose first wife was a drug addict in SPIDER'S WEB. He truly appreciates the joy and peace which his second wife, Clarissa HAILSHAM-BROWN, has brought into his life, but he wishes that she would restrain her imagination.

Hailsham-Brown, Pippa The lanky, twelve-year-old daughter of Foreign Service diplomat Henry HAILSHAM-BROWN in SPIDER'S WEB, she is happy with her imaginative stepmother and wants to stay with her.

Hale, Captain Bingo A semipermanent houseguest of Sir Arthur and Lady Vere MERIVALE, he has no moral scruples about having an affair with Lady Vere in "FINESSING THE KING" and "THE GENTLEMAN DRESSED IN NEWSPAPER." He dresses as "the gentleman dressed in newspaper" from *Alice in Wonderland* at the Three Arts Ball, and claims that he

received a note warning him not to meet Lady Vere at the Ace of Spades on the night she is killed.

Hall, Dr. Owner and operator of a private Bournemouth nursing home, he treats Jane FINN, who suffers amnesia and can no longer speak English in THE SECRET ADVERSARY.

Halliday, Mr. A British scientist who conducts experiments with wireless energy, he disappears while en route to Paris to meet Madame OLIVIER in THE BIG FOUR.

Halliday, Mrs. Married to a British scientist in THE BIG FOUR, she is "a tall, fair woman, nervous and eager in manner" who waits for word about her vanished husband.

Halliday, Arthur An egotistical, wealthy man in "NEXT TO A DOG," his persistence in asking Joyce LAMBERT to marry him seems to have finally paid off when she agrees, but she changes her mind when her beloved dog dies.

Halliday, Ebenezer A large, heavyset man with piercing eyes in "THE PLYMOUTH EXPRESS," he is an American millionaire who hires Hercule POIROT to find the murderer of his daugher, The Honourable Flossie CARRINGTON.

Halliday, Helen Spenlove Kennedy A highly attractive woman in SLEEPING MURDER, she makes enemies of most women but captivates every man she meets. Twenty-years after she disappears, her stepdaughter buys the house in which they lived and discovers the secret of her disappearance.

Halliday, Major Kelvin James A widower in SLEEPING MURDER, he marries an attractive and philandering woman as his second wife. When she disappears, he sends his daughter (Gwenda REED) to live with relatives in New Zealand and signs himself into an insane asylum, where he commits suicide two years later, obsessed with the thought that he murdered his wife. His self-view contrasts greatly with that of his psychiatrist, who views him as a gentle, kindly man.

Hallowe'en Party   Mystery novel.

The novel contains a number of contemporary, late 1960s references to sexual mores, drugs and the clothing of the time. The plot centers on efforts to locate the murderer of two adolescents, one of whom claimed to have witnessed a murder.

PUBLISHING AND DRAMATIZATION HISTORY

The novel was published in 1969 by William Collins Sons and Company, Ltd., in London, and by Dodd, Mead and Company in New York.

The novel has not been adapted for stage or screen.

CHARACTERS

Beatrice ARDLEY, Judith BUTLER, Miranda BUTLER, Hugo DRAKE, Rowena Arabella DRAKE, Miss EMLYN, Dr. FERGUSON, Lesley FERRIER, Jeremy FULLERTON, Michael GARFIELD, Mrs. GOODBODY, Mrs. HARGREAVES, Desmond HOLLAND, Harriet LEAMAN, Mrs. LLEWELLYN-SMYTHE, Elspeth McKAY, Mrs. Ariadne OLIVER, Hercule POIROT, Inspector Henry Timothy RAGLAN, Nicholas RANSOME, Mrs. REYNOLDS, Ann REYNOLDS, Joyce REYNOLDS, Leopold REYNOLDS, Olga SEMINOFF, Superintendent Bert SPENCE, Janet WHITE, Elizabeth WHITTAKER

PLOT SYNOPSIS

Chapters 1–4

Mrs. Ariadne Oliver joins two friends in giving a Hallowe'en party for adolescents at The Elm School in Woodleigh Common. At the party, Joyce Reynolds tells the mystery writer that she once witnessed a murder without realizing it at the time. No more is said, and the party continues. Before the evening ends, Joyce is found drowned in a tub of water used for bobbing for apples. A few days later, Mrs. Oliver visits Poirot, tells him about Joyce's death and claims that she believes the girl did witness a murder. Poirot

agrees to examine the case, and tells her that the name of Woodleigh Common sounds familiar to him.

Chapters 5–8

Poirot recalls that Superintendent Spence has retired and lives in Woodleigh Common, so he meets with him to discuss the case. Spence mentions the names of two boys at the party who have a history of assault: Nicholas Ransome and Desmond Holland. The detective speaks with Rowena Drake and learns that she seems to have strongly disliked the victim. With Mrs. Oliver, he also visits the murdered girl's mother, who claims that she never heard Joyce mention witnessing a murder, a claim with which both Joyce's younger brother and older sister agree. When Poirot once again speaks with Spence, he and his sister reveal that four unsolved murders have occurred in the recent past in the area of Woodleigh Common. They also provide him with a list of the guests at the Hallowe'en party and suggest that he speak with Dr. Ferguson, Joyce's doctor.

Chapters 9–11

After speaking with Ferguson, Poirot visits Miss Emlyn, headmistress of The Elms, to discuss Joyce's boasting about the murder and to learn more about a former teacher who had been strangled on her way home from working at the school. Although she tells him nothing new, Elizabeth Whittaker, a teacher at The Elms, states that Mrs. Drake had been startled by seeing someone at the party and dropped a vase of autumn leaves and flowers as she descended the stairs. Afterwards, Poirot speaks with Michael Garfield, who designed the quarry garden for the late Mrs. Llewellyn-Smythe, and inherited her house and garden. He learns nothing new there, and returns for tea to the Butler house, where Mrs. Oliver is staying.

Chapters 12–14

Poirot speaks with attorney Jeremy Fullerton to learn more about Mrs. Llewellyn-Smythe and a murdered former employee, Lesley Ferrier. Fullerton asserts that his late client simply overstressed a weak heart, and he observes that Ferrier was probably killed by a jealous husband or boyfriend. Poirot also questions him about Olga Seminoff, the au pair girl who had forged a codicil to Mrs. Llewellyn-Smythe's will and then disappeared before the case was heard in court. When Poirot later speaks with Rowena Drake, she ignores his question regarding the broken vase; they speak, instead, about her late husband Hugo, a disabled man who was killed in a hit-and-run accident. At the mention of the forged codicil, she suggests that Olga must have had help from a young man who worked in a law office. Later, Poirot stops by Hugo's grave and speaks with the caretaker, who tells him that he believes that Rowena will be leaving the area soon.

Chapters 15–19
Poirot questions others connected with the case. He speaks with the two boys who were present at the party, but both deny overhearing Joyce's remark about the murder. Mrs. Goodbody, a cleaning lady thought by townspeople to be a witch, tells him that she does not believe Joyce's story but that Leopold is a blackmailer. Mrs. Oliver also continues to interview people, speaking with Harriet Leaman, Mrs. Llewellyn-Smythe's maid, and gardener who witnessed the codicil to the will. Harriet claims that the codicil was placed in a book by her former employer. When Poirot and Mrs. Oliver compare notes, they determine that there were two codicils. Harriet had told Mrs. Oliver that the other codicil had been placed in the Quarry House library in a book entitled *Enquire Within Upon Everything*.

Chapters 20–24
While taking a shortcut through the quarry, Poirot meets Michael Garfield, who is sketching Miranda Butler. He learns that Garfield plans to leave the area. Information arrives from Mr. Goby suggestive of foul play regarding the missing au pair girl, and Joyce's brother, Leopold, is found drowned in the brook. Poirot speaks with Miss Emlyn, who reassures him that he can trust Nicholas and Desmond, whom he needs to help him to unmask the murderer. The authorities seal off the quarry, search it and find Olga's body. Fearful for Miranda's safety, he wires Mrs. Oliver to take the girl and her mother to London, but kidnappers manage to take her anyway.

Chapters 25–26
The final chapters present a startling reason for the murders and kidnapping, involving witchcraft, human sacrifice and greed. Poirot learns that Miranda, not Joyce, had witnessed a murder in the quarry and she told Joyce, who immediately used the story to make herself seem important. An unexpected parent-

child relationship is revealed, and readers learn that two murderers committed the crimes. At the end, one of the murderers drinks the golden goblet of poison that had been intended for the human sacrifice victim, and Miranda is rescued.

CRIME NOTES
The novel contains two murders and also mentions four others that occured before the story opens. Two victims die from knife wounds, two are drowned, a fifth is strangled and a sixth dies of heart failure induced by unidentified means.

Hamer, Silas A millionaire in "THE CALL OF THE WINGS," he experiences a spiritual rebirth one evening while walking home from dinner at a friend's house. He hears the sound of a flute, which makes him want to shed his wealth and possessions. He gives his wealth to a mission for the poor, and sets out to help others, but dies while rescuing a child from the subway tracks.

Hamilton Clipp, Mrs. An unlikely spy because of her short, birdlike appearance, she has had an active life "jumping from boats into aeroplanes and from aeroplanes into trains." She poses as the wife of George HAMILTON CLIPP and pretends to have broken her arm in order to hire Victoria JONES as her traveling companion in THEY CAME TO BAGHDAD.

Hamilton Clipp, George A member of an espionage network in THEY CAME TO BAGHDAD, he is a tall, thin, gray-haired American whose complacent exterior and languorous movements belie his dangerous occupation. He hires Victoria JONES to act as a traveling companion to the woman who poses as his wife.

Hammond, Mr. Small and withered in appearance, he is Roger ACKROYD's solicitor in THE MURDER OF ROGER ACKROYD. His "aggressive chin and sharp grey eyes" reveal his astuteness.

Hannah A fanatically religious maid in "THE HOUSE OF THE LURKING DEATH," she attempts to set on fire the woman whom she suspects of killing her employer.

Hardcastle, Claudia The half-sister of the highly talented and eccentric architect, Rudolf SANTONIX, and a horse enthusiast, she dies soon after Ellie ROGERS because she knows too much in ENDLESS NIGHT.

Hardcastle, Detective Inspector A tall, poker-faced man, he is in charge of the murder investigation in THE CLOCKS. He has a good memory for facts and a habit of following through on all aspects of a case.

Hardcastle, Mrs. A middle-aged woman with a harsh face, she replaces personal secretary Miss GROSVENOR in A POCKET FULL OF RYE. Other characters refer to her behind her back as "Gorgon" and "Horseface Hetty."

Hardcastle, Midge A poor relation of Lady Lucy ANGKATELL, she works in a dress shop to support herself in THE HOLLOW. Although she is very much in love with her fiancé, she breaks the engagement, following which she prevents him from committing suicide.

Harden, Grete A double agent who was sent to infiltrate a group of subversives but finds herself captured and replaced with Victoria JONES in THEY CAME TO BAGHDAD.

Harding, Carol See DAVIS, CAROL.

Harding, Jane A tall and beautiful singer, she provides straightforward and practical encouragement to Vernon DEYRE in GIANT'S BREAD. Strongly aware of the young composer's musical intensity and drive, she sacrifices her voice to launch his first opera, and helps him to make the requisite financial and professional connections. She drowns while returning from Russia by ocean liner.

Hardman, Cyrus Bethman Viewed by Hercule POIROT as the personification of "the true Western spirit of hustle," he is an American detective disguised as a typewriter ribbon salesman in MURDER ON THE ORIENT EXPRESS (1). He is badly dressed and exhibits habits which identify him as common.

Hardman, Marcus An "elderly social butterfly," he owns an extensive collection of valuable jewels. When a priceless emerald necklace disappears one evening during a party attended by socially prominent guests, he hires Hercule POIROT to discreetly locate the stolen necklace in "DOUBLE CLUE."

Hardt, Elsa Implicated in a murder in "THE ADVENTURE OF THE CHEAP FLAT," she poses as a concert singer but is really a German spy. She bides her time and waits to sell stolen naval plans to the highest bidder.

Harfield, Jane An elderly woman in THE MYSTERY OF THE BLUE TRAIN, she chooses to leave her fortune to her nurse-companion, Katherine GREY, rather than to the distant relatives who believe they are her beneficiaries.

Harfield, Mary Anne A vicious woman in THE MYSTERY OF THE BLUE TRAIN whom another character labels "a perfectly poisonous person," she seeks to overturn her late cousin's will and to inherit the large fortune.

Hargraves, Laura See UPWARD, LAURA.

Hargreaves, Mrs. The wife of the church organist in HALLOWE'EN PARTY, she might have prevented a murder if others had accepted her offer of the large green plastic pail for apple dunking.

Hargreaves, Lois One of the murder victims in "THE HOUSE OF THE LURKING DEATH," she becomes frightened after eating poisoned chocolates, and contacts Tommy and Tuppence BERESFORD for help. Before they can intervene, Lois is poisoned when ricin is placed in fig paste sandwiches.

Harker, Captain A villain who attempts to kidnap Tuppence BERESFORD in "BLINDMAN'S BLUFF," his plans are disrupted by the loyal ALBERT.

"Harlequin's Lane" Mystery short story.

The story presents figures from the commedia dell'arte in a mystery involving the mysterious Mr. QUIN.

PUBLISHING AND DRAMATIZATION HISTORY

The story appeared in the short story collection, THE MYSTERIOUS MR. QUIN, published in 1930 by William Collins Sons and Company, Ltd., in London, and by Dodd, Mead and Company in New York.

The story has not been adapted for stage or screen.

CHARACTERS

Anna DENMAN, John DENMAN, Prince ORANOFF, Mr. Quin, Lady ROSCHEIMER, Mr. SATTERTHWAITE, Molly STANWELL, Claude WICKHAM

PLOT SYNOPSIS

Mr. Satterthwaite reluctantly visits the home of Anna and John Denman, whom he views as dull "Philistines." He is pleasantly surprised to find an acquaintance, Mr. Harley Quin, also in attendance. The weekend is to include a ballet performance which will include Harlequin, Columbine, Pierot and Pierrette, and the parts of Harlequin and Columbine are to be danced by professionals who will arrive with Prince Oranoff. A minor automobile accident injures the professional dancers, and Anna Denman decides to dance again for the first time since she left her native Russia and lover Oranoff behind ten years ago. Mr. Quin becomes her partner as Harlequin. The story takes a bizarre twist as old loves emerge, present loves fade and new alliances are forged.

CRIME NOTES

Mr. Quin takes on a new aspect of character in this story, that of Death.

"Harlequin Tea Set, The"   Mystery short story.

The story reunites Mr. Harley QUIN and Mr. SATTERTHWAITE after many years, to investigate a crime of falsified identity.

PUBLISHING AND DRAMATIZATION HISTORY

The story was first anthologized in *Winter Crimes 3,* published by Macmillan London Ltd. in 1971. It later appeared in *Ellery Queen's Magazine,* in 1973, and was included in the twenty-ninth annual *Ellery Queen's Murdercade,* published in 1975 by Random House in New York.

The story has not been adapted for stage or screen.

CHARACTERS

Tom ADDISON, Beryl GILLIAT, Lily GILLIAT, Roland (Eden) GILLIAT, Simon GILLIAT, Timothy GILLIAT, Dr. HORTON, Inez HORTON, Mary HORTON, Mr. Quin, Mr. Satterthwaite

PLOT SYNOPSIS

Many years have passed since Mr. Satterthwaite's last meeting with the mysterious Mr. Harley Quin, but a delay in a small village caused by car trouble leads to the Harlequin Cafe and a reunion. Mr. Satterthwaite relates that he intends to visit a very wealthy childhood friend who now shares his home with son-in-law Simon Gilliat, the son-in-law's second wife Beryl, a grandson, and a stepgrandson. After listening closely, and after the two men meet Beryl, who enters the combined cafe and shop to purchase a coffee mug to replace one which she had supposedly broken earlier, Mr. Quin prepares to leave, uttering only one word to Mr. Satterthwaite: "Daltonism."

Once at Tom Addison's home, Mr. Satterthwaite notices that his friend wears two different colored slippers, and he remembers that Tom is color-blind. He then remembers the meaning of Mr. Quin's whispered warning. When he meets Roland and Timothy, he is struck by the fact that Tom's supposed grandson Roland looks nothing like his grandfather, while Beryl's son from her previous marriage has most of Tom Addison's physical characteristics. The boys are the same age and had been only three or four months old when their widowed parents met and decided to marry. When Timothy shows a clear sign of color-blindness, Mr. Satterthwaite suspects the truth, and acts swiftly to prevent Timothy's murder by his stepmother, who had hoped to make her natural son a wealthy heir.

CRIME NOTES

The author adds supernatural effects to the story in the form of scarecrow who resembles Mr. Quin and in the ghostly figure of the dead mother whose son's life is saved by Mr. Satterthwaite.

Harmon, Diana (Bunch)   The favorite among Miss Jane MARPLE's godchildren, she is a high-spirited young woman married to the Reverend Julian

HARMON. She helps her godmother solve the murder of Rudy SCHERZ in A MURDER IS ANNOUNCED and uncover the facts behind the mysterious death in her husband's church in "SANCTUARY."

Harmon, Reverend Julian   A highly educated man whose knowledge extends far beyond church lore, he is married to Diana (Bunch) HARMON. He remains an onlooker when murders are committed in A MURDER IS ANNOUNCED and "SANCTUARY," while his wife helps her godmother, Miss Jane MARPLE, solve the mysteries.

Harper, Mr.   A pleasant-looking young man in "THE ADVENTURE OF THE EGYPTIAN TOMB," he serves as the American secretary to Mr. BLEIBNER on the Men-her-Ra archaeological expedition.

Harper, Superintendent   A member of the Glenshire Police Force who investigates the murder of Ruby KEENE in THE BODY IN THE LIBRARY, his apparently superficial preliminary questioning of suspects is deceptive, lulling them into a false sense of security.

Harris, Myrna   A waitress at the Royal Spa Hotel who had dated Rudy SCHERZ, she has information that leads the police to change their verdict from suicide to murder in A MURDER IS ANNOUNCED.

Harrison, Mrs.   A pleasant and helpful landlady in ONE, TWO, BUCKLE MY SHOE, she assists Hercule POIROT and Inspector JAPP as they search for clues in the rooms of her murdered lodger, Mabelle SAINTS-BURY SEALE.

Harrison, Nurse   A woman scorned, she falls in love with her employer, Dr. OLDFIELD, and expects to marry him when his wife dies. He is not interested in her, so she spreads rumors which implicate Dr. OLDFIELD and Jane MONCRIEFF in his wife's death in "THE LERNEAN HYDRA."

Harrison, Dr. Arthur   The physician to the late Jane HARFIELD, he vouches with certainty that she was mentally competent when she made her will in THE MYSTERY OF THE BLUE TRAIN. He urges Katherine GREY to ignore threats from the old woman's relatives, and assures her that she is completely entitled to the inheritance.

Harrison, John   An unfortunate young man with only a few months to live, he plots to end his life in a way that will put the blame on his fiancée's former fiancé in WASPS' NEST.

Harrogate   The site of the Hydropathic Hotel in England where Agatha Christie stayed when she disappeared on December 3, 1926. (See DISAPPEARANCE OF AGATHA CHRISTIE.)

Harry   When he fails to help his fiancée Lily PRICE, who almost falls from a window in THE MIRROR CRACK'D FROM SIDE TO SIDE, Miss Jane MARPLE immediately becomes suspicious.

Harte, Mrs.   Manager of the Balaclava Private Hotel in "THE NEMEAN LION," she graciously presses Hercule POIROT to rent a room but fails in her endeavor.

Harter, Mary   An eccentric widow in "WHERE THERE'S A WILL," she clings strongly to the past, and suspects most visitors of plotting to steal her silver. The one man whom she tolerates is her nephew Charles RIDGEWAY, in whose favor she changes her will. Death seems imminent when she begins to hear her dead husband's voice speaking through her radio.

Hartigan, Tom   A sharp observer, he contacts the police when he notices that Alexander Bonaparte CUST has been at each place and time a murder was committed in THE A.B.C. MURDERS.

Hartington, Jack   A golf fanatic who hears the faint cry of "Murder—help! Murder" each morning at 7:25 A.M. in THE MYSTERY OF THE BLUE JAR. While on the golf course, he learns that the sounds emanate from a cottage with a mysterious history.

Hartnell, Amanda   A woman whose reputation for truth is questionable, she is Miss Jane MARPLE's next-door neighbor in ST. MARY MEAD. She is a hearty old woman with a no-nonsense attitude who plays a minor role in four adventures: MURDER AT THE VICARAGE, THE BODY IN THE LIBRARY, "THE TAPE-MEASURE MURDER" and "THE CASE OF THE PERFECT MAID."

Harvey, George   A friend of the accused murderer Leonard VOLE in "WITNESS FOR THE PROSECUTION," he informs Vole of Emily FRENCH's great wealth.

Harvey, Jim   An automobile mechanic in MURDER IS EASY, he quarrels with his fiancée Amy GIBBS, shortly before she is found dead.

Harwell, Eleanor   See LE CONTEAU, ELEANOR.

Harwell, Captain Richard   See MATHIAS, JOHN.

Hassan   A dedicated native servant in "THE ADVENTURE OF THE EGYPTIAN TOMB," he helps Hercule POIROT to identify the murderer of his employer, Sir John WILLARD.

Hastings, Captain Arthur, O.B.E.   A longtime friend and trusted aide of Hercule POIROT in cases that appear in eight novels and twenty-one short stories (see CATEGORICAL APPENDIX), he not only works as an investigator with Poirot but also serves a literary function in putting these cases on paper. Captain Hastings is first seen in THE MYSTERIOUS AFFAIR AT STYLES, set in 1916, shortly after convalescing from wounds suffered at the front in World War I. He accepts an invitation from a childhood friend to complete his convalescence at Styles, where he becomes reacquainted with Poirot, whom he had known before the war while working for Lloyd's of London. Thanks to his involvement in rescuing a kidnapped Prime Minister, he moves from a recruitment post with the War Office to the role of private secretary to a Member of Parliament. He and Poirot share an apartment for a time as they work together on various cases in which the methods of the great detective contrast sharply with those of his more gullible friend Hastings. In many instances, Poirot remarks upon Hastings' talent for missing the obvious and his disorganized approach to investigation. Whenever Hastings becomes too assured of his own detecting abilities, Poirot is deft at deflating his ego and pointing out his errors in logic. Despite his own frequent lack of modesty, Hastings is highly amused by Poirot's ego.

The stories reveal something of Hastings's personality and personal life. Women are his weakness, especially those with auburn hair, and several times he becomes particularly enamored of one. He has two

Captain Hastings, played to great success by Hugh Fraser, is the ever-bumbling but always-ready assistant to the great detective Hercule Poirot.   (Photo courtesy of London Weekend Television)

sisters whose names we never learn, as well as a wife and four children. His marriage to Dulcie DUVEEN occurs at the close of the case in MURDER ON THE LINKS, and the two leave for Argentina to manage a ranch. He fathers two daughters, Grace and Judith, and two sons whose names we are not told. After his marriage, Hastings returns to London several times, and helps his old friend in various cases. In the final Poirot case, CURTAIN, Hastings has become a widower and has relocated to England, where he joins his old friend in one last adventure.

Hastings, Dulcie Duveen   An American-born vaudeville entertainer, she has spent most of her life in England with her twin sister, Bella, who is the other half of The Dulcibella Kids. When she and Captain Arthur HASTINGS first meet in MURDER ON THE LINKS, she teasingly tells him that her name is Cinderella, which later earns her the nickname "Cinders," and she tries to break through his very reserved demeanor. She marries Hastings at the end of the case, moves to Argentina with him, and bears two daughters and two sons. Dulcie dies before her husband, leaving him a widower.

Hastings, Judith   The daughter of Captain Arthur HASTINGS and Dulcie Duveen HASTINGS, she is a research assistant who works with Dr. FRANKLIN, a specialist in tropical diseases. Captain Hastings observes in CURTAIN that she had always been his favorite child, although her interests and behavior have always puzzled him. She eventually marries Dr. Franklin and joins him in researching tropical diseases in Africa.

Hautet, Monsieur   The examining magistrate in MURDER ON THE LINKS, he earns the scorn of Hercule POIROT, who pronounces him to be a "famous old imbecile."

"Have You Got Everything You Want?" Mystery short story.

The story concerns a young wife who is convinced that her husband is plotting against her.

PUBLISHING AND DRAMATIZATION
HISTORY
The story appeared in the short story collection, PARKER PYNE INVESTIGATES, published in 1934 by William Collins Sons and Company, Ltd., in London, and, under the title, MR. PARKER PYNE, DETECTIVE, by Dodd, Mead and Company in New York.

The story has not been adapted for stage or screen.

CHARACTERS
Edward JEFFRIES, Elsie JEFFRIES, Mr. Parker Pyne, Madame SUBAYSKA

PLOT SYNOPSIS
While traveling on the Simplon Express enroute to Trieste, a young woman named Elsie Jeffcries consults Mr. Parker Pyne about a message she had read on the ink blotter at home. Her husband, Edward, had written the words "wife . . . Simplon Express . . . just before Venice would be the best time." Mr. Parker Pyne calms her and promises to stay with her. Just before the train reaches Venice, smoke erupts in the train corridor and chaos breaks out, after which Elsie finds that she has been robbed of her jewels. After several well-chosen questions and a telegram at Trieste, Mr. Parker Pyne not only solves the mystery of the missing jewels but also assures the romantic future of Edward and Elsie Jefferies.

CRIME NOTES
Mr. Parker Pyne insists in this story that he is not a detective, and that his aim is to help people who are unhappy.

Havering, Roger   The heir to a substantial fortune in "THE MYSTERY OF HUNTER'S LODGE," he dies soon after he receives the inheritance from his uncle Harrington PACE, who had lived with Roger and his wife for three years.

Havering, Zoe   A stage actress, she dies with her husband in a plane crash in "THE MYSTERY OF HUNTER'S LODGE" soon after they receive a substantial inheritance from his uncle.

Hawker, Dr.   An admirer of the intellectual powers of Hercule POIROT, this bachelor doctor lives a few streets away from the detective, whom he sometimes visits in the evenings in "THE ADVENTURE OF THE ITALIAN NOBLEMAN."

Hawker, Anthony   A disreputable-looking drug dealer in "THE HORSES OF DIOMEDES," he is shot by his girlfriend, Patience GRACE, while she is under the influence of cocaine.

Hawkes, Mr.   Despite his High Church views and pious fasting on Fridays, the new curate in ST. MARY MEAD embezzles church funds in MURDER AT THE VICARAGE. His superficial devoutness does not endear him to the vicar of St. Mary Mead, Leonard CLEMENT, who finds his behavior suspicious.

Hawkins, Edward   Pseudonym of ROBERT JONES.

Haworth, Alistair   A startlingly beautiful woman in "THE GIPSY," she possesses second sight, which she seems to have inherited from her mother, a well-known psychic medium. She foresees her own demise and is found dead the day after telling Mr. MacFARLANE that they would not meet again.

Hay, Sergeant   A stolid and thorough assistant to the inspector in charge of the murder investigation in A POCKET FULL OF RYE, he discovers the rye in Rex FORTESCUE's pocket.

Haydock, Captain   An old friend of the investigator in charge of the murder case in "ACCIDENT," he tries to keep Inspector EVANS from pursuing the investigation.

Haydock, Commander   A spy of several disguises in N OR M?, he is also known as "N" and Dr.

BINION. He plays the patriot as Commander Haydock, but he is a leader of the Fifth Column as "N." In the guise of Dr. Binion he attempts to interrogate Tuppence BERESFORD.

Haydock, Dr. The Police Surgeon in ST. MARY MEAD and a next-door neighbor of Miss Jane MARPLE, he makes an appearance in six cases: MURDER AT THE VICARAGE, THE BODY IN THE LIBRARY, THE MIRROR CRACK'D FROM SIDE TO SIDE, SLEEPING MURDER, "THE CASE OF THE CARETAKER" and "DEATH BY DROWNING." Contrary to prevailing theories, he believes that criminal behavior results from a physical malfunction that should be treated as one might treat a physical ailment.

Haydon, Elliot Stabbed in the shoulder during a fancy dress party he survives only to die later while on an expedition to the South Pole in "THE IDOL HOUSE OF ASTARTE."

Haydon, Sir Richard A longtime admirer of Diana ASHLEY, he trips and falls during her performance as Astarte and dies when a long thin knife pierces his heart in "THE IDOL HOUSE OF ASTARTE."

Hayes, Sergeant In charge of investigating the death of Walter ST. JOHN in Reverend HARMON's church, he too readily accepts a woman's claim of being the dead man's sister in "SANCTUARY."

Hayes, Mary Sweet and well-mannered but dull, she is selected to be the main character's companion in UNFINISHED PORTRAIT.

Haymes, Phillipa (Pip) A widow who works as an assistant gardener in A MURDER IS ANNOUNCED, she and her sister Emma STAMFORDIS stand to inherit a substantial fortune if Letitia BLACKLOCK, the woman with whom she boards, should die.

Hayward, Sir Arthur An Assistant Commissioner of Scotland Yard and Charles HAYWARD's father in CROOKED HOUSE, he is affectionately referred to as "the Old Man" by his son and subordinates. Despite an emotionless exterior, Sir Arthur loves his son deeply and is very concerned about his involvement in the LEONIDES case. He is also a very perceptive man who respects his son and who knows exactly what each man under his command is doing.

Hayward, Charles The son of an Assistant Commissioner of Scotland Yard, he met Sophia LEONIDES, the woman whom he wants to marry, while serving with her in the Diplomatic Service in Egypt, but tragedy separates them when they return to England in CROOKED HOUSE. He is aware of the suspicions under which all Leonides family members are placed after the death of the family patriarch, and he is determined to clear Sophia's name.

Hazy, Lady Selina An elderly guest at Bertram's Hotel, she is in London to consult Harley Street specialists about her arthritis and teeth in AT BERTRAM'S HOTEL. Because of vision problems, she continuously mistakes strangers for acquaintances, occasionally with annoying results.

Hearn, Detective Inspector Skilled in working with French law enforcement officials in "THE GIRDLE OF HIPPOLYTA," he is a valuable ally for Hercule POIROT in solving a mystery.

Heath, Dr. A fussy, elderly physician and a fan of Hercule POIROT, he is called to examine the dead body of Carlotta ADAMS in LORD EDGWARE DIES.

Heavyweather, Sir Ernest Known throughout England as an attorney who mercilessly bullies witnesses in the courtroom, he is the pompous, egotistical defender of John CAVENDISH, on trial for murdering his stepmother in THE MYSTERIOUS AFFAIR AT STYLES.

Heilger, Romaine See VOLE, ROMAINE.

Helier, Jane A popular actress, also known as Jane HELMAN, her strength lies in her beauty, not her intellect, in "THE AFFAIR AT THE BUNGALOW." She also appears briefly in "STRANGE JEST," referring two young people to seek help from Miss Jane MARPLE.

Hellin, Marie The former maid to Katrina SAMOUSHENKA, she might be the woman sought by Hercule POIROT as he tries to reunite two lovers in "THE ARCADIAN DEER." Once he meets with her and observes her sharp tongue and unpleasant demeanor, he concludes that she could not be the woman for whom Ted WILLIAMSON pined.

Helman, Jane   See HELIER, JANE.

Hemming, Mrs.   A quaint, old-fashioned woman in THE CLOCKS, she lives next to the house in which the first murder occurs, and keeps twelve cats to whom she speaks as if they were human beings able to answer her.

Hemmingway, Gerald   A young actor who plays the role of STEPHENS the window washer in CARDS ON THE TABLE, he helps Hercule POIROT to force Dr. ROBERTS to admit his guilt in Mrs. LORRIMER's death.

Henden   An unscrupulous-looking butler in DEAD MAN'S FOLLY, he is at his best when banging the dinner gong, which he does with a flourish and obvious delight.

Henderson, Dr.   As the Bishop of Northumbria, he is a highly credible witness who aids in saving the reputation of Dagmar FERRIER in "THE AUGEAN STABLES." He testifies that she was staying with him and his wife at the time that the libelous *X-Ray News* claimed she had a rendezvous with an Argentine gigolo.

Henderson, Deidre   A plain young woman who takes little care with her appearance, she also pays no attention to social graces in MRS. MCGINTY'S DEAD. Due to the generosity of an aunt from whom she inherited a large sum of money, Deidre has financial control over her mother and stepfather.

Henderson, Ellie   A never-married woman of forty-five in "PROBLEM AT SEA," she freely admits to both her age and her fascination with scandals. She impresses Hercule POIROT with her ability to manipulate an irritable old general to obtain information regarding Colonel CLAPPERTON, a man with whom she falls in love while en route to Egypt.

Hendon   The butler at Nasse Hall in DEAD MAN'S FOLLY.

Henet   One of several murder victims in DEATH COMES AS THE END, she is the completely devoted

housekeeper of IMHOTEP, whom she obeys without question. She has an unattractive personality, and dies after being suffocated and swathed in linen.

Hengrave, Mrs.   A widow in SLEEPING MURDER, she has unusual tastes in interior design which include mustard-colored walls and a wisteria frieze in the drawing room.

Henry   The appearance and manner of this robust and courtly butler at Bertram's Hotel seem out of place in modern London. He is the perfect butler who is at once sympathetic and efficient, and he has an uncanny ability to sense a guest's needs in AT BERTRAM'S HOTEL.

Hensley, Mr.   An employee of the Baghdad Public Works, he becomes a murder suspect despite his close friendship with the victim in "THE GATE OF BAGHDAD." He is incriminated by having sat behind the murdered man on the journey and by the sand found in his pocket which may be linked with the suspected weapon, a sandbag.

Henson, Reverend Eustace   A young, thin curate, he presides over the christening of Shirley, the third child of Mr. and Mrs. FRANKLIN in THE BURDEN.

"Herb of Death, The"   Mystery short story.
   The story focuses on the death that occurs when foxglove is mixed with sage in the roast duck stuffing.

PUBLISHING AND DRAMATIZATION HISTORY
The story appeared in the short story collection, THE THIRTEEN PROBLEMS published in 1932 by William Collins Sons and Company, Ltd., in London, and, under the title, *The Tuesday Club Murders*, by Dodd, Mead and Company in 1933 in New York.
   The story has not been adapted for stage or screen.

CHARACTERS
Dolly BANTRY, Sir Ambrose BERCY, Mrs. Adelaide CARPENTER, Sylvia KEENE, Jerry LORIMER, Miss MARPLE, Maude WYE

PLOT SYNOPSIS

Dolly Bantry tells the Tuesday Night Club the story of a fatal dinner she attended some months earlier during which a young woman died. All of the guests had become extremely ill after eating the duck, which included sage stuffing, but Sir Ambrose's ward, Sylvia Keene, died. Investigators found that poisonous foxglove leaves had been picked with the sage and included in the fatal stuffing. Six months after Sylvia's death, her fiancé, Jerry, married Maud, who stands to inherit a fortune. Miss Marple becomes suspicious after pondering the marriage and the fact that only Sylvia died, even though everyone had eaten the stuffing.

CRIME NOTES

The victim dies of poisoning from ingesting foxglove leaves, which are made more potent by the addition of digitalin.

Hercule Poirot's Christmas Mystery novel.

The novel is prefaced by the epigram from *Macbeth*, "Yet who would have thought the old man to have had so much blood in him?" The plot of this locked-room mystery centers on the effort of Hercule POIROT to identify the murderer of patriarch Simeon LEE, who has called his family together during the Christmas holidays in order to taunt them.

PUBLISHING AND DRAMATIZATION HISTORY

The novel was published in 1938 by William Collins Sons and Company in London, and, under the title, *Murder for Christmas,* by Dodd, Mead and Company in 1939 in New York.

The novel has not been adapted for stage or screen.

CHARACTERS

Gladys BEST, Mr. CHARLTON, Stephen (Farr) GRANT, Sydney HORBURY, Colonel JOHNSON (1), Queenie JONES, Joan KENCH, Adelaide LEE, Alfred LEE, David LEE, George LEE, Harry LEE, Hilda LEE, Lydia LEE, Magdalene LEE, Simeon LEE, Conchita LOPEZ, Beatrice MOSCOMB, Hercule Poirot, Emily REEVES, Gladys SPENT, Superintendent SUGDEN, Edward TRESSILIAN

PLOT SYNOPSIS

Part 1

The novel opens as Stephen Farr and Conchita Lopez, traveling as Pilar Estravados, meet on a train on their way to visit family for the holidays. In England, the members of Simeon Lee's extended family discuss the upcoming Christmas holiday, during which all are expected to gather at the family home at the patriarch's command. Their reactions to the invitation vary, revealing the individual relationships between family members. Simeon has also invited the child of his late daughter and a Spanish artist. Prodigal son Harry will also be present, as well as his more stable and respectable brothers. As he ponders the events to come, Simeon opens his safe and takes out a bag of uncut diamonds, to which he talks as he runs his fingers through them.

Part 2

Harry Lee arrives, and he is met by his sister-in-law Lydia and niece. Simeon shows the uncut diamonds to his counterfeit granddaughter, telling her that they are worth ten thousand pounds. David Lee recalls his late mother reading to him when he was young; he plays a song at the piano for a short while before bringing his hands down on the keys with a crash. Stephen Farr, whose father knew Simeon in South Africa, also arrives and surprises the false Pilar.

Part 3

Simeon begins to taunt his sons, telling each of them something he is sure will irritate. Not content to insult them, Simeon also berates his sons, saying that their mother had the "brains of a louse," before sending them out of his sight. Soon after, Superintendent Sugden arrives, collecting for the police orphanage. Dinner is served, but Simeon fails to join his family, and soon a scream and a crash are heard from his room upstairs. Family members break into the room and find Simeon dead in a pool of blood. Local law enforcement arrives, and Hercule Poirot, a holiday guest of Colonel Johnson, joins the investigation. Alerted by Superintendent Sugden that Simeon's diamonds have been stolen, Poirot questions the family members to determine which of them had the motive and the opportunity to commit the crime. He also asks what kind of man Simeon had been when young, and learns that he was a womanizer who drank a bit, and that he had a sense of humor that was more than tempered by a vengeful streak. The safe is examined, and a fifteen-year-old will is found in which Simeon left half of his estate to his son Alfred and directed that the remaining half be divided among the four remaining children.

Part 4

Magdalene Lee, Simeon's daughter-in-law, tells Poirot that Pilar picked up something right after the murder was discovered and gave it to Sugden. Speaking with Sugden, Poirot also learns that two family members were not speaking on the phone near the time of the murder, as they had claimed. Two other daughters-in-law of the murder victim speak with Poirot to tell him that their husbands are victims of the dead man, but not his murderers. While looking at a garden constructed by Lydia Lee, Poirot recognizes that the pebbles which are used in the Dead Sea motif are really the missing diamonds.

Part 5

As Poirot delves further into the secrets of each family member, he uncovers unsavory, previously hidden details. Alfred approaches the detective and asks him to stay and to solve the case, a request which Poirot must consider. Later, as he examines family portraits hanging in the corridor, he is met by the false Pilar, whom he observes would be a bad enemy, with her volatile mix of Spanish, Irish, English and gipsy blood. He tells her that the police want to see her passport and, while she goes to get the passport, Poirot attempts an experiment to determine who could have heard Simeon's scream. Satisfied with the results of the experiment, Poirot accepts the case, then asks Alfred for a picture of Simeon as a young man.

Part 6

Mr. Charlton reads the will, which leads to some disagreement within the family regarding whether or not Simeon's granddaughter should receive her mother's share of the estate. As the family discusses this, Poirot returns and learns from Tressilian that a cannonball from the front entrance of the house is missing. He also receives a telegram which verifies that the real Stephen Farr died two years previously. Before he can act on his new knowledge, a thud and an ear-piercing scream are heard. Poirot and Sugden rush to false Pilar's room, where they learn that the cannonball had been balanced on top of the door to her room and that it had fallen and nearly struck her.

Unnerved by the experience, she admits that she is an imposter, and states that the real Pilar was killed in a bombing in Spain. She took the passport because she bore a likeness to Pilar. Stephen admits that he had known the Farrs in South Africa and that he decided to pass as Stephen to get to know Pilar better. He is also Simeon's illegitimate son. Poirot finds that he has all the pieces to the puzzle; he unmasks the murderer and explains the elaborate murder plan.

Part 7

After the murderer is taken away by the authorities, the family says its farewells, and tentatively plans to hold Christmas on the Riviera the following year.

CRIME NOTES
The sole murder victim in this novel dies when his throat is cut.

Hercule Poirot's Early Cases   See POIROT'S EARLY CASES.

Hermanstein, Ikey   See ISAACSTEIN, HERMAN.

Heroulde, M.   A sinister figure whose respectable appearance masks the fact that he is a counterfeiter in "THE CRACKLER."

Hersheimmer, Julius P.   A caricature of the rough-and-ready, brash American, he carries a gun named "Little Willie," and his favorite expression is "Put me wise." The wealthy cousin of Jane FINN, he offers one million pounds to locate her and her family in THE SECRET ADVERSARY, and briefly becomes enamored with Tuppence BERESFORD, whom he half-heartedly asks to marry him.

Hetherington, Janet   While she appears to be a typical middle-aged English lady whose favorite pastimes are knitting and gossip, she is really an intelligence agent whose territory consists of Spain and Morocco in DESTINATION UNKNOWN. To complete her disguise, she socializes only with English and American guests "of a certain social standing," and voices the appropriate disapproval when an unmarried celebrity couple checks into the Hotel St. Louis.

Hickory Dickory Death   See HICKORY DICKORY DOCK.

Hickory Dickory Dock   Mystery novel.

The novel concerns a series of very complicated occurrences in a youth hostel. The plot centers on the efforts of Hercule POIROT to discover the perpetrator of petty yet bizarre crimes, which hide an even greater evil.

PUBLISHING AND DRAMATIZATION HISTORY

The novel was published in 1955 by William Collins Sons and Company, Ltd., in London, and, under the title, HICKORY DICKORY DEATH, by Dodd, Mead and Company in New York.

The novel has not been adapted for stage or screen.

CHARACTERS

Mr. AKIBOMBO, Achmed ALI, Celia AUSTIN, Leonard BATESON, Sergeant BELL, Nigel CHAPMAN, Mr. ENDICOTT, Sally FINCH, GERONIMO, Valerie HOBHOUSE, Mrs. HUBBARD, Elizabeth JOHNSTON, Chandra LAL, Patricia LANE, Miss Felicity LEMON, Colin McNABB, Mrs. NICOLETIS, Hercule Poirot, Inspector SHARPE, Jean TOMLINSON

PLOT SYNOPSIS

Chapters 1–2

Hercule Poirot is shocked when his usually meticulous secretary Miss Lemon makes three mistakes in typing the same letter. She tells him that she is worried about her sister, the manager of a youth hostel that has been the site of a series of petty thefts. The detective suggests that Miss Lemon invite her sister, Mrs. Hubbard, to tea so that he may speak with her. He is puzzled when he learns that all of the items stolen, aside from a diamond ring, had little financial value.

Chapters 3–6

When Mrs. Hubbard returns to the hostel, she learns that one of the students plans to leave because of the thefts, and another complains that someone poured green ink over her study sheets. Perturbed, Mrs. Hubbard calls Poirot and asks him to speak with the students. After discussing his methods, the detective shocks those present by suggesting that they call the police, a tactic which leads to Celia Austin's confes-

sion to some of the thefts. Psychiatry student Colin McNabb is intrigued by Celia Austin's "problem," and asks her to marry him so that he can study her at close range.

Chapters 7–10

Celia is found dead, an apparent suicide from an overdose of morphine. The suicide note found near the body is not in her handwriting, and Poirot believes that she was murdered. Investigators learn that Celia had obtained the drug from her job at St. Catherine's Hospital, but they identify several suspects. They interview Nigel Chapman, who asserts that Celia was a kleptomaniac. The police suspect him because he served her coffee and the drug was traced to her coffee cup. Under pressure, Chapman admits that he took Bateson's stethoscope and that he has three types of poison in his drawer, but he swears that he is not guilty.

Chapters 11–13

Inspector Sharpe questions other students and learns from Sally Finch that the day before her death, Celia had said something about an electric bulb and a passport. Elizabeth Johnston, whose study sheets were ruined when green ink was poured over them, claims that she dislikes Sally, but gives no reason. A frustrated Sharpe plans to get a search warrant, which upsets the owner of the hostel, Mrs. Nicoletis. Poirot asks Mrs. Hubbard to list the stolen items in the order in which they disappeared. He also asks Geronimo, an Italian-born servant in the house, about the electric bulb. He learns from Sharpe that several of the students have an unsavory history.

Chapters 14–16

Mrs. Nicoletis becomes anxious about the proceedings, and begins to drink liquor, but she soon becomes ill, passes out, and dies. An inquest is planned, and an autopsy is arranged. During this time, Poirot discovers that the diamond in the ring that had been stolen then returned is fake. The students believe that Mrs. Nicoletis was murdered, and Patricia Lane reveals that she replaced the morphine in Chapman's drawer with a harmless substance, but the real morphine has now disappeared. As tension builds, Chapman learns that his father is dying but refuses to visit because his father may have murdered his mother. The students begin to accuse each other of the murders.

Chapters 17–19
Patricia calls Chapman, asking him to visit her, but she is dead when he arrives. The investigators suggest, based on their evidence, that a woman killed Patricia. Mr. Akibombo tells the investigators that he had an upset stomach a few days earlier and took what he thought was sodium bicarbonate from Patricia's room, but it turned out to be boracic acid in the bottle Patricia thought she had filled with morphine taken from Nigel's drawer.

Chapters 20–23
Investigators learn that Valerie works in a store that is a cover for a phony passport business, and they also learn that Mrs. Nicoletis is her mother. Other information is discovered regarding Chapman which complicates the case. Poirot finally sorts through the clues to uncover the murderers and solve the case. At the end, Miss Lemon tells the detective that her sister has resigned from her job, and is taking a long cruise.

CRIME NOTES
The novel contains three murders. Two victims are poisoned with morphine tartrate, and a third victim is hit on the back of the head with a sock containing a heavy paperweight.

Hicks, Anthony   The second husband of Agatha Christie's only child, Rosalind, who married him five years after the World War II death of her first husband. HICKS was trained as a barrister and called to the Bar, and he also studied Sanskrit and Tibetan. Both Christie and her second husband, Sir Max MALLOWAN, write that he was one of the kindest people they had ever known.

Hicks, Rosalind Christie Prichard   Born in 1919, she is the only child of Agatha Christie and the product of the author's first marriage to Colonel Archibald CHRISTIE. She was widowed when her first husband, Hubert PRICHARD, was killed in World War II; she married Anthony HICKS in 1949. She is the mother of Christie's only grandchild, Mathew PRICHARD, born on September 21, 1942.

Hickson, Joan   A British actress born in 1906, she has been hailed as the quintessential Miss MARPLE for her portrayal of the sleuth in the 1984 through 1989 television adaptations of the following

Christie novels: AT BERTRAM'S HOTEL, THE BODY IN THE LIBRARY, THE CARIBBEAN MYSTERY, 4.50 FROM PADDINGTON, THE MOVING FINGER, MURDER AT THE VICARAGE, A MURDER IS ANNOUNCED, NEMESIS, A POCKETFUL OF RYE and SLEEPING MURDER.

Higgins, Bill   A stoic deep-sea diver hired by John NEWMAN to search for the sunken gold cargo of the wrecked *Juan Fernandez* in "INGOTS OF GOLD."

Higgins, Mary   See SKINNER, EMILY.

Higgs, William   Despite his small stature and rat-like appearance, this Cockney dog trainer seems to work miracles in leading the intimidating guard dog, Cerberus, from the nightclub, Hell, to police headquarters in "THE CAPTURE OF CERBERUS." When asked to explain his method, he tells the Countess Vera ROSSAKOFF that it was something that he would " 'Ardly like to say afore a lady," and adds that such methods would not work with female dogs.

Higley, Milly   A buxom waitress lacking common sense, she worked at the Ginger Cat with the second victim in THE A.B.C. MURDERS, Elizabeth BARNARD. Hercule POIROT charms her into speaking with him by pointedly paying attention to her physical charms.

Hill, Mr.   A man who looks like "a white worm," he is singer Jane HARDING's piano accompanist in GIANT'S BREAD.

Hill, Florence   Despite her intimidating appearance, the former maidservant of Miss Jane MARPLE is fiercely protective of her old employer in 4.50 FROM PADDINGTON. She now runs a lodging house, but gladly looks after Miss MARPLE while Lucy EYELESBARROW works on assignment at Rutherford Hall.

Hill, Gladys   The parlourmaid in "THE AFFAIR OF THE PINK PEARL," she finds the pendant with the missing pearl.

Hill, Mary   A chambermaid in "MISS MARPLE TELLS A STORY," she is the last person to see the murdered Mrs. RHODES alive.

Hillingdon, Colonel Edward   A botanist and colleague of the Dysons, with whom he and his wife travel each year to the West Indies, he is also an unfaithful husband who had an affair with his traveling companion's second wife, Lucky DYSON in A CARIBBEAN MYSTERY. After the affair ends, Lucky manipulates him with reminders of his role in helping her to remove the first Mrs. DYSON.

Hillingdon, Evelyn   Married to Colonel Edward HILLINGDON and herself a botanist, she journeys yearly with her husband and the Dysons to the West Indies in A CARIBBEAN MYSTERY. She knows about her husband's affair with Lucky DYSON, but attempts to forget the past when he ends the affair and vows to make their marriage work.

Hinchcliffe, Miss   A stern-faced woman with a stoic attitude, she lives with the feather-brained Amy MURGATROYD on a small pig and poultry farm in A MURDER IS ANNOUNCED. Despite reservations, she is convinced by her friend to become an onlooker to the murder which is advertised in the local paper.

Hobhouse, Valerie   She is the daughter of Mrs. NICOLETIS, who runs the youth hostel in HICKORY DICKORY DOCK, and she works in the Sabrina Fair beauty parlor. Her elegant appearance belies her illegal inclinations, which include a very profitable smuggling business and the underworld contacts which she makes under the guise of many aliases: Mrs. DA SILVA, Sheila DONOVAN, Miss Irene FRENCH, Mrs. Olga KOHN, Miss Nina LE MESURIER, Madame MAHMOUDI, Miss Moira O'NEELE and Mrs. Gladys THOMAS.

Hod   A "stupid but honest-looking" medical orderly, he is entrusted with the safety of Nick BUCKLEY, who is confined to a clinic in PERIL AT END HOUSE. That trust seems misplaced when he delivers a box of poisoned chocolates to his charge.

Hodgson, Mr.   A partner in the firm of solicitors who represent Hercule POIROT, he speaks with respondents when Poirot places an advertisement for information regarding Claud DARRELL in THE BIG FOUR.

Hoffman, Robert   A seemingly respectable diamond merchant, he and his brother have been involved in questionable activities in other areas of Europe in the past. A suspicious Chief Inspector Fred DAVY delves deeply into Hoffman's business in AT BERTRAM'S HOTEL and learns that the Hoffman brothers are the actual owners of the hotel.

Hogben, Superintendent   See JIM.

Hogg, Doris   A domestic staff member at the elite girls' school, Meadowbrook, she has no information and no opinions when questioned by police about the murder of Miss SPRINGER in CAT AMONG THE PIGEONS.

Hogg, Frederick   A self-important young man, he is the only person to see Major EUSTACE leave the apartment of the murdered Barbara ALLEN in MURDER IN THE MEWS.

Hoggin, Sir Joseph   A philandering husband who hires Hercule POIROT to find his wife's kidnapped Pekinese Shan Tung in "THE NEMEAN LION," he is carrying on an affair with his glamorous blonde secretary.

Hoggin, Lady Milly   A "stout, petulant-looking woman with dyed henna red hair" in "THE NEMEAN LION," she cares more for her dog than for the feelings of the humans in her life. When her Pekinese Shan Tung is kidnapped and the ransom note warns her that the dog's ears and tail will be cut off if she goes to the police, she berates her husband into retaining a private detective, and he hires the best, Hercule POIROT.

Hohenbach Salm, Princess Sasha   A dark and mysterious Russian noblewoman in ABSENT IN THE SPRING, she inspires the main character to reveal her hidden feelings about family and self.

Hollaby, Mr.   A partner in Sessle's Porcupine Assurance Company, he is the last identified person to see Anthony SESSLE alive and the only witness to his partner's strange behavior on the golf course in "THE SUNNINGDALE MYSTERY."

Holland, Desmond   He is a seventeen-year-old in HALLOWE'EN PARTY whose psychiatric record marks him as a possible murder suspect in the death of Joyce REYNOLDS. Questioned by Hercule POIROT, he suggests a range of other suspects for which he presents highly original justifications. The detective believes him to be innocent, and requests that he and Nicholas RANSOME protect Miranda BUTLER.

Holland, Elsie   A nursery governess in THE MOV-ING FINGER whose exquisite features, shapely body, and breathtaking beauty captivate every man she meets. Her one flaw is her "flat, competent voice." She is one of the recipients of the poisoned pen letters which plague the village.

Hollow, The   Mystery novel.

The author describes the novel in AN AUTOBIOG-RAPHY as the one "I had ruined by the introduction of Poirot," in this, his twenty-second appearance in a novel. The plot centers on Hercule POIROT's efforts to identify the murderer of a prominent physician, whose personal life is decidedly less admirable than his professional one.

PUBLISHING AND DRAMATIZATION HISTORY

The novel was published in 1946 by William Collins Sons and Company, Ltd., in London, and, under the title, *Murder After Hours*, by Dodd, Mead and Company in New York.

The novel was adapted for the stage by the author, and the play opened at the Fortune Theatre in London on June 7, 1951. The character of Hercule Poirot was omitted from the cast.

CHARACTERS

ALBERT, Madame ALFREDGE, David ANGKATELL, Edward ANGKATELL, Sir Henry ANGKATELL, Lady Lucy ANGKATELL, Gerda CHRISTOW, Dr. John CHRISTOW, Zena CHRISTOW, Beryl COLLINS, Mrs. CRABTREE, Veronica CRAY, Inspector GRANGE, Mr. GUDGEON, Midge HARDCASTLE, Elsie PATTERSON, Hercule Poirot, Doris SAUNDERS, Henrietta SAVERNAKE

PLOT SYNOPSIS

Chapters 1–3

Lady Lucy Angkatell awakens Midge Hardcastle early one morning at The Hollow, in order to plan the upcoming weekend. As Lady Lucy obsesses about her guest list, Henrietta Savernake works in her sculpting studio with model Doris Saunders, aiming to capture just the right spirit in her work. As she reaches her goal, Henrietta destroys the work

through unspoken frustration. Later that day, Dr. John Christow completes a day of seeing patients and thinks about a former lover, the actress Veronica Cray. He looks forward to the weekend at The Hollow, where he will again see his current love, Henrietta.

Chapters 4–5

The doctor daydreams about Henrietta, and recalls that she once asked his wife Gerda to sit for a sculpture. The results were two figures, a statuette for Gerda, and another, for his eyes only, of a figure worshipping an unseen deity, which Henrietta said was the doctor. As John arrives home late for dinner, he reflects upon his "horrible" house, in which his wife agonizes over her ruined dinner and his precocious nine-year-old daughter Zena reads his future in the cards with frightening accuracy.

Chapters 6–9

The guests arrive at The Hollow, and various secrets are revealed. Edward Angkatell arrives with Henrietta, and asks her to marry him. She refuses, and he says that she would probably marry him if there were no John Christow in her mind. Veronica Cray is the Angkatell's neighbor. She and John meet that night in a small pavilion near the swimming pool, and Gerda pretends not to notice when he sneaks home hours later.

Chapters 10–12

Veronica wants John to become her lover again. John refuses her, so she threatens him. John is later shot at the poolside, just as Hercule Poirot arrives to see Gerda standing over John, holding a revolver. She claims to have picked up the revolver after finding him lying on the ground. Inspector Grange is convinced that she is the murderer.

Chapters 13–15

Henrietta becomes distraught at John's death, and Edward tries to comfort her. The household is in turmoil, and Midge calls the dress shop to explain that she cannot go to work because of the murder. Grange and Poirot find Veronica Cray's fur cape in the pavilion, as well as six boxes of matches that she borrowed from the Angkatells the night before. Grange questions why Veronica went to the Angkatells' house a half-mile away for matches.

Chapters 16–18

Grange questions those present during the murder. Everyone has a different theory. Henrietta admits that she had been the victim's mistress for six months, but the *real* woman in his life most recently was Mrs. Crabtree, a patient who is valiantly fighting Ridgeway's disease. She also tells Poirot about the rendezvous with Veronica Cray.

Chapters 19–21
One of the maids reports that the butler was in the hall with a revolver in his hand. When questioned, he claims that he found the revolver lying on the hall table, and replaced it in the master's collection. Lady Lucy contradicts Gudgeon, after thanking him for trying to spare her trouble. She says that she placed the gun on the table but cannot remember why.

Chapters 22–24
Veronica approaches Poirot, and lies to him about what passed between John and her on their night together. After the inquest, Henrietta returns to her sculpting, and Midge returns to work in the dress shop. When Edward goes to the shop to take Midge to lunch, he tells her that she deserves better, and asks her to marry him and live with him on the family estate. She agrees.

Chapters 25–27
Lady Lucy immediately begins to plan the wedding. Poirot finds the gun missing from the master's collection in the hedges, and Lady Lucy tells him that she knows who committed the murder and will tell him if he drops the investigation, but he refuses. Midge imagines that Edward still loves Henrietta, and she breaks off their engagement.

Chapters 28–30
A distraught Edward attempts to commit suicide by turning on the gas and placing his head in the oven, but Midge breaks the kitchen window and saves him. Later in the day, Gerda and Henrietta meet for tea, but Poirot walks in and recommends that the tea remain untouched. Despite his warning, the murderer drinks the tea, which has been poisoned, and dies. The motive for the crime was the victim's rendezvous with Veronica Cray.

CRIME NOTES
The sole murder in the novel results from a gunshot wound. The poison in the tea, which the murderer drinks at the end of the novel, is not identified.

Holmes, Mr. (1)   A well-trained butler, he follows the orders of his eccentric employer, Mr. FARLEY, without question in "THE DREAM."

Holmes, Mr. (2)   See OBOLOVITCH, PRINCE MICHAEL.

Holmes, Gladys (Gladdie)   A solidly built girl with a nervous giggle and an even temperament, she is a cousin of Miss Jane MARPLE's maid, Emily, in "THE CASE OF THE PERFECT MAID." Gladdie is opinionated and adenoidal, but she is basically honest, despite her employers' charge that she stole a brooch.

Honeycott, Mrs.   A violent opponent of the Roman Catholic Church who refers to the church as "The Scarlet Woman," she suspects the intent of convents with their "quantities of beautiful young girls shut up there." Gilda GLEN is murdered in her home in "THE MAN IN THE MIST."

Hood, Miss   A governess in UNFINISHED PORTRAIT, she becomes part of the family.

Hope, Evelyn (1)   An accused murderess whose real name is Eva Kane, she moves to Australia and changes her name after being cleared of guilt in the notorious Craig trial in MRS. McGINTY'S DEAD. She names her son with the same first name as hers.

Hope, Evelyn (2)   See UPWARD, ROBIN.

Hope, Mrs. Gerald   One of the wealthy mothers of students at the very exclusive Meadowbrook School, she becomes irate when the school refuses to allow her daughter to leave midterm for a vacation in CAT AMONG THE PIGEONS. She is easily appeased by Miss BULSTRODE's flattering words regarding her newest designer suit.

Hope, Mildred   One of two young women in "THE THIRD-FLOOR FLAT," she was given the apartment key for safekeeping but lost it on the way home.

Hopkins, Jessie   A District Nurse in SAD CYPRESS who takes an inordinate interest in the disposition of Laura WELMAN's estate, she writes an anonymous letter telling Elinor CARLISLE that someone is flattering her aunt to obtain the inheritance. She later convinces Laura Welman's heir, Mary GERRARD, to leave her money to an aunt in New Zealand.

Hopkinson, Mr. Precise and businesslike, he is legal advisor to Mary HARTER and has guided her in creating each of her wills in "WHERE THERE'S A WILL."

Horbury, Lady Cicely A clever and manipulating former chorus girl in DEATH IN THE CLOUDS, she is married to Lord Stephen HORBURY, who wants a divorce which she has refused to grant him. Her cocaine addiction and gambling obsession have made her an expensive embarrassment, and Lord HORBURY regrets his marriage. She is present on the *Prometheus* flight when Madame GISELLE is murdered.

Horbury, Lord Stephen An English aristocrat in DEATH IN THE CLOUDS, he falls in love with a glamorous and beautiful chorus girl and marries her, then soon regrets the marriage. He later falls in love with the Honourable Venetia KERR but remains silent about his love to protect his family honor and to prevent his wife from gaining grounds for divorce.

Horbury, Sydney A male nurse with an unctuous manner in HERCULE POIROT'S CHRISTMAS, he is furtive in his movements and disconcerts the family of his charge, Simeon LEE, with his lurking and slinking in the shadows.

Horder, Mr. A gnarled and elderly retired gardener in post–World War II England, he works for Laura FRANKLIN out of a respect for her gardening sense in THE BURDEN.

Hori The chief advisor and confidant to Egyptian ruler IMHOTEP, he acts as a steadying influence on the royal household when the murders begin in DEATH COMES AS THE END. He accurately assesses the pattern of the murders and saves the life of IMHOTEP's daughter RENISENB, later marrying her.

Horlick A young and nervous gardener who expects to be married soon, he asks Elinor CARLISLE to recommend him for the post of main gardener to the new owner when she sells Hunterbury Hall in SAD CYPRESS. His distinguishing characteristic is his Adam's apple, which moves rapidly up and down his neck as he speaks.

Horriston, Dr. Viewed by Tommy BERESFORD as unpleasant-looking and shifty-eyed, the doctor operates a weight control clinic in "THE CASE OF THE MISSING LADY."

Horsefall, Pamela A caricature of a woman reporter with her "tall, manly-looking" features, heavy drinking and smoking habits and hard-edged manner, she writes the article about women involved in murder cases which makes at least one woman in MRS. MCGINTY'S DEAD nervous—and dangerous.

Horsefield, Sir Roderick An aged former army man who is currently writing his memoirs, he consults Hercule POIROT when some politically sensitive papers disappear in THIRD GIRL. He has poor eyesight, and doctors have cautioned him that his health is frail, yet Sir Roderick continues to enjoy a whiskey whenever possible.

"Horses of Diomedes, The" Mystery short story.

The plot focuses on cocaine use among the wealthy, and presents an unexpected source of the substance.

PUBLISHING AND DRAMATIZATION HISTORY

The story appeared in the short story collection, THE LABOURS OF HERCULES, published in 1947 by William Collins Sons and Company, Ltd., in London, and by Dodd, Mead and Company in New York.

The story has not been adapted for stage or screen.

CHARACTERS

Lady CARMICHAEL, Patience GRACE, General GRANT, Pam GRANT, Sheila GRANT, Anthony HAWKER, Mrs. Beryl LARKIN, Hercule POIROT, Dr. Michael STODDART

PLOT SYNOPSIS

The story opens when Hercule Poirot is summoned by physician Michael Stoddart, who is treating two women suffering from the effects of cocaine use during a wild party in London the night before. The physician is infatuated with the young, seemingly innocent Sheila Grant, whom he had met before in Mertonshire. Poirot agrees to return to Mertonshire and investigate the stories of drug use in the region and the involvement of the four wild daughters of the retired General Grant. He uncovers a sophisticated drug-dealing operation and a surprising source of the drug.

CRIME NOTES
The mythological Hercules dealt with the human-flesh-eating horses of Diomedes, but Hercule Poirot deals with the cocaine-consuming young women in the story, who are dangers to themselves and to others.

Horsham See CRISPIN, ANGUS.

Horsham, Henry A highly placed security man in PASSENGER TO FRANKFURT, his security clearance grants him admittance to extremely confidential meetings, especially those in which Project Benvo is discussed. He also has access to classified information and knows highly placed individuals in the British Intelligence community.

Horton, Dr. A solid and reliable general practitioner, he is called upon by Mr. SATTERTHWAITE to analyze the presumed poison in the teacup in "THE HARLEQUIN TEA SET."

Horton, Major A former British officer in India, he is now retired yet continues the same regimented existence in MURDER IS EASY. Henpecked by his wife, Lydia HORTON, this man with the stiff moustache and protruding eyes commends such behavior and expresses the view that a man needs a wife to keep him in line. "Otherwise he gets slack—yes, slack." He appears to suffer a great loss when Lydia Horton dies of gastroenteritis.

Horton, Inez A beautiful, dark-haired young woman, approximately twenty years of age, she is the granddaughter of Thomas ADDISON in "THE HARLEQUIN TEA SET." She and her father live in the house next to Addison's.

Horton, Lydia A difficult woman in MURDER IS EASY who runs her household like a military camp, she goes through fifteen cooks and parlourmaids in a year. Married to Major HORTON, she nags him incessantly, and others view her as the most disagreeable woman alive. She dies of gastroenteritis shortly after eating hothouse grapes.

Horton, Maria The late daughter of Thomas ADDISON and wife of Dr. HORTON in "THE HARLEQUIN TEA SET," she dies while giving birth to her daughter Inez.

Hoskins, Robert (Bob) A police constable in DEAD MAN'S FOLLY, he doggedly patrols his territory and makes notes of everything that occurs.

"Hound of Death, The" Mystery short story.
The story centers on a mysterious Belgian nun who possesses supernatural powers that may threaten the world.

PUBLISHING AND DRAMATIZATION HISTORY
The story appeared in the short story collection, THE HOUND OF DEATH AND OTHER STORIES, published in 1933 by William Collins Sons and Company, Ltd., in London.
The story has not been adapted for stage or screen.

CHARACTERS
Sister Marie ANGELIQUE, Mr. ANSTRUTHER, Dr. ROSE, William P. RYAN

PLOT SYNOPSIS
The story is related by Mr. Anstruther who, just before leaving London for a visit with his sister to a small village in Cornwall, learns from an American reporter that a Belgian nun who had worked a miracle now lives in the same village. During World War I, the nun lived in a convent that exploded spontaneously when German soldiers threatened to enter it. The rubble of the convent had formed the shape of a hound. Currently under the care of Dr. Rose, the nun now speaks of strange dreams in which she is a high priestess and a new savior, and holds the secret to signs which mark the fate of the world and the secret of the Power of Destruction. She is also fearful that Dr. Rose seeks her secrets.
At the close of the story, Mr. Anstruther learns that Dr. Rose's wealthy uncle has died, the victim of lightning on an otherwise calm night, and left his substantial fortune to the doctor. This occurs on the same night that the doctor's cottage is destroyed by a landslide, taking with it both the doctor and the

nun and leaving a pile of debris, again in the form of a hound.

Hound of Death and Other Stories, The
Mystery short story collection.

The majority of the twelve stories in the volume relate supernatural incidents rather than murder mysteries or other crimes requiring solutions. The most famous among them is "WITNESS FOR THE PROSECUTION" which became a successful stage play and then a movie. The remaining stories in the collection deal with psychic experiences, the occult and the unexplainable, as well as with individuals who take advantage of those who believe in the supernatural.

PUBLISHING AND DRAMATIZATION HISTORY
The Hound of Death and Other Stories was published in 1933 by William Collins Sons and Company, Ltd., in London.

"Witness for the Prosecution" was adapted for the stage by Agatha Christie for a 1953 London production, and the American production made its debut in 1954. The story appeared in three different adaptations for American television in 1949, 1950 and 1953. In 1957, the film version was released, and a television adaptation using the stage adaptation was presented in 1982. "THE RED SIGNAL" was adapted for television in 1949 and later filmed again by Thames Television as part of the 1982 series THE AGATHA CHRISTIE HOUR, which also broadcast "THE MYSTERY OF THE BLUE JAR" and "THE FOURTH MAN." In 1984, "THE LAST SEANCE" was adapted by Thames Television.

TITLES IN THE COLLECTION
The Hounds of Death and Other Stories contains the following short stories: "THE HOUND OF DEATH," "The Red Signal," "The Fourth Man," "THE GIPSY," "THE LAMP," "WIRELESS," "Witness for the Prosecution," "The Mystery of the Blue Jar," "THE STRANGE CASE OF SIR ARTHUR CARMICHAEL," "THE CALL OF THE WINGS," "The Last Seance" and "S.O.S."

CRIME NOTES
In "Witness for the Prosecution," the most famous story in the collection, the criminal avoids punishment, but the author changed the ending to include punishment for the murderer when she wrote the stage adaptation twenty years after the original story was published.

"House at Shiraz, The" Mystery short story.

The plot centers on the desire of a young German pilot to unravel the mystery of a long-ago love.

PUBLISHING AND DRAMATIZATION HISTORY
The story appeared in the short story collection, PARKER PYNE INVESTIGATES, published in 1934 by William Collins Sons and Company, Ltd., in London.

The story has not been adapted for stage or screen.

CHARACTERS
Lady Esther CARR, Muriel KING, Mr. PARKER PYNE, Herr SCHLAGAL

PLOT SYNOPSIS
The story concerns the efforts of Mr. Parker Pyne to uncover the secret of a young British aristocrat who secludes herself in a house in Persia. While en route to Shiraz, he speaks to a young German pilot who recalls flying two English women, Lady Esther Carr and her maid, to the same city several years earlier. The pilot had fallen in love with the maid, but Lady Esther had fallen in love with him. Before a relationship could develop, the maid died, and Lady Esther secluded herself in her home.

"House of the Lurking Death, The" Mystery short story.

The plot takes Tommy and Tuppence BERESFORD to a gloomy old mansion where poison and murder lurk.

PUBLISHING AND DRAMATIZATION HISTORY
The story appeared in the short story collection, PARTNERS IN CRIME, published in 1929 by William Collins Sons and Company, Ltd., in London, and by Dodd, Mead and Company in New York.

The story was adapted for television in 1984 by London Weekend Television in England, and was also shown on the Public Broadcasting Service in the U.S.

A disguise is needed for Tommy and Tuppence Beresford to solve the mystery of "The House of the Lurking Death." (Photo courtesy of London Weekend Television)

CHARACTERS

Tommy Beresford, Tuppence Beresford, Dr. BURTON, Mary CHILCOTT, HANNAH, Lois HARGREAVES, Miss LOGAN, Esther QUANT, Dennis RADCLYFFE

PLOT SYNOPSIS

The International Detective Agency becomes involved in a murder by poisoning when Lois Hargreaves approaches the Beresfords for help. Chocolates containing arsenic have been received at the house and several occupants have become ill. Before the detectives begin their investigation, two people die of poisoning and a third becomes seriously ill. Before they can identify the murderer, the two detectives must learn who stands to benefit from the deaths.

CRIME NOTES

This story is another in a series of Tommy and Tuppence Beresford stories in which the author parodies popular fictional detectives of her day. In this story, Tommy imitates French Sûreté detective Gabriel Hanaud, and Tuppence enacts the role of his sidekick Mr. Ricardo, both characters created by mystery writer Alfred Edward Mason (1865–1948).

"How Does Your Garden Grow?" Mystery short story.

The story places Hercule POIROT in the unpleasant situation of responding too late to a client's request for help.

The simple pleasures of a flower show lead to a murder investigation for Hercule Poirot (David Suchet) in "How Does Your Garden Grow?" (Photo courtesy of London Weekend Television)

PUBLISHING AND DRAMATIZATION HISTORY

The story appeared in the short story collection, THE REGATTA MYSTERY AND OTHER STORIES, published in 1939 by Dodd, Mead and Company in New York.

The story was adapted for television in 1991 by London Weekend Television in England and was also shown on the Public Broadcasting Service in the U.S.

CHARACTERS

Mary DELAFONTAINE, Felicity LEMON, Hercule Poirot, Katrina RIEGER, Inspector SIMS

PLOT SYNOPSIS

Hercule Poirot receives a letter from an old woman, who requests that he meet with her to discuss several concerns. He receives no acknowledgment of his reply and learns five days later that the old woman died soon after sending her original letter. Curious about her sudden death, Poirot travels to Charman's Green, where he meets both the victim's niece and the Russian girl, Katrina, to whom the dead woman had left a considerable sum of money. When the postmortem report indicates that death was due to strychnine poisoning, Poirot puts his "little gray cells" to work to uncover the murderer.

CRIME NOTES

This story marks the first appearance of Miss Felicity Lemon as secretary to Hercule Poirot.

Howard, Evelyn (Evie) Viewed by Hercule POIROT as "an excellent specimen of well-balanced English beef and brawn" in THE MYSTERIOUS AFFAIR AT STYLES, she is equally admired by others in the novel. She is the companion to Emily INGLETHORPE and a level-headed addition to the household at Styles.

Howell, Mrs. A dignified if somewhat aged housekeeper at Chimneys in THE SEVEN DIALS MYSTERY, she knows a good deal about what has gone on within the household in years past. Her demeanor frightens her current employer, Lady COOTE, but she warms completely to the easy charm of Bundle BRENT, who finds "Howelly" to be a storehouse of valuable information.

Hubbard, Mrs. A plump, round-faced, softer version of Miss Felicity LEMON, her sister and secretary to Hercule POIROT, she is widowed and back in England after years of living in Singapore. As the manager of Mrs. NICOLETIS' youth hostel in HICKORY DICKORY DOCK, she becomes alarmed when a series of thefts occur at the hostel, and contacts POIROT for advice.

Hubbard, Caroline Martha A formerly famous stage actress whose real name is Linda ARDEN, she retired from the theater after family tragedy struck. In MURDER ON THE ORIENT EXPRESS (1), she pretends to be traveling to visit her daughter and son-in-law who teaches at an American university in Smyrna. She is really the mother of Sonia ARMSTRONG and the grandmother of Daisy ARMSTRONG, and a source of many misleading statements regarding the murder.

Hudd, Gina A beautiful young woman whose Italian parentage provides an exotic tinge to her appearance, she flaunts her youth and beauty and has led most of the men at Stoneygates to fall in love with her in THEY DO IT WITH MIRRORS.

Hudd, Walter (Wally) A big, brash American in THEY DO IT WITH MIRRORS, he is married to Gina HUDD, whose family makes him uncomfortable. He strongly desires to take Gina home with him to America.

Huish, Superintendent A tall, melancholy-appearing police superintendent assigned to the ARGYLE murder case in ORDEAL BY INNOCENCE, he is "the life and soul of a children's party" who loves to make jokes and perform amateur magic tricks.

Humfries, Mr. The smooth-talking manager of Bertram's Hotel, he is a chameleon among his guests, and adapts his conversation and interests to suit their every taste. Chief Inspector DAVY distrusts him and views him as a "smarmy sort of chap" who is hiding something in AT BERTRAM'S HOTEL.

Humbleby, Jessie Rose She grieves extensively when her husband Dr. HUMBLEBY dies and others suspect that he was murdered in MURDER IS EASY. Retired policeman Luke FITZWILLIAM visits her and finds her huddled up in her chair; she tells him there is a great deal of evil in the town of Wychwood.

Humbleby, Dr. John Ward   An old-fashioned country doctor, he is a victim in MURDER IS EASY, leaving behind his grieving widow, Jessie Rose HUMBLEBY, and daughter, Rose HUMBLEBY, who wants to marry her father's partner, Dr. THOMAS. Dr. Humbleby dies of acute septicaemia, but others in the town believe he was marked for death by the Wychwood murderer.

Humbleby, Rose   In love with Dr. THOMAS, her father's partner in practice, she yields to her father's disapproval of the relationship while he is still alive. After Dr. HUMBLEBY dies in MURDER IS EASY, she plans to marry Dr. THOMAS, but waits until a respectable amount of time passes for the period of bereavement.

Hunt, Verity   Orphaned when her parents die in a plane crash in Spain, she is raised by her appointed guardian and her parents' good friend, Clothilde BRADBURY-SCOTT. She is believed to have been murdered by Michael RAFIEL when the disfigured body of another woman is identified as hers in NEMESIS.

Humfries, Mr.   The hotel manager in AT BERTRAM'S HOTEL, he is a fifty-year-old man who has all the right information for his guests, whatever their needs might be.

Hunter, David   He creates a very complicated deception in TAKEN AT THE FLOOD when he convinces a young woman to impersonate his late sister, Rosaleen CLOADE, and claim her inheritance. He falls in love with Lynn MARCHMONT and jeopardizes his position, but the most dangerous threat is a letter signed by "Enoch ARDEN" who threatens to reveal Rosaleen's first, still-valid marriage.

Hunter, Megan   A tall, awkward girl, she finds the body of Agnes WODDELL and helps the police to identify the killer in THE MOVING FINGER. She accompanies Jerry BURTON to London to visit his sister's dressmaker and hairdresser, and the result is renewed self-esteem for the newly attractive young woman.

Hurst, Jim   A secretary to the wealthy Mr. Caleb BLUNDELL, from whom he was once caught stealing, he and his employer's daughter want to marry, but her father has another man in mind as prospective son-in-law in THE PEARL OF PRICE.

Hydropathic Hotel   The resort where Agatha Christie stayed in HARROGATE during the ten days she disappeared in 1926. (See DISAPPEARANCE OF AGATHA CHRISTIE.)

I

"Idol House of Astarte, The" Mystery short story.

The story is another of the previously unsolvable mysteries recounted at a meeting of the Tuesday Night Club to which Miss Jane MARPLE finds a solution.

PUBLISHING AND DRAMATIZATION HISTORY

The story appeared in the short story collection, THE THIRTEEN PROBLEMS, published in 1932 by William Collins Sons and Company, Ltd., in London, and, under the title, *The Tuesday Club Murders,* published in 1933 by Dodd, Mead and Company in New York.

The story has not been adapted for stage or screen.

CHARACTERS

Diana ASHLEY, Elliot HAYDON, Sir Richard HAYDON, Dr. PENDER

PLOT SYNOPSIS

The story, told by Dr. Pender, relates the story of a murder that occurred on the night that a costume party was held at the home of Sir Richard Haydon, who was a rival of his cousin Elliot for the affections of the lovely Diana Ashley. Sir Richard's estate contains the grove of Astarte with a mysterious stone summer house, rumored to have been the site of numerous sacred rites in years long past. In a surprise move, Diana enacts the role of Astarte and startles Sir Richard, who stumbles and falls when he moves toward her. When others reach his body, he is found dead of a knife wound to the heart, but no one except Miss Marple can determine either the motive or the murderer.

CRIME NOTES

The murder occurs by stabbing.

Imhotep A mortuary priest in DEATH COMES AS THE END who maintains the Temple of Meripath, he is also the father of four children by his late wife. He infuriates his family when he brings home the nineteen-year-old concubine, NOFRET, and makes her his heir. Tensions mount even more as he refuses to make his sons partners in his profession and, instead, treats them more like slaves than free men. He is largely to blame as his household is rapidly decimated by death.

"In a Glass Darkly" Mystery short story.

The plot focuses on a murder, which is prevented by a supernatural occurrence.

PUBLISHING AND DRAMATIZATION HISTORY

The story appeared in the short story collection, THE REGATTA MYSTERY AND OTHER STORIES, published in 1939 by Dodd, Mead and Company in New York.

The story was adapted for television in 1982 by Thames Television in England.

CHARACTERS

Alan CARSLAKE, Sylvia CARSLAKE, Charles CRAWLEY, Derek WAINWRIGHT

PLOT SYNOPSIS

As a houseguest of an old friend, the unnamed narrator has a vision in the mirror of a man with a scar strangling a beautiful young woman. At dinner, he meets the people of his vision, his best friend's sister, Sylvia, and her fiancé, Charles, who bears a scar. He tells Sylvia of his vision, and he learns later that she has broken off her engagement. After being injured

Sylvia and Matthew (unnamed in Christie's story), played by Emma Piper and Nicholas Clay, share a wistful moment in the Thames Television production of "In a Glass Darkly." (Photo courtesy of Thames Television)

in the war, he visits Sylvia and they fall in love and marry, but the anonymous narrator is a jealous husband who drives his wife slowly away from him. When she leaves him and returns to her family home, he follows and nearly strangles her in his jealousy but stops in time to learn a frightening truth.

Inch The older women of ST. MARY MEAD have long referred to Inch's Taxi Service as simply "Inch," even after Mr. Inch is succeeded by Mr. Roberts and the company functions under new ownership. Miss Jane MARPLE goes "in Inch" in THE MIRROR CRACK'D FROM SIDE TO SIDE and in NEMESIS.

"Incredible Theft, The" Mystery short story.
The plot of this lengthy story focuses on the disappearance of diagrams for a new military bomber, and the threat to national security.

PUBLISHING AND DRAMATIZATION HISTORY
The story appeared in the short story collection, MURDER IN THE MEWS, published in 1937 by William Collins Sons and Company, Ltd., in London, and, under the title, *Dead Man's Mirror and Other Stories,* by Dodd, Mead and Company in New York.

The story was adapted for television in 1989 by London Weekend Television in England, and was also shown on the Public Broadcasting Service in the U.S.

CHARACTERS
Air Marshall Sir George CARRINGTON, Lady Julia CARRINGTON, Reggie CARRINGTON, LEONIE (1), Mrs. MACATTA, Lord Sir Charles McLaughlin MAYFIELD, Hercule POIROT, Mrs. VANDERLYN

PLOT SYNOPSIS
Plans for a secret military bomber disappear from the desk of the Minister of Defence during a weekend

The theft of bomber airplane plans and the threat to national security require the discreet services of Hercule Poirot (David Suchet) in "The Incredible Theft." (Photo courtesy of London Weekend Television)

conference at his estate. The guests include not only government officials but a woman of dubious reputation who has been married to three men of different nationalities and who has developed an extensive network of espionage contacts. When the plans disappear, the officials call in Hercule Poirot to find them. After scrutinizing the activities of all the guests, the detective comes to a very interesting conclusion before locating the plans and saving the fate of England.

CRIME NOTES
The story is an expanded version of a significantly shorter story entitled "THE SUBMARINE PLANS."

Ingles, John   An expert in Chinese politics and personalities in THE BIG FOUR, he disappears from the S.S. *Shanghai* soon after the ship leaves the port of Marseilles, and his Chinese servant is murdered. Hercule POIROT had consulted with him to learn if the Big Four gang is connected to the opium trade in the Chinese underworld.

Inglethorpe, Alfred   Perceived by Hercule POIROT to be a "man of method," he is a fortune hunter in THE MYSTERIOUS AFFAIR AT STYLES who marries a much older, wealthy widow.

Inglethorpe, Emily Agnes   An energetic woman of more than seventy years of age, she is a wealthy woman who supports many charities in THE MYSTERIOUS AFFAIR AT STYLES. One of her charitable projects is Leastways Cottage, which houses Belgian refugees displaced by World War I, and Hercule POIROT is one of the boarders. She marries her former secretary, a marriage of which her stepchildren strongly disapprove. Emily dies a painful, convulsive death after being poisoned by strychnine, and POIROT repays her kindness to him and his countrymen by investigating the case and apprehending the murderer.

Inglewood, Sir Mortimer   A dignified and powerful attorney in "THE AUGEAN STABLES," he prosecutes the libel suit against the *X-Ray News*. His rhetoric is peppered with references to national security and the need to oppose the Fascists and Communists who use such methods "to undermine Democracy by every unfair machination known."

"Ingots of Gold"   Mystery short story.
The story centers on the treasure of a wrecked Spanish ship and its dangerous allure.

PUBLISHING AND DRAMATIZATION HISTORY
The story appeared in the short story collection, THE THIRTEEN PROBLEMS, published in 1932 by William Collins Sons and Company, Ltd., in London, and, under the title, *The Tuesday Club Murders,* by Dodd, Mead and Company in 1933 in New York.

The story has not been adapted for stage or screen.

CHARACTERS
Inspector BADGWORTH, Mr. KELVIN, Miss Jane MARPLE, John NEWMAN, Raymond WEST

PLOT SYNOPSIS
The story told by Raymond West to The Tuesday Night Club details his visit to John Newman, a friend who is searching for the Spanish ship *Otranto*, which was wrecked on the Serpent Rocks off the coast of Cornwall. While en route, West had engaged in conversation with Inspector Badgworth, who was extremely knowledgeable about the shipwreck and the disappearance of its bullion. Newman disappeared before West arrived in Cornwall, then reappeared a few days later, claiming that he had been abducted by thieves who had stripped the *Otranto* of its bullion. He claims that the landlord of the local pub had worked with the robbers. As she listens to the story, Miss Marple solves the mystery that has puzzled her nephew.

Ingrid   A large-boned, blonde, German girl who learns English from her employer's adolescent daughter in THE CLOCKS, she is tricked by the girl into saying "get the hell out of here" when she wishes to say the English equivalent of *Auf Wiedersehen.*

Instow, Jean   In love with the married George PRITCHARD in "THE BLUE GERANIUM," she views his wife, Mary PRITCHARD, as a miserable woman who should die.

Ipy   The son of IMHOTEP and his mistress IPI, he is Imhotep's high-spirited third son who views himself as smarter than the other household members in

DEATH COMES AS THE END. He is murdered, his body found face down in a stream.

Isaacstein, Herman   One of the "strong, silent yellow men of finance" in THE SECRET OF CHIMNEYS, he will lend money to Herzoslovakian Prince Michael OBOLOVITCH in return for oil concessions. Also identified as "Ikey HERMANSTEIN," "Nosystein" and "FAT IKEY," he is implicated in the Prince's death when the murder weapon is found in his suitcase.

Ivanovitch, Boris   A little man with a ratlike face who appears in both THE SECRET ADVERSARY and THE MYSTERY OF THE BLUE TRAIN, he poses as Count STEPANOV, a member of a Bolshevist gang, in the first book. He assumes the identity of Monsieur KRASSINE in the second book and steals the Heart of Fire rubies with Olga DEMIROFF.

Ivanovitch, Sergius   See ORANOFF, PRINCE SERGIUS.

J

Jackson, Arthur   Nurse, valet and masseur to the very rich but exasperating old Mr. Jason RAFIEL, he was formerly employed in the pharmaceutical industry, and knows the names and dangers of the drugs contained in Molly KENDALL's cosmetics in A CARIBBEAN MYSTERY.

Jacobs, Miss   A level-headed elderly woman, she calls the police emergency number when another tenant in her building discovers a woman with a bloody knife standing over the body of David BAKER in THIRD GIRL.

Jacques   A surly and suspicious servant at the Hotel Rochers Neige in "THE ERYMANTHIAN BOAR."

James   See DARRELL, CLAUD.

James, Caroline   An excellent cook married to the inept gardener in THE MAN IN THE BROWN SUIT, she is the only reason that her employer, Sir Eustace PEDLER, keeps her husband on his payroll.

Jameson, Commissionaire   The law enforcement officer in Doncaster, he discovers the fourth victim and the railway guide under the seat in THE A.B.C. MURDERS.

Jameson, Mrs.   A hair stylist in THE MIRROR CRACK'D FROM SIDE TO SIDE, her clientele is made up of solid, middle-aged women who have not changed their hair styles in decades and who see no reason for ever doing so. She provides Miss Jane MARPLE with copies of movie magazines in which to read about movie star Marina GREGG.

Jameson, Richard   A boring man who lectures his fellow tourists about the fine points of architecture on the tour of famous houses and gardens of Great Britain in NEMESIS. Even Miss Jane MARPLE finds her patience strained by his monotonous tone of superiority.

Jane   A friend of Tuppence BERESFORD, she provides four photographs in the unsuccessful attempt to break Una DRAKE's alibi in "THE UNBREAKABLE ALIBI."

"Jane in Search of a Job"   Mystery short story.

The plot focuses on one woman's adventures as she impersonates a Grand Duchess.

PUBLISHING AND DRAMATIZATION HISTORY

The story appeared in the short story collection, THE LISTERDALE MYSTERY, published in 1934 by William Collins Sons and Company, Ltd., in London.

The story was adapted for television in 1982 by Thames Television in England.

CHARACTERS

Jane CLEVELAND, Detective-Inspector FARRELL, Colonel KRANIN, Grand Duchess PAULINE, Princess POPORENSKY, Count STYLPTITCH

PLOT SYNOPSIS

The story focuses upon the adventures of Jane Cleveland, who has recently lost her job and has the seeming good fortune to receive an offer of two thousand pounds to impersonate a grand duchess. The royal retainers tell Jane that the job will be dangerous because attempts may be made on Grand Duchess Pauline's life, and this makes the offer even more attractive to her. Dressed initially as an American

The danger is real for Jane, played by Elizabeth Garvie, in "Jane in Search of a Job."   (Photo courtesy of Thames Television)

journalist, Jane must arrive at a formal affair, then change clothes and leave as the duchess. Everything proceeds according to plan, until Jane wakes up after being kidnapped and drugged. With the help of Detective-Inspector Farrell, she learns that she has been the dupe for a gang of jewel thieves.

Janet (1)   An elderly, grim-faced housemaid in AFTER THE FUNERAL, she thoroughly enjoys her continued disputes with the ninety-year-old butler of Enderby Hall, LANSCOMBE. She proves to be his ally in their shared disapproval of the modern generation of servants.

Janet (2)   The eleven-year-old granddaughter of Tommy and Tuppence BERESFORD in POSTERN OF FATE.

Janet (3)   A frightened, girlish lady's maid in "THE LOVE DETECTIVES," she fears that her lover, the valet, will become a murder suspect.

Japp, Chief Inspector James   His association with Hercule POIROT precedes their first recorded case, as hints in the eight novels and seven short stories in which he appears indicate (see CATEGORICAL APPENDIX). The two met in 1904 while Poirot was still a member of the Belgian police force and Japp was only a detective at Scotland Yard. Their two early cases, the Abercrombie forgery case and the Baron Altara case, are referred to, though they remain unrecorded, but these early experiences instilled in both men a strong respect for each other despite their differences in method. Although their investigations seem to become a battle between the "little gray cells" and presumed scientific methods, Japp often turns to Poirot for assistance in sorting through confusing evidence.

Jarrold, Detective Inspector   A member of Scotland Yard, this small man with ginger-colored hair and moustache is assigned in "THE GIRL IN THE TRAIN" to shadow a known spy named MARDENBERG.

He nearly fails in his mission, but then he notices that George ROWLAND is also following the spy.

Jarrow, Dorothea (Dolly)   The twin sister of Molly RAVENSCROFT, she had been the first object of General Alistair RAVENSCROFT's affections in ELEPHANTS CAN REMEMBER. When her sister dies, Dorothea uses wigs to disguise herself as Molly and takes her sister's place in the Ravenscroft household.

Jeanne   Dresser to the elegant Parisian dancer Madame NADINA in THE MAN IN THE BROWN SUIT.

Jefferson, Adelaide   Widowed and in a precarious financial position due to her second husband's losses on the stock market, she is a devoted mother who will do anything to prevent her son, Peter CARMODY, from being deprived of his inheritance in THE BODY IN THE LIBRARY. Courted by both Hugo McLEAN and Raymond STARR, she agreed to marry the blindly devoted McLean.

Jefferson, Conway   Permanently confined to a wheelchair due to a plane crash which also killed his wife, son and daughter, he remains an intellectually vital man in THE BODY IN THE LIBRARY. He plans to adopt Ruby KEENE and make her his heir, a move which would deprive his stepnephew, Peter CARMODY, of the inheritance.

Jeffries, Edward   A straitlaced, sober American man with a strongly puritanical streak in "HAVE YOU GOT EVERYTHING YOU WANT?" whose kindness in having allowed an abused wife to stay one night at his home haunts him now that he is married. When he speaks to Mr. PARKER PYNE about this seeming indiscretion, Mr. Parker Pyne advises him that women love a scoundrel, and that his wife will desire Edward all the more if she believes that he has a slightly indiscreet past.

Jeffries, Elsie   A young American wife who confides in Mr. PARKER PYNE about her suspicions regarding her husband's past in "HAVE YOU GOT EVERYTHING YOU WANT?," she is robbed of her jewelry while traveling on a train. Mr. Parker Pyne manages to allay her fears and recover her jewels.

Jenkins, Miss   A physically unattractive and apparently unintelligent secretary to realtors Gable and Stretcher in DUMB WITNESS, she incorrectly relays a message containing an important four-digit number to her boss.

Jenkins, Sister   A dour, pessimistic army hospital nurse in GIANT'S BREAD.

Jennings   Once dismissed for stealing, he is the valet of a murdered man in "THE LOVE DETECTIVES." A maid in the household tries hard to protect him, but Mr. SATTERTHWAITE recognizes Jennings' ruthless qualities and views him as a strong suspect in the murder of Sir James DWIGHTON.

Jennson, Miss   A thin, dark girl who wears glasses and projects a particularly unattractive appearance, she is a key worker in Mr. ARISTIDES' Brain Trust in DESTINATION UNKNOWN. Andrew PETERS finds her very attractive because she is completely knowledgeable about the operation of the trust.

Jesmond, Mr.   A member of the Foreign Office, he asks Hercule POIROT to locate a stolen ruby for Prince ALI in "THE THEFT OF THE ROYAL RUBY." To lure Poirot to the estate of Kings Lacey, he speaks of the numerous modern conveniences that have been installed there.

Jessop, Mr.   A secretive man whose role as a member of a special Intelligence unit has brought him into contact with agents in the United States, in the Mediterranean and on the Continent. After preventing Hilary CRAVEN's suicide, he recruits her to help the British government and to infiltrate Mr. ARISTIDES' Brain Trust in DESTINATION UNKNOWN.

Jethroe, Johnny   A photographer's assistant in THE MIRROR CRACK'D FROM SIDE TO SIDE, he is an exuberant young man who suggests to Scotland Yard Inspector Dermot CRADDOCK that a murder case resembles a photograph in the way it "develops."

"Jewel Robbery at the Grand Metropolitan, The"   Mystery short story.
   The story features the theft of pearls and an all-too-obvious suspect.

PUBLISHING AND DRAMATIZATION HISTORY

The story appeared in the short story collection, POIROT INVESTIGATES, published in 1924 by John Lane in London, and in 1925 by Dodd, Mead and Company in New York.

The story was adapted for television in 1993 by London Weekend Television in Britain, and was also shown on the Public Broadcasting Service in the U.S.

CHARACTERS

CELESTINE, Captain Arthur HASTINGS, Mrs. OPALSEN, Ed OPALSEN, Hercule POIROT

PLOT SYNOPSIS

Hercule Poirot and Captain Hastings are on holiday at the opulent Grand Metropolitan Hotel in Brighton, where they meet the wife of a wealthy stockbroker. As they discuss the jewels worn by Mrs. Opalsen, the great detective relates his experiences in cases which have concerned some of the best-known jewels in the world. Excited by his anecdotes, the wealthy matron eagerly offers to show him a very expensive pearl necklace, but when she goes to retrieve it, she discovers that it has been stolen. When the police arrive and question both the hotel chambermaid and Mrs. Opalsen's personal maid, Celestine, they find the pearls under Celestine's mattress. Although the police are ready to charge her, Poirot knows the identity of the real thief, which he soon reveals.

Jim One of three children in a notorious child neglect case, as an adult he poses as both Superintendent HOGBEN and Sergeant TROTTER in his plot to gain revenge for the death of his brother, Georgie, in "THREE BLIND MICE."

Jobson, Mr. An old taxi driver with a ragged moustache, spectacles and hoarse voice in LORD EDGWARE DIES, his information destroys the alibis of Geraldine and Ronald MARSH who claimed to be at the opera during the murder.

John (1) One of several aspiring young mediums in "THE BIRD WITH THE BROKEN WING," he owns the Ouija board through which Mr. Harley QUIN sends a message to Mr. SATTERTHWAITE regarding Madge KEELEY.

John (2) A young squadron leader who provides Nurse LEATHERAN with information regarding the American expedition at Tell Yarimjah in MURDER IN MESOPOTAMIA, he was once infatuated with her new employer, Mrs. LEIDNER, of whom he now speaks as being "long in the tooth."

John (3) The father in UNFINISHED PORTRAIT, he is a big, jolly man who dies when the main character is eleven, leaving the family in dire financial straits.

Johnson (1) The well-trained butler of Sir Alington WEST in "THE RED SIGNAL," he overhears an argument between his employer and the man's nephew Dermot WEST, and later discovers that his master has been shot through the heart.

Johnson (2) The constable who assists Inspector JAPP in conducting the investigation in BLACK COFFEE.

Johnson, Colonel (1) The Chief Constable for the village of Middleshire in HERCULE POIROT'S CHRISTMAS, he is consulted by Hercule POIROT when Simeon LEE is brutally murdered on Christmas Eve.

Johnson, Colonel (2) An old friend of Mr. SATTERTHWAITE, he is the Chief Constable of Yorkshire, who is in charge of the investigation in THREE-ACT TRAGEDY. He expresses the view that most criminals are "chicken-livered."

Johnson, Constable An assistant in the investigation headed by Inspector BADGWORTHY when murder occurs in the hamlet of Market Basing in THE SECRET OF CHIMNEYS, he is excited by his first murder investigation and looking forward to a hanging.

Johnson, Miss (1) A plump girl with fair hair who works at a tavern named the Crown and Feathers in Croyden, she is romantically linked with Albert DAVIS, the second steward on the *Prometheus*, in DEATH IN THE CLOUDS.

Johnson, Miss (2)　The school matron in CAT AMONG THE PIGEONS, she viewed Meadowbank School as her family.

Johnson, Miss (3)　See WILLETT, VIOLET.

Johnson, Mr.　One of the witnesses to Aristide LEONIDES' secret will, unknown to both the old man's family and lawyer in CROOKED HOUSE, he has the most to lose when Leonides dies because he receives an annual bonus with significant yearly increases instead of a bequest.

Johnson, Mrs. (1)　See BLIGH, GERTRUDE.

Johnson, Mrs. (2)　See WILLETT, MRS.

Johnson, Anne　One of the nontechnical personnel on the American expedition at Tell Yarimjah in MURDER IN MESOPOTAMIA, she is murdered when someone replaces her glass of water with a glass of hydrochloric acid. Hercule POIROT obtains his most important clue from her when she identifies for him the architecture of the house.

Johnson, Elizabeth　A proud young woman nicknamed "Black Bess" by the boarders with whom she shares Mrs. NICOLETIS' youth hostel in HICKORY DICKORY DOCK, she is said to have "the ego of a Napoleon." She is a member of the Communist Party, and arrogant in her politics.

Johnson, Victoria　When she discovers the owner of the bottle of pills in Major PALGRAVE's room after he is found dead in A CARIBBEAN MYSTERY, this Golden Palm Hotel maid decides to attempt blackmail. She is soon stabbed to death, leaving behind her common-law husband and two children.

Joliet, Madame　The formidable manager of the Ballet Maritski in Paris whom the police contact for information regarding Anna STRAVINSKA, she is brisk with the police inspectors in 4.50 FROM PADDINGTON, and blames men for the defection of girls from her dance company.

Jonathan, Caleb　An old-fashioned lawyer in FIVE LITTLE PIGS who heads the law firm which rep-

resents the CRALE family, he has the depth of character, eccentricities and quality vintage port that appeal to Hercule POIROT.

Jones　A valet to Lord Edward CAMPION, he is in the vicinity when the Rajah of Maraputna's emerald disappears in "THE RAJAH'S EMERALD." He assumes the disguise of Detective Inspector MERRILEES to question James BOND, but foolishly uses a cycling club medallion as his fake badge.

Jones, Constable　A member of local law enforcement who aids in the murder investigation in SPIDER'S WEB.

Jones, Detective Sergeant　Assigned to the case when Lady TRESSILIAN is murdered in TOWARDS ZERO, he manages to locate and identify the fingerprints of the murderer.

Jones, Mr.　The village bank manager in MURDER IS EASY, he is questioned with other suspects by retired police officer Luke FITZWILLIAM. He identifies two characters who were not in Wychwood on the day that Miss FULLERTON is murdered in London.

Jones, Mrs.　An ordinary forty-five-year-old woman in "THE TUESDAY NIGHT CLUB," her death is wrongly blamed on botulism poisoning from spoiled canned lobster.

Jones, Albert　The salesman for a chemical manufacturing firm in "THE TUESDAY NIGHT CLUB," he plays the role of the grieving widower and inherits eight thousand pounds after his wife dies. No one knows that he fathered a child by Gladys LINCH, who died in childbirth.

Jones, Policewoman Alice　She fakes drowning in DEAD MAN'S FOLLY to prove that Lady Hattie STUBBS could have drowned as a tourist boat passed nearby.

Jones, Gwyneth　Prone to seizures, she had been ordered not to take a job working with children. Her loss of consciousness during a seizure causes a house fire that almost kills the children in THE BURDEN.

Jones, Mary　The daughter of the innkeeper in "AT THE 'BELLS AND MOTLEY,'" she believes in the innocence of her fiancé, Stephen GRANT, despite the strength of public opinion against him.

Jones, Montgomery Hoping to win a bet with Una DRAKE and to capture her heart, this wealthy young man contacts Tommy and Tuppence BERESFORD for help in "THE UNBREAKABLE ALIBI."

Jones, Queenie A member of Simeon LEE's household staff, she is the kitchenmaid in HERCULE POIROT'S CHRISTMAS.

Jones, Robert (Bobby) The fourth son of the Vicar of Marchbolt and an inventive young man, he assumes several disguises in tracking down a murderer with his close friend, and the woman he loves, Lady Frances DERWENT, in WHY DIDN'T THEY ASK EVANS? He discovers the body at the outset of the novel, then begins his investigation, posing at various times as a chauffeur, lawyer and businessman. After successfully identifying the murderer, he marries his love and plans their move to Kenya to manage a coffee plantation.

Jones, Reverend Thomas The Vicar of Marchbolt in WHY DIDN'T THEY ASK EVANS? and the father of several sons, he disapproves of his son Bobby's activities and friends, but prefers to view Bobby's behavior as a burden to be borne stoically, though it upsets his digestion greatly.

Jones, Victoria Lighthearted and adventurous, she is often at odds with her employers. After she loses her job for performing exaggerated imitations of her employer's wife, she blithely falls in love with criminal mastermind Edward GORING and follows him to Baghdad, where she works for him until she learns the true nature of his operation in THEY CAME TO BAGHDAD. She then works for Mr. DAKIN in Intelligence by spying on Goring, and finally manages

to help her country and herself when she falls in love with Richard BAKER.

Jones, William Proprietor of the Bells and Motley and father of Mary JONES in "AT THE 'BELLS AND MOTLEY,'" he provides Mr. QUIN and Mr. SAT TERTHWAITE with details in the story of the disappearance of Captain Richard HARWELL.

Jordan, Mary A long-dead member of British Intelligence in POSTERN OF FATE, she posed as a nursery governess while investigating suspicious political activities in the village of Hollowquay during World War I. Mary died after ingesting foxglove leaves, mistakenly mixed in a salad.

Joseph, Franz See ARGUILEROS, KARL.

Josephine (Jehoshaphat) A mild-tempered cat, she is used by the main character of THE BURDEN in an attempt to smother a baby, a plot in which the cat refuses to cooperate.

Juanita See CORTMAN, MILDRED JEAN.

Judd, Henry Married to actress Rosina NUNN, he caters to her every whim. He becomes part of a group of strangers who huddle together for shelter from a sudden snowstorm during which secrets are uncovered in "THE WORLD'S END."

Judy The daughter of the main character in UNFINISHED PORTRAIT, she distances herself from her mother.

Jules The maitre d'hotel at the elite Chez Ma Tante in "DEATH ON THE NILE" (1), he recognizes the refined palate of Hercule POIROT, and flatters the detective by creating a special meal which the restaurant proprietor describes as "positively a poem!"

K

Kait A devoted mother in DEATH COMES AS THE END, her maternal ministrations mask a shrewd mind and a strong will to ensure her children's future when her father-in-law, IMHOTEP, disinherits them in favor of his latest concubine. She is contemptuous of the faithlessness of most men, including her husband SOBEK, and believes that women provide the strength to continue the race, while men are needed only for breeding. At the end of the novel, she is one of the few members of the royal family to survive the murders.

Kameni He resembles the late husband of RENISENB in DEATH COMES AS THE END, but his love songs and attractiveness are not enough to convince her to marry him.

Kane, Sergeant A member of Scotland Yard, he recalls seeing an advertisement for Monkswell Manor, the proposed site of further murders in "THREE BLIND MICE."

Kane, Eva See HOPE, EVELYN (1).

Kane, Norton An awkward young man, he attracts the attention of Hercule POIROT while on a journey by motorcoach because of his very sparse moustache, which the detective compares with his own. Kane is blamed when another passenger complains that valuable miniatures have been stolen in "DOUBLE SIN."

Karl, Prince Cousin of the Grand Duchess ANASTASIA, and the man whom her uncle tries to make her marry in "THE GIRL IN THE TRAIN," he is "a horrid, pimply person" whom Anastasia despises. He attempts a duel with George ROWLAND, whom Anastasia favors, and, when he is refused, pulls

George's nose. This leads to a fist fight, which the prince loses, and he also loses Anastasia to George.

Kate A placid, robust cook in UNFINISHED PORTRAIT, she never follows recipes.

Kate, Killer See LANCASTER, JULIA.

Keane, Marcia A horsewoman and a close friend of Margery GALE, she does not agree with her friend that ghosts haunt Abbot's Mead and congenially teases her about the perceived apparitions. Nonetheless, she agrees to participate in a seance to please Margery in "THE VOICE IN THE DARK."

Keble, Ellen The very awkward companion of Mrs. SAMUELSON, she is victim of a dognapping while walking her employer's Pekinese Nanki Poo in "THE NEMEAN LION." When questioned about the incident, she blushes and stammers as she explains that she was cooing over a baby in a carriage as the dog was taken.

Keeley, David A brilliant mathematician in "THE BIRD WITH THE BROKEN WING," he is also a man of little personal magnetism or vigor, and believes that Mabelle ANNESLEY committed suicide. He shows Mr. SATTERTHWAITE the body.

Keeley, Madge Intrigued when Mr. SATTERTHWAITE visits her home in "THE BIRD WITH THE BROKEN WING" after he receives a message from a Ouija board, she is the daughter of David KEELEY and his complete opposite in personality. She exhibits an infectious enthusiasm for life but is unable to prevent her fiancé, Roger GRAHAM, from becoming infatuated with Mabelle ANNESLEY.

Keen, Dr. A young, self-important doctor in GIANT'S BREAD, he is wounded in World War I.

Keene, Sergeant Unusually knowledgeable about gipsy lore and customs, he is the head of law enforcement in Kingston Bishop, and Michael ROGERS consults him in ENDLESS NIGHT about a curse placed on Gipsy's Acre.

Keene, Geoffrey The shy, awkward secretary to Hubert Lytcham ROCHE, he is used by Diana CLEVES to mislead her father into believing that she has given up her desire for the man of whom her father disapproves in "THE SECOND GONG."

Keene, Ruby An eighteen-year-old, platinum blonde-haired dancer whose real name is Rosy LEGGE, she has had a difficult life and takes advantage of any and all possibilities for obtaining security. When Conway JEFFERSON becomes her benefactor and decides to adopt her, her future appears secure, but she is murdered before she can enjoy her new found security in THE BODY IN THE LIBRARY. Investigators first identify the body found in Arthur BANTRY's library as hers, but later find her badly burned body in George BARTLETT's stolen automobile.

Keene, Sylvia The fiancée of Jerry LORIMER in "THE HERB OF DEATH," she dies after eating a salad that includes foxglove leaves.

Kellett, Billy See DAVENHEIM, MR.

Kelly, Sheila See GRANT, SHEILA.

Kelsey, Detective Inspector A perceptive man in charge of investigating the murders at the elite Meadowbank School in CAT AMONG THE PIGEONS, he is highly efficient and willing to follow all promising leads. He had worked with Hercule POIROT many years earlier.

Kelsey, Inspector A source of humorous relief in his mimicry of the more annoying mannerisms of witnesses, he works with Inspector CROME in THE A.B.C. MURDERS.

Kelsey, Major A member of the Tell Yarimjah expedition, he and his wife hire Nurse LEATHERAN to accompany Mary KELSEY to Baghdad and to care for their new baby in MURDER IN MESOPOTAMIA.

Kelsey, Mary The essentially nice but very nervous wife of Major KELSEY, she is a new mother accompanied to Baghdad by Nurse LEATHERAN in MURDER IN MESOPOTAMIA.

Kelvin, Mr. The dark, dangerous-looking owner of the Three Anchors in "INGOTS OF GOLD," he appears to be constantly avoiding the scrutiny of others.

Kemp, Chief Inspector A Scotland Yard detective, he works with Colonel RACE in solving the Barton murders in SPARKLING CYANIDE.

Kench, Joan A member of Simeon LEE's household staff, she is the between-maid in HERCULE POIROT'S CHRISTMAS.

Kendall, Molly Half-owner with her husband in the Golden Palm Hotel, she is an attractive, likable, blonde woman in her early twenties who suffers from nightmares, hallucinations and blackouts. Drugs placed in her cosmetics are causing these reactions, which drive her to madness in A CARIBBEAN MYSTERY.

Kendall, Tim With his wife, Molly KENDALL, he is half-owner in the Golden Palm Hotel in A CARIBBEAN MYSTERY. Lean, dark and attractive, he follows his wife's advice to flatter the female guests, and he is especially solicitous to Miss Jane MARPLE.

Kennedy, Dr. James The village physician of Dillmouth and a self-admitted straitlaced man, he speaks with disapproval of his half-sister's twenty-year absence in SLEEPING MURDER. Despite his reputation for being a highly skilled and intelligent physician, he fails to question whether foul play was involved in the disappearance of Helen Spenlove Kennedy HALLIDAY.

Kent, Captain Possessed of an impassive face which looks more as if it was carved out of wood than made of flesh, he is a member of the United States Secret Service who is sent to investigate the disappearance of Mr. HALLIDAY in THE BIG FOUR.

Kent, Charles A drug addict who is nearly implicated in a murder, he is the illegitimate son of Roger

ACKROYD's housekeeper, Mrs. RUSSELL, in THE MUR-DER OF ROGER ACKROYD. He claims that he was simply visiting his mother on the night the murder occurred.

Kent, Dr. Marcus   The physician who treats Jerry BURTON for war wounds, he recommends that the former pilot find a quiet village in which to recuperate, but his patient finds small-town gossip and murder in THE MOVING FINGER.

Kerr, Dr.   The brisk and decisive police surgeon called to examine the body of the first victim in THE A.B.C. MURDERS, he feels that the murder is not a woman's crime.

Kerr, Mary   The name given by actress Jane HEL-IER to the woman whom she believes has stolen her husband in "THE AFFAIR AT THE BUNGALOW," Kerr is said to be living a life of luxury.

Kerr, The Honourable Venetia Anne   In love with Lord Stephen HORBURY in DEATH IN THE CLOUDS, she views his wife Cicely as "a little tart." She believes that Horbury and his wife are separated and is shocked by their joint appearance after Madame GISELLE's death. Due to the intervention of Hercule POIROT, Lady Cicely is eventually able to marry her love.

Kettering, Derek   A man known for his many affairs in THE MYSTERY OF THE BLUE TRAIN, he expects to inherit his father's title and become Lord Leaconbury, but he is penniless without his wife's money. He has an affair with a dancer and falls in love with yet another woman, even as his wife threatens divorce.

Kettering, Ruth   The former Ruth VAN ALDIN, she marries impoverished nobleman and philanderer Derek KETTERING for his future title in THE MYSTERY OF THE BLUE TRAIN. She agrees with her father's demand to divorce Derek for his unfaithfulness, and she appears to be conducting an affair with the Comte Armaud DE LA ROCHE. Soon after receiving the famous Heart of Fire rubies as a gift from her father, she is murdered while aboard the *Blue Train,* on the way to a rendezvous with DE LA ROCHE.

Kharsanova, Anna   See DENMAN, ANNA.

Khay   The deceased husband of RENISENB in DEATH COMES AS THE END.

Kidd, Gracie   See MASON, JANE.

Kidd, Kitty   See MASON, ADA BEATRICE.

Kiddell, Mrs.   A haphazard housekeeper in MRS. MCGINTY'S DEAD, she horrifies the meticulous Hercule POIROT by the pride she takes in living in a house in which a notorious murder once occurred, and she seems to have erased permanently all traces of the formerly spotlessly maintained home.

Kidder, Mrs.   A better gossip than she is a cleaning woman in 4.50 FROM PADDINGTON, she is careless in completing tasks and highly suspicious. She also appears to know something about the murders and is overheard muttering "Nasty things, mushrooms."

Kidderminster, Lady Victoria (Vicky)   A large woman with a face like a horse, she is a well-known public figure in SPARKLING CYANIDE. She considers her son-in-law to be politically useful and, when her son-in-law's mistress is found dead, has not the slightest doubt that her daughter is capable of murder.

Kidderminster, Lord William   Well-known in political circles as a powerful influence, he is a strong personality in SPARKLING CYANIDE who appears to be an even match for his equally forceful wife. He also approves of his daughter's choice of Stephen FARRA-DAY as a husband.

"Kidnapped Prime Minister, The"   Mystery short story.

The story takes place near the end of World War I. Hercule POIROT is called upon to avert an international crisis by locating the kidnapped prime minister before a crucial conference convenes.

PUBLISHING AND DRAMATIZATION HISTORY
The story appeared in the short story collection, POIROT INVESTIGATES, published in 1924 by John

Lane in London, and in 1925 by Dodd, Mead and Company in New York.

The story was adapted for television in 1990 by London Weekend Television in England, and was also shown on the Public Broadcasting Service in the U.S.

CHARACTERS
Captain DANIELS, Bernard DODGE, Bertha EBENTHAL, Lord ESTAIR, Captain Arthur HASTINGS, Detective-Inspector JAPP, David MacADAM, O'MURPHY, Hercule POIROT

PLOT SYNOPSIS
When British Prime Minister David MacAdam disappears on the eve of an extremely important conference of world powers in the waning days of World War I, an important member of the House of Commons turns to Hercule Poirot to find him. The detective learns that an assassination attempt was made on the prime minister some months before, and that he has now been kidnapped in France, somewhere between Boulogne and Paris. His secretary is found chloroformed, and the chauffeur disappears with the prime minister. While the authorities discreetly interrogate everyone connected with the case, Poirot deduces the startling fact that the prime minister actually never left England. He solves the mystery in time to avert a political crisis.

CRIME NOTES
Chloroform is used to temporarily disable the prime minister in this story.

Kimble, Lady Abbot Intrigued when she reads Gwenda REED's call for information about Helen Spenlove Kennedy HALLIDAY in SLEEPING MURDER, the former parlourmaid for the missing woman responds eagerly. She is murdered while on her way to meet with Dr. KENNEDY, Helen's half-brother, despite her husband's warning not to do so.

King, Alix See MARTIN, ALIX.

King, Amelie A former debutante in GIANT'S BREAD, she married an impoverished man for love; her sad life is a warning to others.

King, Beatrice A housekeeper who is dismissed by the family when Mrs. OLDFIELD dies, she denies that she overheard an incriminating conversation between Dr. OLDFIELD and Jean MONCRIEFFE in "THE LERNEAN HYDRA."

King, Muriel A former lady's maid who was taken to Persia by her mistress, Lady Esther CARR, as a young and ignorant girl, she assumes CARR's identity when her mistress dies. To protect her secret, she plays the role of an eccentric who rejects everything British and who becomes totally immersed in native ways in "THE HOUSE AT SHIRAZ."

"King of Clubs, The" Mystery short story.

In this story, Hercule POIROT becomes an advisor to royalty in matters of love and murder.

PUBLISHING AND DRAMATIZATION HISTORY
The story appeared in the short story collection, THE UNDER DOG AND OTHER STORIES published in 1951 by Dodd, Mead and Company in New York.

The story was adapted for television in 1989 by London Weekend Television in England, and was also shown on the Public Broadcasting Service in the U.S.

CHARACTERS
Captain Arthur HASTINGS, Mr. and Mrs. OGLANDER, Miss OGLANDER, Prince PAUL of Mauriania, Hercule Poirot, Henry REEDBURN, Valerie SAINTCLAIR, Madame ZARA

PLOT SYNOPSIS
Hercule Poirot is asked by Prince Paul of Mauriania to solve a murder which involves Valerie Saintclair, the famous dancer to whom he has recently become engaged. The only witnesses to the dancer's distress after the murder are a family of four who claim to have been playing bridge near an open window when she staggered in, crying "Murder." As he delves into the lives and activities of all those concerned with the crime, Poirot learns that the victim, Henry Reedburn, had been blackmailing the dancer, and that Valerie Saintclair and the Oglander family share a secret. Although Poirot deduces the true identity of the murderer, he compassionately considers the circumstances, and places the blame on the illusory tramp of whom he says "I doubt if that tramp will ever be found."

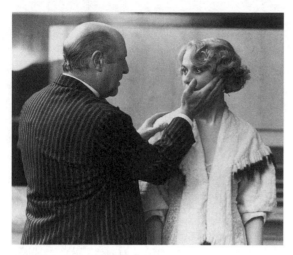

Impressario Henry Reedburn (David Swift) threatens dancer Valerie Saintclair (Niamh Cusack) in "The King of Clubs." (Photo courtesy of London Weekend Television)

CRIME NOTES
Despite his reputation for self-aggrandizement, Poirot chooses compassion over ego when he refrains from identifying the murderer in this story.

King, Sarah A young woman touring Jerusalem in APPOINTMENT WITH DEATH, she takes a strong interest in the highly dysfunctional Boyton family, particularly in Raymond BOYNTON. She has just completed her medical studies, and is called upon to ascertain Mrs. BOYNTON's time of death.

King, Winnie While en route to Miss POPE's exclusive school for girls in Neuilly, France, she is kidnapped in "THE GIRDLE OF HIPPOLYTA." No ransom is demanded because the kidnapper, James ELLIOT, is more concerned with smuggling a stolen Rubens painting into France, for which Winnie's luggage is useful.

Kingston Bruce, Beatrice The daughter of Colonel and Mrs. KINGSTON BRUCE, she consults Tommy and Tuppence BERESFORD at the International Detective Agency when her houseguest, Mrs. BETTS-HAMILTON, reports her pink pearl stolen in "THE AFFAIR OF THE PINK PEARL." Her obvious bad humor may be traced to her romance with the left-leaning Mr. RENNIE, whom her parents despise.

Kingston Bruce, Colonel Charles and Mrs. Owners of the Laurels and the parents of Beatrice KINGSTON BRUCE, they suspect her socialist boyfriend, Mr. RENNIE, when a prominent guest in their home reports her pearl pin missing in "THE AFFAIR OF THE PINK PEARL."

Kirkwood, Frederick A partner in the law firm of Walters and Kirkwood, he is Captain TREVELYAN's lawyer, and handles the details of the late man's will in THE SITTAFORD MYSTERY.

Kleek, Sir James (Jamie) A nervous man with eyes that dart about in sharp, suspicious glances, he is the son of one of Lord Edward ALTAMOUNT's closest friends, but plots against the well-respected statesman in PASSENGER TO FRANKFURT.

Knight, Miss An annoying nurse-companion provided for Miss Jane MARPLE by her nephew Raymond WEST in THE MIRROR CRACK'D FROM SIDE TO SIDE, she often finds herself outsmarted by the sprightly elderly lady, who sends the companion on lengthy errands, then escapes for her own adventure. Her attempts to make Miss MARPLE comfortable are more aggravating than helpful.

Knighton, Major An international jewel thief known as Monsieur LE MARQUIS in THE MYSTERY OF THE BLUE TRAIN, he has a passion for historically important jewels, and he now has his eye on the Heart of Fire rubies. To accomplish his task, Knighton becomes the secretary to Rufus VAN ALDIN, owner of the rubies.

Knox, Dr. Llewellyn A mere youth when he received the call to religious missionary work and evangelism, he carries with him a vision of a dark-haired, tragic-eyed woman in THE BURDEN. After years of devotion to his calling, Knox has a physical and emotional breakdown that forces him to retire from life.

Kochter, Monsieur A piano instructor in a French finishing school in UNFINISHED PORTRAIT, he tells the main character that she is not talented enough to be a concert pianist.

Kohn, Olga   See HOBHOUSE, VALERIE.

Kramenin   A Socialist fanatic in THE SECRET ADVERSARY, he is known as "Number One," and credited with being the force behind the Russian Revolution. His unprepossessing appearance masks his great ability to foment rebellion, although a strong suggestion of his power shows in his eyes, which have a "burning presence."

Kranin, Colonel   The first interviewer in "JANE IN SEARCH OF A JOB," he assesses Jane CLEVELAND before sending her to meet with Count STYLPTITCH to make the final decision as to her fitness to impersonate the Grand Duchess PAULINE.

Krapp, Charlotte   See VON WALDSAUSEN, THE GRAFIN CHARLOTTE.

Krassine, Monsieur   See IVANOVITCH, BORIS.

L

Labours of Hercules, The Mystery short story collection.

The book consists of an introductory chapter and twelve stories in which Hercule POIROT takes on twelve cases that correspond in the contemporary world to the twelve labors of Hercules, the hero of Greek mythology. The stage is set in the introductory chapter, in which a dinner guest compares the labors of Poirot to those of his mythological counterpart, and the great detective is not amused. Poirot has already decided to retire, but first he will take on twelve monumental cases as a suitable farewell. Each of the cases reflects in some manner the labors accomplished by Hercules.

PUBLISHING AND DRAMATIZATION HISTORY
The Labours of Hercules was first published in 1947 by William Collins Sons and Company, Ltd., in London, and by Dodd, Mead and Company in New York.

None of the stories has been adapted for stage or screen.

TITLES IN THE COLLECTION
The Labours of Hercules contains the following short stories: "THE NEMEAN LION," "THE LERNEAN HYDRA," "THE ARCADIAN DEER," "THE ERYMANTHIAN BOAR," "THE AUGEAN STABLES," "THE STYMPHALEAN BIRDS," "THE CRETAN BULL," "THE HORSES OF DIOMEDES," "THE GIRDLE OF HYPPOLITA," "THE FLOCK OF GERYON," "THE APPLES OF THE HESPERIDES" and "THE CAPTURE OF CERBERUS."

CRIME NOTES
Hercule Poirot once again meets the love of his life, Countess Rossakoff, in the final story of the collection.

Lacey, Colin Heir to the Kings Lacey estate upon his grandfather's death, the fifteen-year-old joins his close friend and cousin in planning a Boxing Day surprise for Hercule POIROT in "THE THEFT OF THE ROYAL RUBY."

Lacey, Em Hostess at Kings Lacey, she persuades Hercule POIROT to help expose a fortune hunter who is preying upon her granddaughter, Sarah LACEY, in "THE THEFT OF THE ROYAL RUBY."

Lacey, Colonel Horace Lord of the Kings Lacey estate, he is an old-fashioned former military man who strongly disapproves of the fortune-hunting Desmond LEE-WORTLEY in "THE THEFT OF THE ROYAL RUBY."

Lacey, Sarah A young heiress, she is described by her grandmother, Em LACEY, as being a modern girl who lives in "two rather unpleasant rooms in Chelsea down by the river and wears these funny clothes that they like to wear, and black stockings or bright green ones." She also makes plans to elope with fortune hunter Desmond LEE-WORTLEY in "THE THEFT OF THE ROYAL RUBY."

Laidlaw, Major Suspected of counterfeiting by Scotland Yard in "THE CRACKLER," he requests assistance from Tommy and Tuppence BERESFORD.

Laidlaw, Marguerite The young and attractive French wife of Major LAIDLAW, she falls under suspicion after being found with counterfeit money three times in "THE CRACKLER."

Lake, Captain John Quiet and mild-mannered, he is an intelligent and candid man in "DEAD MAN'S

MIRROR" who is well-liked by others and serves as the estate agent for his father-in-law, Sir Gervaise CHEVENIX-GORE.

Lal, Chandra   A medical student of Indian extraction who boards at Mrs. NICOLETIS' hostel in HICKORY DICKORY DOCK, he is a secret subversive obsessed with politics and possessed of a persecution complex.

Lal, Ram   A young Hindu student who assaults the prime minister in ONE, TWO, BUCKLE MY SHOE, he is described as "a bit excitable but he feels the wrongs of India very keenly."

Lamb, Detective-Sergeant   An efficient, if unimaginative, police sergeant, he arrests Brenda LEONIDES and Laurence BROWN for murder in CROOKED HOUSE, despite his misgivings.

Lamb, Colin   A special agent working under an assumed name and posing as a police constable in THE CLOCKS, he falls in love with suspect Sheila WEBB. He later marries her and becomes a marine biology instructor at an Australian university.

Lambert, Joyce   An impoverished young widow with an intense desire to keep her dog from starving leads her to accept a marriage proposal from a man whom she hates in "NEXT TO A DOG." When the dog dies, she escapes the intended marriage and leaves England as a governess to Mr. ALLABY's son.

"Lamp, The"   Non-mystery short story.

The plot centers on a haunted house, and the way in which it changes the lives of its new inhabitants forever.

PUBLISHING AND DRAMATIZATION HISTORY
The story appeared in the short story collection, THE HOUND OF DEATH AND OTHER STORIES, published in 1933 by William Collins Sons and Company in London.

The story has not been adapted for stage or screen.

CHARACTERS
Mrs. LANCASTER, Geoffrey LANCASTER, Mr. RADDISH, Mr. WINBURN

PLOT SYNOPSIS
This ghost story opens as the widowed Mrs. Lancaster surveys a somewhat grim-looking house which has been on the market for a long time. The price is low, but the house agent insists that there is nothing wrong with the house aside from some rumors that previous occupants have heard crying, but "there's nothing *seen*." Mr. Raddish explains that thirty years previously a wanted criminal with a young son had rented the house, killed himself while away and left his son to starve to death inside. Since then, occupants had reported sobbing sounds in the night. Undaunted by the story, the practical widow purchases the house and moves in with her father and young son, both of whom soon hear the ghost. Young Geoffrey also sees the spirit, and tries to befriend it. Only the unimaginative Mrs. Lancaster hears nothing. Within months of moving into the house, Geoffrey becomes seriously ill, and the doctor expresses no hope because the child has had serious lung trouble for a long time. In his delirium, he speaks continuously of the ghostly little boy and, just before dying, calls out "All right, I'm comin'." As Geoffrey dies, Mrs. Lancaster and Mr. Winburn hear childish laughter and the sound of two sets of feet running off into the distance.

Lancaster, Mrs.   A middle-aged widow with a no-nonsense attitude, she buys a house that is haunted by the spirit of a young boy and eventually loses her own son to the ghost in "THE LAMP."

Lancaster, Geoffrey   The young son of Mrs. LANCASTER and grandson of Mr. WINBURN, he claims to meet a small boy in various parts of the house his mother has just purchased in "THE LAMP." When he becomes very ill and dies, his mother hears, faint, childish laughter, and two sets of footsteps running away from the sickroom.

Lancaster, Julia   A woman with numerous pseudonyms and a very checkered past in BY THE PRICKING OF MY THUMBS, she is an elderly nursing home resident whose abandoned, unwed mother committed suicide soon after her birth. Under the name of Killer KATE, she had been a mentally unbalanced member of a wild gang. She was also the wife of a nobleman who committed her to various rest homes. When Tuppence BERESFORD finally traces her, Mrs. LANCASTER is living at Watermead, but she dies soon afterwards of poisoning.

Lane, Patricia   A physically unattractive archaeology student who boards at Mrs. NICOLETIS' youth hostel in HICKORY DICKORY DOCK, she is robbed of her diamond solitaire ring and later knocked out with a blow from a paperweight encased in a sock.

Lane, Reverend Stephen   A clergyman in EVIL UNDER THE SUN, he is obsessed with the devil, "especially the Devil in the guise of a woman—scarlet woman—whore of Babylon." Two women are strangled within twelve miles of his home before Arlene MARSHALL, a woman whom he labeled as embodying all the "evil under the sun," meets a similar fate.

Lang, Dr.   A tall, untidy, slouching man with long nervous fingers, he is, despite his ruthless and sarcastic demeanor, a clever army surgeon beloved by the nurses in GIANT'S BREAD.

Langdon, Miss   Manager of the Golf Hotel in "THE UNDER DOG," she becomes appropriately flustered when meeting Hercule POIROT.

Langton, Claude   The former fiancé of Mary DEANE who claims to seek a reconciliation with her in "WASPS' NEST," he tells Hercule POIROT that he is going to use gasoline to destroy a wasps' nest at the home of her current male friend.

Lanscombe   The intensely loyal, ninety-year-old butler in the Abernethie household who despises the laxity of the current generation of servants in AFTER THE FUNERAL, he seeks to maintain ancient standards of service in the household and would do anything necessary to protect those whom he serves.

Lansquenet, Cora Abernethie   The widowed youngest sibling of Richard ABERNETHIE in AFTER THE FUNERAL, she exhibits little judgement and only a rudimentary understanding of human nature. Her chance remark that her brother may have been murdered motivates an investigation, and causes her death soon afterwards.

La Paz, The Mistress of   A mysterious woman with a tragic history whose presence is rejuvenating

to Mr. SATTERTHWAITE in "THE MAN FROM THE SEA," she first marries a sadistic English swimmer who dies tragically and later has an affair with the sole purpose of conceiving a child.

Larkin, Mrs.   A woman with the appearance of a gipsy in THE CLOCKS.

Larkin, Beryl   Involved with a drug pusher, Anthony HAWKER, she hosts drug parties in "THE HORSES OF DIOMEDES" where cocaine is freely available.

La Roche, Mademoiselle   A highly feminine individual whose fashion sense has been honed by years of employment in the Parisian high fashion industry, she works at the Brain Trust complex in DESTINATION UNKNOWN, where she must guide the fashion sense of the female scientists. Her task is difficult, for "these scientific ladies often take very little interest in *la toilette*."

Larraby, Dr.   A usually good-humored physician, he refuses to consider that Richard ABERNETHIE was murdered in AFTER THE FUNERAL.

Larraby, J.   The narrator of UNFINISHED PORTRAIT, he was a promising portrait painter until he lost his hand in World War I, leaving him with only a stump. He intervenes to save the main character from suicide.

"Last Seance, The"   Non-mystery short story.

The story focuses on a successful medium who seeks to retire but who conducts one last fatal seance as a favor to a friend.

PUBLISHING AND DRAMATIZATION
HISTORY
The story appeared in the short story collection, THE HOUND OF DEATH AND OTHER STORIES, published 1933 by William Collins Sons and Company in London.

The story has not been adapted for stage or screen.

CHARACTERS
Raoul DAUBREUIL, ELISE (1), Madame EXE, Madame SIMONE

PLOT SYNOPSIS

The story concerns the highly successful medium, Madame Simone, who has promised to conduct one last seance before retiring forever to peaceful married life. Her fiancé, Raoul Daubreuil, appears to indulge her wishes, but he pointedly remarks that her fears and exhaustion are the price which all "martyrs to Science" have paid throughout the ages, and asks that she not be too hasty in her decision. The final seance will once again call forth the spirit of Madame Exe's daughter, a spirit which has taken increasingly solid form in preceding seances. Although frightened by Madame Exe, an extremely large woman who is heavily draped in mourning, Madame Simone is persuaded by her fiancé that she must show compassion to the grieving mother. The duplicitous Madame Exe cares only to regain her daughter and, on the pretext of guaranteeing that the seance proceeds honestly, she demands to bind Raoul's hands and feet with rope so that he is unable to move. Once her daughter is called forth and takes fleshly form because the spirit has drawn on the essence of the medium, Madame Exe escapes with the child and leaves behind the desiccated body of the dead Madame Simone.

CRIME NOTES

The author takes pains to make the character of Raoul Daubreuil produce a scientific explanation of the phenomenon of materialization, as he refers to a future in which "Science" will be able to test and weigh ectoplasm believed to issue from the medium during a seance.

Latimer, Edward (Ted) A disreputable character in TOWARDS ZERO, he is an opportunist whose profuse charm fails to mask his ruthless nature.

Laurier, Henri The contact agent between the Brain Trust complex and recruits in DESTINATION UNKNOWN, he conducts his shadowy business while playing the role of a French commercial traveler.

Laverton-West, Charles Viewed by Inspector JAPP as a "bit of a stuffed fish," he is an ambitious man in "MURDER IN THE MEWS" who seeks to improve his public speaking skills and to rise in British government. Although he looks a little like "a boiled owl," his fiancée, Barbara ALLEN, loves him deeply.

Lavigny, Father See MENIER, RAOUL.

Lavington, Mr. A member of a gang of jewel thieves in "THE VEILED LADY," he pretends to blackmail the false Lady Millicent Castle VAUGHN, who then ensnares Hercule POIROT in the plan. Lavington later double-crosses the gang, thus accidentally leading to their capture.

Lavington, Dr. Ambrose A self-proclaimed doctor of the soul in "THE MYSTERY OF THE BLUE JAR," he suggests that a seance be held when another guest claims to hear mysterious voices every morning at 7:25 A.M. With fellow guests at the small Stourton Heath hotel, he hopes to contact the ghost of a woman murdered at Heather Cottage.

Lawes, Esther Tall and exotic in appearance, she is engaged to Dickie CARPENTER in "THE GIPSY." Soon after his return from the sea, she mysteriously terminates their engagement.

Lawes, Rachel A childlike woman with "honest brown eyes" in "THE GIPSY," she is the "truer and sweeter" sister of Esther LAWES, who is engaged to Mr. MACFARLANE.

Lawson, Edgar An insignificant-appearing man in THEY DO IT WITH MIRRORS, he is Lewis SERROCOLD's illegitimate son who pretends to suffer from schizophrenic paranoia. He drowns after moving to his father's estate, Stoneygates.

Lawson, Wilhelmina The beneficiary of her employer's will after years of slavish devotion in DUMB WITNESS, she is an enthusiastic spiritualist who worked hard to prevent Miss ARUNDELL from rewriting the will during her last illness. After her employer's death, "Mina" feels guilty, and eagerly shares her inheritance with the Arundell heirs.

Lawton, Mrs. Sheila WEBB's aunt in THE CLOCKS, she informs the police that Sheila's mother is still alive.

Laxton, Harry Indulged by the local villagers despite his wild youth spent breaking windows, running up debts and sowing wild oats, he is the son of an army major and owner of Kingsdean House in

"THE CASE OF THE CARETAKER." He grows up, becomes a wealthy man through hard work and marries a pleasant young woman who dies soon after they settle down.

Laxton, Louise   Her good looks and comfortable family background are the envy of villagers in her husband's hometown in "THE CASE OF THE CARETAKER." Their bad wishes come to fruition when she dies after being thrown by her horse.

Lazarus, Jim   A wealthy friend of Nick BUCKLEY, he is co-owner with his father of a Bond Street art gallery in PERIL AT END HOUSE.

Lazenby, Dr.   A police surgeon in TOWARDS ZERO, he identifies the murder weapon as a golf club and suggests that a left-handed person murdered Lady TRESSILIAN.

Lazenby, Cedric   Subject to extensive stress during the heyday of the Youth Movement and increasing student unrest, he is the Prime Minister of England in PASSENGER TO FRANKFURT. Despite a public persona of extreme optimism, he experiences apprehension for the fate of England.

Leach, Inspector James   A member of Scotland Yard and the nephew of Superintendent BATTLE, he refuses to believe that a fine sportsman might also be a murderer in TOWARDS ZERO.

Leadbetter, Mr.   Present at the fourth murder in THE A.B.C. MURDERS, he is annoyed rather than alarmed when the murderer strikes, and fails to observe any significant details.

Leadbetter, Mrs.   A guest at the Stag Hotel in "THE GOLDEN BALL," she visits annually on the anniversary of her husband's death. Her nocturnal observations prove valuable to Hercule POIROT on the night of the murder.

Leadbetter, Ephraim   A rich businessman in "THE GOLDEN BALL," he fires his nephew for being lazy, then regrets his error.

Leaman, Harriet   Witness to the codicil of her employer's will, this cleaning lady in HALLOWE'EN PARTY consults Ariadne OLIVER after Mrs. LLEWELLYN-SMYTHE dies.

Leason, Claud   See AVERBURY, CLAUD.

Leathern, Miss   The most virulent of the village gossips in "THE LERNEAN HYDRA," she falls prey to the brilliance of Hercule POIROT, who masquerades as a Home Office investigator and uses her to spread the rumor that a suspected murder victim will be exhumed.

Leathern, Amy   An agreeably plump woman with kind and thoughtful eyes in PASSENGER TO FRANKFURT, she is the paid companion of Lady Matilda, who views her as "a nice, faithful, kindly sheep."

Leathern, Nurse Amy   Hired first to care for a newborn baby, then to serve as companion to Louise LEIDNER in MURDER IN MESOPOTAMIA, she views Hercule POIROT as a comic character until murder strikes. She then overcomes her bias, and joins POIROT in the search for the murderer.

Leathern, Eve   The daughter-in-law of AMALFI, the famous jewel thief, she is a twenty-seven-year-old woman who masquerades as a teenager in "THE REGATTA MYSTERY." Really Maria AMALFI, she tricks a wealthy merchant out of a diamond worth thirty thousand pounds, but the authorities catch her.

Leathern, Samuel   Head of an international gang of jewel thieves, his real name is AMALFI, but he masquerades as a wealthy American businessman in "THE REGATTA MYSTERY" as he plots to steal the valuable Morning Star diamond.

Leblanc, Monsieur   Designated to locate and expose Aristides' Brain Trust Complex in DESTINATION UNKNOWN, the French agent views scientists as being temperamental and difficult to control.

Lebrun, Madame   An old woman with white hair and claw-like hands who is a piano teacher in UNFINISHED PORTRAIT.

Leckie, Martha   The cook in Sir Bartholomew STRANGE's household in THREE-ACT TRAGEDY, she is horrified by the nature of the police investigation into her employer's murder.

Lecky, Mr.   The last man to see the murder victim alive in "THE SUNNINGDALE MYSTERY."

Le Conteau, Eleanor   A member of an acrobatic troupe that specializes in the theft of valuable art objects in "AT THE 'BELLS AND MOTLEY,' " she poses as a Canadian, Eleanor HARWELL, and claims to have been deserted by her new husband when they returned from their honeymoon.

Lee, Adelaide   The late wife of Simeon LEE in HERCULE POIROT'S CHRISTMAS, she is said to have died of a broken heart due to her husband's extensive philandering.

Lee, Alfred   The dull, eldest son of Simeon LEE who, although married, lives with and devotes his life to his father in HERCULE POIROT'S CHRISTMAS. Both his father and brother Harry despise Alfred.

Lee, David   The youngest of Simeon LEE's sons in HERCULE POIROT'S CHRISTMAS, he bears a grudge against his father for making his mother die of a "broken heart." He has been away from home for twenty years, living as an artist in London.

Lee, Dinah   A heavily made-up platinum-blonde in THE BODY IN THE LIBRARY who is really married to Basil BLAKE, she pretends to be his mistress simply to stimulate gossip in ST. MARY MEAD.

Lee, Esther   A frightening old woman known as a witch and a fortune teller in ENDLESS NIGHT, she sends ominous warnings of impending doom to the inhabitants of Gipsy's Acre. Suspected by the authorities of sending the anonymous messages, "Old Mother Lee" is found dead in a quarry soon after Ellie ROGERS' murder.

Lee, George   A boring, penny-pinching and dull-witted Member of Parliament, he is Simeon LEE's second-eldest son in HERCULE POIROT'S CHRISTMAS. Barely tolerated by Simeon, George only pretends affection for his father.

Lee, Henry (Harry)   The disreputable yet favored third son of Simeon LEE in HERCULE POIROT'S CHRISTMAS, he left the family home to roam the world after forging his father's signature on a check. Harry reconciles with his father years later after being summoned home, and learns that Simeon plans to leave the bulk of the estate to him.

Lee, Hilda   A stout, dumpy, middle-aged woman with a forceful personality, she is married to Simeon LEE's youngest son, David, in HERCULE POIROT'S CHRISTMAS. She is forced to deal with her husband's obsession with his dead mother.

Lee, Lydia   Married to Simeon LEE's eldest son, Alfred, in HERCULE POIROT'S CHRISTMAS, she is a "lean greyhound of a woman" admired by her father-in-law for her spirit. Lydia despises Simeon because he belittles her husband and manipulates them both.

Lee, Magdalene   The much-younger, platinum-blonde wife of Simeon LEE's second son, George, in HERCULE POIROT'S CHRISTMAS, she thrives on the attention of men. Although she pretends otherwise, she lived for a while with one man before her marriage, and presently meets others secretly. Her smooth, egglike face and plucked eyebrows create a masklike appearance on a face that is often devoid of expression.

Lee, Simeon   Found brutally murdered in HERCULE POIROT'S CHRISTMAS, he is the patriarch of a family that contains four legitimate sons and one legitimate daughter, as well as two illegitimate sons. Known to have driven his late wife, Adelaide, to her death, he delights in harassing his remaining family, whom he calls together at Christmas in order to torment them as a group. He has also treated business acquaintances badly, and an old injustice resurfaces to threaten his life.

Leech, Andrew   Known as "the old devil" to his employees in DEATH IN THE CLOUDS, he is the owner of a beauty salon, where he is known as Monsieur ANTOINE, and employs Jane GREY.

Lee-Wortley, Desmond   A young fortune hunter in "THE THEFT OF THE ROYAL RUBY" who is known to prey on young heiresses, he arrives at Kings Lacey with the goal of ensnaring the naïve Sarah LACEY.

Legge, Alec   A moody and obsessed atomic scientist in DEAD MAN'S FOLLY, he becomes an espionage agent with the aim of curing injustice in the world. His mean-tempered behavior drives his wife, Sally, away from him.

Legge, Rosy   See KEENE, RUBY.

Legge, Sally   An intelligent and attractive university graduate who once had an art studio in Chelsea, she is the unhappy wife of Alec in DEAD MAN'S FOLLY. After three unhappy years of marriage, she leaves her husband for an old admirer.

Legge, Sir Thomas   Despite his years of experience with Scotland Yard, the Assistant Commissioner finds the deaths of ten people on Indian Island "fantastic—impossible" in AND THEN THERE WERE NONE.

Leicester, Marjory   Friend and roommate of Una DRAKE in "THE UNBREAKABLE ALIBI," she testifies that Una was in the apartment on the night of the bet.

Leidner, Dr. Eric   A former German spy named Frederick BOSNER who has undergone reconstructive surgery and created a new life for himself as a distinguished archaeologist in MURDER IN MESOPOTAMIA, he is passionately in love with his wife Louise. Head of the expedition at Tell Yarimjah, he hires Nurse LEATHERN to care for his wife, who shows signs of mental imbalance.

Leidner, Louise   Contradictory in behavior, she is both a "champion liar" and "a mass of affectation," as well as a woman who could inspire obsessive devotion in men in MURDER IN MESOPOTAMIA. She turned her first husband in to the authorities when she learned that he was a German spy responsible for the loss of hundreds of lives, and married Dr. Eric LEIDNER, unaware that he was her first husband, who had undergone reconstructive surgery and a change of identity. She is murdered by a blow to the head after weeks of being terrorized by threatening letters.

Leith, Duchess of   An old noblewoman who wears her numerous valuable diamond brooches pinned haphazardly on her dresses in "THE WORLD'S END," she makes friends with the socially conscious Mr. SATTERTHWAITE. Her eccentricities amuse him, and she convinces him to leave Cannes for Corsica with her.

Lejeune, Inspector   A quietly capable police inspector in THE PALE HORSE, he is an imaginative man who looks beyond the obvious in solving crimes.

Lemaitre, Charles   See MARTIN, GERALD.

Leman, Anne Morisot   See MORISOT, ANNE.

Lemarchant, Carla   Unable to marry while uncertain whether her mother actually did murder her father, she contacts Hercule POIROT to uncover the truth of the murder in FIVE LITTLE PIGS.

Le Marchant, Jimmy   The young man who verifies that Una DRAKE had dinner with him at the Savoy on the night of the bet in "THE UNBREAKABLE ALIBI," he also reports that his friend had seen Una in Torquay on the same day.

Le Marquis, Monsieur   See KNIGHTON, MAJOR.

Lementeuil, Commissionaire   An old friend and colleague of Hercule POIROT in "THE ERYMANTHIAN BOAR," he is the Swiss Commissionaire of Police who supplies information about the murderer MARRASCAUD. He arrives by helicopter at the Rochers Neige resort to make the arrest.

Lemesurier, Hugo   Obsessed with the family curse that decreed first-born Lemesurier sons do not live to inherit, he takes steps in "THE LEMESURIER INHERITANCE" which seem designed to thwart the curse.

Lemesurier, Major Roger   A distant cousin not subject to the fate of the cursed branch of the Lemesurier family in "THE LEMESURIER INHERITANCE," he explains the curse in detail to Hercule POIROT.

Lemesurier, Ronald   Claimed as the first-born son and heir to the Lemesurier fortune in "THE LEMESURIER INHERITANCE," the eight-year-old boy was really fathered by Hugo LEMESURIER's secretary,

John GARDINER. Despite his lineage, Ronald suffers several suspicious accidents which mark him for death.

Lemesurier, Sadie   Unhappily married to Hugo LEMESURIER, she has a son by her husband's secretary in "THE LEMESURIER INHERITANCE" and marries him after her husband's death.

Lemesurier, Vincent   Shell-shocked from the war, Hugo LEMESURIER's nephew is highly fearful of the family curse in "THE LEMESURIER INHERITANCE." His mental stability is further threatened when his father is nearly killed by a fall from a horse.

"Lemesurier Inheritance, The"   Mystery short story.

The plot centers on a family curse which decrees that no first-born Lemesurier son will live to inherit the family holdings.

PUBLISHING AND DRAMATIZATION HISTORY

The story appeared in the short story collection THE UNDER DOG AND OTHER STORIES, published in 1951 by Dodd, Mead and Company in New York.

The story has not been adapted for stage or screen.

CHARACTERS

John GARDINER, Captain Arthur HASTINGS, Hugo LEMESURIER, Major Roger LEMESURIER, Ronald LEMESURIER, Sadie LEMESURIER, Vincent LEMESURIER, Hercule POIROT

PLOT SYNOPSIS

The story recounts a series of past deaths attributed to the centuries-old Lemesurier curse, which has barred first-born sons from claiming their inheritance. Hercule Poirot becomes suspicious when murder is once again attempted, this time in the guise of a series of accidents and, finally, through a purported bee sting. He sets the trap and, with the help of Hastings, catches the very unexpected murderer.

CRIME NOTES

An injection of formic acid, a carboxylic acid originally obtained by distilling ants, is the means of one attempted and one actual murder in the story. Other murders are due to falls from a horse and a train.

Lemoine, Monsieur   A notorious jewel thief known as King VICTOR to his gang in Paris, he masquerades under this name as an inspector from the Sûreté in Paris in THE SECRET OF CHIMNEYS. In this one of many disguises, he wears a black, pointed beard and clothes which give him a foppish appearance. (See King VICTOR.)

Lemon, Felicity   Highly efficient and passionate about order, she is Mr. PARKER PYNE's secretary in two cases, "THE CASE OF THE MIDDLE-AGED WIFE" and "THE CASE OF THE DISTRESSED LADY," before working for Hercule POIROT in eight cases: "HOW DOES YOUR GARDEN GROW?," "THE NEMEAN LION," "THE CAPTURE OF CERBERUS," HICKORY DICKORY DOCK, DEAD MAN'S FOLLY, "THE MYSTERY OF THE SPANISH CHEST," THIRD GIRL and ELEPHANTS CAN REMEMBER. Described as "unbelievably ugly" yet "incredibly efficient," she is a tall and angular woman, who follows Poirot's orders precisely and mirrors his passion for order. Aside from the introduction of her sister, Mrs. HUBBARD, in *Hickory Dickory Dock*, nothing is revealed about Miss Lemon's personal life, except that she dreams of creating the perfect filing system, "besides which all other filing systems should sink into oblivion."

Leonides, Aristide   The elderly patriarch of the Leonides family whose fortune supports them all, he dies at the age of eighty-four when someone replaces his insulin with eserine in CROOKED HOUSE. He is a wealthy Greek businessman, "a gnome—ugly little fellow—but magnetic," whose second marriage, at the age of seventy-four, was to a woman fifty years his junior, a waitress in one of his restaurants. He leaves a will that makes his granddaughter Sophie the beneficiary over his dependent sons, daughters-in-law and grandchildren. He places on her the burden of maintaining the family income.

Leonides, Brenda   A large-eyed, flat-voiced woman with a sleepy smile who resembles "a big purring lazy cat," she was a twenty-four-year-old waitress when she married her wealthy employer, Aristide LEONIDES in CROOKED HOUSE. Her passion for Laurence BROWN, her stepchildren's tutor, places her under suspicion when Aristide is murdered.

Leonides, Clemency   Obsessively protective of her husband, Roger LEONIDES, she is a scientist studying radiation effects in CROOKED HOUSE. Her personal surroundings and her personality are austere, and her only indulgence seems to be the love she lavishes on her husband, who "made up her whole existence."

Leonides, Eustace   The moody and arrogant sixteen-year-old grandson of Aristide LEONIDES and son of Philip and Magda in CROOKED HOUSE, he walks with a halting gait as the result of polio, and dislikes being tutored with his younger sister Josephine. Aristide viewed Eustace as indolent and too easily influenced by others.

Leonides, Josephine   A precocious eleven-year-old in CROOKED HOUSE who distinctly resembles her grandfather, Aristide LEONIDES, more than her parents Philip and Magda, she knows everything that occurs in the house. Her inquisitiveness may be the reason that three attempts are made on her life.

Leonides, Magda   An actress under the stage name of Magda West who is married to Philip LEONIDES, she is given to dramatic exits and entrances and "absolute orgies of emotion" in CROOKED HOUSE. She liked her late father-in-law Aristide LEONIDES, but her self-absorbed nature makes her worry more about her waning career than about identifying the murderer.

Leonides, Philip   An apparently emotionless man who has written numerous books that remain unread, he is husband to Magda LEONIDES and father to Sophia, Eustace and Josephine in CROOKED HOUSE. Independently wealthy because his father settled money upon him years before, he lacks confidence in himself, and has long craved his father's love and attention.

Leonides, Roger   Hopeless in business transactions, he is the companionable eldest son of Aristide LEONIDES in CROOKED HOUSE. Despite his longing to match his father's business success, Roger has no ability. His continued failures make him an object of pity and resentment to other family members, but his wife Clemency fiercely protects him from their criticism.

Leonides, Sophia   A courageous and independent young woman who meets her fiancé Charles HAYWARD while the two serve in Egypt during the war, this daughter of Philip and Magda LEONIDES is given control of the entire estate in Aristide LEONIDES' will in CROOKED HOUSE. Her grandfather perceives her as having the necessary brains, judgment and generosity of spirit to manage the inheritance.

Leonie (1)   The flirtatious French maid of Mrs. VANDERLYN in "THE INCREDIBLE THEFT," she first claims to have seen a ghost but later admits to Hercule POIROT that she invented the story. She screamed because her employer's boyfriend had surprised her on the stairs and hugged her, and she assures Poirot that she would not scream if *he* surprised her on the stairs.

Leonie (2)   The flirtatious French maid of Mrs. CONRAD in "THE SUBMARINE PLANS," she claims to have screamed because she saw a ghost on the stairs. To Hercule POIROT, she admits the truth, that she screamed when Leonard WEARDALE surprised her on the stairs and kissed her.

"Lernean Hydra, The"   Mystery short story.

The plot centers on Dr. OLDFIELD, targeted by village gossip as having poisoned his wife, who asks for Hercule POIROT's assistance in clearing his name.

PUBLISHING AND DRAMATIZATION HISTORY

The story appeared in the short story collection THE LABOURS OF HERCULES, published in 1947 by William Collins Sons and Company in London, and by Dodd, Mead and Company in New York.

The story has not been adapted for stage or screen.

CHARACTERS

GEORGES, GLADYS (4), Nurse HARRISON, Beatrice KING, Miss LEATHERAN, Jean MONCRIEFFE, Dr. Charles Oldfield, Hercule Poirot

PLOT SYNOPSIS

Dr. Charles Oldfield contacts Hercule Poirot and asks him to prove the doctor innocent of murdering his wife to stop the vicious rumors. When Poirot challenges his visitor to tell the whole truth, the doctor balks, then reveals that he is in love with his dispenser and the two would have married long before, had the gossip not continued. Poirot takes the case, and orders the exhumation of Mrs. Oldfield, which reveals that she was poisoned. Given the easy access to poison of three individuals, the detective must weigh carefully the evidence, as well as each person's motive, before identifying the murderer.

CRIME NOTES

The murder in this story results from arsenic poisoning.

The story is a modern retelling of the second labor of the Greek mythological figure Hercules, who was required to destroy the many-headed Hydra of the Lernean swamp. The many-headed monster of this story is gossip.

Lessing, Ruth The loyal and efficient secretary of murder victim George BARTON in SPARKLING CYANIDE, she has a cool exterior hiding a passionate nature.

Lester, Charles A young bank clerk who is falsely accused of murdering Chinese merchant WU LING while on board the S.S. *Assunta* in "THE LOST MINE."

Lestrange, Miss An amiable woman with a smile and a twinkle in her eyes, she rents the newlyweds their first apartment in UNFINISHED PORTRAIT.

Lestrange, Mrs. An enigmatic presence in St. Mary Mead in MURDER AT THE VICARAGE, she is really Colonel PROTHEROE's first wife, and mother of Lettice PROTHEROE. She secretly meets her former husband the night before his murder.

Letardeau, Raoul A mysterious traveler in a train compartment containing three English travelers in "THE FOURTH MAN," he provides missing clues in their puzzled discussion of Felicie BAULT and her multiple personalities.

Leverson, Charles Young and hotheaded, he quarrels with his uncle Sir Reuben ASTWELL shortly before murder occurs and becomes a suspect in "THE UNDER DOG."

Levinne, Mr. and Mrs. Described in GIANT'S BREAD as "a very Christian brand of Jew," their purchase of an English country estate and the expensive improvements they make provide gossip for the local inhabitants.

Levinne, Sebastian A young Jewish boy in GIANT'S BREAD when he first meets the protagonist, he must deal with the anti-Semitism of his English neighbors. He becomes a lifelong friend of Vernon DEYRE, and provides the financial support to produce Vernon's musical compositions.

Li Chang Yen Viewed by Poirot as "the finest criminal brain ever known," he is "Number One" in the Big Four gang and the most intelligent member of the group in THE BIG FOUR.

Linch, Gladys A young maid whose story provides a mystery puzzle in "THE TUESDAY NIGHT CLUB," she dies in childbirth after her lover, Albert JONES, deserts her.

Lindstrom, Kirsten (Kirsty) A woman who is "as plain as a currant bun," she is a Swedish nurse and masseuse at the wartime nursery run by Rachel ARGYLE in ORDEAL BY INNOCENCE. Devoted to her employer, she remains as housekeeper after Rachel is murdered.

Lingard, Miss Hired as an assistant to Sir Gervase CHEVENIX-GORE, who is writing a family history in "DEAD MAN'S MIRROR," she disguises her identity as his brother Anthony's former mistress and the mother of Ruth, fathered by Anthony and adopted by Sir Gervase and his wife.

Lionel, Sir Angered by the thought that the murderer in THE A.B.C. MURDERS might work his way through to "Z," the Assistant Commissioner of the Central Intelligence Division at Scotland Yard furiously resists the possibility that the guilty party might be declared insane and placed into a nursing home rather than prosecuted.

Lippincott, Andrew P. The attorney to heiress Ellie ROGERS in ENDLESS NIGHT, he suspects that his ward might be in danger, and hires two private investigators disguised as a cook and a butler to work in her household as protection.

Lippincott, Beatrice Manager of the inn in Warmsley Vale where the mysterious "Enoch Arden" attempts to blackmail David HUNTER in TAKEN AT THE FLOOD, she reports what she hears to Rowley CLOADE, who then takes action.

Lipscomb Faithful assistant to the unscrupulous Dr. ANDERSEN who leads a religious cult in "THE FLOCK OF GERYON," he is a crude and primitive man who is devoted to his employer.

Liskeard, Professor Responsible for the authenticity of design of the Countess ROSSAKOFF's nightclub, Hell, in "THE CAPTURE OF CERBERUS," he is a meek archaeologist and innocent bystander.

Listerdale, Lord A wealthy nobleman in "THE LISTERDALE MYSTERY" (2) who desires to repent for his earlier selfish life, he assumes his butler's identity and rents out his house to Mrs. ST. VINCENT, an impoverished widow, her daughter and her son. After serving them for a time, he is unmasked, and asks Mrs. St. Vincent to marry him.

Listerdale Mystery, The (1) Mystery short story collection.

The twelve stories in the collection do not contain any of the familiar detectives of other works by Agatha Christie, and only seven of the stories contain a crime that must be solved. The remaining five stories contain deceptions, but the emphasis is upon romance, and the author uses a lighthearted tone in arranging for her characters to meet and then to fall in love.

PUBLISHING AND DRAMATIZATION
HISTORY
The Listerdale Mystery was first published by William Collins Sons and Company, Ltd., in London in 1934, but there have been no American editions of the intact collection. Each of the stories except "SING A SONG OF SIXPENCE" has been published in one of the American collections WITNESS FOR THE PROSECU-

TION AND OTHER STORIES, THE GOLDEN BALL AND OTHER STORIES and SURPRISE! SURPRISE!

Several of the stories have been adapted for stage or screen. "PHILOMEL COTTAGE" was adapted for the stage as "LOVE FROM A STRANGER" and opened in London and New York in 1936. Films made of this adaptation appeared in 1937 and 1947. Thames Television adapted "THE GIRL IN THE TRAIN," "JANE IN SEARCH OF A JOB" and "THE MANHOOD OF EDWARD ROBINSON" for television in 1983.

TITLES IN THE COLLECTION
The Listerdale Mystery contains the following short stories: "THE LISTERDALE MYSTERY" (2), "Philomel Cottage," "The Girl in the Train," "Sing a Song of Sixpence," "The Manhood of Edward Robinson," "ACCIDENT," "Jane in Search of a Job," "A FRUITFUL SUNDAY," "MR. EASTWOOD'S ADVENTURE," "THE GOLDEN BALL," "THE RAJAH'S EMERALD" and "SWAN SONG."

"Listerdale Mystery, The" (2) Mystery short story.

The plot centers on a missing aristocrat and the good fortune of an impoverished family who rent his elegant town house.

PUBLISHING AND DRAMATIZATION
HISTORY
The story appeared in the short story collection THE LISTERDALE MYSTERY (1), published in 1934 by William Collins Sons and Company, Ltd., in London.

CHARACTERS
Colonel Maurice CARFAX, Lord LISTERDALE, QUENTIN, Mrs. ST. VINCENT, Barbara ST. VINCENT, Rupert ST. VINCENT

PLOT SYNOPSIS
The story tells of impoverished yet genteel widow Mrs. St. Vincent, who is faced with increasing financial strains that will force her to move with her son and daughter into surroundings even shabbier than those they presently inhabit. Good fortune in the form of a rental ad for an elegant home with servants available at a nominal rent saves the family's image and provides the appropriate setting for Barbara St. Vincent to ensnare a comfortably well-off fiancé. The former resident disappeared abruptly and Quentin,

the butler, seems to act suspiciously, so Rupert St. Vincent investigates the situation and uncovers the truth of Lord Listerdale's whereabouts.

Litchfield, Elizabeth   See COLE, ELIZABETH.

Littledale, James Arthur   The chemist who identifies the exact drug used to poison Mary GERRARD in SAD CYPRESS.

Littleworth, Mr.   See SANDERS, JACK.

Livingstone, Miss   The replacement for Ariadne OLIVER's former secretary, Miss Sedgwick, in ELEPHANTS CAN REMEMBER, she proves to be inefficient when asked to locate her employer's birthday book and old address books.

Llewellyn, Evan   A dark and wolfish-looking writer in "THE REGATTA MYSTERY," he has the misfortune to win a substantial amount of money at the racetrack on the day that a guest is robbed of a highly valuable diamond.

Llewellyn-Smythe, Mrs.   A wealthy but extremely short-tempered woman in HALLOWE'EN PARTY, she uses her will as a means of controlling her relatives. After a fight with her nephew, Hugo DRAKE, she disinherits him, but the codicil naming her au pair as the new heir is found to be a forgery after both aunt and nephew die.

Lloyd, Dr.   A member of the Tuesday Night Club, he tells the story of "THE COMPANION" as his offering to the group.

Lloyd, Mrs.   An exotic-looking medium brought to Abbot's Mead to conduct a seance in "THE VOICE IN THE DARK," she wears a chain of moonstones and numerous rings. Before conducting each seance, she eats only fruit.

Lloyd, Gerald (Gerry)   Perpetually down on his luck, he appears to be weak-willed and ineffectual until his love for Sarah PRENTICE in A DAUGHTER'S A DAUGHTER forces him to use his inner strength to save her.

Lloyd, Stanford   An investment banker who managed investments for heiress Ellie ROGERS in

ENDLESS NIGHT, he is fired by Ellie's husband when he gets too close to the truth.

Loftus, Squadron Leader   See LONG, SAMUEL.

Logan, Miss   Formerly the companion of the late Lady Radclyffe, she is the housekeeper for Lois HARGREAVES, Lady Radclyffe's niece, in "THE HOUSE OF THE LURKING DEATH." She dies of shock after an arson attempt.

Lollipop, Baron   See LOLOPRETJZYL, BARON.

Lolopretjzyl, Baron   A member of the Herzoslovakian entourage in THE SECRET OF CHIMNEYS, the baron maneuvers to obtain the memoirs of the late Count STYLPTITCH but fails.

Lomax, The Honourable George   Undersecretary of State for Foreign Affairs in THE SECRET OF CHIMNEYS and THE SEVEN DIALS MYSTERY, he is a physically unattractive man whose protruding, fish-like eyes give him the nickname of "Codders." One of his assistants describes him as "a disgusting windbag, an unscrupulous, hypocritical old hot-air merchant—a foul, poisonous self-advertiser."

Lombard, Captain Philip   A bloodthirsty soldier of fortune accused of murdering twenty-one members of an East African tribe, he is the ninth victim on Indian Island in AND THEN THERE WERE NONE.

Long, Samuel   Traveling from Damascus to Baghdad under the identity of Squadron Leader Loftus in "THE GATE OF BAGHDAD," he is really "a great criminal" whose exploits have made many people suffer.

Longman, Professor   A scientific investigator interested in the paranormal in "MOTIVE VERSUS OPPORTUNITY," he is retained to expose spiritualist Eurydice SPRAGG as a fraud.

Lonsdale, Susan   Young and brazen, she confronts her lover's wife in THE BURDEN and demands a divorce that her lover has no intention of pursuing.

Lopez, Conchita   An imposter who assumes the identity of her dead friend to obtain an inheritance in HERCULE POIROT'S CHRISTMAS, she is found out by Hercule POIROT, who observes that her brown eyes could not have resulted from two blue-eyed parents.

Lord, Inspector   The head of the murder investigation in SPIDER'S WEB, he refuses to believe Clarissa HAILSHAM-BROWN when she tells the truth, but sympathizes with her when she lies.

Lord, Dr. Peter   A physician whose interest is curing people of disease in SAD CYPRESS, he retains Hercule POIROT to clear Elinor CARLISLE of murder charges.

Lord Edgware Dies   Mystery novel.

The novel concerns a murder which could only have been committed if one person were able to be in two places at the same time. The plot centers on the efforts of Hercule POIROT both to identify a murderer and to determine how the seemingly impossible could occur.

PUBLISHING AND DRAMATIZATION HISTORY

The novel was published in 1933 by William Collins Sons and Company, Ltd., in London, and by Dodd, Mead and Company in New York, under the title *Thirteen at Dinner*.

The first film version of the novel was released in 1934 by Real Arts in England, starring Austin Trevor in his third appearance as Hercule Poirot, with the following additional cast members: Jane Carr, Richard Cooper, Michael Shepley and John Turnbull.

The novel was adapted in 1985 as a 90-minute movie named *Thirteen for Dinner*, made by Warner Brothers especially for television. The story was modified to open with Hercule Poirot appearing on the David Frost television show, where he meets the actress Jane Wilkinson. The production starred Peter Ustinov as Hercule Poirot, as well as Jonathan Cecil, Faye Dunaway, Lee Horsley and David SUCHET as Inspector Japp, prior to the actor's own success as Poirot. The production was broadcast in 1986 on British television by London Weekend Television.

CHARACTERS

Carlotta ADAMS, ALTON, Alice BENNET, Miss CARROLL, Sir Montague CORNER, Jenny DRIVER, ELLIS, Captain Arthur HASTINGS, Dr. HEATH, Chief Inspector James JAPP, George Alfred St. Vincent MARSH (the fourth Baron Edgware), Geraldine MARSH, Captain Ronald MARSH (the fifth Baron Edgware), Brian MARTIN, Dowager Duchess of MERTON, Duke of MERTON, Hercule Poirot, Donald ROSS, Mrs. WILBURN, June WILKINSON

PLOT SYNOPSIS
Chapters 1–3
Poirot and Hastings attend a performance by celebrity impersonator Carlotta Adams and later have supper at the Savoy, where actress Jane Wilkinson, the present Lady Edgware, asks Poirot for help. She wants to marry the Duke of Merton, but Lord Edgware refuses to grant her a divorce. Poirot agrees to intervene, and is approached by her dinner companion, who tells him that Lady Edgware is capable of anything—even murder.

Chapters 4–6
Poirot meets with Lord Edgware, who claims that he consented to the divorce in a letter sent six months previously. Late that night, Lord Edgware is killed. Poirot reads an account in the paper that Jane was at a dinner party that night, which provides her with a solid alibi. Jane admits that she did not want to attend the dinner party and went only at her maid's insistence. While at the party, she received a telephone call which was disconnected before the caller was identified. Privately, Brian Martin insists to Poirot that Jane had threatened Lord Edgware's life, and he believes that she committed the murder.

Chapters 7–9
Questioned by Poirot, Lord Edgware's secretary claims that Jane, dressed in black, had entered the house on the night of the murder, but Poirot challenges her, and states that she could not have seen Jane's face from where she stood. Recalling Carlotta Adams' impersonation of Jane, Poirot suspects that she might be in trouble, and goes to her house. He is too late, as he learns that she has died of a veronal overdose, despite her maid's insistence that Carlotta never took more than one veronal pill.

Chapters 10–13
After searching Carlotta's home, Poirot finds veronal in an expensive trinket box that is inscribed "C.A. from D. Paris Nov. 10—Sweet Dreams." He

interviews Jenny Driver about their luncheon the previous day, and she tells him that Carlotta hinted at being involved in an elaborate practical joke. When Poirot speaks with Jane, he finds that she is no longer concerned with Lord Edgware's death, and is already planning her wedding, which will take place in four or five months. Poirot questions Geraldine, Lord Edgware's daughter, who admits that she never really loved him. He also questions Ronald Marsh, about to become the next Lord Edgware, and learns that Marsh is acquainted with Carlotta, and is shocked at her death.

Chapters 14–17

Poirot sorts out the information gathered to date, and finds that he has more questions than answers at this point. He speaks with the Widburns' butler about the telephone call, and learns that the caller hung up when Jane identified herself as Lady Edgware. Despite her death, Carlotta remains the only suspect in Inspector Japp's mind, and he tries to solve the additional mystery of the missing one hundred pounds which Lord Edgware's secretary claims to have left on the table the night of his death. Japp tells Poirot that Lord Edgware's butler has left without a word.

Chapters 18–21

Poirot questions the Duke of Merton, who refuses to commit himself regarding an upcoming marriage to Jane, but Poirot surreptitiously reads a love letter lying on Merton's desk. When the Dowager Duchess of Merton contacts Poirot to ask for his help in preventing her son from marrying Jane, the detective tells her that her son is old enough to make his own decisions. Japp contacts Poirot to show him a letter Carlotta had sent her sister, in which she stated that Marsh promised her ten thousand pounds to dress up as Jane to fool Lord Edgware. Marsh denies the charge, and tells the authorities that he and Geraldine returned to the house on the night of the murder to obtain her pearls, which she is giving him to raise the money he needs.

Chapters 22–25

Poirot suspects that Carlotta received the expensive trinket box more recently than November. Although the police arrest Ronald Marsh, Poirot realizes that one page has been taken from Carlotta's letter to implicate Marsh. Geraldine asks Poirot to clear Marsh.

A significant clue emerges during a luncheon, when Donald Ross comments about "the judgment of Paris," and Jane thinks that he is speaking about the city rather than the Trojan War. Ross calls Poirot, but the call ends before he can speak with the detective.

Chapters 26–29

Ross is murdered, and Poirot begins a second round of questioning. He switches glasses with Lord Edgware's secretary and finds that she really needs her glasses to see. He questions Jane's maid and learns that Martin was madly in love with Jane, but she would rather have Merton's title. When Poirot switches glasses with the maid, she does not notice a difference. Poirot learns that Brian suppressed the letter from Lord Edgware in which he approved the divorce because she had turned her affections toward Merton. The detective also learns that the missing page of Carlotta's letter implicated a "she" rather than a "he."

Chapters 30–31

Poirot reveals what really happened in the affair, and he names an unexpected murderer. He explains, in detail, the way in which the murderer managed to carry out the crimes, then receives a letter from the individual who confesses everything.

CRIME NOTES

The novel contains three murders. The first and third victims die when they are stabbed with a corn knife in the base of the skull. The second victim is poisoned with an overdose of veronal.

Lorimer, Mrs. One of the invited guests at Mr. SHAITANA's dinner and bridge party in CARDS ON THE TABLE, she is a suspect in his murder, but later is murdered with an overdose of Evipan.

Lorimer, Dr. George A physician and the nephew of Anthony and Henry GASCOIGNE in "FOUR-AND-TWENTY BLACKBIRDS," he fails to notice changes in his Uncle Henry's diet.

Lorimer, Jerry Engaged to Sylvia KEENE, whose uncle initially opposed the match in "THE HERB OF DEATH," he is seen kissing another woman soon before Sylvia dies of poisoning.

"Lost Mine, The" Mystery short story.

The plot centers on the murder case that provided Hercule POIROT with fourteen thousand shares of Burma Mines, Ltd. stock.

PUBLISHING AND DRAMATIZATION HISTORY

The story appeared in the short story collection, POIROT INVESTIGATES, published in 1924 by John Lane in London, and in 1925 by Dodd, Mead and Company in New York.

The story was adapted for television in 1990 by London Weekend Television in England, and was also shown on the Public Broadcasting Service in the U.S.

CHARACTERS

DYER, Captain Arthur HASTINGS, Charles LESTER, Inspector MILLER, Mr. PEARSON, Hercule Poirot, WU LING

PLOT SYNOPSIS

The story recounted is a warning to Captain Hastings after his suggestion that Hercule Poirot invest three hundred pounds in Porcupine Oil Fields. Poirot's cautionary tale is of a case in which he was retained to locate the murderer of a Chinese man who had journeyed to London bearing the only known record of a fabulously rich mine in Burma. When Wu Ling is found dead, Poirot goes to work and solves the crime, which nets him fourteen thousand shares of mine stock and the conviction to stay only with safe investments.

CRIME NOTES

The victim is murdered by being drowned in the Thames River.

"Love Detectives, The" Mystery short story.

The plot centers on the efforts of Mr. SATTERTHWAITE to uncover the true murderer in a love triangle.

PUBLISHING AND DRAMATIZATION HISTORY

The story appeared in the short story collection, THREE BLIND MICE AND OTHER STORIES, published in 1950 by Dodd, Mead and Company in New York.

The story has not been adapted for stage or screen.

Diabolical forces, one played by Hi Ching, contrive to prevent an Asian businessman from profiting from a very valuable map in "The Lost Mine." (Photo courtesy of London Weekend Television)

CHARACTERS

Inspector CURTIS, Paul DELANGUA, Sir James DWIGHTON, Lady Laura DWIGHTON, JANET, JENNINGS, Colonel MELROSE, MILES, Mr. Harley QUIN, Mr. Satterthwaite

PLOT SYNOPSIS

Mr. Satterthwaite is present when Colonel Melrose is summoned to investigate the murder of Sir James Dwighton. Admissions of guilt by both the victim's widow and a young man recently ejected from his house clash with suspicion of the valet, who was fired the same morning. Two smashed timepieces add to the confusion, but Mr. Harley Quin sorts out the clues and leads Mr. Satterthwaite to the correct conclusion as they save a pair of innocent lovers.

CRIME NOTES
The victim is murdered by a blow to the back of the head with a bronze figure of Venus, which is two feet in height.

Love from a Stranger See "PHILOMEL COTTAGE."

Lowen, Mr. A financial speculator in "THE DISAPPEARANCE OF MR. DAVENHEIM," he is accused of murder.

Lucas, Harry A diamond prospector victimized by the seductive Anita GRUNBERG in THE MAN IN THE BROWN SUIT, he escapes into the army, where he dies trying to regain his honor.

As the scheming husband in *Love from a Stranger*, Basil Rathbone plots to murder yet another wife. (Photo courtesy of The Museum of Modern Art, Film Stills Archive)

Basil Rathbone and Ann Harding appear in the 1937 United Artists motion picture, *Love from a Stranger*, based on "Philomel Cottage." (Photo courtesy of The Museum of Modern Art, Film Stills Archive)

Lucas, Dr. Mark A research chemist in DESTINATION UNKNOWN, he is among the last three people known to have seen the missing Thomas BETTERTON alive.

Luke, Mrs. The local grande dame of country society in UNFINISHED PORTRAIT, she offers extensive matchmaking advice.

Luscombe, Colonel Derek A good-hearted but obtuse man in AT BERTRAM'S HOTEL, he attempts to raise Elvira BLAKE and act as her godfather, guardian and manager of her trust after her father dies. Despite his affection for her, he is unable to communicate with her.

Luttrell, Claude An employee of Mr. PARKER PYNE who appears in "THE CASE OF THE MIDDLE-AGED WIFE" and "THE CASE OF THE DISTRESSED LADY," his talents lie in reuniting unhappily married women with their husbands. He is "one of the handsomest specimens of lounge lizard to be found in England."

Luttrell, Daisy (Mrs. Colonel) A sharp-tongued wife and owner of Styles Court whose curt, irritable manner in CURTAIN leads Hercule POIROT to say that he would take a hatchet to her if he were her husband. She plays bridge ruthlessly and without regard for the rules, and she humiliates her husband in public. After being shot accidentally by Colonel LUTTRELL, who claims to have mistaken her for a rabbit, she becomes a sweet and gentle person.

Luttrell, Colonel George (Toby)   A former military man once stationed in India and now owner of Styles Court, he is often publicly humiliated by his wife in CURTAIN.

Luxmore, Mrs.   Attracted to John DESPARD, she fabricates a story that he shot her husband because he loves her in CARDS ON THE TABLE.

Lyall, Captain   An officer of the Royal Flying Corps in "THE KIDNAPPED PRIME MINISTER," he flies the released Prime Minister, David MacADAM, to the Court of Versailles.

Lyall, Pamela   A talkative and nosy guest at the hotel in Rhodes where Valentine CHANTRY and Douglas GOLD begin their affair in "TRIANGLE AT RHODES," she thrives on gossip.

Lyon, Maureen   As Maureen Gregg, she was a defendant in a famous case of criminal child neglect of wartime evacuees in "THREE BLIND MICE." When she is strangled to death, the murderer identifies her as "The Farmer's Wife" in the song that he uses as his signature.

Lytcham Roche, Hubert   The tyrannical lord of the manor in "THE SECOND GONG" who demands that his guests be punctual to meals or forever be banished from his table, he is shot through the head and left to die with a note containing one word, "Sorry," beside him.

Lytton Gore, Hermoine (Egg)   Nicknamed "Egg" because of her shape as a toddler, she joins Sir Charles CARTWRIGHT and Mr. SATTERTHWAITE in uncovering the murderer in THREE-ACT TRAGEDY. She feigns a crush on Sir Charles to mask her real passion for Oliver MANDERS.

Lytton Gore, Lady Mary   The mother of Hermoine "Egg" LYTTON GORE, she is a fifty-five-year-old widow who interferes in her daughter's love life in THREE-ACT TRAGEDY.

M

"M" See SPROT, MILLICENT.

Maberly, Diana The fiancée of Hugh CHANDLER in "THE CRETAN BULL," she turns to Hercule POIROT when Chandler breaks off their engagement because he fears the curse of mental illness in the Chandler family has struck him.

MacAdam, David Kidnapped only a day before he is expected to address the Allies Conference in Versailles in "THE KIDNAPPED PRIME MINISTER," "Fighting Mac" sets off a panic among highly placed British politicians. As the Prime Minister of England during World War I, he was more than a politician—"he *was* England."

MacAllister, Dr. A physician in PERIL AT END HOUSE and the uncle of Commander George CHALLENGER, he is a cocaine supplier.

MacAndrews, Dr. Attending physician in "FOUR-AND-TWENTY BLACKBIRDS" when Henry GASCOIGNE dies, he provides Hercule POIROT with information to distinguish between twin brothers.

MacArthur, General John Gordon, C.M.G., D.S.O. The third of the guests on Indian Island to die in AND THEN THERE WERE NONE, he succumbs when his skull is crushed by a blow with a heavy object. Unlike the others, he is glad for the release from thirty years of guilt and torment.

Macatta, Mrs., M.P. Despite her important role in British government, she is interrogated by Hercule POIROT when bomber plans disappear in "THE INCREDIBLE THEFT." When cornered, she deftly turns the conversation to a discussion of the negative effects of gambling and the observation that increasing numbers of women have gained leadership roles in government.

Mace, Albert Although he testified that he had sold strychnine to Alfred INGLETHORPE in THE MYSTERIOUS AFFAIR AT STYLES, the young chemist's assistant nervously admitted that he had never met the man in question.

MacFarlane, Mr. Possessed of second sight, he is "a dour Scot, with a Celtic imagination hidden away somewhere" in "THE GIPSY."

MacKenzie, Helen Bitter because she believed that her late husband was cheated out of a fortune by Rex FORTESCUE and left to die in A POCKET FULL OF RYE, she has instilled hate in her children for Fortescue, and made them promise to kill him. She commits herself to the Pinewood Private Sanatorium as a voluntary patient.

MacKenzie, Janet Elderly maid to the murdered Emily FRENCH in "WITNESS FOR THE PROSECUTION," she claims that her employer was a competent financial manager who did not need the assistance of Leonard VOLE.

MacKenzie, Ruby Despite her mother's attempts to instill vehement hatred of the Fortescue family in A POCKET FULL OF RYE, she marries Percival FORTESCUE and suffers being ostracized by her mother, Helen MACKENZIE.

MacKintosh, Miss The awe-inspiring proprietor of a dancing school in UNFINISHED PORTRAIT.

MacMaster, Dr. When Dr. CALGARY becomes involved in the murder of Rachel ARGYLE in ORDEAL

BY INNOCENCE, he turns to this retired colleague for information regarding her family.

MacNaughton, Elsie   Largely unsympathetic to her patient, Lady Ariadne GRAYLE in "DEATH ON THE NILE" (1), whose illnesses she believes to be nonexistent, the travelling companion and nurse suggests that a busier schedule would be therapeutic.

MacQueen, Hector Willard   Private secretary to the murdered Samuel RATCHETT in MURDER ON THE ORIENT EXPRESS, he mistakes Hercule POIROT for "a woman's dressmaker." His connection to the Armstrong case is through his father, the district attorney who handled the case.

MacRae, Margaret   A childhood friend of the main character in UNFINISHED PORTRAIT, her lack of front teeth makes her lisp.

MacWhirter, Andrew   Hired by Lord CORNELLY because of his honesty in TOWARDS ZERO, this "damned pig-headed Scot" who once tried to commit suicide clears Audrey STRANGE of suspicion with his evidence.

Madeleine   See MORISOT, ANNE.

"Magnolia Blossoms"   Non-mystery short story.

The plot centers on the choices to be made by a runaway wife who learns that her husband's business firm has collapsed.

PUBLISHING AND DRAMATIZATION HISTORY
The story appeared in the short story collection, THE GOLDEN BALL AND OTHER STORIES, published in 1971 by Dodd, Mead and Company in New York.

The story was adapted for television in 1982 by Thames Television in England, and was also shown on the Public Broadcasting Service in the United States.

CHARACTERS
Richard DARRELL, Theodora DARRELL, Vincent EASTON

Theodora Darrell, played by Ciaran Madden, is the alluring wife in "Magnolia Blossoms" whose unscrupulous husband uses her to save his business reputation.   (Photo courtesy of Thames Television)

PLOT SYNOPSIS
The story focuses on Theodora Darrell, who leaves her husband Richard but returns when she learns that his business has collapsed. At first, he seems grateful for her presence, but he soon asks her to obtain incriminating papers and to use any means necessary to do so. She retrieves the papers, but realizes that Richard had been willing to sell her honor to save himself, so she leaves him for good.

Mahew, George   A solicitor who meets with Hercule POIROT in FIVE LITTLE PIGS and "THE UNDER DOG," he is "a thin, dry, cautious gentleman" who is more clever than he appears.

Mahmoud   The dragoman in the trip to Petra in APPOINTMENT WITH DEATH.

Mahmoudi, Madame   See HOBHOUSE, VALERIE.

Maine, Inspector   The Scotland Yard inspector who conducts a background check of the murder victims in AND THEN THERE WERE NONE.

Maitland, Captain   Placed in charge of the investigations in the murders of Louise LEIDNER and Anne JOHNSON in MURDER IN MESOPOTAMIA, he is captain of the police in the Tell Yarimjah archaeological site.

Maitland, Ellie   Nearly six feet tall, she marries "a merry little fellow" whom her family views as a sensible choice until he leaves her ten years later for a woman he meets on a cruise ship in UNFINISHED PORTRAIT.

Maitland, Peter   His years abroad in the military have developed in him an easygoing attitude toward life which does not impress the main character of UNFINISHED PORTRAIT, whom he wishes to marry.

Malinowski, Ladislaus   A world champion race car driver in AT BERTRAM'S HOTEL whose gun is used to murder Micky GORMAN, he juggles love affairs with both Lady Bess SEDGWICK and her daughter, Elvira BLAKE.

Mallaby, Mrs.   One of three characters who discover the murdered Lord CRONSHAW in "THE AFFAIR AT THE VICTORY BALL," she appeared in the costume of Pulcinella at the Victory Ball.

Mallowan, Barbara Parker   A secretary to Max MALLOWAN on many of the Middle Eastern archaeological digs on which Agatha Christie accompanied him, she is described as "a woman of dauntless courage" in *Mallowan's Memoirs.* Not only did she perform the usual secretarial duties, but she was also "expected to do everything, especially to take the blame when things went wrong." She became Mallowan's second wife in the year following the author's death.

Mallowan, Sir Max   Fourteen years Agatha Christie's junior, he became her second husband in 1930, less than a year after the two met when the author was visiting renowned English archaeologist

Leonard Woolley and his wife Katherine. He was assigned by the imperious Katherine to escort the already-famous mystery writer on a tour of the surrounding desert sights. After their marriage, the two remained together for seasons in the Middle East, on digs where the author would spend her days cleaning and photographing pottery and other artifacts, and her nights typing her novels on a portable typewriter placed on often-makeshift tables. During their over forty years together, Mallowan became an eminent archaeologist and Middle Eastern scholar. In 1948, he became Professor at the Institute of Archaeology at London University, occupying the Chair of Western Asiatic Archaeology. That same year, he also embarked upon the most important dig of his life, at Nimrud. In 1968, he was knighted for his accomplishments and service to the British Empire. He died in 1978.

Maltravers, Mrs.   A beautiful, substantially younger wife in "THE TRAGEDY AT MARSDEN

Sir Max Mallowan and Agatha Christie in 1950, leaving for the archaeological dig at Nimrud. (Photo courtesy of Popperfoto)

MANOR," she is left the family estate by her heavily insured husband who dies after only a year of marriage.

Manders, Oliver   Viewed by Hercule POIROT as the most likely suspect in the murders of Reverend Stephen BABBINGTON and Sir Bartholomew STRANGE in THREE-ACT TRAGEDY, he is a twenty-five-year-old man with an unusual background. In addition to foreign roots, he is an avowed Communist with a pronounced inferiority complex.

Manelli, Giuseppe   Murdered when he tried to blackmail Virginia REVEL in THE SECRET OF CHIMNEYS, he is a member of the Comrades of the Red Hand, and his official mission was to steal the memoirs of Count STYLPTITCH.

"Man from the Sea, The"   Non-mystery short story.

The plot centers on two lonely people who are given a second chance at happiness through the efforts of Mr. Harley QUIN and Mr. SATTERTHWAITE.

PUBLISHING AND DRAMATIZATION
HISTORY
The story appeared in the short story collection, THE MYSTERIOUS MR. QUIN, published in 1930 by William Collins Sons and Company, Ltd., in London, and Dodd, Mead and Company in New York.

The story has not been adapted for stage or screen.

CHARACTERS
Anthony COSDEN, Mr. Harley Quin, Mr. SATTERTHWAITE, unnamed woman

PLOT SYNOPSIS
The story relates the past of an unnamed woman who lives in seclusion in a green, shuttered villa on the island of La Paz, and of a man who has returned to the island to die. Mr. Satterthwaite thwarts their separate plans of suicide, and learns that they share a long-held secret. Through his efforts, aided by Harley Quin, both gain new reasons to live.

"Manhood of Edward Robinson, The"   Short story.

The plot centers on the transformation that occurs when a mild-mannered store clerk wins a newspaper contest.

PUBLISHING AND DRAMATIZATION
HISTORY
The story appeared in the short story collection, THE LISTERDALE MYSTERY (1), published in 1934 by William Collins Sons and Company, Ltd., in London.

The story was adapted for television in 1982 by Thames Television in England, and was also shown on the Public Broadcasting Service in the United States.

CHARACTERS
Lady Noreen ELLIOT, MAUD, Edward ROBINSON

PLOT SYNOPSIS
Sane and sensible Edward Robinson secretly dreams of fast cars, adventurous women and danger, but his fiancée, Maud, keeps him grounded in reality. When Edward wins five hundred pounds in a newspaper contest, he immediately buys the sleek red car of his dreams, without telling Maud. Adventure follows, as he is mistaken for a bored playboy and lured into a high society game of burglary involving a valuable diamond necklace and a reckless society girl. After his evening of adventure, Edward assumes an air of self-confidence, returns to his fiancée, and establishes the new boundaries of their relationship.

Man in the Brown Suit, The   Mystery novel.

The novel contains an unusual structure—narrative chapters are alternated with chapters identified as "Extracts from the diary of Sir Eustace, M.P." and "Anne's Narrative Resumed." The plot centers on the efforts of a young woman to locate a murderer and the mysterious man in the brown suit.

PUBLISHING AND DRAMATIZATION
HISTORY
The novel was published in 1924 by John Lane in London, and by Dodd, Mead and Company in New York.

The novel was adapted for television by CBS Television in 1989, and featured Edward Woodward, Tony Randall, Rue McClanahan and Ken Howard in major roles. The film updated the setting and characters to a contemporary period.

CHARACTERS
BATANI, Anne BEDDINGFELD, Mrs. Suzanne BLAIR, L.B. CARTON, Mr. FLEMMING, Mrs. FLEMMING,

A wild night of danger and intrigue with Lady Noreen Elliot, played by Cherie Lunghi, gives Edward Robinson, played by Nicholas Farrell, a new outlook on life in "The Manhood of Edward Robinson." (Photo courtesy of Thames Television)

Anita GRUNBERG, Mrs. Caroline JAMES, JEANNE, Harry LUCAS, Detective-Inspector MEADOWS, Arthur MINKS, Lord NASBY, Guy PAGETT, Count Sergius PAULOVITCH, Sir Eustace PEDLER, Miss PETTIGREW, Colonel Johnny RACE, Harry RAYBURN

PLOT SYNOPSIS
Prologue
Count Paulovitch is impressed by Nadina, the Russian dance sensation in Paris. She tells him that she's being spied upon because she has taken some of the DeBeers diamonds. "The Colonel" is identified as Nadina's husband.

Chapters 1–2
Anne Beddingfeld has spent years working with her anthropologist father, and she feels set adrift when he dies of double pneumonia. Her father's former solicitor and his wife invite her to live with them in London and welcome her with kindness. Unwilling to accept the offer, yet without an alternative plan, Anne walks to the tube station, and watches in hor-ror as a man falls backwards onto the track and dies. A man wearing a brown suit rushes forward, claims to be a doctor and pronounces the fallen man dead. As he rushes away, a piece of paper bearing the words "17–122 Kilmorden Castle" falls to the ground. The same day, a woman is found stabbed to death in Mill House. Inspector Meadows questions all connected with the deaths, and concludes that the man who claimed to be a doctor and pronounced L.B. Carton dead wasn't really a doctor.

Chapters 5–7
Scotland Yard declares the tube station death accidental, but Anne suspects murder and is determined to uncover the truth. She rushes into press tycoon Lord Nasby's office and convinces him that he should hire her to investigate the case. He agrees to hire her if she uncovers important information, so Anne studies the scrap of paper found at the tube station, then visits Mill House, where she finds a roll of film with a date on it. She later buys a first-class ticket on the steamship *Kilmorden Castle*.

Chapters 8–11

In an extract from his diary, Sir Eustace Pedler, M.P., owner of Mill House, writes that he wants to eliminate Guy Pagett and muses about the murder which took place in his house. He intends to go to South Africa. When Anne's narrative resumes, she is on the boat and learns the meaning of the numbers on the paper found at the station, but her cabin is ransacked.

Chapters 12–16

In an extract from his diary, Sir Eustace notes that there is something odd about Cabin 17, and he invites Mrs. Blair to join him in South Africa, where there are a lot of diamonds and theft. Anne opens the roll of film she found at Mill House and finds diamonds inside, a discovery which she and Suzanne Blair realize can be dangerous to her health. Later, in a series of confused actions, Anne learns that the numbers 17–122 were really instructions that the film was to be dropped at Cabin 71 at 1 A.M. on January 22.

Chapters 17–20

In an extract from his diary, Sir Eustace recounts his relief to be off the ship and considers the possibility that Harry Rayburn is the man in the brown suit. Anne's resumed narrative relates that she is now in South Africa. She receives a note from a museum curator, but realizes that she is in the hands of the enemy when she arrives at her destination. She struggles and finally frees herself, but she fails to reach the *Kilmorden Castle* before it leaves. Stranded, Anne decides to go to Durban, but Sir Eustace doesn't like the thought of her going alone.

Chapters 21–24

Fearful that something very strange is happening, Anne speaks with Colonel Race. In his diary, Sir Eustace notes that he has hired Anne as his temporary secretary and is taking her with him to Rhodesia. Harry Rayburn may be there, and Anne still needs to find him if she is going to be hired by the *Daily Budget*. In a later conversation with Colonel Race, she tries to learn more about him and realizes that he is in love with her. When he asks her to marry him, Anne refuses and tells him that she loves someone else.

Chapters 25–29

Lured to an isolated spot by a note signed by Harry Rayburn, Anne falls and is knocked unconscious. She awakens with Rayburn present, and he tells her that he did not write the note. The two talk, and he admits his real name and tells Anne what he knows about the deaths. They fall in love, and Anne decides that he is the man she will marry. Meanwhile, Sir Eustace learns that Anne is missing from her room, yet he cannot delay his trip to Johannesburg.

Chapters 30–34

Anne's resumed narrative details that she and Mrs. Blair suspect Colonel Race of being the killer, and they refer to him in code as "Eric." Anne receives instructions to go to Johannesburg, where she learns that "the Colonel" is really Sir Eustace. He admits that he had tried to throw her overboard. Cornered when Harry enters the room, Sir Eustace makes his escape in the mass confusion that occurs when a bomb is thrown in the town, creating a blaze, but Harry manages to obtain the diamonds.

Chapters 35–36

Harry admits that his real name is John Harold Eardsley and that he had been framed years before by Sir Eustace and Nadina. He and Anne marry and, two years later, they receive two letters. Mrs. Blair writes to wish the couple the greatest in happiness, and Sir Eustace Pedler sends her his diary and promises her that it explains everything.

CRIME NOTES

The novel contains two murders. The first victim dies when he is pushed onto the third rail of the subway and electrocuted, while the second victim is stabbed to death.

"Man in the Mist, The"   Mystery short story.

The plot focuses on a glamorous actress whose secret past results in her murder. This is another in a series of Tommy and Tuppence BERESFORD stories, in which Agatha Christie parodied popular fictional detectives of the 1920s.

PUBLISHING AND DRAMATIZATION HISTORY

The story appeared in the short story collection, PARTNERS IN CRIME, published in 1929 by William Collins and Sons, Ltd., in London, and by Dodd, Mead and Company in New York.

The story was adapted for television in 1984 by London Weekend Television in England, and was shown on the Public Broadcasting Service in the United States.

CHARACTERS
Tommy Beresford, Tuppence Beresford, ELLEN (3), Mervyn (Bugler) ESTCOURT, Gilda GLEN, Mrs. HONEYCUTT, Mr. MARVELL, James REILLY

PLOT SYNOPSIS
Tommy and Tuppence Beresford have cocktails at the Grand Aldington Hotel, commiserating over a bungled case, and they are introduced to a glamorous actress, Gilda Glen. They learn that she plans to marry a wealthy lord and that she is also being followed by a jealous admirer. When the partners receive a request from the actress to meet at The White House on Morgan's Avenue, they find the actress dead, her head bloody and crushed.

CRIME NOTES
In this story, Tommy wears a clerical collar and imitates the style and mannerisms of the fictional detective created by G.K. Chesterton (1874–1936), Roman Catholic priest Father Brown, whose defining characteristics are his clerical collar and his shabby umbrella.

Mannheim, Professor A research chemist in DESTINATION UNKNOWN, he is the former father-in-law of the missing Thomas BETTERTON.

Mannheim, Elsa A research chemist in DESTINATION UNKNOWN, she is the first wife of Thomas BETTERTON. She is murdered for her professional secrets.

Manning (1) A witness to Emily INGLETHORPE's new will in THE MYSTERIOUS AFFAIR AT STYLES, he had long been the head gardener at Styles Court.

Manning (2) Hired by Miss MARPLE to assist the octogenarian gardener at Hillside house in SLEEPING MURDER, he is a seventy-five-year-old gardener who is also asked to gather information about the Kennedy family.

"Man Who Was No. 16, The" Mystery short story.

The final case in the series of parodies of popular fictional detectives of the 1920s provides substantial peril for Tommy and Tuppence BERESFORD, who must confront a secret adversary.

PUBLISHING AND DRAMATIZATION HISTORY
The story appeared in the short story collection, PARTNERS IN CRIME, published in 1929 by William Collins and Sons, Ltd., in London, and by Dodd, Mead and Company in New York.

The story has not been adapted for stage or screen.

CHARACTERS
ALBERT, Tommy Beresford, Tuppence Beresford, Mr. A. CARTER, Mrs. Cortlandt VAN SNYDER, Paul de VAREZ, Prince VLADIROFFSKY

PLOT SYNOPSIS
The story concerns the impending arrival of a Russian agent, identified only by the code number 16, who is expected to contact the managers of the International Detective Agency. The Chief of Intelligence warns Tommy and Tuppence that this man is dangerous, and that they must remain on their guard. When No. 16 arrives under the name of Prince Vladiroffsky, he wines and dines the couple, then disappears with Tuppence, despite heavy surveillance by intelligence agents. Undeterred by a decoy, Tommy locates Tuppence, and government agents capture No. 16. Tommy proposes that the pair retire from detective work, and Tuppence surprises him with her ready agreement. She tells him that they are embarking on a more exciting adventure—parenthood.

CRIME NOTES
In this story, Agatha Christie parodied her own creation, as Tommy imitates the style and mannerisms of Hercule POIROT, with Tuppence acting as the faithful Captain Arthur HASTINGS.

Marbury, Lily The daughter of Alexander Bonaparte Cust's landlady in THE A.B.C. MURDERS.

March, Cicely Proprietor of a beauty salon, she responds to an advertisement placed by Tommy and Tuppence BERESFORD to locate Eileen O'Hara, who had pretended illness outside the Ambassador's cabin in "THE AMBASSADOR'S BOOTS." In reality, she is herself Eileen O'Hara, and runs a beauty salon as a front organization for a drug smuggling ring.

Marchaud, Felice   A young and attractive woman in "THE MYSTERY OF THE BLUE JAR," she lives in a cottage that is haunted by the ghost of a murdered woman.

Marchington, Lord   The gout-ridden and wealthy father of Lady Frances (Frankie) DERWENT in WHY DIDN'T THEY ASK EVANS?

Marchmont, Adela   A widow whose financial difficulties after World War II forced her to borrow money from a woman masquerading as her sister-in-law in TAKEN AT THE FLOOD.

Marchmont, Lynn   A young woman in TAKEN AT THE FLOOD who develops a disturbing passion for stranger David HUNTER, leading her to break off her engagement to Rowley CLOADE. She nearly dies when her former fiancé attempts to strangle her, but Hercule POIROT arrives in time.

Mardenberg   A German spy in "THE GIRL IN THE TRAIN," he tries to smuggle defense plans for Portsmouth harbor out of England by disguising them in a love letter written in code.

Margaret, Sister   Volunteers at Town Hospital in GIANT'S BREAD describe her as "a holy terror," but she is a highly efficient nursing supervisor.

Margrave, Lily   Paid companion to Lady Nancy ASTWELL in "THE UNDER DOG," she is really a spy for her brother, Captain Humphrey NAYLOR, who was cheated by Sir Reuben ASTWELL in a mining deal. She forged her references to obtain the post.

Marguerite   See VANDEMEYER, RITA.

Marie   Personal maid to Linnet DOYLE in DEATH ON THE NILE (2), she resents her employer's revelation that her lover, Mr. FLEETWOOD, a ship engineer, is a married man with three children.

"Market Basing Mystery, The"   Mystery short story.

The plot centers on the death of a man who found that life in a small town can be dangerous.

PUBLISHING AND DRAMATIZATION
HISTORY
The story appeared in the short story collection THE UNDER DOG AND OTHER STORIES, published in 1951 by Dodd, Mead and Company in New York.

The story has not been adapted for stage or screen.

CHARACTERS
Miss CLEGG, Dr. GILES, Captain Arthur HASTINGS, Chief Inspector JAPP, Mr. and Mrs. PARKER, Hercule POIROT, Constable POLLARD, Walter PROTHEROE

PLOT SYNOPSIS
Chief Inspector Japp convinces Hercule Poirot and Captain Hastings to join him for a peaceful weekend in the country, far from the pressures of London. True to Poirot's warning that no place is free from crime, Japp is soon approached by the local police, who ask his help in unraveling the confusing clues regarding a local murder. With the assistance of Poirot's keen powers of perception, a blackmail plot is uncovered, and the true killer is unmasked.

CRIME NOTES
The sole murder victim in this story dies from a gunshot wound to the head.

Marks, Miss   An attractive and amiable dental assistant in "THE CORNISH MYSTERY," she marries her employer only months after his wife dies.

Marle, Iris   The prime suspect in the poisoning murder of her sister in SPARKLING CYANIDE, she is the chief beneficiary of a large fortune upon her sister's death. Only one man realizes that she is also in danger.

Marple, Miss Jane   An elderly, unmarried lady who was between 65 and 70 years of age when she made her first appearance in THE MURDER AT THE VICARAGE in 1930. She appeared in twelve novels and twenty short stories over a period of forty-one years. The author had not planned so long a relationship with her detective, and often regretted having made Miss Marple so old at the outset, because she

Miss Marple (Joan Hickson) proves repeatedly that human nature is the same everywhere. (Photo courtesy of Plunkett Green)

would have been 115 years old by 1971, had she aged, when she appeared in NEMESIS, the last book written with her as detective. Although SLEEPING MURDER was published in 1976, the author had written it during World War II and placed it in a vault to be published should she die during the war. Agatha Christie lived, and Miss Marple's last adventure remained locked away for more than three decades.

In appearance, she is a tall, thin woman whose snowy white hair is piled upon her head in an old-fashioned manner, below which are her pink, wrinkled face and pale blue eyes. Her innocuous appearance and ever-present knitting needles mislead people into underestimating her and viewing her as simply a "dithering old maid," an image which she encourages with her often aimless talk about her hobbies of bird-watching and gardening. Still, those who really know her recognize that she is a sharp observer of human nature, and they assert that "she

has got an uncanny knack of being always right." In spite of her innocent appearance and life in the seemingly dull ST. MARY MEAD, she is quite worldly in her recognition and acceptance that evil is all around and that "you simply cannot afford to believe everything that people tell you." Moreover, she is also quick to point out that her village and its environs contain every type of character trait and evil in human nature that are to be found in big-city residents. Thus, her method of detection consists in finding parallels between life and people in St. Mary Mead and happenings in the outside world, no matter how gruesome. (See CATEGORICAL APPENDIX.)

Marrascaud An extremely dangerous killer in "THE ERYMANTHIAN BOAR," he has eluded the police for many years. When angered, his response is primal, like that of "a wild boar, ferocious, terrible, who charges in blind fury." Hercule POIROT tracks him to the Swiss Rochers Neige resort, where the criminal expects to meet his gang, and the two match wits when an avalanche seals off routes to the resort.

Marriot, Inspector A member of Scotland Yard, he asks for the help of Tommy and Tuppence BERESFORD in destroying a counterfeiting ring in "THE CRACKLER," and he is also part of the action with the Beresfords in "THE UNBREAKABLE ALIBI," "THE ADVENTURE OF THE SINISTER STRANGER" and "THE AFFAIR OF THE PINK PEARL."

Marsden, Chief Inspector A member of Scotland Yard in SAD CYPRESS, he is convinced that Elinor CARLISLE committed murder, and assures himself that he has "a clear conscience" in this case for he is certain that he has the right person.

Marsdon, Antony (Tony) Viewed as "one of the most brilliant beginners in the coding department" of British Intelligence in N OR M?, he shows great promise in government service.

Marsh, Andrew Although he made Violet MARSH his heir in "THE CASE OF THE MISSING WILL," he disapproved of her lifestyle and modern ways, so he made her work for her inheritance by hiding the will and leaving clues to be followed after his death.

Marsh, Geraldine (Dina) Abandoned by her mother and mistreated by her father as a child, she is an emotionally cold woman in LORD EDGWARE DIES. At her father's death she is without grief, and tells Hercule POIROT that she is actually grateful to the unknown murderer.

Marsh, George Alfred St. Vincent, the Fourth Baron Edgware   A bitter and sadistic man in LORD EDGWARE DIES, his obsession with wreaking revenge on the world for his first wife's faithlessness borders on madness. At his death—one welcomed by many—visitors observe works by the Marquis de Sade in his library.

Marsh, Captain Ronald, the Fifth Baron Edgware   A pleasant man with nondescript features in LORD EDGWARE DIES, he is a great contrast to the previous Lord Edgware, his late uncle George MARSH.

Marsh, Violet   The heir to a vast estate in "THE CASE OF THE MISSING WILL," she contacts Hercule POIROT to help her find her uncle's hidden will.

Marshall, Andrew   Legal advisor to the Argyle family in ORDEAL BY INNOCENCE, he views his clients with cynicism and suggests that their home was well served by its original name, Viper's Point.

Marshall, Arlena   A glamorous and self-centered actress in EVIL UNDER THE SUN, she is the former Helen Stuart, whose stage career has brought her wealth and fame. Now married to Captain Kenneth MARSHALL, she continues her outrageous flirting, and she is murdered while on vacation in Leathercombe Bay.

Marshall, Edward John   A witness in the trial of Elinor CARLISLE in SAD CYPRESS, the former New Zealand resident identifies Nurse Jessie HOPKINS as the victim's aunt, who has a financial stake in the murder of Mary GERRARD.

Marshall, Captain John   The true object of Diana CLEVES's affections in "THE SECOND GONG," he was considered to be an unsuitable match for the heiress.

Marshall, Captain Kenneth   Despite his poor judgment in marrying the glamorous actress, Arlena Stuart, in EVIL UNDER THE SUN, he is basically a good man who has the bad habit of "making unfortunate marriages." After Arlena is murdered, he proposes marriage to childhood friend Rosamund DARNLEY.

Marshall, Linda   The unhappy and unattractive stepdaughter of glamorous stage actress, Arlena MARSHALL, in EVIL UNDER THE SUN, she hates her stepmother and wishes her dead. When Arlena dies after Linda creates what appears to be a voodoo doll and sticks it with pins, Linda attempts suicide.

Marston, Anthony James (Tony)   The first of the ten victims to die on Indian Island in AND THEN THERE WERE NONE, he is a remorseless young man whose crime was running over two young people with his car years before.

Martha   Cook, maid and housekeeper for thirty years to Lily CRABTREE, she was devoted to her murdered mistress in "SING A SONG OF SIXPENCE." As the last person to see the victim alive, she is an important witness who, her devotion not withstanding, has her own secrets to hide.

Martin, Miss   The secretary of soap king Abe RYLAND in THE BIG FOUR.

Martin, Alix   A normally cautious young woman, she falls madly in love with Gerald MARTIN in "PHILOMEL COTTAGE," and marries him without learning anything about his past. She becomes suspicious of her new husband when he tells the gardener that Alix is going to London, when she has made no plans to do so, and when she learns that Gerald gave the real estate agent only two thousand pounds for the cottage, rather than the three thousand pounds that she had lent him.

Martin, Brian   An actor jilted by Jane WILKERSON for the Duke of MERTON in LORD EDGWARE DIES, he remains heartbroken.

Martin, Elizabeth   A determined American tourist in "THE SOUL OF THE CROUPIER," she is methodically " 'doing Europe' in a stern conscientious spirit." Mr. SATTERTHWAITE invites her to be his guest at a party arranged in Monte Carlo.

Martin, Gerald Pictured in old newspaper photographs as a "long-bearded, scholarly-looking gentleman" named Charles LeMaitre who was charged in America with murdering several wives, he assumed a new identity and a new appearance before arriving in England. He lies to his new wife, Alix, making her fear for her life in "PHILOMEL COTTAGE."

Martin, Gladys A former maid to Miss Jane MARPLE, Gladys is a half-witted parlourmaid in the Fortescue household who is used as an accomplice to murder in A POCKET FULL OF RYE. She has sent Miss Marple a photograph of herself with "Bert Evans," and her former employer investigates the tragedy when Gladys is found strangled to death wearing a clothespin on her nose.

Martindale, Hilda See BLAND, VALERIE.

Martindale, Katherine A formidable woman, she is the proprietor of the Cavendish Secretarial and Typing Bureau whose employees refer to her as "Sandy Cat" behind her back in THE CLOCKS.

Marvel, Sir Donald A member of the tourist party travelling to Petra in "THE PEARL OF PRICE," he is "a tired-looking Englishman" who wants to marry Carol BLUNDELL.

Marvell, Mr. The lawyer representing suspected murderer James REILLY in "THE MAN IN THE MIST."

Marvell, Mary An American film star in "THE ADVENTURE OF 'THE WESTERN STAR,' " she owns a great diamond called the "Western Star."

Mary A housemaid at the Keston Spa Hydro in "A CHRISTMAS TRAGEDY," she dies of an infected finger.

Mary Ann See ZERKOWSKI, COUNTESS RENATA.

Mason, Ada Beatrice An actress and impersonator in THE MYSTERY OF THE BLUE TRAIN, also known as Kitty Kidd, she is a partner of jewel thief Major KNIGHTON, and plays the role of Ruth KETTERING's maid in a plot to steal the Heart of Fire rubies.

Mason, Jane An impersonator whose real name is Gracie Kidd, she poses as the maid of The Honourable Flossie CARRINGTON in "THE PLYMOUTH EXPRESS." Jane plans to steal her employer's jewels and sell them through a jewel fence.

Massingham, Mrs. Referred to as "The Mem Sahib" in A DAUGHTER'S A DAUGHTER, she is a thin, stringy woman who lived in India for many years.

Massington, Mrs. A good friend to Iris WADE in "THE CASE OF THE DISCONTENTED HUSBAND," this nosy woman is married to a man who enjoys sports and talks "stocks and shares and golf alternately."

Masterman, Edward Henry Valet to Samuel Edward RATCHETT in MURDER ON THE ORIENT EXPRESS (1), he was an aide to Colonel ARMSTRONG during World War I.

Masterton, Connie A large, officious woman in DEAD MAN'S FOLLY, she is the power behind her husband's political success. To Hercule POIROT she looks like a bloodhound, with her "full underhung jaw and large, mournful, slightly bloodshot eyes."

Matcham, Mrs. A valuable source of information in ELEPHANTS CAN REMEMBER, she is Ariadne OLIVER's old nanny, and provides an intriguing piece of information regarding the twin sisters, Dolly JARROW and Molly RAVENSCROFT.

Mathias, John A member of a traveling acrobatic troupe that moonlights as art thieves in "AT THE 'BELLS AND MOTLEY,' " he plays the dual role of gardener and dashing, daredevil Captain Richard Harwell, who later disappears.

Maud An exacting and highly practical woman in "THE MANHOOD OF EDWARD ROBINSON," she "was always right about everything," a quality which greatly disturbed her fiancé, Edward, who longed for adventure.

Mauhourat, Mademoiselle A tall, clumsy French woman whom the main character in UNFINISHED PORTRAIT refuses as her tutor.

Maverick, Dr. Branded by Miss Jane MARPLE as being "distinctly abnormal," for his view that "We're all mad. . . . That's the secret of existence," he is the chief psychiatrist at a home for delinquent boys in THEY DO IT WITH MIRRORS.

Mayerling, Mr.   Missing for five years in the Soviet Union, he is a British Secret Service agent in THE BIG FOUR who dies shortly after providing Hercule POIROT with information regarding the Big Four gang.

Mayfield, Lord, Sir Charles McLaughlin Plans for a new bomber disappear from the library of his country estate in "THE INCREDIBLE THEFT."

Mayherne, Mr.   Convinced of his client's innocence in "WITNESS FOR THE PROSECUTION," he manages to undermine the testimony of the defendant's hostile wife and gain an acquittal for his client.

Mayhew, Mr.   The solicitor representing Charles LEVERSON in "THE UNDER DOG," he is a "dry, cautious gentleman."

McCrae, Detective Constable   A seemingly humorless but thorough police officer, he investigates the occurrences at the Hickory Road Hostel in HICKORY DICKORY DOCK.

McGillicuddy, Elspeth   While en route to visit Miss MARPLE after a day of Christmas shopping in 4.50 FROM PADDINGTON, she sees what appears to be a murder on a train going in the opposite direction.

McGinty, Mrs.   A washerwoman and cleaning lady who had heard too much for her own good in MRS. MCGINTY'S DEAD, she dies after a blow to the back of the head with a heavy object.

McGrath, Jimmy   A young adventurer in THE SECRET OF CHIMNEYS, he convinces his old friend, Anthony CADE, to act as courier from Africa to England for a manuscript and a packet of letters.

McKay, Elspeth   A perceptive observer of life in HALLOWE'EN PARTY, she is the widowed sister of retired police official Superintendent SPENCE, an old friend of Hercule POIROT.

McLaren, Commander Jock   An old friend to the Clayton family in "THE MYSTERY OF THE SPANISH CHEST," he has secretly adored Margharita CLAYTON for years.

McLaughlin, Sir Charles   See MAYFIELD, LORD, SIR CHARLES MCLAUGHLIN

McLean, Hugo   Deeply in love with Adelaide JEFFERSON in THE BODY IN THE LIBRARY, he is a "tall, middle-aged man with a thin, brown face" who will do whatever his love commands.

McNabb, Colin   One of the students in Mrs. NICOLETIS' student hostel in HICKORY DICKORY DOCK, he is taking a postgraduate course in psychiatry. Celia AUSTIN is murdered on the night he proposes to her.

McNaughton, Mrs.   An unreliable witness in THE CLOCKS, she claims to have seen the murdered man, but the investigating detective recognizes that she is a type of witness who "just wants to think she's seen him."

McNaughton, Angus   Next-door neighbor to the murder victim in THE CLOCKS, he is a retired professor whose love is his garden.

McNeil, Mr.   A partner in Hercule POIROT's firm of solicitors, McNeil and Hodgson, in THE BIG FOUR.

McNeil, Sir Andrew   A prison governor in NEMESIS, he refuses to believe that Michael RAFIEL is guilty of murdering Verity HUNT.

Meadows, Detective Inspector   A Scotland Yard detective in THE MAN IN THE BROWN SUIT, he investigates the death of L.B. CARTON.

Meadows, Dr.   A quiet and efficient army doctor in GIANT'S BREAD.

Meadows, Inspector   A member of Scotland Yard in THE BIG FOUR, he heads the investigation in the Whalley case.

Meauhourat, Mademoiselle Zellie   A French governess in ELEPHANTS CAN REMEMBER, she aids Hercule POIROT in revealing the secrets surrounding the deaths of General Alistair and Lady Molly RAVENSCROFT.

Melchett, Colonel   A resident of Much Benham and Chief Constable for Radfordshire, he appears in MURDER AT THE VICARAGE, "DEATH BY DROWNING," THE BODY IN THE LIBRARY and "THE TAPE-MEASURE MURDER." He is a "dapper little man who had a habit of snorting suddenly and unexpectedly." His territory includes ST. MARY MEAD.

Melford, Mildred   She is of no assistance at all as a witness in AT BERTRAM'S HOTEL, because she is both "fearfully easy to deceive" and extremely unobservant. A cousin of Colonel Derek LUSCOMBE, she is also a guardian of Elvira BLAKE.

Melrose, Colonel   An old friend of Lord CATERHAM and a frequent visitor to Chimneys, he is Chief Constable for the region that includes Market Basing and King's Abbot. He appears in THE SECRET OF CHIMNEYS, THE SEVEN DIALS MYSTERY and "THE LOVE DETECTIVES."

Menier, Raoul   Apprehended in Baghdad with his colleague in MURDER IN MESOPOTAMIA, he is a clever thief who specializes in stealing art objects from museums and exhibitions. At Tell Yarimjah, he poses as the priest Father LAVIGNY, and substitutes electroplated copies for valuable archaeological finds.

Merall, Major   A law enforcement official in DEAD MAN'S FOLLY, he heads the investigation into the Tucker murder case.

Mercado, Joseph   A secret drug addict whose craving has reached a peak in MURDER IN MESOPOTAMIA, he is in his second year with the Tell Yarimjah expedition.

Mercado, Marie   A wildly jealous woman, she is also maternally protective of her husband and aids him in concealing his drug addiction in MURDER IN MESOPOTAMIA. She is particularly fearful that her husband will be drawn to the "calamitous magic" of fellow traveler Louise LEIDNER.

Merdell   A ninety-two-year-old man who works at the ferry docks in DEAD MAN'S FOLLY, he is murdered by being pushed into the river.

Meredith, Anne   A guest at Mr. SHAITANA's dinner party in CARDS ON THE TABLE, she drowns while trying to kill her housemate, Rhoda DAWES.

Merivale, Sir Arthur   Costumed as a seventeenth-century executioner at the Three Arts Ball in "THE GENTLEMAN DRESSED IN NEWSPAPER," he is the cuckolded husband of the murdered Lady MERIVALE.

Merivale, Lady Vere   Wife of one man and mistress of another in "THE GENTLEMAN DRESSED IN NEWSPAPER," she is murdered when a jewelled dagger is plunged through her heart at the place where she had planned a rendezvous with her lover.

Merrilees, Detective Inspector   See BOND, JAMES.

Merrion, Miss   A shrill woman who affects a "high, distressing gentlewoman voice" in THE A.B.C. MURDERS, she is the proprietor of the Ginger Cat cafe.

Merrowdene, George   The trusting second husband of Margaret MERROWDENE and a former chemistry professor in "ACCIDENT," he has recently complied with his wife's request that he take out a large insurance policy.

Merrowdene, Margaret   A happily married woman in "ACCIDENT," she was once charged with the arsenic poisoning murder of her first husband, soon after he took out a large insurance policy on his life. She was acquitted of that charge, and after six years of marriage to her second husband she urges him to take out a large insurance policy.

Merrypit, Mrs.   A valuable source of information in NEMESIS, she runs a wool shop in Carristown, helps Miss MARPLE to match yarn, and provides the detective with information regarding the Verity HUNT case and the BRADBURY-SCOTT family.

Mersu, Divine Father   A highly skilled physician in DEATH COMES AS THE END, he tries vainly to save SOBEK's life after the wine is poisoned.

Merton, Dowager Duchess of   An overbearing woman whom Hercule POIROT views as wishing "to arrange the universe to her manner of thinking," she tries to enlist the detective in her effort to end a love affair between her son and Jane WILKINSON in LORD EDGWARE DIES.

Merton, Duke of   A religious fanatic who scorns marriage to a divorcée yet becomes infatuated with the extremely modern Jane WILKINSON, he is an unlikely looking noble in LORD EDGWARE DIES. More like a "weedy young haberdasher than like a duke," he resists his mother's attempts to end his engagement.

Merton, Mrs.   A talkative woman with sharp, black eyes and an elaborate hairdo in ONE, TWO, BUCKLE MY SHOE, she gives Hercule POIROT and Inspector JAPP important information regarding the mysterious Mr. Chapman.

Merton, Milly   See CROFT, MILLY.

Mesnard, Virginie   A poor but honest cousin in the Deroulard residence in "THE CHOCOLATE BOX," she has lived with the family for three years, during which time Paul DEROULARD has tried to become intimate with her. After consulting Hercule POIROT about Paul's death and receiving answers, she enters religious service.

Metcalf, Dr.   A physician in THE BODY IN THE LIBRARY, he advises his patient, Conway JEFFERSON, to begin living life rather than wasting life by fearing death.

Metcalf, Major   See TANNER, INSPECTOR.

Meynell, Dr.   The physician to Mrs. HARTER in "WHERE THERE'S A WILL," he performs the autopsy which reveals that she would have lived only a few months more had she not been murdered.

Michael   A member of a traveling repertory group in MRS. MCGINTY'S DEAD, the actor told Maude WILLIAMS of an Australian playwright whose birth name had been Evelyn HOPE.

Michel, Pierre   A train conductor in both THE MYSTERY OF THE BLUE TRAIN and MURDER ON THE ORIENT EXPRESS, he discovers the bodies of the murder victims in both novels.

Miklanova, Anna   See DENMAN, ANNA.

Miles   The elderly butler of the Dwighton manor in "THE LOVE DETECTIVES."

Miller, Inspector   A member of Scotland Yard, he forms an uneasy alliance with both Captain HASTINGS and Hercule POIROT, and appears in "THE DISAPPEARANCE OF MR. DAVENHEIM," "THE UNDER DOG," "THE MYSTERY OF THE SPANISH CHEST" and "THE LOST MINE."

Miller, Clara Boehmer   Agatha Christie's mother, with whom she had a very close and trusting relationship. When Clara died in 1926, the author lost her confidante and chief supporter. Clara had been the one certainty for the author, a source of unconditional love, and her loss was overwhelming.

Miller, Frederick Alvah   Agatha Christie's father, who died when she was eleven. His father was an American, of New England stock, and his mother was British. Before his marriage, Frederick had been a man about town whose listing in the Social Register had made him a very eligible bachelor. Described in AN AUTOBIOGRAPHY as "not trained for anything," he was unable to manage his own father's fortune, and left his family in dire financial straits at his sudden death.

Miller, Louis Montant (Monty)   Agatha Christie's brother, who was ten years her senior. Reckless, eccentric, and given to calling the author "a scrawny chicken" in his youth, he was described by a fellow soldier as being courageous but "mad as a hatter," and by his sister as someone whose "life had been a disaster." Although his constant debt and grandiose schemes aggravated his family, he was a charming scoundrel who always found someone to take care of him when he was ill or penniless.

Miller, Margaret West   "Auntie-Grannie" to the child Agatha Christie, she was actually the author's step-grandmother and the second wife to Frederick Miller's father, Nathaniel. The relationship becomes even more complicated than that of stepmother to the author's father, because Margaret's sister Polly was widowed young and left with four children to raise. At Margaret's request, Polly gave up one of her children to be adopted by Margaret and Nathaniel. That child was the author's mother, Clara, who was raised by "Auntie-Grannie" in the household where she met her future husband and Margaret's stepson, Frederick MILLER. The pain which Clara felt throughout her life over having been given up made the author's relationship with "Auntie-Grannie" closer than the one she had with her natural maternal grandmother, Polly Boehmer, who became known as "Grannie B."

"Million Dollar Bond Robbery, The"   Mystery short story.

The plot centers on Hercule POIROT's attempt to identify the thief of one million dollars in Liberty Bonds and to save a young banker's career.

PUBLISHING AND DRAMATIZATION HISTORY
The story appeared in the short story collection, POIROT INVESTIGATES, published in 1924 by John Lane in London, and in 1925 by Dodd, Mead and Company in New York.

The story was adapted for television in 1991 by London Weekend Television in England, and was shown on the Public Broadcasting Service in the United States.

CHARACTERS
Miss Esmee FARQUHAR, Captain Arthur HASTINGS, Hercule Poirot, Mr. Philip RIDGEWAY, Mr. SHAW, Mr. VAVASOUR

PLOT SYNOPSIS
The story concerns Hercule Poirot's efforts to help a young woman who approaches him for assistance in clearing her fiancé of suspicion in the robbery of one million dollars in Liberty Bonds, which he had been responsible for transferring from London to New York City. The detective traces the route of the bonds, and learns the identities of all who had keys to the locked trunk that held the bonds. He solves the crime, and uncovers an unexpected perpetrator.

Milly   Ariadne OLIVER's maid in THE PALE HORSE.

Seasickness is no excuse for Hercule Poirot (David Suchet) and Captain Hastings (Hugh Fraser) to shirk responsibility in "The Million Dollar Bond Robbery." (Photo courtesy of London Weekend Television)

Milray, Mrs.   An unappealing woman in THREE-ACT TRAGEDY, she is an overweight, "immense dumpling of a woman" who uses her invalid condition to tyrannize her daughter Violet. She reluctantly agrees to be interviewed by Sir Charles CARTWRIGHT and "Egg" LYTTON GORE regarding the murder of Reverend BABBINGTON.

Milray, Violet   Secretly in love with her employer, Sir Charles CARTWRIGHT, who views her as "the perfect robot," she is a plain-featured woman who has worked for him for six years in THREE-ACT TRAGEDY.

Milson   See WEST, DERMOT.

Minks, Arthur   A master of disguise in THE MAN IN THE BROWN SUIT, he pretends to be Count Sergius Paulovitch, the Reverend Edward Chichester and Miss Pettigrew to obtain information from a range of other characters.

Minton, Sophia   An incompetent bridge player in N OR M?, she is "the *compleat* British spinster."

Mirabelle   The ostentatious new mistress of the king of Bosnia, she appears in Monte Carlo and excites jealousy in the king's previous paramour in "THE SOUL OF THE CROUPIER."

Mirelle   A dancer who is Derek KETTERING's fickle mistress in THE MYSTERY OF THE BLUE TRAIN, she is on the train when Ruth KETTERING is killed.

Miriam   Young, intelligent and full of vitality, she serves as the anchor of her daughter's life in UNFINISHED PORTRAIT, and sacrifices everything to keep the family home and give her daughter a good life.

Mirotin   See GREY, MARY.

Mirror Crack'd, The   See THE MIRROR CRACK'D FROM SIDE TO SIDE.

Mirror Crack'd from Side to Side, The   Mystery novel.

The novel is the last to take place entirely in the village of ST. MARY MEAD; later Miss MARPLE mysteries take place elsewhere, and provide only brief views of this microcosm of good and evil. The plot centers on efforts to determine the murderer of a woman poisoned at a fund-raiser hosted by a movie star.

PUBLISHING AND DRAMATIZATION HISTORY

The novel was published in 1962 by William Collins Sons and Company, Ltd., in London, and, under the title, *The Mirror Crack'd*, by Dodd, Mead and Company in New York.

The novel was adapted by EMI as a film (*The Mirror Crack'd*) released in 1980, starring Angela Lansbury as Miss Marple, with Elizabeth Taylor and Kim Novak as the rival actresses, in addition to an all-star cast. The plot remained similar to that of the novel, but the casting of Lansbury in the detective's role strained believability, because the actress was nearly thirty years too young for the role. The novel was remade for television by the BBC in 1992, and starred Joan Hickson as a more believable Miss Marple. This production appeared under the title "The Mirror Crack'd from Side to Side."

CHARACTERS

Arthur BADCOCK, Heather BADCOCK, Mary BAIN, Cherry BAKER, Jim BAKER, Mrs. Dolly BANTRY,

Two fading screen stars (Kim Novak and Elizabeth Taylor) with their film director (Rock Hudson) invade the quiet village of St. Mary Mead in *The Mirror Crack'd*.   (Photo © 1980 Associated Film Distribution)

Margot BENCE, Lola BREWSTER, Chief Inspector CRADDOCK, Gladys DIXON, Ardwyck FENN, Dr. GILCHRIST, GIUSEPPE, Marina GREGG, Dr. HAYDOCK, Mrs. JAMESON, Miss KNIGHT, Miss Jane Marple, Hailey PRESTON, Jason RUDD, Dr. SANFORD, Detective-Sergeant William (Tom) TIDDLER, Ella ZIELENSKY

PLOT SYNOPSIS

Chapters 1–3

Miss Marple resents the fussing of Miss Knight, the live-in nurse-companion provided by her increasingly successful nephew Raymond WEST. She sends Miss Knight out to do an errand, then slips out herself simply to walk around. While walking through the nearby development, Miss Marple falls, and is rescued by Heather Badcock, who speaks with her about the new owner of Gossington Hall. She then visits Dolly Bantry, the previous owner of Gossington Hall, where she learns that the movie star, Marina Gregg, has bought the place. Miss Marple takes the taxi back to St. Mary Mead and calls Dr. Haydock, who finds that she is fine, despite the fall, and prescribes a nice "juicy murder" to lift her spirits.

Chapters 4–6

Mrs. Bantry and others attend a benefit at Gossington Hall to raise money for the St. John's Ambulance Brigade. Heather Badcock monopolizes Marina

Gregg, telling her that they met many years before, when Heather was in the military and escaped quarantine for German measles just to meet Marina. As Heather speaks, Marina's eyes fix for a long moment on the wall, midway up the stairs, then drop. The party continues, but Heather has a sudden seizure and dies. Cherry Baker gives Miss Marple the news, and Dolly Bantry stops by to ask her old friend for an opinion regarding the murder. Miss Marple answers that Heather might have said something dangerous without realizing it.

Chapters 7–10

An autopsy determines that Heather was poisoned with six times the normal dosage of a product named Calmo, a sedative. Craddock visits Miss Marple, who tells him to see Mrs. Bantry and ask her about the look that she had noticed on Marina's face. He questions Marina's entourage at Gossington Hall, and learns that the house contains a large quantity of Calmo. He also notices a portrait of the Madonna and Child on the wall, midway up the stairs, the spot where Marina had fixed her gaze at the party. Craddock learns of Marina's previous meeting with Heather, and that both Marina and Jason assume that Marina was the true murder target.

Chapters 11–14

Craddock questions Ella, who tells him that Marina is difficult to work for, especially because she cannot bear to see children or to hear that anyone is pregnant. Craddock and Miss Marple review their clues to date, and narrow their suspects to two: Jason Rudd and Ella. Craddock and Cornish add Ardwyck Fenn and Lola Brewster to the suspect list. Craddock learns from Marina that she has received written death threats, and she explains his questions regarding her fixed stare at the party as being simply "a wave of tiredness." An interview with Lola reveals that she had once threatened to shoot Marina for stealing her husband.

Chapters 15–18

Craddock interviews Margot Bence, who photographed the party, and learns that she is one of four children adopted by Marina and then abandoned to foster homes, and that Marina had not recognized Margot at the party. Marina's coffee on the movie set is poisoned, and an analysis shows that the coffee contained arsenic. Ella is twice seen making phone calls from a public telephone, and she later dies when her hay fever flares up and she uses her nasal spray. The medication in the atomizer had been replaced by cyanide. Giuseppe, the butler at Gossington Hall, is shot to death after he returns from a trip to London.

Chapters 19–22

Cherry tells Miss Marple that Gladys Dixon, hired to serve food at the event, saw Heather purposely spill her drink. Fearful for Gladys' safety, Miss Marple sends her away on a trip to Bournemouth. Craddock informs Miss Marple that Giuseppe deposited five hundred pounds in the bank when he visited London, and he shows her the picture of Marina staring at the wall during the party. Miss Marple thinks that the look is more of apprehension than doom. She decides to speak with Marina's husband, but Dr. Gilchrist tells her that Marina has died in her sleep, "an overdose of sleeping stuff."

Chapter 23

Miss Marple insists on speaking with Rudd, and she informs him that Badcock was Marina's first husband, Alfred Beadle. She examines each of the deaths, identifying the motives and the murderer.

CRIME NOTES

The novel bears a strong similarity to an incident that occurred in actress Gene Tierney's life, which she recounted in her 1979 autobiography, *Self-Portrait*. During World War II, the actress gave birth to a daughter, who was soon diagnosed as hearing- and sight-impaired as well as mentally retarded, conditions which resulted from the German measles that Tierney had contracted early in the pregnancy. Some years later, the actress met a young woman who said that she was a former marine and had met Tierney during a World War II appearance at the Hollywood Canteen. She told the actress that she was such a great fan that, even though the women's camp was under strict quarantine for German measles, she had sneaked out of camp to meet and shake hands with Tierney.

The novel contains three murders. One victim is shot to death, a second dies from an overdose of Calmo, a sedative of indeterminate chemical composition, and a third is poisoned when cyanide is placed in her nasal atomizer.

Miss Marple's Final Cases and Two Other Stories   Mystery short story collection.

The collection is the final book by Agatha Christie. Despite the title, the six Miss MARPLE stories recount cases from the middle of her career, rather than her final adventures, and all are reprinted from earlier collections.

PUBLISHING AND DRAMATIZATION HISTORY
Miss Marple's Final Cases and Two Other Stories was published in 1979 by William Collins Sons and Company, Ltd., in London.

See the original collections for adaptations.

TITLES IN THE COLLECTION
Miss Marple's Final Cases and Two Other Stories contains the following short stories: "MISS MARPLE TELLS A STORY," "IN A GLASS DARKLY" (see THE REGATTA MYSTERY AND OTHER STORIES); "STRANGE JEST," "THE TAPE-MEASURE MURDER," "THE CASE OF THE CARETAKER," "THE CASE OF THE PERFECT MAID" (see THREE BLIND MICE AND OTHER STORIES); "SANCTUARY" and "THE DRESSMAKER'S DOLL" (see DOUBLE SIN AND OTHER STORIES).

"Miss Marple Tells a Story"   Mystery short story.

The plot centers on Miss MARPLE's efforts to save a young husband from a murder charge.

PUBLISHING AND DRAMATIZATION HISTORY
The story appeared in the short story collection, THE REGATTA MYSTERY AND OTHER STORIES, published in 1939 by Dodd, Mead and Company in New York.

The story has not been adapted for stage or screen.

CHARACTERS
Miss CARRUTHERS, Mrs. GRANBY, Mary HILL, Miss Jane Marple, Mr. PETHERICK, Mr. RHODES

PLOT SYNOPSIS
The story is framed as a chatty tale related by Miss Marple to her nephew and his wife, Raymond and Joan West. Consulted by attorney Mr. Petherick for assistance in clearing his client, Mr. Rhodes, of murder charges, Miss Marple questions the men, and learns that Mrs. Rhodes had a dark secret. Through a clever test of their powers of observation, Miss Marple ferrets out the existence of two additional suspects whose presence had been ignored. Using her brilliant intuitive powers, the elderly detective identifies the real killer and the hidden motive.

Mitchell, Henry Charles   Chief steward on board the *Prometheus*, he discovered the body of Madame GISELLE in DEATH IN THE CLOUDS.

Mitchell, Ruth   A provincial woman in DEATH IN THE CLOUDS, she believes that the murder of Madame GISELLE was the result of a communist plot and an especially dirty trick because it occurred on a British airplane.

Mitzi   An hysterical maid known for her temper and reputation for lying, this European refugee was, nonetheless, useful in helping Miss MARPLE set a trap for the murderer in A MURDER IS ANNOUNCED.

Mogson, Mrs.   See VOLE, ROMAINE.

Mohammed   An elevator operator in DESTINATION UNKNOWN, he offers to obtain a disguise and a means of escape for Andrew PETERS in exchange for being set up in a business in Chicago.

Molly   A helpful and observant waitress at the Gallant Endeavour in "FOUR-AND-TWENTY BLACKBIRDS," she provides clues that help Hercule POIROT to solve the murder of Henry GASCOIGNE.

Monckton, Colonel   Present on the night of an old friend's apparent suicide in "THE DEAD HARLEQUIN," he agrees with Mr. SATTERTHWAITE that the circumstances were highly suspicious.

Moncrieffe, Jean   An extremely honest young woman in "THE LERNEAN HYDRA" who served as pharmaceutical dispenser to Dr. OLDFIELD for three years, she refuses to marry him after his wife's death because of rumors that he had murdered his wife.

Monro, Flossie   A heavily made-up, "somewhat lurid-looking lady no longer in her first youth" in THE BIG FOUR, she helped Hercule POIROT to identify her former lover, Claud DARRELL. She is killed by an automobile before she can provide Poirot with a photograph of Darrell.

Montresor, Miss   See CLEVELAND, JANE.

Montresor, Mary   Beautiful and reckless, she intrigues George DUNDAS, sweeping him off his feet and into her sports car in "THE GOLDEN BALL." After testing him in several ways, she agrees to marry him only hours after they first meet.

Montressor, Helen   See GRANT, GERDA.

Montu   In DEATH COMES AS THE END, he is the divine Father of the Temple of Hathor.

Moody, Elizabeth   Once a theater-dresser, she is now a nursing home resident in BY THE PRICKING OF MY THUMBS. She is found dead of morphine poisoning soon after hinting that she had recognized someone from her past.

Mooney, Kitty   One of two young woman aboard ship in "PROBLEM AT SEA," she works hard to make Colonel CLAPPERTON forget both his age and his wife's rules.

Moorhouse, Hannah   See RYMER, AMELIA.

Morales, Pedro   See DRAKE, VICTOR.

Morelli, Tony   See BROWNE, ANTHONY.

Morisot, Anne   The twenty-four-year-old daughter of Madame GISELLE and George Leman, she lives under several names in DEATH IN THE CLOUDS. She poses as Madeleine, a maid for Lady Cicely HORBURY, and later as Anne Richards, the wife of James RICHARDS. She is traveling under this last name when found dead on a train.

Morisot, Marie Angelique   See GISELLE, MADAME.

Morley, Georgina   The heavyset, physically imposing sister of the murdered dentist, Henry MORLEY, in ONE, TWO, BUCKLE MY SHOE, she places the blame on his alcoholic business partner.

Morley, Henry   Murdered while in the office of his dental practice in ONE, TWO, BUCKLE MY SHOE, he is small in stature and belligerent in appearance.

Morris, Dr. (1)   The physician who performs a physical examination of the dead Mabelle ANNESLEY in "THE BIRD WITH THE BROKEN WING," he discovers that she was strangled before being hanged in her room.

Morris, Dr. (2)   Personal physician to Luther CRACKENTHORPE in 4.50 FROM PADDINGTON, he informs the investigating detective about the mental instability of Luther's mother.

Morris, Isaac   Not one of the directly intended victims of the Indian Island party in AND THEN THERE WERE NONE, he makes all arrangements for the purchase of the island, the provision of food and drink and the issuing of invitations. Just before the first guests arrive on the island, he is found dead of a barbiturate overdose.

Morton, Inspector   A member of Scotland Yard investigating the murder of Cora LANSQUENET in AFTER THE FUNERAL, he is a quiet, middle-aged man with an unhurried manner and shrewd eyes.

Mory, Angele   Known under the names of Mademoiselle Genevieve BRUN, Countess Varaga POPO-LEFFSKY, Queen VARAGA of Herzoslovakia and Virginia REVEL, she is a former dancer with the Folies Bergère in THE SECRET OF CHIMNEYS. Approached by a subversive organization to help them trap the King of Herzoslovakia in immoral behavior, she falls in love with him instead and decides to marry him, turning herself into the Countess Popoleffsky in the effort.

Moscomb, Beatrice   A member of Simeon LEE's staff, she is the third housemaid in HERCULE POIROT'S CHRISTMAS.

Mosgorovsky, Mr.   Proprietor of the Seven Dials Club in the SEVEN DIALS MYSTERY, he hired the former footman at Chimneys as a guard at the club at a salary more than three times his previous pay. A Russian emigré, he runs a legal dancing and drinking club with illegal gambling tables.

Moss, Edwin   The phony brother-in-law of murder victim Walter ST. JOHN in "SANCTUARY," he is a criminal who switches suitcases with Bunch HARMON at the train station.

Moss, Mary   Once an exotic dancer who numbered royalty among her fans, the former Zobeida died three years earlier and left a fortune in real emeralds sewn into a costume in "SANCTUARY." Her husband escapes from prison, retrieves the jewels, and tries with difficulty to give them to the caretakers of their little girl.

"Motive Versus Opportunity"   Mystery short story.

The plot centers on the influence of a spiritualist and a will with disappearing ink.

PUBLISHING AND DRAMATIZATION
HISTORY
The story appeared in the short story collection, THE THIRTEEN PROBLEMS, published in 1932 by William Collins Sons and Company, Ltd., in London, and in 1933 under the title *The Tuesday Club Murders* by Dodd, Mead and Company in New York.

The story has not been adapted for stage or screen.

CHARACTERS
Christobel CLODE, George CLODE, Mary CLODE, Simon CLODE, Lucy DAVID, Emma GAUNT, Miss Jane MARPLE, Mr. PETHERICK, Eurydice SPRAGG

PLOT SYNOPSIS
At a meeting of the impromptu crime-solving club, The Tuesday Night Club, attorney Mr. Petherick relates an incident involving the late Simon Clode, a wealthy client. Obsessed with his granddaughter's death despite the presence of his young nephew and niece, Clode turns to spiritualist Eurydice Spragg to contact his granddaughter in the afterlife. He writes a new will, which favors Eurydice to the exclusion of his family. To everyone's surprise, when the envelope containing the will is opened after Clode's death, only a blank piece of paper is found. Despite a paucity of clues, Miss Marple solves the mystery of the blank will and, once again, astonishes the club.

Mountford, Mrs.   Married to Dillmouth's confectioner in SLEEPING MURDER, she is interviewed for information related to Helen HALLIDAY.

Mousetrap, The   Mystery play.

The play has become the longest continuously running stage play in history. The plot centers on a group of snowbound individuals who are terrorized by a murderer whose motive is revenge.

THEATRICAL AND PUBLISHING HISTORY
The play had its beginning as a twenty-minute radio play, entitled *Three Blind Mice,* written in 1947 for the eightieth birthday of Queen Mary at the request of the royal family, and broadcast by the BBC. The play then became the short story, "THREE BLIND MICE," which appeared in the short story collection, THREE BLIND MICE AND OTHER STORIES, published in 1950 by Dodd, Mead and Company in New York. The author then rewrote the short story into a two-act, full-length play, retitled *The Mousetrap,* which opened in London at the Ambassadors Theatre on November 25, 1952, and shortly after moved to the 550-seat St. Martins Theatre. It has become the longest running play in theater history, thanks in good part to American tourists, who have made the play part of their English experience. Although film rights to the play were sold many years ago, the agreement stipulated that a filmed version of the play will not appear until the London stage production ends.

CHARACTERS
Mrs. BOYLE, Mrs. CASEWELL, Mr. PARAVICINI, Giles RALSTON, Molly RALSTON, Major METCALF, Detective Sergeant TROTTER, Christopher WREN

PLOT SYNOPSIS
The story concerns a murderer whose motive is revenge for the abuse of three World War II evacuee children at Longridge Farm, which resulted in one child's death. The perpetrators, John and Maureen Gregg, had been sentenced to prison in 1940. John had escaped from prison, then died; his wife had served her time, and was released to live under the name of Mrs. Lyon. After Mrs. Lyon is found strangled, police find a notebook, dropped by the killer, which contains two addresses. The first address is the victim's and the second is Monkswell Manor, a newly

opened guest house. Scotland Yard places a man incognito at the manor, but one more murder occurs before the now-grown eldest of the three child evacuees is discovered at the guest house.

CRIME NOTES
The two murders occur as the result of strangulation, one using a belt. The author changed the names of the owners of Monkswell Manor from Davis in the short story to Ralston in the play.

Moving Finger, The   Mystery novel.

The novel was one of two on which the author worked simultaneously during World War II while she stayed alone in London. She alternated writing N OR M? and *The Moving Finger* to keep herself "fresh at task." The plot centers on the efforts of Miss MARPLE to uncover the source of the numerous poison-pen letters that terrorize a small village.

PUBLISHING AND DRAMATIZATION
HISTORY
The novel was published in 1943 by William Collins Sons and Company, Ltd., in London, and in 1942 by Dodd, Mead and Company in New York.

The novel was adapted for television in 1985 by the BBC in England, and was also shown on the Public Broadcasting Service in the U.S.

CHARACTERS
Colonel APPLEBY, Emily BARTON, Jerry BURTON, Joanna BURTON, Reverend DANE CALTHROP, Mrs. Maud DANE CALTHROP, Mrs. CLEAT, FLORENCE, Miss GINCH, Inspector GRAVES, Mary GREY, Aimee GRIFFITH, Dr. Owen GRIFFITH, Elsie HOLLAND, Megan HUNTER, Dr. Marcus KENT, Miss Jane MARPLE, Superintendent NASH, Mr. PYE, Mona SYMMINGTON, Richard SYMMINGTON, Agnes WODDELL

PLOT SYNOPSIS
Chapter 1
Jerry Burton is a military pilot on sick leave to recover from crash injuries. His doctor has advised him to find a quiet little town in which to recuperate, and Little Furze seems ideal. He and his sister Joanna rent a home from Emily Barton, but they soon receive an anonymous letter which accuses them of being lovers rather than brother and sister. When he goes to Dr. Griffith for a check up, the doctor reveals that he and others in the town have received similarly poisonous anonymous letters.

Chapter 2
Megan Hunter, stepdaughter of attorney Richard Symmington, shows up on the Burtons' doorstep and invites herself to dinner. Other residents of the town receive poison-pen letters, and the vicar's wife wonders to Jerry why the writer makes up gossip in the letters and never includes real indiscretions. Aimee Griffith claims to have thrown her letter away, but Mrs. Symmington commits suicide when she receives a letter claiming that her second son was not her husband's child.

Chapter 3
The authorities analyze the letters received so far, and determine that the words have been cut from a book printed in approximately 1830. No fingerprints are found on the paper, leading them to deduce that the perpetrator wore gloves. The typeface on the envelopes is identified as having come from a Windsor 7 machine, one which Mr. Symmington donated from his office to the Women's Institute.

Chapter 4
Agnes Woddell, the maid in the Symmington household, calls Mr. Symmington's housekeeper, and the two agree to have tea so that Agnes can ask for advice, but she never arrives. Joanna recalls that Mrs. Symmington committed suicide a week earlier, also on the maid's day off. Jerry becomes worried and calls the Symmington house, but Agnes does not return. Early the next morning, Megan calls the Burtons to tell them that Agnes was found dead under the stairwell. Jerry tells Superintendent Nash that Agnes must have seen who put the letter into the mailbox.

Chapter 5
Superintendent Nash questions Elsie, the Symmingtons' governess, the only one who has not received one of the letters. Emily Barton tells Jerry that she has received several such letters, each accusing her of poisoning different members of her family. Yet she asserts that she does not believe that the murder and the letters are connected.

Chapter 6
Jerry unexpectedly finds a book published in 1840 on his bookshelf, with the middle pages cut. The

only fingerprints on it are his and those of Partridge. He receives a call from Mrs. Dane Calthrop, who invites him to tea to meet someone whom she believes can put a stop to the letters. The Burtons attend tea at the vicarage and meet Miss Jane Marple, with whom they discuss the letters and the murder. A few nights later, he sees someone at the Women's Institute and learns that Superintendent Nash has the place under surveillance in the belief that the letter writer will type there again.

Chapter 7
Jerry goes to London for a physical checkup, and takes Megan with him to have her hair done and buy new clothes. Dr. Kent is pleased with Jerry's recovery, and surprised to hear how exciting the small town has been. Jerry and the "new" Megan go out dining and dancing, and they return late. The next day, Jerry asks Megan to marry him, but she refuses. He speaks to her stepfather, but Symmington says that the decision is Megan's. Joanna takes a walk and comes upon a farmhouse, where she stops for a drink of water. Dr. Griffith is there delivering a baby, and he asks Joanna to help. She is very impressed with him. Later, Superintendent Nash calls Jerry to tell him that Elsie has received a letter. He also says that Aimee Griffith was seen typing letters at the Institute between 11 and 11:30 P.M.

Chapter 8
Jerry sees Miss Marple speak with Megan, then enter the police station. He begins to worry about Megan. That evening, he and Nash watch Megan's house. They see someone carry Megan down the stairs from her room and into the kitchen, where her head is placed into the gas oven. The two men save her, and the perpetrator is arrested. Miss Marple explains how she identified the letter writer and found the connection between the letters and the deaths of Agnes and Mrs. Symmington. The novel ends with the promise of weddings for Joanna Burton to Dr. Griffith and Jerry Burton to Megan Hunter.

CRIME NOTES
The novel contains two murders. The first victim dies when she is hit on the head, then skewered in the base of the skull, while the second victim dies when cyanide is placed in the water with which she takes her back pain pills each evening.

"Mr. Eastwood's Adventure" Mystery short story.

PUBLISHING AND DRAMATIZATION HISTORY
The story appeared in the short story collection, THE LISTERDALE MYSTERY (1), published in 1934 by William Collins Sons and Company, Ltd., in London.

The story has not been adapted for stage or screen.

CHARACTERS
CARMEN, Detective Sergeant CARTER, Anthony EASTWOOD

PLOT SYNOPSIS
The story concerns the misadventures of Anthony Eastwood, a mystery writer who is lured by a phone call to the site of a faked murder. He is then misidentified as Conrad Fleckman, and charged with murder by two individuals masquerading as police officers. When the two phony policemen accompany Mr. Eastwood home, one keeps him occupied in conversation while the other searches the house to locate the writer's valuable collection of miniature paintings, the true goal of the masquerade.

Mr. Parker Pyne, Detective See PARKER PYNE INVESTIGATES.

Mrs. McGinty's Dead Mystery novel.

The novel marks the second appearance of Mrs. Ariadne OLIVER working with Hercule POIROT to solve the crime, fourteen years after they joined forces in CARDS ON THE TABLE. The plot centers on efforts to prove the innocence of a man convicted of the murder of a cleaning lady, despite his failure to defend himself of the charge.

PUBLISHING AND DRAMATIZATION HISTORY
The novel was published in 1952 by William Collins Sons and Company in London, and by Dodd, Mead and Company in New York.

The novel was adapted for film by MGM in 1964, and released under the title *Murder Most Foul*. The character of Hercule Poirot was replaced by Miss Jane MARPLE, played by Margaret RUTHERFORD.

CHARACTERS

James BENTLEY, Bessie BURCH, Joe BURCH, Eve CARPENTER, Guy CARPENTER, EDNA (2), Mrs. ELIOT, Deirdre HENDERSON, Evelyn HOPE, Pamela HORSEFALL, Mrs. KIDDELL, Mrs. McGINTY, MICHAEL, Mrs. Ariadne OLIVER, Hercule POIROT, Dr. RENDELL, Shelagh RENDELL, Superintendent Bert SPENCE, Major Johnnie SUMMERHAYES, Maureen SUMMERHAYES, Mrs. SWEETIMEN, Mrs. Laura UPWARD, Robin UPWARD, Mr. WETHERBY, Mrs. WETHERBY, Maude WILLIAMS

PLOT SYNOPSIS

Chapters 1–3

Superintendent Spence visits Hercule Poirot and asks the detective to help him to prove that James Bentley, recently convicted of killing his landlady, is innocent of murder. Spence admits that all the facts point to Bentley's guilt, but his intuition says otherwise. Intrigued, Poirot agrees to look into the matter, and he decides to take a room in Broadhinny and investigate.

Chapters 4–6

Poirot questions the murder victim's niece, Bessie Burch, and her husband, Joe. He feels that Bessie is a straightforward woman, but Joe is too helpful and seems to be hiding something. The detective gains the impression from his initial investigation that the victim was murdered by someone she trusted. He speaks with Bentley's former employers, and learns that he was a mediocre employee whom they fired. Only Maude Williams, a secretary at Bentley's old place of work, believes in his innocence, and expresses respect for him. Poirot also learns that Bentley is devoted to his mother, and he asks the jailed man if he or his mother have any enemies. Bentley replies that he has no enemies, nor has he any friends.

Chapters 7–10

Poirot visits the woman who found the victim, then talks to the postmistress and learns that Mrs. McGinty bought a bottle of ink two days before she died, but Bessie never received a letter from her aunt. Poirot searches the victim's possessions and finds a newspaper from three days before the murder from which an article has been cut out. Bessie tells him that the police have the article, which was found in the victim's purse. The article deals with women involved in past tragedies and asks the question "Where are they now?" Poirot thinks that Mrs. McGinty either might have been one of the women in the article or might have known one of the women. A reporter with the paper tells Poirot that she received a letter from the victim in which she claimed to know where there was another picture like the one in the paper. Poirot also becomes reacquainted with Mrs. Ariadne Oliver, who is adapting one of her novels into a play with Robin Upward.

Chapters 11–14

Spence and Poirot review the cases of the four women in the newspaper article. Both agree that one of the women must have some connection to one of the victim's employers. Meanwhile, Mrs. Oliver strikes up conversations with several people in town, hoping to gain new information. When she returns to the Upwards' house, she meets Eve Carpenter, who extends an invitation to her party. When the conversation turns to the McGinty murder, Poirot takes the photographs of the four women and places them on the table. Laura Upward recognizes one, but she remains silent.

Chapters 15–18

Maude Williams joins the investigation when Poirot calls her and asks her to take a post as a domestic with the Wetherbys. Robin and Mrs. Oliver go to a show, and they find Mrs. Upward dead when they return home, a lipstick-smeared glass on the table and a heavy scent of perfume in the room. Although the dead woman had telephoned Deirdre Henderson that evening, Deirdre had found the house dark when she arrived, so she had not stayed. She does not wear lipstick or perfume, so someone else must have been there after she left. Poirot visits Bentley and tells him that Spence and Maude are helping in the investigation, and he learns that Mrs. McGinty had told Bentley that one of the women in the picture had a playwright for a son.

Chapters 19–22

Edna, who was cheating on her boyfriend by meeting a married man on the night of Mrs. Upward's murder, saw a fair-haired woman entering the house, but fears to reveal her activities. The police find a book bearing the name "Evelyn Hope" in the Upward home, the name of one of the four women in the article, a fact which upsets Maude.

Chapters 23–27
Poirot learns that Mrs. Upward had called Eve Carpenter and Maureen Summerhayes and had also asked them to visit her on the night she was murdered. When Poirot gathers the people involved to identify the murderer, he notes that the name "Evelyn Hope" is both the name taken by Eva Kane, a woman in the article, and of her child. Mrs. McGinty had come across a picture while cleaning, then decided to extract a price for it. The true identity of the murderer and the reason for it come as a surprise.

Epilogue
The reader learns why Eve Carpenter was reluctant to cooperate with the police, as well as that Dr. Rendell was suspected of killing his first wife and feared a police investigation. The happy note is that the now-freed James Bentley is planning to marry.

CRIME NOTES
The novel contains two murders, one the result of a blow to the head with an ax and the other the result of strangulation.

Mugg, Charles See CARTWRIGHT, SIR CHARLES.

Mullins, Iris Hired by Tuppence BERESFORD to serve as an assistant gardener in POSTERN OF FATE, she incurs the severe dislike of the Beresfords' terrier, Hannibal.

Mundy, Mrs. A woman in Chipping Cleghorn, she raises Jewel ST. JOHN, whose father is murdered in "SANCTUARY."

Murchison, Bianca A member of Aristides' Brain Trust in DESTINATION UNKNOWN, she is an Italian-born woman married to research scientist Simon MURCHISON. She occasionally gives lectures on the subjects of economics and commercial law at the Brain Trust.

Murchison, Dr. Simon A research scientist at Aristides' Brain Trust in DESTINATION UNKNOWN, he is a quaint, old-fashioned, "thin, anaemic-looking man of about twenty-six."

Murder at Hazelmoor See THE SITTAFORD MYSTERY.

Murder Ahoy! Film released in 1964 by Metro-Goldwyn-Mayer. The movie was the fourth in the series starring Margaret Rutherford as Miss MARPLE, but it is not based on a Christie work. Instead, the script was an original story written by David Pursall and Jack Seddon, adapters of earlier novels by the author.

CAST
The cast consists of Margaret Rutherford as Miss Jane Marple, Charles Tingwell as Inspector CRADDOCK, as well as Bernard Adams, Joan Benham, Gerald Cross, Stringer Davis, Terence Edmund, Norma Foster, Roy Holder, Lionel Jeffries, Henry Longhurst, Miles Malleson, Francie Mathews, William Mervyn, Derek Nimmo, Henry Oscar and Tony Quinn.

PLOT SYNOPSIS
The story concerns murder in a nautical setting in a wholly invented plot that places Miss Marple on a navy training ship to investigate murder and blackmail. As far-fetched as the premise might be, the ending is even more fantastic, as the eighty-year-old Margaret Rutherford fights a fencing duel with the murderer in the final scenes of the movie.

PRODUCTION NOTES
The film was a box office failure, and the planned series of Miss Marple movies ended with this fourth effort.

Murder at a Gallop Film released in 1963 by Metro-Goldwyn-Mayer. The movie is very loosely based on the 1953 novel, AFTER THE FUNERAL, by Agatha Christie.

CAST
The cast consists of Margaret Rutherford as Miss Jane MARPLE, and Robert Morley as Hector Enderby, as well as Stringer Davis, Katya Douglas, Gordon Harris, Duncan Lamont, Flora Robson, Charles Tingwell, Robert Urquhart and Robert Villiers.

CHANGES FROM THE ORIGINAL TEXT
The adaptation, written by David Pursall and Jack Seddon, changed not only the setting and plot of the novel but also changed the detective—from Hercule POIROT to Miss Marple. In *After the Funeral*,

Hercule Poirot investigated the death of middle-aged Richard ABERNETHIE, after whose funeral the family gathers at the family estate, where the hint of murder emerges. In the movie, the detective has become Miss Marple, the dead man has become an elderly recluse, and the estate has become a riding academy, complete with a riding school proprietor as the detective's sidekick. The plot called for Rutherford to mingle with the hunting set and actually to ride a horse in one scene.

PRODUCTION NOTES
Agatha Christie did not like the changes made in her story by the scriptwriters, but the public made the film a box office success.

Murder at the Vicarage, The   Mystery novel.
The novel marks the first appearance of Miss MARPLE and the village of ST. MARY MEAD. In creating the white-haired sleuth, the author attracted women readers, who could relate to Miss Marple's shrewd, intuitive approach to crime.

PUBLISHING AND DRAMATIZATION HISTORY
The Murder at the Vicarage was published in 1930 by William Collins Sons and Company, Ltd., in London, and by Dodd, Mead and Company in New York.

The novel was adapted for the stage by Moie Charles and Barbara Toy, and opened on December 14, 1949 at the Playhouse Theatre in London. The novel was adapted for television in 1988 by the BBC in England, and was also shown on the Public Broadcasting Service in the U.S.

CHARACTERS
Dennis CLEMENT, Griselda CLEMENT, Reverend Leonard (Len) CLEMENT, Miss CRAM, GLADYS (GLADDIE), Miss HARTNELL, Mr. HAWES, Dr. HAYDOCK, Mrs. LESTRANGE, Miss Marple, Mrs. PRICE RIDLEY, Anne PROTHEROE, Lettice PROTHEROE, Lawrence REDDING, Dr. STONE, Caroline WETHERBY

PLOT SYNOPSIS
Chapter 1–4
Narrated by Reverand Clement, the novel opens as he and his wife Griselda banter. Their discussion reveals the nature of their marriage and the character of the village. Lettice Protheroe complains that her father is too restrictive, while Griselda prepares a tea party for four ladies of the parish. After evening service, the vicar speaks with Mrs. Lestrange, and wonders why so sophisticated a woman chooses to live in a small village. He stops at Lawrence Redding's studio, and surprises the artist and Mrs. Protheroe in an embrace. She later tells him that she is miserable with her husband and wishes that he were dead. When Redding joins the Clements for dinner that evening, the vicar privately counsels the artist to leave town to stop the gossip.

Chapters 5–7
The vicar meets Redding rushing madly from the vicarage, then comes upon the body of Colonel Protheroe in the study. Redding is arrested and charged with the murder, but Dr. Haydock disputes his guilt and notes a discrepancy between the setting on the clock and the temperature of the dead body. Miss Marple also refuses to believe that Redding is guilty.

Chapters 8–12
Both Anne Protheroe and Laurence Redding individually claim to have committed the murder, and Miss Marple notes that there are at least seven suspects. The investigators observe that the letter Colonel Protheroe was writing at the time of his death has no date on it, and the gun found on the floor in his study belongs to the vicar. Colonel Melchett concludes that Redding cannot be guilty, and he decides to speak with several neighbors of the Protheroes.

Chapters 13–16
Colonel Melchett questions Mrs. Price Ridley, and learns that she recently received a threatening telephone call. He intends to question Mrs. Lestrange, who met with Protheroe on the night before his death. She contacts the vicar and asks for his help, but refuses to reveal the nature of her conversation with the victim. Meanwhile, the suspect list increases, and Miss Marple suggests that anyone might have committed the murder.

Chapters 17–20
The police determine that Anne is not a suspect, but add Gladys Cram to their list. In an effort to close gaps in the investigation, the police speak with household staff members, and learn that Mrs.

Lestrange had threatened to kill Protheroe. Meanwhile, Clement finds an earring in his study that he did not see on the night of the murder.

Chapters 21–24

Miss Marple learns that Dr. Stone is an imposter, and Griselda receives a note from Anne claiming that she needs the vicar's advice. She intends to marry Redding in six months. At the same time, Lettice admits that she planted Anne's earring in the vicar's study in an attempt to frame her stepmother for the murder. While searching through the broken shrubs surrounding his house, the vicar finds a suitcase containing some of Protheroe's belongings. Once inside the vicarage again, he learns from Griselda that, years before their marriage, she had been in love with Laurence.

Chapters 25–28

The clues continue to implicate various suspects, and the investigators learn that Mrs. Lestrange is fatally ill. As the pressure builds, the vicar gives a scathing sermon from the pulpit that shocks his parishioners. Later, he confers with Miss Marple, who seems to be getting closer to solving the case, to the great consternation of Colonel Melchett. The police determine that the note found with Protheroe at his death is not in his handwriting, and they trace the writing to the new curate, Hawes.

Chapters 29–32

The police are too late in contacting Hawes to learn the identity of the murderer, because he is found dead of a drug overdose when they reach his home. Reviewing the evidence again, Miss Marple and the vicar deduce that the call and the fake shot from the woods occurred at the same time. They set a trap for the murderer by having someone warn him, then watch his reaction. The plan succeeds, and the murderer is revealed and brought to justice.

CRIME NOTES

The murder in this novel is the result of a gunshot wound to the head.

Murder for Christmas   See HERCULE POIROT'S CHRISTMAS.

Murder in Mesopotamia   Mystery novel.

The novel is one of several works that emerged from the author's involvement with her husband's archaeological expeditions in the Middle East during

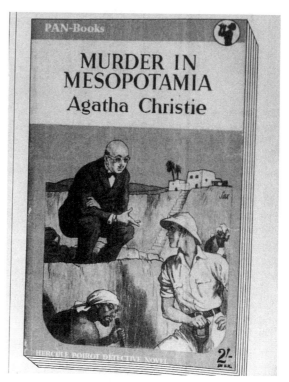

An old paperback cover for *Murder in Mesopotamia* presents one artist's conception of the famed Hercule Poirot.   (Photo courtesy of the R. Gregor Collection)

the 1930s. The plot centers on efforts to identify the murderer of an archaeologist's wife at a dig site along the Tigris River.

PUBLISHING AND DRAMATIZATION HISTORY

The novel was published in 1936 by William Collins Sons and Company, Ltd., in London, and by Dodd, Mead and Company in New York.

The novel has not been adapted for stage or screen.

CHARACTERS

ALI YUSEF, Frederick BOSNER, Richard CAREY, Bill COLEMAN, David EMMOTT, Anne JOHNSON, Major KELSEY, Mary KELSEY, Father LAVIGNY, Amy LEATHERAN, Dr. Eric LEIDNER, Mrs. Louise LEIDNER, Captain MAITLAND, Raoul MENIER, Joseph MERCADO, Marie MERCADO, Major PENNYMAN, Hercule

POIROT, Dr. Giles REILLY, Sheila REILLY, Carl RE-ITER, Monsieur VERRIER

PLOT SYNOPSIS

Chapters 1–4

Nurse Amy Leatheran takes a position with Major and Mrs. Kelsey to accompany them to Iraq and to care for their anticipated baby. When plans change, Amy fears that she will have to return to London, but she learns of a position caring for Dr. Leidner's wife, a hypochondriac who also complains of insomnia. Hired by Dr. Leidner, she travels to the Tell Yarimjah dig to begin work.

Chapters 5–8

During tea, Amy learns that many of the others at the dig site have known each other for years. The topic of conversation seems to be Mrs. Leidner's "nerves," to the point that Mrs. Leidner insists that they talk about something other than her ailments. Father Lavigny shows Amy around the palaces and temples, and confides that Mrs. Leidner is a dangerous and ruthless woman. Amy takes a walk with Mrs. Leidner, and observes that she appears to be terrified of a man wearing European clothes whom they observe looking into one of the windows.

Chapters 9–12

Mrs. Leidner confides to Amy that she is afraid of being murdered, and recounts the story of her first marriage to a German spy, Frederick Bosner, whom she believes to still be alive despite official reports of his death. She claims to receive anonymous threatening letters from time to time, but Amy observes that the handwriting on such letters resembles that of her patient. Mrs. Leidner is found dead in her room, and the police determine that the murderer is one of the members of the expedition. Dr. Reilly announces that Hercule Poirot is expected to pass through the area on his way to Baghdad, and suggests that they ask for his assistance.

Chapters 13–15

Poirot arrives, and questions members of the expedition. Amy tells him about the threatening letters and of Mrs. Leidner's first marriage, and he asserts that the letters are probably genuine and that either Mrs. Leidner's former husband or her brother-in-law may be on the expedition staff. Dr. Leidner tells Poirot that he had not taken the threats seriously because of the similarity of the handwriting. Poirot also learns

that Dr. Leidner will not receive his late wife's considerable estate; it has been bequeathed to the Pittstown Museum.

Chapters 16–18

After examining the crime scene, where he finds a small amount of blood in the washbasin, Poirot asks Amy if anyone did not like the victim. She identifies Mrs. Mercado, Miss Johnson and Mr. Carey. Mrs. Reilly tells Poirot that Mrs. Leidner deserved to be murdered, because she was the kind of woman who did not want to see others happy and she was after every man within her reach, statements with which Amy disagrees.

Chapters 19–21

Amy finds Miss Johnson crying in Dr. Leidner's office, and tries to comfort her. As she straightens up the room, she finds a crumpled piece of paper, which Miss Johnson snatches from her hand and throws into the fire. Amy notices that the writing is the same as that on the death notes. Poirot later goes out to the dig with Amy, where the detective surreptitiously stabs Joseph Mercado with a needle. Amy applies iodine and notices that Mercado has track marks on his arm. In a later discussion, Carey admits to Poirot that he hated Mrs. Leidner.

Chapters 22–25

Poirot finds a mask imprinted with India ink, and Amy tells him that it matches the description of the face which Mrs. Leidner had claimed to see in her window. Amy happens upon Miss Johnson, who is standing on the roof and saying to herself, "I've seen how someone could come in from the outside—and no one would ever even guess." Later that night, Miss Johnson is heard choking in her room, after swallowing corrosive acid. Her final words to Amy are "The window . . . Nurse . . . the window." Captain Maitland finds the weapon that killed Mrs. Leidner under Miss Johnson's bed, and the camp learns that Father Lavigny is missing.

Chapters 26–29

The investigation discloses that Father Lavigny is really an international thief named Raoul Menier, whose plan was to make impressions of valuable finds, create duplicates, and sell the originals to collectors. Mrs. Leidner may have learned the truth and taunted the thief. Another possibility is Mrs. Leidner's first husband, who has undergone plastic surgery and made a new life for himself. Considering that she also liked other women's men, a third possible motive is jealousy. Poirot sorts through the clues and confronts the real murderer, thus revealing the murder of Mrs. Leidner to be a crime of passion. The murder of Miss Johnson occurred because she learned too much about the earlier death.

CRIME NOTES
Two murders occur in the novel. The first results from a blow to the temple with a blunt object, while the second occurs when the victim drinks hydrochloric acid that has been substituted for her water.

Murder in Retrospect   See FIVE LITTLE PIGS.

Murder in the Calais Coach   See MURDER ON THE ORIENT EXPRESS.

Murder in the Mews (1)   Mystery short story collection.

Four novellas comprise this collection, with Hercule POIROT providing the solutions to the mysteries. Also present in the collection are Captain HASTINGS and Inspector JAPP, and Mr. SATTERTHWAITE, who usually appears with Mr. Harley QUIN, is present for one story. Although each story is complete in itself, three have plot similarities to other works by the author, and in one of the novellas, a character quotes lines that become the title of a later novel.

PUBLISHING AND DRAMATIZATION
HISTORY
Murder in the Mews (1) was published in 1937 by William Collins Sons and Company, Ltd., in London, and, under the title, *Dead Man's Mirror and Other Stories,* by Dodd, Mead and Company in New York.

"THE INCREDIBLE THEFT" was produced for radio in America in 1948 as part of the series *The Adventures of M. Hercule Poirot.* "MURDER IN THE MEWS," "THE INCREDIBLE THEFT" and "TRIANGLE AT RHODES" were adapted for television in 1989 by London Weekend Television in England, and were also shown on the Public Broadcasting Service in the U.S.

TITLES IN THE COLLECTION
Murder in the Mews contains the following novellas: "Murder in the Mews," "The Incredible Theft," "Triangle at Rhodes" and "DEAD MAN'S MIRROR"

Chief Inspector Japp (Philip Jackson) and Hercule Poirot (David Suchet) decide if it is murder or suicide in "Murder in the Mews." (Photo courtesy of London Weekend Television)

CRIME NOTES
The American edition of the collection omitted "The Incredible Theft," which has not been published in America.

"Murder in the Mews" (2)   Mystery novella.
The plot centers on the presumed suicide of a woman, but Hercule POIROT suspects murder.

PUBLISHING AND DRAMATIZATION
HISTORY
The novella appeared in the novella collection, MURDER IN THE MEWS (1), published in 1937 by William Collins Sons and Company, Ltd., in London, and,

under the title, *Dead Man's Mirror and Other Stories*, by Dodd, Mead and Company in New York.

The novella was adapted for television in 1989 by London Weekend Television in England, and was also shown on the Public Broadcasting Service in the United States.

CHARACTERS
Barbara ALLEN, Major EUSTACE, Captain Arthur HASTINGS, Chief Inspector JAPP, Charles LAVERTON-WEST MP, Mrs. PIERCE (1), Jane PLENDERLEITH, Hercule Poirot

PLOT SYNOPSIS
The story concerns the shooting death of Barbara Allen in the apartment she shared with Jane Plenderleith. Chief Inspector Japp calls in Hercule Poirot when he realizes that the initial verdict of suicide is doubtful, because the gun was in the dead woman's right hand, but the bullet entered her left temple. The presence of a Turkish cigarette butt and a man's cufflink lend further doubt to the possibility of suicide. After questioning Jane, and a careful examination of the premises, Poirot arrives at the surprising truth.

Murder in Three Acts   See THREE-ACT TRAGEDY.

Murder Is Announced, A   Mystery novel.

The novel introduces Chief Inspector Dermot Eric CRADDOCK, nephew of Miss MARPLE's old friend and fellow member of the Tuesday Night Club, Sir Henry CLITHERING. The plot centers on identifying who placed a newspaper announcement that a murder will occur at a precise time, on a given day and at a specific location, then proceeded to commit murder.

PUBLISHING AND DRAMATIZATION HISTORY
The novel was published in 1950 by William Collins Sons and Company, Ltd., in London, and by Dodd, Mead and Company in New York.

The novel was adapted for the stage, and opened in London at the Vaudeville Theatre on September 21, 1977. The novel was also the first of the Miss Marple mysteries to be adapted for television. The adaptation was presented in a live broadcast on the NBC Television *Goodyear Playhouse* on December 30, 1956, starring Gracie Fields as Miss Marple. The novel was again adapted for television in 1986 by the BBC in England, and was also shown on the Public Broadcasting Service in the U.S.

CHARACTERS
Old ASHE, Charlotte BLACKLOCK, Letitia BLACKLOCK, Dora BUNNER, Johnny BUTT, Sir Henry Clithering, Detective Inspector Craddock, Colonel Archie EASTERBROOK, Laura EASTERBROOK, Sergeant FLETCHER, Belle GOEDLER, Randall GOEDLER, Sonia GOEDLER, Diana "Bunch" HARMON, Reverend Julian HARMON, Myrna HARRIS, Phillipa HAYMES, Miss HINCHCLIFFE, Jim HUGGINS, Miss Jane Marple, MITZI, Amy MURGATROYD, Mr. ROWLANDSON, Chief George RYDESDALL, Rudi SCHERZ, Patrick SIMMONS, Emma STAMFORDIS, Mrs. SWETTENHAM, Edmund SWETTENHAM, TIGLATH-PILESER

PLOT SYNOPSIS
Chapters 1–2
The town on Chipping Cleghorn receives its usual delivery of the *Gazette* on October 29th, and the attention of many readers is drawn to a brief announcement which states: "A murder is announced and will take place on Friday, October 29, at Little Paddocks, at 6:30 p.m. Friends please accept this, the only intimation." Several people decide to attend what they believe to be a murder mystery party. The residents of Little Paddocks also read the article and think that it is silly, but their cook Mitzi takes the announcement seriously and fears that she will be killed.

Chapters 3–5
Miss Blacklock, owner of Little Paddocks, realizes that people will respond to the announcement, even if she did not place it, so she prepares to receive guests. The niece of the former owner of Little Paddocks arrives, as do other residents of Chipping Cleghorn. At 6:30 P.M., the lights all go off, the door swings open, and a voice says "Stick 'em up." Two bullets are fired and several people scream. Then the lights go on and a man unknown to the group is found dead, while Miss Blacklock has been shot in the ear. The police arrive and determine that the dead man is Rudi Scherz, an employee of the Royal Spa Hotel.

Chapters 6–8
Craddock and Fletcher question members of the Little Paddocks household, but no one knew Scherz personally. They also question all of the people present at the murder, but the only suspicious respondent is Mitzi, who seems to be holding back information. Miss Marple sends a letter to Craddock, then suggests to the investigators that Scherz was paid to kill one of the guests. Myrna, Scherz's girlfriend, tells police that Scherz had told her that he had to fake a holdup and that he had shown her the newspaper announcement.

Chapters 9–12
Inspector Craddock questions Mitzi again, and she tells him that she had heard Rudi Scherz speaking with Phillipa Haymes. Craddock also asks about the bolted door, which has been opened recently. Miss Blacklock tells him that she inherited Little Paddocks from her former employer, whose will stated that the estate go first to his wife, then to Miss Blacklock upon his wife's death. Craddock questions Phillipa, and she denies that she had spoken to Scherz before the tragedy. Miss Marple goes to tea at Little Paddocks and learns where everyone was at the time of the incident. At the same time, the police agree that the formerly bolted door had been oiled to open noiselessly when the lights went out. Those present at the murder analyze what little they observed, and Colonel Easterbrook learns that his revolver is missing.

Chapters 13–16
Miss Marple sees Dora Bunner enter the Bluebird Cafe; she sits down with her to talk, hoping to uncover new information. Meanwhile, Craddock visits Sonia Goedler, the late Randall Goedler's sister, who would have inherited Little Paddocks had they not quarreled, and he leaves viewing her two daughters as suspects. Miss Blacklock plans a birthday party for Dora, and Mitzi makes a rich chocolate cake for the party. Patrick unintentionally insults her by calling the cake "Delicious Death." Dora dies after ingesting poisoned aspirin, which may have been tampered with at her birthday party.

Chapters 17–20
The authorities fear that another attempt will be made on Miss Blacklock's life, and the situation becomes more eerie because someone has removed every photograph of Sonia Goedler from Miss

Blacklock's album. Craddock continues to suspect Phillipa, and questions her regarding the death of her husband, as well as about the supposed conversation with Scherz. Miss Hinchcliffe and Miss Murgatroyd argue over the identity of the killer, and Miss Murgatroyd realizes that her housemate was missing from the room at the time of the killing. Later, as Miss Murgatroyd dries her clothes, someone strangles her.

Chapters 21–23
Miss Marple drops out of sight, and Craddock fears that she is in danger. When she reappears, she has startling information for the authorities regarding the murders, the identity of the murderer, and Miss Blacklock. The police learn that Mitzi did have reason to fear the murderer, not them, because she had very damaging information.

Epilogue
In a brief aside, the author shows Edward Swettenham refusing someone's offer of a copy of the *Gazette,* because the article in that paper had created the entire incident.

CRIME NOTES
Two murders occur in the novel. The first victim is shot to death, the second is strangled.

Murder Is Easy   Mystery novel.

The novel concerns the often-hidden evil of the small town, and offers a classic example of the author's fare. The plot centers on the efforts of a retired policeman, recently returned to England from India, to uncover a series of murders in a tranquil English village.

PUBLISHING AND DRAMATIZATION
HISTORY
The novel was published in 1939 by William Collins Sons and Company, Ltd., in London, and by Dodd, Mead and Company in New York.

The novel was adapted for American television by David L. Wolper and Stan Margulies in 1982, and broadcast on the CBS network program, "Saturday Night at the Movies."

CHARACTERS
Mr. ABBOT, Mrs. ANSTRUTH, Superintendent BATTLE, Harry CARTER, Lucy CARTER, Miss CHURCH,

Bridget CONWAY, Lord EASTERFIELD, Mr. ELLS-
WORTHY, Luke FITZWILLIAM, Lavinia FULLERTON,
Amy GIBBS, Major HORTON, Mrs. Lydia HORTON,
Mrs. Jessie Rose HUMBLEBY, Dr. John Ward HUM-
BLEBY, Rose HUMBLEBY, Mr. JONES, Jimmy LOR-
RIMER, Sir William OSSINGTON, Mrs. PIERCE (2),
Tommy PIERCE, Mr. RIVERS, Doctor Geoffrey
THOMAS, Alfred WAKE, Honoria WAYNFLETE

PLOT SYNOPSIS
Chapters 1–3
Luke Fitzwilliam, just retired from a police career in
Asia, meets Mrs. Fullerton on her way to Scotland
Yard to report four murders in the quiet village of
Wychwood. When he reads in the next day's paper
that she is a hit-and-run accident victim, he decides
to investigate the murders. Presenting himself as a
writer, he arranges to live in the village and to pose
as the cousin of Bridget Conway. After his arrival,
Luke learns that still another village resident has
died.

Chapters 4–6
Luke decides to link the deaths and village burial
customs as the theme for his imaginary book.
Bridget introduces him to the vicar, who tells him
about the death of Tommy Pierce, who fell from a
ladder while washing windows, and Amy Gibbs, who
mistakenly swallowed paint instead of cough syrup.
Luke talks with Mr. Abbot, an attorney who employed Tommy Pierce, and Miss Waynflete, who employed Amy, and learns that Major Horton's wife
died of acute gastritis a year before. After spending
time with Luke, Bridget asks him what he is really
doing in Wychwood, and he admits that he is investigating the deaths.

Chapters 7–9
Luke develops possible theories for the murders, but
none satisfy him. He visits Dr. Thomas on the pretext of needing treatment for his knee, and brings up
the deaths, which the doctor does not view as murders. When Luke speaks with the mother of Tommy
Pierce, he learns that her son was dismissed by Mr.
Abbot for reading a private letter out loud. She also
tells him that Abbott quarreled with two others who
died.

Chapters 10–12
Luke learns from Bridget that Mr. Ellsworthy is a
member of a witches' coven, in whose ceremonies

Tommy Pierce once participated. Luke acquaints
himself with other residents, and he meets widower
Major Horton, who praises his dead wife highly. At
a party, Luke learns that Bridget is engaged to the
wealthy, older landowner, Lord Easterfield, and plans
to marry him for financial reasons. Luke tells her that
he loves her and wants to marry her, but she finds
his suggestion humorous.

Chapters 13–15
Luke determines that Miss Waynflete can be very
useful, so he tells her that he is a private investigator.
She claims that Amy was murdered, but she has no
ideas as to who committed the murder. She also
mentions that she had once been engaged to marry
Lord Easterfield. When Luke speaks with Miss
Church, Amy's aunt, he learns that she suspects foul
play in her niece's death. After reviewing all of his
clues, Luke creates a list of suspects, but he realizes
that he lacks evidence.

Chapters 16–18
Luke continues to talk with people, and Miss Waynflete warns him not to reveal his identity to too many
people. Easterfield is upset when Bridget tells him
about the activities of Ellsworthy and his friends in
Witches' Meadows, and he threatens to expose them
in his paper. Luke seizes the opportunity of Ellsworthy's absence to search his home, and finds evidence showing that Ellsworthy had an interest in two
of the victims. The village is shocked when the body
of the chauffeur Rivers is found, only a short while
after being dismissed by Easterfield for drinking and
taking the car without permission. Luke shares his
concerns with Dr. Thomas, who still refuses to consider that the deaths were murder.

Chapters 19–21
Sir William Ossington of Scotland Yard speaks with
Luke about the murders, and tells him that a witness
identified Easterfield's Rolls Royce and license plate
as the car that killed Miss Fullerton, despite the
chauffeur's contention that he was parked outside
Boomington House waiting for his lordship. The
two conclude that Easterfield may be the murderer,
and Luke visits Miss Waynflete to learn why she
broke off her engagement. She tells him that Easterfield wrung the neck of her canary, thus frightening
her with his temper. Bridget falls in love with Luke,
and she tells Easterfield, who threatens that they will

have to pay for their deception. A frightened Luke informs Bridget of his suspicions, but she cannot believe that Easterfield is the murderer.

Chapters 22–24
Bridget stays with Miss Waynflete and has tea, but danger lurks nearby. Several village members express suspicions regarding the murderer's identity, and Luke's suspicions of one individual are confirmed. As he and Superintendent Battle race to apprehend the murderer, Bridget fights for her life. The authorities arrive in time, and save her. After the person responsible for the deaths is led away, Bridget and Luke begin to plan their life together.

CRIME NOTES
Five murders occur before the novel opens, and two occur during the course of the novel. Of the first five, one victim dies from arsenic poisoning, a second is pushed off a cliff, a third is pushed from a building, a fourth victim ingests oxalic acid and a fifth dies of septicemia, after the scratch of a rusty nail turns septic. During the course of action in the novel, one victim is run over with a car and a second is hit on the head with part of a lamppost.

Murder Most Foul   Film released in 1965 by Metro-Goldwyn-Mayer. The movie is based on the 1952 novel, MRS. MCGINTY'S DEAD, but Hercule POIROT in the novel has been replaced by Miss Jane MARPLE in the movie.

CAST
The cast consists of Margaret Rutherford as Miss Marple, as well as Francesca Annis, James Bolam, Anne Cruikshank, Stringer Davis, Megs Jenkins, Ralph Michael, Ron Moody, Dennis Price, Terry Scott, Allison Seebohm and Charles Tingwell.

CHANGES FROM THE ORIGINAL TEXT
The adaptation, written by David Pursall and Jack Seddon, not only changed the title to one the author had identified as a "rotten" title for a mystery story in her own MR. EASTWOOD'S ADVENTURE, but also changed the detective from Poirot to Marple. Rather than being approached by the investigating detective from Scotland Yard, who has doubts about a convicted murderer's guilt (Poirot's experience in the novel), Miss Marple is a juror in a murder trial, and

Margaret Rutherford stars as Miss Marple in the 1965 *Murder Most Foul.* (Photo courtesy of The Museum of Modern Art, Film Stills Archive)

refuses to accept the guilty verdict for the man accused of murdering a blackmailing actress. The film focuses on her investigation of the backstage activities of a third-rate repertory company.

PRODUCTION NOTES
The author was horrified at the extent to which the original novel had been modified.

Murder of Roger Ackroyd, The   Mystery novel.

The novel is the most controversial of the author's many novels—even her locked-room murders—because of her choice of murderer, which broke the rules of traditional mystery writing. The plot centers on the efforts of Hercule POIROT, now retired from detection for a year and cultivating marrows in King's Abbot, to discover the murderer of local squire Roger Ackroyd.

PUBLISHING AND DRAMATIZATION HISTORY
The novel was published in 1926 by William Collins Sons and Company, Ltd., in London, and by Dodd, Mead and Company in New York.

The novel was adapted for the stage as the play *Alibi*, opening at the Prince of Wales' Theatre in London on May 15, 1928, starring Charles Laughton as Hercule Poirot. Laughton also starred in the 1932 American stage production, retitled *The Fatal Alibi*. In 1931, the film *Alibi* was produced by Twickenham Studios in England, and starred Austin Trevor as Hercule Poirot.

CHARACTERS
Mrs. Cecil ACKROYD, Flora ACKROYD, Roger ACKROYD, Ursula BOURNE, Major Hector BLUNT, Colonel CARTER, Mrs. FERRARS, Mrs. Richard FOLLIOTT, Miss GANETT, Mr. HAMMOND, Charles KENT, PARKER, Captain Ralph PATON, Hercule Poirot, Inspector Denis RAGLAN, Geoffrey RAYMOND, Miss RUSSELL, Caroline SHEPPARD, Dr. James SHEPPARD

PLOT SYNOPSIS
Chapters 1–3
Dr. Sheppard's patient, Mrs. Ferrars, dies of an overdose of veronal, an act which his sister Caroline contends is in remorse, for the village believes that Mrs. Ferrars poisoned her husband with arsenic. Villagers had expected Mrs. Ferrars and Roger Ackroyd to marry, but Roger had had reservations. The doctor speaks with his neighbor, the celebrated Hercule Poirot, who is now retired, and the two discuss the engagement between Ackroyd's niece, Flora, and his stepson, Ralph Paton. Caroline claims that she overheard Paton tell Flora that his stepfather intends to cut off his income, and that Paton observed that he would be a very wealthy man if Ackroyd died.

Chapters 4–6
At dinner, Flora announces her engagement; then Roger speaks with the doctor in private. He states that Mrs. Ferrars did poison her husband and that she was being blackmailed, although she had refused to reveal to him the name of the blackmailer. The doctor receives a telephone call at 10:15 P.M., telling him that Ackroyd is dead. When Sheppard arrives at Fernly Hall, the butler claims that he did not call, and assumes that Ackroyd is still in his study. They break down the door, locked from the inside, and discover Ackroyd stabbed to death with an antique knife from his own collection. Aside from the doctor's sighting of a stranger at the front gate at 9 P.M. and the butler's contention that he heard Ackroyd arguing with someone about blackmail, the police have no clues.

Chapters 7–9
Flora asks Poirot to investigate the murder because she fears that Paton will be accused. The detective

agrees, and asks the butler to tell him exactly where everything was in the room when he and the doctor broke in. The police learn that the call to Dr. Sheppard came from the train station, and a witness reports seeing Paton enter the gate of Fernly Hall near the estimated time of death. Poirot overhears Flora tell Major Blunt that Ackroyd left her twenty thousand pounds, making her financially independent.

Chapters 10–12
Poirot learns from the Ackroyd family lawyer that Ralph has inherited a sizable fortune. Delving further into the investigation, Poirot theorizes that the murderer probably wore gloves and pressed the dead man's fingers onto the murder weapon to leave his prints. While the authorities look for the victim's stepson, Flora's mother expresses her happiness that the engagement was not formally announced.

Chapters 13–15
Despite the contention of authorities that Paton has the motives to commit murder, Poirot believes that he has too many motives, and is probably innocent. Mrs. Ackroyd confesses to the doctor that she had been caught by the maid a few days earlier looking through Ackroyd's will. She is desperate for money to cover her large bills. The victim's secretary admits that he owes money and welcomes the five-hundred-pounds bequest.

Chapters 16–18
Poirot locates a ring in the pond inscribed "R. March 13," and he speculates that either Roger Ackroyd or his stepson had already married. A joint funeral is held for Ackroyd and Mrs. Ferrars. Afterward, Mrs. Ferrars' lawyer discovers that she paid out twenty thousand pounds in blackmail money in one year, and the authorities learn that the butler had blackmailed his previous employer and had considered blackmailing Ackroyd. Kent is questioned, and he tells authorities that he left Fernly Hall by 9:25 and went to the Dog and Whistle pub. Poirot learns that Major Blunt is really in love with Flora, and he tells Blunt to reveal his feelings.

Chapters 20–22
Miss Russell admits that Charles Kent is her son and that is why he was at Fernly Hall. He is a drug addict and an alcoholic, and he contacted her for money. Poirot learns that Ursula Bourne and Ralph Paton

were secretly married and that he had had to hide the marriage because Ackroyd would have disinherited him for marrying a penniless woman. The detective also learns that Ackroyd had been pressuring Paton to marry Flora, while Ursula had been pressuring Paton to reveal their marriage.

Chapters 23–25
Poirot meets with all of the suspects, then announces the marriage between Ursula and Paton. He also tells the assembled group that Parker had heard Ackroyd's voice on the dictaphone on the night of the murder. Poirot tells them that the murderer is in the room, and that Captain Raglan will know who it is in the morning.

Chapters 26–27
Poirot reveals the identity of the murderer, who also blackmailed Mrs. Ferrars and pushed her into committing suicide. Poirot details the events of the night of the murder, and explains how the murderer succeeded. At the end, the murderer commits suicide.

CRIME NOTES
In her *An Autobiography,* the author credited both her brother-in-law, James Watt, and Lord Louis Mountbatten for the idea of the unusual choice of murderer. In 1924, Mountbatten (the uncle of Prince Philip, Duke of Edinburgh) was then a young naval officer, who wrote to the author and suggested his idea.

The only murder that occurs in this novel is a fatal stabbing, carried out with an antique knife.

Murder on the Links   Mystery novel.

The novel marks the first meeting of Captain Arthur HASTINGS and his future wife. The plot centers on the efforts of Hercule POIROT to solve a robbery-murder that might have been staged by a member of the household.

PUBLISHING AND DRAMATIZATION HISTORY
The novel was published in 1923 by John Lane in London, and by Dodd, Mead and Company in New York.

The novel has not been adapted for stage or screen.

CHARACTERS
Joseph AARONS, Francoise ARRICHET, Lucien BEX, Madame DAUBREUIL, Marthe DAUBREUIL, Bella DUVEEN, Monsieur GIRAUD, Captain Arthur Hastings, Dulcie Duveen HASTINGS, M. HAUTET, Hercule Poirot, Mrs. RENAULD, Jack RENAULD, Paul T. RENAULD, Gabriel STONOR

PLOT SYNOPSIS
Chapters 1–3
Returning by train from Paris, Captain Hastings feels an attraction for a heavily made-up young woman who identifies herself as "Cinderella." After they part, he joins Poirot in an attempt to assist Paul T. Renauld, but Renauld is already dead. The victim had been abducted from his house, stabbed, and placed face down in an open grave. Mrs. Renauld had been bound and gagged, and left in the house.

Chapters 4–6
The investigating officer gives Poirot a letter found in the dead man's overcoat and written by an English girl named Bella, stating that she would kill any woman who came between them. Poirot later finds a portion of a pink bank check with the name "Duveen" on it. Mrs. Renauld tells the investigators that two men entered their bedroom. One bound and gagged the couple, while the second held a little dagger to her husband's heart and ordered him to go into the next room. She claims that the men spoke "bastard Spanish." A search of the grounds turns up a spade, gloves and a lead pipe.

Chapters 7–9
Investigators learn that Madame Daubreuil has deposited nearly four thousand pounds in her bank account since the arrival of Mr. Renauld. When questioned, she expresses indignation and asks the inspector to leave. Meanwhile, Hastings meets the young woman from the train, who arrives at the murder scene and requests a tour. As no new clues emerge, Poirot ponders the fact that the murderers did not have their own weapons, but used the spade and gloves already on the premises and the paper knife that was in the bedroom.

Chapters 10–12
Poirot learns that Madame Daubreuil was blackmailing Renauld. When the victim's son, Jack, returns, he admits that he and his father fought before he left

because of his desire to marry Marthe Daubreuil. The authorities discover that the murder weapon has disappeared, and Hastings may be at fault because he left the shed unlocked for twenty minutes while he showed "Cinderella" around. Poirot determines that Mrs. Renauld is lying about the time the crime took place, as well as about the two men; yet he believes that she really did love her husband.

Chapters 13–15

As the investigation continues, Hastings attempts to locate his "Cinderella," but she has given hime a false address. At the same time, Poirot travels to Paris to locate a photograph of a murderess named Madame Beroldy, whom he believes to be Madame Daubreuil. Another murder occurs, and the second victim is stabbed with the same dagger. Investigators determine that the man has been dead for forty-eight hours. When Poirot returns from Paris, he examines the second victim and deduces that he died from an epileptic fit and was stabbed after he died.

Chapters 16–18

Poirot reviews the Beroldy case, and learns that the wife in that case claimed that two Russian men bound and gagged the couple, then killed the husband. In that case, Madame Beroldy had a lover, Georges Conneau, whom the police accused of collaborating with the wife in murder. On the stand, Madame Beroldy convinced the jury that Georges alone committed the murders and that she had loved her husband very much, so she was acquitted. Poirot tells Hastings that Madame has no motive in the current crime, but he believes that Jack dug the grave. He sends Jack on an errand to the train station to get him out of the way, then interviews Marthe, who identifies the second victim as a tramp whom she had seen speaking with Mr. Renauld on the morning of the murder. Despite Poirot's protests, the authorities arrest Jack.

Chapters 19–21

Poirot learns that Bella Duveen was in love with Jack, and her letter was found in his overcoat, not his father's. In his haste to leave the house, he had grabbed the wrong overcoat. She had visited Mr. Renauld that night to plead with him, but he wrote her a check, which she tore up. Poirot also reveals that Paul Renauld was really Georges Conneau, and Madame Daubreuil had been blackmailing him for this

reason. When the tramp died of an epileptic fit at his gate, Mr. Renauld decided to fake his own death, so he dressed the tramp in his clothes, stabbed the body and disfigured the face with a lead pipe. When he went to bury the body, someone stabbed him.

Chapters 22–26

When Hastings finds Bella, she claims that she stabbed Renauld by mistake, thinking that she was stabbing Jack. The love-struck Hastings says that he doesn't care because he loves her, and she escapes while he creates an alibi for her. Poirot informs Hastings that there were three knives, not two, and that Jack still has one. Jack lies in court about his whereabouts on the night of the murder, but porters prove him wrong. He is fortunate that Dulcie, posing as sister Bella, appears and clears his name. Later, Dulcie, the real "Cinderella," writes to Hastings and explains that she was only protecting her twin sister.

Chapters 27–28

On the advice of Poirot, Mrs. Renauld pretends to disinherit Jack and tells him to leave the house. The real murderer appears and tries to kill Mrs. Renauld, but Poirot and Hastings are waiting. In the struggle which follows, the murderer falls to the ground and is killed by a blow to the head. As the novel ends, a wedding appears to be imminent for Hastings and Dulcie.

CRIME NOTES

The sole murder which occurs in this novel is the result of a stab wound.

Murder on the Nile   Mystery play.
    See DEATH ON THE NILE (2).

Murder on the Orient Express (1)   Mystery novel.

The novel is based upon actual events that occurred in 1929 and 1932. The plot centers on Hercule POIROT's efforts to discover the murderer of an American businessman while snowbound on the Orient Express.

PUBLISHING AND DRAMATIZATION HISTORY

The novel was published in 1934 by William Collins Sons and Company, Ltd., in London, and, under the title, *Murder in the Calais Coach*, by Dodd, Mead and Company in New York.

The novel was adapted in 1974 by EMI into a celebrity-studded film, starring Albert Finney as Hercule Poirot.

CHARACTERS
Countess Helena Maria ANDRENYI, Count Rudolph ANDRENYI, Colonel ARBUTHNOT, M. BOUC, Dr. CONSTANTINE, Mary DEBENHAM, Princess DRAGO-MIROFF, Lieutenant DUBOSC, Antonio FOSCARELLI, Cyrus HARDMAN, Mrs. HUBBARD, Hector MacQUEEN, Edward Henry MASTERMAN, Pierre MICHEL, Greta OHLSSON, Hercule Poirot, Mr. RATCHETT, Hildegarde SCHMIDT

PLOT SYNOPSIS
Part 1: Chapters 1–3
Hercule Poirot has just completed a successful case in Syria, and he returns to his hotel to learn that he is wanted immediately in London. He meets his friend M. Bouc, director of the train line, and they both board the Orient Express. The train is full, and Poirot is initially unable to obtain a sleeper. When a Mr. Harris fails to appear, Poirot is assigned his upper berth and shares the compartment with Hector MacQueen, secretary to the American philanthropist, Samuel Edward Ratchett, who tries to hire Poirot to serve as his bodyguard.

Chapters 4–5
Mrs. Hubbard confides to Poirot that she thinks Ratchett is a murderer. Later that evening, Poirot hears a loud groan emerging from Ratchett's compartment and a voice responding "It is nothing" in French to the conductor's concerned inquiry. When the detective rings for water the next morning, the conductor informs him that the train has run into a snowdrift and will be delayed. Poirot meets M. Bouc for breakfast, who reveals that Ratchett has been "found dead in his berth!" Dr. Constantine establishes the death at 1:00 A.M., and tells officials that the victim had twelve stab wounds. M. Bouc insists that Poirot take the case.

Chapters 6–7
Poirot questions MacQueen, who tells him that Ratchett had received threatening letters and points out that the victim knew no foreign language. Constantine and Poirot examine the body, which has

wounds varying in size and angle, appearing to have been thrust by the right as well as the left hand. Constantine observes that the condition of the body means that the man may have been already dead before he was stabbed. Poirot finds various clues, including a partially burned paper bearing the following words: "MEMBER LITTLE DAISY ARMSTRONG." The clues lead Poirot to believe that Ratchett was the kidnapper of Daisy Armstrong, an American child who was held for a $200,000 ransom and then found dead. The tragedy had destroyed numerous lives, but the killer, Cassetti, had been released on a technicality. He then changed his name to Ratchett and left America.

Part 2: Chapters 1–3
Poirot questions Pierre Michel, the conductor, who remembers Ratchett calling out. He tells the detective what several other passengers were doing at the time. Poirot questions MacQueen and tells him Ratchett's true identity; then he learns that Ratchett's valet was instructed always to carry a sleeping potion when his employer traveled by train. Masterman claims to have shared his compartment with an Italian man who annoyed him, and to have remained awake with a toothache until four in the morning.

Chapters 4–6
As other travelers are interviewed, Poirot finds that several of them have been associated with the Armstrong family. Mrs. Hubbard claims that she awoke to find a man in her room, and she produces a button from a conductor's uniform as proof. Her maid, Greta Ohlsson, was the last to see the victim alive as she accidentally opened his compartment door and saw him reading a book. The conductor proves that the button does not come from his uniform.

Chapters 7–11
Poirot questions the rest of the passengers, noting whether any smoke a pipe, because a pipe cleaner was found near the victim. He learns that most of the passengers claim to have seen a woman in a scarlet kimono in the corridor, but no one can identify her. Cyrus Hardman, Ratchett's bodyguard, claims not to have known that Ratchett was Cassetti.

Chapters 12–15
Another passenger claims to have seen an unfamiliar conductor in the corridor, and her description

matches Hardman's description of Ratchett's stalker. As Poirot begins to believe that the man described does not exist, Mrs. Hubbard finds the murder weapon in her sponge bag. Poirot first calms down Mrs. Hubbard, then searches through the rest of her luggage. The detective then searches the luggage of the other passengers, and he finds the conductor's uniform in Hildegarde Schmidt's luggage. The pocket of the uniform contains a pass key. Poirot finds the kimono in his own compartment while looking for cigarettes.

Part 3: Chapters 1–7
Poirot realizes that Ratchett spoke no languages other than English, so his murderer must have been the one who answered through the compartment door. He is also puzzled by slight discrepancies among statements by the passengers, and suspects that someone on the train is closely connected with the Armstrong family. His suspicions are proved true as he reviews the evidence with the passengers.

Chapter 8
With the passengers assembled, Poirot tells them that Ratchett was alive until twenty-three minutes to one, but lying in his bed in a drugged state until he was stabbed. The detective solves the crime, but decides to tell the Yugoslavian police that it was a Mafia killing by a stranger who escaped.

CRIME NOTES
The novel is based in part upon the kidnapping of the Lindbergh baby in the United States in 1932, when Charles and Anne Morrow Lindbergh paid a ransom of $50,000, but the baby was murdered nonetheless. The second incident that influenced the plot occurred in 1929, when the Orient Express train crossed the Turkish border and was snowbound for six days.

The sole murder victim in the novel dies of multiple stab wounds.

Murder on the Orient Express (2) Film produced in 1974 by EMI Films. The movie is based on the 1934 novel of the same name.

CAST
The cast consists of Albert Finney as Hercule POIROT, as well as Lauren Bacall, Martin Balsam, Ingrid Bergman, Jacqueline Bisset, Colin Blakely, Jean-

Pierre Cassel, Sean Connery, George Coulouris, John Gielgud, Wendy Hiller, Anthony Perkins, Denis Quilley, Vanessa Redgrave, Rachel Roberts, Richard Widmark and Michael York.

CHANGES FROM THE ORIGINAL TEXT
The adaptation, written by Paul Dehn, remained very close to the original text.

PRODUCTION NOTES
The author was reluctant to allow any more films to be made of her work, and it took the intervention of Lord Louis Mountbatten, former Viceroy to India and uncle to Prince Philip, Duke of Edinburgh, to convince her to take one more chance. The film was lavishly costumed, and real Orient Express cars were borrowed to provide authenticity. The film premiere was held in London, with Queen Elizabeth in attendance. This event marked the final public event of Agatha Christie's life.

The film was a huge box office and critical success, winning the British Film Awards for Best Picture, Best Actor and Best Supporting Actress. In the U.S., the film earned six Academy Award nominations, but won only one, awarded to Ingrid Bergman for Best Supporting Actress.

Murder She Said Film released in 1962 by Metro-Goldwyn-Mayer. The movie is based on the 1957 novel, 4.50 FROM PADDINGTON, by Agatha Christie.

CAST
The cast consists of Margaret RUTHERFORD as Miss Jane MARPLE, as well as Gerald Cross, Stringer Davis, Michael Golden, Joan Hickson, Ronald Howard, James Robertson Justice, Arthur Kennedy, Muriel Pavlow, Conrad Phillips, Ronnie Raymond, Charles Tingwell and Thorley Walters.

CHANGES FROM THE ORIGINAL TEXT
The adaptation, written by David Pursall and Jack Seddon, eliminates the character of Elspeth McGILLI-CUDDY as witness to the murder on a passing train. Instead, Miss MARPLE is the eyewitness who then becomes embroiled in the investigation.

The film was the first of four films made from the author's works to star Margaret Rutherford as Miss Marple.

PRODUCTION NOTES
The film title was changed from that of both 4.50 FROM PADDINGTON, the British title, and WHAT MRS. McGILLICUDDY SAW!, the American title, to attract audiences. When asked about the film, Agatha Christie claimed not to be disappointed by the movie, because she had expected the worst all along.

Murder with Mirrors   See THEY DO IT WITH MIRRORS.

Murdoch, Cynthia   A resident at Styles Court through the good graces of Emily INGLETHORPE, she works in the Red Cross Hospital pharmacy in THE MYSTERIOUS AFFAIR AT STYLES.

Murgatroyd, Mrs.   A former caretaker who hurls threats when told she must leave the ruined house that is to be torn down in "THE CASE OF THE CARETAKER."

Murgatroyd, Amy   A foolish, fat, amiable woman with a messy head of gray curly hair, she eagerly responds to a newspaper advertisement inviting people to witness a murder in A MURDER IS ANNOUNCED. Once at the site of Little Paddocks, she becomes a victim.

Murray, Dr.   Resident physician in the nursing home where Elizabeth MOODY dies in BY THE PRICKING OF MY THUMBS, he performs an autopsy that reveals morphine poisoning.

Mysterious Affair at Styles, The   Mystery novel.

The novel was Agatha Christie's first published work, and it marked the first appearance of Hercule POIROT. Written in 1916, *The Mysterious Affair at Styles* was not published until five years later, after six publishing houses had rejected it. Bodley Head did publish it, but held the manuscript for eighteen months before making its final decision. The plot centers on what developed into a familiar Christie pattern: murder by poison within a family setting.

PUBLISHING AND DRAMATIZATION HISTORY
The Mysterious Affair at Styles was published in 1921 by Bodley Head in London and New York.

The novel was adapted for television in 1990 by London Weekend Television in Britain, and was also shown on the Public Broadcasting Service in the U.S.

CHARACTERS
Dr. BAUERSTEIN, John CAVENDISH, Lawrence CAVENDISH, Mary CAVENDISH, Mr. DENBY, Captain Arthur HASTINGS, Sir Ernest HEAVYWEATHER, Evelyn HOWARD, Alfred INGLETHORPE, Emily Agnes INGLETHORPE, Chief Inspector JAPP, MANNING, Cynthia MURDOCH, Hercule Poirot, Mrs. RAIKES, Superintendent SUMMERHAYE

PLOT SYNOPSIS
Chapter 1
After spending several months in a convalescent home recuperating from war injuries, Captain Hastings meets an old friend, John Cavendish, and receives an invitation to Styles, the family estate. He learns that John's inheritance has been threatened because his stepmother has married a sinister-looking, much-younger man upon whom she dotes. Within hours of his arrival, Hastings feels "a premonition of approaching evil."

Chapter 2
While visiting the dispensary in town where Cynthia Murdoch works, Hastings meets Hercule Poirot, whom he knew from Belgium during the war. Poirot is part of a group of displaced Belgian refugees helped to relocate by Mrs. Inglethorpe. The two agree to meet in a few days.

Chapter 3
Tragedy strikes in the middle of the night when Mrs. Inglethorpe becomes ill, but her locked bedroom door delays help. When family members break in, they find her convulsive and near death. Dr. Bauerstein suspects poison, and Hastings locates a description of strychnine poisoning in a medical book. The dying woman calls out her husband's name.

Chapters 4–5
The suspicion of poison leads Hastings to consult Poirot, who examines the dead woman's room, then interviews the parlourmaid. She claims to have overheard a quarrel between the victim and her husband the day before. When the Cavendish family lawyer

arrives, Poirot surprises everyone by indicating that the victim had made a new will on the day she died, and the gardener, Manning, was one of the witnesses. Although the weight of the evidence seems to be against Alfred Inglethorpe, Poirot proceeds cautiously.

Chapters 6–7
Evidence given at the inquest points strongly to Alfred as the murderer, a conclusion with which Poirot strongly disagrees. When two Scotland Yard men present at the inquest seek to arrest Alfred, Poirot forestalls them because the evidence is too clear-cut and too solid. Poirot points out that each of the witnesses seemed to have slanted the testimony. When all are assembled, he reveals the secret that Alfred has sought to hide, one which proves that he could not have purchased the poison at the hour stated.

Chapters 8–9
Poirot's quick thinking in preventing a false arrest earns him the appreciation of Inspector Japp and Superintendent Summerhaye, and the search for the murderer continues. Poirot questions members of the family and asks that Evelyn Howard, the late Mrs. Inglethorpe's companion, be his ally despite her vehement assertion that Alfred is guilty. After overhearing a quarrel between John and Mary Cavendish over Mary's obsession with Dr. Bauerstein, Hastings transfers his suspicion to the doctor. He is not surprised when he learns that Bauerstein has been arrested.

Chapters 10–11
Dr. Bauerstein is arrested for espionage, not murder, for acting as a spy for Germany. The attention of the authorities turns to the victim's stepsons, and Poirot discovers that a black wig had been sent to Styles only days before the murder. John Cavendish is arrested for the murder and put on trial, but Poirot remains unsatisfied.

Chapters 12–13
Poirot calls together the members of the household to put forth his clues and forces the real murderer to show his hand. In a clever twist, the detective not only brings the killer to justice, but also reunites an estranged husband and wife, and sets the stage for another marriage.

CRIME NOTES
The method of murder is one of slow poisoning, and depends upon a toxic quantity of strychnine settling at the bottom of a bottle to make the final dose lethal.

Mysterious Mr. Quin, The Mystery short story collection.

The twelve stories all feature the mysterious Mr. Harley QUIN, who appears unexpectedly and disappears as suddenly, and his old friend Mr. SATTERTHWAITE, a bachelor in his sixties who has spent his life as a spectator, not a participant. The author considered these stories to be her favorite, and observes in AN AUTOBIOGRAPHY that Mr. Quin was a carryover from her Harlequin and Columbine poems, contained in THE ROAD OF DREAMS, and that both he and "little Mr. Satterthwaite" became favorite characters. In the stories, the two men do not function as a typical detection team; rather, Mr. Quin, dressed in black, mysteriously appears and light cast upon him produces a surreal, colorful image. Through his carefully worded questions and observations, he provides Mr. Satterthwaite with insight that leads to the solution of the mysteries.

PUBLISHING AND DRAMATIZATION HISTORY
The Mysterious Mr. Quin was first published in 1930 by William Collins Sons and Company, Ltd., in London, and by Dodd, Mead and Company in New York. The first story of the collection, "THE COMING OF MR. QUIN," was the first work by Agatha Christie to be made into a movie in Britain. It was adapted into a movie entitled THE PASSING OF MR. QUINN [*sic*] and released in 1928.

The book is dedicated by the author "To Harlequin, The Invisible," which makes it unique; no other Christie book is dedicated to a character.

TITLES IN THE COLLECTION
The Mysterious Mr. Quin contains the following short stories: "The Coming of Mr. Quin," "THE SHADOW ON THE GLASS," "AT THE 'BELLS AND MOTLEY,' " "THE SIGN IN THE SKY," "THE SOUL OF THE CROUPIER," "THE WORLD'S END," "THE VOICE IN THE DARK," "THE FACE OF HELEN," "THE DEAD HARLEQUIN," "THE BIRD WITH THE BROKEN WING," "THE MAN FROM THE SEA" and "HARLEQUIN'S LANE."

"Mystery of Hunter's Lodge, The" Mystery short story.

The plot centers on a murder which Hercule POIROT, too ill to investigate, must solve at second hand, based on information wired to him by Captain Arthur HASTINGS.

PUBLISHING AND DRAMATIZATION HISTORY

The story appeared in the short story collection, POIROT INVESTIGATES, published in 1924 by John Lane in London, and in 1925 by Dodd, Mead and Company in New York.

The story was adapted for television in 1991 by London Weekend Television in Britain, and was also shown on the Public Broadcasting Service in the U.S.

CHARACTERS

Captain A. Hastings, Roger HAVERING, Zoe HAVERING, Inspector James JAPP, Harrington PACE, Hercule Poirot

PLOT SYNOPSIS

The story concerns the murder of a wealthy American, Harrington Pace, at the home of his dissipated, debt-ridden nephew, Roger Havering. Called by Roger to find his uncle's killer, Poirot is too ill with influenza to accept. He sends Captain Hastings in his place, with the demand that Hastings send frequent telegrams to update Poirot on the case. Although not at the site of the crime, the detective dismisses claims that a black-bearded stranger has worked in collusion with the lodge housekeeper. He correctly identifies the murderer, but a lack of evidence prevents a conviction for the crime.

CRIME NOTES

The murder is committed by a gunshot to the back of the victim's head.

"Mystery of the Baghdad Chest, The" Mystery short story.

The plot centers on the murder of a man whose dead body lies in a trunk in the very room where his wife and friends are holding a dance party. The plot is repeated in a slightly expanded version in "THE MYSTERY OF THE SPANISH CHEST."

PUBLISHING AND DRAMATIZATION HISTORY

The story appeared in the short story collection, THE REGATTA MYSTERY AND OTHER STORIES, in 1939 by Dodd, Mead and Company in New York.

The story has not been adapted for stage or screen.

CHARACTERS

BURGOYNE, Lady CHATTERTON, Edward CLAYTON, Marguerita CLAYTON, Major CURTISS, Captain Arthur HASTINGS, Hercule POIROT, Major Jack RICH

PLOT SYNOPSIS

The story concerns a sensational murder case, which Poirot and Hastings first read about in the newspapers. They are later drawn into the case by a plea for help from the victim's wife. Marguerita Clayton admits that she no longer loved her husband, but she fervently asserts that the man she does love, Major Rich, is not the killer, even though the body was found in a trunk in his home. Even more grotesque, the party and dancing the evening before occurred in the same room as the trunk with its murdered contents. Hercule Poirot enters the investigation and learns that the victim had concealed himself to spy on his wife, and that he must have been double-crossed by his accomplice.

CRIME NOTES

The murder weapon in this story is a stiletto knife.

"Mystery of the Blue Jar, The" Mystery short story.

The plot centers on a mysterious Chinese jar and its connection with a murdered woman.

PUBLISHING AND DRAMATIZATION HISTORY

The story appeared in the short story collection, THE HOUND OF DEATH AND OTHER STORIES, published in 1933 by William Collins Sons and Company, Ltd., in London.

The story was adapted for television in 1982 by Thames Television in England, and was shown on Public Broadcasting Service in the United States.

CHARACTERS

Uncle GEORGE, Jack HARTINGTON, Dr. Ambrose LAVINGTON, Felice MARCHAUD, Mrs. TURNER

The Oriental jar holds a well-hidden secret for three people who seek to discover the source of a cry for help in "The Mystery of the Blue Jar." (Photo courtesy of Thames Television)

PLOT SYNOPSIS

The story concerns the attempts of avid golfer Jack Hartington to determine the source of and reason for the mysterious cries for help he hears every morning at the same hour while on the golf course. He speaks with the resident of the cottage from which the cries emanate, and learns that she has had unsettling dreams of a woman with a blue Chinese vase. Acting on the belief that the cries for help are from the ghost of the late Mrs. Turner, former resident of the cottage, Jack asks a psychic investigator to join him in spending a night at the house, a night which has startling results.

Mystery of the Blue Train, The Mystery novel.

The novel takes place on the elegant Blue Train, officially named the Calais-Paris-Nice Express, on which the wealthy travel to spend the winter season on the Riviera. The plot centers on the efforts of Hercule POIROT to identify the murderer of a millionaire's daughter and to solve the disappearance of her priceless Heart of Fire necklace on the Blue Train.

PUBLISHING AND DRAMATIZATION HISTORY

The novel was published in 1928 by William Collins Sons and Company, Ltd., in London, and by Dodd, Mead and Company in New York.

The novel has not been adapted for stage or screen.

CHARACTERS

Joseph AARONS, ALICE, Monsieur CARREGE, Monsieur CAUX, Comte Armand DE LA ROCHE, Olga DE-MIROFF, ELLEN (2), Charles "Chubby" EVANS, Mr. GOBY, Katherine GREY, Boris IVANOVITCH, Derek KETTERING, Ruth KETTERING, Major Richard KNIGHTON, Ada Beatrice MASON, Pierre MICHEL, MIRELLE, Demetrius PAPOPOLOUS, Zia PAPOPOLOUS, Hercule Poirot, The Honourable Lenox TAMPLIN, Viscountess Rosalie TAMPLIN, Rufus VAN ALDIN, Amelia VINER

PLOT SYNOPSIS
Chapters 1–5
The novel opens in a Paris apartment where a package is exchanged for money. An American leaves with the package. A man with white hair questions a passerby about the American, then goes to an antique shop to speak with the owner. His daughter listens at the keyhole, and believes that she hears something about rubies. Later, wealthy American Rufus Van Aldin gives his daughter the famous Heart of Fire rubies to ease her pain over her failing marriage. After she leaves, he contacts Mr. Goby and asks for a complete report on his soon-to-be former son-in-law, Derek Kettering, a titled but penniless English noble.

Chapters 6–10
Kettering visits his lover, dancer Mirelle, who tells him that she needs a man who has money. She points out that he will inherit millions if something happens to his wife Ruth. Meanwhile, in St. Mary Mead, Katherine Grey has just inherited a large sum of money from her former employer, despite efforts from the woman's relatives to contest the bequest. Katherine visits the attorney and arranges to give part of her inheritance to the relatives, then she visits a dressmaker with orders to remake her image. She later books a compartment on the Blue Train, and attracts the attention of Kettering. Before the trip, Van Aldin offers Kettering one thousand pounds to agree to a divorce, but Kettering refuses. Ruth Kettering has also booked a place on the train en route to meeting her lover, and she confides in Katherine while they travel.

Chapters 11–15

Ruth is found strangled on the Blue Train, and her scarlet morocco jewel case is missing. Hercule Poirot handles the investigation and questions other passengers, including Katherine, who will be staying with her cousin Lady Tamplin. Katherine is vaguely disturbed that she saw the same man on the train whom she had seen earlier at the Savoy and at Cook's office. She learns later that he is Ruth's husband. When Van Aldin learns of his daughter's death, Mr. Goby tells him that Kettering and Mirelle were also on the train, and that Ruth had sent her maid to Paris. Poirot learns of a letter from De La Roche, Ruth's former lover, in which he asks Ruth to write about the rubies and their legacy.

Chapters 16–20

Van Aldin tells Poirot that Kettering will inherit two million pounds, and informs the detective of his offer. Poirot questions De La Roche, who is surprised to hear that Ruth was murdered; and Ruth's maid claims that she did not see the man in the compartment. Kettering claims not to have seen Ruth for three weeks. He also decides to break off his relationship with Mirelle and to pursue Katherine. The ever-opportunistic Mirelle meets with De La Roche, and claims that Kettering confessed to her that he murdered Ruth. When Katherine speaks with Poirot, she tells him that she saw Kettering go into Ruth's train compartment, and she tells Van Aldin about her conversation with Ruth.

Chapters 21–25

Poirot informs Van Aldin that the police intercepted a package containing the rubies mailed by De La Roche to a newspaper shop in Paris. The detective tells the millionaire to keep this information a secret. He believes that De La Roche is a thief but not a murderer. Meanwhile, De La Roche attempts to blackmail Kettering for one hundred thousand francs, and claims to have proof of Kettering's guilt. When Mirelle confronts Kettering, she tells him that she wants him back, but he wants to marry Katherine.

Chapters 26–30

Kettering tells Katherine that he did go into his wife's compartment but found her sleeping, so he left. He confesses his love for her, but Knighton, Van Aldin's secretary, arrives and ruins the moment.

Later, Poirot and Knight visit Mirelle, who throws a tantrum about Kettering leaving her, but claims to know nothing about the rubies. She speaks with the authorities and tells them that she knew that Ruth was dead but she will not betray her lover. De La Roche's butler and housekeeper confirm Poirot's suspicions that their master had arrived a day earlier than claimed. Poirot asks Mirelle if she found what she was looking for when she went into Ruth's compartment.

Chapters 31–36

Poirot's friend, Joseph Aarons, tells him about a male impersonator named Kitty Kidd and also says that he saw Mirelle with a "Heart of Fire" ruby on a platinum chain around her neck. After meeting with Katherine, Poirot tells Van Aldin and Knighton that Kettering did not murder his wife. He explains that an actress impersonated Ruth to make it seem that she was alive longer than people knew. He also notes that Knighton is an imposter. Poirot identifies the murderer and wraps up the case, while a reformed Derek Kettering heads for St. Mary Mead to see Katherine.

An unhappy wife (Caroline Langrishe) is under suspicion when her husband is murdered in "The Mystery of the Spanish Chest." (Photo courtesy of London Weekend Television)

CRIME NOTES
The sole murder victim is strangled to death.

"Mystery of the Spanish Chest, The"   Mystery short story.

The plot centers on the murder of a man whose dead body lies in a trunk in the same room in which his wife and friends have a party and dance. The same plot exists in an early story, "THE MYSTERY OF THE BAGHDAD CHEST," but this version is longer, characters' names are spelled differently and several first names are changed.

PUBLISHING AND DRAMATIZATION
HISTORY
The story appeared in the short story collection, THE ADVENTURE OF THE CHRISTMAS PUDDING AND A SE-LECTION OF ENTRIES, published in 1960 by William Collins Sons and Company, Ltd., in London.

The story was adapted for television in 1991 by London Weekend Television in England, and was shown on the Public Broadcasting Service in the United States.

CHARACTERS
William BURGESS, Arnold CLAYTON, Margharita CLAYTON, Miss LEMON, Jack MCLAREN, Major Charles RICH, Jeremy (Jim) SPENCE, Linda SPENCE

PLOT SYNOPSIS
See "THE MYSTERY OF THE BAGHDAD CHEST."

N

Nadina   See GRUNBERG, ANITA.

Nancy   A scheming office worker in "THE CASE OF THE MIDDLE-AGED WIFE," she wore figure-revealing clothing and flashed her most dazzling smiles to attract her boss' attention.

Narracott, Inspector   A quiet and persistent man with a logical mind and a penchant for detail in THE SITTAFORD MYSTERY, he is the police inspector who investigates the Trevelyan murder case.

Narracott, Fred   The close-mouthed boat operator who transported the visitors from the mainland to Indian Island in AND THEN THERE WERE NONE.

Narracott, Gladys   A maid at the Jolly Roger Hotel in EVIL UNDER THE SUN who is asked to identify the owner of the empty pill bottle.

Nasby, Lord   A physically large man in THE MAN IN THE BROWN SUIT, he is also the extremely wealthy owner of the *Daily Budget* who assigns a reporter to cover the "Man in the Brown Suit" mystery.

Nash, Superintendent   Assigned to investigate the poison-pen cases in THE MOVING FINGER, he is a Criminal Investigation Department county superintendent whose straightforward manner and air of easy confidence make him especially effective in the case.

Naylor, Captain Humphrey   A suspect in the murder of Sir Reuben ASTWELL in "THE UNDER DOG," he had been cheated out of a share in an African gold mine by the victim. He stays at a nearby hotel on the night of the murder.

Naylor, Lily   See MARGRAVE, LILY.

Nazorkoff, Paula   See CAPELLI, BIANCA.

Neasdon, Dr.   The police surgeon in EVIL UNDER THE SUN who is called in to the Jolly Roger Hotel when Arlena MARSHALL is murdered.

Needheim, Helga   Possessed of a fascist world vision, she is a prominent endocrinologist in DESTINATION UNKNOWN who eagerly joins Mr. ARISTIDES' Brain Trust.

Neele, Chief Inspector   A member of Scotland Yard and an old friend of Hercule POIROT, he is assigned the Restarick case and handles the investigation into David BAKER's death in THIRD GIRL.

Neele, Inspector   A member of Scotland Yard in charge of investigating the murder of Rex FORTESCUE in A POCKET FULL OF RYE.

Neele, Nancy   The younger woman for whom Archibald CHRISTIE left his wife in 1926. Neele and Christie were married at St. George's Church in Hanover Square, London, and the two remained married until her death in 1959.

Neele, Teresa   The name under which Agatha Christie registered at the HYDROPATHIC HOTEL during her famous disappearance on December 3, 1926. (See DISAPPEARANCE OF AGATHA CHRISTIE.) She claimed to be a widow from Cape Town, South Africa.

Neilson, Dr.   A precise-thinking bureaucrat in DESTINATION UNKNOWN, he is the Deputy Director of the Brain Trust complex.

"Nemean Lion, The"   Mystery short story.

The plot centers on Hercule POIROT's efforts to retrieve a kidnapped Pekinese dog and to end a rash of such crimes.

PUBLISHING AND DRAMATIZATION HISTORY

The story appeared in the short story collection, THE LABOURS OF HERCULES, published in 1947 by William Collins Sons and Company, Ltd., in London, and by Dodd, Mead and Company in New York.

The story has not been adapted for stage or screen.

CHARACTERS

Miss Amy CARNABY, Emily CARNABY, GEORGES, Mrs. HARTE, Sir Joseph HOGGIN, Lady Milly HOGGIN, Miss Ellen KEBLE, Miss LEMON, Hercule Poirot, Mrs. SAMUELSON

PLOT SYNOPSIS

The story concerns a dognapping case, reluctantly undertaken by Hercule Poirot as he begins what he has decided will be his final twelve cases. Contacted by Sir Joseph Hoggin to identify the person who had taken and held for ransom his wife's Pekinese, Poirot at first views the case as beneath his talents. He becomes intrigued when he learns that other Pekinese dogs have been taken and ransomed. As the detective investigates, he learns that a ring of unlikely suspects has cleverly planned and carried out sixteen such dognappings. Poirot solves the crime and returns Sir Joseph's money, but he protects the identity of the perpetrator after extracting the promise that the crimes will cease.

CRIME NOTES

The story is a modern version of the first labor of the Greek mythological figure Hercules, whose task was to kill the lion of Nemea, a beast impervious to all weapons.

Nemesis   Mystery novel.

The novel is the last Miss MARPLE mystery written, but not the last published. That distinction belongs to SLEEPING MURDER, which was published in 1976, although it was written during World War II and then placed in a bank vault for over thirty years. The plot centers on the efforts of Miss Marple, given the name "Nemesis" by Mr. Jason RAFIEL in A CARIBBEAN MYSTERY, to earn a bequest of twenty thousand pounds from Rafiel by solving a crime for which he provides no clues in his will.

PUBLISHING AND DRAMATIZATION HISTORY

The novel was published in 1971 by William Collins Sons and Company, Ltd., in London, and by Dodd, Mead and Company in New York.

The novel was adapted for television in 1987 by the BBC, and was also shown on the Public Broadcasting Service in the U.S.

CHARACTERS

Cherry BAKER, Miss BARROW, Archdeacon BRABAZON, Anthea BRADBURY-SCOTT, Clotilde BRADBURY-SCOTT, Nora BROAD, James BROADRIBB, Mr. CASPAR, Miss COOKE, Miss Joanna CRAWFORD, Lavinia BRADBURY-SCOTT GLYNNE, Verity HUNT, Richard JAMESON, Sir Andrew MCNEIL, Miss Jane Marple, Miss MERRYPIT, Emlyn PRICE, Jason Rafiel, Michael RAFIEL, Mrs. SANDBOURNE, Mr. SCHUSTER, Elizabeth TEMPLE, Mrs. VINEGAR, Esther WALTERS, Professor WANSTEAD

PLOT SYNOPSIS

Chapters 1–4

Miss Marple reads in the paper that millionaire Jason Rafiel has died, and soon after she receives a letter from lawyers requesting that she meet with them. She and Rafiel had solved a mystery years before, at which time he had named her "Nemesis," the Greek goddess of retribution. At his attorneys' office, she is read a letter from Rafiel in which he asks her to perform an investigation for which she will receive twenty thousand pounds, but the letter contains no clues nor further information. To learn more about the mysterious millionaire's family, Miss Marple arranges a "chance" meeting with his former secretary, now married to an engineer. Esther Anderson reveals that Rafiel had two daughters, one of whom died, and a son of whom she knows nothing.

Chapters 5–9

Rafiel had arranged for Miss Marple to go on a tour of famous houses and gardens of Britain, a part of the mystery. She observes the other tour members to determine how they might illuminate her assignment, but remains puzzled. She finds Miss Cooke familiar, but she remembers her with dark, not blond hair. Elizabeth Temple reveals that a pupil of hers was engaged to Rafiel's son, Michael, but died of "love." Later, Miss Cooke tells Miss Marple that she had once been in St. Mary Mead and that the two had met on a footpath. Lavinia Glynne approaches the detective and states that Rafiel had told her prior to his death that Miss Marple would be on the tour, and that he had wanted her to stay with Lavinia and her sisters. Miss Marple agrees to the arrangement. At their house, she takes a tour of the house and garden, noting that Anthea steers her away from the decayed and fallen greenhouse.

Chapters 10–13

The sisters tell Miss Marple the history of the house, as well as their own history. She learns that the former owner left the house to Clotilde, who was later joined by Anthea and then Lavinia after her husband died. When two of her friends died in an airplane crash, Clotilde raised their daughter. The girl fell in love and planned to marry, but when she was found strangled and beaten in a quarry, her fiancé, Michael Rafiel, was the suspect. His rich father paid to get him out of jail. The tour resumes, and Miss Temple is hurt when stones rain down upon her from a cliff; the tour is cancelled for the day. Professor Wanstead speaks with Miss Marple and tells her that Rafiel had told him about her, and had asked him to watch over her. He also provides her with further information regarding Michael Rafiel, and mentions the disappearance of Nora Broad. He later takes Miss Marple to the hospital because Miss Temple has briefly regained consciousness and asked for her. Miss Marple learns about a girl named Verity Hunt who had also died, then Miss Temple passes away.

Chapters 14–17

Eager to see their reaction when she returns to their home, Miss Marple mentions the name Verity Hunt to the three sisters, and learns that she was the girl whom they took into their home after her parents were killed. She speaks with a shopkeeper, and learns that Nora Broad's body was never found, then asks the postmistress about the parcel sent earlier by Anthea, and learns that it was sent to a clothing drive. An inquest rules that insufficient evidence exists in the death of Miss Temple. Miss Marple decides to leave the tour, but she watches carefully to see who attends the funeral service for Miss Temple. She moves into the Golden Boar Inn, then visits Nora Broad's cousin, and learns that the girl accepted a ride from a stranger and was never seen again.

Chapters 18–20

Archdeacon Brabazon conducts the funeral service, and asks to speak with Miss Marple afterwards. He tells her that he had agreed to marry Verity Hunt and Michael Rafiel secretly because he believed that they truly loved each other, but neither appeared at the appointed time. Miss Cooke and Miss Barrow, who were also on the tour, move into the Golden Boar. Anthea meets with Miss Marple, and insists that she move back in with the sisters for the duration of her stay. Miss Barrow and Miss Cooke visit Miss Marple, and they all discuss Miss Temple's death.

Chapters 21–22

Miss Marple stays the night with the sisters. She escapes poison in both her coffee and her warm milk, and accuses her attacker, who also murdered Verity Hunt and Nora Broad. Secret agents Miss Cooke and Miss Barrow arrive in time to save Miss Marple from further harm, after which the murderer drinks the poisoned milk and dies. Miss Marple succeeds in gaining a pardon for Michael Rafiel, who will now begin a new life. She visits the late Mr. Rafiel's attorneys to obtain her twenty thousand pounds, which she intends to enjoy spending.

CRIME NOTES

Three murders occur in this novel. The first victim is strangled, a second victim is poisoned with "some sleeping stuff," and the third victim is crushed by falling rocks.

Neuman, Lisa   Totally devoted to her employer, Robert SHOREHAM, for whom she works as lab assistant and secretary in PASSENGER TO FRANKFURT, she is also very much in love with him.

Neville, Gladys   Beyond reproach in her office manner and skills, she is a secretary to dental partners Morley and Reilly in ONE, TWO, BUCKLE MY SHOE. She is lured away from the office by a telegram on the day that murder occurs.

Newman, John A man with a fabricated past in "INGOTS OF GOLD," he searches for the gold cargo of a shipwreck off the Cornwall coast.

"Next to a Dog" Short story.

The plot centers on a penniless young war widow whose only solace is her aging and blind terrier.

PUBLISHING AND DRAMATIZATION
HISTORY
The story appeared in the short story collection, THE GOLDEN BALL AND OTHER STORIES, published in 1971 by Dodd, Mead and Company in New York.

The story has not been adapted for stage or screen.

CHARACTERS
Mr. ALLABY, Mrs. BARNES, Arthur HALLIDAY, Joyce LAMBERT

PLOT SYNOPSIS
The story concerns Joyce Lambert, who is left destitute when her husband is killed in the war. Her only comfort is Terry, an aging and half-blind terrier, whom she loves dearly because he was given to her by her husband shortly before he reported for military duty. Desperate for a means to support them, Joyce agrees to marry the very wealthy Arthur Halliday, but changes her mind when Terry is badly injured and dies. Freed of her burden of love, Joyce becomes governess to the three-year-old son of the man who helped her to take Terry to the veterinarian.

Nicholas V, Prince Pseudonym of ANTHONY CADE.

Nicoletis, Mrs. Proprietor of a student hostel in HICKORY DICKORY DOCK, she actually makes most of her money through the smuggling operation she runs with her daughter. "Mrs. Nick" dies when her brandy is laced with a dose of morphine.

Nicholson, Dr. Jasper A highly observant physician in WHY DIDN'T THEY ASK EVANS?, he heads a clinic for people recovering from mental stress and drug addiction.

Nicholson, Moira Married to Dr. NICHOLSON, she used the name of Rose Emily Templeton when present at the death of John SAVAGE. She becomes the beneficiary of the will forged by Roger BASSINGTON-FFRENCH in WHY DIDN'T THEY ASK EVANS?

Nimrud The modern name of the ancient military capital of Assyria which A.H. Layard excavated from 1845 to 1851. Sir Max MALLOWAN reopened the excavations in 1949 and in the following ten years made invaluable historical discoveries there that resulted in major contributions to the field of archaeology.

Nina, Aunt She is the protagonist's aunt in GIANT'S BREAD and her weakness for men leads to the ruin of her reputation.

Nofret A nineteen-year-old concubine in DEATH COMES AS THE END who returns unexpectedly with IMHOTEP, motivating anger and hate in the family. She dies when pushed from a cliff.

N or M? Mystery novel.

The novel is one of two which the author worked on simultaneously during World War II while she stayed alone in London. She alternated writing THE MOVING FINGER and *N or M?* to keep herself "fresh at task." The plot centers on the efforts of middle-aged Tommy and Tuppence BERESFORD to aid the government in learning the significance of a dying government secret agent's last words, "N or M Song Susie."

PUBLISHING AND DRAMATIZATION
HISTORY
The novel was published in 1941 by William Collins Sons and Company, Ltd., in London, and by Dodd, Mead and Company in New York.

The novel has not been adapted for stage or screen.

CHARACTERS
APPLEDORE, Albert BATT, Deborah BERESFORD, Derek BERESFORD, Tommy Beresford, Tuppence Beresford, Dr. BINION, Major BLETCHLEY, Alfred CAYLEY, Elisabeth CAYLEY, Mr. GRANT, Commander HAYDOCK, Anthony MARSDON, Sophia MINTON, Mrs. O'ROURKE, Mrs. Eileen PERENNA, Sheila PERENNA, Vanda POLONSKA, Betty SPROT, Mrs. Millicent SPROT, Carl VON DEINIM

PLOT SYNOPSIS

Chapters 1–3

Eager to relive their glory days of World War I when both were actively involved in the war effort, Tommy and Tuppence Beresford feel middle-aged and useless as World War II rages and they remain inactive. Their prospects brighten when Mr. Grant, a member of British Intelligence, visits and asks Tommy to resume his old activities to aid in breaking down the "Fifth Column," the enemy from within. Tuppence is called away, and Tommy appears headed for danger alone until he arrives at his destination, the Sans Souci villa, and finds a disguised Tuppence among the guests. She is "Mrs. Blenkensop," a widow with three sons in military service. The detectives mingle with the other guests to gather information.

Chapters 4–6

Tommy and Tuppence attempt to determine which guest might be the coded "N" or "M." Tuppence picks up a telephone extension and hears a voice say "everything going well. On the fourth, then." After replacing the receiver, she leaves the room and walks up the stairs, followed by Mrs. Perenna, only to find her way blocked by Mrs. O'Rourke. For a moment, Tuppence feels afraid and trapped between the two women, a feeling alleviated only when little Betty runs up to her and embraces her. Tuppence receives letters from her real children, and a fake letter from her imaginary son, Raymond, which she tells others at dinner is written in code. Her "Raymond" letters are read, but the intruder leaves no fingerprints. Tommy demands a room change and moves into the one next to Tuppence. This allows him to watch who sneaks into Tuppence's room after she once more baits the other guests with stories of letters containing military information.

Chapters 7–9

A poorly dressed woman has been seen several times outside the gate. When Betty Sprot disappears, a servant reports that she walked away with the woman. The guests organize a search party and catch up to the woman at the edge of a cliff, where Mrs. Sprot shoots her in the head as she threatens to throw Betty off the cliff. The inquest reveals that the woman was a Polish refugee, and possibly a spy. Soon after, the authorities arrest guest Carl Von Dei-

nim as a spy. The Beresfords send for Albert. Tommy plays golf with Haydock and baits the commander's servant, who appears German to Tommy, by mentioning the letters N and M. Tommy is knocked unconscious when he returns to the villa.

Chapters 10–12

Tommy does not return, and while the other guests laughingly say that he is out womanizing, the disguised Tuppence is worried. Their daughter, Deborah, learns that her mother is not in Cornwall as planned, and becomes worried when she returns home and finds a photograph of her parents missing from her room. She confides her concern to fellow intelligence worker Tony Marsden, who visits Tuppence to speak with her. In the meantime, Tuppence meets with Mr. Grant and learns that the enemy plans to attack on the fourth, a week away. Tuppence tells Albert to plant a letter about "N" and "M" to draw out the enemy. All the while, Tommy is held captive in Haydock's cellar. Luckily for him, Albert suspects Haydock, and stands outside the house humming, to which Tommy replies by snoring "SOS" in Morse code. Albert hears, and taps a code in return.

Chapters 13–16

Marsdon is a traitor who endangers Tuppence's life, but Mr. Grant saves her and returns her to the villa. They later find that Betty's *Little Jack Horner* book contains information regarding all of England's military maneuvers, as well as a list of traitorous members of British Intelligence. An unexpected "M" is unmasked. The reader learns that Betty was really the daughter of the dead Polish refugee, who had first given her up and then wanted her back. As they close out the case, Tommy and Tuppence make plans to adopt the orphaned Betty.

CRIME NOTES

The sole murder in the novel is the result of a gunshot wound to the head.

Norreys, Hugh The narrator of THE ROSE AND THE YEW TREE, he begins his story after an accident with a bus renders him wheelchair-bound.

Norris, Inspector A member of British Intelligence assigned to the Laurels detail in POSTERN OF

FATE, he poses as a local police officer to avert suspicion.

Norris, Sister Nicknamed "Sister Theatre" in GIANT'S BREAD, she is sharp-tongued and short-tempered with subordinate nurses.

Norton, Stephen An amateur naturalist in CURTAIN, he resides at Styles Court and dies from a gunshot to his forehead.

Nunn, Rosina A no-longer-young stage actress in "THE WORLD'S END," she cultivates an image of helplessness and seeks constant attendance from those around her.

Nye, Sir Stafford Despite his solid political and social connections, he is a Foreign Office member who has "failed to fulfill his early promise" in PASSENGER TO FRANKFURT.

O

Obolovitch, Prince Michael Heir to the throne of Herzoslovakia, he eagerly desires freedom of movement and poses both as Count Stanislaus and Mr. Holmes in THE SECRET OF CHIMNEYS. He is eventually murdered while a guest at Chimneys.

Obolovitch, Nicholas Sergius Alexander Ferdinand An alies of Anthony CADE.

O'Connor, Sergeant A handsome, personable, Scotland Yard detective in CARDS ON THE TABLE, he is nicknamed "The Maidservant's Prayer" because of his particular skill in charming female servants into talking.

O'Connor, Derek Sent in CAT AMONG THE PIGEONS to break the news of Mrs. SUTCLIFFE's brother's death to her, he also speaks to her about the jewels that Bob RAWLINSON carried.

Oglander, Mr. And Mrs. Seated at the table next to Una DRAKE and Jimmy LE MARCHANT at the Savoy, they hear the details of the bet in "THE UNBREAKABLE ALIBI" and verify Una's presence for Tuppence BERESFORD.

Oglander, Miss A seemingly unimaginative member of the family in "THE KING OF CLUBS," she plays a major role in designing the drama which covers up a murder.

O'Hara, Eileen See MARCH, CECILY.

Ohlsson, Greta The last person to see the murdered Samuel Edward RATCHETT alive in MURDER ON THE ORIENT EXPRESS, she is a Swedish missionary school matron who had been Daisy ARMSTRONG's nurse.

Oldfield, Dr. Charles A widowed physician in "THE LERNEAN HYDRA," he consults Hercule POIROT to clear his name when townspeople began to suggest that he had murdered his wife.

Olga, Grand Duchess See DE SARA, MADELEINE.

Oliver, Ariadne A successful detective novelist who appears in two short stories, with Mr. PARKER PYNE, and seven novels, of which six are with Hercule POIROT (see CATEGORICAL APPENDIX), she is a middle-aged woman with a penchant for apples. She is described in one of the novels as "handsome in a rather untidy fashion, with fine eyes, substantial shoulders, and a large quantity of rebellious grey hair with which she was continuously experimenting." As the author of "forty-six works of fiction, all best sellers in England and America, and freely translated into French, German, Italian, Hungarian, Finnish, Japanese and Abyssinian," she is also creator of the Finnish detective, Sven Hjerson. Ariadne Oliver expresses feelings toward Sven similar to those her creator had expressed toward Hercule Poirot, once she had come to dislike him: " 'If I ever met that bony, gangling vegetable-eating Finn in real life, I'd do a better murder than any I've ever invented.' " She is also feisty in her view of law enforcement, and believes that Scotland Yard should be lead by a woman because of the effectiveness of female intuition. Overall, she represents something of a caricature of the author, an exaggerated version of detective novelist Agatha Christie.

Olivera, Jane Young, gangly, and politically left, she is the American niece of wealthy banker Alistair BLUNT in ONE, TWO, BUCKLE MY SHOE. She falls under suspicion when Blunt is murdered, both because of her political leanings and because she is heir to much of his vast fortune.

Olivera, Julia   A rude and patronizing woman in ONE, TWO, BUCKLE MY SHOE, she is a niece by marriage to Alistair BLUNT and an heir to his fortune.

Olivier, Madame   A brilliant French chemist, rumored to be "Number Three" in the Big Four gang, she "was one of the most prominent personalities of the day" in THE BIG FOUR.

O'Murphy   An Irish-born member of the Criminal Investigation Department of Scotland Yard, he is temporarily assigned as the chauffeur to the British Prime Minister. When Prime Minister MACADAM is kidnapped in "THE KIDNAPPED PRIME MINISTER," he becomes a prime suspect

O'Neele, Moira   See HOBHOUSE, VALERIE.

O'Neill, Captain   See VICTOR, KING.

O'Neill, Dr.   He is a character in "THE RED HOUSE" who tries to purchase a house and then "haunts" it to drive out the owner.

One, Two, Buckle My Shoe   Mystery novel.

The novel contains ten chapters, each loosely corresponding to a line in the nursery rhyme that precedes the story. The plot centers on the efforts of Hercule POIROT to find the murderer of a dentist and to uncover a greater plot that might topple the government.

PUBLISHING AND DRAMATIZATION HISTORY

The novel was published in 1940 by William Collins Sons and Company, Ltd., in London, and in 1941 by Dodd, Mead and Company in New York.

The novel was adapted for television in 1992 by London Weekend Television in Britain, and was also shown on the Public Broadcasting Service in the U.S.

CHARACTERS

Colonel ABERCROMBIE, Mr. AMBERIOTIS, Reginald BARNES, Alistair BLUNT, Frank CARTER, Agnes FLETCHER, Gerda GRANT, Mr. HARRISON, Inspector JAPP, Ram LAL, Mrs. MERTON, Georgina MORLEY, Henry MORLEY, Gladys NEVILLE, Jane OLIVERA, Julia OLIVERA, Hercule Poirot, Howard RAIKES, Mr. REILLY, Mabelle SAINSBURY SEALE

PLOT SYNOPSIS
Chapters 1–2
Mr. Morley, Poirot's dentist, has a difficult schedule because his assistant Gladys has been called away to tend to an aunt who has had a stroke. He tells the detective that he has a very important patient later that day—Mr. Alistair Blunt, one of the most powerful businessmen in England. That evening, Inspector Japp calls Poirot and tells him that Morley has committed suicide. They identify Morley's enemies, then learn that Gladys was falsely called away. Suspecting that either the murderer was after Blunt or Morley was killed because of something he knew, they question all the dentist's acquaintances and patients. When Poirot arrives at the hotel of Morley's last patient, they learn that Mr. Amberiotis has died.

Chapters 3–4
The next day, Japp tells Poirot that the Morley case is officially a suicide and that Amberiotis died of an overdose of procaine and adrenalin, a local anesthetic placed on the gums by dentists. After interviewing other patients, Poirot learns that one patient walked out of her hotel after dinner the night before and has not been seen since. When Poirot arrives home, Gladys tells him that Morley could not have made a mistake because the anesthesia dosage was routine. When a woman is found dead in King Leopold Mansions, Japp believes it is Mabelle but later concludes that he is wrong. Instead, he identifies the dead woman as Sylvia Chapman, the wife of a secret service agent.

Chapters 5–6
Poirot receives a telephone call warning him to stop interfering with the case. That evening the Prime Minister is shot at as he leaves 10 Downing Street with Alistair Blunt. Blunt invites Poirot to spend the weekend at his estate, where the detective finds Gladys' boyfriend, Frank Carter, working under an assumed name as a gardener. As Poirot walks the grounds with Blunt, a shot rings out, and they come upon Carter struggling with Howard Raikes, an undesirable suitor of Blunt's niece, Jane Olivera. Raikes

claims that Carter fired the shot, but Carter denies this.

Chapters 7–8

Poirot meets Reilly at the counter of a shipping company, where he is making arrangements to go to America to start a new life. Reilly claims that Morley could not possibly have given the wrong dosage to Mr. Amberiotis. In a later conversation, Japp postulates that Carter killed Morley, because the pistol used was a twin of the one that fired on Blunt. Poirot meets with Morley's parlourmaid, Agnes, who tells him that she saw Carter slip furtively down the stairs and walk toward Morley's surgery on the day of the murder. Poirot tells this to Japp, Japp questions Carter, who first denies the report and then admits that he was waiting to speak with Morley, because he believed that the dentist was trying to turn Gladys against him.

Chapters 9–10

The authorities learn that the dead woman really is Mabelle, and Poirot pieces together the clues and comes to a startling conclusion about the murders. The murderer had given the murders political associations, but the true motive lies in a very ordinary domestic situation.

CRIME NOTES

Three murders occur in this novel. The first victim dies from a gunshot wound to the head. The second victim is murdered by the administration of an overdose of procaine and adrenalin. The third victim is bashed on the head and her face disfigured.

Opalsen, Mrs. Married to a wealthy stockbroker in "THE JEWEL ROBBERY AT THE 'GRAND METROPOLITAN,'" she is an imposing woman who hires Hercule POIROT to find her pearl necklace, which she claims has disappeared from her hotel room.

"Oracle at Delphi, The" Mystery short story.

The plot centers on the cleverness of Mr. PARKER PYNE in aiding a distraught mother to retrieve her kidnapped son.

PUBLISHING AND DRAMATIZATION HISTORY

The story appeared in the short story collection, PARKER PYNE INVESTIGATES, published in 1934 by William Collins Sons and Company, Ltd., in London,

and under the title MR. PARKER PYNE, DETECTIVE by Dodd, Mead and Company in New York.

The story has not been adapted for stage or screen.

CHARACTERS

ARISTOPOULOS, Mr. Parker Pyne, Mrs. Willard J. PETERS, Willard PETERS, JR., Mr. THOMPSON

PLOT SYNOPSIS

The story concerns a kidnapping case in Greece, solved by Mr. Parker Pyne, who is traveling incognito. He learns that the wealthy Mrs. Peters has consulted a man claiming to be Mr. Parker Pyne in the effort to free her son, who is being held captive. The ransom demand is Mrs. Peters' diamond necklace, worth one hundred thousand dollars, and the false Parker Pyne suggests that the stones in the necklace be replaced by paste imitations. Without fanfare, the real Parker Pyne rescues the captive and retrieves the real necklace, revealing the subterfuge to a grateful Mrs. Peters.

Oranoff, Prince Sergius A Russian emigre dancer in "HARLEQUIN'S LANE," who is recruited to dance in the Harlequinade, he becomes reacquainted with the woman he lost ten years earlier.

Ordeal by Innocence Mystery novel.

The novel contains a clever and very effective use of amnesia as the basis for a plot designed around a wrongful conviction. The plot centers on the efforts of a geophysicist to exonerate the memory of a man wrongfully jailed for murder.

PUBLISHING AND DRAMATIZATION HISTORY

The novel was published in 1958 by William Collins Son and Company, Ltd., in London, and in 1959 by Dodd, Mead and Company in New York.

The novel was filmed in 1984 by Golan-Gobus Productions in England and starred Donald Sutherland, Sarah Miles and Christopher Plummer. The film adheres closely to the novel.

CHARACTERS

Christina ARGYLE, Hester ARGYLE, Jack "Jacko" ARGYLE, Leo ARGYLE, Michael ARGYLE, Rachel ARGYLE, Dr. Arthur CALGARY, Joe CLEGG, Maureen CLEGG, Dr. Donald CRAIG, Mary DURRANT, Philip

DURRANT, Major FINNEY, Cyril GREEN, Superintendent HUISH, Kirsten LINDSTROM, Dr. MacMASTER, Andrew MARSHALL, Gwenda VAUGHAN

PLOT SYNOPSIS
Chapters 1–3
Dr. Arthur Calgary takes a ferry across the Rubicon River to Sunny Point to speak with the Argyle family. A year before, the matriarch of the family was murdered and a son, Jack, was convicted and sentenced to prison, where he died of pneumonia. He had protested his innocence throughout the case, and asserted that he had been hitchhiking and been picked up by a stranger. The police could not locate the stranger, so Jack's alibi was viewed as a lie. Dr. Calgary is that stranger, and he explains to the Argyles that he was hit by a bus soon after dropping Jack off. Amnesia followed by research in Antarctica had kept him from hearing about the case and coming forward to support Jack's contention. The doctor's revelation has a disturbing effect on the family, because it means that someone else in the family is guilty.

Chapters 4–6
Calgary learns that all of the Argyle children are adopted, and the Argyle family attorney, Andrew Marshall, tells him that Rachel Argyle was devoted to caring for the children. Jack, the accused murderer, was the problem child, whose stealing and misbehaving made him the logical choice as the murderer. The authorities decide to reopen the case, while Calgary visits every member of the family, including Jack's widow, who has remarried.

Chapters 7–9
Dr. MacMasters tells Calgary that Mrs. Argyle pampered her children, and that she also tried to control every aspect of their lives. Despite her obvious material kindness, none of the children appears to have loved the victim, and each resented her for a different reason. The authorities also begin to suspect Leo Argyle, the victim's husband, because he is planning to marry his longtime secretary. They learn that Rachel neglected her role as wife in favor of a highly active role as mother.

Chapters 10–12
Marshall speaks with the Argyles, and Leo recalls that he heard the doorbell ring at 7 P.M. on the night of the murder. The lawyer says that this means that an unknown intruder entered the house, murdered Rachel, and took the money. As the family members think back to the night of the murder and review their later testimony to the police, each learns that he or she has something to hide.

Chapters 13–15
Superintendent Huish questions the family members, and discovers that none of them know the exact time that Jack left, nor can they agree as to whether or not Mrs. Argyle gave Jack money. Although the police decide that their chief suspects are Leo Argyle and Gwenda Vaughan, several other family members also had opportunities to commit the murder. Philip Durrant, confined to a wheelchair, wants to help solve the murder by using his mental abilities, but his wife Mary just wants to go home.

Chapters 16–18
As Philip pursues the case on his own, he learns that Leo really does not want to know who committed the murder. Hester speaks with Philip, and tells him about her attempts at suicide and of the affair with a married man that had left her crushed. She swears that she is innocent, and falls into his lap. As he kisses her, his wife walks in, and becomes very annoyed. When Hester visits Dr. Calgary, she tells him that she is very upset because everyone is accusatory and the family is marked by distrust. He advises that she get away from the family, and plans to have dinner with her in London.

Chapters 19–21
Attention in the case turns to Tina Argyle, whose car was outside the family home at the time of the murder. She claims that she was there but decided not to enter the house. Calgary speaks again with Jack's widow, obtains the name of one of Jack's old girlfriends, and tries to clarify a few points. Concurrently, Philip and Mary discuss Tina's involvement, sure that she knows more than she is telling.

Chapters 22–24
Michael meets Tina placing flowers at Mrs. Argyle's grave. She admits that she went to the family home to discuss a job change. She claims that she heard someone say "Between seven and seven-thirty," "You can trust me," and "And after that, darling, everything will be wonderful." She cannot identify the speaker. When they return to Sunny Point, they learn that Philip has been murdered. Tina faints in Michael's arms, and he realizes that she has also been

stabbed. Huish believes that Michael is responsible for both stabbings, but Calgary disagrees. Instead, Calgary calls everyone together and divulges the name of the murderer, explaining the motive. The novel ends with Michael expected to marry his adoptive sister Tina, and Hester expected to marry Calgary.

CRIME NOTES
The novel contains two murders. The first victim dies of a blow to the head, while the second victim dies of a stab wound to the base of the spine.

O'Rourke, Flight Lieutenant One of twelve people travelling from Damascus to Baghdad in "THE GATE OF BAGHDAD," he is the first to suggest that Captain SMETHURST's death was not an accident.

O'Rourke, Mrs. An obese woman who is "like an ogress dimly remembered from early fairly tales," she eagerly observes everything which occurs at the Sans Souci hotel in N OR M?

O'Rourke, Terence As secretary to Air Minister Sir Stanley DIGBY, he is present at the negotiations for a secret metal formula in THE SEVEN DIALS MYSTERY. He is later drugged and robbed of the papers.

Orwell, Robert Once the partner of Andrew RESTARICK in a Kenyan prospecting operation, he returns to London and assumes his former partner's identity in THIRD GIRL. Orwell seeks to fool the Restarick family and defraud Norma RESTARICK of her inheritance.

Osborne, Zachariah A quaint, old-fashioned chemist in THE PALE HORSE, he is also the owner of the market research firm, Customer's Reactions Classified. In appearance, he is innocuous, "a small, mid-

dle-aged man with a bald domed head," but he is really a shrewd observer of people.

Osric, Prince As guardian to the Grand Duchess ANASTASIA in "THE GIRL IN THE TRAIN," he attempts to arrange a politically suitable marriage for his niece, but fails to convince her to accept Prince KARL.

Ossington, Sir William A well-respected Scotland Yard official in MURDER IS EASY, he is known to longtime colleagues as Billy Bones.

Otterbourne, Rosalie A lonely and unhappy young woman who must contend with her irritable and unpredictable alcoholic mother in DEATH ON THE NILE (2), she bitterly despises the beauty and wealth of Linnet DOYLE, and would love to " 'stamp on her lovely, arrogant, self-confident face.' " After her mother's death, Rosalie and Tim ALLERTON fall in love.

Otterbourne, Salome Secretly a chronic alcoholic in DEATH ON THE NILE (2) who publicly declares that she cannot stand the taste of liquor, she is also the author of steamy, sexually explicit novels. She is murdered just before she can name the murderer of Louise BOURGET.

Owen, Ulick Norman See WARGRAVE, MR. JUSTICE LAWRENCE JOHN.

Owen, Una Nancy See WARGRAVE, MR. JUSTICE LAWRENCE JOHN.

Oxley, Louise An apparent witness to the murder of Miss GREENSHAW while locked in the library in "GREENSHAW'S FOLLY," she is the financially troubled niece of Joan WEST, to whom she owes her present position as editor of Nathaniel Greenshaw's diaries.

P

Pace, Harrington The American uncle of Roger HAVERING in "THE MYSTERY OF HUNTER'S LODGE," he lives with Roger and his wife, Zoe, for three years before dying and leaving them his vast estate.

Packard, Miss The efficient manager of the Sunny Ridge Nursing Home in BY THE PRICKING OF MY THUMBS, she carefully controls her emotions. Even her mourning after Ada FANSHAWE's death has a practiced air, for "she was an expert in the exact amount of condolence which would be acceptable."

Packington, George A philandering husband in "THE CASE OF THE MIDDLE-AGED WIFE," he is a short, bald, middle-aged man who is having an affair with his young secretary, Nancy. When his wife takes up with an attractive man, George becomes jealous, and finds his own affair to be substantially less exciting.

Packington, Maria A formerly sensible "model of economy" in "THE CASE OF THE MIDDLE-AGED WIFE," she transforms herself into a stylish woman who radiates self-confidence after Mr. PARKER PYNE supplies a love interest. She begins to pity her husband George for trying to be young, and her new attractiveness renews his desire for her.

Pagett, Edith The sister-in-law of the confectioner in Dillmouth in SLEEPING MURDER, she is interviewed by Gwenda REED regarding events of twenty years earlier.

Pagett, Guy The highly efficient, hardworking secretary to Sir Eustace PEDLER, M.P., in THE MAN IN THE BROWN SUIT, he aggravates his employer of six years by his zeal and thoroughly admirable behavior. Unknown to Sir Pedler, Pagett has a wife and four children.

Pale Horse, The Mystery novel.

The novel is the only one in which Mrs. Ariadne OLIVER solves a crime in the absence of Hercule POIROT. The plot centers on the efforts of Mrs. Oliver to expose the individuals behind an evil murder-for-hire scheme.

PUBLISHING AND DRAMATIZATION
HISTORY
The novel was published in 1961 by William Collins Sons and Company, Ltd., in London, and in 1962 by Dodd, Mead and Company in New York.

The novel has not been adapted for stage or screen.

CHARACTERS
David ARDINGLY, C.R. BRADLEY, Eileen BRANDON, Dr. Jim CORRIGAN, Katherine (Ginger) CORRIGAN, Reverend Caleb DANE CALTHORP, Maud DANE CALTHORP, Mrs. Jesse DAVIS, Colonel John Hugh DESPARD, Rhoda Dawes DESPARD, Mark EASTERBROOK, Lou ELLIS, Father GORMAN, Thyrza GREY, Detective-Inspector LEJEUNE, MILLY, Mrs. Ariadne OLIVER, Hermia REDCLIFFE, Sybil STAMFORDIS, Pamela (Poppy) STIRLING, Thomasina TUCKERTON, Mr. VENABLES, Bella WEBB

PLOT SYNOPSIS
Chapters 1–3
Mark Easterbrook is in a Chelsea coffeehouse when a fight breaks out between two young women, a blonde and a redhead. The blonde pulls out a handful of red hair before the police arrive, and the owner tells Mark that the redhead is heiress Thomasina Tuckerton. A week later, Mark reads of her death in

a nursing home. In a seemingly unrelated incident, Catholic priest Father Gorman goes to the bedside of a dying woman and leaves with a list of nine names, which he puts into his shoe because he has a hole in his pocket. He is killed on his way home, but the police find both the list and a witness who saw a man following the priest. They learn that all the people on the list are dead.

Chapters 4–6

After viewing a production of *Macbeth*, Mark and his friends discuss witches and murderers. One friend laughingly observes how convenient it would be simply to call upon a murderer when one was needed. Another member of the group, Poppy Stirling, states that this was possible at the Pale Horse inn. Mark hears the name again a few days later when Mrs. Oliver speaks of her book-signing and of Rhoda Despard's party. He also runs into an old school friend, Dr. Jim Corrigan, who is currently a police surgeon. Corrigan shows Mark the list of names, most of whom Mark recognizes. Mark asks Mrs. Oliver's friends about the inn and learns that it is now the home of psychic Thyrza Grey, medium Sybil Stamfordis and witch Bella Webb. Mrs. Oliver takes Mark to the inn, where he speaks with Thyrza about witchcraft and love potions.

Chapters 7–10

After leaving the Pale Horse, Mark learns that two people on the list had stayed at the nearby King's Arms in the past year. He discusses the story with Mrs. Dane Calthrop, and they decide to watch the Pale Horse. Inspector Lejeune continues to investigate Father Gorman's death, and receives a letter that identifies Mr. Venables as the man who followed the priest. Meanwhile, Mark and Corrigan conclude that all the people who died left considerable estates.

Chapters 11–14

Mark and Ginger Corrigan, the doctor's sister, plan to learn more about the connection between the Pale Horse and the deaths. Ginger speaks with Poppy, who gives her the name "C.R. Bradley" and an address through which she can hire the witches. When Mark speaks with Bradley, he is told to view the arrangement as a bet in which Bradley receives five thousand pounds if the person dies, and Mark receives one hundred pounds if the person lives past the appointed date. Mark then speaks with the late Thomasina's stepmother, under the guise of wanting

to buy her house, and watches her become nervous and pale when he mentions the Pale Horse. Mark and Ginger create a plan in which Ginger will pretend to be Mark's wife who has turned up after many years. He will pretend that he wants to eliminate her so that he can marry another woman.

Chapters 15–18

Mark tells Lejeune about his plan, then contacts Bradley with his story. Bradley tells him that the "bet" must be eighteen to one that she will die within a month. Mark is told to take a glove or handkerchief of hers to a seance at the Pale Horse. The morning after the seance, Ginger seems fine.

Chapters 19–22

The next morning, Ginger awakens with a severe sore throat, and Mark insists that she call a doctor. The doctor diagnoses the flu, and Lejeune tells Mark to call a psychiatrist. Ginger's fever is very high and her hair is falling out. Mrs. Oliver speaks with Mark and tells him that a friend of one of the women on the list told her that the late woman also suffered hair loss before her death, as did Mary Delafontaine and Thomasina Tuckerton. She suggests that the doctor test for thallium poisoning.

Chapters 23–25

The authorities discover that the people on the original list were all poisoned with thallium, and the residents at the Pale Horse were employed to add an aura of the occult to the proceedings. Those who benefited from their deaths had made a "bet" with C.R. Bradley, who then dispatched the murderer to introduce the thallium into the intended victim's system. After the arrests are made, Ginger returns to the Pale Horse to clean the sign of the now-vacant inn, and Mark asks her to marry him.

CRIME NOTES

The nine murders, eight of which occur before the novel opens, are all the result of thallium poisoning. The substance is added to a range of foodstuffs, cosmetics and medicines of the victims, and it produces many nonspecific symptoms which appear to be due to a range of diseases. The victims all share the same characteristic hair loss before death.

Palgrave, Major   An elderly man in A CARIBBEAN MYSTERY who is staying at the Golden Palm Hotel, he is "purple of face, with a glass eye, and the general appearance of a stuffed frog." Miss MARPLE sympathetically listens to his stories, but he dies soon after telling her one particular story and showing her a photograph of a wife-murderer with whom he was once acquainted.

Palgrove, Edward (Ted) A poorly paid office clerk in "A FRUITFUL SUNDAY," he purchases an old car to take his girlfriend, Dorothy PRATT, for Sunday drives. He buys a small basket of cherries on one of these drives, and discovers that it contains a missing ruby necklace worth thirty thousand pounds.

Palk, Constable A pleasant-faced law enforcement officer in ST. MARY MEAD, he appears in THE BODY IN THE LIBRARY and "THE TAPE-MEASURE MURDER."

Palliser, Sir Edward A retired attorney in "SING A SONG OF SIXPENCE" who had once been "one of the most eminent criminal barristers of his day." Although reluctant, he agrees to honor an old promise to Magdalen VAUGHAN when she calls upon him to solve the mystery of her great-aunt Lily CRABTREE's death.

Palmer, Mabel Acting in the interests of the Big Four gang, the "pleasant-faced woman of middle-age" who poses as a nurse for the Lark Sisterhood introduces Hercule POIROT to the Templeton case in THE BIG FOUR.

Papopolous, Aristide Headwaiter at the popular nightclub, Hell, in "THE CAPTURE OF CERBERUS," he is "a lean Mephistopheles" suspected by the police of dealing in drugs.

Papopolous, Demetrius An expert diamond cutter and resetter in THE MYSTERY OF THE BLUE TRAIN, he receives the stolen Heart of Fire rubies, and provides Hercule POIROT with a vital clue in gratitude for earlier assistance from the detective.

Papopolous, Zia A diamond cutter's daughter in THE MYSTERY OF THE BLUE TRAIN, she dislikes illegal activity, and informs Hercule POIROT that her father has the Heart of Fire rubies.

Paravincini, Mr. An unlikable elderly man in "THREE BLIND MICE," he arrives at Monkswell Manor with a wallet full of banknotes. The guesthouse hostess observes that his walk is much younger than his apparent age, and he seems to wear makeup. When murder occurs, he seems genuinely amused, and goads the other guests.

Pardoe, William Reuben An older cousin to Ellie ROGERS in ENDLESS NIGHT, he visits her home after her death to comfort her husband Michael.

Pardonstenger, Amy Pseudonym of Bella Wallace. (See WALLACE, BELLA AND RUBE).

Parfitt, Canon A church official known for his "scientific sermons," he joins the three men on the train in "THE FOURTH MAN," and takes a theological stand against Dr. CLARK's discussion of two souls inhabiting one body.

Parker The shifty-eyed butler at the Ackroyd estate in THE MURDER OF ROGER ACKROYD, he has a "fat, smug, oily face," and has worked for Roger ACKROYD for only one year.

Parker, Mr. and Mrs. A larcenous pair in "THE MARKET BASING MYSTERY," they propose to blackmail Walter PROTHERO for an act that occurred while he served in the Royal Navy under another name.

Parker, Bernard A suspect in the theft of the Medici necklace in "DOUBLE CLUE," "this particular young man with his white, effeminate face and affected lisping speech" serves as an assistant to collector Marcus HARDMAN.

Parker, George See JONES, ROBERT (BOBBY).

Parker, Gerald His party provides the setting in which Hercule POIROT first hears the story of the underpriced apartment in "THE ADVENTURE OF THE CHEAP FLAT."

Parker, Harry See RAYBURN, HARRY.

Parker Pyne, Christopher A former government employee who spent thirty-five years compiling statistics, he set up his own detective agency upon retirement. Clients were obtained through an advertisement placed in the "Personals" column of the *Times*, in which Mr. Parker Pyne invited those who were unhappy to contact him at 17 Richmond

Street. Those who contact him are assured of success, and his comfortable bulk and twinkling eyes provide added reassurance. Mr. Parker Pyne's specialty is in reuniting straying husbands and wives or lovers, and he has even kept together young couples whose parents have sought to separate them by using such accomplices as the handsome and well-dressed Claude LUTTRELL and the sexy siren, Madeline DE SARA, in a variety of roles. Mr. Parker Pyne also had the distinction of employing Miss Felicity LEMON before she became Hercule POIROT's secretary, and of working first with Mrs. Ariadne OLIVER. The adventures of Mr. Parker Pyne appear in the short story collection, PARKER PYNE INVESTIGATES, and in two stories in the short story collection, THE REGATTA MYSTERY AND OTHER STORIES: "THE REGATTA MYSTERY" and "PROBLEM AT POLLENSA BAY." (See CATEGORICAL APPENDIX.)

Parker Pyne Investigates   Mystery short story collection.

The twelve stories in the collection offer the reader a detective who is different from Hercule POIROT and Miss MARPLE. Mr. PARKER PYNE, who appears in only two additional stories outside this collection, states quite clearly that he is not a detective but "a heart specialist." He advertises in the newspapers by asking "Are you Happy? If not, consult Mr. Parker Pyne," and his cases all end on a happy note. Deception, accomplices and manipulation are all part of his method of operation; he works to cure unhappiness more frequently than to investigate crime.

The first six stories, all of which are entitled "The Case of. . .," take place in England and focus on Parker Pyne as a detective of the heart. The remaining six stories occur in foreign settings where Parker Pyne is vacationing and unwilling to deal with clients. In these stories, he is confronted with crimes, and must serve as an advisor to individuals in distress.

PUBLISHING AND DRAMATIZATION HISTORY
The short story collection was published in 1934 by William Collins Sons and Company, Ltd., in London, and, under the title *Mr. Parker Pyne, Detective,* by Dodd, Mead and Company in New York in 1934.

Two of the stories, "THE CASE OF THE MIDDLE-AGED WIFE" and "THE DISCONTENTED SOLDIER," were adapted for television in 1982 by Thames Television in England.

TITLES IN THE COLLECTION
Parker Pyne Investigates contains the following short stories: "The Case of the Middle-Aged Wife," "The Case of the Discontented Soldier," "THE CASE OF THE DISTRESSED LADY," "THE CASE OF THE DISCONTENTED HUSBAND," "THE CASE OF THE CITY CLERK," "THE CASE OF THE RICH WOMAN," "HAVE YOU GOT EVERYTHING YOU WANT?," "THE GATE OF BAGHDAD," "THE HOUSE AT SHIRAZ," "THE PEARL OF PRICE," "DEATH ON THE NILE" and "THE ORACLE AT DELPHI."

CRIME NOTES
The collection introduces two characters who later develop a long association with Hercule POIROT. In these stories, Miss Felicity LEMON works as Parker Pyne's personal secretary, and she is later employed by Poirot from "HOW DOES YOUR GARDEN GROW?" onward. Mrs. Ariadne OLIVER assists Parker Pyne in "The Case of the Discontented Soldier," and makes her first appearance in a novel in CARDS ON THE TABLE.

Parkinson, Alexander   A young boy who had died because he knew too much, he leaves an underlined message in a book that leads Tuppence BERESFORD to solve an old case of espionage and murder in POSTERN OF FATE.

Parminter, Inspector   A Scotland Yard official in "THREE BLIND MICE" who is in charge of the investigation of Mrs. LYON's murder.

Parsons   The image of the well-trained butler with a properly emotionless demeanor, he is in service to Sir Reuben ASTWELL in "THE UNDER DOG."

Parsons, Olive   A fair-haired girl with wide-set, blue eyes, she is a thief at Miss AMPHREY's school in TOWARDS ZERO.

Partners in Crime   Mystery short story collection.

The collection features Tommy and Tuppence BERESFORD in a series of interconnected stories which make the work resemble a picaresque novel.

The book is made up of twenty-three individually titled chapters, among which are contained fifteen stories, some made up of two chapters.

Six years have passed since the Beresfords first began their sleuthing partnership and marriage in THE SECRET ADVERSARY, and both are ready for new adventures. At the outset, the author has given Tommy a desk job with the British Secret Service, and has placed Tuppence at home. Both are ready for danger when the chief of British Intelligence calls upon them to take over the International Detective Agency, which has been a tool of the Bolsheviks, involved in spying activities. Tommy poses as Mr. Blunt, the former head of the agency, who has been incarcerated for espionage, and Tuppence as his secretary, but both take active roles in solving cases.

PUBLISHING AND DRAMATIZATION HISTORY
Partners in Crime was published in 1929 by William Collins Sons and Company, Ltd., in London, and by Dodd, Mead and Company in New York.

"THE CASE OF THE MISSING LADY" was first adapted for television in 1950. The first adaptation of the entire book, in 1953, was made by BBC radio, which produced a thirteen-part series starring Richard Attenborough and his wife Sheila Sim in the title roles. In 1984, London Weekend Television adapted ten of the stories for a series starring James Warwick and Francesca Annis as the Beresfords.

TITLES IN THE COLLECTION
Partners in Crime contains the following short stories: "A FAIRY IN THE FLAT," "A POT OF TEA," "THE AFFAIR OF THE PINK PEARL," "THE ADVENTURE OF THE SINISTER STRANGER," "FINESSING THE KING/ THE GENTLEMAN DRESSED IN NEWSPAPER," "The Case of the Missing Lady," "BLINDMAN'S BUFF," "THE MAN IN THE MIST," "THE CRACKLER," "THE SUNNINGDALE MYSTERY," "THE HOUSE OF LURKING DEATH," "THE UNBREAKABLE ALIBI," "THE CLERGYMAN'S DAUGHTER/THE RED HOUSE" and "THE AMBASSADOR'S BOOTS."

CRIME NOTES
The stories contain parodies of fictional detectives who were well-known to readers of the 1920s. Tommy and Tuppence assume the mannerisms and methods of a different detective or detective team in each story.

Partridge, Mr. James   The last person to see Alice ASCHER, the first victim of the A.B.C. murderer, alive in THE A.B.C. MURDERS.

Passenger to Frankfurt   Mystery novel.
The novel concerns a conspiracy to attain world control through the manipulation and arming of the planet's youth. The plot centers on efforts to defeat a rising tide of anarchy and the need to crush what promises to be a resurgence of Nazi domination.

PUBLISHING AND DRAMATIZATION HISTORY
The novel was published in 1970 by William Collins Sons and Company, Ltd., in London, and by Dodd, Mead and Company in New York.

The novel has not been adapted for stage or screen.

CHARACTERS
Lord Edward ALTAMOUNT, Squadron Leader ANDREWS, Karl ARGUILEROS, Clifford BENT, Admiral Philip BLUNT, Jim BREWSTER, Lady Matilda CHECKHEATON, Gordon CHETWYND, Mildred Jean CORTMAN, Sam CORTMAN, Dr. DONALDSON, Professor ECKSTEIN, Professor GOTTLIEB, Monsieur le President GROSJEAN, Henry HORSHAM, Sir James KLEEK, Cedric LAZENBY, Amy LEATHERAN, Lisa NEUMANN, Sir Stafford NYE, Colonel Ephraim PIKEAWAY, Eric PUGH, Dr. REICHARDT, Mr. ROBINSON, Robert SHOREHAM, Herr Heinrich SPIESS, Signor VITELLI, the Grafin Charlotte VON WALDSAUSEN, Countess Renata ZERKOWSKI

PLOT SYNOPSIS
Chapters 1–3
While diplomat Sir Stafford Nye waits in the Frankfurt air terminal for the plane to London, a young woman approaches him and tells him that her life is in danger. She asks him to deliberately drink a drugged beer so that she can take his cloak and passport, then pass through disguised as Nye. Back in London, he learns from diplomatic colleagues that his actions saved the mysterious woman's life and have added some luster to his generally undistinguished diplomatic career.

Chapters 4–5
In London, Nye is nearly run over by a car that appeared to be headed directly for him. The "stolen" passport arrives in his mail, and he decides to find the young woman known as "Mary Ann" through an advertisement in the "Personals" column of the newspaper. He receives a response, and meets a woman on the Hungerford Bridge, where he is passed a ticket for the production of Wagner's opera *Siegfried* the next evening. A woman arrives after intermission and asks to borrow his program, signs "the young Siegfried" at one point, then returns the program when she leaves. He finds that she penciled in words from the Siegfried motif. He decides to visit his politically connected Aunt Matilda immediately.

Chapters 6–8
Nye discusses politics with Aunt Matilda, and she mentions a new hero of the youth movement, who calls himself "young Siegfried." A few days later, he attends a dinner at the American Embassy, where, in a room filled with diplomats, FBI agents and secret service agents, he sees "Mary Ann." Outside, an anti–Vietnam War demonstration turns violent, and police arrive to quell the disturbance. Mildred Cortman, wife of the ambassador, is disgusted by these occurrences. After dinner, "Mary Ann," really the Countess Renata Zerkowski, offers Nye a ride home, but she first takes him to a large house in the countryside.

Chapters 9–11
Several high ranking members of the British Foreign Service meet with Nye and inform him that he will undertake an investigation for a committee of inquiry of worldwide significance. He will be given his instructions on a need-to-know basis, but the goal is to stop a growing movement of violence for its own sake, involving youth and drugs. Nye and Renata head for Bavaria the next day, to attend the Festival Youth Theater. The next morning, they drive to a small country inn for lunch, and Renata tells Nye that he will meet the "Master of Assassins," who plies his followers with drugs to keep them under his control. She also tells him that one of the committee members is a traitor. When they arrive at their destination, a great castle, Nye meets the Countess von Waldsausen, known as "Big Charlotte" in diplomatic circles, a grotesquely fat woman who claims to know Aunt Matilda. At dinner, Wagnerian music plays, and

the guests salute each other with a Nazi-like "Heil." While horseback riding the following day, he learns that the Countess is a very powerful and wealthy woman who finances youth groups with the aim of taking over the world. She is the force behind the young, blond, muscular Franz Joseph, a great orator who is known as "the young Siegfried." Nye realizes that Renata is a double agent, but cannot be sure where her real loyalty lies.

Chapters 12–15
Renata takes Nye to a large mountain stadium where Franz Joseph speaks, and they see the frenzy he creates. Secret conferences are called in Paris and London to combat the growing threat, and top security man Henry Horsham outlines the group's breakdown of power. Fear spreads as pockets of power, "Black Power," "Red Power" and others, seem to be supportive of the movement. Conference members report that large tracts of land in France are under the domination of youth power troops, financed by the financial genius, Big Charlotte. They conclude that "There's fighting in some parts of every country." Aunt Matilda decides to take a hand in the action, and she makes a visit to her old schoolfriend, Big Charlotte, to whom she hints that Nye is a malcontent in the diplomatic service. Big Charlotte promises to make him the spearhead of the movement in England.

Chapters 16–18
The news worldwide is bad, and world upheaval is imminent. Dr. Reichardt reveals that the real Hitler had been confined to a mental asylum with numerous Hitler lookalikes, all claiming to be him. Identities were switched, and the real Hitler escaped to Argentina, where he married a fair-haired Aryan woman, with whom he produced a fair-haired son who was branded with a swastika on one foot. The child, named Karl Arguileros, is Franz Joseph or the "Young Siegfried," leader of the New World State.

Chapters 19–22
Three students visit Nye, and ask for his assistance in ending the violence and producing change. Lady Matilda informs the authorities about a drug invented by Professor Shoreham that makes suicidal people become relaxed and benevolent. Officials learn that the professor destroyed all notes for his Project Benvo three weeks before his stroke because

of its dangerous side effects. In desperation, the inscrutable Mr. Robinson and two high-ranking British government officials visit Shoreham and convince him to reconstruct his experiment.

Chapter 23
The officials hope to use the formula on the Revolution of Youth members. Shoreham agrees, if Lord Altamount will head the project. Lord Altamount's assistant, James Kleek, jumps forward and tries to inject him with strychnine, but he is restrained. Lord Altamount dies, nonetheless.

Epilogue
Arrangements are made for Nye to marry the vindicated Renata.

CRIME NOTES
The two murders in this novel result from gunshot wounds.

Passing of Mr. Quinn, The   Film released in 1928 by Strand Films. The movie is based on the short story, "THE COMING OF MR. QUIN," which was first published in *Pearson's Magazine*.

CAST
The cast consists of Stewart Rome as Harley QUINN [*sic*], as well as Trilby Clark and Ursula Jeans.

CHANGES FROM THE ORIGINAL TEXT
In addition to changing the spelling of Mr. Harley Quin's last name and changing the title, the adaptation, written by Leslie Hiscott, also completely rewrote the story. Mr. SATTERTHWAITE is eliminated from the story, which becomes a tale of the investigation to save a woman whose evil professor husband has been poisoned after having had an affair with their maid.

PRODUCTION NOTES
Despite high expectations for the film, it had only moderate success at the box office. To promote the film, Strand Films commissioned writer G. Roy McRae to write a full-length novelization of the film, which was published by The Novel Library and had no connection to Agatha Christie.

Paton, Captain Ralph   The stepson of Roger ACKROYD who had left home six months earlier after

Popular matinee idol Stewart Rome played the enigmatic Mr. Quin in the 1928 film, *The Passing of Mr. Quinn [sic]*. (Photo courtesy of the National Film Archive)

an argument, he was in the vicinity on the night of the murder in THE MURDER OF ROGER ACKROYD. According to Hercule POIROT, he is " 'unusually good-looking for an Englishman,' " and he is secretly married to the parlourmaid, Ursula BOURNE.

Paton, Mrs. Ralph   See BOURNE, URSULA.

Patriotic Murders, The   See ONE, TWO, BUCKLE MY SHOE.

Patterson, Elsie   Despite her dislike of her sister Gerda, she moves in with her after the death of her brother-in-law to run the household in THE HOLLOW.

Patterson, Janet   A pleasant, fifteen-year-old girl in UNFINISHED PORTRAIT, she has "that mysterious thing—a figure" which the main character envies.

Patterson, Phyllis   The fiancée of Arthur CARMI-CHAEL, she remains devotedly near while he suffers through being possessed by the spirit of a grey Persian cat in "THE STRANGE CASE OF SIR ARTHUR CARMICHAEL."

Paul, Prince of Maurania   A nobleman who occasionally poses as Count Feodor, he loves Valerie SAINTCLAIR, and desires to protect her from scandal in "THE KING OF CLUBS," calling upon Hercule POIROT for assistance.

Pauline, Grand Duchess   An imposter in "JANE IN SEARCH OF A JOB" who tricks Jane CLEVELAND into posing in public as the Grand Duchess on the pretext that assassins are near. The imposter knows that the real Pauline has already eloped with the chauffeur, but she is a member of a gang of robbers who dupe Jane and leave her to take the blame.

Paulovitch, Count Sergius   See MINKS, ARTHUR.

Pauncefoot Jones, Dr. John (Pussyfoot)   Senior member of the archaeological dig at the ancient city of Murik in THEY CAME TO BAGHDAD, he is a learned and respected archaeologist.

Pavlovitch, Count Alexis   A dilettante and old friend of Hercule POIROT, he is a reliable source of information regarding everyone and everything in the artistic world in "THE ARCADIAN DEER."

Payne, Maisie   An American girl with a drawl, she helps CELIA to feel at home at the French finishing school in UNFINISHED PORTRAIT.

Paynter, Mr.   Wealthy, well-read and well-traveled, he is a man of about fifty-five years of age whose manuscript on the topic of covert activities in China disappears when he is found dead in THE BIG FOUR.

Paynter, Gerald   A young artist and nephew to a murdered man in THE BIG FOUR, he has an alibi for the night of the murder.

Peabody, Caroline   A willing source of information when Hercule POIROT attempts to learn more about the Arundell family in DUMB WITNESS, she was a close friend of the murdered Emily ARUNDELL.

Peake, Mildred   A big, jolly-looking woman in her forties who is fond of tweeds and rubber boots, she is the housekeeper with an arch manner in SPIDER'S WEB who is also referred to as "the Amazon." Her real name is Mrs. Brown; she seeks to identify the person who murdered her business partner.

"Pearl of Price, The"   Mystery short story.

The plot centers on the recovery of a valuable pearl earring among a company of tourists in the African desert.

PUBLISHING AND DRAMATIZATION HISTORY
The story appeared in the short story collection, PARKER PYNE INVESTIGATES, published in 1934 by William Collins Sons and Company, Ltd., in London and under the title, *Mr. Parker Pyne, Detective,* by Dodd, Mead and Company in New York.

The story has not been adapted for stage or screen.

CHARACTERS
Mr. Caleb BLUNDELL, Carol BLUNDELL, Dr. CARVER, Colonel DUBOSC, Abbas EFFENDI, Jim HURST, Sir Donald MARVEL, Mr. PARKER PYNE

PLOT SYNOPSIS
The story concerns the disappearance of a pearl earring purported to be worth forty thousand dollars. Its owner, Mr. Blundell, asks Mr. Parker Pyne to clear a young man of suspicion. Called upon to determine the guilty party, the detective recalls with suspicion Mr. Blundell's vehement emphasis upon the value of the earrings. Mr. Parker Pyne considers the possible motives and rightly identifies the least likely individual as the thief.

Pearson, Mr.   The member of a bank board of directors, he is among those interested in investing in a Burmese mine said to contain fabulous riches in "THE LOST MINE." He hires Hercule POIROT to locate missing courier WU LING, who was expected to deliver vital papers containing the mine location. When the detective suggests that answers may be found in an opium den frequented by another bank official, he has the audacity to suggest that Poirot shave his mustache so that the two can enter the opium den incognito.

Pearson, Mrs. Spoken of as "Mrs. Funnyface" by another character in THE BIG FOUR, she is Hercule POIROT's landlady at 14 Farraway Street.

Pearson, Brian A resident of Australia in recent years, the younger brother of James PEARSON returns to England shortly before his uncle, Captain TREVELYAN, is murdered in THE SITTAFORD MYSTERY.

Pearson, James Viewed by his attorney, Mr. DACRES, as not having a "very high standard of commercial honesty," he falls under suspicion when his uncle, Captain TREVELYAN, is murdered in THE SITTAFORD MYSTERY.

Pebmarsh, Millicent A blind schoolteacher in THE CLOCKS, she finds the murder victim and several unfamiliar clocks in her home when she returns from shopping.

Pedlar, Sir Eustace, M.P. A man who functions on both sides of the law in THE MAN IN THE BROWN SUIT, he is both the highly efficient criminal mastermind, the "Colonel," and a Member of Parliament. The "Colonel" has a talent for organization and the ability to make his illegal plans work. In his everyday role as an M.P., he commands respect, and professes, "My only object in life is to be thoroughly comfortable."

Pendar, Dr. A member of the Tuesday Night Club, he is an elderly clergyman in ST. MARY MEAD who joins in the spirit of helping to solve the crimes that other members bring to club meetings in THE THIRTEEN PROBLEMS.

Pengelly, Mrs. She believes that her "gastritis" attacks occur because her husband is poisoning her, and she consults Hercule POIROT too late in "THE CORNISH MYSTERY."

Pengelly, Edward A dentist in "THE CORNISH MYSTERY," he marries his assistant soon after the death of his wife, whom he is suspected of poisoning.

Penn, Elizabeth A woman in "DOUBLE SIN" who owns an antique shop in Ebermouth, she sends her niece, Mary DURRANT, with miniatures to sell to collector J. Baker WOOD.

Penn, Major General Sir Josiah (Old Josh) An old man with a double chin, bald head, bushy eyebrows and enormous paunch, he is a former suitor of Tommy BERESFORD's Aunt Ada in BY THE PRICKING OF MY THUMBS. He might have been Tommy's uncle had he not gone to India decades before. Despite being "extremely deaf, half-blind, crippled with rheumatism," he remains a highly effective and respected member of the International Union of Associated Security.

Pennington, Andrew The scheming American trustee of Linnet DOYLE's estate in DEATH ON THE NILE (2), he arrives in Egypt with papers for her to sign that would aid him in bilking her out of her estate.

Pennyfeather, Canon An absentminded cleric in AT BERTRAM'S HOTEL who is also a scholar of Hebrew and Aramaic, he is missing for five days before the police contact his housekeeper, Mrs. MacRAE. He is in London to attend a conference on the Dead Sea Scrolls, but arrives on the wrong day. When he returns to his hotel room, he is knocked unconscious, and placed on a country road, to be found by Emma WHEELING and her husband.

Pennyman, Major The atmosphere at the Tell Yarimjah disturbs this elderly retired army officer who now lives in Baghdad in MURDER IN MESOPOTAMIA. While he cannot identify exactly what seems unnatural at the site, he states that he "got a queer impression of something being wrong . . . they all passed the butter to each other too politely."

Penrose, Dr. Consulted by Gwenda REED about the suicide of a former patient—her father, Major Kelvin HALLIDAY—he is the psychiatrist and superintendent of the Saltmarsh House nursing home in SLEEPING MURDER. His appearance prompts Gwenda to feel that the doctor is himself somewhat mentally unbalanced.

Pentemian, Mrs. One of the tourists in "THE GATE OF BAGHDAD," she is really the mother of Signor POLI.

Percehouse, Caroline A wealthy invalid who uses her potential inheritance as a means of making people obey her in THE SITTAFORD MYSTERY, she is not impressed by her spineless nephew, Ronald GARFIELD. As the owner of five cats, she is just as likely to leave her fortune to an animal shelter as to her relatives.

Perenna, Eileen Widow of an IRA agitator and the manager of the San Souci guest house in N OR M?, she is suspected of subversive activities.

Perenna, Sheila The daughter of a slain IRA agent in N OR M?, she is bitterly opposed to patriotic activity and all forms of propaganda. The beautiful young woman is very upset when her lover is arrested and charged with possessing sabotage plans.

Peril at End House Mystery novel.

The novel concerns a series of attempts on the life of the young and pretty mistress of an eerie and imposing family mansion. The plot centers on Hercule POIROT's efforts to unmask whomever is trying to murder Nick BUCKLEY.

PUBLISHING AND DRAMATIZATION HISTORY

The novel was published in 1932 by William Collins Sons and Company, Ltd., in London, and by Dodd, Mead and Company in New York.

The novel was adapted for the stage by Arthur Ridley, and opened at the Vaudeville Theatre in London on May 1, 1940, starring Francis L. Sullivan as Hercule Poirot.

The novel was later adapted for television in 1990 by London Weekend Television in England and presented in a two-hour production, the first of a new series to mark the centenary year, starring David SUCHET as Hercule Poirot.

CHARACTERS

Reverend Giles BUCKLEY, Jean BUCKLEY, Maggie BUCKLEY, Nick Buckley, Commander George CHALLENGER, Bert CROFT, Milly CROFT, Dr. GRAHAM, Captain Arthur HASTINGS, Chief Inspector JAPP, Jim LAZARUS, Dr. MacALLISTER, Hercule Poirot, Mr. RICE, Frederica RICE, Charles VYSE, Dr. WHITFIELD, Ellen WILSON

PLOT SYNOPSIS
Chapters 1–3
Poirot and Hastings are vacationing in St. Loo, where they meet the lovely young Nick Buckley, who has had three "accidents" that look suspiciously like murder attempts to Poirot. A wasp annoys Nick as she sits with the detectives, and Poirot finds a bullet on the ground and a bullet hole in the hat she leaves behind. He visits her at End House, and tells her that he fears for her safety. After learning that her real name is Magdala, and that she is called Nick after her grandfather, he asks who might benefit from her death. The visit ends as Poirot offers to protect Nick.

Chapters 4–6
Concerned that someone will murder Nick, Poirot questions the mechanic who worked on her car after the brakes failed, as well as her cousin, Charles Vyse, and friends. At End House, Poirot shows Hastings how easily someone could have accomplished the accidents. He later suggests that Nick invite her cousin Maggie Buckley to stay with her.

Chapters 7–9
Nick invites Poirot to watch the fireworks from the promontory at End House, and he meets Maggie who, like Nick, is dressed in black. The difference is that Nick has draped a red Chinese shawl across her shoulders to enliven the black. As they watch the fireworks, Maggie returns to the house for a coat, but she is shot and dies. She is found lying on the ground, wearing Nick's red shawl. Three bullets are found in the body.

Chapters 10–12
Poirot attempts to learn who called Nick during dinner, and discovers that her former fiancé, pilot Michael Seton, is listed in the newspaper as dead. He also learns that the still-married Frederica Rice has been having an affair with Jim Lazarus. Eager to protect Nick, Poirot takes her to a nursing home where no visitors are allowed. Nick reveals that her engagement to Michael Seton had been kept a secret,

Inspector Japp (Philip Jackson), Hercule Poirot (David Suchet), Captain Hastings (Hugh Fraser) and Felicity Lemon (Pauline Moran) in a group portrait at the end of the 1990 television film, *Peril at End House.* (Photo courtesy of London Weekend Television)

because his Uncle Matthew would have disinherited him. Poirot asks her permission to search End House for her will. He now suspects Charles Vyse and Freddie Rice, who stand to inherit millions if Nick were to die.

Chapters 13–16
Poirot does not find the will at End House, but he does find Seton's love letters to Nick. When questioned, Nick remembers that she had asked her neighbor, Bert Croft, to mail the will to Charles Vyse. Vyse claims that he never received the will, and Croft claims that he mailed it. In a visit to Freddie, the detective observes that she picks up a watch from George, and he becomes suspicious that it may be carrying cocaine. The circle of friends has all the

signs of cocaine use. Poirot cautions Nick to not eat anything from the outside, and, to cheer her up, he sends her flowers with the card signed "with the compliments of Hercule Poirot." Soon after, Nick is poisoned by cocaine which had been placed in chocolates accompanied by Poirot's card from the flowers. He decides to let everyone think that Nick has died to see what the murderer will do next.

Chapters 17–19
Vyse receives Nick's will in the mail, and they plan a reading at End House. Poirot desires to hold a seance before the reading, using Hastings as the medium. Nick appears at the seance, and they realize that she is still alive. Japp enters End House after the seance and unmasks a well-known forger.

Chapters 20–22
A gun is found in Freddie's coat pocket, but she is later shot, the bullet grazing her shoulder. The gunman is her cocaine-addicted husband, whom the police shoot dead. As Nick's friends and family are gathered, Poirot reveals the murderer. The police take away the murderer, who is seen by Poirot taking one of the cocaine-filled watches as a "souvenir," which he expects will be used to commit suicide. At the end, Freddie and Lazarus make plans to marry.

CRIME NOTES
The sole murder victim in this novel dies from three gunshot wounds.

Perrot, Jules   An airline employee who accepted a bribe to delay the departure of a passenger until the flight on which she is murdered, he is unable to withstand the scrutiny of Hercule POIROT in DEATH IN THE CLOUDS.

Perry, Alice and Amos   An unusual couple who were the caretakers of Julia LANCASTER in her final days, they live in a home that appears prominently in a painting in BY THE PRICKING OF MY THUMBS. Mr. Perry is harmless but mentally unstable, while his wife evokes the image of a witch, with long, straggly hair and "a kind of steeple hat perched on her head."

Perry, Percy   The editor of the *X-Ray News* in "THE AUGEAN STABLES," he prints gossip and innuendo about the government as news in the effort to sell papers. He justifies the stories by the assertion that he wants to clean up Parliament with the "purifying flood of public opinion."

Peters, Andrew   See GLYDR, MAJOR BORIS ANDREI PAVLOV.

Peters, Mrs. Willard J.   A widow who tours the Greek ruins as a concession to her son's strong interest in antiquity in "THE ORACLE AT DELPHI," she is more at home in Paris, London or the Riviera. When kidnappers take her son and demand her diamonds as ransom, she consults Hercule POIROT.

Peters, Willard J., Jr.   The pampered and smothered eighteen-year-old son of a widowed mother in "THE ORACLE AT DELPHI," he is kidnapped by Greek jewel thieves and held for ransom. His mother refers to him as "her pet, her delicate serious Willard."

Petherick, Mr.   An attorney who handles Miss MARPLE's legal affairs, he is a member of the Tuesday Night Club and a man who placed all of his trust in facts alone in "MOTIVE VERSUS OPPORTUNITY." His son takes over the practice after his death.

Pettigrew, Miss   See MINKS, ARTHUR.

Phelps, Hayward   An American journalist whom Bundle BRENT watches closely at the Seven Dials meeting, he is also known under the names of Number Four and Four O'clock in THE SEVEN DIALS MYSTERY.

Phillips, Sergeant   A police officer in EVIL UNDER THE SUN, he assists in the murder investigation.

Phillpot, Major   A friend of Michael and Ellie ROGERS and Claudia HARDCASTLE, he is viewed by the inhabitants of Kingston Bishop as "God locally" in ENDLESS NIGHT. He has a special connection with the gipsy, Esther (Old Mother) LEE.

Phillpot, Gervase   The invalid wife of Major PHILLPOT in ENDLESS NIGHT, she wants to know whom Michael ROGERS knows among society.

"Philomel Cottage"   Mystery short story.
The plot centers on a young woman's fear of her new husband's past, and the threat posed to her life.

PUBLISHING AND DRAMATIZATION HISTORY
The story appeared in the short story collection, THE LISTERDALE MYSTERY (1), published in 1934 by William Collins Sons and Company, Ltd., in London.

The story was adapted in 1936 into a play named *Love from a Stranger*, which opened in London at the New Theatre on March 31, 1936. In 1937, a film dramatization under the same name, starring Ann Harding and Basil Rathbone, was released by United Artists in England, the first film to be made of an Agatha Christie work in England. In 1947,

Eagle Lion Studios in Hollywood remade the film, using a new screenplay written by American mystery writer Philip MacDonald. The film, which starred John Hodiak and Sylvia Sidney, was renamed *A Stranger Walked In.*

CHARACTERS
Mr. AMES, GEORGE, Alix King MARTIN, Gerald MARTIN, Dicky WINDYFORD

PLOT SYNOPSIS
The story concerns a young woman's fears which arise when she suspects that her new husband is really a bigamist, swindler and murderer. Dicky Windyford has long loved Alix, but he wanted to make his fortune before making a commitment, and his reticence increases when Alix inherits two thousand pounds. She unexpectedly meets and marries a stranger, Gerald Martin, thus dashing Dicky's hopes forever, but the new bride soon feels uneasy. Her feelings are heightened by her discovery of old American newspapers and a diary which reveal Gerald's dark past. Frightened, she contacts Dicky for help, but his delay in responding forces Alix to defend herself in a clever manner before help arrives.

Philpotts, Eden A British author and neighbor of the Millers at Ashfield, he was famous for his Dartmoor novels. At Clara MILLER's suggestion, Agatha Christie showed her early writing to him. He not only provided her with constructive criticism, but recommended her to his own literary agent, Hughes Massie.

Pierce, Constable A young constable in THE CLOCKS, he nervously refers a woman to his supervisor for an interview only a short time before she becomes the second murder victim.

Pierce, Mrs. (1) An elderly, heavyset woman in "MURDER IN THE MEWS" (2) who cleaned house for Miss PLENDERLEITH and Mrs. ALLEN, she is an unreliable woman who often arrives long after the appointed hour of 9 A.M.

Pierce, Mrs. (2) Manager of a tobacco and stationery store in MURDER IS EASY, she is the mother of eight children. Luke FITZWILLIAM speaks with her, and learns about the death of her son, Tommy.

Pierce, Amabel A tourist in Jerusalem in APPOINTMENT WITH DEATH, she is a former nursery governess who is deathly afraid of heights.

Pierce, Tommy One of eight children of a tobacco and stationery shop manager in MURDER IS EASY, he is an opportunist and an acolyte in Mr. ELLSWORTHY's satanic coven. He dies after falling from the third-story window of Wych Hall while washing windows.

Pierre A nervous and unsure waiter at the exclusive Luxembourg restaurant in SPARKLING CYANIDE, he is the headwaiter's nephew and "a frightened white rabbit of sixteen." When he retrieved Iris MARLE's purse and placed it at the wrong place at the table, he moved all members of the party over by one seat.

Pike, Albert and Jessie Witnesses to Andrew MARSH's only valid will in "THE CASE OF THE MISSING WILL."

Pikeaway, Colonel Ephraim A man of great bulk and inscrutable appearance, he is head of the Special Branch of British Intelligence and appears in CAT AMONG THE PIGEONS, PASSENGER TO FRANKFURT and POSTERN OF FATE.

Plenderleith, Jane A truly dedicated friend to Barbara ALLEN in "MURDER IN THE MEWS" (2), she dislikes both Barbara's fiancé, Charles LAVERTON-WEST, and Major EUSTACE.

"Plymouth Express, The" Mystery short story.
The plot centers on the murder of a wealthy young heiress whose body is left stuffed under the seat of a railroad carriage. The plot appeared in expanded form in THE MYSTERY OF THE BLUE TRAIN.

PUBLISHING AND DRAMATIZATION
HISTORY
The story appeared in the short story collection, THE UNDER DOG AND OTHER STORIES, published in 1951 by Dodd, Mead and Company in New York.
The story was adapted for television in 1991 by London Weekend Television in England, and was

shown on the Public Broadcasting Service in the United States.

CHARACTERS
The Honorable Flossie CARRINGTON, Rupert CARRINGTON, Count Armand DE LA ROCHEFOUR, Ebenezer HALLIDAY, Captain Arthur HASTINGS, Inspector James JAPP, Jane MASON, Hercule POIROT, Lieutenant Alec SIMPSON, R.N.

PLOT SYNOPSIS
The story concerns the death of a wealthy American industrialist's daughter and the disappearance of over one hundred thousand dollars in jewels. When Ebenezer Halliday's daughter's body is found stuffed under a train seat, he hires Hercule Poirot to locate the murderer. The likely suspects are the dead woman's disreputable husband, and a former lover with whom she had recently renewed contact. As Poirot interviews the dead woman's personal maid, he realizes that certain clues seem to have been planted. Using his "little gray cells," he surprises Inspector Japp with the solution to the mystery.

CRIME NOTES
The victim in this story is first rendered unconscious with chloroform and then stabbed with a knife.

Pocket Full of Rye, A Mystery novel.
The novel concerns a family murder that loosely follows the nursery rhyme, "Sing a Song of Sixpence." The plot centers on the efforts of Miss MARPLE to reveal a murderer who has killed three people, one of whom is her former parlourmaid.

PUBLISHING AND DRAMATIZATION HISTORY
The novel was published in 1953 by William Collins Sons and Company, Ltd., in London, and in 1954 by Dodd, Mead and Company in New York.

The novel was adapted for television in 1986 by the BBC in England, and was also shown on the Public Broadcasting Service in the U.S.

CHARACTERS
Mr. ANSELL, Mr. BILLINGSLEY, Mr. CRUMP, Mrs. CRUMP, Mary DOVE, Vivian DUBOIS, ELLEN (4), Albert EVANS, Adele FORTESCUE, Elaine FORTESCUE, Jennifer FORTESCUE, Lancelot FORTESCUE, Patricia FORTESCUE, Percival FORTESCUE, Rex FORTESCUE, Miss GRIFFITH, Mrs. GROSVENOR, Inspector Sergeant HAY, Helen MACKENZIE, Ruby MACKENZIE, Miss Jane Marple, Gladys MARTIN, Inspector NEELE, Miss Effie RAMSBOTTOM, Gerald WRIGHT

PLOT SYNOPSIS
Chapters 1–3
Miss Grosvenor, personal secretary to wealthy industrialist Rex Fortescue, takes tea to her employer. When he falls ill, she panics and calls a doctor. Inspector Neele is called to Fortescue's office to investigate, and he learns from the doctor that Fortescue has died of poisoning. He interviews the head typist, and learns of the victim's black market connections. He also questions Miss Grosvenor about the rye grain found in the victim's jacket pocket, but she knows nothing about it.

Chapters 4–7
At Yewtree Lodge, the Fortescue home, Neele questions the staff but learns little of interest, aside from the fact that one of the victim's long-absent sons will be arriving soon. When the victim's wife, Adele, arrives home, Neele informs her of her husband's death, and he is shocked to note a faint smile.

Chapters 8–10
Neele and Inspector Sergeant Hay learn that another of the victim's sons, Percival, will return immediately to London. They question the housemaid, Ellen, who tells them that Fortescue would have applied for a divorce if he had not died. When they interview the victim's sister-in-law, Miss Ramsbottom, she tells them that he was a sinful man whom she never liked. The only family member who seems honestly to mourn the victim is his daughter, Elaine. Although the authorities are puzzled, they believe that Adele is the killer.

Chapters 11–12
Adele and Vivian Dubois discuss the murder, and Vivian asks Adele to burn his letters so that he will not be incriminated. At tea, Lancelot appears and discusses the murder with Adele, while Jennifer makes the observation that one good aspect of the housekeeper, Mary Dove, is that she "knows her place." When he speaks with his Aunt Effie, Lance realizes that she is fully aware of Adele's affair. The

authorities learn that Gladys is to be married in the spring to a man named Bert, whose letters they find in her room among newspaper clippings about unidentified flying objects and truth drugs used by the Russians. Adele dies after eating half a scone and tea, and Neele believes that she has been poisoned.

Chapters 13–16
After Gladys Martin is found dead, Miss Marple enters the case, because she is the young woman's former employer. She speaks with Neele, and asks him to look into the question of blackbirds, because the murders follow the pattern in the nursery rhyme. When Neele follows her lead, he learns that someone had placed four dead blackbirds on the victim's desk. He speaks with Elaine, who can now marry Gerald Wright, whom her father had opposed. Lance tells the detective about the Blackbird Mine in Africa, in which Rex Fortescue may have left someone to die.

Chapters 17–20
Neele contacts Mr. Ansell, the attorney who drew up Adele's will, and learns that she left everything to Vivian Dubois. When he speaks with Gerald Wright, Neele finds that blackbirds were put in a pie one night as a joke. Neele follows his intuition in contacting another attorney, who points out that Adele had nothing to leave because she did not survive Rex for a month. Therefore, that estate goes to Percival. In searching for more information about the Blackbird Mine, Neele speaks with Helen MacKenzie, widow of Rex Fortescue's late partner. She states that she raised her children to promise revenge on Rex Fortescue, but she has ended her relationship with her daughter Ruby.

Chapters 21–23
Miss Marple speaks with Percival's wife, who is extremely frightened. When Miss Marple speaks with Patricia, she observes that there will be no more deaths, because the murderer has accomplished his purpose. Lance goes to the family business office and tries to work, but Neele arrives, and the two discuss the case. When Percival arrives, the brothers argue, because Percival does not agree that the MacKenzies are back for revenge.

Chapters 24–28
Neele speaks with Miss Marple about the rhyme, which suggests that the maid is the murderer. They search the bushes and find a jar of marmalade con-

taining the slow-acting poison that killed Rex Fortescue. Miss Marple concludes that Gladys Martin killed Rex Fortescue by putting taxine in the marmalade, after being told to do so. The same person strangled her later. After speaking with Miss Ramsbottom, Miss Marple is certain of the name of the murderer. She unearths a letter of confession and apology from the late Gladys, with a picture enclosed showing Gladys with the murderer.

CRIME NOTES
Three murders occur in this novel. The first victim is poisoned with marmalade containing slow-acting taxine, a substance extracted from the leaves and berries of the yew tree. The second victim is strangled with a nylon stocking. The third victim is poisoned by potassium cyanide placed in her tea.

Poems Poetry collection.
The two-volume collection includes THE ROAD OF DREAMS as the first volume of the collection, with twenty-seven additional verses collected in the second volume.

PUBLISHING AND DRAMATIZATION HISTORY
The collection was published in 1973 by William Collins Sons and Company, Ltd., in London, and by Dodd, Mead and Company in New York.
The collection has not been adapted for stage or screen.

TITLES IN THE COLLECTION
The collection is divided into two volumes. Volume I consists of the author's early collection, *The Road of Dreams*, published in 1924, which is divided into four parts: "A Masque from Italy," "Ballads," "Dream and Fantasies" and "Other Poems." The ten poems in "A Masque from Italy" are created around the theme of the *commedia dell'arte,* and focus on the character of Harlequin, a precursor of Mr. Harley QUIN in her short stories. The seven ballads in "Ballads" contain romantic stories of knights, ladies and death in childbirth. In "Dreams and Fantasies," the seven poems contain nebulous references to dream- and nightmare-like states. The final section of Volume I, "Other Poems," is the miscellany of eleven poems that the section title implies.

Volume II of the collection contains twenty-seven poems of more recent composition, in sections entitled "Things," "Places," "Love Poems and Others" and "Verses of Nowadays." The four poems of "Things" contain ruminations on beauty, water, sculptors and tunes for wandering. In the section entitled "Places," the author writes of five locations ranging from the Middle East to Dartmoor, and delves into the religious past of Calvary. "Love Poems and Others" contains eleven passionate calls for love, including a lament of women and a lament of the tortured lover. The four poems of "Verses of Nowadays" contain nostalgia for lost childhood innocence and a dead love, and a prosaic rendering of a picnic alongside the road.

Pointz, Isaac   A wealthy diamond merchant who keeps a diamond worth thirty thousand pounds with him at all times as good luck in "THE REGATTA MYSTERY," he is duped into a bet that nearly costs him the stone.

Poirot, Achille   A subject of conjecture, this reputed twin brother of Hercule POIROT appears in only one adventure, THE BIG FOUR, and is mentioned in the "Foreword" to THE LABOURS OF HERCULES. When Hercule tells Hastings that he will have to bring his twin brother into the case, Captain HASTINGS is understandably surprised, because this is the first time he has heard of a twin brother's existence. Before Achille appears, Hercule described him as living a life of complete indolence near Spa in Belgium, despite possessing highly refined skills in detection. When Achille appears, it is after Hastings and the Countess Vera ROSSAKOFF believe that Hercule has died in an explosion after trying to light a fire in a fireplace. Achille is remarkably similar to Hercule in appearance, except that his voice is different, his eyes are dark, his moustache is a fake, and he has a scar on his upper lip. As Achille attempts to escape from Felsenlabyrnth, their surroundings explode and Hastings wakes up in bed with Hercule standing by his side. To Hastings' question about Achille, Hercule replies that his brother has returned "to the land of myths," and he assures his old friend that he was disguised as Achille. He claims that he darkened his eyes with drops of belladonna and had inflicted an actual scar on his upper lip two months previously. The second mention of Achille occurs in the "Foreword" to THE LABOURS OF HERCULES, when Dr. BURTON asks Hercule why his mother had chosen the classical name for her son, and notes that the detective had a brother named Achille. To this, Hercule replies "Only for a short time."

Poirot, Hercule   The only fictional character ever to be honored with an obituary on the front page of *The New York Times*, the detective had a long and glorious career in thirty-three novels and sixty-five short stories. Created in 1916 as the detective star of the author's first novel, *The Mysterious Affair at Styles*, which was not published until 1921, Poirot entered literature as a Belgian refugee who had retired in 1904 from the Belgian police force. Through various novels, readers learned that Poirot had moved quickly through the police ranks until he became their most successful detective. After retirement from the force, Poirot built a reputation throughout Europe as the most celebrated sleuth on the Continent. In these years, before his adventures were recorded by Agatha Christie, the sleuth became acquainted with Inspector James JAPP, first in the Abercrombie forgery case in Brussels and later in the Baron Altara case in Antwerp. He also became acquainted with Arthur HASTINGS in the years before World War I, when the man who would later become his trusted sidekick was still working for Lloyd's of London. These early adventures appear as references or footnotes in later Poirot adventures, chronicled by Hastings and authored by Agatha Christie.

The physical Poirot is as unusual in appearance as he is in detecting talent. Green-eyed and standing five feet, four inches tall, he is a meticulously dressed man who usually wears patent leather shoes, and whose head is shaped like an egg. He is fastidious in his habits, and he takes great pride in his luxuriant moustache. Although other detectives might spend their time hunting down footprints and looking for clues, Poirot uses "the little gray cells," and does his most effective detecting work while sitting in an easy chair.

Hastings and Poirot meet again at Styles Court, after their initial involvement in a case related to Lloyd's of London, and decide to take rooms together at 14 Farraday Street after the case in *The Mysterious Affair at Styles*. Some years later, after Hastings marries and moves away, Poirot relocates to Whitehaven Mansions, which he chooses because it

Of all the actors who have attempted the role of Hercule Poirot, David Suchet has created the definitive characterization of the Belgian sleuth. (Photo courtesy of London Weekend Television)

is new and constructed symmetrically in exactly proportioned units. He had retired for a time to the country to grow vegetable marrows, but he welcomed a return to London to work as a private investigator. His telephone, number Trafalgar 8137, was soon busy with the calls of potential clients and requests for help from Inspector Japp. In his new quarters, he also employed the perfect gentleman's gentleman, GEORGE, referred to in some stories as Georges, and he hired Miss Felicity LEMON as his secretary, whose most recent previous employer was Mr. PARKER PYNE. Although he never married, Poirot became passionately attached to Countess Vera ROSSAKOFF, who remained the love of his life throughout three decades.

By his final appearance in CURTAIN, Poirot was confined to a wheelchair, his body crippled by arthritis. His mind and those little gray cells were as sharp as ever as he solved his final and most challenging case. Poirot engineered his own demise as he stoically pushed out of reach the medicine which could have saved his life. On August 6, 1975, *The New York Times* reported on page one the following headline: "Hercule Poirot Is Dead; Famed Belgian Detective." As he said in his letter, delivered posthumously to Hastings, he lived his days well and "They have been good days."

Poirot Investigates   Mystery short story collection.

The first story collection published by Agatha Christie, her fourth book contains twelve short stories which were originally published in *Sketch*. The editor, Bruce INGRAM, approached the relatively new author and told her that he would like to publish a series of short stories starring Hercule POIROT. The publication of the first story, on March 7, 1923, included the first illustration of the Belgian detective. The author first titled the book *The Curious Disappearance of the Opalsen Pearls,* then *The Jewel Robbery at the Metropolitan*; the publisher suggested *The Gray Cells of Monsieur Poirot* and *Poirot Investigates*.

PUBLISHING AND DRAMATIZATION HISTORY
Poirot Investigates was published in 1924 by John Lane in London and in 1925 by Dodd, Mead & Co. in New York.

All of the stories in the collection have been adapted for television by London Weekend Television and also shown on the Public Broadcasting Service in the U.S.

TITLES IN THE COLLECTION
Poirot Investigates contains the following short stories: "The Adventure of 'The Western Star'," "THE TRAGEDY AT MARSDEN MANOR," "THE ADVENTURE OF THE CHEAP FLAT," "THE MILLION-DOLLAR BOND ROBBERY," THE MYSTERY OF HUNTER'S LODGE, THE ADVENTURE OF THE EGYPTIAN TOMB, THE JEWEL ROBBERY AT THE GRAND METROPOLITAN, "The Kidnapped Prime Minister", "THE DISAPPEARANCE OF MR. DAVENHEIM", THE ADVENTURE OF THE ITALIAN NOBLEMAN, THE CASE OF THE MISSING WILL, "THE VEILED LADY", "THE LOST MINE", "THE CHOCOLATE BOX."

Poirot Loses a Client   See DUMB WITNESS.

Poirot's Early Cases   Mystery short story collection.

The eighteen stories in the collection span the career of Hercule POIROT. They have been drawn from five earlier short story collections.

PUBLISHING AND DRAMATIZATION
HISTORY
Poirot's Early Cases was published in 1974 by William Collins Sons and Company in London, and, under the title of *Hercule Poirot's Early Cases,* by Dodd, Mead & Company in New York.

See earlier collections for adaptations.

TITLES IN THE COLLECTION
Poirot's Early Cases contains the following short stories: "THE LOST MINE," "THE CHOCOLATE BOX," "THE VEILED LADY" (see POIROT INVESTIGATES), "PROBLEM AT SEA," "HOW DOES YOUR GARDEN GROW" (see THE REGATTA MYSTERY AND OTHER STORIES), "THE ADVENTURE OF JOHNNIE WAVERLY," "THE THIRD FLOOR FLAT" (see THREE BLIND MICE AND OTHER STORIES), "THE AFFAIR AT THE VICTORY BALL," "THE ADVENTURE OF THE CLAPHAM COOK," "THE CORNISH MYSTERY," "THE KING OF CLUBS," "THE LEMESURIER INHERITANCE," "THE PLYMOUTH EXPRESS," "THE SUBMARINE PLANS," "THE MARKET BASING MYSTERY" (see THE UNDER DOG AND OTHER STORIES), "THE DOUBLE CLUE," "DOUBLE SIN" and "WASPS' NEST" (see DOUBLE SIN AND OTHER STORIES).

Poli, Signor   An Italian traveler in "THE GATE OF BAGHDAD," he meets Mr. PARKER PYNE on the boat to Beirut, but has difficulty understanding the English gentleman.

Pollard, Constable   A local police officer in Market Basing, he approaches the vacationing Hercule POIROT for assistance in a mysterious case of murder in "THE MARKET BASING MYSTERY."

Pollock, Sergeant   A local police officer assigned to the murder investigation in THE SITTAFORD MYSTERY, he is a cautious man who does not voice his theories regarding the murder until he has evidence.

Pollock, Alfred   The illegitimate, lazy half-cousin of the murder victim, Miss GREENSHAW, in "GREENSHAW'S FOLLY," he might have been arrested for the murder by bow and arrow had he not left work early on that day to spend lunchtime at the local pub.

Polonska, Vanda   A Polish refugee in N OR M? who had arrived penniless in England during World War II, she sold her infant daughter to Millicent SPROT. Later, she was apprehended and shot through the head when she tried to retrieve her child.

Pope, Lavinia   The headmistress of an exclusive school for girls in Neuilly, France, she is a formidable woman who controls every aspect of the operation in "THE GIRDLE OF HIPPOLYTA." She aids Hercule POIROT in identifying why Winnie KING has been kidnapped, as well as in uncovering a stolen priceless painting.

Popoleffsky, Countess Varaga   See MORY, ANGELE.

Poporensky, Princess Anna Michaelovna   Member of a gang of thieves in "JANE IN SEARCH OF A JOB," she poses as the lady-in-waiting to the imposter Grand Duchess PAULINE.

Portal, Alec   An unimaginative man of "the usual good, sound English stock," he suspects that his wife murdered her first husband in "THE COMING OF MR. QUIN." Only the intervention of Mr. Harley QUIN sets his mind at ease.

Portal, Eleanor   Acquitted of the murder of her first husband "more through the lack of evidence against her than from any overwhelming proof of innocence," she despairs of ever being free of suspicion, and contemplates suicide in "THE COMING OF MR. QUIN." Her lover, Derek CAPEL, had committed suicide, and her first husband's body was found to contain strychnine when exhumed. Only after Mr. Harley QUIN examines every detail of the case is she finally free of suspicion.

Porter, Major George Douglas   A staid, old army type with a guilty secret in TAKEN AT THE FLOOD, he is "the club bore" of the Coronation

Club. When he inadvertently reveals his acquaintance with Rosaleen CLOADE and Robert UNDERHAY, her first husband, he sets off a chain of events that ends in death. He accepts a bribe to identify someone else's dead body as that of Underhay, then commits suicide as the result of guilt over his false testimony.

Porter, Major John, D.S.O. Years before, while on safari, both he and his host, Richard SCOTT, had fallen in love with Iris STAVERTON. Now, both men, Iris, Scott's wife Moira and a young army officer are spending a weekend together at the Scotts' home, Greenways House, in "THE SHADOW ON THE GLASS." Porter fears that old rivalries will emerge, but he does not expect death.

Postern of Fate   Mystery novel.

The novel, the last written by the author, concerns a murder-in-retrospect and espionage. The plot centers on the efforts of Tommy and Tuppence BERESFORD to solve a sixty-year-old murder, and to discover how espionage of the past impacts on the present.

PUBLISHING AND DRAMATIZATION HISTORY

The novel was published in 1973 by William Collins and Sons and Company, Ltd., in London, and by Dodd, Mead and Company in New York.

The novel has not been adapted for stage or screen.

CHARACTERS

ANDREW, Colonel ATKINSON, Albert BATT, Deborah BERESFORD, Tommy BERESFORD, Tuppence BERESFORD, Henry BODLICOTT, Isaac BODLICOTT, Miss COLLODON, Angus CRISPIN, Mr. DURRANCE, Miss GRIFFIN, GWENDA, JANET, Mary JORDAN, Miss Iris MULLINS, Inspector NORRIS, Alexander PARKINSON, Colonel Ephraim PIKEAWAY, Mr. ROBINSON, ROSALIE

PLOT SYNOPSIS
Book 1: Chapters 1–4
Tommy and Tuppence Beresford have retired and moved to a house in the resort town of Hollowquay. As Tuppence sorts through children's books left by previous residents, she sees letters underlined in Robert Louis Stevenson's *The Black Arrow*, which bears the nameplate of Alexander Parkinson. When

placed together, the letters form the following message: "Mary Jordan did not die naturally. It was one of us. I think I know which one." She looks for Mary Jordan's grave in the local churchyard, but she finds only Alexander Parkinson's grave, and learns that he died at the age of fourteen. Eager to learn more, she goes to the white elephant sale preparations at the vicarage.

Chapters 5–8
Tuppence returns from the vicarage to find Tommy looking through more of the books. He has also found Alexander's tombstone, and both find the early death disturbing. They learn from their maid that Mrs. Griffin is Alexander's godmother. Tuppence meets Mrs. Griffin at the vicar's tea party. She tells Tuppence that she has heard of Mary Jordan, and remembers that the Parkinsons were mixed up in some sort of trouble related to naval secrets.

Book 2: Chapters 9–12
The happenings of sixty years before remain legend in the village. Tuppence learns from Gwenda, who works in the post office, that Mary Jordan was an *au pair* living with the Parkinsons who died of poisoning when she accidentally ate foxglove leaves. Isaac Bodlicott, the gardener, shows Tuppence the greenhouse where the children kept their toys, but remembers nothing about Mary Jordan. While Tommy goes to London to speak with an old friend from British Intelligence, Tuppence is nearly struck by a pane of glass that falls in the greenhouse.

Chapters 13–14
Tuppence finds a birthday book, and plans to ask Mrs. Griffin if she recognizes any of the names. Tommy learns that Hollowquay had been involved in a scandal in which submarine plans were sold to either the Russians or the Japanese. He also meets with the inscrutable Mr. Robinson, who tells him that foxglove alone would not kill a person, and suggests that a digitalin alkaloid may have been added to Mary's coffee to kill her. He also tells Tommy that Mary was a member of British Intelligence.

Book 3: Chapters 15–18
Mrs. Griffin tells Tuppence that Alexander died of food poisoning contracted at a local picnic, and she sends Tuppence to speak with a much older Hollowquay resident. Tuppence believes that Alexander was murdered because he knew too much. She and

Tommy decide to take apart the rocking horse found in the greenhouse, and they find a note which reads "Meeting Place changed. Kens. Gardens near Peter Pan. Wed. 25th, 3:30 P.M."

Chapters 19–22
Tommy meets with Colonel Pikeaway, who suggests that old espionage secrets still haunt highly placed government officials, and that the old scandal in Hollowquay is still important. At the same time, Tuppence visits the photographer in the village, and attempts to locate photographs of the principal players in that old drama. When she returns home, she find Isaac lying dead on her doorstep.

Chapters 23–26
Their late gardener's grandson Henry and his friend join the Beresfords in searching for clues, as they inspect the inside of the china stool that Tuppence calls the Cambridge. Their terrier Hannibal becomes upset and growls, only moments before two shots are heard and a bullet grazes Tuppence's shoulder. A doctor is called to tend to the wound, and Tommy calls Colonel Pikeaway, who has already heard about the incident. Tommy takes the metal box found inside the Cambridge to Pikeaway, who tells him to be aware that British Intelligence sometimes used the name Solomon as a code, and to trust Inspector Norris.

Chapters 27–29
A Miss Mullins appears and offers her services as gardener, but Hannibal does not like her. Later, a young man named Angus Crispin appears and asks about the gardening position. He says that he worked at the house years before when a Mr. Solomon owned it. The next morning, Miss Mullins arrives early with a book about gardening for Tuppence. As soon as he can get to her, Hannibal bites Miss Mullins, giving Crispin enough time to apprehend her as the person who shot Tuppence.

Chapters 30–31
Deborah visits her parents and brings her three children with her. They all decide that "Postern of Fate" would be a good name for the house. When Tommy and Tuppence have dinner with Mr. Robinson, they learn that the Fascist movement, which had a center in Hollowquay more than sixty years before, had begun to form there again. Old secrets were likely to

emerge which many people wanted hidden, and the resurgence of activity might be exposed.

CRIME NOTES
The two murders which occurred in the distant past are suspected poisonings, although no definite substance is identified in either case.

"Pot of Tea, A"   Mystery short story.
The plot centers on the efforts of Tommy and Tuppence BERESFORD to locate a man's missing love.

PUBLISHING AND DRAMATIZATION HISTORY
The story appeared in the short story collection, PARTNERS IN CRIME, published in 1929 by William Collins Sons and Company, Ltd., in London, and by Dodd, Mead and Company in New York.

The story has not been adapted for stage or screen.

CHARACTERS
ALBERT, Tommy Beresford, Tuppence Beresford, Janet SMITH, Lawrence ST. VINCENT

PLOT SYNOPSIS
The story concerns the first case undertaken by the Beresfords under the auspices of the fledgling Blunt's International Detective Agency. A well-dressed young gentleman approaches the detectives and asks them to locate a missing young woman in whom he has an interest and who works in Madame Violette's hat shop. Eager to build the agency, Tuppence promises results in twenty-four hours for double the usual fee, and Lawrence St. Vincent readily agrees. While Tommy anxiously combs the hospitals in London to locate the girl, Tuppence calmly remains in the office, having solved the crime long before.

Potts, Gladys   Greedy and unpopular with her coworkers in GIANT'S BREAD, she is a lazy Red Cross volunteer who steals food rations from the others.

Power, Emery   An avid collector of rare antiquities in "THE APPLES OF THE HESPERIDES," he desires to obtain a chalice decorated with a scene of golden apples that is rumored to have belonged to the Borgias. He retains Hercule POIROT to find the chalice.

The great detective succeeds, then convinces Power to donate it to a convent in exchange for daily masses for his soul.

Pratt, Dorothy Jane While on a Sunday drive with her boyfriend in "A FRUITFUL SUNDAY," she finds a ruby necklace in a small basket of cherries bought at a roadside stand.

Pratt, Rose See CHUDLEIGH, ROSE.

Prentice, Ann Forty-one years old and widowed for sixteen years, her deep love for her daughter makes her give up her chance for happiness with Richard CAULDFIELD in A DAUGHTER'S A DAUGHTER. Plagued by her sacrifice, she is transformed from a placid and gentle woman to one who is unfeeling and brittle, until she realizes the self-destructiveness of such behavior, and accepts life as she has made it.

Prentice, Sarah Headstrong and accustomed to receiving all her mother's attention, she refuses to accept the depth of her mother's love for Richard CAULDFIELD in A DAUGHTER'S A DAUGHTER. Sarah marries a corrupt aristocrat, and becomes addicted to alcohol and cocaine. She is fortunate that her old love, Gerry LLOYD, reappears and places her in a detoxification program, then takes her with him to start a new life in Canada. Before they leave, she acknowledges her love for her mother and her sorrow for the pain she has caused.

Prescott, Joan Despite her protestations to the contrary, this cleric's sister in A CARIBBEAN MYSTERY delights in gossip, and eagerly tells Miss MARPLE about the bizarre behavior of Molly KENDALL.

Preston, Hailey The garrulous assistant to Jason RUDD in THE MIRROR CRACK'D FROM SIDE TO SIDE, he plays the concurrent roles of public relations man, personal assistant and private secretary. Despite his "willowy" and "elegant" appearance, the police inspector characterizes him as "an efficient and voluble gas bag."

Price, Emlyn A member of the tour of famous houses and gardens of Great Britain in NEMESIS, he is one of two people who witness the murder of Elizabeth TEMPLE.

Price, Lily While looking at homes with her fiancé, Harry, in THE MIRROR CRACK'D FROM SIDE TO SIDE, she nearly falls out of a second-story window, and Harry does nothing to help her. Miss MARPLE sees the occurrence and warns Lily to rethink her relationship, counseling that "You want someone whom you can rely upon if you're in danger."

Price Ridley, Martha The most vicious gossip in the tiny village of ST. MARY MEAD, she has no concern for whom she might hurt, and her self-righteous behavior infuriates many. She appears in MURDER AT THE VICARAGE and THE BODY IN THE LIBRARY.

Prichard, Hubert Married to Agatha Christie's only daughter in 1940, he was killed in action in France in 1944. He was of Welsh descent, a major in the regular army and a friend of the author's nephew Jack. Rosalind met him at the home of her aunt and uncle, Madge (Punkie) and James WATTS. He is also the father of the author's much-beloved only grandchild, Mathew PRICHARD, who inherited the Prichard family estate, Pwllywrach, in South Wales.

Prichard, Mathew Caradoc Thomas The only grandchild of Agatha Christie, he was born on September 21, 1943, to the author's only daughter Rosalind and her first husband, Hubert PRICHARD. His father was killed in action in France in 1944, and he lived with his mother on the Prichard family estate, Pwllywrach, in South Wales until his mother married Anthony HICKS in 1949. The author has described her grandson in AN AUTOBIOGRAPHY as being a handsome, active, sociable and confident young man with whom she delighted to converse. When Mathew Prichard was nine years old, the author signed over to him the royalties to THE MOUSETRAP, which no one at the time predicted would become the longest-running stage play in history. He attended Eton, where he was captain of the cricket team, and later Oxford. After completing his education, he worked with Penguin Books, and was later appointed chairman of the authors division at Booker McConnell. He also has the distinction of being the last High Sheriff of Mid Glamorgan, a position to which he was appointed in 1976.

Priestman, Marguerite An American girl who speaks with a twang in UNFINISHED PORTRAIT.

Primer, Detective Inspector A mild-mannered law enforcement officer investigating the murder of Lily KIMBLE in SLEEPING MURDER, he expresses great admiration for Miss MARPLE's crime-detecting skills.

Pritchard, Alex A.k.a. ALAN CARSTAIRS.

Pritchard, George Ordered around by his invalid wife who constantly grumbles in "THE BLUE GERANIUM," he patiently attends to her needs, but he is in love with another woman.

Pritchard, Mary A complaining, unreasonable, demanding semi-invalid in "THE BLUE GERANIUM," she is never happy with anything that her husband does for her. After her death, observers agree that no one could have blamed her husband if he had murdered her.

"Problem at Pollensa Bay" Mystery short story.

The plot centers on Mr. PARKER PYNE's efforts to set a mother's mind at ease by saving her son from "an unsuitable young woman."

PUBLISHING AND DRAMATIZATION HISTORY
The story appeared in the short story collection, THE REGATTA MYSTERY AND OTHER STORIES, published in 1939 by Dodd, Mead and Company in New York.

The story has not been adapted for stage or screen.

CHARACTERS
Mrs. Adela CHESTER, Basil CHESTER, Betty GREGG, Mr. Parker Pyne, Madeleine de SARA, Mina WYCHERLEY

PLOT SYNOPSIS
The story concerns a possessive mother who asks a vacationing Mr. Parker Pyne to interfere in the love life of her son, Basil. Mrs. Chester disapproves of her son's recent engagement to Betty Gregg, an artist whose bohemian existence appalls the straitlaced English matron. After determining that the two young lovers are well suited to each other, Mr. Parker Pyne devises a plan that changes Mrs. Chester's perception of Betty. He arranges for the appearance of a flamboyant seductress to seemingly sweep Basil off his feet, thus making Betty appear innocuous by comparison. Faced with her son's new infatuation, Mrs. Chester readily promotes his earlier love as a better choice, and the story ends happily for all.

"Problem at Sea" Mystery short story.

The plot centers on the murder of a rich and bossy woman in an apparently locked room.

PUBLISHING AND DRAMATIZATION HISTORY
The story appeared in the short story collection, THE REGATTA MYSTERY AND OTHER STORIES, published in 1939 by Dodd, Mead and Company in New York.

A ventriloquist's doll holds a vital clue for Hercule Poirot (David Suchet) in "Problem at Sea." (Photo courtesy of London Weekend Television)

The story was adapted for television in 1989 by London Weekend Television in Britain, and was also shown on the Public Broadcasting Service in the U.S.

CHARACTERS
Adeline CLAPPERTON, Colonel John CLAPPERTON, Pam CREGAN, General FORBES, Miss Ellie HENDERSON, Kitty MOONEY, Hercule POIROT

PLOT SYNOPSIS
The story concerns the murder of Mrs. Adeline Clapperton, a rich industrialist's widow now married to a former music hall entertainer. The generally ill-tempered woman was disliked by most of the guests on board the ship, but her husband remained oblivious to her sharp comments. When she is found stabbed through the heart with a string of beads on the floor near her bed, everyone but Hercule Poirot comes to the wrong conclusion.

CRIME NOTES
The murder is committed with a dagger.

Proctor, Dr.   An impatient physician in AFTER THE FUNERAL, he is visibly irritated by being called to examine Miss GILCHRIST.

Prothero, Walter   Once a Royal Navy lieutenant named Wendover, he is a recluse who becomes the target of a blackmail scheme in "THE MARKET BASING MYSTERY."

Protheroe, Anne   The much younger wife of a country squire in ST. MARY MEAD and stepmother to his teenage daughter, Lettice, she is having an affair with an artist. Both confess to the crime when her husband is murdered in MURDER AT THE VICARAGE.

Protheroe, Lettice   When her father is murdered, she tries to place the blame on her hated stepmother, Anne PROTHEROE, in MURDER AT THE VICARAGE. She plans to leave ST. MARY MEAD with her mother, Mrs. LESTRANGE.

Protheroe, Colonel Lucius   The village magistrate of ST. MARY MEAD and owner of Old Hall, he is a pompous man who has made significant enemies in MURDER AT THE VICARAGE. He has a meeting with his first wife only hours before his death.

Pryce, Netta   One of a party of twelve traveling from Damascus to Baghdad in "THE GATE OF BAGHDAD," she is a popular and charming young woman who delights in flirting.

Pugh, Eric   A closemouthed man who has been friends with Sir Stafford for many years in PASSENGER TO FRANKFURT, he is a keen observer who knows a lot more than others realize.

Purdy, Professor   An elderly archaeologist in THE CLOCKS, he hires Sheila WEBB from the Cavendish Secretarial and Typing Bureau, and frequently keeps her working long past the assigned time.

Purvis, William   A partner in the respectable law firm of Purvis, Purvis, Charlesworth and Purvis in DUMB WITNESS, he represents the interests of Emily ARUNDELL, whom he is unable to stop from revising her will.

Pye, Mr.   One of the recipients of the poison-pen letters in THE MOVING FINGER, he is a wealthy collector of antiques and a "lady-like plump little man" who, with his high-pitched voice, resembles "a middle-aged spinster."

Q

Quant, Esther A parlourmaid in "THE HOUSE OF THE LURKING DEATH," she dies of poisoned fig sandwiches.

Quentin (1) Now retired, he was a butler in Lord LISTERDALE's service for many years before his master took the butler's place in his own household in "THE LISTERDALE MYSTERY" (2). Rupert ST. VINCENT locates him and takes him to the Listerdale residence to unmask the imposter.

Quentin (2) See LISTERDALE, LORD.

Quentin, Dr. See DARRELL, CLAUD.

Quimper, Dr. A family physician with "a casual off-hand, cynical manner," in 4.50 FROM PADDINGTON, he is unmoved when his wife is found dead in a sarcophagus on a neighbor's estate.

Quin, Harley A highly unusual character who appears in the fourteen stories in the short story collection THE MYSTERIOUS MR. QUIN, in "THE LOVE DETECTIVES," and in "THE HARLEQUIN TEA SET," he is an important presence who takes no active part in the proceedings. In AN AUTOBIOGRAPHY, Agatha Christie observed that her Mr. Quin stories were her favorites, and she proved this by making Mr. Harley Quin the only character to whom she dedicated a book: at the beginning of THE MYSTERIOUS MR. QUIN, she writes "To Harlequin The Invisible."

Rather than a fully realized character, he is "a catalyst, no more—his mere presence affected human beings." She planned him to be consistent in what he stood for: "he was a friend of lovers, and connected with death." The character first appears in a series of poems about *commedia dell'arte* figures that appeared in THE ROAD OF DREAMS, in particular "Harlequin's Song," in which the author writes "And nobody ever sees Harlequin, 'Happy go lucky' Harlequin." In the stories, he appears at critical moments, in the sparkle of sunshine or sitting beneath a stained glass window, so that the multiple colors of the harlequin always seem to surround him. Teamed with Mr. SATTERTHWAITE, from whom he elicits information and whom he guides in providing solutions, he works to reveal to Mr. Satterthwaite the significance of what is plainly seen. When his work is done, the unobtrusive Mr. Quin disappears, as if by magic.

R

Race, Colonel Johnny A member of the British Secret Service, he was "usually to be found in one of the outposts of the Empire where trouble was brewing." He is a man of action who appears in four novels, three of them with Hercule POIROT. He tracks the charming Sir Eustace PEDLER, known to the world of organized crime as a criminal mastermind, the "Colonel," in THE MAN IN THE BROWN SUIT. In CARDS ON THE TABLE, the novel in which he first meets Poirot, he is one of four law enforcement agents invited to Mr. SHAITANA's dinner and bridge party. He later works with Poirot in DEATH ON THE NILE (2) and SPARKLING CYANIDE, playing a supporting role to that of the great detective. Single by circumstance, not necessarily by choice, he proposed marriage to Anne BEDDINGFIELD, but was turned down. He remains a bachelor throughout his four appearances.

Radclyffe, Dennis The third victim to die by ingesting ricin in "THE HOUSE OF THE LURKING DEATH," his earlier behavior marked him as a more likely suspect than victim. Disinherited by his aunt after a disagreement over his debts, he loses his inheritance to his cousin, Lois HARGREAVES, who makes him the beneficiary of her will. Soon after, he dies after being poisoned by ricin in his cocktail.

Raddish, Mr. A rental agent in "THE LAMP," he hesitates to tell a client that the house she likes is haunted by a child's spirit.

Radley, General A guest of Bertram's Hotel whom Chief Inspector Davy interviews regarding the disappearance of Canon PENNYFEATHER, he is a very old and very gruff former military man in AT BERTRAM'S HOTEL.

Radmaager, Herr A famous composer in GIANT'S BREAD, he encourages Vernon DEYRE to continue to experiment with musical form.

Radnor, Jacob A deceptive suitor to both Mrs. PENGELLEY and her niece, Freda STANTON, in THE CORNISH MYSTERY, he pursues Freda because she will inherit a substantial estate from her uncle.

Radzky, Countess, Anna See ST. MAUR, BABE.

Rafiel, Jason An extremely rich old man who is "semi-paralyzed and looked like a wrinkled old bird of prey," he joins Miss MARPLE in solving the mystery of the murders at the Golden Palm Hotel in A CARIBBEAN MYSTERY. When his son is arrested for murder, Rafiel arranges for Nemesis, his name for Miss Marple, to learn the truth in NEMESIS, even after his own death.

Rafiel, Michael In trouble with the law for much of his life, the son of Jason RAFIEL is imprisoned for the murder of his fiancée, Verity Hunt, but his father's will arranges for Miss MARPLE to uncover the truth in NEMESIS.

Ragg, Gordon See EASTERFIELD, LORD.

Raglan, Inspector A member of the investigation in THE MURDER OF ROGER ACKROYD, he is "a horrid, weaselly little man" whose appearance is "black as thunder" to observers.

Raglan, Inspector Henry Timothy Respectful of the detection skills of Hercule POIROT, the local law enforcement official of Woodleigh Common recommends that the detective be consulted after Joyce REYNOLDS is murdered in HALLOWE'EN PARTY.

Raikes, Mrs.   The source of gossip because of her meetings with Alfred INGLETHORPE, she is a "pretty young woman of gipsy type" in THE MYSTERIOUS AFFAIR AT STYLES.

Raikes, Howard   A strong advocate of leftist economic theories, he is an American suspected of murder when his girlfriend's conservative and wealthy uncle, Alistair BLUNT, is murdered in ONE, TWO, BUCKLE MY SHOE.

"Rajah's Emerald, The"   Mystery short story.

The plot centers on an underpaid clerk named James BOND whose social importance increases when he accidentally locates a valuable stolen emerald.

PUBLISHING AND DRAMATIZATION HISTORY
The story appeared in the short story collection, THE LISTERDALE MYSTERY (1), published in 1934 by William Collins Sons and Company, Ltd., in London.

The story has not been adapted for stage or screen.

CHARACTERS
James Bond, Lord Edward CAMPION, GRACE, JONES, Claud SOPWORTH

PLOT SYNOPSIS
The story concerns James Bond, an underpaid clerk who is tricked by his girlfriend of three years into taking a seaside vacation. Once at their destination, she stays with wealthy friends at the upscale Esplanade Hotel, while he rooms at an obscure boarding-house. Through a trick of fate, and the dishonesty of Lord Campion's valet, Jones, James rescues an emerald and becomes the guest of a rajah.

Ramone, Delores   See DE SARA, MADELEINE.

Ramsbottom, Effie   An eccentric, religious maniac in A POCKET FULL OF RYE, she is the sister of Rex FORTESCUE's first wife, and lives with the Fortescue family after her sister's death and the remarriage of Rex.

Ramsey, Ted   One of two highly energetic schoolboys in THE CLOCKS, he and his brother Bill find a Czechoslovakian coin in blind Mrs. PEBMARSH's garden and influence investigator Colin LAMB to consider a communist connection.

Randolph, Myrna   Young and attractive, she is rumored to have had an affair with Rodney SCUDAMORE in ABSENT IN THE SPRING.

Ransome, Nicholas (Nicky)   One of two young men whom Hercule POIROT asks to protect Miranda BUTLER in HALLOWE'EN PARTY, he has a lively imagination, and suggests that the murder has a sexual basis: "I mean, there's always got to be a sex background to these things."

Ratchett, Samuel Edward   A traveler in MURDER ON THE ORIENT EXPRESS whose role as a rich American businessman is merely a cover for his real identity, the kidnapper and extortionist Cassetti. He had been arrested for the kidnapping and murder of Daisy ARMSTRONG, but was acquitted. He offers Hercule POIROT twenty thousand dollars to be his bodyguard, but the detective refuses. A short while later, he is murdered, the victim of multiple stab wounds.

Rathbone, Dr.   An enthusiastic distributor of books, he opens bookshops in many remote places, but he falls prey to blackmail when he takes for his personal use a percentage of the donations and grants given to his peace institute in THEY CAME TO BAGHDAD.

Rathbone, Dennis   A faithful suitor in CAT AMONG THE PIGEONS, he proposes marriage to but is continually refused by Ann SHAPLAND, who considers him too dull.

Rattery, John   A young man in FIVE LITTLE PIGS engaged to Carol LEMARCHANT, whose mother was imprisoned for murdering her father.

Ravel, Annette   One of several children raised at Miss Slater's English home for destitute children in "THE FOURTH MAN," she is a famous singer, also known as Annette RAVELLI, who holds the key to understanding the multiple personalities of Felice BAULT.

Ravelli, Annette   See RAVEL, ANNETTE.

Ravenscroft, General Alistair   Once in love with Dolly JARROW, he later fell in love with and married her sister Molly in ELEPHANTS CAN REMEMBER. After Molly's death, he agreed to allow the emotionally unstable Dolly to impersonate her late sister and to seek refuge at his home. He is the father of Edward and Celia RAVENSCROFT.

Ravenscroft, Celia   The goddaughter of Ariadne OLIVER, she is surprised when her godmother reveals in ELEPHANTS CAN REMEMBER the request of Mrs. BURTON-COX, mother of Celia's fiancé, Desmond, in ELEPHANTS CAN REMEMBER. She is unable to supply Mrs. Oliver with information about her parents' deaths, because she was away at school when they died.

Ravenscroft, Lady Margaret (Molly)   A former schoolmate of Ariadne OLIVER in ELEPHANTS CAN REMEMBER, she is the mother of Edward and Celia RAVENSCROFT and the wife of General Alistair RAVENSCROFT. Her death motivates curious questions about four wigs.

Rawlinson, Dr.   The elderly Denman family doctor in "THE THUMB MARK OF ST. PETER," he is described by Miss MARPLE as being old and doddering, "so short-sighted as to be pitiful, slightly deaf and, withal, touchy and sensitive to the last degree."

Rawlinson, Squadron Leader Bob   Private pilot to the prince of the wealthy but war-torn nation of Ramat in CAT AMONG THE PIGEONS, he dies in a plane crash while trying to smuggle over a half million pounds of jewels out of the country at the request of the prince.

Rayburn, Harry   Identified as the "Man in the Brown Suit" by Anne BEDDINGFIELD in THE MAN IN THE BROWN SUIT, he is the son of Sir Laurence Eardsley and a relative of Colonel RACE. He is also known variously as John Eardsley, Harry Lucas and Harry Parker. After school at Cambridge, he and a friend, Harry LUCAS, traveled to British Guiana, where they discovered a rich diamond deposit. Later tricked out of his holdings, he is framed as possessing diamonds stolen from the DeBeers diamond merchants, but his father uses his influence to quash the charges. He serves in World War I, but his friend Lucas is killed while wearing Eardsley's identification tags. Thus, while officially dead, he assumes the name of Harry Parker and works to clear his real name. He meets Anne Beddingfeld several times, and the two eventually marry.

Raymond, Geoffrey   As secretary to Roger ACKROYD for two years, he is aware of his master's many secrets in THE MURDER OF ROGER ACKROYD. He receives five hundred pounds in the will after Ackroyd's murder.

Raynes, Roger   A rotund professional singer in UNFINISHED PORTRAIT, he seeks to marry CELIA.

Raynor, Edward   An unremarkable, twenty-eight-year-old man in BLACK COFFEE, he is a personal secretary to research scientist Sir Claud AMORY.

Read, Miss Vera   A pale girl with an efficient manner in "SWAN SONG," she is the personal secretary of temperamental opera star Madame NAZORKOFF.

Redcliffe, Hermia   Romantically involved with Mark EASTERBROOK in THE PALE HORSE, she loses him to Katherine CORRIGAN.

Redding, Lawrence   A "clever painter in the modern style" in MURDER AT THE VICARAGE, he is romantically involved with Anne PROTHEROE, the wife of the unpopular local magistrate.

Redfern, Christine   The seemingly neglected wife of Patrick REDFERN in EVIL UNDER THE SUN, she is a guest at the Jolly Roger Hotel whose lack of a tan makes her appear to be "a bit uncooked" in appearance.

Redfern, Patrick   Married to Christine REDFERN in EVIL UNDER THE SUN, he attracts the attention of Arlena MARSHALL, to the distress of his wife. Viewed by Hercule POIROT as an "'adventurer who makes his living one way or another, out of women,'" his real name is Edward Corrigan, a man whose first wife was strangled; the killer was never found.

"Red House, The"   Mystery short story.

Tommy and Tuppence BERESFORD expose phony poltergeists and find a fortune hidden in the grounds of their client's house, allowing her to keep her home.

PUBLISHING AND DRAMATIZATION HISTORY

The story appeared in the short story collection, PARTNERS IN CRIME, published 1929 by William Collins Sons and Company, Ltd., in London, and by Dodd, Mead and Company in New York.

The story was combined with THE CLERGYMAN'S DAUGHTER and adapted for television in 1984 by London Weekend Television in England; it was shown on the Public Broadcasting Service in the U.S.

CHARACTERS

Tommy Beresford, Tuppence Beresford, CROCKETT, Monica DEANE, Dr. O'NEILL

PLOT SYNOPSIS

The Beresfords pose as prospective house buyers, hoping to uncover the involvement of the maid Crockett or her nephew in the "haunting" of Monica Deane's home. After questioning the gardener and accumulating verbal clues, the detectives uncover a fortune buried in the garden, which enables Monica to keep the Red House.

CRIME NOTES

The clues to the story are buried in a biblical verse and a rather obscure rhyme.

"Red Signal, The"   Mystery short story.

The plot centers on an ominous warning of death, which emerges during a seance.

PUBLISHING AND DRAMATIZATION HISTORY

The story appeared in the short story collection, THE HOUND OF DEATH AND OTHER STORIES, published in 1933 by William Collins Sons and Company, Ltd., in London.

The story was adapted for television in 1982 by Thames Television in England, and was also shown on the Public Broadcasting Service in the United States.

CHARACTERS

Mrs. Violet EVERSLEIGH, JOHNSON, Mrs. THOMPSON, Claire TRENT, Alington WEST, Dermot WEST

PLOT SYNOPSIS

The story concerns a murder that occurs after participants in a seance have been warned that one man is in danger. The group had been invited to dinner to allow psychiatrist Sir Alington West the opportunity of discreetly examining one of those present for signs of mental illness. Dermot West is in love with the hostess, Clair Trent, but his uncle warns that Claire will never be free to marry Dermot. Late that night, Aldington is found murdered, and Dermot is the prime suspect. When the police finally identify the real murderer, carefully concealed secrets are exposed.

CRIME NOTES

The murder in this story results from a gunshot wound to the heart.

Reece-Holland, Claudia   The secretary to Andrew RESTARICK, she is the first girl in THIRD GIRL to rent the flat she later shared with Frances CARY and her boss's daughter, Norma RESTARICK.

Reed   See LAVINGTON, MR., Reed's pseudonym.

Reed, Giles   A distant relative of Joan WEST, wife of Miss MARPLE's nephew Raymond, Giles has traveled extensively because of his job. He is a great fan of detective stories, and when his new bride Gwenda identifies a mystery in their new home in SLEEPING MURDER, he eagerly joins her in uncovering the details.

Reed, Gwenda   A young bride in SLEEPING MURDER, she has moved from New Zealand to England, but psychic impressions imply that she has a strong physical connection to her new home. With her husband, she tries to locate her stepmother, said to have deserted Gwenda's father eighteen years earlier, and

to learn more about her father, who committed suicide in an insane asylum.

Reedburn, Henry   A famous impresario in "THE KING OF CLUBS," he is found dead in his library, "the back of his head cracked open like an eggshell."

Rees-Talbot, Mary   The new employer of parlourmaid Betty ARCHDALE, who once worked for the late Rosemary BARTON in SPARKLING CYANIDE, she is an old friend of Colonel Race.

Reeves   An unctuous butler in the employ of Colonel PROTHEROE in MURDER IN THE VICARAGE, his emotionless face disguises his stormy relationship with the Colonel.

Reeves, Inspector   A police inspector investigating the death of Hubert LYTCHAM ROCHE in "THE SECOND GONG," his lack of imagination prevents him from seeing beyond a decision of suicide as the cause of death.

Reeves, Emily   A member of Simeon LEE's household staff, she is the cook in HERCULE POIROT'S CHRISTMAS.

Reeves, Pamela (Pamie)   An unfortunate victim of circumstance, while on the way to a Girl Guide rally in THE BODY IN THE LIBRARY, she was approached by a stranger who asked if she wanted to be in the movies. She is murdered, and the police misidentify her body disguised as that of Ruby KEENE.

"Regatta Mystery, The"   Mystery short story.

The plot centers on a young woman's bet that she can make a diamond disappear in front of witnesses, and her later inability to make it reappear.

PUBLISHING AND DRAMATIZATION HISTORY
The story appeared in the short story collection, THE REGATTA MYSTERY AND OTHER STORIES, published in 1939 by Dodd, Mead and Company in New York.

The story has not been adapted for stage or screen.

CHARACTERS
Eve LEATHERN, Mr. Samuel LEATHERN, Evan LLEWELLYN, Sir George and Lady Pamela MARROWAY, Mr. Isaac POINTZ, Mr. PARKER PYNE, Mrs. Jane RUSTINGTON, Mr. Leo STEIN

PLOT SYNOPSIS
The story concerns the disappearance of a diamond worth thirty thousand pounds, after a young woman makes a playful bet with diamond merchant Isaac Pointz. Eve Leathern succeeds in making the stone disappear without a trace, leading all Pointz's guests to search the dining area thoroughly, but no stone is found. Retained by a young man upon whom suspicion for the theft has fallen, Mr. Parker Pyne uncovers the true identity of a gang of thieves, and retrieves the diamond.

Regatta Mystery and Other Stories, The   Mystery short story collection.

The nine stories in this volume were especially assembled for publication in the United States. They represent three of the best-known Christie detectives. Five of the stories feature Hercule POIROT, two feature Mr. PARKER PYNE and one features Miss Jane MARPLE. The collection also contains a tale of the supernatural. All of the stories, aside from "YELLOW IRIS," also appeared in other short story collections published later in Britain.

PUBLISHING AND DRAMATIZATION HISTORY
The Regatta Mystery and Other Stories was published by Dodd, Mead and Company in New York in 1939; there has been no British edition of the intact collection.

"IN A GLASS DARKLY" was adapted for television in 1982 by Thames Television. London Weekend Television adapted "PROBLEM AT SEA" for broadcast in 1989 and "HOW DOES YOUR GARDEN GROW?" in 1991.

TITLES IN THE COLLECTION
The Regatta Mystery and Other Stories contains the following short stories: "THE REGATTA MYSTERY," "THE MYSTERY OF THE BAGHDAD CHEST," "How Does Your Garden Grow?" "PROBLEM AT POLLENSA BAY," "Yellow Iris," "MISS MARPLE TELLS A STORY,"

Dermot West and Sir Alington West, played by Richard Marand and Alan Badel, argue in "The Red Signal" shortly before Sir Alington is found stabbed to death. (Photo courtesy of Thames Television)

"THE DREAM," "In A Glass Darkly" and "Problem at Sea."

"Problem at Sea" has also appeared under the title of "Crime in Cabin 66" as a separate sixteen-page booklet published by Vallency Press, Ltd., in London in 1944. Miss Felicity LEMON makes her first appearance as Hercule POIROT's secretary in "How Does Your Garden Grow?"

Reichardt, Dr.   Director of a large mental institution in PASSENGER TO FRANKFURT that contains several patients suffering from the delusion that they are Hitler, he believes that one of the patients might actually be Hitler, living in seclusion.

Reid, Major   A British army officer stationed in Iraq, he is involved in a scandal with Barbara WRAY, the main character's daughter, in ABSENT IN THE SPRING.

Reilly, Mr.   The last person to see Mr. MORLEY alive on the day when the murder occurred in ONE, TWO, BUCKLE MY SHOE, he is a partner of the murdered dentist but has no reason to wish Morley harm.

Reilly, Dr. Giles   A member of the archaeological expedition at Tell Yarimjah in MURDER IN MESOPOTAMIA, he asks Hercule POIROT to investigate the murder of Louise LEIDNER.

Reilly, James   A man of violent passions and even more violent appearance, with his "flaming red hair, pugnacious jaw and appallingly shabby clothes" in "THE MAN IN THE MIST," he is arrested for the murder of his former love, Gilda GLEN.

Reilly, Sheila   The attractive and strong-willed daughter of Dr. Giles REILLY in MURDER IN MESOPOTAMIA, she is surrounded by admiring males at the Tell Yarimjah archaeological site, and eventually marries archaeological assistant David EMMOTT.

Reiter, Carl   A photographer with the archaeological expedition at Tell Yarimjah in MURDER IN MESOPOTAMIA, he looks "just a little like a pig." He becomes infatuated with Louise LEIDNER, who embarrasses him in front of others on the expedition by mocking his social awkwardness.

Remembered Death   See SPARKLING CYANIDE.

Renauld, Madame   A woman with a formidable presence in MURDER ON THE LINKS, she is the mother of Jack RENAULD and wife of the murdered Paul T. RENAULD.

Renauld, Paul T.   A wealthy businessman with a very dark secret in MURDER ON THE LINKS, he sends for Hercule POIROT for help, but the detective arrives too late to prevent Renauld's murder.

Rendell, Dr.   A physician for whom the unfortunate Mrs. MCGINTY has worked in MRS. MCGINTY'S DEAD, he is the recipient of anonymous letters which claim that his first wife's death was not an accident.

Rendell, Shelagh   The suspicious second wife of physician Dr. RENDELL in MRS. MCGINTY'S DEAD, she believes that Hercule POIROT is investigating the death of her husband's first wife.

Renisenb   A young widow in DEATH COMES AS THE END, she is the daughter of IMHOTEP and the mother of Teti. She chooses to marry HORI rather than KAMENI, who resembles her late husband.

Rennie, Mr. An outspoken and offensive political radical in "THE AFFAIR OF THE PINK PEARL," he is outspoken and offensive in his views. He loves Beatrice KINGSTON despite her father's objections.

Restarick, Alexis A very successful actor and playwright in THEY DO IT WITH MIRRORS, he guesses too accurately the identity of the murderer, and becomes the second victim.

Restarick, Andrew The long-dead father of Norma RESTARICK in THIRD GIRL, his identity is assumed by Robert ORWELL, who sought to bilk the Restarick family of their estate.

Restarick, Mary A fortune hunter whose real name is Frances CARY, she met Robert ORWELL in Africa, and the two developed a plan to obtain the Restarick fortune in THIRD GIRL.

Restarick, Norma Convinced that she had caused the death of her father's lover in THIRD GIRL, she contacts Mrs. Ariadne OLIVER and asks her for the name of a detective. When she and Hercule POIROT meet, the exceedingly thin girl with the stringy hair thinks that he is too old to help her. After a series of harrowing adventures, she is headed for marriage with the physician who saves her from suicide, Dr. STILLINGFLEET.

Revel, The Honourable Mrs. Timothy See REVEL, VIRGINIA.

Revel, Virginia The widowed daughter of a lord, a very slim, beautiful woman with "a delicious and quite indescribable mouth" in THE SECRET OF CHIMNEYS, she is used by her cousin as bait to obtain the memoirs of Count STYLPTITCH.

Reynolds, Mrs. The mother of murder victims Joyce and Leopold REYNOLDS in HALLOWE'EN PARTY.

Reynolds, Ann A tall, willowy, sixteen-year-old girl in HALLOWE'EN PARTY, she is the older sister of the murdered Joyce and Leopold REYNOLDS.

Reynolds, Joyce A loud, obnoxious, thirteen-year-old girl in HALLOWE'EN PARTY, she attempts to impress Mrs. Ariadne OLIVER when they first meet by announcing that she had once witnessed a murder. Murdered shortly afterwards, she is drowned in the tub where the children were to bob for apples.

Reynolds, Leopold The self-centered brother of the murdered Joyce REYNOLDS and Ann REYNOLDS in HALLOWE'EN PARTY, he tries to profit from his sister's murder by blackmail. His amateur attempt at extortion seals his fate when he is drowned in a nearby stream.

Rhodes, Mr. When he is suspected of murdering his wife in "MISS MARPLE TELLS A STORY," he turns to Miss Marple for help in stopping the gossip.

Riccovetti One of the thieves in "THE APPLES OF THE HESPERIDES," he drives the getaway car in the robbery of the Borgia goblet.

Rice, Inspector A member of Scotland Yard, he joins the constable and the physician to initiate an investigation when Mrs. Ernestine GRANT is found dead in "THE THIRD-FLOOR FLAT."

Rice, Mr. Killed by the police after attempting to murder his wife, Frederica RICE, in PERIL AT END HOUSE, he is a drug addict who bullied his estranged wife to provide him with cocaine obtained from drug supplier Commander CHALLENGER.

Rice, Mrs. An extortionist in "THE STYMPHALEAN BIRDS," she poses as the mother of Elsie CLAYTON, and the two simulate a scenario with a phony jealous husband to blackmail a politically ambitious young man.

Rice, Dicky A dutiful nephew to an aging aunt in "THE UNBREAKABLE ALIBI," he sees Una DRAKE in Torquay at the same time that she is having supper with Mr. LE MARCHANT, miles away in London.

Rice, Frederica (Freddie) A best friend of Nicky BUCKLEY, of whose will she was beneficiary and whom she provided with cocaine, she has the appearance of a "weary Madonna" in PERIL AT END

HOUSE. The murderer attempts to frame her by placing the murder weapon in her pocket.

Rich, Eileen　An excellent teacher at the Meadowbank School in CAT AMONG THE PIGEONS, she once gave birth to an illegitimate stillborn child while on a one-term leave from school. When Miss BULSTRODE retires, she is named headmistress of the exclusive school for girls.

Rich, Major Charles　A close friendship with Arnold CLAYTON does not prevent Rich from desiring Margharita CLAYTON in "THE MYSTERY OF THE SPANISH CHEST," and he falls under suspicion when Clayton's stabbed body is found in a Spanish chest in his living room.

Rich, Major Jack　A close friend of Arnold CLAYTON in "THE MYSTERY OF THE BAGHDAD CHEST," he is in love with Marguerita CLAYTON and will do anything to have her for himself. Arnold Clayton's stabbed body is found in the Baghdad chest in Rich's living room.

Richards　Extremely observant, he is valet to Ambassador Ralph WILMOTT in "THE AMBASSADOR'S BOOTS." He supplies Tommy and Tuppence BERESFORD with details regarding the missing attaché case and a description of Eileen O'HARA, who feigned illness outside the ambassador's door.

Richards, Anne　See MORISOT, ANNE.

Richards, Ernestine　Former secretary to Lady Naomi DORTHEIMER in "THE CASE OF THE DISTRESSED LADY," she consults Mr. PARKER PYNE about a stolen ring. The former Daphne St. John has made a marvelous transformation, the result of dyeing her hair dark brown and parting it differently.

Richards, James　See GALE, NORMAN.

Richetti, Signor Guido　Posing as an archaeologist in DEATH ON THE NILE (2), he overdoes his part and makes Hercule POIROT suspicious because "he was almost too word perfect in his role."

Riddell, Albert　First person to enter Alice ASCHER's tobacco shop after her murder in THE A.B.C.

MURDERS, he provides the police with a time frame for her death.

Riddle, Major　Convinced that the CHEVENIX-GORE death is suicide in "DEAD MAN'S MIRROR," the Chief Constable of Westshire resents the assertion by Hercule POIROT that murder has occurred.

Ridgeway, Dr.　A physician who lives near Hercule POIROT and Captain Arthur HASTINGS in THE BIG FOUR, he provides medical assistance to Mr. MAYERLING, Hastings and Poirot after an explosion.

Ridgeway, Charles　A patient and persistent young nephew in "WHERE THERE'S A WILL," he is beneficiary of his aunt's will and impatient to inherit the estate. He uses ingenuity to bring about death by natural causes, but receives a bitter surprise.

Ridgeway, Linnet　See DOYLE, LINNET.

Ridgeway, Philip　Despite taking every precaution in "THE MILLION DOLLAR BOND ROBBERY," he suffers the loss of one-million-dollars-worth of Liberty Bonds while traveling aboard the *Olympia*.

Rieger, Katrina　Suspected of murdering her employer when authorities find a packet of strychnine under her mattress, she is a "miserable little cornered rat" in "HOW DOES YOUR GARDEN GROW?" Hercule POIROT clears her of murder charges.

Rigg, Dr.　A physician in THE CLOCKS, he serves as the coroner at the inquest for "R.H. Curry."

Riley, Mary　See DRAPER, MARY.

Rival, Merlina　Found stabbed to death in Victoria Station shortly after identifying the murdered "R.H. CURRY" as her former husband, she is a friend of Miss MARTINDALE in THE CLOCKS.

Rivers, Mr.　The seventh victim of the Wychwood murderer in MURDER IS EASY, he is Lord EASTERFIELD's chauffeur.

Rivington, Mrs.　Interviewed regarding the death of John SAVAGE in WHY DIDN'T THEY ASK EVANS?, she impresses the investigating officer as being "a woman of more looks than brains."

Road of Dreams, The   See POEMS.

Robbins, Miss   Dull and colorless, she is a nursery governess in GIANT'S BREAD.

Robert (1)   A disguised police officer whose real name is Inspector DROUET, he is imprisoned and murdered by the master criminal MARRASCAUD at the Swiss Rochers Neige resort in "THE ERYMANTHIAN BOAR."

Robert (2)   An art expert in BY THE PRICKING OF MY THUMBS, he identifies a certain artist by a picture that Tommy BERESFORD shows him. He hopes devoutly that Tommy will not take up art himself.

Roberts, Dr.   A physician in CARDS ON THE TABLE whose commonsense attitude and pleasant manner set individuals at ease, he is one of four bridge players with a hidden past at Mr. SHAITANA's card party.

Roberts, Mr.   A middle-aged government employee in "THE CASE OF THE CITY CLERK," he consults Mr. PARKER PYNE with the desire to gain adventure in his life. The detective affords him the opportunity to meet a Grand Duchess, deal with secret plans and the Russian crown jewels and become involved in international espionage.

Roberts, Gladys   The former parlourmaid named Evans in WHY DIDN'T THEY ASK EVANS?, now married and in service in the vicarage in Marchbolt, her name is mentioned by the dying Alan CARSTAIRS.

Robinson, Mr.   A shadowy figure whose exact affiliation is never explained, he is a member of an organization named the Arrangers that controls events in the world of international finance. Although Hercule POIROT, Miss MARPLE, Tommy and Tuppence BERESFORD and Scotland Yard consult him at different times in CAT AMONG THE PIGEONS, PASSENGER TO FRANKFURT, POSTERN OF FATE and AT BERTRAM'S HOTEL, he is not a finely drawn character. Described as being "fat and well-dressed, with a yellow face, melancholy dark eyes, a broad forehead, and a generous mouth that displayed rather over-large very white teeth," he is not identified by nationality. In the same manner, he vaguely describes his role as be-

ing that of "just a man who knows about money," as well as someone who knows about "people and their idiosyncracies and their practices in life."

Robinson, Edward   Quiet, hardworking and thrifty, his life changes in "THE MANHOOD OF EDWARD ROBINSON" when he wins five hundred pounds in a newspaper contest and uses the money to buy a sports car without consulting his practical-minded fiancée. The adventures that follow change his personality forever.

Robinson, John   See GALE, NORMAN.

Robinson, Stella   The underpriced apartment in the normally expensive Montagu Mansions was a blessing in disguise for this financially strapped young woman in "THE ADVENTURE OF THE CHEAP FLAT," but Hercule POIROT becomes suspicious.

Robson, Cornelia Ruth   Companion to the irritable Mrs. VAN SCHUYLER, she is a poor American relative who travels with her cousin to Egypt in DEATH ON THE NILE (2). On board the ship, she meets Dr. BESSNER, whom she later marries.

Rockford, Sterndale   An American trustee of the Linnet DOYLE's business interests in DEATH ON THE NILE (2), he schemes with his business partner, Andrew PENNINGTON, to defraud their client.

Rogers, Mrs.   A tall and angular woman in ENDLESS NIGHT, with a "mouth like a rattletrap and eyes that were eternally suspicious," her son, Michael ROGERS, marries an American heiress and inherits vast holdings.

Rogers, Ellie   An American heiress whose maiden name is Ellie Guteman, she met her husband, Michael ROGERS, on the cursed land, Gipsy's Acre, and they eloped without informing her family in ENDLESS NIGHT. Michael is named her beneficiary, and she dies soon after their marriage after a fall from her horse.

Rogers, Ethel and Thomas   The second and fourth victims on Indian Island, they were hired to serve as the butler and the cook to the rest of the house party in AND THEN THERE WERE NONE. Their deaths, hers from an overdose of a sleeping potion and his from being hacked to death with a hatchet, fulfill the rhyme in which one Indian boy "overslept himself" and "one chopped himself in halves."

Rogers, Michael   A handsome and charming man with few ties and little desire for a stable life in ENDLESS NIGHT, his happiness in life lies in "seeing the world, and getting off with good-looking girls." He charms the sheltered American heiress, Ellie Guteman, then inherits her large fortune when she dies after a fall from a horse soon after their marriage.

Rolf, Gregory B.   A good-looking American movie star in "THE ADVENTURE OF THE 'WESTERN STAR,' " he once had an affair with Lady YARDLY, who gave him a valuable diamond named the Star of the East. He renames the diamond the Western Star and gives it to his new wife, Mary MARVEL, as a wedding present.

Ronnie   See GOODMAN, ADAM.

Rosalie   The seven-year-old granddaughter of Tommy and Tuppence BERESFORD in POSTERN OF FATE, she is their daughter Deborah's child.

Roscari, Signor   Prepared to sing the role of Scarpia in a performance of *Tosca,* he suffers a mild case of poisoning on the day of the performance, so that Edouard Breon is forced to take his place in "SWAN SONG."

Roscheimer, Lady   A strong-willed philanthropist who supports the artistic efforts of numerous young men and girls of the village in "HARLEQUIN'S LANE," she arranges the ballet performance in which Madame NAZORKOFF is reunited with her long lost love.

Rose, Dr.   An investigator into the occult in "THE HOUND OF DEATH," he is the nephew of a man who died when a bolt of lightning struck and left a mark in the shape of a hound on his body. As village doctor in Folbridge, Cornwall, he becomes acquainted with Sister Marie ANGELIQUE, from whom he learns the secrets of the house of Crystal. He dies when an avalanche pushes his cottage over a cliff.

Rose and the Yew Tree, The   Non-mystery novel.

The novel is the fourth written under the pseudonym of Mary WESTMACOTT. The title is derived from the "Little Gidding" section of *The Four Quartets* by T.S. Eliot, which states that "the moment of the rose and the moment of the yew tree are of equal duration."

PUBLISHING AND DRAMATIZATION HISTORY
The novel was published in 1948 by William Heinemann and Company in London, and by Holt, Rinehart and Winston in New York.

The novel has not been adapted for stage or screen.

CHARACTERS
Doctor BURT, Milly BURT, Captain CARSLAKE, Mrs. Bigham CHARTERIS, Isabella CHARTERIS, Father CLEMENT, John GABRIEL, Anne MORDAUNT, Hugh NORREYS, Lady Adelaide ST. LOO, Rupert ST. LOO, Lady TRESSILIAN, Catherine YOUGOUBIAN

PLOT SYNOPSIS
Prelude
The narrator is approached by a female visitor who begs him to follow her to the bedside of a dying man named John Gabriel. The narrator refuses vehemently, for the man named Gabriel, whom he had known earlier, had been a womanizing drunkard and opportunist whose only concern had been for himself. As the woman pleads for the narrator to follow her, she states that Gabriel is Father Clement, a man who had courageously helped many people during the dark years after World War II. Intrigued, the narrator agrees to go to the man responsible for the death of a woman they had both loved. Thus begins the story of their shared past.

Chapters 1–3
Hugh Norreys describes his meeting and falling in love with a woman on a train. They plan to fly off together, but Hugh is in an accident and lands in the hospital. Afterwards, the severely injured man is visited by his love, and he realizes that she bores him. Their attraction was "the attraction of the flesh only." With his brother and sister-in-law, Norreys moves to the fashionable seaside resort of St. Loo,

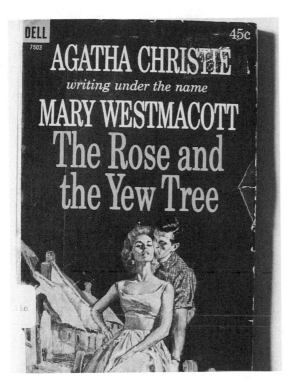

An early paperback cover of *The Rose and the Yew Tree,* **one of the romance novels written under the pseudonym of Mary Westmacott.** (Photo courtesy of the R. Gregor Collection)

which contains a thriving artist's colony whose politics are "definitely pink if not red."

Chapters 4–6

As he recuperates from his injuries, Norreys becomes immersed in the politics of St. Loo, in which the general concern is to get the Conservative candidate, John Gabriel, elected. Although Gabriel is "of the new school," Conservative supporters recognize that they must forget old ideas of "the ruling class" or they will be left behind. Gabriel confesses that he has no strong political beliefs other than wanting to be on the winning side. He exploits his heroism in war and in the recent incident in which he saved a small child from drowning. Even if the local aristocrats do not like the him, they realize his value to their cause.

Chapters 7–10

Isabella visits Norreys and aids him in hiding the morphine tablets he has collected to commit suicide.

Surprised by his sister-in-law, they feign conversation, and Isabella mentions her cousin, Rupert St. Loo, whom she hopes to marry. Lady Tressilian tells Norreys that Isabella's marriage would keep the castle in the family. Gabriel's political career is given another boost when he helps Mrs. Charteris, whose dog is hit by a car. He takes the dog to the veterinarian, where he meets abused wife Milly Burt. A few days later, she joins the campaign to elect Gabriel.

Chapters 11–14

Isabella looks forward to the imminent arrival of her cousin, Rupert, but a chance encounter with Gabriel shocks Norreys, when Gabriel tests Isabella's ability to withstand pain. Milly Burt admits that her husband is a sadistic brute, but cries that she has no possible way to leave her marriage. When Gabriel chivalrously offers her a ride home, gossip erupts and endangers his political ambitions.

Chapters 15–18

Sympathetic to Milly Burt's position, Norreys tells her about the gossip in St. Loo regarding her friendship with John Gabriel. Milly professes innocence, and decides to avoid the politician until after the election. At a fund-raising event, Gabriel sneaks away with Isabella and returns with the gleeful news that "she's human all right—as human as any little piece you pick up on a Saturday night." Isabella is unaffected by their lovemaking, but Gabriel is infuriated by her indifference.

Chapters 19–21

Rupert St. Loo comes home on leave, he and Isabella become engaged, and Lady St. Loo is relieved that St. Loo Castle will now be saved. The drama increases when a drunken James Burt pursues Milly and she runs for protection to John Gabriel. The election seems lost until Lady St. Loo steps in and invites Milly to stay at the castle, safe from the drunk and abusive James Burt. Attempts to repair the damage to Gabriel's campaign yield limited results; the election is close.

Chapters 22–Epilogue

Isabella shocks her family when she announces that she is leaving St. Loo with Gabriel, who gives up his seat in Parliament. Two years later, Norreys travels to Zagrade, where a new surgical technique provides him with the ability to walk on crutches. He meets Gabriel at an outdoor cafe and learns that Isabella is also in the city and that the two are not married. He visits Isabella and finds her living in a squalid apartment, yet she has no desire to leave. Days later, Isabella is dead, having stepped in front of Gabriel when a crazed student shot at him. At the end, Norreys realizes that Isabella's death had resulted in a spiritual awakening for Gabriel who had then assumed the role of Father Clement.

Rosen, Dr.   A man of German background whose efforts helped to destroy the Schwartze Hand in "THE FOUR SUSPECTS," he lives in hiding.

Rosen, Greta   Once a member of the blackmail and terrorist organization, the Schwartze Hand, she is the niece of the man who helped to destroy the organization in "THE FOUR SUSPECTS."

Rosentelle, Madame   Owner of Eugene and Rosentelle, a fashionable London hairdressing shop in ELEPHANTS CAN REMEMBER, she made the four wigs used by Dolly JARROW to impersonate Molly RAVENSCROFT.

Ross, Miss   An extremely attractive, red-haired secretary and dental assistant in DEATH IN THE CLOUDS, her employer viewed her as "frightfully competent."

Ross, Donald   A self-centered actor who became the thirteenth guest at the dinner party given by Sir Montagu Corner in LORD EDGWARE DIES, he is murdered because he is too observant a listener. When he meets the real Jane WILKINSON and she confuses the Paris of Greek mythology with the city of Paris, France, he realizes that the woman posing as Jane at the dinner party was an imposter.

Rossakoff, Countess Vera   A flamboyant Russian emigrant who may or may not really be a countess, she is the only woman to capture the heart and mind of Hercule POIROT, who views her as "a remarkable woman." The two first meet in "DOUBLE CLUE," when she swoops into the detective's office, "bringing with her a swirl of sables . . . and a hat rampant with slaughtered ospreys." She contacts Poirot to ask his assistance in clearing Bernard PARKER of jewel theft charges. His investigation leads Poirot to the realization that the countess is well

connected to the criminal underworld and that she is a jewel thief, but his admiration continues. The two next meet in THE BIG FOUR, in which the countess works as a secretary to Big Four gang member, Madame OLIVIER, under the name of Inez Veroneau. She is also the mother of a son, Niki, who is kidnapped, thus sending the countess to her admirer Poirot for help. After a touching ending in *The Big Four,* in which the possibility of a continued romance is hinted, Poirot and the countess remain apart for twenty years, until they meet accidentally while riding escalators going in opposite directions in "THE CAPTURE OF CERBERUS." She is now the proprietor of a popular new nightclub named Hell, which her partner in the operation is using as a site for the sale of narcotics. Poirot clears the countess of culpability in the illegal operation, then sends her roses, only in part as congratulations for the engagement of her son.

Rossiter, Edward   Engaged to his cousin, Charmain STROUD, he expects to receive a windfall when his uncle, Mathew STROUD, dies in "STRANGE JEST," but he discovers that the estate contains no money. Undaunted, the "fair-haired amiable young giant" contacts Miss Jane MARPLE for help.

Rouncewell, Mrs. (Rouncey)   An enormous, calm woman in UNFINISHED PORTRAIT, she treats cooking as a ritual.

Rouselle, Madamoiselle (Maddy)   Former governess to the twins, Celia RAVENSCROFT and Dolly JARROW, she reveals to Hercule POIROT that one of her former charges in ELEPHANTS CAN REMEMBER was an extremely jealous individual.

Rowan, Miss   Despite the evidence that fellow instructor Miss SPRINGER at the Meadowbank School in CAT AMONG THE PIGEONS was shot from a distance of more than four feet, this intense schoolmistress, who holds a degree in psychology, insists that the cause is suicide.

Rowe, Janet   Convinced that the Communists or the Catholics were behind the death of Aristide LEONIDES in CROOKED HOUSE, she dies when she accidentally drinks a cup of cocoa containing digitalin that had been meant for Josephine LEONIDES.

Rowland, George After being fired by his uncle for not taking his job seriously enough in "THE GIRL IN THE TRAIN," he heads for the village of Rowland's Castle because the name seemed to promise him a new fate. On the way, he meets the Grand Duchess ANASTASIA, whom he helps to hide from her guardian and an eager suitor. By the end of the day, after helping Scotland Yard to retrieve harbor defense plans, his proposal of marriage is accepted by Anastasia, and his fortune has turned.

Rowlandson, Mr. The manager of the Royal Hotel Spa in A MURDER IS ANNOUNCED, he provides information about his murdered employee, Rudi SCHERZ.

Royde, Thomas The partner in a Malaysian plantation in TOWARDS ZERO, he is a quiet man who is called "Silent Thomas" and "Taciturn Thomas." He has also earned the nickname of "Hermit Crab" because he walks with a sideways motion like a crab, the result of an accident in which he was jammed in a door during an earthquake.

Rubec, Dr. A member of Mr. ARISTIDES' Brain Trust in DESTINATION UNKNOWN, he is a psychologist in charge of administering psychological tests to new employees.

Rudd, Jason (Jinks) A physically unattractive man who is the fifth husband of movie star Marina GREGG in THE MIRROR CRACK'D FROM SIDE TO SIDE, he is also an extremely successful film director.

Rudge, Franklin A crude yet likeable American tourist in Monte Carlo in "THE SOUL OF THE CROUPIER."

Rumbolt, Mr. The very gloomy-looking, cross gardener in UNFINISHED BUSINESS, he hangs himself in the stable after others learn of his extramarital affair.

Rumbolt, Mrs. She appeals to the master of the house in UNFINISHED PORTRAIT to help her find her husband.

Runcorn, Lady A middle-aged woman in "DOUBLE CLUE," she is present during the jewel theft at the home of Marcus HARDMAN.

Russell, Barton The widower of Iris RUSSELL in "YELLOW IRIS," he reenacts the night of her murder four years later but finds an unexpected addition to the guest list: Hercule POIROT.

Russell, Iris Murdered with strychnine at a dinner party, she is a wealthy heiress in "YELLOW IRIS" whose estate is jointly left to her sister, Pauline WEATHERBY, and her husband, Barton RUSSELL.

Russell, Miss The highly efficient housekeeper in THE MURDER OF ROGER ACKROYD whose "pinched lips and an acid smile" graced the Ackroyd mansion for five years, she inherits one thousand pounds from her employer.

Rustington, Janet A writer of "high-brow sort of stuff" in "THE REGATTA MYSTERY," she is a guest of Isaac POINTZ and the object of Evan LLEWELLYN's affections.

Rustonbury, Lady A philanthropic woman who uses her wealth to sponsor artists in productions at the family castle in "SWAN SONG."

Ryan, William P. The former war correspondent in "THE HOUND OF DEATH," he tells Mr. ANSTRUTHER the story of Sister Marie ANGELIQUE and her strange powers.

Rycroft, Mr. A follower of spiritualism and a member of the Psychical Research Society, he attends the seance on the night of Captain TREVELYAN's murder in THE SITTAFORD MYSTERY. He is an "elderly, dried-up man" who lives in a bungalow on the Sittaford estate; he is also an amateur criminologist who investigates the murder.

Ryder, Hank P. A wealthy American in "THE CRACKLER," he becomes enamored with Marguerite LAIDLOW and seeks to help her to escape her financial difficulties.

Ryder, James Bell En route to Paris to negotiate a loan to bail out his financially troubled company, he has the good fortune to sit in front of the murdered Madame GISELLE in DEATH IN THE CLOUDS. He sells his eyewitness account to reporters for enough money to eliminate the need for the loan.

Rydesdale, Chief George The chief constable of Middleshire, he aids in the investigation in A MURDER IS ANNOUNCED.

Ryland, Abe A member of the Big Four gang in which he is designated by the symbol of a dollar sign with a star and two stripes. He was known by most people as the American Soap King and is viewed as the "the richest man in the world, richer even than Rockefeller" in THE BIG FOUR. He hires Hercule POIROT to conduct business for him in Rio de Janeiro.

Rymer, Amelia A wealthy widow in "THE CASE OF THE RICH WOMAN," she is a one-time farmhand whose husband grew successful as a button shank manufacturer. Unhappy despite her wealth, she consults Mr. PARKER PYNE for advice, and he retains physician Dr. CONSTANTINE to drug her and take her to a Cornish farmhouse, where she is led to believe that she is Hannah Moorhouse, a farm servant. While on the farm, she meets and falls in love with another farmhand, Joe Walsh.

S

Sad Cypress   Mystery novel.

The novel is the only one which the author claimed that she ruined by putting Hercule POIROT in it. The plot centers on the efforts of Poirot to free a young woman falsely charged with murder.

PUBLISHING AND DRAMATIZATION HISTORY

The novel was published in 1940 by William Collins Sons and Company, Ltd., in London, and by Dodd, Mead and Company in New York.

The novel has not been adapted for stage or screen.

CHARACTERS

Mr. ABBOT (2), Inspector BRILL, Sir Edwin BULMER, Elinor CARLISLE, Mary DRAPER, Ephraim GERRARD, Mary GERRARD, Jessie HOPKINS, HORLICK, James Arthur LITTLEDALE, Dr. Peter LORD, Chief Inspector MARSDEN, Nurse O'BRIEN, Hercule Poirot, Alfred James WARGRAVE, Laura WELMAN, Roderick WELMAN

PLOT SYNOPSIS

Prologue

The novel opens with the trial of Elinor Carlisle, accused of killing Mary Gerrard. Elinor pleads "not guilty" to the charge. As the prosecuting attorney presents his case, she reviews in her mind the events that led to her arrest.

Chapters 1–5

The chapters are a flashback recounting the anonymous letter that first motivated Elinor and her boyfriend Roddy to visit Laura Welman, Elinor's aunt and the widow of Roddy's uncle, and the string of events which followed. The letter states that some-one has been manipulating herself into Aunt Laura's good graces to the point that Elinor's and Roddy's expected large inheritances might be endangered. The two visit Aunt Laura, who suffered a stroke sometime earlier and has two nurses caring for her. While there, they meet Mary Gerrard, daughter of the groundskeeper. Roddy finds her very attractive. Aunt Laura has a second stroke and dies in her sleep shortly after, without having made a will. Nurse Hopkins finds a dose of morphine missing from her medical case. Elinor inherits everything. She is generous to the staff and also gives Mary two thousand pounds, prompting Nurse Hopkins to suggest that Mary should make a will. In her will, Mary leaves everything to her Aunt Mary Riley of New Zealand. Elinor also makes a will, leaving everything to Roddy, although she has broken off their engagement because of his interest in Mary.

Chapter 6

The chapter is composed of letters from all involved. The nurses learn that Laura Welman and a mysterious man in a photograph found in her bureau were romantically linked. Elinor sells the house, while Roddy vacations to sort out his feelings. Mary's father dies, and she asks to stay with Elinor for a time.

Chapter 7

On the way to the house to clean out Laura's personal effects, Elinor stops at the store for fish paste to make sandwiches. At the same time, Mary and Nurse Hopkins go through Mary's late father's effects, and learn that Mary was not his biological daughter. At Laura's house, Elinor invites Nurse Hopkins and Mary to join her for sandwiches, then Elinor and the nurse go upstairs to begin work while Mary stays in the kitchen to wash up. They descend later and find Mary dying of poison.

Chapters 8–13
Peter Lord, the doctor who attended Laura Welman, consults Hercule Poirot and asks for help in proving Elinor innocent of Mary's murder. Poirot does not offer much hope, but he questions people close to Mary Gerrard and Laura Welman, as the police exhume Laura's body to learn if she was also poisoned. Poirot questions Roddy, and implies that either Roddy or Elinor could have poisoned Laura for her money.

Chapters 14–17
Everything that Poirot learns points to Elinor's guilt, but he continues to pursue clues. He is particularly interested in the missing dose of morphine reported by Nurse Hopkins.

Chapters 18–19
Poirot questions Elinor, who contends that she did not kill either her aunt or Mary. She recounts in careful detail all of the events that occurred on the day that Mary died, and remembers that Nurse Hopkins had a small mark on her wrist, which she claimed was a scratch from a thorn. Dr. Lord and the detective speak with the gardener, who recalls seeing a car similar to Lord's in the driveway on the day of the murder and finding matches in the bushes outside the window of the house.

Chapters 20–22
Nurse Hopkins reveals to Poirot that Laura Welman was Mary's biological mother, conceived in an extramarital affair. The gardener insists that the car in the driveway was Dr. Lord's and will swear to the plate numbers. Faced with this information, Poirot rehashes all of the evidence and questions additional witnesses.

Chapters 23–26
Elinor takes the stand and denies taking the morphine and killing Mary or Laura. Two witnesses are called and they reveal shocking information regarding Nurse Hopkins's true identity. Poirot introduces a torn pharmacy label to show that apomorphine, a morphine antidote, was present at the scene of Mary's death. With the assistance of Hercule Poirot, Elinor is judged innocent. She goes to a sanitarium to recuperate. When she has recovered, she will marry Dr. Lord. The guilty party is brought to justice.

CRIME NOTES
The two murders in this story are the result of poisoning with morphine hydrochloride.

Sainsbury Seale, Mabelle　A former actress who later works as a teacher in India, she is the third murder victim in ONE, TWO, BUCKLE MY SHOE.

Saintclair, Valerie　Engaged to Prince PAUL OF MAURANIA, who believes that she is descended from Russian royalty, this famous dancer in "THE KING OF CLUBS" is really a daughter in the British middle class Oglander family. She becomes enveloped in scandal when a male acquaintance is murdered in her home.

Salmon, Sir Joseph　A major figure in Jane HELIER's scheme to expose her former husband's new wife in "THE AFFAIR AT THE BUNGALOW," she protects his identity by naming him Sir Herman Cohen when she relates the plan.

Samoushenka, Katrina　Born the daughter of a Leningrad taxi driver, she is a world-famous Russian ballet dancer in "THE ARCADIAN DEER" who develops tuberculosis and retires to a Swiss sanatorium. In the search for Ted WILLIAMSON's lost love, Hercule POIROT contacts the dancer for information.

Sampson, Mr.　A feisty, elderly resident of ST. MARY MEAD who boasts of being the oldest man in the village at ninety-six in THE MIRROR CRACK'D FROM SIDE TO SIDE, he prophetically proclaims that "there'll be a lot of wickedness" at the fund-raising benefit for St. John's Ambulance Brigade held in Gossington Hall.

Samuelson, Mrs.　One of several wealthy women in "THE NEMEAN LION" whose Pekinese pets are kidnapped and then ransomed, she pays the three-hundred-pound ransom. Once Nanki Poo is returned, she attempts to retrieve the package of money but finds only blank sheets of paper in the parcel.

Sanchia　See DE SARA, MADELEINE.

"Sanctuary"　Mystery short story.
The plot centers on the discovery of a bloody and dying man in a church, and his sole utterance, "Sanctuary."

PUBLISHING AND DRAMATIZATION HISTORY

The story appeared in the short story collection, DOUBLE SIN AND OTHER STORIES, published in 1961 by Dodd, Mead and Company in New York.

The story has not been adapted for stage or screen.

CHARACTERS

Police Constable ABEL, Inspector Dermot CRADDOCK, Mr. ECCLES, Pam ECCLES, Dr. GRIFFIN, Mrs. Diana (Bunch) HARMON, Reverend Julian HARMON, Sergeant HAYES, Miss Jane MARPLE, Edwin MOSS, Jewel ST. JOHN, Walter ST. JOHN, ZOBEIDA

PLOT SYNOPSIS

The story concerns the murder of a stranger found in a church by the vicar's wife, Diane "Bunch" Harmon, as she prepares the flowers for the weekly service. No one in the small village of Chipping Cleghorn recognizes him, and the mystery deepens when a couple appears, pretending to be relatives. Through clever sleuthing, and with the help of her aunt, Jane Marple, Bunch discovers a suitcase containing valuable emeralds that also reveals the reason for the stranger's desperate journey.

CRIME NOTES

The murder in this story is the result of a gunshot wound to the chest.

Sandbourne, Mrs.   A hearty and caring woman who is as much social director as guide on the tour of famous houses and gardens of Great Britain in NEMESIS, she excels in making certain that no one in her group feels alone.

Sandbourne, William   See ST. JOHN, WALTER EDMUND.

Sandeman, Sir Edwin   Called by Rex FORTESCUE's secretary when her boss has a seizure in A POCKET FULL OF RYE, this Harley Street physician is too late to reverse the effect of the poison.

Sanderfield, Sir George   A wealthy scoundrel, "rolling in money," he is "a short square man with dark coarse hair and a roll of fat in his neck" who has an affair with the prima ballerina Katrina SAMOUSHENKA in "THE ARCADIAN DEER."

Sanders, Gladys   Still a newlywed when she dies in "A CHRISTMAS TRAGEDY" after being hit over the head with a sandbag, she had a comfortable income from a trust fund, which is willed to her husband, Jack SANDERS.

Sanders, Jack   The epitome of a good-natured, popular man, he is the husband of the murdered Gladys SANDERS in "A CHRISTMAS TRAGEDY." Observers commented that "nobody could have been pleasanter to his wife than he was," but they did not know about the telephone call that he made as "Mr. Littleworth."

Sandford, Dr.   The young and modern physician who joins Dr. HAYDOCK's practice in ST. MARY MEAD, he earns the disapproval of Miss MARPLE in THE MIRROR CRACK'D FROM SIDE TO SIDE. Unimpressed with his up-to-date reliance on modern pharmacology, she feels that "the younger doctors are all the same. . . . Medicine nowadays is just like a supermarket—all packaged up."

Sandford, Rex   Adamant in his claim that the murdered Rose EMMOTT had aggressively pursued him, then become pregnant with his child in "DEATH BY DROWNING," he is a young architect whose creations are "full of new-fangled stuff."

Sanseverato, Rebecca   The second wife of Alistair BLUNT in ONE, TWO, BUCKLE MY SHOE, she does not realize that her marriage to the politically powerful man is bigamous.

Santonix, Rudolf   A young, famous architect in ENDLESS NIGHT, he is in great demand by wealthy clients, but chooses to design only houses that please him. His best work is the house on Gipsy's Acre, commissioned by Michael and Ellie ROGERS, which he completes shortly before his death.

San Veratrino, Marchese di   The owner of the Borgia goblet in "THE APPLES OF THE HESPERIDES," he loses the goblet when it is stolen from his palace on the night it is sold to Emery POWERS.

Sarah (1)   A young spiritualist in "THE BIRD WITH THE BROKEN WING," she conducts a Ouija session which helps Mr. SATTERTHWAITE to make an important decision when Harley QUIN breaks in with his own message.

Sarah (2)   In UNFINISHED PORTRAIT, she is the faithful cook whose secret of a daughter born sixty years before dies with her.

Satipy   The second death in DEATH COMES AS THE END, she is the wife of YAHMOSE and the mother of two young sons. Although she is "handsome in a hard, commanding kind of way," she is also an acid-tongued shrew who finds fault with everyone and everything.

Satterthwaite, Mr.   An elderly man who sometimes regrets his role in life as an onlooker with "neither chick nor child," he appears in the twelve stories in the short story collection, THE MYSTERIOUS MR. QUIN; the short stories, "DEAD MAN'S MIRROR," "THE LOVE DETECTIVES" and "THE HARLEQUIN TEA SET" and the novel, THREE-ACT TRAGEDY. Unlike other recurring characters, he clearly ages during the stories, from sixty-two years of age to sixty-nine. An old friend of Hercule POIROT, who observes that "he has the sense of atmosphere," Mr. Satterthwaite usually depends upon Mr. Harley QUIN to appear and help him interpret what he has already seen yet failed to understand fully. A connoisseur of the arts, he draws his acquaintances from the upper levels of society, and he especially likes the company of nobility. He is an amateur photographer and a published author of *Homes of My Friends*.

Saunders, Doris   A sculptor's model in THE HOLLOW, she is "a common mean spiteful little piece," but her beautiful eyes make up for her personality.

Savage, John   An apparent suicide in WHY DIDN'T THEY ASK EVANS? who is fatally ill with cancer, he is an extremely wealthy man whose old friend Alan CARSTAIRS refuses to accept the official ruling of his death as a suicide.

Savaronoff, Dr.   See DARRELL, CLAUD.

Savernake, Henrietta   A sculptress in THE HOLLOW whose work includes both the traditional and the *avant garde*, she uses her work to escape grief

when John CHRISTOW, her lover, is found dead of a gunshot wound.

Sayers, Maggie   See DE SARA, MADELEINE.

Scheele, Anna   Confidential secretary of Otto MORGANTHAL and sister-in-law of Dr. John PAUNCE-FOOT JONES in THEY CAME TO BAGHDAD, she gathers information about a subversive group that diverts money, jewels and people to accomplish its evil aims.

Scherz, Rudi   Suspected of stealing money from his employer, the Royal Spa Hotel, he is "a very ordinary pleasant young chap" in A MURDER IS ANNOUNCED. He is found dead of a gunshot wound at Little Paddocks a short time after placing a newspaper advertisement announcing a murder at a specific date and time.

Schlagal, Herr   A German-born pilot now working for an air service in Baghdad in "THE HOUSE AT SHIRAZ," he relates to Mr. PARKER PYNE how he fell in love years before with Muriel KING, but lost her to death.

Schlieder, Anna and Freda   They are the Dutch mother and daughter who risk their own safety to shelter an escaped English prisoner of war in GIANT'S BREAD.

Schmidt, Fraulein Hildegarde   Formerly the cook in the household from which Daisy ARMSTRONG was kidnapped, she is the maid of Princess DRAGOMIROFF in MURDER ON THE ORIENT EXPRESS (1).

Schneider, Mr.   One of the casualties of the presumed curse in "THE ADVENTURE OF THE EGYPTIAN TOMB," he is a representative of the Metropolitan Museum of New York on the Menher-Ra expedition. He dies of tetanus at the excavation site.

Schuster, Mr.   A young attorney in NEMESIS, he views the provisions in Mr. RAFIEL's will as extremely odd, especially those which relate to Miss MARPLE.

Schwartz, Gertrud   An old German servant who had been with Dr. ROSEN for forty years in "THE FOUR SUSPECTS," she is one of the suspects in his murder.

Schwartz, Mr.   An American tourist staying at the Rochers Neige resort in "THE ERYMANTHIAN BOAR," he saves Hercule POIROT's life when MARRASCAUD's gang members attempt murder.

Scotswood   The name of the large, Victorian country house in Sunningdale, divided into four flats, in which Archie and Agatha Christie made their home.

Scott, Moira O'Connell   A beautiful young newlywed in "THE SHADOW ON THE GLASS" whose golden red hair "stood out round her small face like a saint's halo," she is shot to death in the garden of Greenways House while embracing a man other than her husband.

Scott, Richard   The husband of Moira O'Connell SCOTT in "THE SHADOW ON THE GLASS," he is a guest with his new bride at Greenways House, which he had previously visited and whose legend he knew.

Scudamore, Joan   The main character in ABSENT IN THE SPRING, she is an interfering, controlling, middle-aged woman who is blind to others' dislike of her. Stranded in Mesopotamia for five days, she examines her past and dislikes what she learns about herself. Although she vows to be more yielding and sympathetic to others when she returns home, she fails to keep that promise, for she lacks the courage needed to change her behavior.

Scudamore, Rodney   Quiet and agreeable, he has allowed his wife Joan to dominate his life in ABSENT IN THE SPRING. He has always wanted to be a farmer, yet he complies with his wife's insistence that he remain a lawyer despite his deep feelings of revulsion for the profession.

Scudamore, Tony   Despite his mother's attempts to dominate his life in ABSENT IN THE SPRING, he refuses to give up his dream of farming, and moves to South Africa to run an orange tree farm in defiance of his mother.

Scuttle, Mr.   Head of the real estate firm for which accused murderer James BENTLEY had once worked in MRS. MCGINTY'S DEAD, he mistakes Hercule POIROT for either a restaurant proprietor or a hotel manager.

"Second Gong, The"   Mystery short story.

The plot centers on a murder that occurs in an apparently locked study with only the victim present. The plot is nearly identical to that of "DEAD MAN'S MIRROR."

PUBLISHING AND DRAMATIZATION HISTORY
The story appeared in the short story collection, WITNESS FOR THE PROSECUTION, published in 1948 by Dodd, Mead and Company in New York.

The story has not been adapted for stage or screen.

CHARACTERS
Joan ASHBY, Gregory BARLING, Diana CLEVES, Harry DALEHOUSE, Mr. DIGBY, Geoffrey KEENE, Mr. Hubert LYTCHAM ROCHE, Captain John MARSHALL, Hercule POIROT

PLOT SYNOPSIS
The story is concerned with the murder of Mr. Hubert Lytcham Roche, an autocratic man in whose home a dinner gong is sounded twice each night to call guests to dinner. Those who fail to arrive at the table soon after the second gong are never again invited to social events at his home. When Poirot discovers the murdered man alone in the study, with both windows and doors locked, he faces the difficult task of finding the murderer. Although all four household members seem to have alibis for the time of the murder, one must be guilty.

CRIME NOTES
The murder in this story is the result of a gunshot wound to the head.

Secret Adversary, The   Mystery novel.

The novel is the second by the author and the first adventure to star Tommy and Tuppence BERESFORD. The story mixes their courtship with espionage. The plot centers on an international adventure sparked by Tuppence's inadvertent use of a dangerous alias.

PUBLISHING AND DRAMATIZATION HISTORY
The novel was published in 1922 by John Lane in London, and by Dodd, Mead and Company in New York.

George Baker and Francesca Annis star in the 1983 television film version of *The Secret Adversary.* (Photo courtesy of London Weekend Television)

The novel was adapted in 1928 by the Fox Film Corporation in Germany for the first screen version of an Agatha Christie work in *Die Abenteur G.m.b.H.*, which translates into *Adventure, Inc.* (See DIE ABENTEUR GmbH.) The novel was also adapted for television in 1985 by London Weekend Television in England and shown on the Public Broadcasting Service in the U.S.

CHARACTERS
ANNETTE, Albert BATT. Tommy Beresford, Tuppence Beresford, Mr. BROWN, A. CARTER, Sir James Peel EDGERTON, Jane FINN, Dr. HALL, Julius P. HERSHEIMER, Boris IVANOVITCH, KRAMENIN, Marguerite VANDEMEYER, Edward WHITTINGTON

PLOT SYNOPSIS
Chapters 1–3
Childhood friends Tommy Beresford and Prudence (Tuppence) Cowley meet again after World War I, and share their frustrations over the lack of employment opportunities in England. They decide to form a business called "Young Adventurers," and advertise that they will go anywhere and do anything. In a restaurant, they are overheard by Edward Whittington, who sits at a nearby table. He quickly approaches Tuppence and asks her to meet him at his office the following day. She gives her name as "Jane Finn" and he hires her to enroll in a Parisian girls' school. She receives her retainer of fifty pounds and agrees to meet the next day, but the office is locked and empty when she keeps the appointment.

Chapters 4–6
The newspaper advertisement draws two responses, one of which Tommy recognizes as being from an official in British Army Intelligence. A. Carter tells them that Intelligence will hire the young sleuths to find the real Jane Finn, who had been entrusted with highly sensitive government documents, including a treaty, by an Intelligence agent on the S.S. *Lusitania* just before it was torpedoed. The plot is complicated when Julius P. Hersheimer appears and asks for assistance in locating his cousin, Jane Finn, upon whom he wants to bestow part of his fortune. He claims that an Inspector Brown from Scotland Yard spoke with him and obtained a photograph of Jane, but the Yard has no inspector of that name. Tommy and Tuppence begin their investigation by tracking down all surviving passengers of the *Lusitania*, to learn what they can about Jane's fate.

Chapters 7–9
The pair observe Whittington and another man leaving South Audley Mansions, the home of one of the passengers, Marguerite (Rita) Vandemeyer. Tommy follows the unknown man to a house in Soho, where he hears and uses the secret knock and the password, "Mr. Brown." Once in the house, Tommy looks around for a place to hide and listen for information. He hears conversations about labour parties, a revolution and a strike, as well as references to a document held by a girl who must be made to talk. He is then knocked unconscious by a blow to the head. Still at South Audley Mansions, Tuppence speaks with the young elevator operator, later their trusted accomplice, Albert, and asks for his assistance in getting a job with Rita. He tells her that the woman's parlourmaid is leaving and that he will recommend Tuppence.

Chapters 10–13

Tuppence gets the job and immediately begins to eavesdrop. She sees Rita meet with Boris, the unknown man whom Tommy had followed, and hears his reprimand against allowing a visit from an old friend and famous criminologist, Sir James Peel Edgerton. Tuppence meets with Hersheimer, and learns that he had trailed Whittington to a nursing home, where the man visited his niece Edith. They worry because Tommy has sent no word, so they visit Edgerton and ask his help in getting information from Rita. When Tuppence returns to her employer, Rita threatens her with a gun, which Tuppence wrests from her as Rita passes out. Edgerton, Julius and Tuppence remain at the apartment all night, but Rita is found dead of a chloral overdose the next morning.

Chapters 14–17

The three visit Dr. Hall at the nursing home to learn if Jane Finn were there. They find that a woman answering her description had been committed to care by Rita, who took her away four days earlier. Just as the case seems to have hit a dead end, Tuppence receives a telegram signed by Tommy. Although he did not send the telegram, he has escaped from his captors through the assistance of Annette, a young woman who takes his food to him. Once free, Tommy tells Carter everything he heard while captive, then returns to the Ritz to learn that Tuppence checked out fifteen minutes earlier.

Chapters 18–21

Tommy contacts Hersheimer and learns what has happened in his absence. They find the crumpled telegram and learn that Tuppence has been lured to the Moat House in Yorkshire, but they arrive too late, and find only her brooch on the ground. They stay a week, searching the area and waiting for word, then Hersheimer contacts Scotland Yard. Tommy responds to a telegram from Edgerton who has found Jane Finn. She has regained her memory, and has informed him that, before losing her memory, she hid the papers under a boulder near the sea. Tommy and Hersheimer locate the spot, but the oilskin pouch contains only blank papers. When heated, one of the papers yields the message "With the compliments of Mr. Brown." Tommy learns that a barely identifiable body wearing Tuppence's clothes has washed up on the Yorkshire coast.

Chapters 22–24

Tommy traces the telegram found in Tuppence's room and learns that it was a plant: really she has been lured to Astley Priors in Kent. Tommy and Hersheimer plan a rescue, and learn that Annette is with Tuppence. Hersheimer demands at gunpoint to know the exact location of the women. After the rescue, they drive off in a blaze of gunfire, as Annette is revealed to be Jane Finn.

Chapters 25–28

Jane and Tuppence arrive safely at Edgerton's house, where Jane reveals that she fooled her captors by speaking fluent French and feigning memory loss. She had hidden the real papers in a magazine in her Soho room, and placed the blank papers in the oilskin pouch under the boulder. They arrive at the Soho room to retrieve the papers and are met by an unexpected perpetrator who threatens their lives before committing suicide. The novel ends as the vital documents are found, Julius and Jane discuss marriage and Tommy and Tuppence firmly decide to marry.

CRIME NOTES

The sole death in this novel is a suicide committed by the ingestion of cyanide.

Secret of Chimneys, The Mystery novel.

The novel marks the first appearance of Inspector BATTLE, who would appear in four later novels. The plot of this thriller concerns a missing packet of letters, and their connection to murder and control of the throne of Herzoslovakia.

PUBLISHING AND DRAMATIZATION HISTORY

The novel was published in 1925 by John Lane in London, and by Dodd, Mead and Company in New York.

The novel has not been adapted for stage or screen.

CHARACTERS

Boris ANCHOUKOFF, Chief Inspector BADGWORTHY, Inspector Battle, Clement Edward Alistair BRENT, Daisy BRENT, Dulcie BRENT, Lady Eileen (Bundle) BRENT, Anthony CADE, Dr. CARTWRIGHT, DUTCH PEDRO, Bill EVERSLEIGH, Hiram FISH, Herman

ISAACSTEIN, Constable JOHNSON, Monsieur LEM-OINE, Baron LOLOPRETJZYL, Honourable George LOMAX, Guiseppe MANELLI, Jimmy MCGRATH, Colonel MELROSE, Angele MORY, Prince Michael OBO-LOVITCH, Virginia REVEL, Count STYLPTITCH, TREDWELL, King VICTOR, Professor WYNWOOD

PLOT SYNOPSIS
Chapters 1–3
Adventurer Jimmy McGrath asks his old friend, Anthony Cade, to deliver the memoirs of Count Stylptitch to a publisher. McGrath has been promised a thousand pounds if the manuscript arrives by a specific date, and he offers Cade two hunderd and fifty pounds to take his place. The memoirs are of concern to Allistair Brent and George Lomax, who want their publication delayed at least a month for editing. McGrath also asks Cade to return some letters in his possession, which have been used to blackmail a woman named Virginia Revel.

Chapters 4–6
Anthony Cade arrives in England, and is approached by Baron Lolopretjzyl, a representative of the London Loyalist Party of Herzoslovakia. He fears that the memoirs are scandalous, and offers to purchase them for fifteen hundred pounds, but Cade refuses. Shortly afterward, a member of the Red Hand organization threatens Cade with a gun and demands the memoirs, but Cade knocks the gun from his hand and throws him out of the room. Hours later, hotel employee Giuseppe Manelli awakens Cade, who struggles and beats him off, saving the memoirs, but the letters are taken. Manelli locates Virginia Revel to extort a thousand pounds for the letters, but she is the wrong Virginia Revel.

Chapters 7–10
The publishers contact Cade. They arrange to send a messenger for the manuscript and give him a check for a thousand pounds. Soon after the exchange is made, he receives a document from Alistair Brent demanding that he hold the manuscript until after they have talked, and inviting him to a weekend party at the stately mansion Chimneys. He refuses, because the manuscript has already been delivered. Cade visits Virginia, who has also been invited to Chimneys, and he arrives as she discovers Manelli dead in her study, shot above the heart. They find a note in the dead man's pocket which reads "Chimneys, 11:45,

Thursday." After putting Manelli's body in a trunk and dumping it along a lonely stretch of road, Cade goes to Chimneys. As he arrives, he sees a light on in only one room, and he hears a shot. Prince Michael of Herzoslovakia is found dead, and Lomax calls in Battle of Scotland Yard.

Chapters 11–14
The investigation reveals footprints in the mud and a report that a car was outside the estate moments before the shot. Battle locates Cade, who reveals what he saw and tells them the story of his mission for McGrath. Cade views the body of Prince Michael and identifies him as the publisher's representative who had retrieved the memoirs from him. Scotland Yard demands that no one leave Chimneys until after the inquest, and various motives for the crime are examined.

Chapters 15–18
Cade identifies the inhabitant of the sole room with a light on during the murder as recently hired governess, Mademoiselle Brun. He questions Baron Lolopretjzyl as to what Prince Michael planned to do with the memoirs after reading them. He refuses to believe that they were to be burned. To his great surprise, the Prince's valet approaches him and tells him that he will serve Cade faithfully and without pay. Cade leaves for Paris to learn more about the Seven Dials group and learns that a current guest at Chimneys, Bill Eversleigh, is a member. When Cade returns, Battle meets him at the train station, and tells him about a hidden jewel sought by the notorious King Victor and about the body found along a deserted roadway. That evening, Eversleigh, Cade and Virginia lie in wait for the intruder. They capture someone, but his identification proves that he is M. Lemoine, an inspector from the Sûreté in Paris, who claims to have seen the intruder chased off the previous night.

Chapters 19–21
The letters signed by "Virginia Revel" were actually written in code to King Victor by a Parisian actress named Angele Mory, who had assumed a royal title and married King Nicholas IV. Both were presumed killed in the revolution, but Mory hid the priceless Koki-noor jewel before her death. Cade tells Battle that he dumped Manelli's body on the roadside. Later he finds the missing letters on his bedside

table. Alistair Brent invites the guests to stay longer, even though Scotland Yard says that they can leave. Isaacstein insists that he must leave and hurries out with his suitcases. One case falls open and a revolver drops out, but Lemoine carefully picks it up with a handkerchief and returns it to the case.

Chapters 22–24
Cade tells Virginia that he loves her, and Bundle reveals a secret passage through the council chamber which leads from Chimneys to Wyvvern Abbey. When Cade walks in the rose garden, he asks Hiram Fish for a match but does not light it. He later learns that Fish is a special agent assigned to shadow King Victor. Cade demands that everyone return to Chimneys and meet in the council chamber at nine in the evening. He tells them that clues point to the jewels being hidden in the library, and Battle accuses him of being King Victor. They hear a whistle, and rush to the library, where they find the governess shot to death by Boris.

Chapters 28–31
Cade reveals that the governess was really Angele, and that Lemoine is an imposter. The jewel is found in the rose garden, the memoirs are located intact, and Cade's true identity is revealed, for a surprise ending for both Cade and Virginia Revel.

CRIME NOTES
The two murder victims in the novel die of gunshot wounds.

Sedgwick, Miss   Secretary to the mystery writer, Mrs. Ariadne OLIVER, in ELEPHANTS CAN REMEMBER.

Sedgwick, Lady Bess   A fearless adventurer in AT BERTRAM'S HOTEL, she was married three times but only once legitimately. Well-known to the public, she has made a career of daring danger, but her daughter Elvira BLAKE has only read about her mother, because Lady Bess has never felt quite capable of assuming the maternal role. When her first, and only legitimate, husband reenters her life, she becomes distraught. He is later shot to death and she confesses, then drives her car at ninety miles per hour into a railing along the side of the highway.

Sedley, Amelia Mary   A witness at the trial of Elinor CARLISLE in SAD CYPRESS, she reveals that the

woman who called herself Nurse Jessie Hopkins was really Mary DRAPER, the aunt of the murdered young woman.

Selkirk, Eve   See CARPENTER, EVE.

Seminoff, Olga   Identified as beneficiary to Mrs. LLEWELLYN-SMYTH's estate in a forged codicil to the original will in HALLOWE'EN PARTY, she stubbornly refuses to relinquish her claim, despite the invalidity of the document.

Serakis, Catherine   A woman of melancholy appearance, she is the secretary of the Olive Branch and romantically involved with Edward GORING in "THEY CAME TO BAGHDAD."

Serrocold, Carrie Louise   The mistress of the Stoneygates estate, which becomes a home for delinquent boys in THEY DO IT WITH MIRRORS, she ignores all evil that goes on around her, even when murder occurs.

Serrocold, Lewis   A man who is constantly involved in one cause or another in THEY DO IT WITH MIRRORS, he turns the family estate, Stoneygates, into a home for delinquent boys, and dies while trying to save his son from drowning.

Sessle, Captain Anthony   The partner in an insurance firm in "THE SUNNINGDALE MYSTERY," he is a former soldier who is found dead on the seventh tee after an afternoon of golf. The cause of death is a hatpin through his heart.

Settle, Dr.   The physician who first attends Sir Arthur CARMICHAEL when he loses his power of speech and most human characteristics in "THE STRANGE CASE OF SIR ARTHUR CARMICHAEL," he later calls in Dr. Edward CARSTAIRS for a consultation on the case.

Seven Dials Mystery, The   Mystery novel.
   The novel provides a return to Chimneys, the country house that served as the setting for THE SECRET OF CHIMNEYS, and the reappearance of many characters from that earlier novel. The plot concerns a mysterious organization and the deaths linked with it.

PUBLISHING AND DRAMATIZATION HISTORY

The novel was published in 1929 by William Collins Sons and Company, Ltd., in London, and by Dodd, Mead and Company in New York.

The novel was adapted for television in 1981 by London Weekend Television in England, and was also shown on the Public Broadcasting Service in the U.S. Sir John Gielgud played the role of Alistair Brent.

CHARACTERS

ALFRED, Count ANDRAS, Rupert BATEMAN, Superintendent BATTLE, John BAUER, Clement Edward Alistair BRENT, Lady Eileen "Bundle" BRENT, Marcia BRENT, Dr. CASSELL, Lady Maria COOTE, Sir Oswald COOTE, Vera "Socks" DAVENTRY, Ronny DEVEREAUX, Sir Stanley DIGBY, Herr EBERHARD, Bill EVERSLEIGH, George LOMAX, Colonel MELROSE, Mr. MOSGOROVSKY, Terence O'ROURKE, Howard PHELPS, Countess RADZKY, Gerald ST. MAUR, Mr. STEVENS, Jimmy THESIGER, TREDWELL, Gerald WADE, Loraine WADE

PLOT SYNOPSIS

Chapters 1–3

Sir Oswald and Lady Maria Coote invite a group of young adults as guests for their last party at Chimneys. Gerry Wade is a late riser, and the others decide to play a joke on him. The eight friends buy eight alarm clocks and set them to go off one after another, starting at 6:30 A.M. The clocks fail to wake him, and Gerry is found dead of a chloral overdose. After informing his sister, Loraine, of the death, Thesiger and Devereaux go to his room, but only seven clocks are on the mantelpiece.

Chapters 4–6

Lord Caterham and his daughter, Lady Eileen "Bundle" Brent, return to Chimneys, where Bundle finds a letter written by Gerry Wade to his sister Loraine. The letter mentions the Seven Dials, a slum district of London. When Bundle drives to town, a man who falls onto the road. She stops to help him, finds that he has been shot and hears him mumble, "Seven dials—tell Jimmy Thesiger." The man is Ronny Devereaux.

Chapters 7–9

Bundle gives Thesiger the news that Devereaux is dead. Loraine Wade is also present, and the three decide that they are going to unmask the murderer. Thesiger tells them that the Seven Dials is the headquarters of organized crime. Bundle later learns that Lomax has had a letter from Seven Dials, and that he is hosting a party the following week. Convinced that Devereaux and Wade were in the Secret Service, Thesiger uses Eversleigh, whom he believes also to be involved, to gain entry to the party.

Chapters 10–12

Bundle visits Superintendent Battle and asks for a list of secret societies, then asks about Seven Dials, which he refuses to discuss. Eversleigh tells her that Seven Dials is a nightclub, and she insists on going there. The entertainment includes dining, dancing and gambling, and Bundle spots her former footman, Alfred, in the club. She visits her Aunt Marcia the following day, and manages to obtain an invitation to Lomax's party as Marcia's guest.

Chapters 13–15

Bundle returns alone to the nightclub and speaks with Alfred, who tells her that the Seven Dials meet at the club after it closes. She hides in a cupboard, and Alfred locks her in. At the meeting, people are wearing clock masks, each set at a different time. Bundle listens as they discuss Lomax's party and consider the value of Eberhard's invention. After Alfred lets her out of the hiding place the next morning, Bundle relates her adventure to Thesiger, who tells her that Eberhard's invention is a formula for making a steel wire that is as strong as a bar of steel.

Chapters 16–20

Bundle attends Lomax's party, and Battle is undercover as a footman. After the party, Thesiger and Eversleigh take turns standing guard, with Thesiger taking the first watch. He hears noise in the library and goes to investigate, but sees nothing. Meanwhile, Bundle climbs out of her window, but Battle catches her and makes her return to her room. She walks past Thesiger's post and Eversleigh's room, but both are empty. More noises and two shots are heard in the library. Battle finds Thesiger lying wounded on the library floor, and O'Rourke is found drugged in his room, with valuable papers missing.

Chapters 21–26

Battle finds Loraine Wade outside the house, holding the brown packet containing the papers. The confusion in the library is sorted out and Battle finds

Countess Radzky collapsed in a heap behind a large screen. Sir Oswald Coote was outside during the confusion but claims to have seen no one, prompting Battle to state that Thesiger's attacker either was an excellent runner or had re-entered the house after the attacks. Lady Coote invites Thesiger to Chimneys for the following weekend, despite her husband's objections.

Chapters 27–29
Thesiger searches Coote's study, but finds no reference to the Seven Dials. Caught downstairs by Bateman, he lies, saying he was hungry. Bundle and Loraine visit Chimneys the next morning and play golf with O'Rourke and Bateman to give Thesiger more time to search the house. Eversleigh contacts Thesiger and tells him that he has received a letter from Devereaux with instructions to follow if he were to die suddenly.

Chapters 30–34
Bundle receives a call from Thesiger, who asks her to bring Loraine to the Seven Dials and to get rid of Alfred. She does so, and they go upstairs with Thesiger. Eversleigh is found drugged in the car, and when Bundle goes for smelling salts, she is hit on the head and knocked out. When she awakens, Mr. Mosgorovsky summons her to a meeting of the Seven Dials, where she learns that they are a peace-loving organization formed to improve the world. Battle is the leader, number 7, the late Gerry Wade was number 1 and Devereaux was number 2. The murderer is unmasked as the methods used to dispose of Wade and Devereaux are revealed. At the end of the novel, Bundle tells her father that she is marrying Eversleigh.

CRIME NOTES
The first victim dies from ingesting hydrochloride of morphia in his whiskey, and the second victim dies of a gunshot wound.

"Shadow on the Glass, The" Mystery short story.

The plot centers on a mysterious double murder committed with only one bullet.

PUBLISHING AND DRAMATIZATION HISTORY
The story appeared in the short story collection, THE MYSTERIOUS MR. QUIN, published in 1930 by William Collins Sons and Company, Ltd., in London, and by Dodd, Mead and Company in New York.

The story has not been adapted for stage or screen.

CHARACTERS
Captain Jimmy ALLENSON, Lady Cynthia DRAGE, Major PORTER, Mr. Harley QUIN, Mr. SATTERTHWAITE, Moira SCOTT, Richard SCOTT, Mrs. Iris STAVERTON, Mr. UNKERTON, Mrs. UNKERTON

PLOT SYNOPSIS
The story concerns a double murder that occurs at a mansion which contains a haunted window. Despite having been replaced numerous times, the glass pane in this window continues to develop a stain in the image of a Cavalier wearing a plumed hat. The legend combined with amatory jealousy among the guests lead Mr. Satterthwaite to fear impending tragedy. When Captain Allenson and Moira Scott are shot, Mr. Quin appears to provide the needed hints to clarify the situation, so that Mr. Satterthwaite can solve the crime.

CRIME NOTES
The murder in this story is the result of a single gunshot which passes through two closely situated bodies.

Shaista, Princess An imposter in CAT AMONG THE PIGEONS, she claims to have been betrothed to the late Prince Ali YUSEF, but disappears before her presumed uncle, Emir Ibrahim, visits.

Shaitana, Mr. A mysterious and sinister man in CARDS ON THE TABLE, he invites four law enforcement officials and four individuals with something to hide to a dinner and bridge party. Most people feel that he "knew a little too much about everybody." He dies at his own party when he is stabbed with a jewel-handled stiletto.

Shane, Michael A man who acts in a suspicious manner in AFTER THE FUNERAL, he is the husband of actress Rosamund Abernethie SHANE, but the lover of Sorrell DAINTON. An observer views him as "something of a dark horse" because he is ambitious "and also a man of overweening vanity."

Shane, Rosamund Abernethie An actress and the only individual who perceived that Hercule

POIROT was playing a role while disguised as Monsieur Pontarlier in AFTER THE FUNERAL, she is often described as "not conspicuous for brains."

Shannon, Christine   An empty-headed "blond lovely" who is seated at a table next to George BARTON's on the night that he is murdered in SPARKLING CYANIDE, she is "dumber than you'd believe possible except where money is concerned."

Shapland, Ann   A cabaret dancer in CAT AMONG THE PIGEONS, also known as Angelica or Senora Angelica de Toredo, she chooses to work as Miss BULSTRODE's secretary at the Meadowbank School. Pursued by Dennis RATHBONE for years, she does not want to hurt his feelings, "but it would be very dull to be married to Dennis."

Sharpe, Inspector   A member of Scotland Yard in HICKORY DICKORY DOCK, he works with Hercule POIROT in solving the mysterious murders at the youth hostel.

Shaw, Dr.   An old-fashioned village doctor known by inhabitants as "Leave-it-to-Nature-Shaw" in ENDLESS NIGHT, he is called first to treat Ellie ROGERS's sprained ankle and then to determine her time of death.

Shaw, Mr.   A joint manager of the London and Scottish bank in "THE MILLION DOLLAR BOND ROBBERY," he schemes to steal the Liberty bonds being transported to New York by bank employee Philip RIDGEWAY.

Sheldon, Rose   Questioned about the disappearance of Canon PENNYFEATHER in AT BERTRAM'S HOTEL, she is a former actress now working as a chambermaid. Her "calm and competent" manner masks a web of lies.

Sheppard, Caroline   A physician's sister in THE MURDER OF ROGER ACKROYD, she lives with her brother in a cottage next to that of Hercule POIROT, and involves herself in everyone's business.

Sheppard, Dr. James   A friend and physician to Roger ACKROYD, he replaces the absent Captain HASTINGS as chronicler of Hercule POIROT's victory in THE MURDER OF ROGER ACKROYD. He is the brother of Caroline SHEPPARD, whose questions he avoids whenever possible.

Sherston, Captain Charles   A disreputable but charming man in ABSENT IN THE SPRING, he goes to prison for embezzling money from the bank where he works.

Sherston, Leslie   Described as being untidy and unpunctual by Joan SCUDAMORE in ABSENT IN THE SPRING, she is the wife of an embezzler who is imprisoned. Rodney SCUDAMORE praises her to his wife as being a courageous woman who refuses to give up, and he mourns her sincerely when she dies of cancer after being worn out by life.

Shoreham, Robert (Robbie)   A brilliant physicist in PASSENGER TO FRANKFURT, he develops Project Benvo, a gas which permanently changes peoples' natures to be benevolent and passive. He freely gives his latest discovery to the British government.

Shrivenham, Lionel   A man who can afford no more mistakes if he wants to keep his job, he is a member of the British Embassy in "THEY CAME TO BAGHDAD" who has suffered a series of misfortunes.

"Sign in the Sky, The"   Mystery short story.
   The plot centers on a murder conviction that Mr. SATTERTHWAITE believes should be overturned.

PUBLISHING AND DRAMATIZATION HISTORY
The story appeared in the short story collection, THE MYSTERIOUS MR. QUIN, published in 1930 by William Collins Sons and Company, Ltd., in London, and by Dodd, Mead and Company in New York.
   The story has not been adapted for stage or screen.

CHARACTERS
Sir George BARNABY, Lady Vivien BARNABY, Louisa BULLARD, Sylvia DALE, Mr. Harley QUIN, Mr. Satterthwaite, Martin WYLDE

PLOT SYNOPSIS
The story concerns the murder of a married woman whose lover had tried to end the relationship. The

lover is tried and sentenced to death for the murder, but Mr. Satterthwaite is dissatisfied. He carefully examines the motives and lives of the other people associated with the victim and her accused murderer to determine the truth. When he learns that a housemaid has relocated to Canada, Mr. Satterthwaite journeys there to question her, and he learns that she saw smoke from a distant train form a giant grasping hand in the sky at the time of the murder. Mr. Satterthwaite does not recognize the significance of her responses until he speaks with the enigmatic Mr. Quin.

CRIME NOTES
The murder in this story is the result of a gunshot to the head.

Simmons, Archdeacon   A friend of Canon PENNYFEATHER in AT BERTRAM'S HOTEL, he at first feels that the canon had merely lost his way or forgotten to come home, but eventually realizes that the police must be called in.

Simmons, Julia   See STAMFORDIS, EMMA JOCELYN.

Simmons, Patrick   A tall, handsome engineering student in A MURDER IS ANNOUNCED, he is a cousin of the owners of Little Paddocks, and lives there while at college.

Simone, Madame   The object of numerous studies, she is the most successful psychic of her generation. Her materializations have made her a celebrity, but they have also weakened her considerably. Despite warnings about her health, she agrees to undertake one more seance for Madame EXE in "THE LAST SEANCE," to materialize Madame Exe's daughter.

Simpson, Mr.   A bank clerk and boarder in the home of Mr. and Mrs. TODD in "THE ADVENTURE OF THE CLAPHAM COOK."

Simpson, Lieutenant Alec, R.N.   An officer in the Royal Navy he discovers the body of The Honourable Flossie CARRINGTON under his train seat in "THE PLYMOUTH EXPRESS."

Simpson, Alexander   Owner of an art gallery in "THE GIRDLE OF HIPPOLYTA," he consults Hercule POIROT when thieves steal a Rubens from his gallery.

Sims, Inspector   An even-tempered police inspector in "HOW DOES YOUR GARDEN GROW?," he investigates the Barrowby case, and sympathizes with the plight of Katrina RIEGER.

Sims, Mr.   A middle-aged man with a husky, persuasive voice in SLEEPING MURDER, he is hired by Gwenda GLEN to redecorate her newly purchased home.

Sims, Doris   A model for Ambrosine, Ltd., a dressmaking company owned by Cynthia DACRES in THREE-ACT TRAGEDY, she provides Hercule POIROT with information about her employer.

"Sing a Song of Sixpence"   Mystery short story.
The plot centers on the murder of an eccentric, elderly woman and the suspicions cast on members of her household.

PUBLISHING AND DRAMATIZATION HISTORY
The story appeared in the short story collection, THE LISTERDALE MYSTERY (1), published in 1934 by William Collins Sons and Company, Ltd., in London, and in the short story collection, WITNESS FOR THE PROSECUTION AND OTHER STORIES, published in 1948 by Dodd, Mead and Company in New York.
The story has not been adapted for stage or screen.

CHARACTERS
BEN, Emily CRABTREE, Miss Lily CRABTREE, William CRABTREE, MARTHA, Sir Edward PALLISER, Magdalen VAUGHAN, Matthew VAUGHAN

PLOT SYNOPSIS
The story concerns the murder of Mrs. Lily CRABTREE, who left an estate of eighty thousand pounds. The circumstances of the murder make suspects of her four heirs, but the police have no evidence. One upset heir, Magdalen Vaughan, seeks to expose the murderer and calls upon retired barrister Sir Edward Palliser for assistance. After careful

examination of the limited facts and questioning of the suspects, Sir Edward identifies the murderer, a character who is introduced very late in the story.

CRIME NOTES
The murder is the result of a crushing blow to the back of the head with a heavy paperweight.

Sittaford Mystery, The   Mystery novel.
The novel is the first in which the author incorporates the supernatural into one of her long works. The plot concerns the attempt to discover the murderer of a man whose death was foretold to the hour by the spirits in a series of rappings.

PUBLISHING AND DRAMATIZATION HISTORY
The novel was published in 1931 by William Collins Sons and Company, Ltd., in London, and under the title of *Murder at Hazelmoor* by Dodd, Mead and Company in New York.

The novel has not been adapted for stage or screen.

CHARACTERS
Mrs. BELLING, Major John Edward BURNABY, Mr. CURTIS, Amelia CURTIS, Mr. DACRES, Martin DERING, Sylvia DERING, Mr. DUKE, Charles ENDERBY, Rebecca EVANS, Robert Henry EVANS, Jennifer GARDNER, Captain Robert GARDNER, Ronald GARFIELD, Constable GRAVES, Mr. KIRKWOOD, Inspector NARRACOTT, Brian PEARSON, James PEARSON, Caroline PERCEHOUSE, Sergeant POLLOCK, Mr. RYCROFT, Emily TREFUSIS, Captain Joseph Arthur TREVELYAN, Dr. WARREN, Mrs. WILLETT, Violet WILLETT, Captain WYATT

PLOT SYNOPSIS
Chapters 1–6
During a party hosted at Sittaford House by Mrs. Willett and her daughter Violet, the guests decide to hold a seance. They receive read a frightening message: "Trevelyan Dead—Murder." A concerned Major Burnaby calls the police and the doctor, and they arrive at Trevelyan's home and find him dead. The death occurred the precise time predicted at the seance. The investigators learn that Trevelyan owns Sittaford House, which Mrs. Willett rented through an agent. She has never met the victim. The police discover that a man registered at the Three Crowns

inn that day, left the inn at 4:30 P.M. and returned at 6:20 P.M.

Chapters 7–12
Inspector Narracott speaks with Trevelyan's lawyer and learns that the victim died a very rich man. He also questions Burnaby about the time of death and learns of the "table turning" that occurred at the party. News reporter Charles Enderby arranges with Burnaby for an exclusive story, then speaks with the victim's servants. Investigators interview the victim's relatives to learn who would profit from the death, and they learn that his nephew, James Pearson, had checked into the Three Crowns, making him a suspect. When the police arrest Pearson, his fiancée, Emily Trefusis, defends him. She enlists Enderby in her effort to clear him, and the two pretend to be cousins.

Chapters 13–18
Narracott speaks with Mrs. Willett and Violet to learn about the seance, and Violet faints when he mentions James Pearson. Emily is convinced that someone at the table planned the murder and deliberately conveyed the message, but learning who is the problem. Mr. Rycroft, another participant in the seance and an expert in psychic phenomena, offers his services. Emily visits Violet and finds her very upset over the seance. She leaves her gloves, so she returns, and overhears Mrs. Willett and Violet talking and one saying, "Will tonight ever come?"

Chapters 19–24
Emily shares her information with Enderby, then visits another of Trevelyan's relatives who, she learns, had asked the victim's attorney for an advance on her inheritance. Enderby spies on Sittaford House and watches as Violet walks out to the gate at 11:40 P.M. and whistles. A man appears and attacks Enderby. The attacker is Brian Pearson, another of Trevelyan's nephews. The two enter the house and talk. Burnaby and Trevelyan's valet Evans sort through the victim's belongings, and Evans approaches Burnaby for a job. Narracott questions the arrest of Pearson, doubtful that he has the right man, and pursues Martin Dering, who did not attend a literary dinner as he had claimed.

Chapters 25–28
Emily and Enderby meet at a cafe in Exeter and share information as they review the alibis offered by each suspect. Several of the alibis remain

unsupported, and Narracott receives information which leads him to believe that the Willetts are using assumed names. The proprietor of the Three Crowns contacts Narracott to tell him that Trevelyan's man-servant discovered a pair of boots missing from among the victim's effects. An increasingly suspicious Emily searches Enderby's rooms at Hazelmoor and finds the boots wrapped in newspaper and stuffed in the chimney.

Chapters 29–31
Mrs. Willett tells her houseguests that a servant problem forces her to ask them to leave, but they hold a seance before departing. Narracott surprises the group by knocking loudly, then stepping in and charging the murderer with the crime. As the case winds up, Enderby tells Emily that he loves her, but she still loves James Pearson, whom she worked to free.

CRIME NOTES
The sole murder in the novel is the result of a blow to the head with a sandbag used to keep out drafts.

Skinner, Emily   A woman who plays two roles in "THE CASE OF THE PERFECT MAID," she is really the younger sister of Lavinia SKINNER and her accomplice in a very clever scheme. She lives as an invalid, confined to her bed, her hair a mess of tangles. Her masquerade as Mary HIGGINS fools the other tenants of the flats in Old Hall, as she represents "the perfect maid" in appearance and behavior.

Skinner, Lavinia (Lavvie)   The only one of the Skinner sisters in "THE CASE OF THE PERFECT MAID" whom tenants of Old Hall really come to know, because younger sister Emily SKINNER is confined to her bed. She fires Gladdie HOLMES when a brooch is discovered missing. She later lets it be known that she has hired a new maid, Mary HIGGINS, who is "the perfect maid."

Slack, Inspector   An official with the Much Benham police department, he is an energetic man who accomplishes his aims, yet his manner is "rude and overbearing in the extreme." A man of action, he finds Miss MARPLE's approach to crime-solving quaint, and only barely tolerates her involvement in cases. He appears in two novels and two short stories: MURDER AT THE VICARAGE, THE BODY IN THE LIBRARY, "THE TAPE-MEASURE MURDER" and "THE CASE OF THE PERFECT MAID."

Sleeping Murder   Mystery novel.
The novel chronicles the last case of Miss Jane MARPLE, although the author wrote it during World War II and kept it in a vault until its publication more than thirty years later. The plot concerns a murder in retrospect with a connection to *The Duchess of Malfi*, in which the following line is uttered: "Cover her face; mine eyes dazzle: she died young." Hearing this line revives the memory of a young women who witnessed a crime years before but had not recognized it as such.

PUBLISHING AND DRAMATIZATION HISTORY
The novel was published in 1976 by William Collins Sons and Company, Ltd., in London, and by Dodd, Mead and Company in New York.

The novel was adapted for television in 1987 by the BBC in Britain, and was also shown on the Public Broadcasting Service in the U.S.

CHARACTERS
Dorothy AFFLICK, Jackie AFFLICK, Colonel Arthur BANTRY, Dolly BANTRY, Mrs. COCKER, Major ERSKINE, Eleanor FANE, Walter FANE, Mr. GALBRAITH, Helen Spenlove Kennedy HALLIDAY, Major Kelvin James HALLIDAY, Dr. HAYDOCK, Mrs. HENGRAVE, Dr. James KENNEDY, Lady Abbot KIMBLE, MANNING, Miss Jane Marple, Edith PAGETT, Dr. PENROSE, Detective Inspector PRIMER, Giles REED, Gwenda REED, Mr. SIMS, Joan WEST, Raymond WEST

PLOT SYNOPSIS
Chapters 1–4
Newlywed Gwenda Reed has moved to England from New Zealand with her husband, Giles. While her husband is away on business, she views and buys Hillside, a house reputed to be haunted. As Gwenda walks the grounds and inhabits the house, strange images flash into her mind, leading her to believe the stories about the haunting. For a change of scene, she visits her friends, Raymond and Joan West, who introduce her to Raymond's aunt, Jane Marple. The four attend a play, from which Gwenda runs out screaming. She later tells Miss Marple that she has seen Helen dead, then questions why the name came up, because she does not know anyone named

Helen. Miss Marple suggests that Gwenda may be having memories of her childhood, and asks her if she has ever been to England before.

Chapters 5–8
Gwenda's aunt tells her, in response to her inquiry, that Gwenda had been in England for a short while as a child, and Gwenda is convinced that she once witnessed a murder. Giles fails to believe that his wife had actually witnessed a murder, but he joins her in visiting the real estate agent to ask if someone named Helen had ever lived in Hillside. They are referred to Mr. Galbraith, who remembers Gwenda as a child. This leads to a visit to the records department to learn Helen's surname, and they find that a Major Kelvin James Halliday married Helen Spenlove Kennedy. The couple place an advertisement in the newspaper to which Dr. Kennedy, Helen's brother, responds. Gwenda questions her uncle and learns that her father had claimed to have murdered Helen, then he was placed in a sanitorium, and died.

Chapters 9–12
Gwenda visits the sanitorium and speaks with Dr. Penrose, who does not believe that Halliday was the killer. He turns Halliday's diary over to her, and she reads that he questioned whether or not he had strangled Helen. Miss Marple arrives at South Devon to partake of the sea air and to investigate the possible crime. She reads the diary and questions whether Helen was even killed, and they attempt to sort out Helen's jealous lovers.

Chapters 13–16
Gwenda consults Mr. Fane to make a will, and learns that he was once engaged to Helen. She then visits Edith Pagett, who speaks freely with her and stirs up memories in Gwenda. Giles learns the names and addresses of former servants in Helen's household, and the young couple decide to visit them for information. At the same time, Miss Marple learns more about Walter Fane by speaking with his mother, who tells Miss Marple that Walter was very much in love with Helen. She also learns that he had once tried to kill his brother with a poker.

Chapters 17–20
Gwenda and Giles speak with Major Erskine, a former lover of Helen's, who tells them that he was once madly in love with her but does not know what happened to her. His wife remains jealous and speaks

bitterly of the old affair. Miss Marple speaks with Dr. Kennedy, who gives her a letter written to him by Helen. Some distance away, Helen's former maid, Lily Kimble, now Lady Abbot Kimble, argues with her husband, who feels that she should not respond to the call for information. Miss Marple tells the Reeds that another of Helen's former lovers, Jackie Afflick, lives nearby, and their gardener works at his address.

Chapters 21–24
Dr. Kennedy calls the Reeds to inform them that Lily Kimble had written. He expresses displeasure when they mention Jackie Afflick. A handwriting expert certifies that Helen's letter to Dr. Kennedy is authentic, thus proving that she was alive after her husband was institutionalized. Lily is murdered when she arrives in Dillmouth to see the Reeds, and the police question Kennedy and other suspects. Miss Marple arrives at Hillside and tells the Reeds her theory that Helen's body must have been buried on the grounds, and the housekeeper tells them that Fane and Afflick had stopped by to speak with them. Inspector Primer orders his men to dig up the garden, and they unearth Helen's remains. Later, poison is detected in a decanter of brandy. Miss Marple reveals the murderer, and the remaining pieces of the puzzle are found. Giles and Gwenda can now live happily in their home, knowing that it is no longer haunted in any way.

CRIME NOTES
Both the murder in retrospect and the later murder in the novel are the result of strangulation.

Slicker, Mr. A partner in the Market Basing real estate firm, Messrs. Lovebody and Slicker, in BY THE PRICKING OF MY THUMBS, he is the "tweed-suited young man in horsy checks" who provides Tuppence BERESFORD with information about the house in the painting, "House by a Canal."

Smethurst, Captain An unpopular member of a group traveling from Damascus to Baghdad in "THE GATE OF BAGHDAD," who is murdered.

Smith, Ivor A bushy eyebrowed investigator in BY THE PRICKING OF MY THUMBS, he is a friend who provides Tommy BERESFORD with valuable information regarding the criminal activities of the seemingly respectable Mr. ECCLES.

Smith, Nurse Janet   A former war colleague of Tuppence BERESFORD in "A POT OF TEA," she now works in Madame Violette's hat shop, and desires to shock the passive Lawrence ST. VINCENT into finally proposing to her. To that end, she pretends to disappear so that St. Vincent will contact the Beresfords to find her.

Snell   A condescending butler in "DEAD MAN'S MIRROR."

Sobek   Murdered with poisoned wine in DEATH COMES AS THE END, he is the second eldest son of IMHOTEP and the husband of KAIT. His wife considered him "a handsome braggart" and a man whose constant unfaithfulness leaves her remorseless at his death.

Solomon, Mr.   An elderly man "with a flat face like a stuffed fish" in THE CLOCKS, he runs a bookstore that serves as the front for Colonel Beck's Special Branch of British Intelligence.

So Many Steps to Death   See DESTINATION UNKNOWN.

Somers, Miss   A recently hired typist at Rex FORTESCUE's Consolidated Investments Trust in A POCKET FULL OF RYE, she is a middle-aged woman with "a mild worried face like a sheep" and little typing skill.

Sonia   A young secretary ostensibly hired to help Sir Rodney HORSEFIELD write his memoirs in THIRD GIRL, she is really stealing World War II secrets from his files and giving them to agents representing Herzogovinia. When the excitement of espionage passes, she looks to the future, accepts Sir Rodney's marriage proposal and plans to settle down to a life of wealth.

Sopworth, Claud   A wealthy young man who is a rival for the affections of James BOND's girlfriend, GRACE, in "THE RAJAH'S EMERALD," he is a man "of no moral worth whatsoever."

S.O.S.   Mystery short story.

The plot centers on the meaning of a cry for help scrawled in dust on a bedroom nightstand.

PUBLISHING AND DRAMATIZATION HISTORY
The story appeared in the short story collection, THE HOUND OF DEATH AND OTHER STORIES, published in 1933 by William Collins Sons and Company, Ltd., in London.

The story has not been adapted for stage or screen.

CHARACTERS
Mortimer CLEVELAND, Mr. DINSMEAD, Charlotte DINSMEAD, Johnnie DINSMEAD, Magdalen DINSMEAD, Maggie DINSMEAD

PLOT SYNOPSIS
The story concerns the efforts of a psychic researcher, Mortimer Cleveland, to discover the mystery of the Dinsmead family and thus to prevent a murder. Stranded when his car breaks down, Cleveland is given shelter by the Dinsmead family. He finds the letters "SOS" scrawled in the dust on the bedroom nightstand, and his intuition leads him to believe that adopted Dinsmead daughter, Charlotte, left the message. The mystery deepens when, through subterfuge, he learns that Charlotte's natural father had recently died and left her an inheritance of sixty thousand pounds, although she has not been told about the inheritance. Cleveland leaves the house but makes a surprise return visit, during which he tests the tea served at dinner and finds a large dose of poison in one cup.

CRIME NOTES
The means of attempted murder in this story is poisoning through the use of arsenic.

"Soul of the Croupier, The"   Mystery short story.

The plot centers on a love triangle in Monte Carlo, and the mysterious actions of a croupier.

PUBLISHING AND DRAMATIZATION HISTORY
The story appeared in the short story collection, THE MYSTERIOUS MR. QUIN, published in 1930 by

William Collins Sons and Company, Ltd., in London, and by Dodd, Mead and Company in New York.

The story has not been adapted for stage or screen.

CHARACTERS

Countess CZARNOVA, Elizabeth MARTIN, Mr. Harley QUIN, Mr. SATTERTHWAITE, Pierre VAUCHER

PLOT SYNOPSIS

The story concerns the reunion of an estranged couple after many years. Vacationing in Monte Carlo, Mr. Satterthwaite observes the growing jealousy of a young American woman, Elizabeth Martin, as her companion becomes increasingly friendly with the glamorous Countess Czarnova. The countess is rumored to have been the mistress of the King of Bosnia in years past, but to Mr. Satterthwaite's perceptive eyes she is a desperate woman whose beauty and wealth are dimming. When the croupier mistakenly gives Mr. Satterthwaite's winnings to the countess, a long-hidden secret is revealed.

Southwood, The Honourable Joanna A bored young woman in DEATH ON THE NILE (2) whose desire for excitement once involved her in a series of society robberies, she is tall and thin, "with a clever face and freakishly plucked eyebrows." Not the loyal type, she states that she always drops her friends immediately whenever they have any misfortune.

Spalding, Caroline   See CRALE, CAROLINE.

Sparkling Cyanide   Mystery novel.

The novel contains the fourth and last appearance of Colonel Johnny RACE. The plot concerns the death by poisoning of an heiress, and the efforts to determine which of many suspects has the strongest motive.

PUBLISHING AND DRAMATIZATION HISTORY

The novel was published in 1945 by William Collins Sons and Company, Ltd., in London, and, under the title *Remembered Death*, by Dodd, Mead and Company in New York.

The novel was adapted for television in 1983 by CBS Television in the U.S.

CHARACTERS

Betty ARCHDALE, Giuseppe BALSANO, George BARTON, Rosemary BARTON, Patricia BRICE-WOOD-WORTH, Anthony BROWNE, CHARLES, Lucilla DRAKE, Victor DRAKE, Lady Alexandra FARRADAY, Stephen FARRADAY, Chief Inspector KEMP, Lady Victoria (Vicky) KIDDERMINSTER, Lord William, Earl of KIDDERMINSTER, Ruth LESSING, Iris MARLE, Colonel Johnny Race, Mary REES-TALBOT, Chloe Elizabeth WEST

PLOT SYNOPSIS

Book I: Chapters 1–6

Iris Marle thinks with sadness of her late sister Rosemary, who she believes committed suicide nearly a year earlier. Before her death, Rosemary had written a will, and Iris found love letters to "Leopard" soon after Rosemary's death, which she keeps in the belief that they might be needed someday. George Barton, Rosemary's husband, believes that his wife was murdered by someone at her birthday party. Several possibilities loom. Ruth Lessing, Barton's secretary, and Victor Drake both disliked Rosemary, and Anthony Browne had warned Rosemary to forget that she ever heard the name of Tony Morelli, his alter ego. Stephen Farraday, the "Leopard" of the love letters, had been Rosemary's lover. He fell in love with another woman and wanted to end the affair, but she objected and threatened to destroy him. His wife, Alexandra, also disliked her, and she is the last to give Rosemary a drink before her death. Even Barton himself felt animosity toward his wife, after discovering her affair with Farraday. A year later, he wants to reenact the crime.

Book II: Chapters 1–6

Barton makes plans at the Luxembourg restaurant to reenact the night of the murder, but he seems upset in some manner. The Farradays are hesitant to attend. Browne seeks out Iris and asks her to marry him, but she refuses because she is not of age and Barton is her guardian. Barton discusses Rosemary's death with Secret Service agent Colonel Johnny Race, and tells him that it was murder, not suicide. Race is invited to the reenactment party, and Barton tells his guests that "something important" will happen at 9:30 P.M. After all of the guests but Race arrive, the lights are lowered, a stage appears, and music plays. The guests toast Rosemary's memory, and Barton slumps forward, dead.

Book III: Chapters 1–7
Chief Inspector Kemp joins Race in questioning all the guests and waiters, and they create a list of suspects. Iris decides that she will marry Browne, and she shows Rosemary's love letters to Kemp, who takes them for evidence. Browne's sinister past emerges in Race's interview with Betty Archdale, who sat at a table nearby on the night of Rosemary's murder. She relates that Rosemary mentioned the name of Tony Morelli, and that Browne threatened her.

Chapters 8–14
The authorities are surprised by the appearance of Miss Chloe West, who tells Kemp that she had been hired by Barton to pretend to be Rosemary at the party. The suspicion shifts from one member of the party to another, as first Farraday, and then Browne appear to implicate himself or others. Iris is frightened when she learns that a packet of cyanide was found under her chair at the table, and the discovery places suspicion upon her. She is later discovered trying to take her life. The investigation yields a pair of murderers and the surprising conclusion that the glasses at the table were switched around, making the last death a mistake. The crime is solved, and Iris and Browne make plans to marry.

CRIME NOTES
The two murders in the novel are the result of poisoning by ingesting cyanide.

Speeder, Carol   A member of a vaguely identified United Nations group in DESTINATION UNKNOWN, she is among the last three people who see Thomas BETTERTON before his disappearance.

Spence, Mrs.   One of the guests at Major Jack Rich's party in "THE MYSTERY OF THE BAGHDAD CHEST," she danced with the other guests as Edward CLAYTON lay dead in the trunk.

Spence, Superintendent   Chief investigator in the death of "Enoch ARDEN" in TAKEN AT THE FLOOD, he heads the Oatshire police department.

Spence, Superintendent Bert   A good, old-fashioned police officer, honest and dependable, he heads the Kilchester police and appears in MRS. MCGINTY'S DEAD, HALLOWE'EN PARTY and ELEPHANTS CAN REMEMBER. An old friend of Hercule POIROT, with whom he is said to have worked on numerous early and unreported cases, he refuses to allow an innocent man to be executed, and contacts Poirot in *Mrs. McGinty's Dead* to clear James BENTLEY, who has already been convicted of murder.

Spence, Jeremy (Jim)   A guest at Major Charles RICH's party in "THE MYSTERY OF THE SPANISH CHEST," he is married to Linda SPENCE. He joins other guests having a good time in the same room in which Arnold CLAYTON lay dead in a trunk.

Spence, Linda   Married to Jeremy SPENCE, she is with him as guests at Major Charles RICH's party in "THE MYSTERY OF THE SPANISH CHEST" on the night Arnold CLAYTON is murdered. She has "a pair of shrewd eyes" that watch Hercule POIROT carefully as she candidly tells him that she thinks that her host and the dead man's wife were having an affair. Her "little idea" in her allusion to *Othello* provides Poirot with the clue to solve the mystery.

Spender, Mr.   An acquaintance of the widower in "A CHRISTMAS TRAGEDY," he provides Jack SANDERS with an alibi for the time of Gladys SANDERS' death.

Spenlow, Mrs.   Former owner of a successful London florist shop, she is murdered after she moves with her husband to ST. MARY MEAD in "THE TAPE-MEASURE MURDER."

Spenlow, Arthur   A middle-aged jeweller in "THE TAPE-MEASURE MURDER" whose wife is murdered, he claims to have moved to ST. MARY MEAD to indulge his love of gardening, but Miss MARPLE observes that he is ignorant in this area.

Spenser, Miss   An employment counsellor at Guildric's Agency in "THEY CAME TO BAGHDAD," she works with Victoria JONES to find her a permanent position.

Spent, Gladys The head housemaid in HERCULE POIROT'S CHRISTMAS.

Spider's Web Mystery play.

This comedy-thriller was the author's last big success in the theater. The plot centers on the efforts of a Foreign Office diplomat's wife to identify the murderer of a body which appears in her drawing room, as she also attempts to disguise the fact that a murder has occurred.

PUBLISHING AND DRAMATIZATION
HISTORY
The play was written in 1954 to provide a role for actress Margaret Lockwood, who confided to the author during lunch that she had tired of her usual *femme fatale* roles. The play opened at the Savoy Theatre in London on December 14, 1954.

The film version was released in England in 1960 by United Artists, and starred Glynis Johns in the role of Clarissa, with the following other cast members: Cicely Courtneidge, Ronald Howard, Jack Hulbert, John Justin and David Nixon. In 1983, the BBC adapted the play for television in Britain.

CHARACTERS
Hugo BIRCH, Oliver COSTELLO, Sir Rowland (Roly) DELAHAYE, ELGIN, Clarissa HAILSHAM-BROWN, Pippa HAILSHAM-BROWN, Constable JONES, Inspector LORD, Mildred PEAKE, Jeremy WARRENDER

PLOT SYNOPSIS
Act 1
The play opens with Sir Rowland Delahaye and Hugo Birch testing wines, as an out-of-breath Jeremy Warrender runs into the room. Delahaye and Birch have each bet that he has the more refined palate and can distinguish the "local grocer's special" from the two more costly wines. Each believes that he has identified three different wines correctly, but Clarissa informs them that they are disagreeing over the same wine in all three instances because she simply poured wine from the same bottle into three glasses. Jeremy learns that Clarissa has also fooled him into racing back and forth to the lodge gates to beat the record she claimed had been set by the Herzoslovakian minister. Pippa shows Jeremy a se-

cret passage which leads from the drawing room to the library. As the others leave the room, Sir Rowland warns her not to fall in love with Jeremy. Oliver Costello later arrives and tells Clarissa that her husband's former wife, now married to Costello, wants Pippa to live with them. Pippa becomes upset and makes Clarissa promise that this will never happen, and Clarissa promises "over his dead body." When Henry arrives home, he tells Clarissa that they are to be hosts to a top secret conference that evening with a foreign official to be called "Mr. Jones." While Henry prepares to leave, Oliver sneaks into the empty drawing room and is hit over the head as he steals something from the secret drawer of the desk. Clarissa later finds his dead body behind her sofa, and Pippa appears to confess.

Act 2
Clarissa asks her friends to help her to dispose of the body, and she resists Sir Rowland's suggestion to call the police. She overcomes his objections by telling him that Pippa is the murderer. As they move the body, the police arrive and inform them that someone had telephoned the station with news of a murder. The butler, who has the night off, appears unexpectedly and complicates Clarissa's plans. The police inspector tells Clarissa that the former owner of the house, Mr. Sellon, was involved in shady business deals, and warns her that something may be hidden in the house. The police search the house for the body, but Clarissa has hidden it in the secret passage. When Mrs. Peake arrives, she insist that the police look in the secret passage, and they find the body. They question Clarissa alone, then the guests are questioned separately to compare their stories. When the police press for the truth, Clarissa tells them, but they do not believe her, so she makes up a story which they do believe. Returning to the secret passage, they find that the body has disappeared.

Act 3
The body is missing when the police surgeon arrives. While the police search the grounds, Mrs. Peake tells Clarissa that she hid the body under the bolster in the spare room bed because women have to "stand by your own sex." Pippa thought that she killed Oliver because she had created a wax effigy of him and stuck needles in it. As Clarissa ponders the turn of events, she suggests that the former home owner's

partner, Mrs. Brown, is now masquerading as Mrs. Peake. She had been trying to find her late partner's murderer. The real murderer is exposed, and the motive is revealed as pure greed. Henry Hailsham-Brown arrives home after the police leave and, despite the previous excitement, the highly secret conference occurs as planned.

CRIME NOTES
The only murder in this play occurs when a man is hit over the head with a golf club.

Spiess, Herr Heinrich   Concerned with international youth activity, he is the Chancellor of Germany in PASSENGER TO FRANKFURT who meets with British officials to deal with a crisis.

Spragg, Eurydice   A spiritualist in "MOTIVE VERSUS OPPORTUNITY," this flamboyantly dressed, middle-aged woman is highly respected by Simon CLODE, who makes her his heir after she attempts to contact his late granddaughter, Christobel CLODE.

Spragge, Frederick   An attorney and senior partner in a prestigious law firm in WHY DIDN'T THEY ASK EVANS? who uses his persuasive charm to obtain highly confidential information from his clients, he knows and uses many dark secrets about the noble families he represents.

Sprig, Mr.   An elderly real estate agent in BY THE PRICKING OF MY THUMBS, he barely conceals his contempt for "the foolishness of women" when Tuppence BERESFORD questions him about Watermead House.

Springer, Grace   The first of the murder victims at Meadowbank School in CAT AMONG THE PIGEONS, she is the school's physical education director and a woman who has "the manners of a pig." Her colleagues live in fear of her prying, because she delights in revealing any embarrassing secrets from their pasts.

Sprot, Betty   See BERESFORD, BETTY.

Sprot, Millicent   A seemingly maternal woman devoted to her adopted daughter Betty in N OR M?,

this woman with the "pale gooseberry eyes" and "slightly adenoidal voice" is actually "M," a powerful figure in Fifth Column activities in Britain.

Stamfordis, Emma Jocelyn   The niece of wealthy widow Belle GOEDLER and sister of Phillipa HAYMES in A MURDER IS ANNOUNCED, she disguises herself as Julia Simmons to become closer to the rivals for her inheritance, Letitia and Charlotte BLACKLOCK. She will inherit half of her late uncle's fortune if his former secretary dies before their great-aunt Belle.

Stamfordis, Pip   See HAYMES, PHILLIPA.

Stamfordis, Sybil Diana Helen   A psychic medium who lives with spiritualist Thyrza GREY and reputed witch Bella WEBB at The Pale Horse inn, she is a woman "with dark, rather greasy hair, a simpering expression, and a fish-like mouth" in THE PALE HORSE.

Stanislaus, Count   See OBOLOVITCH, PRINCE MICHAEL.

Stanley, Nigel   One of the boarders in Mrs. NICOLETIS' youth hostel in HICKORY DICKORY DOCK, he is the son of Sir Arthur Stanley, but he uses the name Nigel Chapman as he pursues studies in the Bronze Age and Medieval and Italian history. His father never reveals that Nigel murdered his mother with an overdose of medinal.

Stanton, Freda   When she becomes engaged to Jacob RADNOR in "THE CORNISH MYSTERY," Mrs. PENGELLEY resents the relationship because of her own feelings toward Jacob. The ensuing animosity forces Freda to leave the Pengelley house.

Stanwell, Molly   A young ingenue in "HARLEQUIN'S LANE," her married lover, John DENMAN, wants her to dance the role of Pierette in the Harlequinade being presented to guests by Lady ROSCHEIMER.

Star Over Bethlehem   Poetry and short story collection.

The collection is the author's only book for children. It contains six short stories and five poems of a religious nature.

PUBLISHING AND DRAMATIZATION
HISTORY
The book was published in 1965 by William Collins Sons and Company, Ltd., in London, and by Dodd, Mead and Company in New York.

The book has not been adapted for stage or screen.

TITLES IN THE COLLECTION
The brief, seventy-nine-page book contains the following titles: "A Greeting," "Star Over Bethlehem," "A Wreath for Christmas," "The Naughty Donkey," "Gold, Frankincense and Myrrh," "The Water Bus," "In the Cool of the Evening," "Jenny by the Sky," "Promotion in the Highest," "The Saints of God" and "The Island."

Starke, Sir Philip   A dignified, seventy-two-year-old botanist, industrialist and author in BY THE PRICKING OF MY THUMBS, he loves children, but falls under suspicion of being a child murderer.

Starr, Raymond   A tennis professional and professional dancer at the Majestic Hotel in THE BODY IN THE LIBRARY, he pretends to be impoverished gentry in order to attract the rich patrons of the hotel. He is the dance partner of cousins Ruby KEENE and Josephine TURNER, but he really wants to marry widow Adelaide JEFFERSON.

Starkwedder, Michael   An active, tough-looking man with an outdoorsy appearance in THE UNEXPECTED GUEST, he is a shrewd thinker who creates a plan to help a presumed murderer avoid detection. He holds a dark secret that links him with the victim.

Stavansson, Gabriel   A well-known explorer, he consults Tommy and Tuppence BERESFORD when he returns after two years at the North Pole and learns that his fiancée is missing in "THE CASE OF THE MISSING LADY." Unknown to him, his belief that "fat women and fat dogs are an abomination unto the Lord" is behind the disappearance.

Staverton, Iris   Discovered holding the murder weapon when Jimmy ALLENSON and Moira SCOTT are shot in "THE SHADOW ON THE GLASS," she is the former lover of Richard SCOTT, and "the sort of woman who'd stick at nothing."

Steadman, Mrs.   Warmhearted and talkative, she teaches the new bride housekeeping skills in UNFINISHED PORTRAIT.

Steene, Lawrence   Handsome, charming and rich, he is a corrupt aristocrat in A DAUGHTER'S A DAUGHTER who indulges in drugs, orgies and drunken binges. He encourages his wife, Sarah PRENTICE, to participate fully in his dissolute activities and nearly destroys her.

Stein, Leo   Present when the Morning Star diamond disappears in "THE REGATTA MYSTERY," he is the partner of diamond merchant Isaac POINTZ.

Stella   A member of the art community on Pollensa Bay, she is married to an artist. The couple host her sister, Betty GREGG, who is on vacation in "PROBLEM AT POLLENSA BAY."

Stengelberg, Nurse   See OHLSSON, GRETA.

Stepanov, Count   See IVANOVITCH, BORIS.

Stepanyi, Count Paul   A man employed by Mr. PARKER PYNE, he assumes the identity of a count in "THE CASE OF THE CITY CLERK" to make the official presentation of the Order of St. Stanislaus to Mr. ROBERTS.

Stephens   See HEMMINGWAY, GERALD.

Stevens, Mr.   An intellectually sharp manservant in THE SEVEN DIALS MYSTERY, he impresses his employer, Jimmy THESIGER, with the many correspondence courses he takes. He is married to the household cook.

Stillingfleet, Dr. John   A physician and friend of Hercule POIROT, he calls in the detective to investigate after finding a note from the presumed suicide victim, Benedict FARLEY, to Poirot in "THE DREAM." He also appears in THIRD GIRL, in which he cares for Norma RESTARICK, then marries her and goes with her to Australia.

Stirling, Pamela (Poppy) The latest girlfriend of David ARDINGLY in THE PALE HORSE, she is "extremely silly," and is also frightened of someone or something.

St. John, Jewel (Jill) The daughter of now-dead exotic dancer, Mary MOSS, and an incarcerated robber in "SANCTUARY," she lives with Mrs. MUNDY in Chipping Cleghorn. Her father, Walter ST. JOHN, escaped from prison to take her mother's emeralds to her.

St. John, Walter Edmund Found dying of a gunshot wound in the church by Bunch HARMON, the minister's wife, he escaped from prison where he was serving time for jewel theft to take his daughter's legacy to her in "SANCTUARY." Mr. and Mrs. ECCLES appear and claim that the dead man is Mrs. Eceles' brother, Walter Sandbourne, who had recently been depressed and in poor health.

St. Loo, Lady Adelaide An impoverished old aristocrat in THE ROSE AND THE YEW TREE, she recognizes nobility when she sees it, and yearns for the "old ruling class."

St. Loo, Rupert An aristocrat who serves in Burma during World War II in THE ROSE AND THE YEW TREE, he is the hereditary owner of Castle St. Loo and the nephew of Lady Adelaide ST. LOO.

St. Mary Mead The fictional village inhabited by Miss Jane MARPLE, it is situated approximately twenty-five miles from London and twelve miles from the English coast. Residents use the train station in Much Benham, two miles away, to travel to and from their picturesque surroundings. Although the village is mentioned several times in THE MYSTERY OF THE BLUE TRAIN, the first novel to take place in St. Mary Mead is THE MURDER IN THE VICARAGE in 1930. During the next three decades, and through the last Marple story set there (THE MIRROR CRACK'D FROM SIDE TO SIDE, 1962), the village undergoes a change in social structure that mirrors the changing structure of English society.

St. Maur, Babe An actress who becomes involved in political intrigue in THE SEVEN DIALS MYSTERY, she is a member of the Seven Dials Group, and uses the alias of Countess Radzky. She becomes Number One, or One O'clock, after the death of Gerald WADE.

Stoddart, Dr. Michael A hardworking and shrewd young physician in "THE HORSES OF DIOMEDES," he is a friend of Hercule POIROT who is called to attend to a gunshot victim at Patience GRACE's cocaine party. There he meets Sheila GRANT, with whom he falls in love.

Stoddart-West, James A young schoolboy home on vacation in 4.50 FROM PADDINGTON, he is thrilled when he and his friend Alexander EASTLEY are permitted to view the body found in the sarcophagus at Rutherford Hall.

Stoddart-West, Lady Martine The mother of James STODDART-WEST and wife of Sir Robert STODDART-WEST, she was born Martine Dubois, and had known Edmund Crackenthorpe. The body in the sarcophagus found at Rutherford Hall in 4.50 FROM PADDINGTON is first identified as hers.

Stokes, Dr. A physician in AT BERTRAM'S HOTEL who loses his license to practice for performing illegal abortions, he attends to Canon PENNYFEATHER when the Wheelings bring the wounded man to him.

Stone, Dr. The real Dr. Stone is a respected archaeologist, but the man who appears in THE MURDER IN THE VICARAGE is an imposter whom Raymond WEST exposes to both his aunt, Miss Jane MARPLE, and to the vicar, Leonard CLEMENT.

Stonor, Gabriel A man who has traveled all over the world, he has been Paul RENAULD's secretary for two years in MURDER ON THE LINKS.

Strange, Audrey Married in the past to Nevile STRANGE for eight years in TOWARDS ZERO, she visits Lady TRESSILIAN, the widow of Nevile's late guardian, at the same time each year. When her former husband arranges to visit Gull's Point with his new wife at the same time as Audrey, Lady Tressilian is murdered and Audrey becomes the prime suspect.

Strange, Sir Bartholomew (Tollie) Longtime friend and physician to Sir Charles CARTWRIGHT, the intelligent and kindhearted Tollie is present when Reverend BABBINGTON is murdered in Sir Charles' house in THREE-ACT TRAGEDY. He later dies suddenly from nicotine poisoning.

Strange, Kay An aggressive woman, "a tartar—devil of a temper" who manipulates Nevile STRANGE into divorcing his first wife Audrey and marrying her in TOWARDS ZERO. Her husband asks her for a divorce while the two are visiting Gull's Point at the same time as his first wife.

Strange, Nevile A well-known sports figure whose main game is tennis, he tries to assuage his guilt over his first divorce by arranging for his former and present wives to become friends in TOWARDS ZERO. Money left to him by his late guardian, Sir Matthew TRESSILIAN, remains in trust to Lady TRESSILIAN during her lifetime, and it is at her home, Gull's Point, that Nevile wants everyone to congregate, even though she does not approve of his intentions.

"Strange Case of Sir Arthur Carmichael, The" Mystery short story.

The plot centers on the strange behavior of a young heir to a title, and his stepmother's involvement with the occult.

PUBLISHING AND DRAMATIZATION HISTORY
The story appeared in the short story collection, THE HOUND OF DEATH AND OTHER STORIES, published in 1933 by William Collins Sons and Company, Ltd., in London.

The story has not been adapted for stage or screen.

CHARACTERS
Lady CARMICHAEL (2), Sir Arthur CARMICHAEL, Dr. Edward CARSTAIRS, Miss Phyllis PATTERSON, Dr. SETTLE

PLOT SYNOPSIS
The story concerns an unusual case related by the psychologist, Dr. Edward Carstairs. Consulted by a colleague about the mute and catlike behavior of the twenty-three-year-old Sir Arthur Carmichael, Carstairs is the only person who sees a grey Persian cat,

said to have died on the same day Arthur began his strange behavior. Lady Carmichael, Arthur's stepmother, who deals in the supernatural, is clawed nearly to death, and the impaired young man falls into a pond and nearly drowns. When Arthur regains consciousness, his memory and human behavior return, and the shock causes Lady Carmichael's death.

CRIME NOTES
The attempted murder of Arthur, which results in the cat's murder in this story, is the result of arsenic poisoning.

"Strange Jest" Mystery short story.

The plot centers on a hidden inheritance left to a young woman and her fiancé by her uncle, a man who loved practical jokes.

PUBLISHING AND DRAMATIZATION HISTORY
The story appeared in the short story collection, THREE BLIND MICE AND OTHER STORIES, published in 1950 by Dodd, Mead and Company in New York.

The story has not been adapted for stage or screen.

CHARACTERS
Jane HELIER, Miss Jane MARPLE, Edward ROSSITER, Charmian STROUD, Mathew STROUD

PLOT SYNOPSIS
The story concerns the hidden legacy of wealthy Mathew Stroud, left to his great-grand-niece and grand-nephew without a clear indication of its location. Stumped by the cryptic hints he gave shortly before his death, the heirs contact Miss Marple on the advice of their friend Jane Helier. Using her powers of association, Miss Marple recalls her own bachelor uncle's eccentric behavior, and locates a secret desk drawer that reveals the unusual inheritance.

Stranger Walked In, A See "PHILOMEL COTTAGE."

Stranleigh, Lady Discovered murdered in her bath in "THE VOICE IN THE DARK," the four-times-married mother of Margery GALE had asked Mr. SATTERTHWAITE to investigate her daughter's claims that the house was haunted by ghostly voices.

Stravinska, Anna A former ballet dancer and devout Catholic who refused her husband a divorce, she is strangled on a train, and her body is hidden in a sarcophagus at Rutherford Hall and not discovered until three weeks later in 4.50 FROM PADDINGTON.

Streptitch, Count Feodor Alexandrovitch An imposter who posed as the secretary to Grand Duchess PAULINE in "JANE IN SEARCH OF A JOB," he is really a member of a gang that burglarizes Lady Ancester's house during a bazaar for refugees.

Strete, Mildred A bitter and disappointed woman in THEY DO IT WITH MIRRORS, she is the widow of Canon Strete and the younger daughter of Carrie Louise SERROCOLD, who has permitted her second husband to turn the family home into a home for delinquent boys.

Stroud, Charmian Heir, with her cousin and fiancé Edward ROSSITER, to their great-uncle Mathew STROUD's fortune in "STRANGE JEST," the two find that they must solve a puzzle to obtain their inheritance, so they consult Miss MARPLE.

Stroud, Mathew An eccentric bachelor uncle in "STRANGE JEST," he leaves his fortune to his niece and nephew, but they must solve a puzzle to obtain it.

Stuart, Arlena See MARSHALL, ARLENA.

Stuart, Helen See MARSHALL, ARLENA.

Stubbs, Lady Hattie The real Lady Hattie Stubbs disappears in DEAD MAN'S FOLLY soon after marrying James FOLLIAT, and her place is assumed by ELSA, his Italian wife. The false Lady Stubbs plays the part of someone having subnormal intelligence, but many of the household staff see through the act. The fake Lady Stubbs vanishes during a celebration, and is presumed drowned.

Stubbs, Sir George A large man with a red face, he is really James FOLLIAT, an army deserter presumed dead in Italy. He returns to England under an assumed name, and his mother, Amy FOLLIAT, arranges for him to marry her mentally challenged but wealthy ward, Hattie, in DEAD MAN'S FOLLY. He bilks his wife out of her estate, then substitutes ELSA, his Italian wife, for Hattie.

St. Vincent, Mrs. A member of the impoverished gentility, she is a widow in "THE LISTERDALE MYSTERY" (2) who feels good fortune in being offered the tenancy of Lord LISTERDALE's townhouse at a nominal rent. She gradually comes to know and like QUENTIN, Lord Listerdale's butler, who is really Listerdale in disguise. The two agree to marry after the disguise is revealed.

St. Vincent, Barbara (Babs) The daughter of a widowed mother in a family that experiences grave financial difficulty in "THE LISTERDALE MYSTERY" (2), she is embarrassed by her family's reduced circumstances. When the family moves into Lord LISTERDALE's townhouse, she receives a marriage proposal from a wealthy young man whom she met in Egypt while traveling as her cousin's companion.

St. Vincent, Lawrence A wealthy young heir to an earl's fortune in "A POT OF TEA," he consults the International Detective Agency for help in finding his girlfriend, Janet SMITH. He is manipulated into proposing to her once they are reunited. Tommy and Tuppence BERESFORD later use him as a means of infiltrating high society in "THE CRACKLER."

St. Vincent, Rupert Suspicious when his mother is able to rent Lord LISTERDALE's townhouse for a nominal amount in "THE LISTERDALE MYSTERY" (2), he investigates, and discovers that QUENTIN the butler is really Lord Listerdale in disguise.

Stylptitch, Count Known variously as a great statesman, a villain, a dictator and a patriot, he was actually "a perfect king of intrigue" who wrote down all the interesting details in his memoirs. In THE SECRET OF CHIMNEYS, he left the memoirs to Jimmy McGRATH, who had once saved his life, but there were forces who did not want to see those memoirs published.

"Stymphalean Birds, The" Mystery short story.

The plot centers on two unexpected blackmailers who take advantage of a young man's political aspirations.

PUBLISHING AND DRAMATIZATION HISTORY

The story appeared in the short story collection, THE LABOURS OF HERCULES, published in 1947 by William Collins Sons and Company in London, and by Dodd, Mead and Company in New York.

The story has not been adapted for stage or screen.

CHARACTERS

Elsie CLAYTON, Hercule POIROT, Mrs. RICE, Harold WARING

PLOT SYNOPSIS

The story concerns the near-disaster which befalls English politician Harold Waring, vacationing in Herzoslovakia, where he meets and befriends an attractive married woman, Elsie, and her mother, Mrs. Rice. He develops an aversion to two hawk-nosed women, also guests of the hotel, whom he believes to be spies. When Elsie's husband appears and is killed after being hit by a paperweight she throws, Harold is approached by Elsie's mother for financial assistance to bribe local officials. He accedes to the request, but is saved by Hercule Poirot from blackmail at nearly the last minute.

CRIME NOTES

The story is a modern version of the sixth labor of the Greek mythological figure, Hercules, whose task was to kill the Stymphalean birds, devourers of human flesh.

Subayska, Madame
A woman in "HAVE YOU GOT EVERYTHING YOU WANT?" who stops a train by releasing a smoke bomb, she is found in Mrs. JEFFRIES' compartment at the time some jewels disappear.

"Submarine Plans, The"
Mystery short story.

The plot centers on stolen submarine plans, and Hercule POIROT's success in removing a threat to national security.

PUBLISHING AND DRAMATIZATION HISTORY

The story appeared in the short story collection, THE UNDER DOG AND OTHER STORIES, published in 1951 by Dodd, Mead and Company in New York.

The story has not been adapted for stage or screen.

CHARACTERS

Lord ALLOWAY, Mrs. CONRAD, Mr. FITZROY, Captain Arthur HASTINGS, LEONIE, Hercule Poirot, Sir Harry WEARDALE, Leonard WEARDALE, Lady Juliet WEARDALE

PLOT SYNOPSIS

The story concerns the disappearance of secret plans, and a plea for assistance from the future Prime Minister of England. Lord Alloway calls Hercule Poirot to his home when submarine plans, slated to be used to develop British defense, are stolen. After questioning the guests, and puzzling over Lord Alloway's insistence upon certain facts, Poirot discovers that a well-known German counterspy is among those present. Despite this, the obvious person is not the thief, as the story takes a surprise twist in revealing what has really happened to the plans.

Suchet, David
Acclaimed by critics as the definitive Hercule Poirot, the actor has become familiar to fans worldwide through the *Poirot* series produced by London Weekend Television. Suchet prepared carefully for the role by reading all the short stories to gain a feeling for the character as written by the author, and he also read everything that Agatha Christie wrote about her creation. His aim was to produce a faithful portrait of the Belgian detective, with all of his intelligence and idiosyncrasies intact. Although Suchet has become identified closely with the character of Poirot, his acting credits beyond this one character are widespread and impressive. A stage veteran, he has enjoyed strong recognition for his work with the Royal Shakespeare Company. In 1984, Suchet gave a masterful performance as Sigmund Freud in the BBC miniseries, *Freud*. In 1986, he was awarded the Best Actor of the Year award given by the Royal Television Society for his portrayal of Blott in the popular farce, *Blott on the Landscape*. Following this role, Suchet began filming the first season of the *Poirot* series in 1988. During the fourth year of the series, 1992, he also appeared as Adolf Verlac in the Masterpiece Theater adaptation of Joseph Conrad's *The Secret Agent*. As Poirot, however, the actor has received high accolades and the devotion of fans of Agatha Christie.

Sugden, Superintendent The secret illegitimate son of Simeon LEE and superintendent of the Middleshire police in HERCULE POIROT'S CHRISTMAS, he is considered by his superior to be a man without imagination. To Hercule POIROT, the aquiline nose, pugnacious jaw, and chestnut-colored moustache recall images of a young Simeon LEE.

Summerhayes, Superintendent A member of Scotland Yard, he investigates the murder in THE MYSTERIOUS AFFAIR AT STYLES.

Summerhayes, Major John (Johnnie) A former army officer who has turned his decaying family estate into a guest house in MRS. MCGINTY'S DEAD, he has a terrible temper.

Summerhayes, Maureen The wife of Major John SUMMERHAYES and comanager of a guest house in MRS. MCGINTY'S DEAD, she is clearly incapable of cleaning or cooking for her guests.

"Sunningdale Mystery, The" Mystery short story.

The plot centers on the murder of a golfer stabbed through the heart with a hatpin.

PUBLISHING AND DRAMATIZATION HISTORY

The story appeared in the short story collection, PARTNERS IN CRIME, published in 1929 by William Collins Sons and Company, Ltd., in London, and by Dodd, Mead and Company in New York.

The story was adapted for television in 1984 by London Weekend Television in England, and was shown on the Public Broadcasting Service in the United States.

CHARACTERS

Major BARNARD, Tommy BERESFORD, Tuppence BERESFORD, Doris EVANS, Mr. HOLLABY, Mr. LECKY, Inspector MARRIOT, Captain SESSLE

PLOT SYNOPSIS

The story concerns a crime which the Beresfords solve while having lunch. They read about the murder of Captain Sessle, who was stabbed through the heart with a hatpin while on the golf course. The young woman accused of the crime claims to have

Dressed casually for a round of golf, Tommy and Tuppence Beresford are tracking "The Sunningdale Mystery." (Photo courtesy of London Weekend Television)

been lured to Sunningdale by Sessle with romantic promises, and other golfers report that the victim had met a tall and mysterious woman on the course at twilight. Police reports reveal that the Porcupine Assurance Company, in which the victim was a partner, has been bankrupted by embezzlement, and the remaining partners are bereft of funds. Using only clues published in the newspaper, the Beresfords develop a logical, if surprising, solution, to the great appreciation of Inspector Marriot, who is enjoying lunch at a nearby table.

CRIME NOTES

This story is another in a series in which the author parodies fictional detectives popular in her time. Tommy and Tuppence Beresford assume the mannerisms and relationship of the Old Man in the Corner and Polly Burton, a detective and his assistant created by Baroness Emmuska Orczy (1865–1947). The style of the Old Man in the Corner was to sit in the corner of a tea room and solve cases based on information brought by his assistant.

Surprise! Surprise! Mystery short story collection.

All of the stories in this collection appeared in previous volumes.

PUBLISHING AND DRAMATIZATION
Surprise! Surprise! was published by Dodd, Mead and Company in New York in 1965. There was no British edition.

See original collections for adaptations.

TITLES IN THE COLLECTION
Surprise! Surprise! contains the following short stories: "THE CASE OF THE PERFECT MAID," THE THIRD-FLOOR FLAT," "THE ADVENTURE OF JOHNNIE WAVERLY" (see THREE BLIND MICE AND OTHER STORIES); "DOUBLE SIN" (see DOUBLE SIN AND OTHER STORIES), "THE ARCADIAN DEER" (see THE LABOURS OF HERCULES); "WHERE THERE'S A WILL" (see THE HOUND OF DEATH AND OTHER STORIES); "GREENSHAW'S FOLLY" (see THE ADVENTURE OF THE CHRISTMAS PUDDING AND A SELECTION OF ENTREES); "AT THE 'BELLS AND MOTLEY'" (see THE MYSTERIOUS MR. QUIN); "THE CASE OF THE DISTRESSED LADY" (see PARKER PYNE INVESTIGATES); "THE PLYMOUTH" (see THE UNDER DOG AND OTHER STORIES).

Sutcliffe, Angela (Angie) An actress in THREE-ACT TRAGEDY who delights in declaring that she is "appallingly indiscreet," she once had an affair with Sir Charles CARTWRIGHT, and now thinks it a compliment to be suspected of murder.

Sutcliffe, Joan The elder sister of Bob RAWLINSON, she and her daughter are used by her brother to smuggle the jewels of Prince Ali Yusef out of the country in CAT AMONG THE PIGEONS. Because he cannot trust her discretion, her brother hides the jewels in his niece's tennis racket without warning.

"Swan Song" Mystery short story.

The plot centers on a murder committed to revenge a cruel act many years earlier.

PUBLISHING AND DRAMATIZATION HISTORY
The story appeared in the short story collection, THE LISTERDALE MYSTERY (1), published in 1934 by William Collins Sons and Company in London.

The story has not been adapted for stage or screen.

CHARACTERS
Blanche AMERY, Edouard BREON, Mr. COWAN, ELISE (2), Madame Paula NAZORKOFF, Miss Vera READ, Lady RUSTONBURY, Signor ROSCARI

PLOT SYNOPSIS
The story concerns the murder of an aging baritone during a private performance of the opera *Tosca* at the country estate of Lord and Lady Rustonbury. Famed opera star Madame Paula Nazorkoff, whose real name is Bianca Capelli, agrees to perform, but she insists that the opera should be *Tosca*, not Lady Rustonbury's original request of *Madame Butterfly*. The baritone chosen to play Scarpia becomes ill on the day of the performance, so retired opera singer Edouard Breon is asked to step in. Only Madame Nazorkoff knows the old and tragic bond she shares with him.

CRIME NOTES
The murder in this story is committed with a knife.

Sweeny, Mrs. A hearty, "clean, wholesome-looking woman" in THE SECRET ADVERSARY, she holds the keys to Moat House, where Tommy BERESFORD is led to search for Tuppence.

Sweetiman, Mrs. As postmistress in Broadhinny, she presides over the nerve center of the village, her sweet shop that doubles as a post office, and knows much of what occurs among its inhabitants in MRS. MCGINTY'S DEAD. She provides Hercule POIROT with the important clue that Mrs. MCGINTY had bought a bottle of ink on the day before her murder.

Swettenham, Edmund A solemn young man "with an anxious face" in A MURDER IS ANNOUNCED, he is an aspiring writer who is compelled to go with

his mother to see the murder Rudi SCHERZ advertised in the newspaper. He later marries Phillipa HAYMES.

Swinton, Sybil   A dull, unimaginative girl in UNFINISHED PORTRAIT, she has a dilettante's interest in art.

Symmington, Brian   The offspring with his brother Colin of his mother's second marriage in THE MOVING FINGER, he is better loved than his half-sister from his mother's first marriage, Megan HUNTER.

Symmington, Mona   A nervous woman whose ill health and hysteria mask a deliberately selfish and grasping nature in THE MOVING FINGER, she dies of poison, but the death is viewed as a suicide.

Symmington, Richard   Married to Mona SYMMINGTON, he is a partner in the law firm of Messrs. Galbraith, Galbraith and Symmington in THE MOVING FINGER. One of the anonymous letters suggests that he and his secretary Miss GINCH are having an affair, but observers noted that he was "not one to set the pulses madly racing."

T

Taken at the Flood Mystery novel.

The title of the novel is taken from William Shakespeare's *Julius Caesar*, Act V, Scene III, in which Brutus tells Cassius:

There is a tide in the affairs of men,
Which, taken at the flood, leads on to fortune (ll. 218–9).

The plot concerns the efforts of Hercule POIROT to solve one murder and to prevent further murders in a family whose eldest and wealthiest member marries a young widow and then dies, leaving his entire fortune to her.

PUBLISHING AND DRAMATIZATION HISTORY

The novel was published in 1948 by William Collins Sons and Company, Ltd., in London, and, under the title, *There Is a Tide*, by Dodd, Mead and Company in New York.

The novel has not been adapted for stage or screen.

CHARACTERS

Frances CLOADE, Gordon CLOADE, Jeremy CLOADE, Katherine (Kathie) CLOADE, Dr. Lionel CLOADE, Rosaleen CLOADE, Rowland CLOADE, Eileen CORRIGAN, David HUNTER, Mrs. LEADBETTER, Beatrice LIPPINCOTT, Adela MARCHMONT, Lynn MARCHMONT, Hercule Poirot, Major George Douglas PORTER, Superintendent SPENCE, Charles TRENTON, Captain Robert UNDERHAY

PLOT SYNOPSIS
Book I: Chapters 1–3

Hercule Poirot is at his club when he overhears Major Porter remark upon the death of Gordon Cloade and the effect on the family fortune of Cloade's recent marriage to young widow Rosaleen Underhay.

Months later, Katherine Cloade consults the detective and asks him to prove that Gordon is still alive, but she does not have sufficient money for Poirot's services. The family of the late Gordon Cloade builds up resentment against Rosaleen, because they had expected to inherit his money and they were accustomed to obtaining loans from him. They must now ask his widow for funds.

Chapters 4–6

Several members of the Cloade family visit Rosaleen and her brother David Hunter to arrange loans. Mrs. Marchmont, the late man's sister, asks for five hundred pounds, and informs Rosaleen that her late husband used to pay all of the bills for Mrs. Marchmont and her daughter Lynn. Frances Cloade requests a loan of ten thousand pounds, but Hunter intervenes and states that he has to protect his sister from the "Harpies." He warns her to watch out for herself, should he ever be absent.

Chapters 7–9

Mrs. Marchmont gets the money, then hints to Lynn that Rosaleen and Hunter are not really brother and sister. Rosaleen spends an afternoon on the farm with Rowley Cloade, stirring reminders of her early life in Ireland. As she leaves for home, a stranger appears to ask about accommodations, and gives his name as Enoch Arden. The stranger contacts Hunter with news that Rosaleen's first husband, Captain Underhay, is still alive, but he is ill and has numerous medical bills. Through this roundabout form of blackmail, Arden asks for twenty thousand pounds, but settles for ten thousand. Unknown to them, Beatrice Lippincott overhears their conversation through the communicating door of her room.

Chapters 10–13

David and Rosaleen determine that they can raise five thousand pounds by the following Tuesday, while Beatrice eagerly tells Rowley Cloade what she overheard. Lynn argues with her mother over the need for another gardener, then takes a walk to ease the tension and to think about her relationship with Rowley Cloade. She and Hunter meet and kiss, then, as she turns toward home, he says he will call her.

Chapters 14–17
Hunter calls Lynn, tells her to forget him and advises her to marry Rowley. Meanwhile, Beatrice finds Arden dead in his room, and the police question Rowley, who states that the man had tried to blackmail the Cloade family when he visited him early in the evening. The police find several clues at the murder site; then Spence visits Rosaleen and Hunter. He asks Rosaleen to identify the body, on the premise that if Arden knew Underhay she might know him. She claims that she has never seen him before.

Book II: Chapters 1–4
Rowley contacts Poirot for help in identifying the man, convinced that Arden is an alias and sure that Rosaleen recognizes him. The detective shows a picture of the dead man to Major Porter, who identifies him as Robert Underhay. This news is important to the Cloade family, because this means that Rosaleen was never legally married to Gordon Cloade. As Hunter gets ready to attend the inquest, he swears to Rosaleen that he did not kill the man. The inquest reveals that Arden was hit on the head with a large pair of tongs, and a charge of willful murder is established against David Hunter.

Chapters 5–7
Poirot confers with Spence and expresses grave doubts about the inquest's findings because too many questions are unanswered. When he comes upon Rosaleen crying in church, he asks her what Underhay was like, and she runs away. He meets Rowley and Lynn at the inn, and she expresses doubt that Hunter is guilty. When he visits Dr. Lionel Cloade, the physician claims that the murder weapon was more likely something sharp-edged like a brick, but states that he did not contradict the police surgeon, who is satisfied with the suggested weapon.

Chapters 8–10
Poirot asks family members if Gordon might have made another will, but they deny the possibility. While in London to investigate, he stops to visit Major Porter, but learns that Porter has shot himself to death. When Poirot returns, Frances Cloade tells him that the dead man was her cousin Charles Trenton, and she is puzzled that Porter identified his picture as that of Underhay.

Chapters 11–14
Poirot cannot understand why Hunter was blackmailed so easily, nor why Rosaleen seems to be so afraid. As the detective delves deeper into Cloade family secrets, he learns that Lionel Cloade is a morphine addict, and that is why Kathie needs money desperately. Rosaleen dies in her sleep, leaving behind a note in which she claims to be very wicked, and the authorities believe that she committed suicide due to guilt over murdering Arden.

Chapters 15–17
Lynn finally decides that she cannot marry Rowley, and he goes into a rage and nearly chokes her to death. He confesses that he killed Arden by accident, when Arden hit his head on a marble piece of the fireplace after Rowley punched his jaw. He also confesses that he put Porter up to identifying the picture as that of Underhay, but the army veteran refused to give false testimony at a murder trial and preferred to shoot himself. Poirot identifies the murderer of Rosaleen, who was really an Irish housemaid named Eileen Corrigan posing as a woman who had actually been killed in enemy action two years earlier. The murderer escapes for a time, but is eventually caught. At the end, Lynn and Rowley plan their wedding.

CRIME NOTES
In the novel, one victim is an accidental homicide, resulting from hitting his head on a marble section of the fireplace, while the second victim is murdered when a lethal amount of morphine is substituted for the bromide in a sleeping powder.

Tamplin, The Honourable Lenox   A blunt young woman, the daughter of Lady Rosalie TAMPLIN in THE MYSTERY OF THE BLUE TRAIN, she possesses a sardonic wit that makes her mother very uncomfortable. A chance comment of hers leads Hercule POIROT to take the correct direction in solving the puzzling murder.

Tamplin, Lady Rosalie   A well-known member of British society in THE MYSTERY OF THE BLUE TRAIN, she finds her daughter Lenox TAMPLIN difficult to bear. Lady Rosalie has been married four times, although she tends to discount her first marriage as a simple legal mistake. Her second husband was a button manufacturer who died after three years; her third husband was Viscount Tamplin, whom she married for the title; and her final husband is Charles "Chubby" Evans, whom her daughter Lenox views as "an expensive luxury."

Tanios, Bella   A pathetic and envious woman in DUMB WITNESS who is "always wanting what she hadn't got," she is married to a physician, and is the mother of two children. The niece of Emily ARUNDELL, she loses her inheritance through her husband's bad investments.

Tanios, Dr. Jacob   A man of great charm, married to Bella TANIOS in DUMB WITNESS, his Greek nationality has made him an outcast in the Arundell family.

Tanner, Inspector   A member of Scotland Yard in "THREE BLIND MICE," he assumes the name of Major Metcalf when he conducts an investigation at Monkswell Manor.

"Tape-Measure Murder, The"   Mystery short story.

The plot centers on the murder of an unlikely victim in ST. MARY MEAD.

PUBLISHING AND DRAMATIZATION HISTORY
The story was published in 1950 by Dodd, Mead and Company in New York in the short story collection, MISS MARPLE'S FINAL CASES AND TWO OTHER STORIES.

The story has not been adapted for stage or screen.

CHARACTERS
Gladys BRENT, Ted GERARD, Miss HARNELL, Miss Jane MARPLE, Colonel MELCHETT, Miss POLITT, Inspector SLACK, Mrs. SPENLOW, Arthur SPENLOW

PLOT SYNOPSIS
The story concerns the murder of Mrs. Spenlow, whose husband immediately becomes the object of suspicion to both the law enforcement officials and the people of the village of St. Mary Mead. Rumors abound because Mrs. Spenlow was wearing a kimono at the time of her death in the middle of the day, and she had recently become close to Ted Gerard, the young, handsome representative of a religious group. Unfazed by gossip, Miss Marple investigates the murder victim's past, and discovers an unexpected motive.

CRIME NOTES
The victim in this story is strangled with a tape measure.

Tavener, Chief Inspector   A shrewd member of Scotland Yard who heads the investigation into the death of Aristide LEONIDES in CROOKED HOUSE, he joins Detective Sergeant LAMB in arresting Brenda LEONIDES and Laurence BROWN for the murder.

Teeves, Dr.   An agent for the Big Four gang in THE BIG FOUR, he is the physician who attends Mr. TEMPLETON.

Temple, Miss   The maid in THREE-ACT TRAGEDY who unknowingly served the poisoned cocktail to Reverend Stephen BABBINGTON, she must reenact the episode for Hercule POIROT.

Temple, Elizabeth   A fellow traveler of Miss MARPLE's on the tour of famous houses and gardens of Great Britain in NEMESIS, she had once discussed the sad fate of Verity HUNT with the detective. During the tour, someone deliberately dislodges a boulder, which hits her and causes her to lapse into a coma.

Templeton, Charles   An undercover agent in "THE FOUR SUSPECTS" who works for Sir Henry CLITHERING, he poses as a secretary to Dr. ROSEN.

Templeton, Mr. and Mrs.   Agents of the Big Four, the two are investigated by Hercule POIROT, who is especially interested in the circumstances surrounding the supposedly dying Mr. Templeton in THE BIG FOUR.

Templeton, Edgar   See CAYMAN, LEO.

Templeton, Micky   See DARRELL, CLAUD.

Templeton, Rose Emily See NICHOLSON, MOIRA.

Ten Little Indians   See AND THEN THERE WERE NONE.

Tenterden, Miss An anxious-looking dance teacher with no personality who dances extremely well in UNFINISHED PORTRAIT.

"Theft of the Royal Ruby, The"   See "ADVENTURE OF THE CHRISTMAS PUDDING, THE."

Theodofanous,   Daphne See ZERKOWSKI, COUNTESS RENATA.

There Is a Tide   See TAKEN AT THE FLOOD.

Hercule Poirot (David Suchet) examines the valuable gem in "The Theft of the Royal Ruby." (Photo courtesy of London Weekend Television)

Therese, Sister In collusion with the criminal mastermind, Edward GORING, in "THEY CAME TO BAGHDAD," she travels on the flight to Baghdad with Victoria JONES.

Thesiger, Jimmy The best friend of murdered Gerald WADE in THE SEVEN DIALS MYSTERY, he poses as a wealthy playboy to investigate the murder.

They Came to Baghdad   Mystery novel.

The novel is set in the exotic and politically dangerous city of Baghdad, a place in which the author and her husband Max MALLOWAN maintained a house for many years. The plot concerns the efforts to prevent the sabotage of a secret meeting between leaders of the Communist and the capitalist powers.

PUBLISHING AND DRAMATIZATION HISTORY
The novel was published in 1951 by William Collins Sons and Company, Ltd., in London, and by Dodd, Mead and Company in New York.

The novel has not been adapted for stage or screen.

CHARACTERS
ANDRE, Richard (Owl) BAKER, Mr. BOLFORD, Dr. Alan BRECK, Mrs. CARDEW TRENCH, Henry (Fakir) CARMICHAEL, Sir Rupert CROFTON LEE, Captain CROSBIE, Mr. DAKIN, Edward GORING, Mrs. HAMILTON CLIP, George HAMILTON CLIPP, Victoria JONES, Dr. John (Pussyfoot Jones) PAUNCEFOOT JONES, Dr. RATHBONE, Anna SCHEELE, Catherine SERAKIS, Lionel SHRIVENHAM, Marcus TIO, Sheik Hussein el ZIYARA

PLOT SYNOPSIS
Chapters 1–3
The novel opens in a small office in the Middle East, in which two men, Captain Crosbie and Mr. Dakin, trade comments regarding an upcoming summit meeting between major world powers. Seemingly nondescript, they nonetheless have their fingers on the pulse of international affairs and appear to hold responsibility for the safety of those who will attend the meeting. Their conversation hints of espionage and secret treaties. Thousands of miles away, Anna Scheele, the highly efficient office manager of an international banking firm in New York, requests of

her employer three weeks' absence to visit her sister in London. Her name is written among the doodlings on Mr. Dakin's office blotter. In London, Victoria Jones is fired after being caught doing impressions of her boss's wife. While having lunch in a park, she meets Edward Goring, who is leaving for Baghdad within a few days to work with Dr. Rathbone. He asks if he can take her picture, claiming that he now wishes that he were staying in England, but he takes several poses of her face, both profile and full face. A smitten Victoria vows that she will find a way of following Goring to Baghdad.

Chapters 4–6

Victoria manufactures employment references and invents family ties to a bishop and a famed archaeologist to obtain a job as nurse-companion to a woman traveling to Baghdad. In that city, a British Intelligence agent has obtained vital information which must be given to the proper authorities, but he is pursued by a knife-wielding thug. Fakir Carmichael manages to reach the British Consulate and slips a coded message into the pocket of a former Eton classmate before he is attacked.

Chapters 7–9

Victoria travels by plane to Baghdad with Mrs. Hamilton Clipp, her new American employer. The world-renowned Sir Rupert Crofton Lee, a buccaneerlike figure in a swirling cape, is also on the plane, and is treated as a celebrity. During a stopover at a hotel in Cairo, Victoria hears someone who seems to be a flight attendant request Sir Rupert's presence at the B.O.A.C. office three doors down the hall. When she must later straighten out with B.O.A.C. a problem of excess baggage for Mrs. Hamilton Clipp, Victoria finds that the office is larger and is situated in a different location from the one she had seen Sir Rupert enter.

Chapters 10–12

Once in Baghdad, Victoria registers at the Tio Hotel and attempts to find a means of supporting herself, and she aims to find Edward Goring. She questions the hotel proprietor regarding Dr. Rathbone, then attempts to maneuver herself through the crowded streets of Baghdad to find The Olive Branch, the bookstore that is the headquarters of the peace effort. Once there, she views as overly optimistic Dr.

Rathbone's contention that translating literature into numerous languages will further world peace. Back at the hotel, while she worries about her dwindling money, Dakin and Crosbie set up listening posts to receive information from Fakir Carmichael.

Chapters 13–17

As Victoria prepares to go to bed, Carmichael appears at her door, begging her to hide him. When the police arrive, Victoria plays the helpless woman, and soon sends them away. She finds that Carmichael is dead, and she is surprised when she hears her door open and Dakin walk through. He creates a cover story and, with the hotel proprietor, removes the body. Dakin tells her that Carmichael had obtained highly secret information about the disappearance of numerous scientists, technical experts and other ambitious young professionals. Dakin enlists Victoria's help, sending her to the city of Basrah and to Goring. When she tells Goring about her recent adventure, she senses a change in his demeanor and wonders how much he really knows about The Olive Branch. She hears on the radio that the body of Sir Rupert has been fished out of the Nile with a stab wound to the heart. When she returns to Baghdad, Goring obtains for her a low-paying job at The Olive Branch, where she is supposed to see what she can find out, and report to Dakin. When she discovers something important about Sir Rupert, Victoria is drugged and kidnapped.

Chapters 18–21

When Victoria awakens, she devises a means of escape and disguises herself in Arab dress to avoid her captors. She is fortunate that archaeologist Richard Baker, on his way to join Dr. Pauncefoot Jones, sees her on the roadway and gives her a ride. She lies and says that she is the niece of the prominent archaeologist and expects to be unmasked. Pauncefoot Jones mistakes her for an anthropologist named Venetia, who is supposed to join the dig in a few weeks. Through a chance remark, Victoria realizes that Baker was in the Consulate when Carmichael was attacked, and she tells him what transpired at the Tio Hotel. As she entertains herself by reading anything available in the dig house, Victoria realizes that the dying Carmichael had murmured not "Lefarge," as he thrust his knitted scarf into her hands, but "Defarge," in reference to the knitting Madame Defarge in Dickens' *A Tale of Two Cities*. A few days later, she is back in Baghdad and telling her story to Dakin, who is highly interested in a possible code knitted into the red scarf.

Chapters 22–25
Reunited with Edward, Victoria pours out her whole story, then realizes that something does not quite fit. She learns that she must impersonate Anna Scheele, who has acquired important facts about the international plot of world domination in which Edward is involved. Disguised as a member of a religious order, she is led onto a plane, then made up to look like Anna. Thugs accost the disguised Victoria and believe that they have kidnapped the real Anna, in time to prevent her from appearing at the international conference, but they are fooled. Anna lives to present evidence at the conference about the vast installations and underground laboratories functioning in remote areas of China and other nations. The villains are curtailed at the end of the novel, and Victoria seems headed for the altar with Richard Baker.

CRIME NOTES
The two deaths in the novel are due to stab wounds through the heart.

They Do It with Mirrors   Mystery novel.
    The novel is set in a typical small English village setting, but the postwar period depicted contains modern trends and new problems which undermine the old values and ideas of the author's generation and social class. The plot concerns the efforts of Miss Jane MARPLE to solve the murder of a visitor to Stonygate, a home for delinquent boys.

PUBLISHING AND DRAMATIZATION
HISTORY
The novel was published in 1952 by William Collins Sons and Company, Ltd., in London, and, under the title, *Murder With Mirrors*, by Dodd, Mead and Company in New York.
    The novel was adapted for television in 1985 by CBS Television in the U.S., and starred Helen Hayes as Miss Marple in a production entitled *Murder with Mirrors*. The BBC in England adapted the novel for television in 1992 in a production which starred Joan Hickson as Miss Marple and which retained the orig-

inal British title of the novel. The production, entitled *They Do It with Mirrors*, was also shown on the Public Broadcasting Service in the U.S.

CHARACTERS
Juliet BELLEVER, Inspector CURRY, Ernie GREGG, Christian GULBRANDSEN, Gina HUDD, Wally HUDD, Edgar LAWSON, Miss Jane Marple, Dr. MAVERICK, Alex RESTARICK, Carrie Louise SERROCOLD, Lewis SERROCOLD, Mildred STRETE, Ruth VAN RYDOCK

PLOT SYNOPSIS
Chapters 1–3
Miss Jane Marple visits her American friend Ruth Van Rydock in England and learns that Ruth is concerned about her sister Carrie Louise, who lives in England and whom she has not seen in twenty years. Miss Marple agrees to visit Carrie Louise at Stonygate, her home in Market Kimble, and Ruth relates her sister's marital and maternal history. Carrie Louise is presently married to Lewis Serrocold, who has converted the family mansion into a reform school for delinquent boys. Gina, granddaughter of Carrie Louise and married to an American, meets Miss Marple at the train station and takes her back to Stonygate.

Chapters 4–6
Edgar Lawson, a resident of Stonygate who professes to be the son of Winston Churchill, is upset that Gina picks up Miss Marple without informing him first. Gina's husband, Walter Hudd, expresses his unhappiness with life to Miss Marple and tells her that everyone in the house has ample money, but the house is falling apart, they eat off cracked dishes, and they wear darned clothes. When institute trustee Christian Gulbrandsen visits, he questions Miss Marple about Carrie Louise's health, placing particular emphasis upon her heart.

Chapters 7–9
Lawson confronts Miss Marple again, claiming that Serrocold is his father and spies on him. After dinner in the Great Hall, Gulbrandsen retires to his room to type a letter, and Lawson enters Serrocold's study, where the two engage in a heated argument behind the closed door. One shot is heard, then two more sound, and Serrocold tells Lawson to put the gun

down. The office door opens, and the other guests learn that Lawson's shots had entered books on the shelf and that he had used Hudd's gun. Moments later, the housekeeper calls the police, because Gulbrandsen has been shot to death in his room. The paper on which he had been typing is no longer in the typewriter.

Chapters 10–12
Inspector Curry learns that Serrocold believes that his wife is being slowly poisoned with arsenic, because she has complained of difficulty in walking and of stomach discomfort. Serrocold also claims to have identified arsenic in her medicine. When Curry consults Miss Marple, she says that she believes the fight between Lawson and Serrocold was contrived.

Chapters 13–17
Family members and juvenile residents are questioned by the authorities. Resident Ernie Gregg brags that he can sneak out of Stonygate without anyone knowing, and he implies that he saw the murderer do the same. His comments and those of other residents prompt Miss Marple to view the Great Hall as a stage, and she is convinced that an illusion was created on the night of the murder to divert attention from the murder of Gulbrandsen. She says, "They do it with mirrors."

Chapters 18–21
Gina fears that her husband will be accused of the murder, and he wants to return to America. Gregg is missing from roll call, and he is later found with Alex Restarick in the school's theater, their skulls crushed by a counterweight. Miss Marple comforts Carrie Louise, then informs Curry that she strongly suspects Serrocold.

Chapter 22–Epilogue
Written in the form of a letter, Chapter 22 reveals that Lawson tried to flee in a boat on the lake but drowned, and Serrocold also drowned trying to save him. The murderer is unmasked, and Miss Marple reveals that Gulbrandsen was murdered because he discovered that the murderer was embezzling money from the school. Alex Restarick was murdered because he had taken nail clippings from Carrie Louise, which he planned to have analyzed for evidence of arsenic. At the end, justice is served and Gina returns with her husband to America.

CRIME NOTES
Three murders occur in the novel. The first victim is shot to death, and the two later victims die when their skulls are crushed by a heavy, blunt object.

Thibault, Maitre Alexandre Attorney for the murdered Madame GISELLE in DEATH IN THE CLOUDS, he identifies her body and provides details of her business to the inquest.

"Third-Floor Flat, The" Mystery short story.
The plot centers on the discovery of a murder by two couples who use a coal lift to reach a young woman's apartment.

PUBLISHING AND DRAMATIZATION HISTORY
The story appeared in the short story collection, THREE BLIND MICE AND OTHER STORIES, published in 1950 by Dodd, Mead and Company in New York.

The story was adapted for television in 1989 by London Weekend Television in England, and was shown on the Public Broadcasting Service in the United States.

CHARACTERS
Donovan BAILEY, Jimmy FAULKENER, Patricia GARNETT, Mrs. Ernestine GRANT, Captain Arthur HASTINGS, Mildred HOPE, Hercule POIROT

PLOT SYNOPSIS
The story concerns the discovery of a murdered woman by two young couples whose lighthearted evening soon takes on a serious note. Patricia Garnett is locked out, so the four young friends decide that the two men will take the coal lift from the basement to Pat's fourth-floor apartment. In their excitement, Jimmy and Donovan miscount the floors and enter a third-floor apartment. After stumbling in the dark, they recognize their mistake and take the lift one floor higher to Pat's apartment, where Donovan finds his hands are covered with blood. They return to the floor below and find the murdered Mrs. Grant. As they call the police, Hercule Poirot appears at Pat's door and tells them that he has taken the apartment above, under the assumed name of Mr. O'Connor. As the police search for "John Fraser," whose handkerchief and note are found in the victim's apartment, Poirot deduces the true killer.

CRIME NOTES
The murder is the result of a gunshot wound to an unspecified part of the victim's body.

Third Girl   Mystery novel.

The novel pairs Mrs. Ariadne OLIVER with Hercule POIROT in a mystery peopled by modern youth, with their long and scraggly hair, ragtag clothing and nasty habits of "swallowing L.S.D." or "using hemp." The plot concerns the efforts of both detectives to help a young woman learn if she really did murder her stepmother.

PUBLISHING AND DRAMATIZATION HISTORY
The novel was published in 1966 by William Collins Sons and Company, Ltd., in London, and in 1967 by Dodd, Mead and Company in New York.

The novel has not been adapted for stage or screen.

CHARACTERS
David BAKER, Mr. BASCOMB, Miss BATTERSBY, Louise BIRELL, Peter CARDIFF, Frances CARY, Mrs. Louise CHARPENTIER, GEORGE, Mr. GOBY, Sir Roderick HORSEFIELD, Miss JACOBS, Miss Felicity LEMON, Inspector NEELE, Ariadne Oliver, Robert ORWELL, Hercule Poirot, Claudia REECE-HOLLAND, Andrew RESTARICK, Mary RESTARICK, Norma RESTARICK, SONIA, Dr. John STILLINGFLEET

PLOT SYNOPSIS
Chapters 1–5
Norma Restarick consults Hercule Poirot because she believes that she may have committed a murder but, concluding that he is too old to understand, she walks out. When Mrs. Oliver learns of Norma's visit, she goes to the apartment Norma shares with two other girls, making her the "third girl," and learns that no one knows Norma's whereabouts. Poirot goes to the Restarick home and learns that no one is aware that Norma is missing, but he meets her boyfriend, David Baker, gives him a ride home, and obtains information from him about the girl.

Chapters 6–10
Poirot engages Mr. Goby to obtain information about the Restarick family. He learns that Norma is the only "problem" in the successful and wealthy family. Mrs. Oliver follows one of Norma's roommates to work, then stops in a cafe for tea and sees Norma sitting with David. Eavesdropping, she learns that Norma has periods of time for which she cannot account. Mrs. Oliver calls Poirot, who arrives at the cafe and speaks with Norma. He suggests that she see a doctor, but she refuses. Meanwhile, Mrs. Oliver follows Baker, but he sneaks up on her. She hurriedly tells him that she is a mystery novelist gathering material for a book. They go to his friend Peter's loft, where Norma's roommate, Frances, is posing. When Mrs. Oliver leaves, she follows Baker's directions, and she is attacked. Norma wanders into traffic. Dr. Stillingfleet saves her and takes her to a nursing home for safety.

Chapters 11–15
Poirot receives a letter from Norma's father, Andrew, asking for his help in locating her, but the man denies that he sent it. He tells Poirot about his bad first marriage, and suggests that Norma has been slowly poisoning her stepmother, his second wife. The detective learns from sources that Baker, whom Mrs. Oliver believes to have "coshed" her, has been on probation twice, prefers girls who have money, has been paid off by fathers, and does not like the rough life. Goby also reports that Andrew Restarick had a brother who died suddenly, making him heir to the fortune. Mrs. Oliver informs Poirot that a woman in her fifties threw herself out of the window of a seventh-floor apartment of the Borodene Mansions, where Norma lives, and that may be the murder which she believes she committed.

Chapters 16–20
At the Borodene Mansions, Poirot learns that the suicide victim's name was Mrs. Louise Charpentier, and that she drank heavily because she believed that she had cancer. He also learns that she had been the mistress of the father of one of Norma's roommates, Claudia Reece-Holland. Poirot begins to question why Restarick moved his portrait from his home to his office. He also recalls seeing a check for a large sum lying on Restarick's desk, made out to David Baker.

Chapters 21–25
Poirot learns that Restarick had originally left his family for a woman named Louise, and he suspects that Louise Charpentier is that woman. He learns

from Dr. Stillingfleet that Norma has escaped from the nursing home. He later hears that Baker was found dead of a stab wound in Norma's apartment and that she was in the room, clutching the knife. Dr. Stillingfleet assures Poirot that Norma is sane, but someone has been feeding her a combination of drugs which leave her in a confused state. Poirot sorts out the clues, and discovers that the Restaricks are not whom they claim to be. He also uncovers a drug-smuggling operation. At the end, Dr. Stillingfleet asks Norma to marry him and to go with him to Australia.

CRIME NOTES
Two murders occur in the novel. One victim is pushed from a seventh-floor window, and the other victim is stabbed with a knife.

Thirteen at Dinner   See LORD EDGWARE DIES.

Thirteen Clues for Miss Marple   Mystery short story collection.

All thirteen of the stories in this collection appeared in previous collections.

PUBLISHING AND DRAMATIZATION HISTORY
The collection was published in 1966 by Dodd, Mead and Company in New York.

See the original collections for adaptations.

TITLES IN THE COLLECTION
The collection contains the following short stories: "THE BLOODSTAINED PAVEMENT," "MOTIVE VERSUS OPPORTUNITY," "THE THUMB MARK OF ST. PETER," "THE BLUE GERANIUM," "THE COMPANION," "THE FOUR SUSPECTS," "THE HERB OF DEATH" (see THE THIRTEEN PROBLEMS); "STRANGE JEST," "THE TAPE-MEASURE MURDER," "THE CASE OF THE PERFECT MAID," "THE CASE OF THE CARETAKER" (see THREE BLIND MICE AND OTHER STORIES); "GREENSHAW'S FOLLY" (see THE ADVENTURE OF THE CHRISTMAS PUDDING AND A SELECTION OF ENTREES); "SANCTUARY" (see DOUBLE SIN AND OTHER STORIES).

Thirteen for Luck   Mystery short story collection.

All thirteen stories in this collection appeared in previous collections.

PUBLISHING AND DRAMATIZATION HISTORY
Thirteen for Luck was published in 1961 by Dodd, Mead and Company in New York.

See the original collections for adaptations.

TITLES IN THE COLLECTION
The collection contains the following short stories: "THE NEMEAN LION," "THE GIRDLE OF HYPPOLITA" (see THE LABOURS OF HERCULES); "THE BLUE GERANIUM," "THE FOUR SUSPECTS" (see THE THIRTEEN PROBLEMS); "THE BIRD WITH THE BROKEN WING," "THE FACE OF HELEN" (see THE MYSTERIOUS MR. QUIN); "THE REGATTA MYSTERY," "PROBLEM AT POLLENSA BAY" (see THE REGATTA MYSTERY AND OTHER STORIES); "THE VEILED LADY" (see POIROT INVESTIGATES); "THE MARKET BASING MYSTERY" (see THE UNDER DOG AND OTHER STORIES); "THE TAPE-MEASURE MURDER" (see THREE BLIND MICE AND OTHER STORIES); "THE UNBREAKABLE ALIBI" (see PARTNERS IN CRIME); "ACCIDENT" (see THE LISTERDALE MYSTERY [1]).

Thirteen Problems, The   Mystery short story collection.

The unifying premise for the collection is the Tuesday Night Club, six people who meet socially one evening at the home of Miss Jane MARPLE and then decide to meet regularly each Tuesday night to solve a mystery which a group member must relate. Members of the original group are Miss Marple, her nephew novelist Raymond WEST, painter Joan LEMPRIERE, clergyman Dr. PENDER, solicitor Mr. PETHERICK and retired Scotland Yard Commissioner Sir Henry CLITHERING. The friends meet at Miss Marple's house for the first six stories. In the remaining stories in the collection, the meetings take place at the home of Colonel and Dolly BANTRY, who join Miss Marple, Sir Henry Clithering, physician Dr. LLOYD and actress Jane HELIER. Miss Marple provides solutions to all the mysteries related by the other members.

PUBLISHING AND DRAMATIZATION HISTORY
The Thirteen Problems was published in 1932 by William Collins Sons and Company, Ltd., in London,

and, under the title, *The Tuesday Club Murder,* by Dodd, Mead and Company in New York.

The stories have not been adapted for stage or screen.

TITLES IN THE COLLECTION
The collection contains the following short stories: "THE TUESDAY NIGHT CLUB," "THE IDOL HOUSE OF ASTARTE," "INGOTS OF GOLD," "THE BLOOD-STAINED PAVEMENT," "MOTIVE VERSUS OPPORTUNITY," "THE THUMB MARK OF ST. PETER," "THE BLUE GERANIUM," "THE COMPANION," "THE FOUR SUSPECTS," "A CHRISTMAS TRAGEDY," "THE HERB OF DEATH," "THE AFFAIR AT THE BUNGALOW" and "DEATH BY DROWNING."

The book was dedicated to Leonard and Katharine WOOLLEY, who had introduced the author to Max Mallowan two years earlier. Also of note is that this collection marks the last time that Miss Marple appears until a decade later.

Thomas, Dr.   One of two men who discover the body of Alex PRITCHARD at the bottom of a cliff in WHY DIDN'T THEY ASK EVANS?, he later examines the body to determine the cause of death.

Thomas, Inspector   A middle-aged police officer with a poker face and a dryly sarcastic personality in THE UNEXPECTED GUEST, he is dogged in his search for the murderer.

Thomas, Gladys   See HOBHOUSE, VALERIE.

Thompson, Dr.   A well-known psychologist consulted at the outset in THE A.B.C. MURDERS, he admits the possibility of coincidence in the case but strongly suggests that the murderer has an "alphabetical complex."

Thompson, Mrs.   A medium of proven powers in "THE RED SIGNAL," she conducts the seance during which guests are warned of "Danger! Blood!" and the threat of foul play to one individual present.

Three-Act Tragedy   Mystery novel.

The novel pairs Hercule POIROT with Mr. SATTERTHWAITE, a character usually found in the company of the mysterious Mr. Harley QUIN. The plot concerns the efforts of the detectives to unmask the murderer of a man who is poisoned and dies in front of a dining room full of guests.

PUBLISHING AND DRAMATIZATION HISTORY
The novel was published in 1935 by William Collins Sons and Company, Ltd., in London, and in 1934, under the title, *Murder in Three Acts,* by Dodd, Mead and Company in New York.

The novel was adapted by Warner Brothers in 1986 into a 105-minute movie retitled *Murder in Three Acts,* starring Peter Ustinov as Hercule Poirot, Jonathan Cecil as Captain Arthur HASTINGS and Tony Curtis as Charles CARTWRIGHT. The movie changed the setting from England to Acapulco, and Poirot uses a word processor to write his memoirs.

CHARACTERS
Anthony ASTOR, Reverend Stephen BABBINGTON, Sir Charles CARTWRIGHT, Doris COCKER, Superintendent CROSSFIELD, Cynthia DACRES, Freddie DACRES, Margaret DE RUSHBRIDGER, Aristide DUVAL, John ELLIS, Colonel JOHNSON, Hermione "Egg" LYTTON GORE, Lady Mary LYTTON GORE, Oliver MANDERS, Mrs. MILRAY, Violet MILRAY, Hercule Poirot, Mr. Satterthwaite, Sir Bartholomew (Tollie) STRANGE, Angela SUTCLIFFE, Miss TEMPLE, Muriel WILLS

PLOT SYNOPSIS
Act I: Chapters 1–5
Retired actor Charles Cartwright hosts a dinner party during which the Reverend Babbington takes one drink and dies from what is assumed to be a seizure. Hercule Poirot and Mr. Satterthwaite are among the guests. The cocktail is tested and contains no poison, thus natural causes are assumed. Mr. Satterthwaite has tea with Egg Lytton Gore and her mother. He learns that Egg is infatuated with the much-older Cartwright, who, in turn, believes that she is in love with Oliver Manders, prompting Cartwright to decide to sell his estate and move to the South of France.

Act II: Chapters 6–10
At another dinner party where Egg is present, physician Bartholomew Strange dies; the cause of death is nicotine poisoning. Satterthwaite contacts Poirot,

telling him about the second death and assuring him that Cartwright and he will return to investigate. They learn that the physician's butler ran away during the night. When they search his room, they find no evidence of his guilt.

Chapters 11–12

Cartwright remembers seeing an ink stain on the floor of the butler John Ellis's room. He and Satterthwaite deduce that Ellis must have been writing something, then shoved the papers into the fireplace when he heard someone coming, and dropped the fountain pen. The two men return to London and report what they found. Egg joins them, and the three decide that they must go back to the scene of the first death if they are to solve either murder.

Act III: Chapters 13–18

Mrs. Babbington claims that her late husband had no enemies, and there seems to be no motive for his murder. Mr. Satterthwaite speaks with Lady Mary Lytton Gore, and learns that Oliver Manders did not get along well with the reverend, and Strange thought Babbington to be an "interesting study." As the others hunt for clues, Poirot uses the process of elimination to determine the identity of the murderer. "Egg" questions Mrs. Dacres, a dress designer whose young lover had been ordered by Dr. Strange to take a sea voyage. She is known to have a wicked temper.

Chapters 19–25

Cartwright, Egg and Mr. Satterthwaite question others who were guests at the first dinner party, but no important information emerges. Poirot decides to host a sherry party, to which he invites all of the original guests. During the party, Cartwright feigns death after taking a drink, and Poirot points out that the feigned death diverted their attention from another incident in the room. Poirot leaves the party early because he receives a telegram regarding a mysterious nursing home patient who claims to have information about Strange's death. He is too late. Mrs. De Rushbridger is already dead, after ingesting poisoned chocolates.

Chapters 26–27

Manders helps Poirot keep an eye on Cartwright's housekeeper and prevents her from destroying his experimental machine, which extracts alkaloids from a plant food; nicotine is used on roses. Poirot reveals the identity of the murderer and explains the reasons for each of the three murders. As the case ends, Egg and Oliver Manders make plans to marry.

CRIME NOTES

The novel contains three murders. The first murder victim ingests nicotine in a cocktail, the second ingests nicotine in a glass of port and the third victim consumes nicotine in chocolates. The murderer has extracted the nicotine from a rose-spraying solution. Nicotine is a highly toxic substance which can produce respiratory failure and death within minutes after the administration of forty to sixty milligrams.

"Three Blind Mice" Mystery short story.

The plot centers on a psychopathic killer who threatens residents of a guest house who are trapped by a snowstorm.

PUBLISHING AND DRAMATIZATION HISTORY

The story was published in 1950 by Dodd, Mead and Company in New York in the short story collection, THREE BLIND MICE AND OTHER STORIES.

The story had its beginning as a twenty-minute radio play, entitled *Three Blind Mice,* written in 1947 for the eightieth birthday of Queen Mary, at the request of the royal family, and broadcast by the BBC. The play then became the short story, "Three Blind Mice." The author rewrote the short story into a two-act play, retitled *The Mousetrap,* which opened in London at the Ambassadors Theatre on November 25, 1952, and which has become the longest running play in English theater history.

CHARACTERS

Mrs. BOYLE, Mrs. CASEY, Giles DAVIS, Molly DAVIS, Detective Sergeant KANE, Mrs. LYON, Major METCALF, Inspector PARMINTER, Mr. PARAVICINI, Sergeant TROTTER, Christopher WREN

PLOT SYNOPSIS

The story concerns a murderer whose motive is revenge for the abuse of three World War II evacuee children at Longridge Farm, which resulted in one child's death. The perpetrators, John and Maureen Gregg, had been sentenced to prison in 1940. John had escaped from prison and then died. His wife had served her time, and was released to live under the name of Mrs. Lyon. After Mrs. Lyon is found strangled, the police find a notebook, dropped by the killer, which contains two addresses. The first address is the victim's and the second is Monkswell Manor, a newly opened guest house. Scotland Yard places a man incognito at the manor, but one more murder occurs before the now-grown eldest of the three child evacuees is discovered.

CRIME NOTES
The two murders occur as the result of strangulation, one using a belt.

Three Blind Mice and Other Stories   Mystery short story collection.

The stories in this collection contain three of Agatha Christie's most beloved detectives: Hercule POIROT, Miss Jane MARPLE and Mr. SATTERTHWAITE. Poirot appears in three stories, Miss Marple in four and Mr. Satterthwaite in one. The title story was adapted from the twenty-minute radio play written in 1947 for the eightieth birthday of Queen Mary, who was a fan of Agatha Christie.

PUBLICATION AND DRAMATIZATION HISTORY
Three Blind Mice and Other Stories was published intact only in the United States by Dodd, Mead and Company in New York in 1950, although most of the stories were published later in Britain in several different collections.

"Three Blind Mice" was first written as a radio play, then adapted as a short story. It was finally adapted for the stage as THE MOUSETRAP, and became the longest running English play.

TITLES IN THE COLLECTION
Three Blind Mice and Other Stories contains the following short stories: "Three Blind Mice," "STRANGE JEST," "THE TAPE-MEASURE MURDER," "THE CASE OF THE PERFECT MAID," "THE CASE OF THE CARETAKER," "THE THIRD-FLOOR FLAT," "THE ADVENTURE OF JOHNNIE WAVERLY," "FOUR-AND-TWENTY BLACKBIRDS" and "THE LOVE DETECTIVES."

CRIME NOTES
The short story "Three Blind Mice" has not appeared in any British collection, nor has "The Love Detectives."

"Thumb Mark of Saint Peter, The"   Mystery short story.

The plot centers on Miss Jane MARPLE's efforts to clear the name of a woman accused of murdering her husband.

PUBLISHING AND DRAMATIZATION HISTORY
The story appeared in the short story collection, THE THIRTEEN PROBLEMS, published in 1932 by William Collins Sons and Company, Ltd., in London, and under the title, *The Tuesday Club Murders,* in 1933 by Dodd, Mead and Company in New York.

The story has not been adapted for stage or screen.

CHARACTERS
Sir Henry CLITHERING, Mr. DENMAN, Geoffrey DENMAN, Mabel DENMAN, Joyce LEMPRIERE, Miss Jane Marple, Dr. PENDER, Mr. PETHERICK, Raymond WEST

PLOT SYNOPSIS
The story concerns a murder fifteen years earlier which Miss Marple relates to the Tuesday Night Club members. Mabel Denman, her niece, had been recently widowed, and the police suspected murder. Because the marriage had been unhappy, and the late Geoffrey Denman had been a violent, abusive man, the authorities suspected Mabel. After reviewing the facts, Miss Marple had cleared her niece of suspicion and identified the true perpetrator.

CRIME NOTES
The murder in this story is the result of poisoning by the ingestion of atropine sulfate, a chemical found in eyedrops, which produces symptoms similar to those of ptomaine poisoning.

Tiddler, Detective Sergeant William (Tom)
An assistant investigator in THE MIRROR CRACK'D FROM SIDE TO SIDE, he joins Detective Inspector Dermot CRADDOCK in investigating murder in ST. MARY MEAD. Craddock admires him because he is both a competent detective and a link to the filmmaking community.

Tiglath-Pileser   A cat with an Assyrian name who belongs to the Reverend Julian HARMON and his wife

"Bunch," he provides Miss MARPLE with a clue in A MURDER IS ANNOUNCED.

Tio, Marcus   A charming and childlike hotel proprietor in THEY CAME TO BAGHDAD, his circumlocutive conversations annoy Victoria Jones, who feels that "every topic found them returning to the point of departure."

Todd, Mr. and Mrs.   A couple whose cook disappears in "THE ADVENTURE OF THE CLAPHAM COOK," they first approach Hercule POIROT for assistance in finding her, and then terminate his services.

Tomlinson, Mr.   A member of the temporarily stranded picnic party in "THE WORLD'S END," he is a retired Indian judge who reveals the hidden compartment in Rosina NUNN's Indian box containing the long-lost opal.

Tomlinson, Jean   A straitlaced physiotherapist in HICKORY DICKORY DOCK, she is a boarder at Mrs. NICOLETIS' youth hostel, and is a strong believer in law and order.

Torquay   The birthplace of Agatha Christie, it is a seaside resort in Devon. Once known as the "English Riviera," where the upper classes maintained large villas, the winter resort became a haven for sunbathers in the 1920s.

Tosswill, Dr.   A member of the Men-her-Ra expedition in "THE ADVENTURE OF THE EGYPTIAN TOMB," he is a minor-level official of the British Museum who severely criticizes Hercule POIROT's lecture on magic and superstition.

Towards Zero   Mystery novel.

The novel shares a theme with the short story, THE MAN FROM THE SEA, in which suicide is used as a plot device. It chronicles the last of five novels featuring Superintendent BATTLE. The plot concerns the effort to identify a psychopathic killer who has murdered an old woman without apparent motivation. The novel is constructed in a manner different from most written by the author, because it is not divided into numbered chapters, but into four separately titled sections.

PUBLISHING AND DRAMATIZATION HISTORY

The novel was published in 1944 by William Collins Sons and Company, Ltd., in London, and by Dodd, Mead and Company in New York.

The novel was adapted for the stage by Agatha Christie with Gerald Verner, and the play opened at the St. James's Theatre in London in 1956.

CHARACTERS

Mary ALDIN, Miss AMPHREY, George BARNES, Jane BARRETT, Superintendent Battle, Sylvia BATTLE, Alice BENTHAM, Lord CORNELLY, Allen DRAKE, Detective Sergeant JONES, Edward (Ted) LATIMER, Dr. LAZENBY, Inspector James LEACH, Andrew MacWHIRTER, Thomas ROYDE, Audrey STRANGE, Kay STRANGE, Nevile STRANGE, Mr. TRELAWNY, Lady Camilla TRESSILIAN, Mr. TREVES, Emma WALES

PLOT SYNOPSIS

Prologue

Highly respected attorney Mr. Treves speaks with other lawyers about a recent, sensational murder case. He considers that the events leading to any crime actually begin years before, starting with seemingly insignificant actions that generate other actions that eventually converge at the zero point, murder. Plagued by a slight heart condition, the eighty-year-old man prepares to relax at home, then opens a letter that changes his plans entirely.

Open the Door and Here Are the People

Diverse individuals are described in incidents which seem to have no relation to each other, but all of the participants will soon meet at Saltcreek. Andrew MacWhirter is in the hospital after a failed suicide attempt, and Lord Cornelly offers him a job in South Africa. He must leave in one week, so he decides to vacation at Saltcreek. Superintendent Battle investigates a charge that his daughter has admitted to pilfering items at her boarding school. He learns when he speaks with her that she confessed to stop the badgering by school administrators. He intends to go to Saltcreek. Tennis professional Nevile Strange and his former and present wives will visit Lady Tressilian at Gull's Point, despite concerns that trouble might erupt between the two women. Gull's Point is near Saltcreek. Thomas Royde, a cousin of Audrey Strange who was raised with Royde, plans to visit, and so does Ted Latimer, an old friend of Kay Strange. Other characters are identified, and all have plans which eventually take them to Saltcreek and the vicinity.

Snow White and Rose Red

Many of the already-named characters arrive at Gull's Point, including Kay and Audrey Strange, despite the misgivings of their hostess, Lady Tressilian. Nevile Strange's kindness to Audrey in giving her the Illustrated Review section of the paper is countered by his present wife's dancing with old friend Latimer. Royde and Treves discuss the nature of the justice system in cases of murder, and Treves tells the story of a child who was killed while playing bows and arrows with another child. Royde expresses the belief that people should take justice into their own hands if the system fails. The following day, news arrives that Treves has died of a heart attack after climbing three flights of stairs because the elevator falsely bore an "out of order" sign. The same day, Nevile speaks with Audrey, and tells her that he has always loved her, but Kay overhears him and threatens murder. Lady Tressilian speaks with Nevile and reminds him of his responsibility to Kay. Hours later, Lady Tressilian is found dead, hit on the head with a heavy object.

A Fine Italian Hand

Inspector Battle and Inspector Leach are called to the murder scene, and find one of Nevile's golf clubs near Lady Tressilian's body. Nevile inherits the estate, but others also benefit from legacies. The authorities question everyone staying at Gull's Point, and several come to Nevile's defense. Others remember Treves' story about the child murderer, wondering if Treve had recognized someone. Although he had not identified the killer by sex, he did say that a definite peculiarity marks the now-grown child. Mr. Trelawny, Lady Tressilian's lawyer, reveals that her estate is inherited jointly by Nevile and Audrey. Their divorce does not affect the terms of the will. Clues emerge that point to Audrey as the murderer and the police arrest her, but MacWhirter locates proof to contradict this decision.

Zero Hour

Battle takes the remaining suspects out on a boat to explain the case. He tests the swimming skill of one individual, and challenges the pat answers of the oth-

ers. He then explains the manner in which the murderer entered the house and killed Lady Tressilian. Audrey had confessed to the murder, but Battle saw in her eyes the same look that he had seen in his daughter's eyes when she admitted to stealing just to stop the badgering. At the end of the novel, Audrey and Andrew prepare to marry.

CRIME NOTES

The first murder is accomplished by forcing a man with a weak heart to walk three flights of stairs. The second murder occurs when the victim is hit over the head with an extremely heavy doorknob.

"Tragedy at Marsden Manor, The" Mystery short story.

The plot centers on the sudden death of a man whose estate was nearly bankrupt and who had recently taken out a very large insurance policy.

PUBLISHING AND DRAMATIZATION HISTORY

The story appeared in the short story collection, POIROT INVESTIGATES, published in 1924 by John Lane in London, and in 1925 by Dodd, Mead and Company in New York.

The story was adapted for television in 1991 by London Weekend Television in England, and was

Hercule Poirot (David Suchet) must determine if a centuries-old curse or a modern-day murder is responsible for the death in "The Tragedy at Marsden Manor." (Photo courtesy of London Weekend Television)

shown on the Public Broadcast Service in the United States.

CHARACTERS
Dr. Ralph BERNARD, Captain BLACK, Mr. EVERETT, Captain Arthur HASTINGS, Inspector James JAPP, Mr. MALTRAVERS, Mrs. MALTRAVERS, Hercule POIROT

PLOT SYNOPSIS
The story concerns a murder disguised as a suicide, until Hercule Poirot investigates as a representative of the company that insured the victim. Related by Captain Hastings, the story includes a heavily insured, aging country squire whose estate is in financial ruin, a young and beautiful wife and a handsome young military officer. Poirot reconstructs conversations of the day preceding the death, and correctly identifies the murderer.

CRIME NOTES
The murder is the result of a gunshot with a small-caliber rook rifle to the mouth at an angle that lodged the bullet in the brain and simulated the appearance of a hemorrhage as blood oozed onto the victim's lips.

Tredwell   The epitome of the well-trained butler, he is in service to Lord CATERHAM at Chimneys, and appears in THE SECRET OF CHIMNEYS and THE SECRET ADVERSARY.

Trefusis, Emily   An assertive and clever woman in THE SITTAFORD MYSTERY, she steps in and works to clear her fiancé of suspicion when his uncle is murdered. Despite his apparently spineless behavior, she anticipates a future with James PEARSON because she is able to "run him" and expects to "make something of him."

Trefusis, Owen   The seemingly meek and subservient secretary to Sir Reuben ASTWELL in "THE UNDER DOG," he is "a prim, proper young man" who falls under suspicion when his employer is murdered.

Trelawny, Mr.   The attorney for the estate of Lady TRESSILIAN in TOWARDS ZERO, he provides Superintendent BATTLE with the information that the estate is to be divided between the deceased nephew and his former wife, not his present wife, as might be expected.

Trent, Claire   A woman of almost perfect beauty with whom Dermot WEST falls in love in "THE RED SIGNAL," she is "a thing of gold and ivory and pale-pink coral." He later fears that she is mentally unbalanced.

Trent, Hugo   Present when his uncle Sir Gervase CHEVENIX-GORE is killed in "DEAD MAN'S MIRROR," he is viewed by his fiancée as being "a perfect pet, but he's got absolutely no brains."

Trent, Jack   Married to Claire TRENT in "THE RED SIGNAL," he is the perfect host and no one suspects the dark secret he hides.

Trenton, Charles   A scoundrel and a confidence man in TAKEN AT THE FLOOD, he uses the name Enoch ARDEN when he tries to blackmail David HUNTER and Rosaleen CLOADE. His hints that he has damaging knowledge about Robert UNDERHAY are taken seriously by a killer who murders him in his room at the Stag Inn.

Tressilian   A well-trained and highly loyal butler who has served Simeon LEE for over forty years in HERCULE POIROT'S CHRISTMAS, he is willing to go to any lengths to protect the Lee family.

Tressilian, Lady Camila   The wealthy and spirited elderly widow of Sir Matthew Tressilian in TOWARDS ZERO, she is the owner of Gull's Point and a connoisseur of scandal and gossip. She is murdered in her bed, her head crushed with a heavy blunt object.

Trevelyan, Captain Joseph Arthur   A miser and misogynist in THE SITTAFORD MYSTERY, he is an elderly retired Royal Navy officer who owns Sittaford House. With his close friend, Major BURNABY, he has scaled mountains and braved dangers throughout the world, and "he was a regular philistine in every way—devoted to sport." He is murdered when a killer strikes him over the head with a sandbag, crushing his skull.

Treves, Mr.   A specialist in criminal behavior and a close friend of Lady TRESSILIAN in TOWARDS ZERO, he knows many secrets of the rich, famous and infamous. He scoffs at the usual belief that a murder mystery begins with the murder, and offers, instead, the theory that the drama often unfolds years before, as events and people interact. He dies of a heart attack when he climbs the stairs to his hotel room after someone has placed a false "out of order" sign on the elevator.

"Triangle at Rhodes"   Mystery short story.

The plot centers on the murder of a famed beauty who had encouraged a rivalry for her affections between her moody husband and a handsome younger man. The setting and plot were expanded into the novel, EVIL UNDER THE SUN.

PUBLISHING AND DRAMATIZATION
HISTORY
The story appeared in the short story collection MIRROR IN THE MEWS (1), published in 1937 by William Collins Sons and Company, Ltd., in London, and, in the short story collection, DEAD MAN'S MIRROR, published by Dodd, Mead and Company in New York.

The story was adapted for television in 1989 by London Weekend Television in England, and was shown on the Public Broadcasting Service in the United States.

CHARACTERS
General BARNES, Miss Susan BLAKE, Commander Tony CHANTRY, Mrs. Valentine CHANTRY, Douglas Cameron GOLD, Marjorie GOLD, Miss Pamela LYALL, Hercule POIROT

PLOT SYNOPSIS
The story concerns the poisoning murder of Valentine CHANTRY, an attractive, wealthy, yet empty-headed woman whose flirtatious behavior angers her brutish fifth husband. Guests at the resort on Rhodes clearly see a triangle develop between Valentine, her husband Tony and the young and handsome, if vacuous, Douglas Gold. They also see the apparently brave front enacted by the mousy Mrs. Marjorie Gold. When Valentine is murdered, only Poirot recognizes the real murderer.

The flirtation of two married people (played by John Cartwright and Annie Lambert) becomes deadly in "Triangle at Rhodes." (Photo courtesy of London Weekend Television)

CRIME NOTES
The murder in this story is the result of poisoning by ingestion of strophanthin, a drug prescribed for heart ailments.

Tripp, Isabel and Julia   Involved in activities unusual to women of their age and class, they are "vegetarians, theosophists, British Israelites, Christian scientists, spiritualists and enthusiastic amateur photographers." At their seance in DUMB WITNESS, Miss ARUNDELL appears to be surrounded in a "luminous haze," which later is revealed to signify phosphorous poisoning.

Trotter, Sergeant   See JIM.

Tucker, Marlene   A willing pretend victim in a mock murder hunt organized by Mrs. Ariadne OLIVER in DEAD MAN'S FOLLY, she becomes a real murder victim when someone strangles her with a piece of clothesline during the hunt.

Tucker, Marilyn   Sister of one of the murder victims in DEAD MAN'S FOLLY, she informs Hercule POIROT that her sister spied on people and received gifts to keep their secrets.

Tuckerton, Thomasina Ann (Tommy)   A modern young woman who is part of the "Chelsea crowd" in THE PALE HORSE, she dies less than a week after a very physical fight with Lou ELLIS in a Chelsea espresso bar. The official obituary cites encephalitis as the cause of death, but Mark EASTERBROOK suspects murder.

Tuesday Club Murders, The   See THE THIRTEEN PROBLEMS.

"Tuesday Night Club, The"   Mystery short story.

The plot centers on the attempt of the newly formed Tuesday Night Club to solve a year-old murder.

PUBLISHING AND DRAMATIZATION
HISTORY
The story appeared in the short story collection, THE THIRTEEN PROBLEMS, published in 1932 by William Collins Sons and Company, Ltd., in London, and in the short story collection, THE TUESDAY CLUB MURDERS, published in 1933 by Dodd, Mead and Company in New York.

CHARACTERS
Miss Milly CLARK, Sir Henry CLITHERING, Mr. Albert JONES, Mrs. JONES, Joyce LEMPRIERE, Gladys LINCH, Miss Jane MARPLE

PLOT SYNOPSIS
The story concerns the death of Mrs. Albert Jones, the only person to die after a supper during which three people become ill. Related by Sir Henry Clithering, the facts are that all three ate the same canned lobster and trifle, and their subsequent illness is attributed to botulism blamed on the canned lobster. Through careful questioning, Miss Marple uncovers important information that has been ignored by Sir Henry and the authorities, as she identifies a murderer.

CRIME NOTES
The murder in this story results from poisoning by arsenic which is sprinkled on a sugary trifle dessert.

Turner, Mrs.   A former resident of Heather Cottage in "THE MYSTERY OF THE BLUE JAR," she disappeared without a trace, and Felice MARCHAUD believes that the ghostly cries of "Murder—help!" are hers.

Turner, Josephine (Josie)   A dancer at the Majestic Hotel and secretly the wife of Mark GASKELL in THE BODY IN THE LIBRARY, she impresses Miss MARPLE as possessing "one of those shrewd, limited practical minds that never do foresee the future and are usually astonished by it." She manages to obtain a job for her cousin, Ruby KEENE, a short time before Ruby's murder.

Tyler, Fred   Miss MARPLE's acquaintance from the fish shop, he is not aware of how much he knows in A MURDER IS ANNOUNCED.

U

"Unbreakable Alibi, The" Mystery short story.

The plot centers on the efforts of Tommy and Tuppence BERESFORD to help a young woman prove that she was in two places at the same time.

PUBLISHING AND DRAMATIZATION HISTORY

The story appeared in the short story collection, PARTNERS IN CRIME, published in 1929 by William Collins Sons and Company, Ltd., in London, and by Dodd, Mead and Company in New York.

The story was adapted for television in 1984 by London Weekend Television in England, and was shown on the Public Broadcasting Service in the United States.

CHARACTERS

Tommy Beresford, Tuppence Beresford, Una DRAKE, Mr. Montgomery JONES, Mr. LE MARCHANT, Mr. and Mrs. OGLANDER, Dicky RICE

PLOT SYNOPSIS

The story concerns the attempts of the Beresfords to help Mr. Montgomery Jones to win a bet he made with the woman he loves. Una Drake claims that she was in both Torquay and London at the same time, and she dares Mr. Jones to prove her wrong. After investigating, the Beresfords find that witnesses substantiate Una's presence in both locations, and Tuppence decides that there is only one explanation.

CRIME NOTES

The story is another in a series of Tommy and Tuppence Beresford stories in which the author parodies popular fictional detectives of her day. In this story, Tommy Beresford assumes the mannerisms of In-

Tuppence and Tommy Beresford (Francesca Annis and James Warwick) investigate how one person can be in two places at the same time in "The Unbreakable Alibi." (Photo courtesy of London Weekend Television)

spector Joseph French, a Scotland Yard detective created by Freeman Will Crofts (1879–1957). The style of Inspector French was to discuss cases with his wife, who often provided valuable suggestions.

"Under Dog, The" Mystery short story.

The plot centers on a bludgeoning murder which Hercule POIROT is called upon to solve.

PUBLISHING AND DRAMATIZATION HISTORY

The story appeared in the short story collection, THE UNDER DOG AND OTHER STORIES, published in 1951 by Dodd, Mead and Company in New York, and in the short story collection, THE ADVENTURE OF THE CHRISTMAS PUDDING AND A SELECTION OF ENTREES, published in 1960 by William Collins Sons and Company, Ltd., in London.

The story was adapted for television in 1993 by London Weekend Television in England, and was shown on the Public Broadcasting Service in the United States.

OTHER CHARACTERS
Lady Nancy ASTWELL, Sir Reuben ASTWELL, Victor ASTWELL, Dr. CAZALET, Miss COLE, GLADYS (5), GEORGE/GEORGES, Miss LANGDON, Charles LEVERSON, Lily MARGRAVE, Mr. MAYHEW, Inspector MILLER, Captain Humphrey NAYLOR, Hercule Poirot, Owen TREFUSIS

PLOT SYNOPSIS
The story concerns the murder of the wealthy Sir Reuben Astwell, who is bludgeoned to death in his mansion soon after quarreling with his nephew, Charles. His wife believes that Charles is innocent, and retains Hercule Poirot to identify the murderer. As he investigates, Poirot learns that Sir Reuben had swindled the father of Lily Margrave, Lady Astwell's paid companion, out of a gold mine and that Sir Reuben was also on bad terms with his own brother, Victor. Poirot also learns that Lady Astwell and Charles Leverson stand to inherit Sir Reuben's estate.

CRIME NOTES
The murder in this story results from a blow to the back of the head with a heavy wooden club.

Under Dog and Other Stories, The   Mystery short story collection.

The book contains eight stories first published in British magazines from 1923 through 1926, and one story which was greatly expanded and renamed for inclusion into another collection. All of the stories feature Hercule POIROT with Captain HASTINGS as the chronicler of events.

PUBLISHING AND DRAMATIZATION HISTORY
The Under Dog and Other Stories was published intact only in the United States, by Dodd, Mead and Company in New York in 1951. "THE SUBMARINE PLANS" had been expanded in 1937 into a much longer story and renamed "THE INCREDIBLE THEFT," which appears in the collection, "MURDER IN THE MEWS." All of the stories except for "THE PLYMOUTH EXPRESS" were later published in British collections. "The Plymouth Express" was developed in 1928 into a novel entitled THE MYSTERY OF THE BLUE TRAIN.

"THE UNDER DOG," "The Plymouth Express," "THE AFFAIR AT THE VICTORY BALL," "THE CORNISH MYSTERY," "THE KING OF CLUBS" and "THE ADVENTURE OF THE CLAPHAM COOK" were adapted for television by London Weekend Television in England, and were shown on the Public Broadcasting System in the U.S.

TITLES IN THE COLLECTION
The Under Dog and Other Stories contains the following short stories: "The Under Dog," "The Plymouth Express," "The Affair at the Victory Ball," "THE MARKET BASING MYSTERY," "THE LEMESURIER INHERITANCE," "The Cornish Mystery," "The King of Clubs," "The Submarine Plans" and "The Adventure of the Clapham Cook."

Underhay, Captain Robert   The first husband of Rosaleen CLOADE in TAKEN AT THE FLOOD, he understood his wife's inability to live in Nigeria, and agreed to a divorce. When she returned to England, he pretended to die, and she later remarried, never having been divorced. His existence becomes a threat to Rosemary's inheritance of money from her second, bigamous marriage.

Unexpected Guest, The   Mystery play.
The play concerns the role played by an unexpected visitor who chances upon a domestic murder scene. The plot centers on the efforts to uncover the true murderer of a sadistic, wheelchair-bound husband whose wife is found holding the revolver.

PUBLISHING AND DRAMATIZATION HISTORY
The work is an original play in two acts written in 1958, which opened at the Duchess Theatre in London on August 12, 1958.

CHARACTERS
Henry ANGELL, Miss BENNETT, Sergeant CADWALLADER, Julian FARRAR, Michael STARKWEDDER, Inspector THOMAS, Mrs. WARWICK, Jan WARWICK, Laura WARWICK, Richard WARWICK

PLOT SYNOPSIS
Act 1
Michael Starkwedder stops at a house, after driving for several hours in a fog, and enters an unlocked door to find Richard Warwick dead of a gunshot wound and his wife, Laura, holding the gun. After she tells him that she has hated her husband for years because he drank and was cruel, Michael concludes that he will help her to find an alibi because he doesn't like "to think of an attractive woman being shut up in prison for all the best years of her life." She lists her husband's enemies, and he learns that Richard had killed a child while driving drunk and wildly, but had been exonerated. The child's father had threatened revenge. They concoct a story about a mysterious murderer, and Starkwedder fires a shot to rouse the family. Mrs. Warwick, Richard's mother, calls the police. The police arrive and take fingerprints, then question everyone in the house. The victim's mentally disabled brother Jan brings up incidents from the past showing that household members had reason to hate the victim.

Act 2
The victim's valet-attendant tries to blackmail Julian Farrar, whom he saw leave the house right after the gunshot. Laura panics, and Laura and Julian reveal that each thought the other to be the murderer, but they both claim innocence. Jan enters the room and insists on having his brother's guns now that he is "master of the house," but Laura quiets him down. The police return with the disquieting news that MacGregor died two years previously. As Inspector Thomas speaks with the family, Jan sneaks past with a concealed gun, then brags to the housekeeper, Miss Bennett, that he shot Richard. He runs away as the police try to take him into custody, and accidentally shoots himself through the heart during the pursuit. The police close the case, but the play ends with a startling revelation.

CRIME NOTES
The one murder victim in this play dies of a gunshot wound.

Unfinished Portrait   Non-mystery novel.

The second of the novels written as Mary WEST-MACOTT, this work was described by Sir Max MALLOWAN in his memoirs as being a blend of autobiography and imagination. The plot concerns the rescue of a woman from suicide by an artist who then listens as she relates her life and experiences.

PUBLISHING AND DRAMATIZATION
HISTORY
Unfinished Portrait was first published in 1934 by William Collins Sons and Company, Ltd., in London, and by Doubleday and Company in New York.

The novel has not been adapted for stage or screen.

CAST OF CHARACTERS
AUBREY, Miss BANKS, Monsieur BARRE, Madame BEAUGE, Jeanne BEAUGE, Miss BENNETT, CELIA, Marjorie CONNELL, CYRIL, Major Johnnie DEBURGH, Mary DENMAN, DERMOT, FANNY, GLADYS, Ralph GRAHAM, GRANNIE, Mrs. GRANT, Bernard GRANT, Jim GRANT, GREGG, the GUN MAN, Mary HAYES, JUDY, KATE, Monsieur KOCHTER, J. LARRABY, Miss LEADBETTER, Madame LEBRUN, Miss LESTRANGE, Cousin LOTTIE, Mrs. LUKE, Margaret MacRAE, Miss MacKINTOSH, Janet MAITLAND, Captain Peter MAITLAND, Miss MAUHOURAT, MIRIAM, Janet PATTERSON, Maisie PAYNE, Margaret PRIESTMAN, Roger RAYNES, Mrs. ROUNCEWELL, Mr. RUMBOLT, Mrs. RUMBOLT, Mrs. STEADMAN, SUSAN, Sybil SWINTON, Miss TENTERDEN, Bessie WEST

PLOT SYNOPSIS
Book One–The Island
Former portrait painter J. Larraby climbs a promontory overlooking the sea to be alone on a Spanish island retreat and finds a woman sitting in his usual spot. As he leaves, he realizes that she was too distracted to notice his missing hand and make the usual sympathetic comments. He suspects that she has climbed the hill to commit suicide, so he invites her to dinner, and stays with her as she tells him the story of her life.

Book Two–Canvas
Larraby recounts Celia's story, adding his own editorial comments at several points. Celia had a happy and secure childhood, marred only by a recurring dream about a mysterious man with stumps for hands whom she called the Gun Man.

Celia tells of her early life and loves. Educated at home, Celia lived in a financially secure home until

her father died when she was ten; then money became a problem. Lively and attractive, Celia had a
large number of suitors and marriage proposals. She
chose Dermot, who dazzled her and insisted that she
marry him. Their marriage was happy at first, but
Dermot's jealousy and, later, his infidelity drove
them apart. To assuage her growing loneliness, Celia
began to write imaginative stories, and soon found a
publisher. When Celia's mother died, and Dermot
announced that he wanted a divorce, Celia had a
nervous breakdown and attempted suicide.

Book Three—The Island
When Celia's story is nearly complete, Larraby asks
her several questions, and concludes that her failure
was in being too trusting and too childlike. He learns
that she has spent the ten years since the divorce
traveling and trying to make up to her daughter Judy
for Dermot's abandonment of them.

At seven o'clock in the morning, Celia falls asleep,
exhausted. Larraby awakens her later and takes her
to a departing ship, feeling that she is ready to experience life again, for she has finally confronted her
fears.

Unkerton, Mrs.   The mistress of Greenways
House in "THE SHADOW ON THE GLASS," she replaces the haunted window pane without telling her
husband, Ned UNKERTON, and upsets the plans of a
murderer.

Unkerton, Ned   Owner   of   the   historic
Greenways House in "THE SHADOW ON THE GLASS,"
he plays the incompetent host when he invites a
man, his wife and his former lover to a party at the
house where murder occurs.

Upjohn, Mrs.   A former member of British Intelligence during World War II, she is now the sedate,
middle-aged mother of English schoolgirl Julia UP-
JOHN in CAT AMONG THE PIGEONS. Adventure arises
when she recognizes a dangerous agent whom she
had known during the war.

Upjohn, Julia   The daughter of a former member
of British Intelligence and a student at Meadowbank
School in CAT AMONG THE PIGEONS, she discovers
jewels in the handle of her friend's tennis racket, and
takes them to Hercule POIROT.

Upward, Laura   A former actress and presently
an invalid in MRS. McGINTY'S DEAD, she is the adoptive mother of Robin UPWARD and an employer of
Mrs. McGINTY. A social climber, she tries to surround
herself only with prominent and artistically interesting people. She is strangled on the night her son is
meeting with Mrs. Ariadne OLIVER.

Upward, Robin   Adopted by Laura UPWARD
when he was an infant, his real name is Evelyn Hope
and he is the natural son of a woman once accused
of murder in MRS. McGINTY'S DEAD. He and Mrs.
Ariadne OLIVER are adapting one of her novels for
the stage.

V

Valdez, Lola A flamboyant and famous Peruvian dancer in "YELLOW IRIS," she attracts the attention of Hercule POIROT at the Jardin des Cygnes restaurant. He responds to her energy and asks her to dance, motivating her to proclaim, "You're the cat's whiskers, M. Poirot."

Van Aldin, Rufus The wealthy and powerful father of Ruth KETTERING in THE MYSTERY OF THE BLUE TRAIN, he learns that his daughter has been murdered and her jewelry stolen only days after he buys her the Heart of Fire rubies. The American millionaire hires Hercule POIROT to find Ruth's murderer and to retrieve the rubies.

Vandel, Ambrose A set designer for the ballet in "THE ARCADIAN DEER," he provides Hercule POIROT with information regarding Sir George SANDERFIELD.

Vandemeyer, Janet See FINN, JANE.

Vandemeyer, Marguerite Once a paramour of Sir James Peel EGERTON, "the most celebrated KC in England" and future prime minister in THE SECRET ADVERSARY, she is a Russian spy who tracks the movement of the draft treaty plans by pretending to be Jane FINN's aunt. She dies of a chloral overdose.

Vanderlyn, Mrs. A mercenary woman who is involved in espionage in "THE INCREDIBLE THEFT," she has had Russian, German and Italian husbands, all useful in her line of work. A charming and sympathetic woman, she attracts men but "was usually at a disadvantage when left alone with members of her own sex." When bomber plans are stolen from Lord MAYFIELD's country house, the lingering scent of her perfume provides a distinct clue.

Vane, Clarice Despite her attraction to Harry LAXTON in "THE CASE OF THE CARETAKER," she befriends his new wife, and defends Harry against the village gossip that erupts when the wife dies suddenly.

Van Heidem, Paul (Van) A seemingly genial but really cold man who functions as the official spokesman for Mr. ARISTIDES' Brain Trust complex in DESTINATION UNKNOWN, he finds amusing the thought of using a leper colony as a front for the complex.

Van Rydock, Ruth A former school friend of Miss MARPLE in THEY DO IT WITH MIRRORS, she has been married three times, and has increased her bank account with each divorce. When she suspects that her sister, Carrie Louise SERROCOLD, is in danger, she asks Miss Marple to investigate.

Van Schuyler, Marie An old, crotchety, socially prominent kleptomaniac in DEATH ON THE NILE (2), she is generally disliked and verbally abuses everyone around her.

Vansittart, Eleanor A schoolmistress at Meadowbank School in CAT AMONG THE PIGEONS, she is a perfectly groomed woman who is murdered by a blow to the head with a sandbag.

Van Snyder, Mrs. Cortland In appearance "a middle-aged fashionably-dressed woman from Detroit" in "THE MAN WHO WAS NO. 16," she claims to have been drugged by a man who also drugs and kidnaps Tuppence BERESFORD. In reality, she is the Prince VLADIROFFSKY, a Russian by birth and a master of disguise.

Vanstone, Commander   See CARTWRIGHT, SIR CHARLES.

Van Stuyvesant, Cora   The stepmother of Ellie Guteman ROGERS in ENDLESS NIGHT, she lives on an allowance controlled by her stepdaughter. She pretends to like her son-in-law, Michael ROGERS, although he is obvious in his dislike of her.

Varaga, Queen Of Herzoslovakia   See MORY, ANGELE.

Varesco, Paul   The financial strength behind the Countess Vera ROSSAKOFF's popular nightclub, Hell, in "THE CAPTURE OF CERBERUS," he uses the club as a cover for his dealings in both drugs and stolen jewels.

Varez, Paul de   An accomplice of No. 16 in THE MAN WHO WAS NO. 16, he plays the role of a French invalid accompanied by a hospital nurse, and serves as a decoy to allow No. 16 to escape.

Vassilievitch   A completely evil and very clever Russian agent in "THE CASE OF THE CITY CLERK" who, thanks to Mr. PARKER PYNE, increases the danger in Mr. ROBERTS' adventure.

Vassilovna, Olga   See DEMIROFF, OLGA.

Vaucher, Jeanne   An aging beauty in "THE SOUL OF THE CROUPIER" who has led the world to believe that she is the Countess Czarnova, she was once a poor Parisian girl married to a jeweler whom she left as soon as fortune beckoned.

Vaucher, Pierre   Long estranged from his wife Jeanne VAUCHER, he is a one-time Parisian jeweler who is now a croupier in Monte Carlo in "THE SOUL OF THE CROUPIER." He is united with her due to the efforts of the enigmatic Mr. Harley QUIN.

Vaughan, Gwenda   The longtime secretary to businessman Leo ARGYLE in ORDEAL BY INNOCENCE, she has been in love with him for years, and hopes to marry him when his wife dies.

Vaughan, Magdalen   A tall, dark, twenty-six-year-old woman in "SING A SONG OF SIXPENCE," she

and her twin brother become suspects in the murder of her wealthy great-aunt, Lily CRABTREE.

Vaughan, Matthew   An itinerant journalist in "SING A SONG OF SIXPENCE" who owes a large sum of money and has no stable income, he is the twin brother of Magdalen VAUGHAN, and falls under suspicion when their great-aunt, Lily CRABTREE, is murdered.

Vaughn, Lady Millicent Castle   See GERTIE.

Vavasour, Mr.   A bank manager and the uncle of Philip RIDGEWAY in "THE MILLION DOLLAR BOND ROBBERY," he implicates his nephew in the bond theft.

Vavasour, Roley   Heir to the Stranleigh title after Margery GALE, he is a devious man in "THE VOICE IN THE DARK" whom Margery believes has "always been out for what he can get."

"Veiled Lady, The"   Mystery short story.

The plot centers on the request by a young woman that Hercule POIROT retrieve a letter that she claims could jeopardize her upcoming marriage to a nobleman.

PUBLISHING AND DRAMATIZATION HISTORY
The story appeared in the short story collection, POIROT INVESTIGATES, published in 1924 by John Lane in London, and in 1925 by Dodd, Mead and Company in New York.

The story was adapted for television in 1990 by London Weekend Television in England, and was shown on the Public Broadcasting Service in the United States.

CHARACTERS
GERTIE, Captain Arthur HASTINGS, Inspector JAPP, Mr. LAVINGTON, Hercule Poirot

PLOT SYNOPSIS
The story concerns a plea for help to Hercule Poirot from a jewel thief named Gertie who is masquerading as Lady Millicent. The young woman claims that her impending marriage to a nobleman is in jeopardy because of a letter written to a former lover. She

A woman being blackmailed (Frances Barber) pleads for help from Hercule Poirot (David Suchet) and Captain Hastings (Hugh Fraser) in "The Veiled Lady." (Photo courtesy of London Weekend Television)

claims that a man named Lavington has the letter and is blackmailing her, and she asks Poirot to retrieve the letter. When he chivalrously agrees to do so, he learns that Lady Millicent has more than the letter to hide.

Venables, Mr.   A former world traveler and man of action in THE PALE HORSE, he has polio and is confined to a wheelchair. His confinement fails to mask his essentially dangerous nature, and Mark EASTERBROOK views him as still "predatory—destructive."

Ventnor, Mr.   See SHAW, MR.

Vera   Una Drake's twin sister in "THE UNBREAKABLE ALIBI," she makes Una's bet possible by having dinner in one city while Una is seen in another.

Vereker, Nell   A thin child with scraggly fair hair when she first meets Vernon in GIANT'S BREAD, she is no fun as a playmate because she dresses in frills. Later, she is a sweet and lovely young woman who

desires a wealthy husband and a comfortable life, yet she impulsively marries an impoverished soldier.

Veroneau, Inez   See ROSSAKOFF, COUNTESS VERA.

Verrall, Detective Inspector Joe   Really a member of the Patterson gang in "MR. EASTWOOD'S ADVENTURE," he impersonates a police detective to gain access to Mr. EASTWOOD's home and his valuable antique enamel miniatures.

Verrier, Monsieur   A brief visitor to the archaeological dig in MURDER IN MESOPOTAMIA, he is a French archaeologist whose visit to Dr. LEIDNER occurs right after Mrs. LEIDNER dies. After offering hasty and profuse condolences, he leaves the dig.

Vicar, The (1)   A forgetful man in THE MIRROR CRACK'D FROM SIDE TO SIDE, he assumes duties at the church in ST. MARY MEAD after Leonard CLEMENT dies. He attends the reception at Gossington Hall, and hears Heather BADCOCK admit that she suffered from German measles when she met actress Marina GREGG years before.

Vicar, The (2) By telling Tuppence BERESFORD to search for Lily Waters's tombstone in the churchyard in BY THE PRICKING OF MY THUMBS, he places the detective into grave danger.

Victor, King A world-famous, Paris-based jewel thief in THE SECRET OF CHIMNEYS known variously as Monsieur Chelles, Captain O'Neill, Prince Nicholas and Monsieur LEMOINE. He is exposed when he assumes the identity of Prince Nicholas to obtain money from American businessmen in exchange for oil concessions. He also poses as police inspector Monsieur Lemoine of the Sûreté and a traveling silk salesman named Monsieur Chelles.

Vinegar, Mrs. The sympathetic Carristown postmistress in NEMESIS, she fails to recognize that Miss MARPLE's act of being as "scatty as they make them, poor old creature" was a clever ruse to obtain information. The elderly detective gives this name to the "middle-aged woman with a rather vinegar face," and uses subterfuge to learn the destination of a package of used clothing that is mailed at the Carristown post office.

Viner, Amelia An elderly woman in THE MYSTERY OF THE BLUE TRAIN, she provides Hercule POIROT with an important newspaper clipping containing details of a jewel robbery years before. She claims that her long life is due to a daily slice of brown bread and "taking a little stimulant with her meals."

Vitelli, Signor The Italian representative to the international conference on student unrest in PASSENGER TO FRANKFURT, he views student riots as an intensification of a natural phenomenon, but one complicated by high-level political corruption.

Vladiroffsky, Prince An accomplished linguist, he is also a master of disguise in "THE MAN WHO WAS NO. 16" who can pass for more than half a dozen nationalities and either gender. Posing as the prince, he kidnaps Tuppence BERESFORD, then assumes the role of Mrs. Cortland VAN SNYDER, and pretends to have been drugged and terrorized by Russian agents.

"Voice in the Dark, The" Mystery short story.

The plot centers on a shipwreck tragedy years before that seems to be the cause of mysterious voices heard in the night.

PUBLISHING AND DRAMATIZATION HISTORY

The story appeared in the short story collection, THE MYSTERIOUS MR. QUIN, published in 1930 by William Collins Sons and Company, Ltd., in London, and by Dodd, Mead and Company in New York.

The story has not been adapted for stage or screen.

CHARACTERS

Mrs. CASSON, Alice CLAYTON, Margery GALE, Marcia KEANE, Mrs. LLOYD, Mr. Harley QUIN, Mr. SATTERTHWAITE, Lady Barbara STRANLEIGH, Roley VAVASOUR

PLOT SYNOPSIS

The story concerns the appeal made to Mr. SATTERTHWAITE by Lady STRANLEIGH to investigate a threatening voice heard every night at the family estate. Lady Stranleigh and her family at first view the voice as a hoax, but they take the voice more seriously after a box of poisoned chocolates arrives. The family arranges a seance, and the medium channels the voice of Lady Stranleigh's sister, who died many years before in a shipwreck survived by Lady Stranleigh and her maid Alice. Mr. Satterthwaite resurrects memories which right an old wrong and end the voice in the night.

Vole, Leonard Financial manager, friend and, eventually, heir to the fortune of the elderly Emily FRENCH, he is a much younger man in "WITNESS FOR THE PROSECUTION" who is later charged with her murder. He claims to be innocent, but his mistress, who uses the name of Romaine VOLE, refuses to testify that he was with her on the evening of the murder. Under cross-examination, she changes her testimony, and he is acquitted.

Vole, Romaine A former Viennese actress named Romaine Heilger who still has a husband living in an Austrian mental institute, she is the mistress of Leonard VOLE, whose last name she uses in "WITNESS

FOR THE PROSECUTION." At first, she provides damning evidence against him; then she disguises herself as Mrs. Mogson and offers Leonard's lawyer vital information that should clear him.

Von Deinim, Carl   A British Intelligence agent who assumes the identity of a German refugee chemist in N OR M?, he pretends to continue the man's work, but is arrested as a spy after documents detailing sabotage schemes are found in his possession.

Von Waldsausen, The Grafin Charlotte   A nauseatingly obese woman in PASSENGER TO FRANKFURT, also known as Charlotte Krapp and Big Charlotte, she is "a whale of a woman. . . . A great, big, cheesy-looking woman, wallowing in fat." She is also exceedingly wealthy, and provides the financial support to the Youth Movement from which she derives a sense of power.

Vyse, Mr.   A member of actress Rosina NUNN's entourage in THE WORLD'S END, he is a stage producer who once planned to produce Alec GERARD's play but changed his mind after the playwright was convicted of stealing a prize opal from the actress.

Vyse, Charles   A stiff-backed, poker-faced attorney in PERIL AT END HOUSE, he is a cousin to Nick BUCKLEY and a member of the firm of Vyse, Trevannion and Wynnard.

W

Wade, Gerald (Gerry) A seemingly insignificant young man, he works in the Foreign Office in THE SEVEN DIALS MYSTERY and is also known as Number One. He is murdered on the night that his friends hide a large number of alarm clocks in his room as a prank.

Wade, Iris Estranged from Reginald WADE, her husband in "THE CASE OF THE DISCONTENTED HUSBAND," she agrees to wait six months before remarrying. Once Mr. PARKER PYNE begins to guide her husband, she becomes jealous when another woman enters his life.

Wade, Loraine Gerald WADE's stepsister in THE SEVEN DIALS MYSTERY, she has dark blue eyes and a seemingly innocent manner.

Wade, Reginald An inarticulate man in "THE CASE OF THE DISCONTENTED HUSBAND" who finds emotional expression impossible, he retains Mr. PARKER PYNE to keep his wife from leaving him for another man.

Wagstaffe, Inspector A police inspector in "THE APPLES OF THE HESPERIDES" who claims to "speak a bit of the Italiano, you know," he consults with Hercule POIROT regarding the Borgia goblet theft.

Wainwright, Derek A good-looking, witty man in "IN A GLASS DARKLY," he is the friend to whom Sylvia CARSLAKE runs for comfort when her fiancé's jealousy drives her away.

Waite, Josephine (Joe) An independent young girl in GIANT'S BREAD whose mother abandons her emotionally, she runs away with a married sculptor.

Wake, Alfred The elderly vicar of Wychwood in MURDER IS EASY, he is a good source of facts and gossip regarding Wychwood residents both living and dead.

Wales, Emma An important witness who overheard the argument between Lady TRESSILIAN and Nevile STRANGE on the night of the murder in TOWARDS ZERO, she is the housemaid, a "tall thin bit of vinegar" interviewed by Inspector BATTLE.

Wallace, Bella and Rube Friends of Mary MONTRESOR in "THE GOLDEN BALL," they play a gangster and moll who seem to place her in danger from which she must be rescued.

Walters, Esther Former secretary to Mr. RAFAIEL, she appears in both A CARIBBEAN MYSTERY and NEMESIS. In the first novel, she falls in love with the unscrupulous and married Tim KENDALL, and resents Miss MARPLE for interfering. In the second book, she marries Edmund Anderson, and lives "a presumably happy life."

Wanstead, Professor A confidential adviser to the Home Office in NEMESIS, he is a fellow traveler with Miss MARPLE on the tour of famous houses and gardens of Great Britain. He is assigned by Jason RAFIEL to protect Miss MARPLE on the tour, and he also believes that Michael RAFIEL is innocent of murder.

Warburton, Captain Jim Armed with a false military title, he is a representative of the Masterton interests in DEAD MAN'S FOLLY, and has never served in the military.

Wargrave, Alfred James An expert in the cultivation of roses in SAD CYPRESS, he invalidates Jessie

HOPKINS' claim that she had pricked herself on a rose thorn when he testifies that the roses grown around Hunterbury Hall are thorn-free.

Wargrave, Mr. Justice Lawrence John Known variously as "Ulick Norman Owen" and "Una Nancy Owen," both shortened to U.N. Owen or "unknown," he has built a judicial reputation in AND THEN THERE WERE NONE on being "a hanging judge." He employs an agent to purchase Indian Island and to ready the house for the party.

Waring, Harold An ambitious, if naïve, undersecretary to the Prime Minister in "THE STYMPHALEAN BIRDS," his act of chivalry while on vacation in Herzoslovakia turns into a charge of manslaughter. His political future only survives due to the intervention of Hercule POIROT.

Warren, Dr. A reluctant member of the party gathered to break into Captain TREVELYAN's home when foul play is suspected in THE SITTAFORD MYSTERY, he is the village physician and establishes the time and cause of Trevelyan's death.

Warren, Angela The half-sister of convicted murderer Caroline CRALE in FIVE LITTLE PIGS, she provides Hercule POIROT with an important clue in solving the sixteen-year-old mystery when she recounts her practical joke of putting the evil-smelling herb, valerian, into her late brother-in-law's beer years before.

Warrender, Jeremy A young, carefree visitor in SPIDER'S WEB, he is the private secretary to stamp collector Sir Lazarus Stern.

Warwick, Mrs. A tall, commanding woman with a strong personality in THE UNEXPECTED GUEST, she recognizes that her embittered, invalid son has made life unbearable for his family.

Warwick, Jan The mentally disturbed, young half-brother of the murder victim in THE UNEXPECTED GUEST, he desperately fears being institutionalized by his brother.

Warwick, Laura The attractive, blonde, thirty-year-old wife of cruel, wheelchair-bound Richard WARWICK in THE UNEXPECTED GUEST, she has an affair with a Liberal candidate for Parliament, and later stands accused of her husband's murder.

Warwick, Richard The murder victim in THE UNEXPECTED GUEST, he is a sadistic former big-game hunter, later confined to a wheelchair, who drinks too much and who owns an extensive collection of pistols, air guns and rifles.

"Wasps' Nest" Mystery short story.
The plot centers on the efforts of Hercule POIROT to prevent a murder.

PUBLISHING AND DRAMATIZATION HISTORY
The story appeared in the short story collection, DOUBLE SIN AND OTHER STORIES, published in 1961 by Dodd, Mead and Company in New York.

The story was adapted for television in 1991 by London Weekend Television in England, and was shown on the Public Broadcasting Service in the United States.

CHARACTERS
Molly DEANE, John HARRISON, Claude LANGTON, Hercule Poirot

PLOT SYNOPSIS
The story concerns the love of two men for the same woman, and the ingenious manner in which one man hopes to triumph. Claude Langton had been engaged to Molly Deane until a quarrel separated them, driving Molly into the arms of John Harrison. Hercule Poirot soon notes, as does John, that the old feelings between Molly and Claude remain strong, and they appear ready to reconcile. When Poirot learns that one of the men has bought cyanide of potassium on the pretext of intending to destroy a wasps' nest, he warns the one he believes to be the intended victim. Despite the surprising twist to the plot, Poirot manages to prevent the murder.

CRIME NOTES
The intended murder in this story is unusual in that one character expects to commit suicide by ingesting cyanide of potassium, but he will allow another character to be erroneously arrested and hanged for murder.

Waterhouse, Edith A stiff-backed, middle-aged woman in THE CLOCKS who bullies her brother, James WATERHOUSE, she is "intolerant of nonsense in others."

Waterhouse, James A man in THE CLOCKS whose face continuously wears a look of apology, he lives with his sister in the neighborhood where the first murder occurs.

Waverly, Ada The mother of the kidnapped child in "THE ADVENTURE OF JOHNNIE WAVERLY," she finds that her love for her son competes with her love of money when a ransom is demanded.

Waverly, Johnnie A child of unidentified age who's kidnapped in "THE ADVENTURE OF JOHNNIE WAVERLY."

Waverly, Marcus The father of the kidnapped child in "THE ADVENTURE OF JOHNNIE WAVERLY," he provides Hercule POIROT with the odd information that he had received ransom notes before the kidnapping.

Waynflete, Honoria The librarian and museum caretaker of Wych Hall in MURDER IS EASY, she aids Luke FITZWILLIAM as he investigates the Wychwood.

Weardale, Sir Harry A guest at Lord ALLOWAY's home in "THE SUBMARINE PLANS," he is an admiral and the First Sea Lord, and is present on the night that the submarine plans are stolen.

Weardale, Lady Juliet Married to Sir Harry WEARDALE and the mother of Leonard WEARDALE in "THE SUBMARINE PLANS," she secretly believes that her son has stolen the plans.

Weardale, Leonard The rather "effeminate-looking young man" who is suspected of stealing classified documents in "THE SUBMARINE PLANS," he is the son of Sir Harry and Lady Juliet WEARDALE.

Weatherby, Pauline The younger sister of Iris RUSSELL, who died four years earlier of potassium cyanide poisoning in "YELLOW IRIS," she is present at the memorial dinner hosted by her brother-in-law and guardian, Barton RUSSELL. Halfway through dinner, she collapses as her sister did, and cyanide is found in another guest's pocket.

Webb, Bella An attractive woman in THE PALE HORSE who has "a queer, formless face," she works as the cook at an inn named The Pale Horse, and is thought to be a witch. When a seance is held at the inn, another participant is repulsed by the feel of her hand, which is "cold and boneless—it felt like a slug."

Webb, Sheila Rosemary She is a secretary sent by the Cavendish Secretarial and Typing Bureau to the home of blind former schoolteacher Miss Millicent PEBMARSH in THE CLOCKS. She is unaware that Miss Pebmarsh is her natural mother, for she was adopted years before by Mrs. LAWTON, who is also her aunt. After discovering a murdered man, she rushes out of the house and into the arms of the investigating inspector, Colin LAMB, whom she later marries.

Weekes, Miss She is the dull and uninspiring governess in THE BURDEN.

"Weeping Lady with the Silver Ewer" See GLEN, ASPASIA; CHARNLEY, LADY ALIX.

Welman, Laura Poisoned by morphine in SAD CYPRESS, she is the widow of Henry Welman and the aunt of Elinor CARLISLE and Roderick WELMAN. Once the mistress of Sir Lewis RYCROFT, she is also the highly devoted mother of Mary GERRARD.

Welman, Roderick (Roddy) A suspect in the murder of Elinor CARLISLE, who makes him the sole beneficiary of her will in SAD CYPRESS, he breaks their engagement when he falls in love with Mary GERRARD. A romantic young man, he refers to Mary as "Atalanta" and to Elinor as "la Princesse Lontaine."

Welsh, Joe A farmhand in "THE CASE OF THE RICH WOMAN," he falls in love with Hannah MOORHOUSE, who conceals her true identity, the wealthy widow Amelia RYMER.

Welwyn, David A fanatically clean young man in "THE THEFT OF THE ROYAL RUBY," he is invited to

Kings Lacey as a dinner partner for one of the guests, but really loves Sarah LACEY.

Wendover, Mr. See PROTHERO, WALTER.

West, Sir Alington A famous Harley Street psychiatrist in "THE RED SIGNAL," he argues with his nephew, Dermot WEST, and is found shot through the heart five minutes later.

West, Basil A young man with a disarming smile in DEATH ON THE NILE (1) who serves as the private secretary to Sir George GRAYLE, he is the only person who does not anger Lady Ariadne GRAYLE.

West, Bessie A large, overweight girl in UNFINISHED PORTRAIT, she nearly convinces CELIA to become a hospital nurse.

West, Chloe Elizabeth An actress with a well-articulated voice in SPARKLING CYANIDE, she is hired by George BARTON to impersonate his dead wife, Rosemary, at the memorial dinner.

West, David An employee with British Railways who provides schedules for trains which Mrs. McGILLICUDDY might have seen in THE 4.50 FROM PADDINGTON, he is Miss MARPLE's grandnephew and the second son of Joan and Raymond WEST.

West, Dermot The nephew of famed Harley Street psychiatrist Sir Alington WEST and an admirer of Claire TRENT in "THE RED SIGNAL," he possesses a sixth sense in the form of "the Red Signal," which warns him of impending danger. While attending a seance at the Trent home, he experiences that warning, and later finds himself framed for his uncle's murder.

West, Gillian A very beautiful young woman in "THE FACE OF HELEN," she suffers a history of tragedies caused by her beauty.

West, Joan Married to Miss MARPLE's nephew, Raymond WEST, and the mother of two sons, she appears in the short story collection, THE THIRTEEN PROBLEMS, as well as "MISS MARPLE TELLS A STORY," "GREENSHAW'S FOLLY" and SLEEPING MURDER. When originally created as a member of the Tuesday Night Club, her name was Joyce Lempriere, but the author changed the name in her next appearance. She is the mother of two sons, the aunt of Louise OXLEY and the cousin of Giles REED.

West, Magda See LEONIDES, MAGDA.

West, Maureen An unkempt-looking woman in THE CLOCKS whose hair "suggested she'd been out in a blizzard lately," she is an employee of the Cavendish Secretarial and Typing Bureau, and views her boss Katherine MARTINDALE with contempt.

West, Norma See RESTARICK, NORMA.

West, Raymond The nephew of Miss MARPLE and a celebrated novelist and poet, he assumes a background role in the novels MURDER AT THE VICARAGE and SLEEPING MURDER, the short story collection, THE THIRTEEN PROBLEMS, and the short stories, "MISS MARPLE TELLS A STORY" and "GREENSHAW'S FOLLY." Fond of his Aunt Jane, he provides her with special treats whenever possible, the most welcome being a week at her favorite hotel in AT BERTRAM'S HOTEL. He is married to Joan WEST and has two sons.

Westchester, Bishop of A friend of Miss MARPLE's since he was a child, he is the "handsome and well-gaitered" clergyman in AT BERTRAM'S HOTEL who still greets her as "Aunt Jane."

Westhaven, Sister A tall, thin woman with "a look of permanent disapproval," she is a nurse in GIANT'S BREAD.

Westholme, Lady A Member of Parliament in APPOINTMENT WITH DEATH, she is a loud, domineering American woman married to an English country squire. Despite her political popularity and the expectation that she would be appointed as an undersecretary when her party resumed power, she is a very much disliked woman.

Westmacott, Mary The pseudonym adopted by Agatha Christie and under which she published her six romantic novels: GIANT'S BREAD, UNFINISHED PORTRAIT, ABSENT IN THE SPRING, THE ROSE AND THE YEW TREE, A DAUGHTER'S A DAUGHTER and THE

BURDEN. Hidden behind the pen name, the author revealed her values, her outlook on politics, religion and people, and other aspects of life which her real identity would not permit. She told none of her friends about the pseudonym, and became enraged when her secret was made public in 1946. Christie had worked hard to preserve her secret, even to the point of making her contracts for the Mary Westmacott novels under the additional pseudonym of Daniel West.

Weston, Colonel   Head of the investigation into the death of Arlena MARSHALL in EVIL UNDER THE SUN, he is the Chief Constable whose methodical and unimaginative procedures provide a contrast to the brilliant detecting of Hercule POIROT. The two men also work together in PERIL AT END HOUSE.

Wetherby, Miss   The postmistress of ST. MARY MEAD, she is highly outraged when Emily and Lavinia SKINNER provide the dismissed maid, Gladys HOLMES, with a reference but fail to mention her honesty in "THE CASE OF THE PERFECT MAID."

Wetherby, Mr.   A man in MRS. McGINTY'S DEAD who views his stepdaughter with "cold dislike," he is dependent upon her generosity because she controls the family money through her inheritance.

Wetherby, Mrs.   A former employer of Mrs. McGINTY in MRS. McGINTY'S DEAD, she is the invalid mother of Deidre HENDERSON, and has a distinct fear of open windows.

Wetherby, Caroline   Described by the vicar of ST. MARY MEAD as being "a mixture of vinegar and gush," she is one of the old village gossips in MURDER AT THE VICARAGE and THE BODY IN THE LIBRARY, and she lives two doors from Miss MARPLE.

Weyman, Michael   An old friend and admirer of Sally LEGGE, with whom he later runs away, he is hired by Sir George STUBBS as the architect to design a new tennis pavilion in DEAD MAN'S FOLLY.

Whalley, Jonathan   Fearful of the Big Four, he informed John INGLES that the gang was pursuing him, but he is murdered before Hercule POIROT can begin the investigation in THE BIG FOUR.

Wharton, Colonel   A member of British Intelligence in DESTINATION UNKNOWN who appears to be on the edge of a breakdown, he speaks "with a kind of machine-gun abruptness," and paces furiously, while calling out ideas in a disjointed manner.

What Mrs. McGillicuddy Saw   See 4.50 FROM PADDINGTON.

Wheeling, Emma   A good samaritan in AT BERTRAM'S HOTEL who, with her husband, finds the unconscious Canon PENNYFEATHER alongside the road. She feeds him broth and nurses him until he is well enough to function on his own.

"Where There's a Will"   Mystery short story.

The plot centers on a wealthy semi-invalid who receives messages from her dead husband through her radio.

PUBLISHING AND DRAMATIZATION HISTORY

The story appeared in the short story collection THE HOUND OF DEATH AND OTHER STORIES, published in 1933 by William Collins Sons and Company, Ltd., in London.

The story was adapted for television in 1993 by London Weekend Television in England, and was shown on the Public Broadcasting Service in the United States.

CHARACTERS

ELIZABETH, Mrs. Mary HARTER, Mr. HOPKINSON, Dr. MEYNELL, Charles RIDGEWAY

PLOT SYNOPSIS

The story concerns a trick of fate in which a greedy man finds that his evil plan provides him with no benefit. Charles Ridgeway is made heir to his wealthy aunt's fortune in a will replacing an earlier will leaving her money to a niece, but he is impatient to receive his legacy. When he learns that Mrs. Harter has a weak heart and has been warned against sudden shocks, he decides to hasten her death by broadcasting through her radio his impersonation of her late husband's voice, telling her that she will join him soon. The plan works, and Mrs. Harter dies of shock. As she falls dead to the ground, the only copy of the will naming Charles as heir falls into the fireplace and burns. Thus, Charles is punished, for the old will stands.

CRIME NOTES
The murder in this story is the result of an elderly woman being frightened into a fatal heart attack.

Whistler, Dr. James A police surgeon in DEATH IN THE CLOUDS, he examines the body of Madame GISELLE and determines that the murder occurred one hour previously. He is unable to identify the poison used to kill her.

White, Janet A teacher at The Elm School in HALLOWE'EN PARTY, she is strangled while returning home from school. She had received threats from a former boyfriend, but no one knew his name.

Whitfield, Dr. A valuable source of information to Hercule POIROT in PERIL AT END HOUSE, he is an attorney who reveals the provisions of the wills of both Sir Matthew SETON and Captain Michael SETON.

Whitstable, Dame Laura The sixty-four-year-old psychologist and radio personality is a friend of Ann PRENTICE and godmother to Sarah PRENTICE in A DAUGHTER'S A DAUGHTER. Brusque and authoritative, she hesitates to give advice to friends, but helps them discreetly.

Whittaker, Elizabeth One of the organizers of the Halloween party at which Joyce REYNOLDS is murdered in HALLOWE'EN PARTY, she is a humorless woman who teaches at The Elms, the school where the party occurred.

Whittington, Edward Viewed by Julius HERSHEIMER as "the skunk, with his big sleek fat face" in THE SECRET ADVERSARY, he is a Bolshevist agent implicated in the Draft Treaty case.

Why Didn't They Ask Evans? Mystery novel.
The novel features two young and enthusiastic detectives, Bobby JONES and Lady Frances DERWENT, who might have been successors to the Beresfords had the author chosen to develop them. The plot concerns the efforts to locate the murderer of a man pushed off a cliff, whose dying words are "Why didn't they ask Evans?"

PUBLISHING AND DRAMATIZATION HISTORY
The novel was published in 1934 by William Collins Sons and Company, Ltd., in London, and, under the title, *The Boomerang Clue*, by Dodd, Mead and Company in New York.

The novel was adapted for television in 1981 by London Weekend Television in England, and was also shown on the Public Broadcasting Service in the U.S.

CHARACTERS
Dr. George ARBUTHNOT, Thomas ASKEW, Henry BASSINGTON-FFRENCH, Roger BASSINGTON-FFRENCH, Sylvia BASSINGTON-FFRENCH, Tommy BASSINGTON-FFRENCH, Badger BEADON, Alan CARSTAIRS, Amelia CAYMAN, Leo CAYMAN, Lady Frances (Frankie) Derwent, Robert (Bobby) Jones, Reverend Thomas JONES, Lord MARCHINGTON, Dr. Jasper NICHOLSON, Moira NICHOLSON, Rose Chudleigh PRATT, Mrs. RIVINGTON, Gladys Evans ROBERTS, John SAVAGE, Frederick SPRAGGE, Dr. THOMAS, Inspector WILLIAMS

PLOT SYNOPSIS
Chapters 1–5
Bobby Jones and Dr. Thomas are playing golf when they discover the body of a man at the base of a cliff. The man utters "Why didn't they ask Evans?" before dying. Desperate to keep an appointment, Bobby asks a passerby, Roger Bassington-ffrench, to stay with the body. Days later, he meets childhood friend Frankie Derwent, who shows him an article about the dead man that contains a photograph of his sister, Amelia Cayman. An inquest is held, and the dead man is identified as Alex Pritchard. Bobby and Dr. Thomas give testimony. The jury's verdict is death by misadventure. After the inquest, the dead man's sister and brother-in-law ask if he said anything before dying, but Bobby momentarily forgets. He writes to them with the final words.

Chapters 6–11
Bobby turns down a lucrative job offer in South America, and goes to work with his old friend Badger Beadon in an automotive shop. A few days after

the inquest, Bobby is hospitalized after someone drugs his beer with morphine. While in the hospital, he remembers the picture that he had found in the dead man's pocket and tells Frankie that it is not the same as the sister's photograph in the newspaper. Frankie decides to infiltrate the Bassington-ffrench residence to learn more, so she buys an old car from Beadon, and crashes it outside their home. Her close friend and physician, Dr. Arbuthnot, is conveniently nearby, and he proclaims that she has a concussion and must rest quietly for a day or two at the Bassington-ffrench home.

Chapters 12–16
Frankie learns as much as she can about the Bassington-ffrench family and has the opportunity to meet Dr. Nicholson, who runs a drug treatment center and drives a blue Talbot, the type of car seen in the area when Bobby was poisoned. Staying nearby, Bobby visits the treatment center and meets the young woman whose picture was in the dead man's pocket. He poses as Frankie's chauffeur and drives Frankie home from the Bassington-ffrench house.

Chapters 17–22
From Frankie's investigation, and through information gained in talking with the Rivingtons, the sleuths learn that the dead man is Alan Carstairs, a big-game hunter and explorer from Canada. He had Moira Nicholson's picture in his pocket, and Roger Bassington-ffrench says that he removed it to spare her embarrassment. Moira tells the pair that she is afraid of Nicholson, and believes that he wants to kill her.

Chapters 23–27
Frankie visits Dr. Nicholson to invite Moira to stay with her, but she is told that Moira has gone to London. Her husband claims not to know where she is staying. Frankie then tries to track down the Caymens, and finds that they have moved and left no forwarding address. Her final mission is to learn more about John Savage, a man whom Sylvia Bassington-ffrench has mentioned in connection with Alan Carstairs, and who supposedly committed suicide when he learned that he had cancer. Frankie speaks with her father's lawyer for advice in locating Savage's will, and she is told that there was speculation that Savage had been impersonated. Bobby is hit on the head and knocked out when he returns to The

Grange to find Moira, while Frankie is rendered unconscious with chloroform when she follows directions in a letter signed with Bobby's name.

Chapters 28–35
Bobby and Frankie are tied up by an impostor pretending to be Nicholson, but they do not have to wait long before Badger Beadon arrives to rescue them. Together, he and Bobby jump their captor and rescue Moira, who has been drugged with morphine and opium. Bobby and Frankie question members of John Savage's staff, and learn that the parlourmaid, Gladys Evans, was in the house when the will was made, yet the gardener was called in to witness it. Evans is also the person who found Savage dead. They learn that she is now Mrs. Gladys Roberts, and works at the vicarage in Marchbolt where Bobby's father is the vicar. The two sleuths speak with Evans, uncover the identity of the murderer, and also learn that he had help. After working through the puzzle of explanations, Bobby takes a job to manage a coffee plantation in Kenya. Frankie will marry him and join him there.

CRIME NOTES
The novel contains two murders. The first victim dies when he is pushed over a cliff, while the second is shot to death and labeled a suicide.

Wickham, Claude A composer in "HARLEQUIN'S LANE" who is commissioned by a patron of the arts, Lady ROSCHEIMER, to write the music for her recent project, an amateur Harlequinade.

Widburn, Mrs. Hostess of a dinner party in LORD EDGWARE DIES, she is a friend of Jane WILKERSON. It is at her party that Jane confuses Paris, France, with the Trojan prince, Paris.

Wilbraham, Dr. Big, florid and genial, he is an overworked Army doctor in GIANT'S BREAD.

Wilbraham, Major Charlie Bored with the tameness of life in England after years spent in service in East Africa, he contacts Mr. PARKER PYNE to provide him with adventure in "THE CASE OF THE DISCONTENTED SOLDIER." Through his adventure, he rescues the lovely Freda CLEGG, and dazzles her with his courage.

Wilding, Sir Richard A world traveler, adventurer and author of numerous books, he lives on an island for most of the year in THE BURDEN. Unworldly in regard to women, he is cuckolded by his first wife, and fails in his attempt to provide love and security to his second wife.

Wilkinson, Jane A talented American actress in LORD EDGWARE DIES, she seeks Hercule POIROT's help in divorcing her husband and marrying her "dreamy monk," the Duke of Merton.

Willard, Sir Guy The twenty-two-year-old son of Sir John WILLARD, he is an impulsive young man who joins the archaeological excavation at Men-her-Ra soon after graduation from Oxford in "THE ADVENTURE OF THE EGYPTIAN TOMB." He replaces his father as head of the dig when Sir John dies.

Willard, Sir John A knowledgeable Egyptologist in "THE ADVENTURE OF THE EGYPTIAN TOMB," he oversees the archaeological excavation at Men-her-Ra until his sudden death from heart failure.

Willett, Mrs. Part of a mother-and-daughter team hosting seances in THE SITTAFORD MYSTERY, she is a coarse woman whom Mr. RYCROFT views as "Colonial, of course. No real poise." Inspector NARRACOTT recognizes that she is "an exceedingly clever woman," an observation which is particularly appropriate. After her landlord, Captain TREVELYAN, dies, she travels under the name of Mrs. Johnson.

Willett, Violet A carelessly groomed young woman in THE SITTAFORD MYSTERY, she joins her mother in hosting a seance at Sittaford House at which the murder of Captain TREVELYAN is announced. She uses the name "Miss Johnson" when she books passage from Melbourne to London.

Williams, Constable A young police officer in TOWARDS ZERO who is a part of the investigation into the murder of Lady TRESSILIAN, he finds the bundle of bloody clothes in Nevile STRANGE's closet.

Williams, Inspector A longtime acquaintance of Lady Frances DERWENT in WHY DIDN'T THEY ASK EVANS?, he tells her that only one photograph was found with the body discovered by Bobby JONES.

Williams, Cecilia An elderly, poverty-stricken woman in FIVE LITTLE PIGS, she had lived in the Crale residence when Amyas CRALE was murdered sixteen years before. The "thin, frail and indomitable" woman had seen Caroline CRALE wipe fingerprints off a beer bottle, but she did report that fact at the time because she believed that the murder was justified.

Williams, Maude A woman in her mid-thirties in MRS. McGINTY'S DEAD, she has "determinedly golden hair" and a "full buxom figure that Poirot approved." To aid Hercule POIROT in the murder investigation, she takes a job at the home of the Wetherbys and visits Laura UPWARD on the night that Laura is murdered.

Williamson, Flight Lieutenant One of twelve members of the tour going from Damascus to Baghdad in "THE GATE OF BAGHDAD," he is an Air Force officer who overhears Captain SMETHURST, later murdered, speaking with someone in the dark.

Williamson, Ted A rough, uneducated garage mechanic in "THE ARCADIAN DEER," he approaches Hercule POIROT and asks for assistance in locating his lost love, the maid "Nita."

Willoughby, Dr. A physician in ELEPHANTS CAN REMEMBER whom Hercule POIROT consults in regard to Dolly JARROW.

Wills, Muriel A clever, observant woman in THREE-ACT TRAGEDY whose "rabbit-faced" appearance masks a shrewd and merciless mind which reveals itself in successful and witty plays written under the pseudonym of Anthony ASTOR. She is present when the Reverend BABBINGTON and Sir Bartholomew STRANGE are murdered. She is one of only two people who see through the disguise of Sir Charles CARTWRIGHT.

Wilmott, Ambassador Randolph When his bag is mistakenly exchanged with that of an American senator's in "THE AMBASSADOR'S BOOTS," the U.S. ambassador to the Court of St. James contacts Tommy and Tuppence BERESFORD for assistance.

Wilson, Detective Sergeant Investigator of the murder of Madame GISELLE in DEATH IN THE CLOUDS, he finds behind Hercule POIROT's seat the blowgun used to kill her. His evidence leads to an inquest in which a verdict of willful murder is placed against Poirot, but the coroner dismisses the charge.

Wilson, Ellen The housekeeper at End House, she ignores much of what goes on around her in PERIL AT END HOUSE. She and her husband witness the will of Nick BUCKLEY.

Wilson, Gilmour An American chess player in THE BIG FOUR, he suffers death by electrocution.

Wilson, John A middle-aged, burly Englishman who suffers from a heart condition in "THE CHOCOLATE BOX," he is a close friend of Paul DEROULARD. His heart medicine, trinitrine, is used to murder Deroulard.

Wimbourne, Mr. The Crackenthorpe family lawyer in 4.50 FROM PADDINGTON, he provides valuable information in the investigation.

Winburn, Mr. The grandfather of Geoffrey LANCASTER in "THE LAMP," he hears two sets of footsteps leaving the house after Geoffrey dies.

Windlesham, Mr. Charles The first fiancé of heiress Linnet Ridgeway DOYLE in DEATH ON THE NILE (2), he is jilted by her in favor of Simon DOYLE.

Windyford, Dick An extremely proud man in "PHILOMEL COTTAGE," he is reluctant to propose to the woman he loves when she inherits a small fortune. Later, he responds to her desperate call for help to save her from being murdered by her husband.

Winnie A nursemaid in GIANT'S BREAD, she is sent away after having an affair with her master.

Winterspoon, Henry A chief government analyst and an authority on rare poisons in DEATH IN THE CLOUDS, he analyzes the toxin which kills Madame GISELLE. His dreamy expression and benign attitude hide a highly competent man who identifies the poison as the venom of the boomslang, or tree snake.

Wireless See WHERE THERE'S A WILL.

Withers, Jessie Fired by Mr. WAVERLY after the discovery of a series of prekidnapping ransom notes in "THE ADVENTURE OF JOHNNIE WAVERLY," she is the child's nurse.

"Witness for the Prosecution" Mystery short story.

The plot centers on the murder of a wealthy elderly woman, and the refusal of a woman to corroborate her husband's alibi for the night of the murder.

PUBLISHING AND DRAMATIZATION
HISTORY
The story appeared in the short story collection, THE HOUND OF DEATH AND OTHER STORIES, published in 1933 by William Collins Sons and Company, Ltd., in London.

The short story was first adapted for the stage in a greatly expanded form by Agatha Christie in 1953, and the first production opened that year in London. In 1957, United Artists produced the film version of the story, which was released in theaters and starred Charles Laughton, Marlene Dietrich, Tyrone Power and Elsa Lancaster. The play was adapted for television in England in 1982, and was also shown in the United States on the Hallmark Hall of Fame.

CHARACTERS
Emily FRENCH, George HARVEY, Romaine HEILGER, Janet MacKENZIE, Mr. MAYHERNE, Leonard VOLE

PLOT SYNOPSIS
The story concerns the murder of a wealthy old woman who had foolishly become infatuated with a man forty years her junior, to whom she had turned over control of her financial affairs. Leonard Vole claims to be innocent, and asserts that Romaine Heilger, his mistress, will prove that he returned home before the time the murder is said to have occurred. When Romaine is questioned, she exhibits vehement hatred of Vole, and states that he was not home at the time of the murder. She further implicates Vole by claiming that he came home late on the night of the murder with blood on his clothes. The testimony has a disastrous effect on Vole's case, but his attorney manages to obtain letters which

Tyrone Power and Charles Laughton confront each other in the courtroom in the 1957 United Artists motion picture *Witness for the Prosecution.* (Photo courtesy of The Museum of Modern Art, Film Stills Archive)

show that Romaine had a lover with whom she had planned to frame Vole. Leonard Vole is acquitted of the murder, but justice is not really served at the end of the play.

CRIME NOTES
The murder in this story is the result of a blow to the back of the head with a heavy object.

Witness for the Prosecution and Other Stories Mystery short story collection.

The book is made up of stories which had appeared in earlier short story collections published in England. The collection contains six stories from THE HOUND OF DEATH, three stories from THE LISTERDALE MYSTERY (1), and the early version of one story which appears in MURDER IN THE MEWS.

PUBLICATION AND DRAMATIZATION
HISTORY
Witness for the Prosecution and Other Stories was published intact only in the United States by Dodd, Mead and Company in New York in 1948.

Four of the stories have been adapted for stage or screen.

TITLES IN THE COLLECTION
Witness for the Prosecution contains the following short stories: "WITNESS FOR THE PROSECUTION," "THE RED SIGNAL," "THE FOURTH MAN," "S.O.S.," "WHERE THERE'S A WILL" (named "WIRELESS" in the original collection), "THE MYSTERY OF THE BLUE JAR," "PHILOMEL COTTAGE," "ACCIDENT" and "THE SECOND GONG" (an early version of "DEAD MAN'S MIRROR").

Wizell, Fred The Ravenscrofts' gardener in ELEPHANTS CAN REMEMBER.

Woddell, Agnes A maid in the Symmington house in THE MOVING FINGER, she is murdered before she can speak with someone about something that has disturbed her.

Wood, J. Baker A blustering and noisy American millionaire collector of miniatures in "DOUBLE SIN," he is supposed to purchase the Cosway miniatures, which disappear.

Woolley, Katherine The wife of the famed archaeologist Leonard WOOLLEY, she was a fan of the author's writing, and eagerly welcomed her to stay at the dig when Agatha Christie visited it in the fall of 1928. She is depicted as the difficult and demanding Mrs. LEIDNER, a character in the 1936 MURDER IN MESOPOTAMIA, yet she and her husband maintained a warm relationship with the author before her remarriage, and with the Mallowans in the years following.

Woolley, Sir Leonard Renowned British archaeologist in charge of the excavations at Ur, he invited Agatha Christie to stay at the site during her 1928 visit to the Middle East. The following year, the author returned to Ur, where she met Woolley's young assistant, Max MALLOWAN. Woolley's discoveries provided a vast amount of information about ancient Mesopotamia.

Woolmar, Janet A parlourmaid in CROOKED HOUSE, she gives little assistance in solving the crime.

"World's End, The"   Mystery short story.

The plot centers on the disappearance of a valuable opal, which threatens to destroy the lives of a young couple.

PUBLISHING AND DRAMATIZATION HISTORY

The story appeared in the short story collection, THE MYSTERIOUS MR. QUIN, published in 1930 by William Collins Sons and Company, Ltd., in London, and by Dodd, Mead and Company in New York.

This story has not been adapted for stage or screen.

CHARACTERS

Naomi CARLTON-SMITH, Alec GERARD, Henry JUDD, Duchess of LEITH, Rosina NUNN, Mr. Harley QUIN, Mr. SATTERTHWAITE, Mr. TOMLINSON, Mr. VYSE

PLOT SYNOPSIS

The story concerns the repercussions of a crime that never happened. While vacationing on the island of Corsica with the Duchess of Leith, Mr. Satterthwaite meets the duchess' niece, Naomi, who is despondent because the man she loves, Alec Gerard, was imprisoned a year earlier on the charge of stealing an opal from actress Rosina Nunn. Mr. Quin appears and delays Naomi's intended suicide, and later, unexpected events place them into the company of Rosina Nunn. While sharing shelter from a sudden snowstorm, Rosina takes out an Indian puzzle box which has a false bottom, of which she has been previously unaware. An Indian gentleman releases a hidden catch and the missing opal falls out, thus exonerating Alec Gerard and saving Naomi's life.

Wray, Barbara   A young wife in ABSENT IN THE SPRING, she married to escape her officious mother. Her affair with an army major nearly destroys her marriage.

Wray, William   He is a patient and loving husband in ABSENT IN THE SPRING who works to reconcile with his wife and to rebuild their marriage after scandal almost destroys it.

Wren, Christopher   An obnoxious young architecture student in "THREE BLIND MICE," his shrill laugh and prying comments disconcerted the other guests at Monkswell Manor and led them to dislike him violently.

Wright, Alfred   Director of the Northern Union Insurance Company in "THE TRAGEDY AT MARDSON MANOR," he asks Hercule POIROT to investigate the sudden death of a nearly bankrupt client.

Wright, Gerald   A young teacher in A POCKET FULL OF RYE who has leftist sympathies, he is more interested in his fiancée's money than in her.

Wu Ling   Chinese by birth, he travels to England with records of a lost mine in Burma, hoping to sell them in London in "THE LOST MINE." Before reaching his destination, he is murdered and the maps disappear.

Wyatt, Captain   A seemingly misanthropic former military officer in THE SITTAFORD MYSTERY, he is an invalid who lives with his native servant, Abdul, in a bungalow on the Sittaford estate. Determinedly unsociable and surly, he says he wants to see people only when it is convenient for him.

Wycherly, Nina   An acquaintance of Mr. PARKER PYNE, she gushes over his exploits in "PROBLEM AT POLLENSA BAY," exposing his identity.

Wye, Maud   She is a young woman in "THE HERB OF DEATH" whose fiancé cheats on her, with disastrous consequences.

Wylde, Martin   A man falsely accused of the murder of Lady BARNABY in "THE SIGN IN THE SKY," he is in love with the loyal but not-too-intelligent Sylvia DALE. He is saved by Mr. Harley QUIN and Mr. SATTERTHWAITE from hanging for the murder.

Wynwood, Professor   An expert in breaking codes in THE SECRET OF CHIMNEYS, he manages to decipher the code of the Revel-O'Neill letters before lunch, then lectures that "A banana and a water biscuit is [sic] all any sane and healthy man should need in the middle of the day."

Y

Yahmose A hen-pecked husband in DEATH COMES AS THE END, he is the eldest son of IMHOTEP, and is married to SATIPY. He dies when he is struck by an arrow.

Yardly, Lord An attractive, good-natured man who had served in the Boer War, he is in financial difficulty, and seeks to obtain much-needed cash in "THE ADVENTURE OF 'THE WESTERN STAR.' "

Yardly, Lady Maude The wife of the Tenth Viscount YARDLY in "THE ADVENTURE OF THE 'WESTERN STAR,' " she spent part of the World War I years in California, where she met Gregory ROLF, with whom she had an affair, and to whom she gave the Star of the East diamond.

"Yellow Iris" Mystery short story.

The plot centers on an anonymous summons that takes Hercule POIROT to a restaurant where five people are having a memorial dinner in honor of their friend, who died of poisoning four years earlier. The story was expanded into the 1945 novel SPARKLING CYANIDE.

PUBLISHING AND DRAMATIZATION HISTORY

The story appeared in the short story collection, THE REGATTA MYSTERY AND OTHER STORIES, published in 1939 by Dodd, Mead and Company in New York.

The short story was adapted for television in 1993 by London Weekend Television in England, and was shown on the Public Broadcasting Service in the United States.

CHARACTERS

Stephen CARTER, Tony CHAPPELL, Hercule Poirot, Barton RUSSELL, Lola VALDEZ, Pauline WEATHERBY

Peruvian dancer Lola Valdez (Yolanda Vasquez) insists on dancing with Hercule Poirot, whom she later calls "the cat's whiskers" in "Yellow Iris." (Photo courtesy of London Weekend Television)

PLOT SYNOPSIS

The story concerns Hercule Poirot's attempt to prevent a murder which is expected to occur at a memorial dinner for the late Iris Russell. After receiving a frantic call late one evening to go to the Jardin de Cygnes restaurant, Poirot discovers that the woman died of poisoning four years ago to the day. Her husband has recreated the evening, down to the exact entertainment. When the lights go on after the floor show, another member of the party appears to be dead, but it is only a trick used by Poirot to unmask the true murderer.

CRIME NOTES
The first death and later attempted murder are both the result of poisoning by use of potassium cyanide.

Yoaschbim   A highly talented opera star in "THE FACE OF HELEN," his voice is compared to Caruso's, for it could shatter glass. He avoids definition by the press, and is reported to be variously "a Yugoslav, a Czech, an Albanian, a Magyar and a Bulgarian."

Z

Zara A fortune-teller in "ACCIDENT" who tells retired police Inspector Evans that he will soon be engaged in a life-or-death matter. She warns him to be very careful.

Zara, Madame A clairvoyant in "THE KING OF CLUBS," she warns a beautiful dancer, the fiancée of a prince, to "Beware the King of Clubs."

Zarida See COPLING, NURSE.

Zerkowski, Countess Renata An espionage agent in PASSENGER TO FRANKFURT who was once under the protection of the Grafin Charlotte VON WALDSAUSEN, she also poses as Mary Ann and as Daphne Theodofanous. She is the daughter of an English nobleman and a Greek mother, and she aids Sir Stafford NYE in dismantling the Youth Movement.

Zeropoulos, Monsieur The proprietor of an antique shop which deals in high quality items in DEATH IN THE CLOUDS, he identifies for Hercule POIROT the purchaser of the blowgun and dart which killed Madame GISELLE.

Zielinsky, Ella A sufferer of numerous allergies, Marina GREGG's social secretary in THE MIRROR CRACK'D FROM SIDE TO SIDE relies upon her atomizer for relief. She dies when someone puts prussic acid in the atomizer and she inhales it.

Ziyara, Sheik Hussein el Known primarily throughout the Muslim world as "a Holy Man and a poet," the sheik has also been a longtime friend of Henry CARMICHAEL in THEY CAME TO BAGHDAD. He obtains from Carmichael microfilms of an Asian weapon site, as well as coded messages in a red knitted scarf, and a letter of reference.

Zobeida See MOSS, MARY.

Zuleika, Madame A fortune-teller who appears in DEAD MAN's FOLLY wearing "flowing black robes, a gold tinsel scarf wound round her head and a veil across the lower half of her face." She tells the fortune of Hercule POIROT, who sees through her disguise and recognizes that she is really Sally LEGGE.

WORKS BY AGATHA CHRISTIE

Christie, Agatha. *The A.B.C. Murders.* New York: Putnam Publishing Group, 1985.

Akhnaton: A Play. New York: Dodd, Mead and Company, 1973.

And Then There Were None. New York: Putnam Publishing Group, 1985.

Appointment with Death. New York: Berkley Publishing, 1988.

At Bertram's Hotel. New York: HarperCollins, 1992.

An Autobiography. New York: Dodd, Mead and Company, 1977.

The Big Four. New York: Berkley Publishing, 1984.

Black Coffee: A Play in Three Acts. London: Samuel French, Ltd., 1934.

The Body in the Library. New York: HarperCollins, 1992.

By the Pricking of My Thumbs. New York: HarperCollins, 1992.

Cards on the Table. New York: Berkley Publishing, 1987.

A Caribbean Mystery. New York: HarperCollins, 1992.

Cat Among the Pigeons. New York: Putnam Publishing Group, 1986.

The Clocks. New York: Bantam Books, 1988.

Crooked House. New York: HarperCollins, 1991.

Curtain. New York: HarperCollins, 1993.

Dead Man's Folly. New York: HarperCollins, 1992.

Death Comes As the End. New York: Putnam Publishing Group, 1982.

Death in the Clouds. New York: Berkley Publishing, 1987.

Death on the Nile. New York: Bantam Books, 1983.

Destination Unknown. New York: HarperCollins, 1992.

Double Sin and Other Stories. New York: Berkley Publishing, 1984.

Dumb Witness. New York: Berkley Publishing, 1986.

Elephants Can Remember. New York: Berkley Publishing, 1994.

Endless Night. New York: HarperCollins, 1992.

Evil Under the Sun. New York: Putnam Publishing Group, 1981.

Five Little Pigs. New York: Berkley Publishing, 1985.

4.50 from Paddington. New York: HarperCollins, 1992.

Funerals Are Fatal. New York: Putnam Publishing Group, 1992. (The novel is not currently in print under its original British title, *After the Funeral.*)

The Golden Ball and Other Stories. New York: Bantam Publishing, 1987.

Hallowe'en Party. New York: Berkley Publishing, 1991.

Hercule Poirot's Christmas. New York: HarperCollins, 1992.

Hickory Dickory Dock. New York: HarperCollins, 1992.

The Hollow. New York: Putnam Publishing Group, 1992.

The Hound of Death and Other Stories. New York: Bantam Books, 1990.

The Labors of Hercules. New York: Putnam Publishing Group, 1993.

Lord Edgware Dies. New York: Berkley Publishing Group, 1994.

The Man in the Brown Suit. New York: Berkley Publishing, 1994.

The Mirror Crack'd. New York: HarperCollins, 1992. (The novel is not currently in print under its original British title of *The Mirror Crack'd from Side to Side*.)

The Mousetrap and Other Plays. New York: Putnam Publishing Group, 1978.

The Moving Finger. New York: Berkley Publishing, 1987.

Mrs. McGinty's Dead. New York: Putnam Publishing Group, 1993.

The Murder at the Vicarage. New York: Putnam Publishing Group, 1978.

Murder in Mesopotamia. New York: Berkley Publishing, 1984.

Murder in the Mews and Other Stories. New York: Berkley Publishing, 1994.

A Murder Is Announced. New York: Berkley Publishing, 1991.

Murder Is Easy. New York: Putnam Publishing Group, 1981.

The Murder of Roger Ackroyd. New York: HarperCollins, 1991.

Murder on the Links. New York: Berkley Publishing, 1994.

Murder on the Orient Express. New York: HarperCollins, 1991.

The Mysterious Affair at Styles. New York: Bantam Books, 1983.

The Mysterious Mr. Quin. New York: Berkley Publishing, 1987.

The Mystery of the Blue Train. New York: Bantam Books, 1987.

N or M? New York: Berkley Publishing, 1986.

Nemesis. New York: HarperCollins, 1992.

One, Two, Buckle My Shoe. New York: Berkley Publishing, 1994.

Ordeal by Innocence. New York: HarperCollins, 1991.

The Pale Horse. New York: HarperCollins, 1992.

Parker Pyne Investigates. New York: Berkley Publishing, 1985.

Partners in Crime. New York: Berkley Publishing, 1987.

Passenger to Frankfurt. New York: HarperCollins, 1992.

Peril at End House. New York: Berkley Publishing, 1991.

A Pocket Full of Rye. New York: Berkley Publishing, 1991.

Poems. New York: Dodd, Mead and Company, 1973.

Poirot Investigates. New York: HarperCollins, 1992.

Postern of Fate. New York: HarperCollins, 1991.

The Regatta Mystery and Other Stories. New York: Berkley Publishing, 1987.

Sad Cypress. New York: Putnam Publishing Group, 1982.

The Secret Adversary. New York: Berkley Publishing, 1991.

The Secret of Chimneys. New York: Berkley Publishing, 1984.

The Seven Dials Mystery. New York: Bantam Books, 1983.

The Sittaford Mystery. New York: Berkley Publishing, 1987.

Sleeping Murder. New York: Bantam Books, 1983.

Sparkling Cyanide. New York: HarperCollins, 1992.

Spider's Web: A Play in Three Acts. London: Samuel French, Ltd., 1956.

Star Over Bethlehem. New York: Berkley Publishing, 1991.

Taken at the Flood. New York: Berkley Publishing, 1984.

They Came to Baghdad. New York: Berkley Publishing, 1994.

They Do It with Mirrors. New York: Putnam Publishing Group, 1987.

Third Girl. New York: HarperCollins, 1992.

The Thirteen Problems. New York: Berkley Publishing, 1992.

Three-Act Tragedy. New York: Berkley Publishing, 1986.

Three Blind Mice and Other Stories. New York: Putnam Publishing Group, 1985.

Towards Zero. New York: Berkley Publishing, 1991.

The Under Dog and Other Stories. New York: Bantam Books, 1988.

The Unexpected Guest. London: Samuel French Limited, 1958.

Why Didn't They Ask Evans? New York: Berkley Publishing, 1994.

Witness for the Prosecution and Other Stories. New York: Berkley Publishing, 1994.

Christie, Agatha, and the Detection Club. *The Floating Admiral*. New York: Jove Publications, 1993.

Mallowan, Agatha Christie. *Come, Tell Me How You Live*. New York: Bantam Books, 1985.

Westmacott, Mary (pseud.) *Absent in the Spring.* New York: Arbor House, 1972.

The Burden. New York: Arbor House, 1973.

A Daughter's a Daughter. New York: Arbor House, 1972.

Giant's Bread. New York: Arbor House, 1973.

The Rose and the Yew Tree. New York: Dell Publishing, 1964.

Unfinished Business. New York: Arbor House, 1972.

A CHRONOLOGICAL LISTING OF THE WORKS

Novels, Short Story Collections, Plays, Non-fiction

1920 *The Mysterious Affair at Styles*
1922 *The Secret Adversary*
1923 *Murder on the Links*
1924 *The Man in the Brown Suit*
Poirot Investigates (Short Story Collection)
 "The Adventure of 'The Western Star' "
 "The Tragedy at Marsdon Manor"
 "The Adventure of the Cheap Flat"
 "The Mystery of the Hunters Lodge"
 "The Million Dollar Bond Robbery"
 "The Adventure of the Egyptian Tomb"
 "The Jewel Robbery at the Grand Metropolitan"
 "The Kidnapped Prime Minister"
 "The Disappearance of Mr. Davenheim"
 "The Adventure of the Italian Nobleman"
 "The Case of the Missing Will"
The Road of Dreams
1925 *The Secret of Chimneys*
1926 *The Murder of Roger Ackroyd*
1927 *The Big Four*
1928 *The Mystery of the Blue Train*
Alibi (Play)
1929 *The Seven Dials Mystery*
Partners in Crime (Short Story Collection)
 "A Fairy in the Flat"
 "A Pot of Tea"
 "The Affair of the Pink Pearl"
 "The Affair of the Sinister Stranger"
 "Finessing the King"
 "The Gentleman Dressed in Newspaper"
 "The Case of the Missing Lady"
 "Blindman's Bluff"
 "The Man in the Mist"
 "The Crackler"

"The Sunningdale Mystery"
"The House of the Lurking Death"
"The Unbreakable Alibi"
"The Clergyman's Daughter"
"The Red House"
"The Ambassador's Boots"
"The Man Who Was No. 16"
1930 *The Mysterious Mr. Quin* (Short Story Collection)
 "The Coming of Mr. Quin"
 "The Shadow on the Glass"
 "At the 'Bells and Motley' "
 "The Sign in the Sky"
 "The Soul of the Croupier"
 "The World's End"
 "The Voice in the Dark"
 "The Face of Helen"
 "The Dead Harlequin"
 "The Bird with the Broken Wing"
 "The Man from the Sea"
 "Harlequin's Lane"
Murder at the Vicarage
Giant's Bread
Black Coffee (Play)
1931 *The Sittaford Mystery*
1932 *Peril at End House*
The Thirteen Problems (Short Story Collection)
 "The Tuesday Night Club"
 "The Idol House of Astarte"
 "Ingots of Gold"
 "The Blood-Stained Pavement"
 "Motive versus Opportunity"
 "The Thumb Mark of St. Peter"
 "The Blue Geranium"
 "The Companion"
 "The Four Suspects"

SUGGESTED READING

Aisenberg, Nadya. *A Common Spring: Crime Novel and Classic*. Bowling Green, Ohio: Bowling Green University Popular Press, 1980.

Auden, W.H. "The Guilty Vicarage." In *The Dyer's Hand*. New York: Vintage Press, 1968.

Bargainnier, Earl F. *The Gentle Art of Murder: The Detective Fiction of Agatha Christie*. Bowling Green, Ohio: Bowling Green University Popular Press, 1980.

Barnard, Robert. *A Talent to Deceive: An Appreciation of Agatha Christie*. New York: The Mysterious Press, 1987.

Barnes, Melvyn. *The Best Detective Fiction: A Guide from Godwin to the Present*. Hamden, Conn.: Clive Bingley/Linnet Books, 1975.

Barzun, Jacques, and W.H. Taylor. *A Catalogue of Crime*. New York: Harper & Row, 1971.

Cawelti, John G. *Adventure, Mystery, and Romance: Formula Stories as Art and Popular Culture*. Chicago: University of Chicago Press, 1976.

Craig, Patricia, and Mary Cadogan. *The Lady Investigates: Women Detectives and Spies in Fiction*. New York: St. Martin's Press, 1981.

Feinman, Jeffrey. *The Mysterious World of Agatha Christie*. New York: Grosset & Dunlap, 1975.

Gill, Gillian. *Agatha Christie: The Woman and Her Mysteries*. New York: The Free Press, 1990.

Grossvogel, David I. *Mystery and Its Fictions: From Oedipus to Agatha Christie*. Baltimore: The Johns Hopkins University Press, 1979.

Hart, Ann. *The Life and Times of Miss Jane Marple*. New York: Dodd, Mead and Company, 1985.

———. *The Life and Times of Hercule Poirot*. New York: G.P. Putnam's Sons, 1990.

Haycraft, Howard, ed. *The Art of the Mystery Story*. New York: Carroll and Graf, 1983.

———. *Murder for Pleasure: The Life and Times of the Detective Story*. New York: Carroll and Graf, 1984.

Keating, H.R.F., ed. *Agatha Christie: First Lady of Crime*. New York: Hold, Rinehart and Winston, 1977.

Klein, Kathleen Gregory. *The Woman Detective: Gender and Genre*. Urbana, Ill.: The University of Illinois Press, 1988.

Lask, Thomas. "Hercule Poirot is Dead: Famed Belgian Detective," *The New York Times,* August 6, 1975, p. 1.

Lehman, David. *The Perfect Murder: A Study in Detection*. New York: The Free Press, 1989.

Maida, Patricia D., and Nicholas B. Spornick. *Murder She Wrote: A Study of Agatha Christie's Detective Fiction*. Bowling Green, Ohio: Bowling Green University Popular Press, 1982.

Mallowan, Max. *Mallowan's Memoirs*. New York: Dodd, Mead and Company, 1977.

Mann, Jessica. *Deadlier than the Male: Why Are Respectable Women So Good at Murder?* New York: Macmillan and Company, 1981.

Moers, Ellen. *Literary Women: The Great Writers*. New York: New York: Anchor Doubleday, 1977.

Morgan, Janet. *Agatha Christie: A Biography*. New York: Alfred A. Knopf, 1984.

Murdoch, Derrick. *The Agatha Christie Mystery*. Toronto: Pagurian Press Ltd., 1976.

Osborne, Charles. *The Life and Crimes of Agatha Christie*. New York: Holt, Rinehart and Winston, 1982.

Poovey, Mary. *The Proper Lady and the Woman Writer*. Chicago: The University of Chicago Press, 1984.

Ramsey, G.C. *Agatha Christie: Mistress of Mystery*. New York: Dodd, Mead and Company, 1967.

Reddy, Maureen T. *Sisters in Crime: Feminism and*

the Crime Novel. New York: Continuum Press, 1988.

Robyns, Gwen. *The Mystery of Agatha Christie*. New York: Doubleday and Company, 1978.

Routley, Erik. *The Puritan Pleasures of the Detective Story: Sherlock Holmes to Van der Valk*. London: Victor Gollancz, Ltd., 1972.

Symons, Julian. *Bloody Murder: From the Detective Story to the Crime Novel*. New York: Viking Press, 1985.

Symons, Julian, and Tom Adams. *Agatha Christie: The Art of Her Crimes: The Paintings of Tom Adams*. New York: Everest House, 1981.

Tynan, Kathleen. *Agatha*. New York: Ballantine Books, 1978.

Underwood, Lynn, ed. *AGATHA CHRISTIE: Official Centenary Celebration, 1890–1990*. London: Belgrave Publishing, Ltd., 1990.

Wagoner, Mary. *Agatha Christie*. Boston: Twayne Publishers, 1986.

Winn, Dilys. *Murderess Ink: The Better Half of the Mystery*. New York: Workman Publishing, 1979.

Wynne, Nancy Blue. *An Agatha Christie Chronology*. New York: Ace Books, 1976.

CATEGORICAL APPENDIX

I. The Detectives

A. Works in Which Hercule Poirot Appears (Starred entries [*] include Captain Arthur Hastings and entries followed by a plus sign [+] include Chief Inspector James Japp)

NOVELS
The A.B.C. Murders * +
After the Funeral
Appointment with Death
The Big Four * +
Cards on the Table
Cat Among the Pigeons
The Clocks
Curtain *
Dead Man's Folly
Death in the Clouds +
Death on the Nile
Dumb Witness *
Elephants Can Remember
Evil Under the Sun
Five Little Pigs
Hallowe'en Party
Hercule Poirot's Christmas
Hickory Dickory Dock
The Hollow
Lord Edgware Dies * +
Mrs. McGinty's Dead
Murder in Mesopotamia
The Murder of Roger Ackroyd
Murder on the Links *
Murder on the Orient Express
The Mysterious Affair at Styles * +
The Mystery of the Blue Train
One, Two, Buckle My Shoe +
Peril at End House * +
Sad Cypress

Taken at the Flood
Third Girl
Three-Act Tragedy

SHORT STORIES
"The Adventure of Johnnie Waverly"*
"The Adventure of the Cheap Flat"* +
"The Adventure of the Christmas Pudding"
"The Adventure of the Clapham Cook"*
"The Adventure of the Egyptian Tomb"*
"The Adventure of the Italian Nobleman"*
"The Adventure of 'The Western Star' "*
"The Affair at the Victory Ball"* +
"The Apples of the Hesperides"
"The Arcadian Deer"
"The Augean Stables"
"The Capture of Cerberus" +
"The Case of the Missing Will"*
"The Chocolate Box"*
"The Cornish Mystery"*
"The Cretan Bull"
"Dead Man's Mirror"
"The Disappearance of Mr. Davenheim"* +
"The Double Clue"*
"Double Sin"*
"The Dream"
"The Erymanthian Boar"
"The Flock of Geryon" +
"Four-and-Twenty Blackbirds"
"The Girdle of Hippolyta" +
"The Horses of Diomedes"
"How Does Your Garden Grow?"
"The Incredible Theft"
"The Jewel Robbery at the Grand Metropolitan"*
"The Kidnapped Prime Minister"* +
"The King of Clubs"*
"The Lemesurier Inheritance"*
"The Lernean Hydra"

"The Lost Mine"*
"The Market Basing Mystery"* +
"The Million Dollar Bond Robbery"*
"Murder in the Mews" +
"The Mystery of Hunter's Lodge"* +
"The Mystery of the Baghdad Chest"*
"The Mystery of the Spanish Chest" +
"The Nemean Lion"
"The Plymouth Express"* +
"Problem at Sea"
"The Second Gong"
"The Stymphalean Birds"
"The Submarine Plans"*
"The Theft of the Royal Ruby"
"The Third-Floor Flat"
"The Tragedy of Marsden Manor"*
"Triangle at Rhodes"
"The Under Dog"
"The Veiled Lady"* +
"Wasps' Nest"
"Yellow Iris"

B. Works in Which Miss Jane Marple Appears

NOVELS
At Bertram's Hotel
The Body in the Library
A Caribbean Mystery
4.50 from Paddington
The Mirror Crack'd from Side to Side
The Moving Finger
A Murder Is Announced
The Murder at the Vicarage
Nemesis
A Pocket Full of Rye
Sleeping Murder
They Do It with Mirrors

SHORT STORIES
"The Affair at the Bungalow"
"The Blood-Stained Pavement"
"The Blue Geranium"
"The Case of the Caretaker"
"The Case of the Perfect Maid"
"A Christmas Tragedy"
"The Companion"
"Death by Drowning"
"The Four Suspects"

"Greenshaw's Folly"
"The Herb of Death"
"The Idol House of Astarte"
"Ingots of Gold"
"Miss Marple Tells a Story"
"Motive versus Opportunity"
"Sanctuary"
"Strange Jest"
"The Tape-Measure Murder"
"The Thumb Mark of Saint Peter"
"The Tuesday Night Club"

C. Works in Which Tommy and Tuppence Beresford Appear

NOVELS
By the Pricking of My Thumbs
N or M?
Postern of Fate
The Secret Adversary

SHORT STORIES
"The Adventure of the Sinister Stranger"
"The Affair of the Pink Pearl"
"The Ambassador's Boots"
"Blindman's Bluff"
"The Case of the Missing Lady"
"The Clergyman's Daughter"
"The Crackler"
"A Fairy in the Flat"
"Finessing the King"
"The Gentleman Dressed in Newspaper"
"The House of Lurking Death"
"The Man in the Mist"
"The Man Who Was No. 16"
"A Pot of Tea"
"The Red House"
"The Sunningdale Mystery"
"The Unbreakable Alibi"

D. Works in Which Mrs. Ariadne Oliver Appears

NOVELS
Cards on the Table
Dead Man's Folly
Elephants Can Remember
Hallowe'en Party
Mrs. McGinty's Dead

The Pale Horse (The only novel without Poirot)
Third Girl

SHORT STORIES
"The Case of the Discontented Soldier" (with Mr. Parker Pyne)
"The Case of the Rich Woman" (with Mr. Parker Pyne)

E. Works in Which Superintendent Battle Appears

NOVELS
Cards on the Table (with Poirot, Mrs. Oliver, Colonel Race)
Murder Is Easy
The Secret of Chimneys
The Seven Dials Mystery
Towards Zero

F. Works in Which Colonel Johnny Race Appears

NOVELS
Cards on the Table (with Poirot, Mrs. Oliver, Superintendent Battle)
Death on the Nile (with Poirot)
The Man in the Brown Suit
Sparkling Cyanide

G. Works in Which Mr. Parker Pyne Appears

SHORT STORIES
"The Case of the City Clerk"
"The Case of the Discontented Husband"
"The Case of the Discontented Soldier" (with Mrs. Ariadne Oliver)
"The Case of the Distressed Lady"
"The Case of the Middle-Aged Wife"
"The Case of the Rich Woman" (with Mrs. Ariadne Oliver)
"Death on the Nile"
"The Gate of Baghdad"
"Have You Got Everything You Want?"
"The House at Shiraz"
"The Oracle at Delphi"
"The Pearl of Price"

"Problem at Pollensa Bay"
"The Regatta Mystery"

H. Works in Which Mr. Harley Quin Appears with the Ever-Present Mr. Satterthwaite*

SHORT STORIES
"At the 'Bells and Motley' "
"The Bird with the Broken Wing"
"The Coming of Mr. Quin"
"The Dead Harlequin"
"The Face of Helen"
"Harlequin's Lane"
"The Harlequin Tea Set"
"The Love Detectives"
"The Man from the Sea"
"The Shadow on the Glass"
"The Sign in the Sky"
"The Soul of the Croupier"
"The Voice in the Dark"
"The World's End"

II. Novels Written Under the Pseudonym of Mary Westmacott

Absent in the Spring
The Burden
A Daughter's a Daughter
Giant's Bread
The Rose and the Yew Tree
Unfinished Portrait

III. Means of Murder or Attempted Murder

A. Poison

"Accident"
"Affair at the Victory Ball, The"
After the Funeral
Akhnaton
And Then There Were None
Appointment with Death
The Big Four
Black Coffee

*Mr. Satterthwaite appears with Hercule Poirot in the novel *Three-Act Tragedy* and in the short story "Dead Man's Mirror."

"Blue Geranium, The"
Body in the Library, The
By the Pricking of My Thumbs
Cards on the Table
Caribbean Mystery, A
"Chocolate Box, The"
"Cornish Mystery, The"
"Crooked House, The"
Curtain
Death Comes As the End
Death in the Clouds
Destination Unknown
Dumb Witness
Endless Night
Five Little Pigs
"Four-and-Twenty Blackbirds"
4.50 from Paddington
"Herb of Death, The"
Hickory Dickory Dock
"How Does Your Garden Grow?"
"Lemesurier Inheritance, The"
Lord Edgware Dies
Mirror Crack'd from Side to Side, The
"Miss Marple Tells a Story"
Moving Finger, The
Murder in Mesopotamia
Murder Is Easy
Mysterious Affair at Styles, The
Nemesis
One, Two, Buckle My Shoe
Pale Horse, The
Pocket Full of Rye, A
Postern of Fate
Sad Cypress
Seven Dials Mystery, The
Sparkling Cyanide
"Strange Case of Sir Arthur Carmichael, The"
Taken at the Flood
Three-Act Tragedy
"Thumb Mark of Saint Peter, The"
"Triangle at Rhodes"
"Tuesday Night Club, The"
"Yellow Iris"

B. Gunshot

"The Adventure of the Egyptian Tomb"
And Then There Were None
At Bertram's Hotel
Cards on the Table

Cat Among the Pigeons
Curtain
"Dead Harlequin, The"
"Dead Man's Mirror"
Death on the Nile (2)
"Dream, The"
Elephants Can Remember
Hollow, The
"House of the Lurking Death, The"
"Market Basing Mystery, The"
Mirror Crack'd from Side to Side, The
Murder at the Vicarage
Murder in the Mews (2)
Murder Is Announced, A
"Mystery of Hunter's Lodge, The"
N or M?
One, Two, Buckle My Shoe
Passenger to Frankfurt
Peril at End House
Red Signal, The
"Sanctuary"
"Second Gong, The"
Secret of Chimneys, The
Seven Dials Mystery, The
"Shadow on the Glass, The"
"Sign in The Sky, The"
They Do It with Mirrors
"Third-Floor Flat, The"
"Tragedy at Marsdon Manor, The"
Unexpected Guest, The
Why Didn't They Ask Evans?

C. Stabbing

A.B.C. Murders, The
"Affair at the Victory Ball, The"
Cards on the Table
Clocks, The
Death Comes As the End
Death on the Nile (2)
"Disappearance of Mr. Davenheim, The"
"Erymanthian Boar, The"
"Finessing the King"/"The Gentleman Dressed in Newspaper"
"Greenshaw's Folly"
Hallowe'en Party
"Idol House of Astarte, The"
Man in the Brown Suit, The
Murder of Roger Ackroyd, The
Murder on the Links

Murder on the Orient Express
"Mystery of the Baghdad Chest, The"
"Mystery of the Spanish Chest, The"
Ordeal by Innocence
"Plymouth Express, The"
"Problem at Sea"
"Sunningdale Mystery, The"
"Swan Song"
They Came to Baghdad
Third Girl

D. Blow to the Head

A.B.C. Murders, The
"Adventure of the Italian Nobleman, The"
And Then There Were None
The Big Four
Cat Among the Pigeons
"A Christmas Tragedy"
"The Gate of Baghdad"
Hickory Dickory Dock
"King of Clubs, The"
"Man in the Mist, The"
Moving Finger, The
Mrs. McGinty's Dead
Murder in Mesopotamia
One, Two, Buckle My Shoe
Ordeal by Innocence
"Sing a Song of Sixpence"
Sittaford Mystery, The
Spider's Web
Taken at the Flood
They Do It with Mirrors
Towards Zero
"Under Dog, The"
Witness for the Prosecution

E. Strangling

The A.B.C. Murders
And Then There Were None
"Bird with the Broken Wing, The"
Body in the Library, The
Clocks, The
Dead Man's Folly
Evil Under the Sun
4.50 from Paddington
Hallowe'en Party
Mousetrap, The
Mrs. McGinty's Dead

Murder Is Announced, A
Mystery of the Blue Train, The
Nemesis
Pocket Full of Rye, A
Sleeping Murder
"Tape-Measure Murder, The"
"Three Blind Mice"

F. Falling (Being Pushed)

Death Comes As the End
Elephants Can Remember
Endless Night
"Four Suspects, The"
"Lemesurier Inheritance, The"
Murder Is Easy
Nemesis
Third Girl
Why Didn't They Ask Evans?

G. Drowning

"Blood-Stained Pavement, The"
Cards on the Table
Dead Man's Folly
Death by Drowning
Death Comes As the End
Hallowe'en Party
"Lost Mine, The"

H. Electrocution

Big Four, The
Man in the Brown Suit, The

I. Throat Cut

Big Four, The
Hercule Poirot's Christmas

J. Hit-and-Run Automobile Accident

Big Four, The

K. Immolation

Body in the Library, The

L. Suffocation

Death Comes As the End

INDEX

This index is designed to be used in conjunction with the many cross-references in the A-to-Z entries; it thus does not attempt to be exhaustive. Page references to titles, names and terms that have their own A-to-Z entries are **boldfaced** below; for additional references see their text entries. Other titles, names and terms that are not the subjects of A-to-Z entries are generally given fuller citations here. *Italicized* page references indicate illustrations; *c* following the page locators indicate the chronology.

A

Aarons, Joseph, **1**, 33, 101, 234, 241

Abbot, Mr. (1; *Murder Is Easy*), 111, 230

Abbot, Mr. (2; *Sad Cypress*), 111, 293

A.B.C. Murders, The, **1–3**, 18, 24, 28, 29, 50, 53, 67, 79, 82, 97, 102, 104, 108, 129, 143, 150, 158, 172, 179, 180, 188, 193, 207, 213, 259, 286, 331
film version, 15–16

ABC Rail Guide, The, 1, 2

Abdul, **3**, 21

Abel, Police Constable, 295

Abercrombie, Colonel, **3**, 251

Abernethie, Cora, 11, 12

Abernethie, Helen, **3**, 11, 12

Abernethie, Maude, **3**, 11

Abernethie, Richard, 11, 12, 114, 186, 225

Abernethie, Timothy, 131, 11

Abrams, Dr., 75

Absent in the Spring, **3–4**, 50, 53, 134, 145, 159, 280, 284, 297, 304, 351, 358

"Accident," **4**, 115, 152, 194, 213, 330, 357, 361

Ackroyd, Mrs. Cecil, **4**, 233

Ackroyd, Flora, **4**, 233

Ackroyd, Roger, **4**, 40, 42, 120, 124, 147, 179–80, 233, 257, 261, 281, 304

Adams, Dr., **4**

Adams, Bernard, 224

Adams, Carlotta, **4**, 104, 153, 196

Addison, Thomas, **4–5**, 135, 149

Adventure Inc. See Die Abenteurer G.m.b.H.

"Adventure of Johnnie Waverly, The," **5**, 72, 272, 320, 333, 350, 356

Adventure of M. Hercule Poirot, The (radio series), 228

"Adventure of the Cheap Flat, The," **5**, 47, 148, 257, 271, 287

"Adventure of the Christmas Pudding, The," **5–6**, 44, 102, 184, 189, 350

Adventure of the Christmas Pudding and a Selection of Entrees, The, 5, **6**, 30, 142, 243, 339

"Adventure of the Clapham Cook, The,"
6–7, 20, 106, 272, 305, 334, 340

"Adventure of the Egyptian Tomb, The," **7–8**, 17, 38, 39, 150, 151, 271, 297, 334, 355

"Adventure of the Italian Nobleman, The," **8**, 24, 125, 141, 152, 271

"Adventure of the Sinister Stranger, The," **8**, 31, 72, 107, 209, 259

"Adventure of 'The Western Star,' The," **8–9**, 64, 211, 271, 288, 359

"Affair at the Bugalow, The," **9**, 27, 120, 153, 180, 294, 331

"Affair at the Victory Ball, The," **9–10**, *12*, 31, 75, 79, 85, 97, 203, 272, 340

"Affair of the Pink Pearl, The," **10–11**, 30, 33, 158, 182, 209, 259, 285

Afflick, Dorothy, **11**, 307

Afflick, Jackie, **11**, 307

After the Funeral, 3, **11–12**, 29, 80, 114, 135, 138, 144, 173, 186, 219, 224, 277, 303, 304

Agatha (film), **13**, 99

Agatha Christie Hour, The (television series), 164

Agrondopolous, Mr., **13**, 79

Akhnaton (Egyptian pharaoh), 13–14

Akhnaton (play), **13–14**

Akibombo, Mr., **14**, 157

Albert, **14**, 68, 148, 160, 207, 274

Alcadi, **14**, 96

Aldin, Mary, **14**, 334

Aldini, Carlo, **14**, 97, 98

Alexa. *See* Anastasia, Grand Duchess

Alfred, **14**, 302

Alfredge, Madame, **14**, 160

Ali, Prince, 6, **14**, 174

Ali, Achmed, 14, 157

Alibi (film), **15**, 233; *see also Murder of Roger Ackroyd, The*

Alibi (play), 232

Alice, 15, 241

Ali Yusef, **15**, 226

Ali Yusef, Prince, Hereditary Sheik of Ramat, **15**, 62, 303, 320

Allaby, Mr., **15**, 185, 247

Allan, Elizabeth, 15

Allen, Adrienne, 37, 115

Allen, Barbara, **15**, 159, 187, 229, 267

Allenson, Captain Jimmy, **15**, 303, 314

Allerton, Major, **15**, 78, 81

Allerton, Mrs., 15, 92

Allerton, Rosalie, 254

Allerton, Tim, 92, 254

Alloway, Lord, **15**, 318, 350

Alphabet Murders, The (film), 1, **15–16**

Altamount, Lord Edward, **16**, 182, 259

Alton, **16**, 196

Alverstroke, Lord, **16**

Amalfi. *See* Leathern, Samuel

Amalfi, Maria. *See* Leathern, Eve

"Ambassador's Boots, The," **16–17**, 139, 208, 259, 286, 355

Amberiotis, Mr., **17**, 251

Amery, Blanche, **17**, 320

Ames, Dr., 7

Ames, Mr., **17**, 267

Amory, Barbara, **17**, 36

Amory, Miss Caroline, **17**, 36

Amory, Sir Claud, **17**, 36, 140, 281

Amory, Lucia, **17**, 36, 53

Amory, Richard, 17, 36

Amphrey, Miss, **17**, 258, 334

Anastasia, Grand Duchess, **17**, 131, 137, 178, 254, 291

Anchoukoff, Boris, **17**, 299

H